The Economics of Institutions

The International Library of Critical Writings in Economics

Series Editor: Mark Blaug

Professor Emeritus, University of London
Professor Emeritus, University of Buckingham
Visiting Professor, University of Exeter

This series is an essential reference source for students, researchers and lecturers in economics. It presents by theme an authoritative selection of the most important articles across the entire spectrum of economics. Each volume has been prepared by a leading specialist who has written an authoritative introduction to the literature included.

A full list of published and future titles in this series is printed at the end of this volume.

The Economics of Institutions

Edited by

Geoffrey M. Hodgson

Lecturer in Economics
The Judge Institute of Management Studies
University of Cambridge

An Elgar Reference Collection

Published by
Edward Elgar Publishing Limited
Gower House
Croft Road
Aldershot
Hants GU11 3HR
England

Edward Elgar Publishing Company
Old Post Road
Brookfield
Vermont 05036
USA

1776703

British Library Cataloguing in Publication Data
Economics of Institutions. –
(International Library of Critical
Writings in Economics)
  I. Hodgson, Geoffrey M. II. Series
  330.155

Library of Congress Cataloguing in Publication Data
The Economics of institutions / edited by Geoffrey M. Hodgson.
    p. cm. — (The International library of critical writings in
economics; 33) (An Elgar reference collection)
  Includes bibliographical references and index.
    1. Institutional economics. I. Hodgson, Geoffrey Martin, 1946–   .
II. Series. III. Series: An Elgar reference collection.
HB99.5.E255 1993
330—dc20   93–25993
                                                                        CIP

ISBN 1 85278 764 3

Printed in Great Britain by Galliard (Printers) Ltd, Great Yarmouth

Contents

Acknowledgements

The editor and publishers wish to thank the following who have kindly given permission for the use of copyright material.

Academic Press Ltd. for articles: Geoff Hodgson (1989), 'Institutional Rigidities and Economic Growth', *Cambridge Journal of Economics*, **13** (1), March, 79–101; Ugo Pagano (1991), 'Property Rights, Asset Specificity, and the Division of Labour under Alternative Capitalist Relations', *Cambridge Journal of Economics*, **15** (3), September, 315–42.

American Association for the Advancement of Science for article: Herbert A. Simon (1990), 'A Mechanism for Social Selection and Successful Altruism', *Science*, **250** (4988), 21 December, 1665–8.

American Economic Association for articles: Ronald A. Heiner (1983), 'The Origin of Predictable Behavior', *American Economic Review*, **73** (4), September, 560–95; Jon Elster (1989), 'Social Norms and Economic Theory', *Journal of Economic Perspectives*, **3** (4), Fall, 99–117.

American Political Science Association for article: Robert Axelrod (1986), 'An Evolutionary Approach to Norms', *American Political Science Review*, **80** (4), December, 1095–111.

Association for Evolutionary Economics for articles: Alexander James Field (1979), 'On the Explanation of Rules Using Rational Choice Models', *Journal of Economic Issues*, **XIII** (1), March, 49–72; Lawrence A. Boland (1979), 'Knowledge and the Role of Institutions in Economic Theory', *Journal of Economic Issues*, **XIII** (4), December, 957–72; William T. Waller, Jr. (1982), 'The Evolution of the Veblenian Dichotomy: Veblen, Hamilton, Ayres, and Foster', *Journal of Economic Issues*, **XVI** (3), September, 757–71; Paul D. Bush (1987), 'The Theory of Institutional Change', *Journal of Economic Issues*, **XXI** (3), September, 1075–116; William T. Waller, Jr. (1988), 'The Concept of Habit in Economic Analysis', *Journal of Economic Issues*, **XXII** (1), March, 113–26.

Basil Blackwell Ltd. for articles: Giovanni Dosi (1988), 'Institutions and Markets in a Dynamic World', *Manchester School*, **LVI** (2), June, 119–46; Geoffrey M. Hodgson (1993), 'Institutional Economics: Surveying the "Old" and the "New"', *Metroeconomica*, **44** (1), February, 1–28.

Economic Analysis and Workers' Management for article: Hans G. Nutzinger (1976), 'The Firm as a Social Institution: The Failure of the Contractarian Viewpoint', *Economic Analysis and Workers' Management*, **X** (3–4), 217–36.

Edward Arnold Journals and Viktor Vanberg for article: Viktor Vanberg (1989), 'Carl Menger's Evolutionary and John R. Commons' Collective Action Approach to Institutions: A Comparison', *Review of Political Economy*, **1** (3), November, 334–60.

J.C.B. Mohr (Paul Siebeck) Tübingen for articles: Viktor Vanberg (1988), 'Rules and Choice in Economics and Sociology', *Jahrbuch für Neue Politische Ökonomie*, **7**, 146–67; Richard N. Langlois (1988), 'Economic Change and the Boundaries of the Firm', *Journal of Institutional and Theoretical Economics*, **144** (4), September, 635–57; Brian R. Binger and Elizabeth Hoffman (1989), 'Institutional Persistence and Change: The Question of Efficiency', *Journal of Institutional and Theoretical Economics*, **145** (1), March, 67–84.

Kluwer Academic Publishers BV for article: Ulrich Witt (1989), 'The Evolution of Economic Institutions as a Propagation Process', *Public Choice*, **62**, 155–72.

Kluwer Academic Publishers, Inc. for excerpt: Philip Mirowski (1986), 'Institutions as a Solution Concept in a Game Theory Context', in Philip Mirowski (ed.), *The Reconstruction of Economic Theory*, 241–63.

Macmillan Publishing Company for excerpt: Walton H. Hamilton (1932), 'Institution', in Edwin R.A. Seligman and Alvin Johnson (eds), *Encyclopaedia of the Social Sciences*, **8**, 84–9.

M.E. Sharpe, Inc. for articles: David P. Ellerman (1991), 'Myth and Metaphor in Orthodox Economics', *Journal of Post Keynesian Economics*, **13** (4), Summer, 545–64; Philip Mirowski (1991), 'Postmodernism and the Social Theory of Value', *Journal of Post Keynesian Economics*, **13** (4), Summer, 565–82.

Oxford University Press for article: Ugo Pagano (1992), 'Authority, Co-Ordination and Disequilibrium: An Explanation of the Co-Existence of Markets and Firms', *Structural Change and Economic Dynamics*, **3** (1), 53–77.

Pinter Publishers for excerpt: Fabrizio Coricelli and Giovanni Dosi (1988), 'Coordination and Order in Economic Change and the Interpretative Power of Economic Theory', in Giovanni Dosi, Christopher Freeman, Richard Nelson, Gerald Silverberg and Luc Soete (eds), *Technical Change and Economic Theory*, 124–47.

University of Chicago Press for article: Alexander James Field (1984), 'Microeconomics, Norms, and Rationality', *Economic Development and Cultural Change*, **32** (4), July, 683–711.

U.N.E.S.C.O. for article: Geoffrey Newman (1976), 'An Institutional Perspective on Information', *International Social Science Journal*, **XXVIII** (3), 466–92.

Every effort has been made to trace all the copyright holders but if any have been inadvertently overlooked the publishers will be pleased to make the necessary arrangement at the first opportunity.

In addition the publishers wish to thank the Library of the London School of Economics and Political Science, the Marshall Library, Cambridge University and the Photographic Unit of the University of London Library for their assistance in obtaining these articles.

Introduction

The Renewal of Institutionalism

Up to the 1970s it was a common complaint of critics that mainstream economics ignored social institutions or took them as fixed and for granted. It was said that mainstream economic analysis was concerned wholly with economic behaviour either in an unreal institutional void or in a fixed institutional environment. Institutions themselves were not analysed: the firm in particular was taken as a 'black box'. Clearly this is no longer the case. The work of Douglass North, Mancur Olson, Andrew Schotter, Oliver Williamson and many others has placed the question of the emergence, development, nature and function of social institutions near the topic of the economist's research agenda.

The emergence of the 'new' institutionalism has also inadvertently directed renewed attention at the 'old' institutionalism that was founded by Thorstein Veblen, John Commons and Wesley Mitchell. This school of thought was located almost exclusively in the United States, but is now enjoying a renewal and has spread to Europe and elsewhere. This collection of essays spans both the 'new' and the 'old' institutionalism. It is a selection of works exploring the nature and function of institutions in modern economies.

Today, the subject of economics is conceived by many in narrow analytical terms. According to this view, economics by definition is the application of the specific assumptions of equilibrium and individual maximising behaviour to a wide range of social phenomena. This definition of the subject is not the one intended in the title of this collection. Here, and as in other sciences, it is assumed that economics is the study of a class of real objects. In these terms economics is the analysis of economies and economic phenomena: the exploration of the social relations and processes governing the production, distribution and exchange of the requisites of human life.

Hence 'the economics of institutions' is taken to mean the study of the emergence, development and functions of the institutions that are part of the economic system. Such institutions include markets, firms and the state. The 'economics of institutions' as defined here contains as a subset the analysis of institutions with the orthodox economist's assumptions of equilibrium and maximising behaviour. Such theories are generally regarded as major components of the 'new' institutional economics. In addition, however, authors contributing to the 'economics of institutions' include those who do not adopt this theoretical approach, such as the 'old' institutional economists and also some members of the Austrian School.

Accordingly, both the 'old' and the 'new' institutional economics is represented here.[1] The collection is but a small selection from an enormous field of enquiry. Two earlier compilations published by Edward Elgar include other works of major relevance for the topic. First, the three-volume collection in the 'Schools of Thought in Economics' series entitled *Institutional Economics* and edited by Warren Samuels (1988) includes key writings of the 'old' school of institutional economics.

Second, the volume entitled *Evolutionary Economics* in the present series, edited by

Ulrich Witt (1993), includes several important essays on the economics of institutions. Indeed, there is no clear frontier between evolutionary and institutional economics. Several essays on the evolution of institutions are included in the present volume, to complement those in the Witt collection.

Thorstein Veblen argued that economics should be an 'evolutionary' and 'post-Darwinian' science and his followers have often described their work as 'evolutionary economics'. Indeed, insofar as evolutionary economics involves an appeal to the biological analogy of natural selection, the label is more appropriate for the Veblenian rather than the Schumpeterian school (Hodgson, 1993b).

In addition to the essays reproduced here, there are several seminal and indispensable monographs in the topic area. Firstly, there are the prewar classics of the 'old' institutional economics by Thorstein Veblen, John Commons and Wesley Mitchell. Perhaps the best introductions to this genre are found in Wesley Mitchell (1937) and in the article by K. William Kapp (1976). Overall, the most important theoretical volume is Thorstein Veblen (1919).

Second, and in regard to the 'new' institutionalism, the review essay by Hodgson (1993a) included below gives a fuller list of postwar contributions. It should be emphasised that no library collection in the 'new' institutional economic theory would be complete without, for example, the following monographs: Friedrich Hayek (1982, 1988), Mancur Olson (1965, 1982), Thomas Schelling (1960), Andrew Schotter (1981), Robert Sugden (1986) and Oliver Williamson (1975, 1985). The works of Williamson on the firm, for instance, are a major omission from the present collection. However, as they have received extensive coverage elsewhere the space devoted here to the specific institution of the firm has been devoted to a number of very important but less available essays.

Finally, and apart from the above, an important reference work is being published by Edward Elgar, which covers the area of both the 'old' and the 'new' institutional economics, as well as the related field of evolutionary economics. This volume is edited by Warren Samuels, Marc Tool and the present author (Hodgson *et al.*, 1993).

What are Institutions?

Most theorists working in the area take a broad definition of the term 'institution'. Veblen (1919, p. 239) defined institutions very loosely and broadly as 'settled habits of thought common to the generality of men'. A famous and more exact definition is found in the essay reproduced below by the institutionalist Walton Hamilton (1932, p. 84):

> It connotes a way of thought or action of some prevalence and permanence, which is embedded in the habits of a group or the customs of a people. ... Institutions fix the confines of and impose form upon the activities of human beings.

Three points are worthy of immediate note. First, these extremely broad definitions of an institution are acceptable, but an adequately precise and widely acceptable taxonomy of different types of institution is wanting. The specific characteristics of one type – organizations – are discussed later in this introduction. It is also possible to distinguish between rules or norms on the one hand, and other institutions on the other. Rules or norms can be roughly defined as being more elemental and having a greater generality that other, more specific institutions. To use an analogy, nearly all living organisms are subject to the common rules of DNA coding and replication. Likewise, most capitalist economies have common elements of private property and contract law. Rules may thus be seen as being more general, elemental and constitutive than other institutions. Nevertheless, it is an important and as yet incomplete project to construct a more precise and reasonably comprehensive taxonomy of institutions.

Second, coming from the 'old' institutional school, both Veblen's and Hamilton's definitions of institution see common habits as a key feature. This conception of institutions as the embodiment of habituated group behaviour is a prominent feature of the 'old' institutionalism. In contrast, many 'new' institutional economists, for example Schotter (1981) and Sugden (1986), model institutions as the outcome of rational decision-making by interacting agents.

Third, the conception of an institution advanced here involves a recognition of its self-reinforcing qualities. This recognition is common to the 'new' and the 'old' institutionalism but the descriptions of the processes of institutional self-reinforcement are often different. This and the preceding matter of habit are now examined in turn and in more detail.

From Habits to Institutions

There are varied interpretations of the concept of habit. As William Waller notes in the essay reproduced below, the concept of habit has been forced into an unfavoured position in twentieth-century social science. By habit it is meant 'a more or less self-actuating disposition or tendency to engage in a previously adopted or acquired form of action' (Camic, 1986, p. 1044). Such a definition is compatible with the notion that not all thought involves the same level or degree of deliberation. It is also reasonable to assume that the human brain and nervous system have evolved a hierarchy of habitual procedures so as to cope with the vast amounts of complex information involved in any form of action.

Because thought is no longer seen to be at a single level, with a qualitative continuum from deliberative contemplation to the reflexes of the human nervous system, this concept of habit can undermine the Cartesian division between matter and mind. The anti-Cartesian attitude is a hallmark of the pragmatists philosophers Charles Sanders Peirce, William James and John Dewey, who provided the philosophical foundations for the 'old' institutionalism. As John Commons (1934, p. 150) put it, Peirce dissolved the antimonies of rationalism and empiricism seemingly at a stroke, making "Habit and Custom, instead of intellect and sensations, the foundation of all science."

This concept of habit does not necessarily involve a denial of human purposefulness or will. As John Dewey (1930, p. 42) put it:

> The essence of habit is an acquired predisposition to ways or modes of response, not to particular acts except as, under special conditions, these express a way of behaving. Habit means special sensitiveness or accessibility to certain classes of stimulii, standing predictions and aversions, rather than bare recurrence of specific acts. It means *will*.

The notion of habit that has been incorporated into mainstream economics is of a quite different nature. The preservation of the supreme assumption of rational choice involves the treatment of all habit as the expression of a fixed utility or preference function. Accordingly, founders of neoclassical economics such as Alfred Marshall (1890) and Philip Wicksteed (1910) insisted that habits must directly or indirectly emanate from preferences and choice. More recently, conceptions of habitual action have been developed where habits are governed by a meta preference function to which they eventually adjust through time (Becker, 1992). This rationalist and utilitarian approach still involves a Cartesian separation of matter from mind.

As suggested above, institutions involve congealed habits. Thorstein Veblen (1919, p. 241) wrote:

> institutions are an outgrowth of habit. The growth of culture is a cumulative sequence of habituation, and the ways and means of it are the habitual response of human nature to exigencies.

Habits may be distinguished from routines and institutions. Habits are personal, they relate to single individuals. In contrast, routines may involve a group; they are components of institutions. Thus an institution such as a firm may embody a particular routine, involving several persons, when faced with a given environmental stimulus. In enacting this routine it is, of course, likely that habits will also be involved.

Habits, routines and institutions have a stable and inert quality and tend to sustain and thus 'pass on' their characteristics through time, and from one institution to another. For example, the skills learned by a worker in a given firm become partially embedded in his or her habits. Thus these act as carriers of information, 'unteachable knowledge', and skills. Likewise, the structures and routines of the firm are durable institutions, and may be more difficult to alter than the skills of a single worker. In this respect habits and institutions have a quality analogous to the informational fidelity of the gene. Habits and routines thus preserve knowledge, particularly tacit knowledge in relation to skills, and act through time as their transmission belt.

The Self-Reinforcing Quality of Institutions

Those economists employing the assumptions of rational choice tend to see institutional self-reinforcement as emanating from the rational decisions of agents once institutions are in place. For example, once the convention of driving on the left of the road is established it is clearly rational for all drivers to follow the same rule. Accordingly, the emergent convention is reinforced and institutionalised by imitation.

In contrast, heterodox economists do not confine themselves to the assumption of rationality, partly because they do not take the goals or preference functions of individuals as given and unchanging. As well as the recognition of the rational payoff of following an established convention, there is also stress on the way in which institutions frame the perceptions of agents. The 'habits of thought' feature of institutions is given a cognitive dimension: the acquired conceptual frameworks are seen to reflect culturally-based social norms and rules. Institutions are regarded as imposing form and social coherence upon human activity partly through the continuing production and reproduction of habits of thought and action. This involves the creation and promulgation of conceptual schemata and learned signs and meanings. Institutions are seen as a crucial part of the cognitive processes through which sense-date is perceived and made meaningful by agents. Indeed, rationality itself is regarded as reliant upon institutional props (Hodgson, 1988).

A result of the framing or cognitive effects of institutions is to promote conformism. A key question here is whether conformism results simply from given preferences as a 'rational' strategy or whether institutional culture causes a shift in preference functions as well. It is clear that conformism can also be approached with a rational choice framework; in a world of uncertainty it can be seen to be 'rational' to imitate others and conform to the norm. Yet one effect of institutions may be to generate even stronger forces of emulation – to use Veblen's term – amongst agents. Herbert Simon's (1990) essay, reproduced here, on the evolution of altruism should be examined in this light.

The availability of common cognitive tools, as well as perhaps a congenital or learned disposition for individuals to conform with other members of the same group, work together to mould and harmonise individual goals and preferences. Hence it is arguable that significant preference shifts are involved. Importantly, the emphasis of the traditional economist on individuality and choice may obscure the degree to which conformism or emulation occur in modern economies. Clearly, such outcomes are an important part of the institutional self-reinforcing process.

The Evolution of Institutions

It is this durable quality of habits, routines and institutions that forms the basis of the development of the analogy with natural selection in institutional economics. Habits, routines and institutions are regarded as subject to processes of selection: some grow or multiply and others expire. This evolutionary analogy has been developed by a number of economic theorists (Hayek, 1988; Hodgson, 1993b; Nelson and Winter, 1982; Veblen, 1919).

Nevertheless, the use of the evolutionary analogy in evolutionary economics remains problematic and controversial. Although Veblen wanted to turn economics into an 'evolutionary science' by importing the Darwinian metaphor of natural selection, and Commons too found inspiration in biology, this line of theoretical development was virtually abandoned by subsequent institutional economists of the 'old' school. This neglect suggests a reason why the new wave of evolutionary economists of the 1980s adopted the 'Schumpeterian' label. Yet Schumpeter (1954, p. 789) himself had argued that in economics "no appeal to biology would be of the slightest use."

One of the problems with the Darwinian metaphor is that purposeful behaviour is either excluded or reduced to the functions of a programmed automata. It is argued by numerous social scientists, however, that purposeful or intentional behaviour cannot be incorporated in a deterministic view of the world. Institutionalists such as Veblen and Commons repeatedly emphasised the purposeful character of human behaviour and the place of teleology in social science. This issue has important implications and remains an open problem for evolutionary and institutional economics (Hodgson, 1993b).

Karl Marx argued that a distinction between the human architect and the bee was that the architect first constructed an edifice in his or her mind before it was constructed in the material world. Arguably, the use of the evolutionary analogy should not exclude a distinction between those institutions which emerge as the unintended consequence of individual actions, and those institutions which are designed. The Austrian economist Carl Menger (1981) described the former as 'organic' and the latter as 'pragmatic' institutions. This distinction is raised in regard to the works with Menger and Commons in an essay by Viktor Vanberg (1989). This comparison illuminates different uses and meanings of the term 'evolution' in this context.

Yet as Elias Khalil (1992) argues, the idea of a purely organic social institution may conflate organisation with spontaneity. Whether it was pre-designed or not, a key feature of any organization – in distinction from the spontaneous order of a nest of bees or of a slime-mould – is the incorporation of a principle of sovereignty and of a chain of command. Accordingly, the question can be raised as to whether a hard-and-fast distinction can be made between organic and pragmatic institutions.

Perhaps a more appropriate distinction should be drawn between institutions which function primarily through authority and command, described as organisations, and those which do not, such as language and table manners. But even here the distinction is problematic, notably in regard to the institution of the market. In addition to the laws of property and contract, some markets are clearly organised and regulated whereas others sustain themselves without much overall direction. The market is an institution and no institution is free of elements of compulsion and control. Yet some institutions, such as firms, typically involve a higher degree of authority and command, and others, such as markets, rely more on the undirected interactions of individuals according to prescribed rules.

The Informational Function of Institutions

All institutions have both constraining and enabling qualities. An important enabling function of institutional routines is to do with the information they provide for other agents. Both 'old' and 'new' institutionalists recognise the informational function of institutions. Recognition of this is fundamental to the analysis of all social and economic institutions. All organisations gather and process some amount of information on a day-to-day basis, and this may be available within or outside the institution. However, the informational function of institutions is much wider and deeper than this. Through their very existence, and the established, visible character of much of the associated behaviour, institutions actually create additional information as well.

Institutions establish and reproduce a set of rules and behavioural norms. These are fixed in part by habit, but also typically by tacit or legally supported social acceptance or conformity. These rules and norms are not necessarily inviolable, but the point is that they help agents to estimate the potential actions of others. One early and neglected statement in this regard is as follows:

> One individual can choose or plan intelligently in a group of any size only if all others act 'predictably' and if he predicts correctly. This means, *prima facie*, that the others do not choose rationally but mechanically follow an established and known pattern, or else that the first party has coercive power, through force or deception. (...) Without some procedure for co-ordination, any real activity on the part of an individual, any departure from past routine, must disappoint the expectations and upset the plans of others who count on him to act in a way predicted from his past behaviour. (Knight and Merriam, 1948, p. 60)

The critical point is that both routines and formal institutions, by establishing more or less fixed patterns of human action, actually supply information to other agents. Such inflexibilities or constraints suggest to the individual what other agents might do, and the individual can then act accordingly. Whereas if these rigidities or 'imperfections' did not exist the behaviour of others could change with every perturbation in the economic system, and such frequent adjustments to behaviour might be perceived as random or chaotic.

In other words, institutions and routines, other than acting simply as rigidities and constraints, enable decision and action by providing more-or-less reliable information regarding the likely actions of others. One consequence of this function of institutions is that in a highly complex world, and despite uncertainty, regular and predictable behaviour is possible. The informational function of institutions and routines leads to patterns of action, guided by the information that the institutions provide. This point is made in the essays by Geoffrey Newman (1976) and Lawrence Boland (1979) included here, as well as by Andrew Schotter (1981) in a game-theoretic framework and by Richard Langlois (1986, p. 237).

As a result, institutions, not simply despite but because of their rigidity, act as enablers for human action. It is not always recognised that institutions are not simply constraints. An exception is Commons (1934, p. 73), who clearly saw institutions as a liberating as well as a constraining force. The institution of language, for example, provides us with a limited choice of meaningful utterances, yet in doing this it enables us to communicate an immense variety of statements and feelings. Likewise, in an evolutionary process, both deviation and rigidity can be constructive. Evolution proceeds, not in a mechanical manner, of force against resistance, but through the combination of rigid and durable entities – genes or institutions – with unceasing selection and change.

To some extent, the dual function of institutions as both constraints and enablers is rendered problematic in the particular branch of the 'old' institutionalism that follows Clarence Ayres. Ayres was disposed to emphasise the constraining function of institutions to the exclusion of their role as enablers. Only a subset of institutions were regarded as positive or 'instrumental'. The classificatory distinction between 'ceremonial' and 'instrumental' institutions may obscure the dual quality of every institution. The reader may consider this issue in the light of the essay by Paul Dale Bush (1987) included here.

Prospects for Institutional Economics

There are many reasons for which the analysis of institutions is important. In the first place, all economies work through an institutional fabric. No economy can be institution-free. Even markets are institutions, as Giovanni Dosi (1988), in an essay reproduced here, and others have elaborated. This observation is particularly apposite in the context of the former Soviet economies. In a spectacular demonstration of the appropriateness of institutional economics, since 1989 the idea that complex institutions like markets emerge simply through the interactions of 'free' individuals has been totally confounded.

Second, as 'old' institutionalists such as Veblen insisted, individual behaviour is very much a matter of individual-institutional interaction. Each presupposes the other, each may be moulded by the other and each may alter the other. Arguably, as Anthony Giddens (1984) and others have proposed, this approach provides a means of transcending the old divide between methodological individualism and methodological holism.

Third, the analysis of historical change, including economic history, is very much the analysis of institutional emergence, development and breakdown. Only in the short-run is it justifiable to take institutions as given. Alan Garfinkel (1987, p. 206) writes:

> In a model of cooperations as entrainment global attractors model overall equilibria. Because social conventions (like the working day, driving on the right, feudalism, or speaking English) are essentially coordination equilibria, the topology of various attractors in a given system provides the kinematic foundation for theories of social change. We might say, with apologies to Marx, that all history is the history of phase transitions of coordination equilibria.

But in a modern context there are still more reasons why the study of institutions is important. As Alan Kirman (1989) and others have elaborated, severe difficulties have been discovered in the project to base the entire corpus of economic theory on the 'sound microfoundations' of the rational individual. As Philip Mirowski (1987, p. 1034n) argues, the institution is 'a socially constructed invariant', and institutions can be taken as the units and entities of analysis.

This contrasts with the idea of the individual as the irreducible unit of analysis in neoclassical economics, and applies to both microeconomics and macroeconomics. Accordingly, theories based on aggregates become plausible when based on corresponding social institutions. Money is a legitimate unit of account because money itself is an institutionally sanctioned medium; aggregate consumption functions should relate to a set of persons with strong institutional and cultural links; and so on. Again this contrasts with the approach based on reasoning from axioms based on the supposed universals of individual behaviour. The approach based on institutional specifics rather than ahistorical universals is characteristic of institutional economics, and has parallels in some of the economics of the Marxian and Post Keynesian schools.

This does not mean, of course, that institutions are regarded as immutable. Institutions themselves may change, and they have nothing like the degree of permanence of the gene. What is important is to stress the *relative* invariance and self-reinforcing character of institutions: to see socioeconomic development as marked by periods of institutional continuity punctuated by periods of crisis and more rapid development.

One promise of the revived institutional economics of the 'old' variety is that it may provide a means of overcoming the problem of individualistic reductionism which has bedevilled economics since the 1870s (Hodgson, 1993b). Since the 1960s the attempt to place macroeconomics on such 'sound microfoundations' has pointed to the dissolution of macroeconomics as a relatively autonomous sphere of enquiry. It remains to be seen whether the promise will be fulfilled, and whether the adoption of institutions as units of analysis can lead to the reinstatement of macroeconomic theory. Arguably, it was the work of Mitchell and his followers in the United States in the 1930s on national income accounting that provided the aggregative statistical basis for the Keynesian revolution. In addition to the provision of an alternative approach to the analysis of microeconomic units, a revived institutional economics may have something to contribute to the development of macroeconomics as well.

Note

1. The author is grateful to Robert Sugden and Warren Samuels for helpful suggestions in the compilation of this volume.

References

Ayres, Clarence E. (1944), *The Theory of Economic Progress*, 1st edn., Chapel Hill, NC, University of North Carolina Press.

Becker, Gary S. (1992), 'Habits, Addictions and Traditions', *Kyklos*, **45**, Fasc. 3, 327–46.

Boland, Lawrence A. (1979), 'Knowledge and the Role of Institutions in Economic Theory', *Journal of Economic Issues*, **13** (4), December, 957–72. (Reproduced in this collection.)

Camic, Charles (1986), 'The Matter of Habit', *American Journal of Sociology*, **91** (5), 1039–87.

Commons, John R. (1934), *Institutional Economics – Its Place in Political Economy*, New York, Macmillan. (Reprinted 1990 with a new introduction by M. Rutherford: New Brunswick, Transaction Publishers.)

Dewey, John (1930), *Human Nature and Conduct: An Introduction to Social Psychology*, New York, Random House.

Dosi, Giovanni (1988), 'Institutions and Markets in a Dynamic World', *The Manchester School*, **56** (2), June, 119–46. (Reproduced in this collection.)

Garfinkel, Alan (1987), 'The Slime Mold *Dictosteliam* as a Model of Self-Organization in Social Systems', in F. Eugene Yates (ed.), *Self-Organizing Systems: The Emergence of Order*, New York, Plenum Press, 181–212.

Giddens, Anthony (1984), *The Constitution of Society: Outline of the Theory of Structuration*, Cambridge, Polity Press.

Hayek, Friedrich A. (1982), *Law, Legislation and Liberty*, 3-volume combined edn., London, Routledge and Kegan Paul.

Hayek, Friedrich A. (1988), *The Fatal Conceit: The Errors of Socialism, Collected Works of F.A. Hayek*, Vol. 1, London, Routledge.

Hodgson, Geoffrey M. (1988), *Economics and Institutions: A Manifesto for a Modern Institutional Economics*, Cambridge, Polity Press.

Hodgson, Geoffrey M. (1993a), 'Institutional Economics: Surveying the "Old" and the "New"', *Metroeconomica*, **44** (1), February, 1–28. (Reproduced in this collection.)

Hodgson, Geoffrey M. (1993b), *Economics and Evolution: Bringing Life Back into Economics*, Cambridge, Polity Press.

Hodgson, Geoffrey M., Samuels, Warren J. and Tool, Marc R. (eds) (1993), *The Elgar Companion to Institutional and Evolutionary Economics*, Aldershot, Edward Elgar. (Forthcoming.)

Kapp, K. William (1976), 'The Nature and Significance of Institutional Economics', *Kyklos*, **29**, 209–32. (Reprinted in Samuels, 1988, Vol. 1.)

Kirman, Alan (1989), 'The Intrinsic Limits of Modern Economic Theory: The Emperor Has No Clothes', *Economic Journal (Conference Papers)*, **99**, 126–39.

Khalil, Elias L. (1992), 'Hayek's Spontaneous Order and Varela's Autopoiesis: A Comment', *Human Systems Management*, **11** (2), 49–114.

Knight, Frank H. and Merriam, Thornton W. (1948), *The Economic Order and Religion*, London, Kegan Paul, Trench Trubner.

Langlois, Richard N. (ed.) (1986), *Economics as a Process: Essays in the New Institutional Economics*, Cambridge, Cambridge University Press.

Marshall, Alfred (1890), *The Principles of Economics*, 1st edn., London, Macmillan.

Menger, Carl (1981), *Principles of Economics*, edited by J. Dingwall and translated by B.F. Hoselitz from the German edition of 1871, New York, New York University Press.

Mirowski, Philip (1987), 'The Philosophical Bases of Institutional Economics', *Journal of Economic Issues*, **21** (3), September, 1001–38.

Mitchell, Wesley C. (1937), *The Backward Art of Spending Money and Other Essays*, New York, McGraw-Hill.

Nelson, Richard R. and Winter, Sidney G. (1982), *An Evolutionary Theory of Economic Change*, Cambridge, MA, Harvard University Press.

Newman, Geoffrey (1976), 'An Institutional Perspective on Information', *International Social Science Journal*, **28**, 466–92. (Reproduced in this collection.)

Olson, Mancur, Jr. (1965), *The Logic of Collective Action*, Cambridge, MA, Harvard University Press.

Olson, Mancur, Jr. (1982), *The Rise and Decline of Nations*, New Haven, Yale University Press.

Samuels, Warren J. (ed.) (1988), *Institutional Economics*, 3 vols, Aldershot, Edward Elgar.

Schelling, Thomas (1960), *The Strategy of Conflict*, Cambridge, MA, Harvard University Press.

Schotter, Andrew (1981), *The Economic Theory of Social Institutions*, Cambridge, Cambridge University Press.

Schumpeter, Joseph A. (1954), *History of Economic Analysis*, New York, Oxford University Press.

Simon, Herbert A. (1990), 'A Mechanism for Social Selection and Successful Altruism', *Science*, **250**, 21 December, 1665–8. (Reproduced in this collection.)

Sugden, Robert (1986), *The Economics of Rights, Co-operation and Welfare*, Oxford, Basil Blackwell.

Vanberg, Viktor J. (1989), 'Carl Menger's Evolutionary and John R. Commons' Collective Action Approach to Institutions: A Comparison', *Review of Political Economy*, **1** (3), November, 334–60. (Reproduced in this collection.)

Veblen, Thorstein B. (1919), *The Place of Science in Modern Civilisation and Other Essays*, New York, Heubsch. (Reprinted 1990 with a new introduction by W.J. Samuels: New Brunswick, Transaction Publishing.)

Wicksteed, Philip H. (1910), *The Commonsense of Political Economy*, London, Routledge.

Williamson, Oliver E. (1975), *Markets and Hierarchies: Analysis and Anti-Trust Implications: A Study in the Economics of Internal Organization*, New York, Free Press.

Williamson, Oliver E. (1985), *The Economic Institutions of Capitalism: Firms, Markets, Relational Contracting*, London, Macmillan.

Witt, Ulrich (1993), *Evolutionary Economics*, Aldershot, Edward Elgar.

Part I
Individuals, Institutions and Institutionalism

[1]

Encyclopaedia of the Social Sciences

INSTITUTION is a verbal symbol which for want of a better describes a cluster of social usages. It connotes a way of thought or action of some prevalence and permanence, which is embedded in the habits of a group or the customs of a people. In ordinary speech it is another word for procedure, convention or arrangement; in the language of books it is the singular of which the mores or the folkways are the plural. Institutions fix the confines of and impose form upon the activities of human beings. The world of use and wont, to which imperfectly we accommodate our lives, is a tangled and unbroken web of institutions.

The range of institutions is as wide as the interests of mankind. Any simple thing we observe —a coin, a time table, a canceled check, a baseball score, a phonograph record—has little significance in itself; the meaning it imparts comes from the ideas, values and habits established about it. Any informal body of usage—the common law, athletics, the higher learning, literary criticism, the moral code—is an institution in that it lends sanctions, imposes tabus and lords it over some human concern. Any formal organization—the government, the church, the university, the corporation, the trade union—imposes commands, assesses penalties and exercises authority over its members. Arrangements as diverse as the money economy, classical education, the chain store, fundamentalism and democracy are institutions. They may be rigid or flexible in their structures, exacting or lenient in their demands; but alike they constitute standards of conformity from which an individual may depart only at his peril. About every urge of mankind an institution grows up; the expression of every taste and capacity is crowded into an institutional mold.

Our culture is a synthesis—or at least an aggregation—of institutions, each of which has its own domain and its distinctive office. The function of each is to set a pattern of behavior and to fix a zone of tolerance for an activity or a complement of activities. Etiquette decrees the rituals which must be observed in all polite intercourse. Education provides the civilizing exposures through which the potential capacities of individuals are developed into the abilities for performance, appreciation and enjoyment which are personality. Marriage gives propriety to the sex union, bestows regularity upon procreation, establishes the structure of the family and effects such a mediation as may be between personal ambition and social stability. A number of institutions may combine and compete to impress character upon and give direction to the mass of human endeavor. The state claims primary obedience and imposes a crude order upon the doings of mankind; the law by punishing offenses and settling disputes determines the outmost limits of acceptable actions; morality with neater distinctions and more meticulous standards distinguishes respectable from unconventional conduct. The community is made up of such overlapping provinces of social government. It is the institution in its role of organizer which makes of this a social and not a monadic world.

It is impossible to discover for such an organic complex of usages as an institution a legitimate origin. Its nucleus may lie in an accidental, an arbitrary or a conscious action. A man—savage or civilized—strikes a spark from flint, upturns the sod, makes an image of mud, brews a concoction, mumbles a rigmarole, decides a quarrel or helps himself to what he may require. The act is repeated, then multiplied; ideas, formulae, sanctions and habits from the impinging culture get attached; and gradually there develops a ritual of fire, a hoe and spade agronomy, a ceremonial for appeasing the gods, a cult of healing, a spell for casting out devils, a due process of law or a sound business policy. Even if it is deliberately established an institution has neither a definite beginning nor an uncompromised identity. A religious creed or a legislative statute is compounded of beliefs and ideas which bear the mark of age and of wear; a paper charter and a document engrossed upon parchment are not insulated against the novelties in usage which attend the going corporation and the living constitution. It is impossible even in the most rudimentary culture to find folkways which are simple and direct answers to social necessities. In all societies, however forward or backward, the roots of the most elementary of arrangements—barter, burial, worship, the dietary, the work life, the sex union—run far back into the unknown past and embody the knowledge and ignorance, the hopes and fears, of a people.

In fact as an aspect of a continuous social process an institution has no origin apart from its development. It emerges from the impact of novel circumstances upon ancient custom; it is transformed into a different group of usages by cultural change. In institutional growth the usual may give way to the unusual so gradually as to be almost unnoticed. At any moment the familiar seems the obvious; the unfamiliar appears but a little revealed—an implication in a

Institution

convention which is itself taken for granted, a potentiality slowly quickening into life. So it is that the corporation is still a person, the work of the machine is manufacture, the labor contract concerns masters and servants and industrial accidents are personal wrongs. It often happens that new arrangements spring up under the cloak of an established organization. Thus the empire of the Caesars emerged behind the forms of the republic, the holy Catholic church is nominally the episcopal see of Rome and the British Commonwealth does its business in the name of His Majesty. In like manner in the domain of ideas the novelty in doctrine usually appears as a gloss upon the ancient text; systems of theology are commentaries upon the words of Scripture; Coke and Cooley set down their own understanding of the law upon the authority of Littleton and Blackstone. Thus too so intangible a thing as a social theory or a public policy may emerge from the practical commitments of the moment. A mere expediency, such as the abolition of the corn laws, is abstracted from cause and occasion and becomes a generalized policy of free trade; or a comprehensive scheme of railway regulation, such as obtains in the United States, appears as a by-product of the empirical elimination of specific abuses. In the course of events the fact arrives before the word and new wine must be put up in old bottles. Novelties win a tacit acceptance before their strangeness is noticed and compel before their actuality is appreciated. In institutional life current realities are usually to be found behind ancient forms.

As an institution develops within a culture it responds to changes in prevailing sense and reason. A history of the interpretation of Aristotle or St. Paul or Kant at various periods indicates how easily a document lends itself to successive systems of ideas. The public regulation of business has consistently even if belatedly reflected the prevailing winds of doctrine upon the relation of the state to industry. The pages of the law reports reveal the ingenuity with which, in spite of professions that the law remains the same, old rules and standards are remade to serve changing notions of social necessity. An institution which has enjoyed long life has managed to make itself at home in many systems of thought. The classic example is the Christian Gospel. The simple story of the man Jesus presently became a body of Pauline philosophy; the Middle Ages converted it into an intricate theological system and the rationalization of a powerful ecclesiastical empire; at the individualistic touch of the Reformation it became a doctrine of the personal relationship between man and his maker; it is today patching up a truce with Darwinism, the scientific attitude, relativity and even religious skepticism. In this continuous process of the adaptation of usage and arrangement to intellectual environment an active role is assumed by that body of ideas taken for granted which is called common sense. Because it determines the climate of opinion within which all others must live it is the dominant institution in a society.

In an even broader way an institution is accommodated to the folkways of a culture. As circumstances impel and changing ideas permit, a usage in high esteem, like piracy, may fall from grace; while another under tabu, such as birth control, may first win tolerance and in time general acceptance. As one social system passes into another and the manner of living and the values of life are transformed, one institution gives way to another better adapted to the times. It required a number of changes in use and wont to convert the ordeal by combat into the trial by law; the prestige of the family tie, of blood vengeance, of the magical ritual and of might made right had to decline and a consciousness of the waste and injustice which attended legalized conflict had to become prevalent. An institution that survives, such as matrimony, responds surely even if stubbornly to cultural change. While the basis of Christian marriage is no more than the primitive custom of monogamy, the rigid lines of the institution bear the marks of the mediaeval order. It gave support to a caste system resting upon landed property, elevated the social values of family above the individual values of love, was blessed with the ascetic ideal of otherworldliness and became a sacrament. Companionate marriage is emerging from a different world of fact, appreciation, habit and belief. It reduces to usage an attempt to escape the rigors of matrimony without resort to casual relationships; it reflects the condition of an urban society where blood is no longer blue, life is impersonal, children are a luxury and women must earn their own livings. In a culture which develops slowly enough to allow a graceful accommodation folkways may be drawn together into rich and intricate institutional patterns. In the Middle Ages the usages of the church—the trinity, the creed, the litany, the ecclesiastical empire—were all fused into a single conventional whole, to which unity was given by the idea of the death of the god as a vicarious atonement. In the late eighteenth century politics, law, economics, ethics and theology in separate domains alike attempted to superimpose a symmetrical system of mechanical principles upon the mass of human behavior; the common element was an analogue borrowed from physical science. In the social process the life of an institution depends upon its capacity for adaptation. But always amid the whirl of change elements of disorder are present; and long before a harmony is achieved between unlike conventions disintegration has set in.

Nor is an institution introduced from an alien society immune to this process of development. The act of borrowing merely gives the opportunity for its transformation. The nucleus is liberated from its cultural matrix and takes on the character of the usages among which it is set down. In their native habitat the books of the Old Testament were the literature of a people; in the strange world of the mediaeval schoolmen they became a collection of verses inviting dialectical exposition. In England "the higher law" was invoked to justify a popular revolution against an irresponsible monarchy; in America it has become the sanction for a judicial review of legislative acts. In appropriating the machine process Russia stripped away the enveloping business arrangements and made of it an instrument to serve a national social economy. The act of transplantation may at first retard but eventually is likely to promote growth. It introduces into a culture an unknown usage but allows it to emerge as an indigenous institution.

Its very flexibility makes an institution a creature of social stress and strain. In a stable or slowly changing society it fits rather neatly into the cultural pattern; amid the disorder which change brings its office may be compromised by the inflexibility of its structure. As necessity changes, tradition and inertia may stand in the way of the performance of new duties. A group of usages, for all the new demands upon it, may never quite escape slavery to its past. The shadow of ordeal by combat still hangs heavy over trial by law; the jury decides the contest, the judge is the umpire, the procedures are the rules of the game, the witnesses are clansmen armed with oaths and the attorneys are the champions; an appeal court orders a new trial not primarily for want of justice but because of error in the conduct of the ordeal. The United States Supreme Court has come to be the official interpreter of the constitution; yet by tradition its function is judicial, and it is only as an issue is germane to the disposition of a case that it can declare the meaning of the higher law. Almost every institution—from the superfluous buttons on the sleeve of a coat to the ceremonial electors in a presidential contest—bears the vestigial mark of a usage which is gone.

But its elements of stability may be powerless to prevent the conversion of an institution to a service for which it was never intended. Its existence and repute give it value; it may adventitiously or by design assume a new character and play a new role in the social order. Equity, once an informal method of doing justice, now possesses all the appurtenances of a system of law. The principle of "no liability without fault" was once the basis of an individualistic law of torts; in our times the rules of recovery are being socialized, as, for example, in workmen's compensation, by a mere extension of "fault" to acts involving no personal blame. An institution may even fall into the hands of the enemy and be used to defeat its reputed purpose. Thus a community of ascetics develops into a wealthy monastic establishment; a theory of social contract invented as a justification of monarchy is converted into a sanction for its overthrow; a party dedicated to personal freedom becomes the champion of vested wealth; and a philosophy contrived to liberate thought remains to enslave it. As time and chance present their problems, men meet them with expediencies as best they can; but those who contrive rules and formulae cannot control the uses to which they are put. The proneness of an institution, like a lost sheep, to go astray, has been caught in the sentence: "Saint Francis of Assisi set out to bring people to sweetness and light, and left in his wake a plague of gray friars." The folkways are marked by a disposition of event to belie intent.

In the course of time the function of an institution may be compromised by or perhaps even be lost in its establishment. The spirit may become the letter, and the vision may be lost in a ritual of conformity. In time a way of intellectual inquiry may become a mere keeping of the faith; a nice propriety in social relations may decay into a code of etiquette; or a morality intended to point the way toward the good life may come to impose the duty of doing right. Thus ceremonial replaces purposive action and claims a vicarious obedience. The existence of an informal institution gets buttressed about by prevailing opinion and by personal interest. In legislative "deliberation" statesmen cherish their stock in trade of time honored argument and resent the

Institution

appearance of unfamiliar issues; scholars of re-pute defend the established ways of inquiry and the accepted verities; and social lights conserving the older proprieties against feminism "entrench themselves behind their tea-cups and defend their frontiers to the last calling-card." The persons immediately concerned have their stakes in arrangements as they are and do not wish to have personal position, comfort of mind or social prestige disturbed. As it crystallizes into reputable usages an institution creates in its defense vested interest, vested habit and vested ideas and claims allegiance in its own right.

If an institution becomes formal, an even greater hazard to its integrity is to be found in its organization and its personnel. A need for order finds expression in a government or the demand for justice in a legal system or the desire for worship in a church; and various groups become interested in its structure and offices, its procedures and emoluments, its ceremonials and consolations. A host of officials great and small comes into being, who are as solicitous about the maintenance of the establishment to which they are committed. They possess preferences and prejudices, are not immune to considerations of prestige and place and are able to rationalize their own interests. As the scheme of arrangements grows rigid, "the good of the nation"—or the church or the party or the lodge or whatever it is—tends to become dominant. The lines of activity may be frozen into rigidity and ecclesiasticism, legalism, constitutionalism and ritualism remain as fetishes to be served. An institution when once accepted represents the answer to a social problem. In the maze of advantage, accommodation, sense and reason which grows up about it lies a barrier to the consideration of alternatives. Its successor for better or for worse is likely to prevail only through revolution or by stealth.

In its ideal likeness an institution usually creates its apology. As long as it remains vital, men accommodate their actions to its detailed arrangements with little bother about its inherent nature or cosmic purpose. As it begins to give way or is seriously challenged, compelling arguments for its existence are set forth. The picture-as-it-is-painted is likely to be rather a work of art than a representation of fact, a product rather of rationalization than of reason; and, however adventitious its growth, disorderly its structure or confused its function, the lines of its defense lack nothing of trimness and purpose. The feudal regime was an empirical sort of an affair; men of iron lorded it over underlings as they could, yielded to their betters as they were compelled and maintained such law and order as the times allowed; but with its passing its sprawling arrangements and befuddled functions were turned into office and estate ordained of God. In the days of the Tudors kings were kings without any dialectical to-do about it; the overneat statement of the theory of divine right had to await the decadent monarchy of the Stuarts. The tangled thing called capitalism was never created by design or cut to a blue print; but now that it is here, contemporary schoolmen have intellectualized it into a purposive and self-regulating instrument of general welfare. If it is to be replaced by a "functional society," the new order will emerge blunderingly enough; but acquisition of a clean cut structure and clearly defined purpose will have to wait upon its rationalizers. An assumption of uniformity underlies all apologies; invariably they impose simple, abstract names, such as monarchy, democracy, competition and socialism, upon a mass of divergent arrangements.

In this endowment with neatness and purpose an institution is fitted out with the sanctions and trappings of ancient usage. Republican government harks back to Greece and Rome; the "liberties" for which seventeenth century Englishmen fought were the ancient rights of man. Magna Carta, a feudal document, was remade to serve the cause of Parliament against king; a primitive folk government was discovered in the dim twilight of the German forests to give to English democracy a fountainhead which was neither French nor American; and "the spirit of '76" grew up long after the event to serve the patriotism of another century. In the courts it is a poor rule which cannot find a good reason in former decisions and fit itself out with an ancient lineage. But law does not invoke the sanction of precedent more often than other institutions; the openness of its written records merely makes more evident the essential process. A succession of usages stretching from Aristotle to Calhoun has been justified as expressions of the natural order. Even—or above all—in the church the prevailing dogma is set down as interpretations of the creed of the apostles; and Christian marriage "was instituted by God in the time of man's innocency." As tradition leaves its impress upon fact, fact helps to remake tradition. The thing that is is the thing that always was.

It is only as stability gives way to change that the lines of an institution stand out in sharp re-

88 Encyclopaedia of the Social Sciences

lief. So long as a people is able to do as its fathers did it manifests little curiosity about the arrangements under which it lives and works; the folk of the South Sea Islands can administer justice after their ways, but they can neither give answers to hypothetical cases nor tell in abstract terms what they do. So long as the procedure of a group or a school is unquestioned it is little aware of the conventions and values which give character even to outstanding achievement: Scott had little conscious appreciation of the distinctive qualities of the English novel; Jowett could never have put in terms the peculiar features of Oxford education; and Kant might not have been able to place his own philosophy in time and opinion. But the break of usage from usage within a culture and the resulting maladjustment lead to a discovery of the detail which makes up an institution. A number of crises were required to reveal the customs which are the British constitution; it took a Civil War to make clear the nature of the union between the American states. The appearance of social unrest was essential to an appreciation of the difference between competition and laissez faire and between industry and business. An aesthetic revolt marked by a riding into almost all the winds that blow was requisite to a realization of the distinctive modes and values in classical music and in Gothic architecture and to an appreciation of the molds imposed by acceptable form upon creative effort. For such casual glimpses of the intricacies of social institutions as men are permitted to see they are indebted to the stress and strain of transition.

It follows almost of course that institutional development drives a fault line between current fact and prevailing opinion. Men see with their ideas as well as with their eyes and crowd the novel life about them into outmoded concepts. They meet events with the wisdom they already possess, and that wisdom belongs to the past and is a product of a by-gone experience. As new institutions gradually emerge from the old, men persist in dealing with the unfamiliar as if it were the familiar. A national legislature by the enactment of antitrust laws tries to superimpose the competitive pattern upon the turbulent forces of a rising industrialism; a trade union uses the traditional device of a strike to advance wages in an industry in which the unorganized plants can easily supply the total output; a group of elder statesmen approaches the problems of war debts and reparations with the old formula of protection versus free trade. At a time when a depression bears witness to economic disorder the institution of business is discussed in the outgrown vocabulary of private property, liberty of contract, equality of opportunity and free enterprise; and rugged American individualism is invoked as a way of order for a system which has somehow become an uncontrolled and unacknowledged collectivism. Even the Protestants as often as not turn belief into denial; and heresy shackled to an inherited ideology is merely a reverse orthodoxy. In the flux of modern life the various usages which with their conflicting values converge upon the individual create difficult problems that demand judgment; and in the course of very human events it is the fate alike of individual, group and society to have to meet emerging fact with obsolescing idea.

Thus an institution like the living thing it is has a tangled identity. It cannot be shown in perspective or revealed in detail by the logical method of inclusion and exclusion. It holds within its actuality the vestiges of design and accident, the stuff of idea and custom, from many ages, societies, civilizations and climates of opinion. In any important group of institutions, such as marriage, property, the market or the law, there are to be discovered as inseparable aspects of an organic whole notions, procedures, sanctions and values hailing from cultural points far apart. Each holds within its being elements in idea and in form drawn from the contemporary era of relativity, the rational universe of the eighteenth century, the mediaeval world of absolutes and verities and the folkways of some dim far off era. An institution is an aspect of all that it has met, a potential part of all that it will encounter. It holds many unknown possibilities which a suitable occasion may kindle into life. It may continue to hold sanctions which we think have departed; it may already have come to possess compulsions of which we are still unmindful. The discovery of its meaning demands an inquiry into its life history; but even the genetic method will tell much less than we should like to know of how a thing which cannot for long abide came to be.

Moreover the way of knowledge is itself an institution. The physical world, natural resources and human nature may be elementary things; but we can learn about them only in terms of and to the extent allowed by our prevailing methods of inquiry. The little we understand of the universe is a function of the size of the telescope, the sensitiveness of the photographic plate and the bundle of intellectual

Institution

usages called astronomy. Our national resources are a product of technology, and their catalogues at different times reflect the contemporary states of the industrial arts. It was the steam engine and the machine which made of coal and iron potential wealth; it was not until Faraday and Edison had done their work that electricity became potential energy. The little we understand or think we understand about human nature is an institutional product. The inquiries called physiology, anatomy and neurology—each of them a bundle of intellectual usages—reveal no more than the raw material of personal character; the stuff has ripened into individuality within the matrix of the prevailing folkways. Man and woman are so much creatures of custom and belief that the word innate is most treacherously applied to masculine and feminine traits. In various societies the stages upon which peoples must play their parts are set so differently by social heritage that we can as yet speak with little certainty about racial characteristics. The physical world and the human nature we know are aspects of the prevailing state of culture. In matter and in the chromosome may lie limitless possibilities; the actualities which appear are creatures of social institutions.

Among the ways of knowing is "the institutional approach." Institutes as the ordained principles of a realm of learning or of life have long existed; they are known to theology, law, education and all subjects ruled over by dialectic. About the turn of the last century a genetic study of the folkways began to win academic respectability. It could make little headway so long as the Newtonian concept was dominant; inquirers went in search of laws and uniformities, explanations were set down in mechanical formulae and the end of the quest was an articulate and symmetrical body of truths. The institutional method had to wait until the idea of development was incorporated into academic thought and the mind of the inquirer became resigned to the inconsistency which attends growth. The analogy with a biological organism had to be renounced and a basis in ideology had to be discovered before it could become a fruitful method of study in economics, history, philosophy, law and politics. The practical impulse toward its use came with a change in public opinion; so long as laissez faire dominated our minds, dialectic served well enough to turn out explanatory apologies for the existing social arrangements; when we began to demand that order and direction be imposed upon an unruly

society, a genetic study of how its constituent usages had grown up into an empirical organization seemed proper. An inquiry into institutions may supply the analytical knowledge essential to a program of social control or it may do no more than set adventures for idle curiosity. In either event the study of institutions rests itself upon an institution.

Accordingly an institution is an imperfect agent of order and of purpose in a developing culture. Intent and chance alike share in its creation; it imposes its pattern of conduct upon the activities of men and its compulsion upon the course of unanticipated events. Its identity through the impact of idea upon circumstance and the rebound of circumstance upon idea is forever being remade. It performs in the social economy a none too clearly defined office—a performance compromised by the maintenance of its own existence, by the interests of its personnel, by the diversion to alien purpose which the adventitious march of time brings. It may like any creation of man be taken into bondage by the power it was designed to control. It is a folkway, always new yet ever old, directive and responsive, a spur to and a check upon change, a creature of means and a master of ends. It is in social organization an instrument, a challenge and a hazard; in its wake come order and disorder, fulfilment, aimlessness and frustration. The arrangements of community life alike set the stage for and take up the shock of what man does and what he leaves undone. Institutions and human actions, complements and antitheses, are forever remaking each other in the endless drama of the social process.

WALTON H. HAMILTON

See: CULTURE; SOCIAL PROCESS; CHANGE, SOCIAL; HUMAN NATURE; CUSTOM; FOLKWAYS; FASHION; ASSOCIATION; COLLECTIVE BEHAVIOR; FUNCTIONALISM; ECONOMICS, section on INSTITUTIONAL ECONOMICS.

Consult: Lowie, R. H., *Primitive Society* (New York 1920); Sumner, W. G., *Folkways* (Boston 1906); Sumner, W. G., and Keller, A. G., *Science of Society*, 4 vols. (New Haven 1927–28); Veblen, Thorstein, *The Theory of the Leisure Class: an Economic Study of Institutions* (new ed. New York 1918), *The Theory of Business Enterprise* (New York 1904), and *Absentee Ownership and Business Enterprise in Recent Times* (New York 1923); Cooley, C. H., *Human Nature and the Social Order* (rev. ed. New York 1922), and *Social Process* (New York 1918), especially pt. vi; MacIver, R. M., *Community* (3rd ed. London 1924) bk. ii, ch. iv; Hobhouse, L. T., *Social Development* (London 1924) ch. xi; Cole, G. D. H., *Social Theory* (London 1920) p. 41–44 and ch. xiii; Wallas, Graham, *Our Social Heritage* (New Haven 1921); Dewey, John, *Human Nature and Conduct* (New York 1922).

[2]

JeI *JOURNAL OF ECONOMIC ISSUES*
Vol. XXII No. 1 March 1988

The Concept of Habit in Economic Analysis

William T. Waller, Jr.

The concept of habit has played only a very small role in the social sciences since the 1930s. During the 1930s the concept was relegated to psychology; prior to then it was extensively used in sociology.[1] The concept has never had widespread use in orthodox economics, for reasons we will explore later, but it is found frequently in the early literature of institutional economics, particularly in the works of Thorstein Veblen, John Dewey, and Charles Peirce.[2] The term *habit* seldom occurs in contemporary neoinstitutional writings, but the concept is intimately entwined with the idea of ceremonial aspects of behavior. This article will explore the importance of the concept of habit to both orthodox and institutional economics and suggest how it might be fruitfully employed in future institutional research.

Peirce, Veblen, and Dewey on Habit

The contemporary relevance of the concept of habit for institutionalists lies in its close relationship with the Veblenian dichotomy, particularly, though not exclusively, ceremonial aspects of behavior. This is largely the result of Veblen's use of the concept in *The Theory of the Leisure Class,* published in 1899. The absence of citations in this work of Veblen's leaves the sources of some of his ideas ambiguous. To en-

---

The author is Assistant Professor of Economics, Hobart and William Smith Colleges. *This article was presented at the annual meeting of the Association for Institutional Thought and the Western Social Science Association, 25 April 1987.*

sure this is not a problem with the concept of habit, we will first explore its use by Peirce.

Peirce used the concept extensively in his work; indeed, the concept of habit was central to the formulation of Peirce's pragmatic philosophy. Peirce's first discussion of the concept of habit occurred in his article "The Fixation of Belief" [1877], in which he argued that habitual behavior was a way of addressing familiar circumstances in an effective way.[3] He expanded on this notion in "How to Make Our Ideas Clear" [1878], in which he argued that intellectual activity was directed at removing the discomfort associated with doubt. The process of removing doubt was the establishment of belief. To Peirce, belief is something about which we are aware; it appeases the irritation of doubt, and it "involves establishment in our nature of a rule of action, or, say for short, a *habit."* [4]

Later Peirce assigned even greater importance to habits, arguing that it was the very basis of intelligence. "Intellectual power is nothing but facility in taking habits and in following them in cases essentially analogous to, but in non-essentials widely remote from, the normal cases of connections of feelings under which those habits were formed."[5] Peirce went on to speculate about the physiological basis of habits, but argued that physiological explanations are unlikely to generate anything but probabilistic explanations of habitual behavior. This is of interest only because the other eminent pragmatic philosopher, William James, was one of the strongest proponents of the psychological/-biological definition of habit.[6]

Expanding this notion of habits in his 1892 Lowell Lectures on the History of Science, Peirce argued that the way human thought grows is "by the formation of habits, by the violent breaking up of habits, and by the action of innumerable fortuitous variations of ideas combined with differences in the fecundity of different variations."[7] In Peirce's thinking on habits we see the beginnings of a problem—an apparent contradiction—that confounds institutionalist use of the concept of habit. Specifically, habits are inherently past-oriented (activities that most institutionalists would treat as predominantly ceremonial in character), yet habits conserve on intellectual effort and increase efficiency by allowing individuals to concentrate their efforts on new or unique circumstances (which would seem to be an instrumental function). I will return to this issue later.

Veblen, in contrast to Peirce, focused on the social dimensions of habit, rather than on its individual manifestations. Veblen seemed content to resolve the dispute with regard to the physiological/social character of habits by assigning habit formation, the content of habitual behavior, and the breakdown of habitual behavior to the social realm, leaving the differing aptitudes of individuals with regard to acquiring and giving up of habits to the biological side of the phenomenon. In *The Theory of the Leisure Class,* Veblen discussed the social dimension of habits by treating consumption behavior as the result of cultural norms and status relations within society, rather than as the result of rational individual choice. He literally described conspicuous consumption as habitual expenditures, reflecting his view that, "A standard of living is of the nature of habit."[8]

Veblen was very concerned with the strength and stability, or resistance to change, of different habits. He thought that the length of time an individual had a habit, as well as the role a habit played in that person's life, affected the strength of the habit. He wrote, "In general, the longer the habituation, the more unbroken the habit and the more it nearly coincides with previous habitual forms of the life process, the more persistently will the given habit assert itself."[9] The strength of the habit was increased if it was intimately tied to the life process or "the life history of the race."

The issue of very old societal habits was of particular interest to Veblen as the source of the survival of archaic traits. He noted the relative ease with which very old social habits were temporarily overthrown in the face of problems, only to reassert themselves as soon as the problems were addressed. Thus very old social habits seemed to Veblen a strong and important source of cultural conservatism.

> These habits of life are of too pervading a character to be ascribed to the influence of a late or brief discipline. The ease with which they are temporarily overborne by the special exigencies of recent and modern life argues that these habits are the surviving effects of a discipline of extremely ancient date, from the teachings of which men have frequently been constrained to depart in detail under the altered circumstances of a later time; and the almost ubiquitous fashion in which they assert themselves whenever the pressure of special exigencies is relieved, argues that the process by which the traits were fixed and incorporated into the spiritual makeup of the type must have lasted for a relatively very long time and without serious intermission.[10]

Veblen thought that habits would only change permanently as a response to environmental pressure such as a change in population or the industrial arts. Change might occur as long as some members of the community were willing and able to change their habits of life. He noted that this type of circumstance would be uncomfortable for some since it necessitated the relinquishing of the "right and beautiful habits of life."[11]

116   William T. Waller, Jr.

Veblen's discussion of the role of habits in the conservation of archaic traits and his use of the concept to analyze social and individual
consumption seems to be in the tradition of the broader definitions of
habit as employed by Emile Durkheim, Max Weber, and Peirce.[12] Veblen stressed the difficulty of changing habitual behavior, consistent with
treating habits as ceremonial aspects of behavior, but he seems optimis-
tic that some individuals will be of a bent to treat the need to change
as an exhilarating intellectual challenge. In this he seems to have been
strongly influenced by Peirce. Again we see the tension between treating
habitual behavior as largely ceremonial in character, while acknowledging its role in increasing the efficiency of most mundane human behavior, and freeing the individual to address new or unique
circumstances.

John Dewey made the most extensive use of the concept of habit of
any of the social thinkers discussed so far. He devoted his entire book,
Human Nature and Conduct, to a discussion of the role of habits in
human behavior. More than any other social theorist we have discussed, Dewey was acutely aware of the dual character of habits. Like
Peirce, Dewey saw habitual behavior as necessary to all intellectual activity. He argued that thought was dependent on sensory perceptions
carefully analyzed and that proper interpretation was dependent on
training, skill, and habit.[13] But he was also concerned about the limiting
capacity of other habits. Dewey's optimism with regard to the positive
role of habits is similar to that of Peirce and Veblen. He wrote,

> Habits are conditions of intellectual efficiency. They operate in two ways
> upon intellect. Obviously, they restrict its reach, they fix its bound-
> aries . . . Outside the scope of habits, thought works gropingly, fumbling
> in confused uncertainty; and yet habit made complete in routine shuts in
> thought so effectually that it is no longer needed or possible.[14]

He later reemphasized the positive intellectual function of habits.

> Habit is however more than a restriction of thought. Habits become neg-
> ative limits because they are first positive agencies. The more numerous
> our habits the wider the field of possible observation and foretelling. The
> more flexible they are, the more refined is perception in its discrimination
> and the more delicate the presentation evoked by imagination.[15]

Still, Dewey was very concerned with the negative impact of habits,
specifically the capacity of habits to resist change and the ease with
which conservative customs were surreptitiously transmitted to the
young. He described these negative aspects in terms that immediately
bring to mind what institutionalists call ceremonial aspects of behav-

ior. He referred to institutions, meaning social structures, as "embodied habits." He discussed their stability arguing that,

> Any one with knowledge of the stability and force of habit will hesitate to propose or prophesy rapid and sweeping social changes. A social revolution may effect abrupt and deep alterations in external customs. . . . Political and legal institutions may be altered, even abolished; but the bulk of popular thought which has been shaped to their pattern persists. . . . Habits of thought outlive modifications in habits of overt action.[16]

Dewey thought that the conservative character of habits of thought were particularly important in transmitting customs. He argued that the plasticity and docility of the young made them particularly open to instruction; that adults would be unable to resist the urge to teach their current habits. "Education becomes the art of taking advantage of the helplessness of the young; the forming of habits becomes a guarantee for the maintenance of hedges of custom."[17]

Dewey made an effort to clarify the source of the dual character of habits.

> Even liberal thinkers have treated habit as essentially, . . . conservative. In fact only in a society dominated by modes of belief and admiration fixed by past custom is habit any more conservative than it is progressive. It all depends upon its quality. Habit is an ability, an art, formed through past experience. But whether an ability is limited to repetition of past acts adopted to past conditions or is available for new emergencies depends wholly upon what kind of habit exists. The tendency to think that only "bad" habits are diserviceable and that bad habits are conventionally enumerable, conduces to make all habits more or less bad. For what makes a habit bad is enslavement to old ruts. . . . Habits deprived of thought and thought which is futile are two sides of the same fact.[18]

Dewey's distinction between bad habits—those in the same old rut—and good habits—those helpful in problem solving—is not very satisfying. But a clue to a more satisfying resolution may lie in his discussion of habits and "practical men." Practical men are those who pursue their own advantage. In order to do this effectively they encourage routine in others, under the guise of sustaining an ideal. They encourage loyalty, law and order, devotion, obedience, and the maintenance of the status quo generally while "denounc[ing] as subversive anarchy signs of independent thought, of thinking for themselves, on the part of others lest such thought disturb the conditions by which they profit."[19] This aspect of Dewey's discussion suggests to me that the key to using the concept of habit effectively is differentiating between good and bad habits in a more satisfying way.[20] This possibility will be explored in the next section of this article.

This long discussion of the concept of habit by Peirce, Veblen, and Dewey serves two essential purposes. The first is to illustrate that the concept has been an important part of the tradition of institutional thought. The second is more complex; while habit has been treated as largely ceremonial in character, there has always been an awareness of its important role in increasing the efficiency and effectiveness of human activity. This apparent straddling of the two aspects of the Veblenian dichotomy seems to have made institutionalists hesitant to use this important concept. This ambivalence is illustrated by the following passage from a recent article by Marc Tool.

> The working rules, the contractual agreements, the patterns of marketing, the customary consumption patterns (conspicuous and otherwise) are and must be habit ridden. Habits are essential, of course; they embody prior learning and judgments and thus economize on time, energy, and decision making; but they are conservative. Institutions are constituted of habits. ... Economies operate on expectations grounded in habits, predictions based on experience, and promises that can often be legally enforced.[21]

If the concept is inherently problematic, then leaving it in abeyance would be reasonable. But if this ambiguity could be cleared up, the concept could be profitably employed in institutional analysis.

Habit Reconsidered

In order to reconsider the concept of habit, it is necessary to acknowledge the existence of nonreflective behavior. Habitual behavior is automatic in its performance. The individual involved does not have to make a conscious decision to perform the activity regardless of whether the activity is physical or mental. This rather obvious point is in fact important for two reasons. After the 1930s many sociologists decided that nonreflective behavior was no longer part of the subject matter of their discipline. But they never denied the existence of this type of behavior.[22] This is not the case in economics. Neoclassical microeconomic theory is based on the assumption that individuals are rational maximizing agents whose behavior is characterized by rational— meaning reflective—choice. This assumption is crucial to the internal logic and integrity of all variants of the orthodox tradition in economics; the acknowledgement of habitual behavior is a fatal blow to this assumption. The implications of this point will be discussed in the next section.

In order for the concept of habit to make a contribution to contemporary social science, the use of the broader meaning of habit, in the tradition described in this article, is essential. This means that we must again think of habits as social, as well as individual, phenomena. This will create some overlap between the concept of habit and other concepts such as custom or ritual, but this can be easily clarified by limiting habit to mechanically repeated, nonreflective behavior within these broader categories.

It seems that much of the confusion that led to both the loss of the concept of habit to the social sciences and the ambiguity about the character of the concept, progressive or conservative, was the result of concern over both the creation of habits and the social results of habits. Exploration of the biological and social processes that contribute to the process of creating and transmitting habitual behaviors will provide plenty of interesting research questions for all the relevant disciplines. Of much more interest to economists are the social consequences of habitual behavior. The importance of the consequences is not affected by whether the habitual behavior is physical behavior or habits of thought. What is significant is the impact of the habitual behavior on the continuity of the life process.

The key to resolving the dual character of habits lies in analyzing the entire habitual behavior as a whole in its context, rather than examining each independent component part of the behavior pattern. The Veblenian dichotomy can be used in such an analysis. Habits fall into two general types or categories, though no particular habit is purely of either type. These categories, which are aspects of habitual behavior, are simply special cases of the general categories of ceremonial and instrumental aspects of behavior of the Veblenian dichotomy. The ceremonial aspect of habitual behavior can be described as ritualized habit and the instrumental aspect can be described as routine.

Routine is easily understood. We all have habitual behaviors that allow us to carry out essential tasks very easily. In fact we often work at developing these habits in order to increase the scope of activities we can accomplish with little thought or effort. These range from very simple activities like locking doors in the evening to such complex behaviors as typing a manuscript. What characterizes a habit that is predominantly routine in nature, rather than ritualized, is that the purpose of the routine can be explained on technologically warranted grounds. A routine serves an end in view that contributes to the continuity of the life process. This contribution to the maintenance of life should be verifiable, or at least consistent with the best knowledge available. In any case if a habit is routine, if the circumstances for which the habit developed disappear, the habit should not persist. For example, the habits developed for handwriting manuscripts should disappear when an author begins using a word processor.

Referring to the ceremonial aspects of habits as ritualized habit is not intended to confuse ritualized habit with the existing body of scholarship on rituals, but instead to stress some similarities between these types of habits and rituals. Ritualized habits are ordained from authority and repeated mechanically. They are similar to William Graham Sumner's description of ritual: "Ritual is the perfect form of drill and of regulated habit that comes from drill."[23] Like all ceremonial aspects of behavior, ritualized habits mimic the technological process of establishing their authenticity. Therefore, ritualized habits will be justified by myths that attest to the efficacy of the habits and the dire consequences if any attempt is made to alter or eliminate them. It may be the case that ritualized habits, if social in nature, are closely related to the larger category of rites and ritual. It is not as clear where an individual's ritualized habits would fall.

A simple example will illuminate these differences and possibly shed some light on how habits are transformed from routine to ritualized. Families develop routines for mornings and evenings to ensure that everyone is prepared for the day's activities and gets ample rest. Evening routines, particularly in families with small children, are often highly structured, complex routines to get the children into bed and to sleep. When the routine is followed without variation over time, what Sumner described as a "perfect drill," children may refuse to go to sleep if there is any minor change in the routine.

The example above refers to an individual or family habit. These same phenomena occur with social habits. Many social habits are part of complex rituals, such as religious services or commencement exercises, but there are simpler ones as well. Driving an automobile is an extremely complex set of behaviors, most of which necessarily become habitual so that the driver can pay attention to traffic conditions. This complex set of procedures remains routine; we have all stopped at an intersection and waited for a traffic signal to change even when there was no other automobile in the area.

It is useful to analyze the content of habitual behavior, since this behavior is difficult to change because of its nonreflective character. This resistance to change results in limitations on how policy can be implemented when it requires changes in existing habitual behaviors. In economics, three areas where changes in regulation require the alteration of habitual behaviors are: the regulation of potentially hazardous consumer goods, such as cyclamates, saccharine, and red dye no. 2; occupational safety regulations, when new safeguards and procedures are required on familiar machinery; and changes in the tax code that drastically change recordkeeping requirements or change the deductibility of some popular behavior. In each of the examples cited above the public has strongly reacted to the policy actions, not because they disagree with the goal of the policy, but because of the disruption in habitual behavior patterns required by the policy.

It is certainly reasonable to argue that institutional economists have been concerned with habitual behavior all along, but that, like sociologists, they have not used the term explicitly. The purpose of the suggested dichotomization of the concept of habit intended to clear up any ambiguity with the term "habit," so it can be used explicitly. The reason for doing so is not intuitively obvious. As was mentioned earlier, habitual behavior creates serious problems for orthodox economics. Institutional economics is able to explain a broad range of human activity that is beyond the scope of orthodox economics. The response to this by orthodox economists has been to ignore most of these phenomena, or when they take note of them, to define them as noneconomic. Habitual behavior cannot be ignored or denied by orthodox economists, nor can it be accommodated by their paradigm; habitual behavior is a glaring anomaly.

Habit and Orthodox Economics

The problems created for orthodox economics by habitual behavior all stem from the fact that it is nonreflective, which is to say, nonrational. It is not irrational; it is simply behavior patterns that occur in the absence of conscious decision or choice. Habits are not random in character, so they may not be ignored on the grounds that they cancel rational, reflective behavior as the cornerstone of their theory. The importance of this assumption is obvious in the theory of the consumer, but less so in other areas of orthodox economics. To illustrate just how important this concept is I will briefly explore the importance of the rationality assumption, and consequently the importance of denying the existence of habitual behavior, in three different types of orthodox theory.

General equilibrium theory is central to neoclassical microeconomic theorizing. Institutionalists have long recognized that marginal productivity theory was a justification for the distribution of income, and not an explanation of production. General equilibrium theory serves this same function on a larger scale. This theoretical construct is a moral justification of the market system. Its basic tenets are that through the market mechanism, general equilibrium exists and is attainable, general equilibrium is stable, and general equilibrium is pareto optimal. This state of general equilibrium satisfies all of the marginal conditions

122   William T. Waller, Jr.

that neoclassical economists are so enamored with, and which result in
everyone receiving just compensation for their efforts and expenditures.[24] If one wished to substitute another term for general equilibrium, its major tenets could be equally well expressed by the following
formulation—heaven exists and is attainable, heaven is eternal, heaven
is good—with very little change in meaning. This entire moral justification of the market mechanism rests on a few crucial assumptions,
one of which is that economic behavior is reflective, meaning non-
habitual, in character.

If habits exist in economic activity and are social in character this
entire structure is unsustainable, both as an internally consistent theory
and as a moral justification for the market mechanism. This problem
is noted by some theorists. An interesting article entitled "Satiation and
Habit Persistence (or the Dieter's Dilemma)," in a recent issue of the
Journal of Economic Theory, discusses cyclical consumption behavior.
The author remarks in a footnote that,

> Of course, one could dismiss such behavior as irrational and outside the
> scope of economic theory. But this leads to serious questions about the
> relevance of economic theory. It is not at all clear that all cyclical behavior
> can be dismissed as irrational.[25]

The author does not discuss habitual behavior in this article.

A similar awareness can be inferred by the generally cool reception
the work on behavioral theories of the firm by Henry Simon and Oliver
E. Williamson has received from neoclassical microeconomic theorists.[26] Their alteration of the rationality concept embodied in the term
"bounded rationality," carries the same threat to general equilibrium
theory as habit. As a result these ideas have had minimal impact on
the theory of the firm, despite their rather tame character.[27] To understand this resistance to changing the rationality assumption, consider
the solution proposed by contestable market theory to avoid the problems created by increasing returns to scale and noncompetitive markets
for general equilibrium theory. To get around the mathematical problem of a nonzero excess demand function, you simply add the assumption of perfectly costless, frictionless, and instantaneous entry and exit.
This creates the threat of "hit and run entry" and will cause noncompetitive firms to behave as if they were competitive. This sort of legerde-
main would seem to bring the robustness of general equilibrium theory
into serious question and would explain the reluctance of neoclassical
microeconomic theorists to confront nonreflective behavior.

Austrian economics does not accept the notion of static general equilibrium, and its concept of rationality is different from that of neoclas-

sical theory, but habitual behavior is equally problematic for this variant of orthodoxy. Praxeology explicitly treats all human action as the result of individuals pursuing their self interests. This is how rationality is defined in this tradition, an explicitly tautological definition. Human action is a result of pursuit of self interest, because that is the nature of human action; any action you take must be in your best interest or you would not have taken it. Ludwig Von Mises dealt with the possibility of habitual behavior in two ways. Von Mises relegated most nonreflective behavior, which he thought to be biological in character, to psychology.[28] He argued that the remaining, nonbiological, habitual behavior was reflective in character.

> Most of a man's daily behavior is simple routine. He performs certain acts without paying special attention to them. He does many things because he was trained in his childhood to do them, because other people behave in the same way, and because it is customary in his environment. He acquires habits, he develops automatic reactions. But he indulges in these habits only because he welcomes their effects. As soon as he discovers that the pursuit of the habitual way may hinder the attainment of ends considered as more desirable, he changes his attitude. . . . He will watch himself permanently in order not to hurt himself by indulging unthinkingly in his traditional routine and his automatic reactions. The fact that an action is in the regular course of affairs performed spontaneously, as it were, does not mean that it is not due to a conscious volition and to a deliberate choice.[29]

This is simply to assert that nonreflective behavior is reflective. Clearly Von Mises means something different by his use of the term "automatic reaction" than others who have had occasion to use it. But, since praxeological facts cannot be disproved by observation of empirical reality, this proposition is apodistically true (for Austrian economists).

The problem created by habitual behavior for Austrian economics is, of course, similar to the problems of neoclassical microeconomic theory. Both conceive of economic activity as the result of conscious, deliberative choice on the part of individuals. All their interesting results are predicated on this perspective of human behavior. The possibility that human behavior is characterized to any significant degree by social, nonreflective behavior falsifies many of their results and trivializes their research program. Thus these problems will occur with any characterization of human behavior that is logically dependent on atomistic individuals and requires that individual behavior solely consist of conscious choices, which all orthodox schools of thought do, with the possible exception of post Keynesian macroeconomic thought.

Rational expectations theory, albeit unintentionally, is much more

124   William T. Waller, Jr.

dependent on the rationality assumption than most of the rest of orthodoxy. While many critics of rational expectations have noted the
information requirements of the hypothesis, the problem this creates
can be avoided by carefully stating the hypothesis in probabilistic
terms, as was done in its original formulation by John Muth.[30] A much
more serious problem results if one considers that many decisions
made by economic agents are in fact not conscious decisions but habitual in character. This problem is more serious for rational expectations
because, even if the outcome of the hypothesis is that, on the average,
the impact of human activity is to correctly anticipate and offset the
impact of some policy, it presumes at least three identifiable, necessarily reflective, actions by *every* economic agent. Each economic agent
must consciously reflect on impending changes in the environment or
policy and choose the most likely outcome. Then each agent must consciously reflect on the likely consequences of the change. And finally
each agent must choose a course of action to pursue his/her best interests under the new circumstances, presumably compensating for risk
and uncertainty. It cannot be the case that the results contemplated by
these theorists would be forthcoming if any of these decisions were
affected by habitual behavior. The viability of the rational expectations
hypothesis is based on the assumption that errors in judgment will be
randomly distributed around the average, and that habitual behavior is
nonrandom.

Conclusion

The purpose of this article has been to explore the concept of habit
in economic thought. The concept has never been completely absent
from institutional analysis and I have suggested a refinement of the
concept that might enhance its use. Moreover, differentiating between
routine and ritualized habits, and stressing the social aspects of habitual
behavior may provide a useful additional tool for institutional policy
analysis, especially with regard to policy implementation. Finally, the
special problems the concept of habit creates for orthodox analysis provides an additional incentive to pursue the concept further, since it
brings into question the very core assumptions of orthodox economics.

Notes

1. An excellent discussion of the concept of habit in sociology is "The Matter
   of Habit," by Charles Camic, *American Journal of Sociology* 91 (March
   1986); 1039–87.

2. It should be noted that some classical economists, particularly Malthus, used the concept of habit. I would like to thank my colleague, Geoffrey Gilbert, for pointing this out to me.

3. Charles S. Peirce, "The Fixation of Belief," *Values in a Universe of Chance: Selected Writings of Charles S. Peirce*, ed. Philip P. Wiener (Stanford: Stanford University Press, 1958), pp. 91–112.

4. Peirce, "How to Make Our Ideas Clear," *Values in a Universe of Chance: Selected Writings of Charles S. Peirce*, pp. 113–36, at p. 121.

5. Peirce, "The Architecture of Theories" [1891], *Values in a Universe of Chance: Selected Writings of Charles S. Peirce*, pp. 142–59, at p. 152.

6. James defined habit as "a sequence of behaviors, usually simple, . . . that have become virtually automatic." The significance of James's definition, which appears in *The Principles of Psychology* vol. 1 (New York: Dover, 1950 [1890]) p. 107, is discussed in Camic, "The Matter of Habit," p. 1045.

7. Peirce, "Conclusion of the History of Science Lectures," *Values in a Universe of Chance: Selected Writings of Charles S. Peirce*, pp. 257–60, at p. 257.

8. Thorstein B. Veblen, *The Theory of the Leisure Class* (New York: Modern Library, 1934 [1899]), p. 106.

9. Ibid., pp. 107–8.

10. Ibid., p. 221.

11. Ibid., p. 195.

12. For a discussion of the concept of habit in the works of Durkheim and Weber see Camic, "The Matter of Habit," pp. 1050–66.

13. John Dewey, *Human Nature and Conduct* (New York: Modern Library, 1930 [1922]), p. 31.

14. Ibid., p. 172.

15. Ibid., p. 175–76.

16. Ibid., p. 108.

17. Ibid., p. 64.

18. Ibid., pp. 66–67.

19. Ibid., p. 68.

20. Dewey expresses concerns very similar to those of Weber. See Weber's *Economy and Society*, (Berkeley: University of California Press, 1922), p. 321.

21. Marc R. Tool, *Essays in Social Value Theory: A Neoinstitutionalist Contribution* (Armonk, N.Y.: M.E. Sharpe, 1986), p. 21.

22. See Camic, "The Matter of Habit," pp. 1039–50.

23. William Graham Sumner, *Folkways* (New York: Mentor, 1960 [1906]), p. 67.

24. The classic expositions of these theorems are: Gerald Debreu, *Theory of Value: An Axiomatic Analysis of General Equilibrium*, Cowles Foundation Monograph no. 17 (New Haven: Yale University Press, 1959), pp. 37 and 50; Kenneth Arrow, *Social Choice and Individual Values*, 2d ed., Cowles Foundation Monograph no. 12 (New Haven: Yale University Press, 1963), pp. 2–3 and 19–20. Arrow does discuss the importance of the rationality assumption and seems aware that it is problematic. A more accessible presentation, structured in a way similar to my characterization, is: J. Quirk and R. Saposnik, *Introduction to General Equilibrium Theory and Welfare Economics* (New York: McGraw-Hill, 1969).

25. Robert S. Bordley, "Satiation and Habit Persistence (or the Dieter's Di-

lemma)," *Journal of Economic Theory* 38 (Fall 1986): 178–84. See note 1 on page 178.

26. See Herbert A. Simon, "Theories of Decision-Making in Economics and Behavioral Science," *American Economic Review* 49 (June 1959): 253–83, and Oliver E. Williamson, *Markets and Hierarchies* (New York: The Free Press, 1975). See also Fritz Machlup, "Theories of the Firm: Marginalist, Behavioralist, Managerial," *American Economic Review* 57 (March 1967): 1–33.

27. In this regard see William M. Dugger, "The Transaction Cost Analysis of Oliver E. Williamson: A New Synthesis?" *Journal of Economic Issues* 17 (March 1983): 95–114.

28. Ludwig Von Mises, *Human Action: A Treatise on Human Action,* (New Haven: Yale University Press, 1949), pp. 11–13.

29. Von Mises, *Human Action,* pp. 46–47.

30. John F. Muth, "Rational Expectations and the Theory of Price Movements," *Econometrica* 29 (July 1961): 315–34.

[3]

Carl Menger's evolutionary and John R. Commons' collective action approach to institutions: a comparison

Viktor Vanberg *George Mason University*

This essay examines the relation between Carl Menger's and John R. Commons' approaches to institutional analysis. It draws attention to certain aspects of their respective approaches which are of systematic relevance to the ongoing debate on the direction into which an adequate economic theory of institutions ought to be developed. It is argued that – contrary to a common perception – Menger's and Commons' concepts of institutions represent *compatible* and *complementary* rather than conflicting, alternative theoretical perspectives. It is suggested that the explanatory power of an economics of institutions can be enriched by incorporating both perspectives; Commons' collective action perspective as well as Menger's evolutionary perspective.

Law, language, the state, money, markets, all these social structures . . . are to no small extent the unintended result of social development. The prices of goods, interest rates, ground rents, wages, and a thousand other phenomena of social life in general and of economy in particular exhibit the same peculiarity. Also, understanding of them . . . must be analogous to the understanding of unintentionally created social institutions. . . . For they, too, as a rule are not the result of socially teleological causes, but the unintended result of innumerable efforts of economic subjects pursuing *individual* interests (Carl Menger, 1985: 147, 158).

Collective action, as well as individual action, has always been there; but from Smith to the Twentieth Century it has been excluded or ignored, except as attacks on trade unions or as postscripts on ethics or public policy. The problem now is not to create a different kind of economics – 'institutional' economics – divorced from preceding schools, but how to give to collective action, in all its varieties, its due place throughout economic theory (John R. Commons, 1934: 5).

I Introduction

New institutional economics has become a widely adopted name for a set of interrelated approaches in modern economics which aim at systematically extending economic analysis beyond its conventional scope of application to the study of *institutional* phenomena. In discussions on its intellectual heritage the new institutional economics is commonly contrasted to the

'old' US institutionalist school – in fact, this is the rationale for calling it
new (Furubotn and Richter, 1984; Hutchison, 1984; Langlois, 1986; 1988;
Rutherford, 1989). The major difference between the two 'institutionalisms' is generally seen in the fact that the US institutionalist school
developed, theoretically and methodologically, in *opposition* to the
neoclassical tradition in economics, while the new institutionalism emerges
from *within* this tradition. The latter qualifies as *unorthodox* – compared
to neoclassical mainstream – not in the sense of claiming different
theoretical foundations but rather in the sense of reviving the concerns for
institutional issues that were central to classical *political* economy but have
been largely neglected by neoclassical orthodoxy. As far as potential
connecting links between the new institutional economics and its classical,
eighteenth-century roots are identified, reference is notably made to Carl
Menger and his approach to institutional analysis.

This view is, for instance, articulated by Richard Langlois (1986: 2, 5).
He argues that 'modern "institutionalism" reflects less the ideas of the
early Institutionalists than it does those of their *opponents*', and he suggests
that 'Menger has perhaps more claim to be the patron saint of the new
institutional economics than has any of the original institutionalists.' In a
similar vein A. Schotter (1981: 3) talks about potential precursors of the
new economics of institutions. He specifically contrasts 'two distinct interpretations of the rise of social institutions in economics,' the one being what
he calls 'the "collectivist" explanation' of John Commons, the other being
'the "organic" theory' of Carl Menger. Schotter stresses that his own
conception 'is very close to Menger's'.

To contrast in such manner old and new institutionalism and to associate
the latter with the Mengerian approach to institutional analysis is certainly
appropriate in various regards and useful for certain purposes.[1] It is,
however, equally certain that in doing so one simplifies what, looked at
more closely, is a much more complex issue. The issue is more complex
because, as has been repeatedly noted, neither the new nor the old institutionalisms can really be claimed to represent homogeneous and well-
integrated bodies of thought, but rather comprise a number of more or less
diverse and heterogeneous conceptions. In particular John Commons has
more than once been singled out as somebody whose work not only is
characteristically different in certain respects from that of other major
representatives of US institutionalism like Thorstein Veblen, but in certain
respects comes strikingly close to concepts and ideas which figure prominently in the new institutional economics. Oliver Williamson, for instance,
whose 'transaction cost economics' is a major branch of the new institutionalism, points to Commons as a counterexample to the view that US institutionalists cannot be considered antecedents of modern institutionalist

---

[1] I have, in fact, argued along the same lines in Vanberg, 1983.

336 *Evolutionary and collective action approaches*

economics (Williamson 1984: 187). He explicitly states that the emphasis of his own approach '. . . bears a similarity, which is sometimes quite close, to John R. Commons' study of institutional economics' (1975: 3).[2] In an article on 'John R. Commons's foundations for policy analysis' (1976), Vincent Ostrom has drawn attention to the affinities between Commons' approach and such approaches to a new institutional economics like public choice theory or law and economics. And, in an instructive appraisal of 'J.R. Commons's institutional economics', M. Rutherford (1983: 735) points to differences between Commons and other institutionalists and to similarities 'with the neo-classical approach to institutions' which run counter to the more standard view of the relations between old and new institutionalism.

The present paper is intended to examine more closely the relation between Menger's and Commons' approaches to institutional analysis. My purpose, though, is not so much to contribute to the debate about the intellectual roots of the new institutionalism; nor do I intend to provide a comparative survey of Menger's and Commons' work that could in any sense be claimed to be comprehensive. My purpose is the more limited one of drawing attention to certain aspects of their respective approaches to institutional analysis, aspects which, in my view, are not only relevant for our understanding of both authors' work, but are also of systematic relevance for the ongoing debate on the direction into which an adequate economic theory of institutions ought to be developed. More specifically, and counter to views like the one expressed by A. Schotter, I want to argue that Menger's and Commons' concepts of institutions represent *compatible* and *complementary* rather than conflicting, alternative theoretical perspectives. Accordingly, my conclusion will be that an analytically fruitful and explanatorily powerful *economics of institutions* ought to incorporate both perspectives.

II Carl Menger's individualistic-evolutionist approach

As F.A. Hayck has repeatedly pointed out, Carl Menger has to be credited for having systematically restated – about one century later – the 'general theory of law, morals, money, and the market' which was the great contribution of what Hayek (1978: 265n) refers to as the 'Mandeville-Hume-Smith-Ferguson' tradition.[3]

Central to Menger's approach is his well-known distinction between two

---

[2] See also Williamson (1975: 254; 1985: 3 and 5). It should be mentioned, though, that Williamson's explicit reference to Commons goes hardly beyond these general acknowledgments, crediting Commons for regarding '. . . the transaction . . . as the basic unit of analysis' (1985: 3).

[3] See also Hayek (1973: 22): 'And in the great survey of 1883 of the methods of the social sciences by the founder of the Austrian school of Economics, Carl Menger, the central

ways in which institutions may come into existence. Some are, according to
Menger (1985: 133), '. . . the result of a *common will* directed toward their
establishment (agreement, positive legislation, etc.), while others are the
unintended result of human efforts aimed at attaining essentially *individual*
goals.' The first are, in Menger's terminology, institutions of *pragmatic*
origin, and the second institutions of *organic* origin. Whether an existing
institution belongs in the first or in the second category (or perhaps
combines aspects of both kinds) is, of course, as Menger is well aware, a
question of fact. Accordingly, whether with regard to a particular existing
institution a *pragmatic* or an *organic* explanation is the appropriate one,
depends on the actual history of this institution.

    For Menger it is an obvious fact, scarely in need of being explicitly stated,
that the institutional environment in advanced communities is to a large
extent of pragmatic origin and therefore appropriately to be interpreted in a
pragmatic manner (1985: 225). And he clearly acknowledges that 'for the
understanding of social phenomena in their entirety the *pragmatic*
interpretation is, in any case, just as indispensable as the 'organic' (1985:
135). He expresses the conviction, though, that providing an explanation
for institutions which are the intended result of positive legislation or deliberate agreement, etc. does not lead 'to special difficulties' and 'does not
challenge the sagacity of the scholar unduly' (1985: 223). He does not
bother, therefore, to discuss any further the nature of this mode of explanation but concentrates his attention entirely on what he calls the 'organic
view of social phenomena' (1985: 148). It is, according to Menger (1985:
146), the explanation of social institutions '. . . which to a high degree serve
the welfare of society . . . and yet are not the result of communal social
activity' that poses 'a noteworthy, perhaps the most noteworthy, problem
of the social sciences'. In other words, for Menger (1985: 146) the most
challenging question for the social scientist to answer is, 'how can it be that
institutions which serve the common welfare and are extremely significant
for its development come into being without a *common will* directed toward
establishing them?'

    Though this issue is not explicitly addressed by Menger, his discussion
clearly implies that the question of how institutions originate – 'organically' or 'pragmatically' – and the question of whether they 'serve the
common welfare' or not, are two *separate* questions to which any

position for all social sciences of the problem of the spontaneous formation of institutions
and its genetic character was most fully restated on the continent.' As W.N. Butos (1985:
26n) rightly points out, it is ironic and difficult to understand why Menger (1985: 172)
considered his own approach to the study of institutions to be in opposition to Adam
Smith's thought whom he blames for having a '. . . defective understanding of the unintentionally created institutions and their significance for economy'. Elsewhere (Vanberg, 1975:
80ff) I have discussed this aspect and Menger's place within the Mandeville-Hume-Smith-
Ferguson tradition in more detail.

338   *Evolutionary and collective action approaches*

combination of answers is, in principle, possible. Deliberately created institutions may or may not 'advance the welfare of society', and the same is true for unintentionally grown institutions. The question of their social 'functionality' has, for both of them, to be assessed separately from the question of their origin.[4]

Explaining the origin of unintentionally created social institutions is, as Menger argues, an enterprise fully analogous to explaining the formation of market prices, interest rates, and the like. Both types of phenomena are the 'unintended result of innumerable efforts of economic subjects pursuing *individual* interests' (1985: 158), and both are to be explained '. . . by reducing them to their elements, to the *individual* factors of their causation, and by investigating the laws by which [they] . . . are built up from these elements' (159). It is in this sense that Menger (1985: 159) concludes: 'The methods for the exact understanding of the origin of the "organically" created social structures and those for the solution of the main problems of exact economics are by nature identical.'

It is important to distinguish two aspects of Menger's approach which in discussions on his 'compositive method' are not always sufficiently separated, namely its *methodological individualism* and the fact that it represents what is now often called an *invisible-hand explanation*.[5] Certainly, the two are closely related, but they are by no means identical. The choice between methodological individualism and some potential alternative (whether it is called 'methodological collectivism' or otherwise) is a matter of choice among mutually exclusive theoretical paradigms.[6] The choice between an invisible-hand explanation and, for instance, what Menger calls a pragmatic explanation is, by contrast, a choice not among mutually exclusive theoretical orientations but among explanatory schemes that apply to different kinds of phenomena.[7]

The difference between methodological individualism and invisible-hand explanation has to be kept in mind when claims are made concerning the potential role of Menger's compositive method as a general model for social

---

[4] This simple truth has, admittedly, not always found sufficient explicit recognition within the Smith-Menger-Hayek tradition. On this issue: J.M. Buchanan, 1977.

[5] Both aspects are, for instance, implied in Hayek's (1978: 276) description of Menger's compositive method: 'The consistent use of the intelligible conduct of individuals as the building stones from which to construct models of complex market structures is of course the essence of the method that Menger himself described as 'atomistic' (or occasionally, in manuscript notes, as 'compositive') and that later came to be known as methodological individualism.'

[6] I am well aware of the fact that the concept of 'methodological individualism' has been defined in varying ways. The present context is, however, not the appropriate place to enter the debate on this concept. I have done so in some detail in Vanberg, 1975.

[7] For an excellent discussion of the concept of an "invisible-hand explanation" see E. Ullmann-Margalit, 1978. – Elsewhere (Vanberg, 1984) I have discussed in some detail the scope and limits of an invisible-hand explanation of the emergence and the effects of social rules or norms.

theoretical explanations. The claims that can be made for Menger's specific invisible-hand approach are, necessarily, different and more limited than the claims that can be made for his methodological individualism, a fact that Menger was certainly well aware of as his remarks on the relation between the organic and the pragmatic approach to social institutions clearly indicate.

III Methodological individualism and invisible-hand explanation

In his discussion of the nature of an invisible-hand explanation (or, as he calls it, an organic explanation) Menger takes great care to emphasize that the essential part of this kind of explanation consists in the theoretical reconstruction of the process by which the phenomenon that is to be explained is generated. It is not very illuminating, he argues, merely to state 'that institutions are unintended creations of the human mind', if one does not show '*how* they came about' (1985: 149).[8] What is necessary in order to really provide an explanation is to give an account of the process by which an institution is brought about 'as the unintended result of individual efforts . . . in pursuit of individual interests' (1985: 158).

The general characteristics of an organic or invisible-hand explanation are pragmatically exemplified in Menger's well-known explanation of the origin of money (Menger, 1981: 260f; 1984: 13ff; 1985: 151ff; G.P. O'Driscoll, 1986). It is not an attempt to account for the particular historical record of a specific case, that is, of a concrete historical example of some institution. It is, rather, an attempt to provide some general theoretical understanding of the kind of process by which, in principle, the kind of institution that is to be explained could have emerged under conditions that can plausibly be assumed to have existed. This type of explanation – it corresponds to what Hayek (1967: 22ff; 1973: 24) calls 'pattern predictions' or 'explanations of the principle' and to the Scottish moral philosophers' notion of 'conjectural history'[9] – is not only our principal means to understand the emergence of institutions which are *de facto*, in Menger's terminology, 'of organic origin'; it may also contribute to our understanding of institutions which *de facto* have been deliberately

---

[8] Menger (1985: 223f): 'If the theory of the "organic" origin of law is to be more than an empty phrase . . . [it] is necessary to examine the course of the process by which law appears without positive legislation.'

[9] F.A. Hayek (1967, 75): '[T]he aim of such "conjectural history" is not to account for all particular attributes which a unique event possesses, but only for those which under conditions which may be repeated can be produced again in the same combination. Conjectural history in this sense is the reconstruction of a hypothetical kind of process which . . . would have produced phenomena of the kind we observe.' See also the chapter 'The individualist and "compositive" method of the social sciences' in Hayek (1952: 61–76), where Hayek mentions in a footnote (67: note 4) that he '. . . borrowed the term *compositive* from a manuscript note of Carl Menger'.

340   *Evolutionary and collective action approaches*

created by illuminating the forces that could have generated the respective
kind of institution even in the absence of any deliberate design.

More specifically, an invisible-hand explanation as exemplified by
Menger's evolutionary theory of money, proceeds in the following steps:

> Step 1): An 'original situation' is described in which the institution (i.e., the
> behavioural pattern)[10] that is to be explained does not exist (In Menger's
> money example: a pure-barter economy in which no common medium of
> exchange is used).
> Step 2): The ordinary behaviour is described that, under the stated
> conditions, individuals will typically exhibit in pursuit of their own interest (in
> Menger's example, the effort to improve their position through trade).
> Step 3): It is shown that adopting a particular kind of behaviour (in Menger's
> example, to exchange less marketable for more marketable goods) would
> allow the individuals concerned to better realize their interests.
> Step 4): It is shown to be plausible to assume that, sooner or later, some
> innovative individual(s) will discover this particular behaviour and its
> advantageous consequences (Menger, 1985: 154f).
> Step 5): It is shown that, once the initial discovery has been made, other
> individuals are likely to notice the greater success of the 'pioneers' and they
> will tend to imitate their behaviour (Menger, 1981: 261).
> Step 6): It is shown that as the behaviour spreads out and becomes common
> social practice it will result in the institution (that is, the socially uniform
> pattern of behaviour) that is to be explained (Menger, 1984: 15).

A particularly attractive feature of this explanatory argument is that it
rests on very parsimonious assumptions concerning the process that eventually leads to the institution in question. In order for this process to get
started not more is required than that, at some point in time, at least one
person discovers the advantages that can be realized by practising a certain
kind of behaviour. In order for the process to gain momentum no more is
required than that others notice the success of the original innovators or
pioneers and start to imitate their behaviour.[11]

The process is assumed to be entirely driven by the separate and independent pursuit of individual interests, without any need to rely on deliberate
co-ordination of individual efforts – an assumption which is, in fact, the
central ingredient to an invisible-hand explanation. It is important to realize
that this assumption gives a very specific meaning to the notion that an

---

[10] Without intending to enter here the long-standing debate on the issue of what defines an
institution (on this see, Vanberg, 1983), I want to point out that for Carl Menger 'explaining
an institution' clearly meant to explain how a certain socially uniform pattern of behaviour
emerges. See e.g., Menger's (1985: 152) comment on the explanation of the origin of money:
'The problem which science has to solve here consists in the explanation . . . *of a homogeneous way of acting on the part of the members of a community* for which public motives
are recognizable, but for which in the concrete case individual motives are hard to discern'
(emphasis added).
[11] The same 'parsimonious' structure underlies, and accounts for the attractiveness, of R.
Axelrod's (1984) theory of the evolution of co-operation. For a more detailed discussion of
this aspect see Vanberg and Buchanan (1988).

institution is explained as an *unintended outcome of individual actions*. This notion does not simply mean that an institution is different, to a greater or lesser extent, from what anybody involved in its creation intended. This is probably true for most or even all institutions, including those that clearly are the product of deliberate organized effort and not the spontaneous outcome of separate, unorganized individual actions. That most institutions exhibit, in this broad sense, 'unintended' features does not make them proper candidates for an invisible-hand explanation. The claim of the latter type of explanation is more specific and its applicability therefore more limited.[12]

The specific nature of an *invisible-hand* or, in Menger's terms, an *organic* approach to the study of social institutions and the limits to its applicability that its nature implies have to be remembered when claims are made concerning the potential explanatory range of this approach. As is well known, Menger (1985: 155f.) claimed that the 'origin of a number of other social institutions' can be explained in a similar way as the origin of money. 'One needs only to think', he argued (1985: 130), 'of law, of language, of the origin of markets, the origin of communities and of states, etc.' His discussion of these other cases remains, however, quite sketchy and, more importantly, he passes over relevant differences in the sense in which, for instance, *states* as compared to *money* can be said to arise 'unintentionally'. In his discussion on the 'origin of the state' Menger (1985: 156f) fails to explicitly acknowledge that the emergence of a state necessarily implies – in one way or another – the formation of an *organization*, government, and that, therefore, the origin of states cannot in the same sense be said to be 'unintentional' as the origin of money.[13] Menger's failure explicitly to recognize the special issues that arise when his 'organic approach' is applied to *organizations*, like the state, can be attributed to the fact that he does not carefully enough distinguish between, on the one side, the claim that something emerges as an unintended outcome of separate, not deliberately co-ordinated individual efforts and, on the other side, the claim that something is brought about '. . . without any consideration of public interest, merely through the impulse of *individual* interests and as a result of the activation of these interests' (Menger, 1985: 157). The latter claim is an obvious and direct implication of the standard economic model of

---

[12] The notion of explaining something as an 'unintended outcome of individual actions' is apparently interpreted in a less specific sense if with regard to the explanatory range of 'the organic model' it is argued that even deliberately created institutions, like a firm, '. . . may well work out in a manner quite different from what the founders had intended' (Langlois, 1988: 17; 1986: 19).

[13] F.A. Hayek (1979: 140): 'The state, the organization of the people of a territory under a single government, . . . is yet very far from being identical with . . . the multiplicity of grown and selfgenerating structures . . . that alone deserves the name of society. . . . Societies form but states are made.'

342   *Evolutionary and collective action approaches*

behaviour, if it is consistently applied to all kinds of institutions or social structures, including organizations. If one subscribes to the model of rational, self-interested behaviour, it is no more than a requirement of theoretical consistency to assume that individuals who act in an organizational context, be it a government or a firm, do so in pursuit of their individual interest, '. . . without consideration of public interest'. This is not, however, the same as to assume that an organization emerges 'spontaneously', without deliberate co-ordination of individual efforts. In fact, that there is some kind of deliberate co-ordination of individual actions seems to be the essential definitional attribute of what is commonly called an organization.

It has been a quite common feature of what may be called the post-Mengerian (and this means largely: the Hayekian) tradition of spontaneous order theory to cite Menger's explanation of the origin of money as the paradigmatic example of an organic or invisible-hand explanation and to suppose that other institutions can be explained in the same fashion, without actually providing such explanations and substantiating the claim that these explanations exhibit the same essential features as Menger's original example. In fact, it seems that not much effort has been invested in actually applying an invisible-hand approach to such other institutions and to work out exemplary explanations that are as detailed and as compelling as Menger's theory of money. This is an unfortunate neglect because it encouraged a somewhat superficial interpretation of what an organic or invisible-hand approach is about, and it inhibited a more serious discussion on the actual scope and limits of its explanatory potential.

For the following discussion it will be important to keep in mind that the explanatory scope of an invisible-hand explanation is limited in two ways. First there is, the aspect that has been explicitly stressed by Menger, namely that as a matter of fact many institutions have been deliberately established (i.e., they are, in Menger's terms, of pragmatic origin) and that, therefore, an organic or invisible-hand account cannot be considered to be descriptive of the actual process of their origin. However, as has been argued above, one may claim that an invisible-hand interpretation is of interest even in case of such pragmatic institutions because it can provide information about the general nature of the institution and the forces that support it.

The second, and more fundamental sense in which an invisible-hand approach has a limited application is the following: there are certain institutions (social structures) which because of their very nature do not lend themselves to an invisible-hand explanation in the strict sense. That is, they are not only *de facto* not of organic origin, they cannot even in principle be explained as the outcome of a pure invisible-hand process. This is in particular true for what one may call corporate structures, for arrangements of organized collective action. As I will argue in the following section, it is precisely these structures that John Commons' institutional theory focuses on.

IV John R. Commons' collective action approach

The attempt to compare Carl Menger's and John R. Commons' respective
approaches to the study of institutions has to cope with the difficulty that
the latter is much less systematically explicated than the former. While
Menger states the central assumptions and the overall purpose of his
approach in a quite explicit fashion, it is much more difficult to identify the
overall thrust and the core assumptions of Commons' institutional perspective. In fact, Commons' style of writing has often been censured for being
'too eclectic – even unsystematic' (Langlois, 1988: 6) or 'obscure' (Blaug,
1985: 710) and his work, like that of other old institutionalists, has been
criticized for lack of theoretical focus and for exhibiting a collectivistic
orientation which would seem to put it into a methodological camp directly
opposed to Menger's approach.

Based on the sample of Commons' writings with which I have made
myself familiar, I would certainly agree that his idiosyncratic terminology
and his unsystematic style of reasoning are not particularly conducive to an
understanding of his theoretical concerns. However, I want to argue here
that, in my view, there exists a well identified theoretical perspective which
can be extracted – or reconstructed – out of Commons' work: a theoretical
perspective which, above all, is neither incompatible with Menger's methodological individualism nor in conflict with the broader economic tradition
to which Menger's theory belongs. More specifically, I want to argue that
Commons' approach to institutional analysis deserves particular interest
because it addresses a set of important issues about which Menger's theory
remains silent.

Commons is most often quoted with his definition of an institution as
'collective action in control, liberation, and expansion of individual action'
(Commons 1950: 21). This definition to which Commons returns again and
again throughout his work is exemplary of his general style of writing: it is
not formulated to unambiguously communicate a specific meaning on first
reading. The reader is required to labouriously reconstruct its meaning out
of its broader context. My purpose in this section is to reconstruct what I
consider to be the fundamental structure of Commons' collective action
approach to institutions.

As this paper's introductory quotation from Commons indicates he did
not consider institutional economics in general, nor his own contribution in
particular, to be unorthodox in a fundamental paradigmatic sense. Rather,
he viewed his emphasis on collective action to be complementary to received
economics in the sense of drawing attention to an aspect of social reality
that, in his judgement, had been unduly neglected from Adam Smith to his
contemporaries in mainstream economics. At the very beginning of his
Institutional economics – its place in political economy (1934) he describes
his enterprise as an attempt to develop '. . . a theory of the part played by
collective action in control of individual action', and he states that such a
theory is, in his judgement, 'the contribution of institutional economics to

344   *Evolutionary and collective action approaches*

the whole of a rounded-out theory of Political Economy' (1934: 6). In other words, Commons' declared purpose was to widen the scope of economics by giving 'to collective action its due place in economic theory' (1934: 8).[14]

While the notion of collective action in control of individual action is obviously the core notion of Commons' institutionalist approach, the specific content of this notion is not quite as obvious. In fact, there is a fundamental ambiguity in Commons' discussion on this notion, an ambiguity that becomes apparent as one takes a closer look at his claim '. . . that collective action is the general and dominating fact in social life' (1950: 21), that it:

> '. . . ranges all the way from unorganized Custom to the many organized Going Concerns, such as the family, the corporation, the holding company, the trade association, the trade union, the Federal Reserve System, the 'group of affiliated interests,' the State (1934: 70).[15]

Commons' claim that 'collective action is inclusive' (1950: 21), and a 'universal principle' (1934: 72), can be given two interpretations, both of which are present, but not explicitly separated, in his writings. It can, first, be meant to say that individuals always act within some framework of 'collectively enforced' social rules. And it can, secondly, be meant to say that organizations as units of collective action – or corporate actors – are an omnipresent element in modern social life. Though the two themes are inter-related, they are clearly separable, and I will suggest here that Commons' theory of collective action can be fruitfully interpreted as falling into two parts along these two themes. The one part of Commons' theory focuses on the role of 'collective action' in the development and enforcement of the structure of rights or the framework of rules within which individuals operate and interact with each other. I will call this part *Commons' economics of property rights*. The other part of his theory of collective action focuses on the nature and role of organizations or corporate entities as acting units or *collective actors*. I will call this part *Commons' economics of organization* or, preferably, his *corporate actor theory*.

Before I discuss in more detail the two parts of Commons' theory of collective action it is appropriate briefly to return to his definition of an institution. There are, as Commons (1934: 73) explains, two versions of this

---

[14] J.R. Commons (1936: 241n): 'I do not think that institutional economics, defined as collective action in control of individual action, is contrary to the so-called pure economics of the past, which is individual action without collective control. It is a continuation of pure economics.'

[15] Commons adds to the above quoted statement: 'The principle common to all of them is more or less control of individual action by collective action' (1934: 70). See also Commons (1936: 246): 'I name an institution collective action in control of individual action. It may be unorganized collective action which is the meaning of custom, or organized collective action like that of a corporation, a co-operative, a trade union, or the state itself.'

definition: '(T)he short definition of an institution is collective action in control of individual action, the derived definition is: collective action in restraint, liberation, and expansion of individual action.' The additional components that the 'derived definition' contains can be related to the two parts of Commons' theory. The theory of property rights thematizes how socially enforced rules impose a constraint on the individual but, at the same time, by simultaneously constraining others also 'liberate' the individual by securing a protected domain of action, because, as Commons (1950: 35) argues, '(t)he only way in which "liberty" can be obtained is by imposing duties on others who might interfere with the activity of the "liberated" individual.' The theory of organization thematizes how as a member of an organization the individual is subject to certain rules and constraints while, on the other hand, organized collective action allows individuals to accomplish things and to realize gains which could not be achieved by separate individual effort. In Commons' terms:

> Collective Action is more than restraint and liberation of individual action – it is *expansion* of the will of the individual far beyond what he can do by his own puny acts. The head of a great corporation gives orders which execute his will at the ends of the earth (1950: 35).

V Commons' economics of property rights

Some of the arguments and ideas that Commons advanced concerning the direction into which, in his view, institutional economics ought to extend the scope of traditional economic analysis have a striking similarity to the concerns that have been articulated in the more recent literature on the so-called economics of property rights. It is because of this similarity that I classify the respective part of Commons' theory under the same label. In fact, Commons (1934: 8) used the quite similar label 'proprietary economics'.

Not unlike the fundamental theme in J.M. Buchanan's *Limits of liberty* (1975: 53), Commons censured that standard economic reasoning typically takes for granted what is in need of being explained, namely the existence of a structure of rights or a framework of rules within which individuals are able peacefully and successfully to co-operate.[16] While economists have recognized the fundamental fact of scarcity as well as the crucial role of co-operation in overcoming scarcity, they have not, according to Commons, paid adequate attention to the issue of what makes peaceful co-operation

---

[16] K.H. Parsons (1950: 361): 'It is not an exaggeration to say that the analysis of property relations is an integral part of Commons' thought throughout his formulation. . . . Commons, contrary to the prevailing practice of economic theorists, does not 'assume' private property or ownership as a starting point and then work out the implications of economizing under static conditions. Rather, he sets out to make an analysis of economic process, in which he finds property relations to be an important part.'

346   *Evolutionary and collective action approaches*

possible despite the conflicts of interest that result from scarcity.[17] Considering his own approach to be in the tradition of David Hume,[18] he supposes that the answer to this question has to be found in analyzing the process in which men come to establish and to maintain among themselves a system of rules for regulating these conflicts (Mitchell, 1935: 652). Co-operation, Commons (1934: 6f) argues:

> . . . does not arise from a *presupposed* harmony of interests. . . . It arises from the necessity of *creating a new harmony* of interests – or at least order, if harmony is impossible – out of the conflict of interests among the hoped-for cooperators. . . . [H]armony is not a presupposition of economics – it is a consequence of collective action designed to maintain rules that shall govern the conflicts.

And it sounds like a declaration of his own research programme when Commons (1931: 657) states:

> [T]he natural rights ideas of the economists and lawyers created the illusion of a framework, supposed to be constructed in the past, within which present individuals are supposed to act. It was because they did not investigate collective action. They assumed the fixity of existing rights of property and liberty. But if rights, duties, liberties and exposures are simply the changeable working rules of all kinds of collective action, looking towards the future, then the framework analogy disappears in the actual collective action of controlling, liberating and expanding individual action for the immediate or remote future production, exchange, and consumption of wealth.

Similar to the thrust of the modern economics of property rights, Commons reminded his fellow economists that they ought to take more seriously the fact that the behaviour which they study is not simply about material things and services but about uses and transfers of rights of ownership. In terms that might as well be found in contemporary contributions to the economics of property rights Commons argues that '[w]hat we buy and sell is not material things and services but ownership of materials and services' (1936: 242), that what we call 'exchange' is 'not an exchange of physical products or material services' but involves 'two transfers of two ownerships' (1936: 241n), and that the 'term "property" cannot be defined

---

[17] Commons (1936: 242) acknowledges that Böhm-Bawerk in his 1883 publication on 'Recht und Verhältnisse' paid attention to rights as institutional factors, but – as Commons censures – Böhm-Bawerk thought he could exclude them from his 'pure economics', an undertaking which Commons considers inconsistent: 'But if his pure economic man should go along the street picking up groceries, clothing, and shoes according to their marginal utility to him, he would go to jail. He must first negotiate with an owner to whom the policemen, courts, and constitution have given the right to withhold from him what he wants but does not own, until that owner willingly consents to sell his ownership. This is . . . a part of what I mean by institutional economics' (1936: 242f).

[18] Commons (1934: 71): 'David Hume found the unity of these social sciences in the principle of scarcity and the resulting conflict of interests. . . . Institutional economics goes back to Hume'. See also (Commons, 1934: 6).

except by defining all the activities which individuals and the community are at liberty or required to do or not to do, with reference to the object claimed as property' (1934: 74).[19]

It does not sound all too different from Commons' phrasing when, in the more recent literature on the economics of property rights, one reads that social systems rely on 'rules or customs to resolve conflicts that arise in the use of scarce resources' (Alchian and Demsetz, 1973: 14), that what is 'owned' is not the resource itself but '*rights* to use resources' or, in other words, 'socially recognized rights of action' (Alchian and Demsetz, 1973: 17), that 'property rights do not refer to relations between men and things but, rather, *to the sanctioned behavioral relations among men that arise from the existence of things and pertain to their use*' (Furubotn and Pejovich, 1975: 65), that an 'owner of property rights possesses the consent of fellowmen to allow him to act in particular ways' (Demsetz, 1975: 24),[20] and that when 'a transaction is concluded in the marketplace, two bundles of property rights are exchanged' (Demsetz, 1975: 23). All these statements, the list of which could easily be extended, obviously express concerns similar to those that informed Commons' – admittedly theoretically less focussed – inquiries into the 'legal foundations of capitalism'.

I do not intend further to elaborate here on Commons' economics of property rights except for mentioning that his emphasis on transactions as the ultimate units of economic analysis (Commons 1934: 4) – the aspect that O. Williamson stresses in his reference to Commons – can be under- stood as a derivative of his focus on property rights. The use of the term transaction, instead of, for example, 'exchange' is supposed to indicate that the interaction which the economist studies are about uses and transfers of *rights* instead of simply material goods. Transactions are – according to Commons (1931: 652) – 'not the "exchange of commodities", but the alienation and acquisition, between individuals, of the *rights* of property and liberty created by society.'

What – in the context of this paper – deserves particular interest is an aspect of Commons' property rights perspective that is critical not only for one's understanding of his approach but also for how one views its relation to the Mengerian conception. There is a fundamental ambiguity that in

---

[19] Commons (1934: 75) defines '*property-rights* . . . as the *working rules* enforced by the community upon individuals in their transactions respecting that which is or is expected to be scarce.' See also K.H. Parsons (1950: 357ff).

[20] A. Alchian (1977: 129f): 'The rights of individuals to the use of resources (i.e., property rights) in any society are to be construed as supported by the force of etiquette, social custom, ostracism, and formal legally enacted laws supported by the state's power of violence or punishment. . . . By a system of property rights I mean a method of assigning to particular individuals the "authority" to select, for specific goods, any use from a nonpro- hibited class of uses. . . . A property right for me means some protection against other people's choosing against my will one of the uses of resources, said to be "mine".'

348   *Evolutionary and collective action approaches*

similar ways characterizes Commons' use of such central concepts as 'co-operation', 'collective action', and 'transaction'. Commons uses all these terms in a more general as well as in a more specific sense without explicitly distinguishing between the two. In its general meaning co-operation includes all forms of peaceful and ordered interaction, exchange and trade in markets no less than organized co-operation within corporate units like firms. In its more specific meaning co-operation refers just to the latter, to organized, concerted effort. Similarly, the term collective action is used, on the one hand, in a very general sense meaning social control in all its forms, informal as well as formal. On the other hand it is used in the more specific sense of control by some formal, organized apparatus. The same can be said for Commons' use of the notion of transaction. Without explicitly distinguishing between the two, Commons uses this notion in the general sense of interactions that occur in the context of some structure of socially enforced rules and also in the more specific sense of 'joint action' or organized co-operation; that is, in the sense only of intraorganizational interactions (e.g., Commons, 1950: 21).

The ambiguous use of these terms tends to cause confusion because not all of Commons' arguments which apply to 'co-operation,' 'collective action,' and 'transaction' in their respective general meanings do also apply to their more specific meanings (Commons, 1934: 6, 70; 1936: 246). The ambiguity in Commons' reasoning can, however, be easily remedied and the confusion that it causes be avoided if one uses adequate care in distinguishing between two issues which are central to – but not clearly separated in – Commons' discussion on the role of social rules (Commons prefers the term working rules) in governing individual action. The first issue concerns the ways in which social rules are established and the means by which they are enforced. The relevant distinction here is between, on the one hand, rules that spontaneously evolve and are informally enforced and, on the other hand, rules that are deliberately established and enforced in a formal, organized way.[21] The second issue concerns the 'nature' or character of the rules themselves, as defined separately from their modes of origin or enforcement. The relevant distinction here is between – in Hayek's terminology – general rules of conduct and organizational rules, the first kind of rules being characteristic for spontaneous social orders, the latter for organizations.[22] Stated somewhat differently: It is one question to ask whether certain rules are informally and spontaneously maintained or

---

[21] The two aspects, the mode of emergence and the mode of enforcement, will not be separately discussed here though, of course, they may vary independently from each other, at least to some extent.

[22] I am following here Hayek's distinction between two kinds of social order – spontaneous order and organization – and his corresponding distinction between two kinds of rules, general rules of conduct and organizational rules. In the concluding section I will comment in more detail on the relevance of this distinction for institutional analysis.

whether they are subject to formal, organized enforcement. And it is another question to ask whether certain rules are general rules of conduct on which a spontaneous order is based or whether they are organizational rules which govern organized collective action.

The first question is apparently concerned when Commons (1934: 72) talks about the 'universal principle of collective action in control of individual action by different kinds of sanctions', when he argues that the process of legal formalization gives 'greater precision and organized compulsion to the unorganized working rules of custom or ethics' (1934: 73), or when he describes institutional economics as dealing with, in an integrated way, the various kinds of informal and formal rule-enforcement on which ethics, economics and jurisprudence traditionally focus (1931: 650). By contrast, it is apparently the second question which is concerned when Commons comments on the separation of the word 'law' into the 'two meanings of justice and commands':

> One is related to the ethical idea of that which is right as against that which is wrong. The other is a working rule of a going concern, laid down by authority. One is a purpose of obtaining justice – the other is a process of command and obedience (1968: 332).

And, finally, both questions appear interwoven when Commons (1934: 72) talks about collective action as being 'even more universal in the unorganized form of Custom than . . . in the organized form of Concerns', when he refers to the 'working rules of associations and governments' as the source of the individual's 'rights, duties and liberties, as well as his exposures to the protected liberties of other individuals' (1968: 6), and when he argues that working rules '. . . differ for different institutions', but '. . . have this similarity, that they indicate what individuals can, must, or may, do or not do, enforced by Collective Sanctions' (1934: 71).[23]

VI Commons' corporate actor theory

The second of the two parts that I distinguished above within Commons' collective action approach is what I called his theory of organization or corporate actor theory. This theory is supposed to extend received economics in a direction which is clearly separate from the concerns of Commons' theory of property rights. The focus here is on the role that organizations or corporate actors[24] play in the socioeconomic world, and

---

[23] Commons (1934: 71) specifies this description 'of the operation of working rules on individual action' as follows: 'He "can" or "cannot", because collective action will or will not come to his aid. He "must" or "must not", because collective action will compel him. He "may", because collective action will permit him and protect him. He "may not", because collective will prevent him.'

[24] I adopt the term *corporate actor* from J.S. Coleman (1986) whose theory of *corporate action* has, as I will argue later in this paper, a certain resemblance to Commons' approach.

350   *Evolutionary and collective action approaches*

Commons' reproach is that orthodox economics has failed adequately to account for the role of organized collective action. In a time when '[m]ost Americans must work collectively as participants in organized concerns in order to earn a living,' Commons (1950: 23) argues, it is no longer appropriate to model the world as if it is populated only by individuals as property-owning and trading entities. Economics has to '. . . account for the incoming of corporations, trade unions, voluntary associations of all kinds, . . . as well as the interference of government' (Commons, 1968: 6).[25]

According to Commons (1936: 246f) the 1850's can be considered, for the USA, the beginning of the 'time of the general corporation laws' and the 'beginning of modern capitalism':

> These corporation laws endowed individuals with a new universal right, the right of collective action, previously outlawed as conspiracy, and not previously granted as universal but granted only as a monopolistic special privilege by a special act of the legislature.

The change in the structure of the economy that resulted from this 'new universal right of collective action' renders, Commons argues (1936: 247), the '. . . older individualistic economics . . . obsolete or, rather, subordinate to institutional economics'.

Commons emphasizes the necessity to distinguish between the notion that the state through its corporation laws provides legal recognition to associations, and the view that corporate entities are only 'legal fictions', have existence only 'in contemplation of law'. The latter view is, Commons argues, simply wrong because organized associations of individuals factually exist prior to and independent of the law, no less than natural individuals do.[26] There is, Commons conjectures, in this regard no real difference between natural individuals and associations of individuals: as empirical realities they both exist and as legal persons they are both 'artificial' in that they both exist so far only as they enjoy rights. In Commons' words:

> If the individual lives without rights he is, not a person, but a thing, that can be captured, bred, owned and killed without violating any duty towards him. If an association has no rights, it too is an outlaw and its members may be penalized on the ground of conspiracy. What the state does for each is to

---

[25] Commons (1950: 43): 'Private property, owned by individuals for executing the will of the owners, was assumed and taken for granted, without investigation, by the nineteenth century economists. . . . But the incoming of joint stock corporations, labor unions . . . changed the legal foundations of economics. Corporations now began to own the bulk of corporal property.'

[26] Commons (1968: 143): 'Government finds individuals and associations of individuals, each existing prior to, or at least independent of, any act of law. . . . Men associate in families, partnerships, communities, unions, nations, but the law imputes to their association as a unit many of the legal relations that it attributes to natural persons.'

personify it by granting and imposing rights, duties, liberties, exposures, and
if to do this for an association is to create an artificial being so also is it an
artificial process to do the same for an individual (1968: 143).[27]

Commons typically uses the term *going concern* as a name for what I
have referred to before as organizations or corporate actors,[28] though, here
again, it has to be said that his use of this concept is not totally unambiguous because he also uses it sometimes in a broader sense, referring to
'ongoing social orders' of any kind, including nonorganized networks of
social relations.[29] The ambiguity in Commons' use of the concept of a going
concern is a variation of the previously discussed ambiguity in his writings.
It results from the failure to carefully distinguish between the general notion
that individuals living in a social environment are subject to socially
enforced rules, and the more specific notion that individuals as members of
organizations are subject to particular rule constraints. The crucial difference here is between *general rules of conduct*, to which individuals are
subject just by virtue of their living in a certain social environment, rules
which may be informally enforced or enforced by the organized enforcement apparatus of government, and *organizational rules* to which individuals are subject by virtue of their membership in certain organizations, rules
which define the terms of membership in the respective organization.

The distinction between the two kinds of rules can clearly be reconstructed from Commons' writings but it is sometimes blurred because of his
indiscriminate use of the notion of membership. Commons emphasizes as a
particular characteristic of the institutionalist perspective that it views
individuals not 'in a state of nature' but as 'members of a concern . . .
citizen of an institution' (1934: 74). He does not, however, carefully
separate between what may be considered the standard and more specific

---

27 See also Commons (1936: 247n): 'Even the individual of economic theory is not the natural
individual of biology and psychology; he is that artificial bundle of institutes known as a
legal person or citizen.' The same argument has been stated in very similar terms by J.M.
Buchanan (1975: 10, 12): 'Without some definition of boundaries or limits on the set of
rights to do things and/or to exclude or prevent others from doing things, an individual, as
such, could hardly be said to exist. With such defined limits, however, . . . an individual is
clearly an entity distinct from his fellows, . . . If a person lives in society he is defined by his
"rights" . . . Persons are defined by the rights which they possess and are acknowledged by
others to possess.'

28 See e.g., Commons (1934: 69): 'It is these going concerns, with the working rules that keep
them going, all the way from the family, the corporation, the trade union, the trade association, up to the state itself, that we name Institutions.' See also K.H. Parsons (1950: 355): 'In
most general terms, a going concern is an organization of coordinated activity; it is
collective behavior with a common purpose, and a collective will, governed by common
working rules.'

29 See e.g., Commons (1968: 6), where 'the Working Rules of Going Concerns' are explained
to include 'common law, statute law, shop rules, business ethics, business methods, norms
of conduct, and so on'. See also A.G. Gruchy (1940: 832) who, in summarizing Commons'
thoughts, even refers to "the capitalistic process . . . as a going concern."

352 *Evolutionary and collective action approaches*

use of the notion of membership, namely membership in an organization, and a more general interpretation according to which any kind of 'belonging' to some social network is called membership. With this ambiguity in the use of the notion of membership, there remains necessarily a fundamental ambiguity in Commons' (1936: 248n) suggestion that: 'economic theory should make him [the individual, V.V.] a citizen, or member of the institution under whose rule he acts.'

It is, to be sure, not uncommon to say that an individual is a 'member of society', a statement that sounds just like the claim that an individual is a member of an organization. One should be aware, however, that the notion of membership cannot have the same meaning in both contexts. Society is not an organization or a corporate actor like a firm, a trade union or a government; and an individual is not a member of society in the same sense as he is a member of such organizations. Confusion about this sometimes arises – and seems to arise in Commons' argument – because of the special role of the entity that we call *state*. The state is an organization and individuals are members, i.e., citizens, of a state. The state plays a special role, compared to other organizations, in that it is, on the one hand, an organization in which individuals as members/citizens are subject to certain organizational rules, rules which define the terms of membership: contribution obligations (rules of taxation), participation rights (voting rules), etc., while on the other side, it acts as what Buchanan (1975) has called the protective state, i.e., as the agent who enforces (part of) the rules under which individuals interact 'in society', in their private capacities. In the latter capacity individuals act not as members of the state though they are subject to rules that the state, as protective agent, enforces. The 'order of society' that emerges within these state-enforced rules as well as within other, informally enforced rules is, in Hayek's terms, a *spontaneous* order, not an organization. In this sense, what has to be carefully separated are three things: first, as a member of (private) organizations the individual is subject to certain (organizational) rules which define the terms of his membership in these organizations. Secondly, as citizen, i.e., as a member of that special organization, state, the individual is subject to certain rules (again, organizational rules) which define the terms of his membership in the organization state, and his rights and obligations as citizen. Thirdly, living within a society the individual is subject to a set of rules (more specifically, general rules of conduct) which in part are enforced – and defined – by this special organization the state. The authority of the latter in defining and enforcing certain general rules of conduct typically has a territorial extension, so that the earlier statement may be reformulated as saying that by virtue of living within certain territorial limits the individual is subject to certain rules which are enforced by the state whose jurisdiction covers the respective territory.

The various relations of individuals to organizations that I tried to distinguish above are clearly present and separable – though not separated – in statements like the following:

> The working rules . . . may be laid down and enforced by a corporation, or a cartel, or a holding company, or a cooperative association, or a trade union, or an employers' association, or a trade association, or a joint trade agreement of two associations, or a stock exchange or board of trade, or a political party, or the state itself through the United States Supreme Court in the American system. Indeed, these economic collective acts of private concerns are at times more powerful than the collective action of the political concern, the State (Commons, 1934: 70).

Statements like this are potentially misleading because in listing the state along with organizations like trade unions or political parties they tend to ignore the above distinction between the two roles in which the state imposes rule constraints on individuals. Conversely, the fact that 'ordinary' organizations are, for the reasons stated, different from the organization state tends to be ignored when Commons (1968: 83) argues that a person '. . . is a member of several concerns, or has transactions with members of several concerns, each of which is a government that enforces rules of conduct'. What has to be separated are the three different ways in which individuals can be said to be subject to collective control: as members of private organizations, as citizens of states, and as participants in the spontaneous order 'society' which is based on state-enforced as well as privately enforced rules. When Commons argues that individuals as buyers and sellers are 'members of the same national economy' (1936: 239) one has to remember that individuals are, of course, not members of the spontaneous order economy in the same sense as they are members of an organization and that the collective enforcement to which they are subject as buyers and sellers in a market can only be the enforcement of general rules of conduct by the protective state.[30]

Though, as discussed above, Commons' arguments are not always totally unambiguous in this regard, it is obvious that the focus of his discussion on the role of collective action is on those phenomena that emerge where individuals associate or organize themselves into corporate actors – phenomena that the market-focused neoclassical tradition had left largely unilluminated. The analytical perspective that Commons advances reminds one in some regards of James S. Coleman's (1986) more recent theory of corporate action. It seems to me at least that Commons' perspective can be fruitfully reconstructed or restated in terms of Coleman's theory. This is not the place for a detailed review of Coleman's corporate actor conception

---

[30] Commons (e.g., 1968: 150) recognizes the distinctions made above between society or economy as spontaneous orders and state or government as organizations and between the two roles in which the state acts as a collective enforcer. He does not, however, clearly state these distinctions. For a discussion of the distinction between 'society' as a spontaneous order and 'state' as an organization see Hayek (1973: 48, 124f; 1976: 158).

354   *Evolutionary and collective action approaches*

but it may be helpful to give at least a brief description. Corporate actors, in Coleman's interpretation, are '. . . created when two or more persons combine some portion of their resources to create an acting entity' (1986: 7). For different kinds of corporate actors, e.g., for a family as opposed to a firm or a political party, the relevant resources will be of a different kind. But it is, in each case, the control over some kind of combined resources that constitutes a corporate actor. In Coleman's terms:

> All resources reside in natural persons, and corporate actors gain their resources through resource investments of one sort or another by natural persons. In doing so they establish implicitly or explicitly a constitution, which may well be regarded as a social contract among them. The social contract is one in which each party contracts to invest certain rights and resources in the corporate actor, for which he receives two things in return: partial control over the actions of the corporate actor and an expectation of more beneficial consequences from the corporate actor's actions than he would have had from his own individual actions (1986: 341).

The notions that are implied in Coleman's construction can also be recognized in Commons' arguments. K.H. Parsons (1950: 360) describes Commons' view of the 'relation between persons within a concern' as follows: 'Either party may withhold what the other needs but does not own; the withholding is limited by the resources and alternative opportunities of the bargainers. The concern must depend on the "good will" of the parties for their continued participation.' This statement can well be interpreted as reflecting the notion of organized concerns or corporate actors as being constituted and maintained through individual participants' contributions. This notion seems to be implied, in any case, when Commons' (1950: 34) argues with regard to the 'life' of an organization or, in his terms, a going concern: 'The concern 'goes' as long as the participants earn a living or a profit through collective action; it may die by bankruptcy, be dissolved, or be absorbed by another corporation.'

Commons explicitly criticizes a theoretical approach in which 'corporations are falsely treated as individuals' (1936: 238). The alternative interpretation that he advocates may be called in more modern terms a *coalition theory* of organization. It stresses the notion that the organized unit depends for its continued existence on the continued willingness of participants to make their respective contributions to the collective effort, and that this willingness again depends on their expectation to 'profit' from their continued membership relation to the organization.[31] Similar to Coleman's

---

[31] Commons (1968: 145): 'That which holds the going concern together is these two sets of working rules affording an expectation of a gross income to be obtained jointly while it is being distributed among the members. . . . While the expectation continues, the corporation is "a going concern".'

emphasis on the constitutional foundation of corporate action,[32] Commons interprets organizations or going concerns as what one may call constitutional systems. He explicitly argues that what constitutes an organization as an acting unit, as a corporate actor, are the rules which integrate the actions of the various individual participants into some overall scheme. As Commons (1968: 147) argues, 'the going concern may be looked upon as a person with a composite will, but this so-called "will" is none other than the working rules of the concern operating through the actions and transactions of those who observe the rules.[33] And when Commons criticizes Adam Smith, Herbert Spencer and others for holding an '. . . individualistic notion of the state as a mere sum total of individuals, on the one hand, and an abstract entity, on the other' (1968: 151), he does not at all want to advocate some organistic or collectivistic alternative but, rather, wants to emphasize that in social systems like the state individuals are *de facto* unified or 'held together' by a system of rules.[34]

By way of concluding my description of Commons' corporate actor theory I would like to mention two themes that, again, are addressed in a similar way in Commons' as well as in Coleman's construction. The one concerns the fact that organizations do not 'act' except through natural individuals as agents and that, therefore, we have to distinguish between different capacities in which individuals may be members of a corporate actor, a particularly important distinction being in this regard the distinction between principals and agents (see Commons, 1950: 40; 1968: 146). The second theme concerns the consequences that result for the distribution of power in society when corporate actors operate as legal persons in contractual relations and transactions with natural individuals. Both Commons

---

[32] In Coleman's system corporate actors are based on an explicit or implicit *constitution* – i.e., a set of rules – which defines the terms of corporate membership, 'the relative rights of different persons within' the corporate actor (Coleman, 1986: 148). More specifically, the constitution specifies the terms under which individuals contribute resources and get, in return, partial control over the collectivity's actions and some share in the corporately generated benefits.

[33] Commons (1968: 148): '[The] working rules . . . constitute the so-called "collective will" of any going concern in the sense of the relations between the conduct of the members and the accompanying conduct of the concern as a whole, and they apply to all concerns, whether it be a family, tribe, business or the state.' See also Commons (1968: 146f): 'But practically, as an economic institution, the will of the going concern is the composite will of all to the extent that each has any discretion in his acts . . . The collective will is the organized symposium of all the discretionary acts of all participants as they go along from day to day, according to the rules of the organization.'

[34] Immediately following the statement quoted in the text Commons (1968: 151f) argues: 'And when Spencer destroyed this metaphysical entity there was nothing left for him to hold the parts together except to substitute another entity in the form of an analogy to a biological organism. There was no collective will at all – merely an abstract formula of individual rights by which individuals might hold each other off while a biological analogy held them together. Yet that which held them together was their own working rules.'

356   *Evolutionary and collective action approaches*

and Coleman, suggest that the disproportional distribution of power that may occur in these relations commends the imposition of more restrictive legal constraints on corporate actors than on natural actors.[35]

VII Conclusion

A main purpose of this paper has been to argue that the relation between Menger's evolutionary approach and Commons' collective action approach to institutional analysis can be better understood if adequate attention is paid to two things:

> 1) The distinctiveness of two dimensions along which rules may be classified, the one pertaining to their mode of origin (unintentionally evolved versus deliberately created) and mode of enforcement (spontaneous, informal enforcement versus formal, organized enforcement), the other pertaining to their structural nature (general rules of conduct versus organizational rules). 2) The fact that the location within the space that is defined by these two dimensions[36] has, *per se*, nothing to do with the conflict between methodological individualism and methodological collectivism.

Matrix 1

Mode of origin and enforcement — Character of rules	General rules of conduct ('market' rules)	Organizational rules
Spontaneous evolution/ informal enforcement	A	B
Deliberate creation/ organized enforcement	C	D

---

[35] Commons (1936: 247n): 'This personification of collective action ends in the inequality of treating as equals a concerted thousand or hundred thousand stockholders and bankers acting together as a single person, in dealings with wage earners or farmers or other buyers or sellers, who act separately in their naked individualism of Smith, Bentham, Ricardo, the Austrian economists, the Declaration of Independence.' See also Commons (1936: 243; 1968; 71f). It may be of interest to quote here a statement by Hayek (1979: 89f): 'But "freedom of organization" should no more than "freedom of contract" be interpreted to mean that the activities of organizations must not be subject to rules restricting their methods, or even that the collective action of organizations should not be restricted by rules which do not apply to individuals. The new powers created by the perfection of organizational techniques, and by the right conceded to them by existing laws, will probably require limitations by general rules of law far more narrow than those it has been found necessary to impose by law on the actions of private individuals.'

[36] As noted earlier, the modes of origin and enforcement can, of course, vary independently and should, in a more complete analysis, be treated as two separate dimensions. For the purposes of this paper it seems to be justifiable to combine the two and also to ignore the various other combinations that are conceivable beyond the two that are mentioned.

Menger's approach can be said to have its prime focus on the combination A in the Matrix 1, while the emphasis of Commons' approach may be said to be on combination D. Both recognize, to be sure, the existence of rules or institutions that would fall into other categories than the ones they focus on, and both extend, at least occasionally, their analysis into other 'boxes'. But there is clearly a characteristic difference in emphasis between the two. This difference should, however, not be viewed as reflecting fundamentally conflicting methodologies. Commons' focus on organizations or corporate actors and on the rules for organized collective action does not in the least require him to adopt a nonindividualistic, collectivistic methodology. And in fact, contrary to what A. Schotter (1981: 3) and R. Langlois (1986: 4) impute and agreeing with M. Rutherford's (1983) analysis, I would argue that there is no reason to classify Commons in the methodological collectivists' camp. Where Commons criticizes the 'older individualistic economics' (1936: 247) or 'Adam Smith's mechanical principles of individualism' (1968: 6), this is evidently not meant in a methodological sense. Commons does not want to advocate the adoption of an alternative, 'collectivistic' methodology. Rather, he wants to draw attention to the social reality of collective action, to the role that organizations or corporate actors play as decision-making and acting units in the socioeconomic world.

It is neither adequate nor fruitful to interpret the difference between Menger and Commons as a matter of conflicting methodologies or theoretical perspectives. The two authors' approaches can be more fruitfully read as compatible and complementary contributions to different aspects of institutional reality. There is no reason why Commons' two theories, as reconstructed in this paper, could not be incorporated into a methodologically individualist framework. Commons' corporate actor theory can, indeed, be interpreted as a contribution to a methodologically individualistic theory of collective action, a contribution that, in various respects, is not unlike James Coleman's (1986) more recent outline of an individualistic theory of corporate action. A truly general individualistic theory of institutions ought to account for the collective action part of the institutional spectrum no less than for the – in Menger's terms – 'organic' part. It would hardly make sense to deliberately confine the individualistic research programme to the study of a specific subset of the institutional universe.[37]

Under the influence of F.A. Hayek's emphasis on the 'twin ideas' of spontaneous order and evolution, the attention of those who place themselves into the individualistic tradition of institutional analysis has very much been focussed on the 'unintended outcome versus intentional design'

---

[37] It is sometimes erroneously supposed that analysing corporate actors would somehow require relinquishing the precepts of methodological individualism. E. Ullmann-Margalit (1978: 289), for instance, argues: 'The requirements of methodological individualism may

358 *Evolutionary and collective action approaches*

issue. This has distracted attention from another aspect that is equally fundamental to Hayek's discussion of institutional issues, namely his distinction between two kinds of social order, spontaneous order and organization, and his related distinction between the different kinds of rules upon which these two kinds of order are based, i.e., general rules of conduct and organizational rules.[38] If it is true, as Hayek argues, that 'the rules which determine a spontaneous order differ in important respects from another kind of rules which are needed in regulating an organization' (1973: 43), and that 'the rules which are required to maintain an operating spontaneous order and the rules which govern an organization have altogether different functions' (1976: 47), then the careful study of these differences should be a main concern for a theory of institutions.

I suppose that an institutional theory that pays attention to the study of both kinds of rules or institutions, in some way or another, will have to incorporate both kinds of perspectives that are represented by the two approaches compared in this paper, Commons' as well as Menger's.

VIII References

Alchian, A.A. 1977: Some economics of property rights. In Idem, *Economic Forces at Work*, Indianapolis: Liberty Press, 127–49.

Alchian, A.A. and **Demsetz, H.** 1973: The Property Right Paradigm. *Journal of Economic History*,

Axelrod, R. 1984: *The evolution of cooperation*. New York: Basic Books.

Blaug, M. 1985: *Economic theory in retrospect*, Fourth Edition. Cambridge: Cambridge University Press.

Buchanan, J.M. 1975: *Limits of liberty – between anarchy and Leviathan*. Chicago: University of Chicago Press.

Buchanan, J.M. 1977: Law and the invisible hand. In Idem, *Freedom in constitutional contract*, College Station: Texas A and M University, 25–39.

Butos, W.N. 1985: Menger: a suggested interpretation. *Atlantic Economic Journal*, 13, 21–30.

Coleman, J.S. 1986: *Individual interests and collective action, selected essays*. Cambridge: Cambridge University Press.

---

be relaxed to allow units larger than the single individual, such as households or firms, to be the deliberating, deciding, and ultimately acting participants.' – Following J.S. Coleman's theoretical approach I have attempted in Vanberg (1982) to outline in some detail the general structure of a consistently individualistic theory of corporate action.

[38] Hayek (1973: 2): '[A] selfgenerating or spontaneous order and an organization are distinct, and . . . their distinctiveness is related to the two different kinds of rules or laws which prevail in them.' For a more detailed discussion of the two kinds of order and the two kinds of rules see Hayek (1973: 48ff). It is worth mentioning that O. Williamson (1975: 254) in the context of his reference to Commons talks about the '. . . significant difference between the working rules . . . of markets and internal organizations'.

Commons, J.R. 1931: Institutional economics. *American Economic Review* 21, 648–57.

——1934: *Institutional economics – its place in political economy.* New York: Macmillan.

——1936: Institutional economics. *American Economic Review* 26, Supplement, 237–49.

——1950: *The economics of collective action.* New York: Macmillan.

——1968: *Legal foundations of capitalism.* Madison, Milwaukee, and London: The University of Wisconsin Press.

Coase, R.H. 1984: The new institutional economics. *Journal of Institutional and Theoretical Economics* 140, 229–31.

Demsetz, H. 1975: Toward a theory of property rights. In Manne, H.G., editor, *The economics of legal relationships*, St. Paul et al.: West Publishing Company, 23–36.

Furubotn, E.G. and **Pejovich, S.** 1975: Property rights and economic theory: a survey of recent literature. In Manne, H.G., editor, *The economics of legal relationships*, St. Paul et al.: West Publishing Company, 53–65.

Furubotn, E.G. and **Richter, R.** 1984: The new institutional economics, editorial preface. *Journal of Institutional and Theoretical Economics* 140, 1–6.

Gruchy, A.G. 1940: John R. Commons' concept of twentieth-century economics. *Journal of Political Economy* 48, 823–49.

Hayek, F.A. 1952: *The counter-revolution of science.* Glencoe, Illinois: The Free Press.

——1967: *Studies in philosophy, politics and economics.* Chicago: University of Chicago Press.

——1973: *Law, legislation and liberty*, Volume I, Rules and order. London and Henley: Routledge and Kegan Paul.

——1976: *Law, legislation and liberty*, Volume II, The mirage of social justice. London and Henley: Routledge and Kegan Paul.

——1978: *New studies in philosophy, politics, economics, and the history of ideas.* Chicago: University of Chicago Press.

——1979: *Law, legislation and liberty*, Volume III, The political order of a free people. London and Henley: Routledge and Kegan Paul.

Hutchison, T.W. 1984: Institutionalist economics – old and new. *Journal of Institutional and Theoretical Economics* 140, 20–29.

Langlois, R.N. 1986: The 'new institutional economics': an introductory essay. In Idem, editor, *Economics as a process. Essays in the new institutional economics*, Cambridge: Cambridge University Press, 1–25.

——1988: *What was wrong with the 'old' institutional economics? (And what is still wrong with the 'new'.* Review of Political Economy 1, 272–300.

Menger, C. 1981: *Principles of economics.* New York and London: New York University Press.

——1984: *The origins of money.* Greenwich, CT: Committee for Monetary Research & Education.

360   *Evolutionary and collective action approaches*

——1985: *Investigations into the method of the social sciences with special reference to economics*. New York and London: New York University Press.

Mitchell, W.C. 1935: Commons on institutional economics. *American Economic Review* 25, 635–52.

O'Driscoll, G.P., Junior 1986: Money: Menger's evolutionary theory. *History of Political Economy* 18, 601–16.

Ostrom, V. 1976: John R. Commons's foundations for policy analysis. *Journal of Economic Issues* 10, 839–57.

Parsons, K.H. 1950: John R. Commons' point of view, Appendix iii. In Commons, J.R., *The economics of collective action*, New York: Macmillan, 341–75.

Rutherford, M. 1983: J.R. Commons's institutional economics. *Journal of Economic Issues* 17, 721–44.

——1988: *What is wrong with the new institutional economics (and what is still wrong with the old)?*. *Review of Political Economy* 1, 301–20.

Schotter, A. 1981: *The Economic Theory of Social Institutions*, Cambridge: Cambridge University Press.

Ullmann-Margalit, E. 1978: Invisible hand explanations. *Syntheses* 39, 263–91.

Vanberg, V. 1975: *Die zwei Soziologien – Individualismus und Kollektivismus in der Sozialtheorie*. Tübingen: J.C.B. Mohr (Paul Siebeck).

——1982: *Markt und Organisation – Individualistische Sozialtheorie und das Problem korporativen Handelns*. Tübingen: J.C.B. Mohr (Paul Siebeck).

——1983: Der individualistische Ansatz zu einer Theorie der Entstehung und Entwicklung von Institutionen. *Jahrbuch für Neue Politische Ökonomie* 2, 50–69.

——1984: 'Unsichtbare-Hand Erklärung' und soziale Normen. In Horst T., editor, *Normgeleitetes Verhalten in den Sozialwissenschaften*, Berlin: Duncker and Humblot, 115–46.

Vanberg, V. and **Buchanan, J.M.** 1988: Rational choice und moral order. *Analyse und Kritik* 10.

Williamson, O.E. 1975: *Markets and hierarchies: analysis and antitrust implications*. New York: Free Press.

——1985: Reflections on the new institutional economics. *Journal of Institutional and Theoretical Economics* 141, 187–95.

Witt, U. 1988: *On the evolution of economic institutions*. University of Freiburg, Mimeograph.

[4]

Metroeconomica 44:1 (1993)   pp. 001–028

INSTITUTIONAL ECONOMICS:
SURVEYING THE 'OLD' AND THE 'NEW'

Geoffrey M. Hodgson
University of Cambridge
(April 1991: revised September 1991)

ABSTRACT

This paper surveys and compares the literature on the 'new' institutionalism (North, Williamson, etc.) with that of the 'old' (Veblen, Commons, Mitchell). A criterion for distinguishing these two schools is suggested, along with criticisms of the limitations of each. The 'new' institutionalism is associated with methodological individualism and the idea that the individual should be taken as given. Particular attention is paid to 'new' institutionalist treatments of markets and firms. The paper moves on to examine some 'old' institutionalist criticisms of 'economic man' as well as some negative features of the 'old' institutionalism. On the positive side, the latter is seen to have an 'evolutionary' dimension, related to modern work in the area of technological change.

I. INTRODUCTION

Since the mid-1970s there has been a remarkable growth in what has been dubbed the 'new institutional economics'. Much of this has resulted from work within or close to the mainstream of economic theory. One of the many noteworthy features of this development is that it provides a forceful response to the old allegation that mainstream economists took institutions as given or for granted. Indeed, central concerns of the practitioners of the 'new' institutional economics include the analysis of the emergence of institutions and of their comparative efficiency.

It is also significant that the epithet 'new' was chosen precisely to distinguish the more recent approaches from the 'old' institutionalist

---

[1] In writing this article, the author is grateful for the supportive facilities of the Swedish Collegium for Advanced Study in the Social Sciences. He also wishes to thank Mats Lundahl, Francis Sejersted and many others for helpful discussions, as well as Sergio Parrinello for useful editorial advice.

2 *G. M. Hodgson*

school of Thorstein Veblen, John Commons, Wesley Clair Mitchell and others. Although the 'old' institutionalism was a very prominent paradigm amongst US economists in the 1920s and 1930s, many textbooks and histories of economic thought had provided its obituary by the 1960s. Yet one of the late side-effects of the emergence of the 'new' institutionalism was precisely to revive a debate about the nature and viability of the 'old'.[2]

After the heydey of the 'old' institutionalism, economics was affected not simply by the so-called 'Keynesian revolution', but arguably even more profoundly by the 'formalistic revolution' of the 1930s and 1940s (Ward, 1972). It was largely this increasingly self-confident postwar tendency towards a mathematical formalism based on the mechanistic metaphor taken from nineteenth-century physics (Ingrao and Israel, 1990; Mirowski, 1989) that finally led to the eclipse of the 'old' institutionalism and made it the pursuit of a small and relatively isolated minority.

Such a formalistic theoretical system dominated economics in the 1950s and 1960s. However, the breakdown in the postwar consensus in economic theory in the 1970s, and the perception of growing 'crisis' within the discipline, provided the context in which pronounced developments in the new institutionalism occurred in the 1970s.

Although the label is not always used consistently or unambiguously, a list of contributions within or close to the new institutionalist genre could include the following: Kenneth Arrow (1974) and William Niskanen (1971) on organizations and bureaucracies; Mancur Olson (1965) on collective action; Eirik Furubotn and Svetozar Pejovich (1972, 1974) and James Buchanan et al (1980) on the economics of property rights and rent-seeking; Richard Posner (1973) on economics and law; Friedrich Hayek (1982, 1988) and Robert Sugden (1989) on the emergence of 'spontaneous order'; Bo Gustafsson (1991), Douglass North and Robert Thomas (1973), and Douglass North (1981, 1990) on economic history; Mancur Olson (1982) on economic growth; and Armen Alchian and Harold Demsetz (1972), Masahiko Aoki *et al* (1990), Steven Cheung (1983), Michael Jensen and William Meckling (1976), and Oliver Williamson (1975, 1985) on the theory of the firm. The work of Ronald Coase (1937, 1960) is an important precursor in the areas of

---

[2] For contributions to this debate see, for example, Boettke (1989), Dugger (1983), Field (1979), Hodgson (1988, 1989), Langlois (1989), Leathers (1989, 1990), Mayhew (1989), Mirowski (1981), Rutherford (1989a, 1989b), Samuels (1989b), Vanberg (1989), Wynarczyk (1992). Several of these authors stress points of similarity between the 'old' institutionalism and other schools of thought, as well as key points of difference.

property rights and transaction cost economics. More general analyses of rules, norms and institutions in the new institutionalist vein include Robert Axelrod (1986), Jon Elster (1989), Nicolas Rowe (1989), Andrew Schotter (1981), Robert Sugden (1986), Edna Ullmann-Margalit (1977) and many others.[3]

As discussed below, there is a variety of theoretical approaches represented here. However, most of them address a prominent new institutionalist theme: to explain the existence of political, legal, or more generally, social institutions by reference to a model of individual behaviour, tracing out its consequences in terms of human interactions. For mainstream economics, this clearly implies, as James Buchanan (1991, p. 19) succinctly puts it, a 'shift of focus away from in-period, or within-rules, choices to choices among constraints or sets of rules'.

Whilst it involves much innovative development and major theoretical modifications, it shall be argued below that much of the new institutionalism nevertheless leaves many of the core assumptions of mainstream economics unscathed. The irony, of course, is that the original institutionalism of Veblen and others emerged largely out of a critique of orthodox assumptions.

Hence, to complicate matters still further, there are currently signs of a renewal of the 'old' institutionalism as well. This is shown in a growing number of other recent publications with 'old' institutionalist themes.[4] In addition, there are recent signs that 'old' institutionalism may be spreading to Europe and elsewhere, with several related publications by European writers. This 'European' variant has strong links with other schools of thought, including Post Keynesians, Schumpeterians, Marxists and the French *régulation* school.[5]

---

[3] This list is inevitably partial and fragmentary. Additional, but also incomplete, surveys of this large and rapidly expanding field are found, for instance, in Eggertsson (1990) and Moe (1984). For an important collection of essays described as a contribution to the new institutional economics see Langlois (1986). There are a number of journal symposia on the new institutional economics, for example the March 1990 issue of the *Journal of Institutional and Theoretical Economics* (Vol. 146, No. 1), and the September 1989 issue of *World Development* (Vol. 17, No. 9). Note also that the use of the term 'new institutionalism' is not uniform. For example, March and Olsen (1984) use it in a quite unique sense, claiming some continuity with the 'old' institutionalism.

[4] In 1966 the *Journal of Economic Issues* was launched by the USA-based Association for Evolutionary Economics, the organization of American institutionalists. See also, for instance, Gordon and Adams (1989), Kapp (1976), Myrdal (1976), Samuels (1988), Samuels *et al* (forthcoming) and Tool and Samuels (1989a, 1989b, 1989c).

[5] For recent works in this area by European authors see, for instance, Clark and Juma (1987), Dopfer (1976), Dosi *et al* (1988), Foster (1987), Hanusch (1988) and Hodgson (1988, 1993). In 1988 the European Association for Evolutionary Political Economy was formed, as an association of evolutionary and institutional economists.

4

G. M. Hodgson

Section II of this essay involves a critical review of some aspects of the new institutionalism. On this basis a conceptual distinction between the 'old' and the 'new' institutionalism is proposed, related to the question of methodological individualism. This hinges in part on the choice of factors to be taken as exogenous, and in part on the questions deemed appropriate for study.

Given the huge and rapidly expanding volume of the new institutionalist literature, the approach here has to be selective, paying little attention to several important developments, such as the new institutionalist theories of property rights and law. Instead, particular attention is paid to the new institutionalist treatments of markets and firms.

Section III, on the 'old' institutionalism, has three purposes. The first is to examine some 'old' institutionalist criticisms of 'economic man'. The second is to identify some negative features of the 'old' institutionalism. The third is to comment on its research programme, with particular attention to its 'evolutionary' dimension. The latter involves a brief discussion of 'old' institutionalist approaches to the theory of technological change. Section IV concludes the essay.

II. THE NEW INSTITUTIONALISM

Taking individuals as exogenous

If 'neoclassical economics' is defined as an approach which is based on the assumption of 'rational' individuals and equilibrium-orientated analysis, then not all new institutionalists are neoclassical. Austrian writers such as Hayek, for example, are highly critical of the type of Walrasian theory that has dominated the mainstream since the Second World War. Furthermore, modern developments in game theory venture close to the boundaries of neoclassical theory, and offer, for instance, some challenges to the conventional definition of rationality.

In contrast, some of the other new institutionalist theorists cited above, such as Arrow, Furubotn, Jensen, Meckling, North, Olson, Pejovich, Posner and Williamson are closer to the neoclassical mainstream. Furthermore, there are extensive differences of policy outlook in the new institutionalist camp, with the almost unqualified pro-market stance of Hayek (1982, 1988) on the one hand, and the game-theoretic critique of free-market policies by Schotter (1990) on the other. However, even with the many important differences, and despite the fact that there are non-neoclassical as well as neoclassical members of

Institutional economics   5

the set of new institutionalist writers, it is argued below that all of these
types of new institutionalism share some common premises.

In one sense the adjective is misleading, for all elements of the 'new'
institutionalism are based upon some long-established assumptions concerning the human agent, derived from the influence of classic liberalism. Since its inception in the writings of John Locke and others, classic
liberalism has overshadowed economics. Consequently, it is much easier
to identify the few exceptions amongst economists – such as Karl Marx
and Thorstein Veblen – than the many conformists.

Whilst many different ideas and approaches may be grouped under
this title, including both neoclassical and non-neoclassical theories, a key
common proposition of classic liberalism is the view that the individual
can, in a sense, be 'taken for granted'. To put it another way, the
individual, along with his or her assumed behavioural characteristics, is
taken as the elemental building block in the theory of the social or
economic system.

Strictly, it is not a question of whether or not a theorist is found to
admit that individuals – or their wants and preferences – are changed by
circumstances. Indeed, all intelligent economists, from Adam Smith to
Friedrich Hayek inclusive, admit that individuals might so be changed.
What is crucial is that the classic liberal economist may make such an
admission but then go on to assume, *for the purposes of economic
enquiry*, that individuals and their preference functions should be taken
as given. Thus the demarcating criterion is not the matter of individual
malleability *per se*, but the willingness, or otherwise, to consider this
issue as an important or legitimate matter for economic enquiry.

The oft-repeated statement by orthodox economists that tastes and
preferences are not the *explananda* of economics thus derives directly
from the classic liberal tradition. It involves taking the individual 'for
granted'. Likewise, the post-Robbins conception or definition of economics as 'the science of choice' takes the choosing individual and his or
her preference function as given.[6] The new institutionalism has taken
such presuppositions on board.

The assumption of the abstract individual, which is fundamental to
classic liberalism, is basic to the new institutional economics as well. It is
thus possible to distinguish the new institutionalism from the 'old' by

---

[6] Although there have been occasional attempts by mainstream economists to treat
preference functions as endogenous, preference exogeneity remains a hallmark of neoclassical theory. The obvious problems of mathematical intractability also help to explain the
persistence of this hallmark.

6   *G. M. Hodgson*

means of this criterion. This distinction holds despite important theoretical and policy differences within the new institutionalist camp.[7]

Methodological Individualism

The notion of the abstract individual relates closely to the doctrine of
methodological individualism. From the beginning, several new institutionalist writers (e.g. Furubotn and Pejovich, 1974) made their adherence to this outlook clear. Jon Elster usefully defines it as 'the doctrine
that all social phenomena (their structure and their change) are in
principle explicable only in terms of individuals – their properties, goals,
and beliefs' (Elster, 1982, p. 453). This clear definition is quite adequate
for our purposes here, and it is similar to the classic statement of the
idea in the work of Ludwig von Mises (1949).[8]

Methodological individualists take the individual, along with his or her
assumed behavioural characteristics, as the elemental building block in
the theory of the social or economic system. As Steven Lukes (1973,
p. 73) puts it, 'individuals are pictured abstractly as given, with given
interests, wants, purposes, needs, etc.'. Clearly, assumptions of this type
are typical of neoclassical economics, as well as of the new institutionalism as a whole.

The obvious question to be raised is the legitimacy of stopping short
at the individual in the process of explanation. If individuals are affected
by their circumstances, then why not in turn attempt to explain the
causes acting upon individual 'goals and beliefs'? Why should the
process of scientific enquiry be arrested as soon as the individual is
reached?

Some writers, such as George Shackle (1989, p. 51) and Ludwig
Lachmann (1969, p. 63), suggest that individuals make choices which are

---

[7] It is notable that Eggertsson (1990) does not simply exclude the 'old' institutionalism
from his survey. He makes a further distinction between the 'neoinstitutionalist' and 'New
Institutionalist' economics. Because the latter 'has rejected the postulate of optimization
and replaced it with Herbert Simon's concept of *satisficing*' amounting to 'a rejection of
the "hard core" of the neoclassical research program' (ibid., p. 9), it is denied the central
stage. Amazingly, although Eggertsson makes a few references to Williamson, most of his
attention is directed at a quite restricted class of neoclassical and so-called 'neoinstitutionalist' writers.

[8] It should also be noted that there are 'softer' definitions of methodological individualism, as found in the works of Agassi (1975) and Popper (1945). It is beyond the scope of
this work to examine the meaning and viability of the 'softer' definitions here. For a full
examination see Udéhn (1987). The discussion in this present essay will be restricted to the
definition proposed by Elster and von Mises.

The Economics of Institutions

primary, spontaneous and essentially 'uncaused'. Even if this is accepted, there is no obvious reason to exclude the idea that at least *some* human intentions have *some* prior causes which are worthy of investigation. This conclusion is in fact fatal for methodological individualism, at least as the term is defined by Elster or von Mises.

If there are determinate influences on individuals and their goals, then these are worthy of explanation. In turn, the explanation of those may be in terms of other purposeful individuals. But where should the analysis stop? The purposes of an individual could be partly explained by relevant institutions, culture and so on. These, in their turn, would be partly explained in terms of other individuals. But these individual purposes and actions could then be partly explained by cultural and institutional factors, and so on, indefinitely.

We are involved in an apparently infinite regress, similar to the puzzle 'which came first, the chicken or the egg?' Such an analysis never reaches an end point. It is simply arbitrary to stop at one particular stage in the explanation and say 'it is all reducible to individuals', just as much as to say it is 'all social and institutional.' As Robert Nozick (1977, p. 359) remarks: 'In this apparent chicken and egg situation, why aren't we equally methodological institutionalists?' The key point is that in this infinite regress neither individual nor social factors have legitimate explanatory primacy. The idea that all explanations have to be in terms of individuals is thus unfounded.

Methodological individualism implies a rigid and dogmatic compartmentalization of study. It may be legitimate in some limited types of analysis to take individuals as given and examine the consequences of the interactions of their activities. This particular type of analysis, be it called 'situational logic' or whatever, has a worthy place, alongside other approaches, in social science. But it does not legitimate methodological individualism because the latter involves the further statement that *all* social explanations should be of this or a similar type.

The development of institutions

Having taken the individual 'for granted', the new institutionalists are then set to attempt to explain the emergence, existence, and performance of social institutions on the basis of such assumptions. Such explanations address the functioning of all kinds of social institutions in terms of the interactions between given individuals. Of course, the existence of institutions is seen to affect individual behaviour, but only

8 *G. M. Hodgson*

in terms of the choices and constraints presented to the agents, not by the moulding of the preferences and indeed the very individuality of those agents themselves.

In other words, once institutions have emerged on the basis of individual behaviours, they are seen simply as providing external constraints, conventions or openings to individuals who are taken as given. It is assumed that individual actions lead to the formation of institutions, but institutions do not change individuals, other than by supplying information or constraints. The possibility that individuals themselves may be shaped in some fundamental manner by social institutions is not considered.

These common features of the new institutionalism may be illustrated in a number of ways, and here we must confine ourselves to a few examples. Consider first the largely neoclassical work by North and Thomas (1973) on the rise of Western capitalism. Although many factors are highlighted in their discussion of this transition from feudalism, the emergence of well-defined private property rights is given a central position. It is presumed that with the gradual emergence of private property in medieval England, rational, calculating individuals began to undertake profit-seeking activities, leading eventually to greater economic prosperity for the nation as a whole.

However, despite its value and sophistication, the North-Thomas analysis fails to explain the rational, deliberative and guileful individual which it assumes at the outset. Robert Holton (1985, p. 54) has made this point well in his comprehensive discussion of transition theories: 'As with so much economic theory, the calculative, rational individual is presumed rather than explained.' In this respect at least, the new institutionalist approach of North and Thomas contrasts with the earlier, seminal work of Karl Marx (1973, p. 84) and Max Weber (1930, 1947), who were both keen to explain the origin and development of a culture of self-interested maximizers, composed of individuals acting on the basis of rational calculation. They saw these as specific historical phenomena, rather than as elemental and universal features of human life. Thus Marx and Weber did not presume that such rational, calculating individuals have existed for all historical time. Their emergence had to be explained in terms of such factors as changes in culture and institutions.

Related points are central to Alexander Field's (1979, 1981, 1984) forceful critique of the North-Thomas approach and of associated developments in the game-theoretic approach to institutions. In attempting to explain the origin of social institutions, the new institutional economic history has to presume given individuals acting in a certain context. Along with the assumption of given individuals is the assumption of given rules of behaviour governing their interaction. What is forgotten is that in the original, hypothetical 'state of nature' from which institutions are seen to have emerged, a number of weighty rules, institutions and cultural and social norms have already been presumed.

Consider another important type of new institutionalist theory. Game theorists such as Schotter (1981) also take the individual 'for granted', as an agent unambiguously maximizing his or her expected payoff. Further, in attempting to explain the origin of institutions through game theory, Field points out that certain norms and rules must inevitably be presumed at the start. There can be no games without rules, and thus game theory can never explain the elemental rules themselves. Even in a sequence of repeated games, or of games about other (nested) games, at least one game or meta-game, with a structure and payoffs, must be assumed at the outset. Any such attempt to deal with history in terms of sequential or nested games is thus involved in a problem of infinite regress: even with games about games about games to the nth degree there is still one preceding game left to be explained.

Naturally, all theories must first build from elements which are taken as given, and this is no exception. However, the particular problem of infinite regress that is identified here undermines any 'new institutionalist' claim that the explanation of the emergence of institutions can start from some kind of institution-free ensemble of individuals in which there is supposedly no rule or institution to be explained.

Consequently, the new institutionalist project to explain the emergence of institutions on the basis of given individuals has run into difficulties, particularly in regard to the conceptualization of the initial state from which institutions are supposed to emerge. This is graphically illustrated in regard to the question of the market.

The conceptualization of the market

One of the striking features of neoclassical theory is that it does not normally conceive of the market in institutional terms. It typically presumes that the market is the ether within which the preferences and purposes of free-floating individuals are expressed. The market is not seen as an organised and functional entity, but as an aggregation of mere individual traders and exchanges. The notion of the market as an institution, itself organised to structure – and even to some extent to

10 *G. M. Hodgson*

constrain – economic activity, is missing. In neoclassical theory the 'constraints' relate exclusively to market 'imperfections' of extra-market institutions.

Much new institutionalist writing has this deficiency. In attempting to explain the emergence of specific institutions, it is assumed that the market has a prior existence, as an institution-free 'state of nature'. Thus, for instance, Williamson (1975, p. 20) writes that 'in the beginning there were markets' without noting the problem of examining the origin of market institutions. Likewise, in his discussion of economic growth, Olson (1982) first assumes a market and institution-free 'state of nature', associated with faster economic growth, which is subsequently retarded by the emergence of 'interest groups' and 'institutional sclerosis'. This wrongly suggests that markets themselves can be entirely free of institutional restrictions and coalitions of agents.

In contrast to these authors, a number of other writers have argued that the market is not a natural datum or ether, but it is itself a social institution, governed by sets of rules defining restrictions on some, and legitimating other, behaviours (Dosi, 1988a; Hodgson, 1988; Lowry, 1976). For example, when criticizing the work of Hayek on this issue, Viktor Vanberg (1986, p. 75) points out that the market 'is always a system of social interaction characterized by a specific *institutional framework*, that is, by a *set of rules* defining certain restrictions on the behavior of market participants'. Whether these rules are formal or informal, the result is that there is no such thing as the 'true, unhampered market' operating in an institutional vacuum. 'This raises the issue of what rules can be considered "appropriate" in the sense of allowing for a beneficial working of the market mechanism' (*ibid*, p. 97).

The 'old' institutionalist Karl Polanyi (1944) argued at length that the market is necessarily embedded in other social institutions such as the state, and is promoted or even, in some cases, created by conscious design. It is indeed striking that modern experimental economists, in attempting to simulate the market, have found that they face the unavoidable initial problem of setting up its institutional structure. As Vernon Smith (1982, p. 923) writes: 'It is not possible to design a resource allocation experiment without designing an institution in all its detail.'

This raises the issue of Carl Menger's (1963) distinction between 'organic' social institutions which are unplanned and unintentional, on the one hand, and those 'pragmatic' institutions which result from conscious design, on the other. Nevertheless, the distinction may not be as hard-and-fast as Menger suggests. Just as it is dubious that a purely 'organic' institution has ever existed, or could conceivably do so, it is unlikely that any institution has emerged entirely according to plan. Arguably, most, if not all, institutions result from a combination of both intended plans and unintended consequences.[9]

The theory of the firm

We now consider an important subset of new institutionalist writing, in regard to the theory of the firm and particularly the work of Williamson (1975, 1985). Superficially, his work seems to be a departure from much of orthodoxy. For example, he claims to be influenced by Herbert Simon and the behaviouralist school, and if this influence were substantial, it would suggest a break from the neoclassical axiom of maximizing behaviour based on individual rationality.

However, on closer inspection it is evident that Williamson's break from neoclassical theory is partial and incomplete, and much of the core neoclassical apparatus is retained. In fact, Williamson's claimed departure from orthodoxy sits uneasily alongside his repeated invocation that agents are marked by 'opportunism' (i.e. 'self-interest seeking with guile'). Despite much discussion of 'altruism' by neoclassical economists, self-interest remains a typical assumption of the mainstream of economic theory.

Following Ronald Coase (1937), Williamson argues that the existence of firms and their internal supersession of the market mechanism is due to the significant transaction costs involved in market trading. In Williamson's (e.g. 1985, p. 32) hands this Coasian idea is repeatedly linked with that of Simon: 'Economizing on transaction costs essentially reduces to economizing on bounded rationality'. Essentially, the problem is that Williamson has taken only part of Simon's (1957, 1959) argument on board and he is influenced too much by common, but inaccurate, interpretations of behaviouralism.

Simon's argument, of course, is that a complete or global rational calculation is ruled out, thus rationality is 'bounded'; agents do not maximize, but attempt to attain acceptable minima instead. But it is important to note that this 'satisficing' behaviour does not simply arise because of inadequate information, but also because it would be too

---

[9] Furthermore, as Prisching (1989) and others have pointed out, Menger did not give the unqualified support to the free market that is found in some later Austrian writing.

12   *G. M. Hodgson*

difficult to perform the calculations even if the relevant information
were available.

Given this point, a prevailing orthodox interpretation of Simon's work
can be faulted; the recognition of bounded rationality refers primarily to
the matter of computational capacity and not to additional 'costs'.
Furthermore, 'satisficing' does not amount to cost-minimizing behaviour.
Clearly, the latter is just the dual of the standard assumption of
maximization; if 'satisficing' was essentially a matter of minimizing costs,
then it would amount to maximizing behaviour of the orthodox type.[10]

Basically, Williamson adopts the orthodox, cost-minimizing interpretation of Simon and not the one which clearly prevails in Simon's own
work. In Williamson's work 'economizing on transaction costs' is part of
global, cost-minimizing behaviour, and this is inconsistent with Simon's
idea of bounded rationality. Whilst Williamson recognises some of the
informational problems, the fact that the cost calculus remains supreme
in his theory means that he has not broken entirely from the orthodox
assumption of maximization.

Consistent with the retention of the basic orthodox model of optimizing behaviour, Williamson assumes that individual preference functions
are unchanged by the economic environment and the institutions in
which individuals are located. Williamson's work also retains the orthodox assumption of maximizing (or cost-minimizing) behaviour and
reflects some of the ontological presumptions of classic liberalism.
Despite its apparent novelty, and its refreshing attempt to open up the
'black box' of the firm, Williamson's work lies close to the neoclassical
pole of the new institutionalist spectrum.[11]

It seems, therefore, that all varieties of new institutionalism, despite
big differences in analytical methods and even policy conclusions, are
united by their assumption that individual preferences and purposes are
exogenous. In all cases the processes governing their determination and
change are disregarded.

---

[10] Thus Jensen and Meckling (1976, p. 307n.) are in error when they write that 'Simon's
work has often been misinterpreted as a denial of maximizing behavior . . . His later use of
the term "satisficing" . . . has undoubtedly contributed to this confusion because it suggests
rejection of maximizing behaviour rather than maximization subject to costs of information
and decision making.' Indeed, the misinterpretation of Simon's work is Jensen and
Meckling's. The term 'satisficing' is employed by Simon precisely to distance his conception from 'substantive' rationality and maximizing behaviour. It is symptomatic that
Williamson, for example, uses the term 'bounded rationality' much more often than
'satisficing'.
[11] For fundamental criticisms of Williamson's transaction costs theory of the firm see
Dietrich (1991), Dow (1987), Francis *et al* (1983) and Hodgson (1988).

III. THE OLD INSTITUTIONALISM

The mid-century impasse

It may be stated at the outset that the legacy of Veblen, Commons, Mitchell and other American institutionalists has not been entirely positive. Veblen (1919, p. 68), for instance, felt uneasy with intellectual 'symmetry and system-making.' The degree of imprecision in which Veblen's ideas were termed became an impediment to their theoretical development. Despite his concerns in these areas, no adequate systematic theory of industry, technology or the macro-economy appears in his work. Consequently, the institutionalists had to look elsewhere for a basis for their policy recommendations. It is partly because Veblen addressed economic systems in such complex and dynamic terms that he fails to provide a systemic theory. Thus, without leaving a theoretical system of the stature or scope of that of Marx, Marshall or Walras, he left the door open for an even more impressionistic approach to economics amongst his followers.

As for Commons, although he made major contributions to the theory of institutions (Commons, 1924, 1934, 1950), it is with some justice that Vanberg (1989, p. 343) writes that 'his idiosyncratic terminology and unsystematic style of reasoning are not particularly conducive to an understanding of his theoretical concerns.' Commons attempted to build a theoretical system, but the result does not rank in stature to that of Marx, Walras or Marshall. Mitchell's role in the development of national income accounting is enormous, yet his immersion in the processing of data left the task of theoretical development to others at a critical time.

Thus the 'old' institutionalism established the importance of institutions and proclaimed the need for a genuinely evolutionary economics, but then proceeded in a more and more descriptive direction, leaving many of the core theoretical questions unanswered. After half a century of prominence, even sympathizers such as Gunnar Myrdal (1958, p. 254) saw traditional American institutional economics as marked by a 'naive empiricism'.

The mid-century impasse of the 'old' institutionalism did not mean, however, that its approach to economic theory has become irrelevant or outdated. What marks the 'old' institutionalism is its rejection of the ontological and methodological presumptions of classic liberalism. The individual is no longer taken as given.

Indeed, similar concerns have been expressed by many other modern

14   *G. M. Hodgson*

theorists. For example, the sociologist Anthony Giddens (1984, p. 220) argues that the individual, as a fundamental unit, 'cannot be taken as obvious'. Likewise, the economist Tony Lawson (1987, p. 969) expresses anti-reductionist sentiments when he remarks that 'individual agency and social structures and context are equally relevant for analysis – each presupposes each other. Thus any reductionist account stressing analytical primacy for either individual agents or for social "wholes" must be inadequate'.

Above all, the 'old' warnings about proceeding on classic liberal assumptions should not be ignored. In this respect at least the 'old' institutionalism retains some advantages over the new. In addition, as argued below, there is an implicit research programme in Veblen's writings which connects directly with modern work in evolutionary economics.

It should not be claimed, however, that the 'old' institutionalists have yet overcome the problems of theoretical complexity involved in the treatment of the economy in an organicist manner, in which individuals and their preference functions are shaped by circumstances. All that can be identified are hints and pointers to what seems to be a set of potentially useful lines of enquiry.

Veblen's critique of rational economic man

In his famous critique of economic man as 'a lightning calculator of pleasures and pains', Veblen (1919, p. 73) foreshadowed some of the postwar theoretical critiques of 'rational economic man'. The ironic 'lightning calculator' phrase suggests that the problems of global calculation of maximization opportunities are ignored by the neoclassical theorists. This reminds the modern reader of Simon's idea of limited computational capacity and 'bounded rationality'. In describing economic man as having 'neither antecedent nor consequent' Veblen identified and criticized the uncreative and mechanistic picture of the agent in neoclassical theory.

What is not widely appreciated is that Veblen gave further grounds for rejecting orthodox assumptions, other than on the basis of their apparent unrealism. As Thomas Sowell (1967) points out, Veblen (1919, p. 221) accepted that to be 'serviceable' a hypothesis need 'not be true to fact'. He understood that 'economic man' and similar conceptions were 'not intended as a competent expression of fact', but represented an 'expedient of abstract reasoning' (ibid., p. 142).

Veblen's crucial argument against orthodox theory was that it was inadequate for the theoretical purpose at hand. His intention was to analyze the processes of change and transformation in the modern economy. Neoclassical theory was defective in this respect because it indicated 'the conditions of survival to which any innovation is subject, supposing the innovation to have taken place, not the conditions of variational growth' (Veblen, 1919, pp. 176-7). But what Veblen was seeking was precisely a theory as to why such innovations take place, not a theory which ruminates over equilibrium conditions after technological possibilities are established. 'The question', Veblen (1934, p. 8) wrote, 'is not how things stabilize themselves in a "static state", but how they endlessly grow and change.'

Veblen put stress both on the processes of economic evolution and technological transformation, and on the manner in which action is moulded by circumstances. He saw the individual's conduct as being influenced by relations of an institutional nature, thus suggesting an alternative to orthodox theory with its self-contained, rational individual, with autonomous preferences and beliefs, formed apart from the social and natural world. A 'globule of desire', to use Veblen's (1919, p. 73) famous and satiric phrase.

He rejected the continuously calculating, marginally adjusting agent of neoclassical theory to emphasize inertia and habit instead. 'The situation of today shapes the institutions of tomorrow through a selective, coercive process, by acting upon men's habitual view of things, and so altering or fortifying a point of view or a mental attitude handed down from the past' (Veblen, 1899, pp. 190–1). According to Veblen (1919, p. 239), institutions are 'settled habits of thought common to the generality of men'. They are seen as both outgrowths and reinforcers of the routinized thought processes that are shared by a number of persons in a given society.[12]

It was argued that neoclassical economics had a 'faulty conception of human nature' wrongly conceiving of the individual 'in hedonistic terms; that is to say, in terms of a passive and substantially inert and immutably given human nature' (Veblen, 1919, p. 73). Thus Veblen's critique was directed not only at neoclassical economics, as defined

---

[12] Note also the famous definition of the institution by the later institutionalist writer, Walton Hamilton (1963, p. 84): 'It connotes a way of thought or action of some prevalence and permanence, which is embedded in the habits of a group or the customs of a people. ... Institutions fix the confines of and impose form upon the activities of human beings.' This is to be preferred to Veblen's rather mentalistic definition because of its inclusion of human action as well as thought.

16 *G. M. Hodgson*

above, but at all theories in which the individual is taken as given.

The Veblenian theme of the endogeneity of preferences is persistent in the history of the old institutionalism, up to the present day. For example, the account of the emergence of money, such as developed by Mitchell (1950), suggests that this event cannot be explained simply because it reduced costs or made life easier for traders. The penetration of money exchange into social life altered the very configurations of rationality, involving the particular conceptions of abstraction, measurement, quantification and calculative intent. It was thus a transformation of individuals and their preference functions rather than simply the emergence of institutions and rules. Similar themes are also found in the more recent writings of John Kenneth Galbraith (1958, 1969) with his continuing insistence that tastes are malleable and that the idea of 'consumer sovereignty' is a myth.

Institutionalism and evolutionary economics

Veblen's rejection of the assumption of given individuals is directly connected to his attempt to construct an 'evolutionary' economics. He saw instincts, habits and institutions in economic evolution as analogous to genes in biology. Whilst they are more malleable and do not mutate in the same way as their biological analogue, such structures and routines have a stable and inert quality, and tend to sustain and thus 'pass on' their important characteristics through time.

For Veblen, habits and institutions had a cognitive dimension. 'The situation of today shapes the institutions of tomorrow through a selective, coercive process, by acting upon men's habitual view of things, and so altering or fortifying a point of view or a mental attitude handed down from the past' (Veblen, 1899, pp. 190–1). Furthermore: 'A habitual line of action constitutes a habitual line of thought, and gives the point of view from which facts and events are apprehended and reduced to a body of knowledge' (Veblen, 1934, p. 88).

As I have argued elsewhere (Hodgson, 1988), a number of more recent developments in modern anthropology and psychology also suggest that institutions play an essential role in providing a cognitive framework for interpreting sense data and in providing intellectual habits or routines for transforming information into useful knowledge. Given that it is impossible to deal with and understand the entire amount of sense-data which reaches the brain, we rely on concepts and cognitive frames to select aspects of the data and to make sense of these stimulii. These procedures of perception and cognition are learned and acquired from our social surroundings. As cultural anthropologists argue, social institutions, culture and routines give rise to certain ways of selecting and understanding data.

Reference to the cognitive functions of institutions and routines is clearly important in understanding their relative stability and capacity to replicate. Habits and routines are both durable and present in a variety of forms in any complex economy. As in the case of Darwin's theory, this combination of variety with durability provides a basis for evolutionary selection to work. Often unwittingly and without human design, certain institutions and patterns of behaviour become more effective in the given environmental context. Even without changes in the environment the evolutionary process is unceasing. But environmental changes can accelerate, hinder or disrupt the processes of selection, often in dramatic ways.

The idea that routines within the firm act as 'genes' to pass on skills and information has been adopted more recently by Nelson and Winter (1982, pp. 134–6) and forms a crucial part of their theoretical model of the modern corporation. Despite making no reference to the earlier work of Veblen, their work is much closer to the 'old' institutionalism than to the 'new'.

Economic evolution and cumulative causation

Veblen (1919, pp. 74–5) wrote: 'The economic life history of the individual is a cumulative process of adaptation of means to ends that cumulatively change as the process goes on, both the agent and his environment being at any point the outcome of the last process.' This is a full, phylogenetic conception of evolution, in which all elements may change in a process of cumulative causation. Strikingly, the individual and his or her preferences are not taken as fixed or given.

Veblen adopted a 'post-Darwinian' outlook which put emphasis on 'the process of causation' rather than 'that consummation in which causal effect was once presumed to come to rest.' For Veblen, 'modern science is becoming substantially a theory of the process of consecutive change, realized to be self-continuing or self-propagating and to have no final term' (Veblen, 1919, p. 37). Hence Veblen saw modern science as moving away from conceptualizations of equilibria and comparative statics.

In arguing that economics should be an 'evolutionary science', Veblen

18 *G. M. Hodgson*

(1899, p. 188) wrote: 'The life of man in society, just as the life of other species, is a struggle for existence, and therefore it is a process of selective adaptation. The evolution of social structure has been a process of natural selection of institutions.'

The 'selective, coercive process' of institutional replication is not, however, confined to a fixed groove. Institutions change, and even gradual change can eventually put such a strain on a system that there can be outbreaks of conflict or crisis, leading to a change in actions and attitudes. Thus there is always the possibility of the breakdown of regularity: 'there will be moments of crisis situations or structural breaks when existing conventions or social practices are disrupted' (Lawson, 1985, p. 920). In any social system there is an interplay between routinized behaviour and the variable or volatile decisions of other agents.

Such a tension between regularity and crisis is shown in the following quotation from Veblen: 'Not only is the individual's conduct hedged about and directed by his habitual relations to his fellows in the group, but these relations, being of an institutional character, vary as the institutional scene varies. The wants and desires, the end and the aim, the ways and the means, the amplitude and drift of the individual's conduct are functions of an institutional variable that is of a highly complex and wholly unstable character' (Veblen, 1919, pp. 242–3).

With these ingredients it is possible to envisage processes whereby for long periods the reigning habits of thought and action are cumulatively reinforced. But this very process can lead to sudden and rapid change. Veblen's conception of evolution is thus more like the idea of 'punctuated equilibria' advanced by biologists Niles Eldredge and Stephen Jay Gould (1972, 1977) than orthodox Darwinian gradualism.[13] Crucially, the Eldredge-Gould idea of punctuated equilibria relies on the notion of a hierarchy of both processes and units of replication. Whilst relative stability may arise from sufficient compatibility between the different levels for some time, cumulative disturbances at one or more levels, or exogenous shocks, can lead to a breakdown in the former 'equilibrium' and herald developments along a different path.

In Veblen's view the economic system is not a 'self-balancing mechanism', but a 'cumulatively unfolding process'. It is not well known, but Veblen's idea of cumulative causation was an important precursor of other developments of the very same concept by Allyn Young (1928),

---

[13] For other discussions of punctuated equilibria in an economic context see Mokyr (1990, 1991) and Hodgson (1991c).

Gunnar Myrdal (1939, 1944, 1957), Nicholas Kaldor (1972) and K. William Kapp (1976). Because of the momentum of technological and social change in modern industrial society, and the clashing new conceptions and traditions thrown up with each innovation in management and technique, the cumulative character of economic development can mean crisis on occasions rather than continuous change or advance.

We have noted the imprecision in, and incompleteness of, Veblen's ideas. In part, this stems from the limited development of evolutionary theory in biology at his time. However, despite its limitations, Veblen's writing stands out as the most successful attempt, at least until the 1970s, to incorporate post-Darwinian biological thinking into economics and social science. The principal component of this achievement is its embodiment of the idea of the cumulatively self-reinforcing institution as the socio-economic analogue of the gene, to be subject to the forces of mutation and selection.

In his relative success with the evolutionary metaphor, Veblen speaks more loudly and clearly than Marx, although without the latter's symphonic grandeur (Hodgson, 1992). Alfred Marshall's invocation of biology is famous, but Brinley Thomas (1991) shows that Marshall's adoption of evolutionary ideas was more promise than substance.

Although Joseph Schumpeter (1934, 1976) is often associated with the new wave of evolutionary theorizing since the 1980s, he explicitly rejected the employment of the biological analogy in economics, concluding that 'no appeal to biology would be of the slightest use' (Schumpeter, 1954, p. 789). Throughout his works, Schumpeter most frequently employs the term 'evolution' in a developmental sense, but excluding a Lamarckian or Darwinian process of evolutionary selection. Consequently, Veblen's use of evolutionary thinking from biology was much more extensive than that of Schumpeter. Veblen should thus be placed amongst the founding figures of modern evolutionary economics. Unlike Schumpeter, his implicit research programme is to explore the application of biological ideas to economic science.

Evolutionary theories of technological change

There have been substantial modern developments in the theory of technological change.[14] Although links are claimed with the earlier

---

[14] The conception of the relationship between institutions and technology remains controversial within the 'old' institutionalism. See, for example, Samuels (1977). A useful statement on the nature of technology is also found in Dosi (1988b).

20 *G. M. Hodgson*

theories of Joseph Schumpeter, for the reasons given above the work in this tradition could just as well be regarded as 'old' institutionalist rather than 'neo-Schumpeterian'. Important examples of this genre are found in the works of Norman Clark and Calestous Juma (1987), Giovanni Dosi (1988b) and Giovanni Dosi *et al* (1988).

Some of the links with the 'old' institutionalist tradition are worth spelling out here. First, in attempting to explain technological change, these writers are breaking from the neoclassical and Austrian traditions which have taken technology as exogenous. In doing so they have firmly aligned themselves with the work of Veblen and some of his followers. Although the deterministic modelling or prediction of future technological advance is, in principle, ruled out (Popper, 1960, pp. v-vii), recent work has shown that technology and innovations can be analyzed in terms of a multi-levelled taxonomy of 'paradigms', 'systems', 'paths' or 'trajectories' which are useful both analytically and as a guide to business and government policy.

Second, in using the biological metaphor of evolution, links have again been created with Veblen and the institutionalists. In particular, however, some writers have borrowed ideas from the evolutionary theory found in modern biology to illuminate the processes of change. A good example is Clark and Juma's (1987) use of Conrad Waddington's (1957) biological concept of the 'chreod' to describe a constrained path of technological development.

A chreod is a relatively stable trajectory of development for a species or technology. Although changes and perturbations may occur, past developments ensure that development is channelled along a certain route. A biological example is the survival of the same basic configuration of the skeletal frame amongst mammals, reptiles and birds. Evolution cannot provide a more optimal configuration in every case, as the basic skeletal frame is determined by the history of the species. A technological example is the adoption of the internal combustion engine for the motor car around 1900. Despite its apparent supremacy, with sufficient research and development there still may be other superior alternatives, such as steam or electrical power.

Third, Nelson and Winter (1982) and Dosi (1988b) in particular have stressed the tacit nature of much technical knowledge, and its connection with routinized behaviour within the firm. This connects with Veblen's conception of habit, and the use of habits and routines as the analogue for the gene in economic evolution. The tacitness of knowledge is also tied up with the importance of cognitive frames. Given that the acquisition of the latter is often subtle and lasting, and critical introspection is difficult at such a basic level, such durable habits of thought are tricky to alter or replace.

IV. CONCLUSION: TOWARDS A NEW BEGINNING?

It has been suggested above that the 'old' institutionalism is as alive as the 'new', and is worthy of careful examination. The new institutionalism has put the analysis of the origins and functions of institutions right back near the top of the orthodox theorist's agenda. Having achieved this, the 'old' questions about the original assumptions and the process of the evolution of institutions are also raised.

Further examination of the limits and possibilities of the biological metaphor, as progressing in the above-cited work on the theory of the firm and technological change, would seem at the present time to be the most fruitful basis for the development of 'old' institutionalist theory.[15]

Despite the contributions of the neoclassical subset of the new institutionalists, in neoclassical economic theory structural development is still addressed mainly in terms of comparative statics. The failure to address the processes of long-run economic change remains another neoclassical weakness. However, the dramatic contrast between the preoccupations of general equilibrium theorizing and a real world of rapid and dramatic institutional change has become increasingly clear. Once again this creates an opportunity for all kinds of institutional analysis.

In addition, new results in mathematics have led to questions about the predictive methods that are prominent in economic science. Developments in chaos theory have drawn attention to the limitations of the models involving the kind of linear equations which are widely used in economic theory. Chaos theory shows that apparently random or chaotic behaviour can flow from simple, non-linear models. Furthermore, such models are often so sensitive to initial parameter values that precise prediction is impossible (Gleick, 1988).

Institutionalists have been quick to point out some of the implications of chaos theory for economics (Coricelli and Dosi, 1988; Dopfer, 1988; Radzicki, 1990). The results for science as a whole are likely to be profound. Not only is the common obsession with precise prediction

---

[15] It should be emphasized, however, that modern biology challenges both Panglossian conceptions of evolution and its association with 'progress' (Hodgson, 1991b; Nitecki, 1988).

22   G. M. Hodgson

confounded. In addition, the whole atomistic tradition in science of attempting to reduce each phenomenon to its component parts is placed into question.

Work on complex, non-linear systems suggests the possibility that a 'rich representation of non-linearities leads to a model that is relatively insensitive to parameter values. Being insensitive to parameter values is also a characteristic of most social systems.' Such a system tends 'to move along the changing slopes of its non-linearities until it finds an operating region that is determined more by the structure of the system than by plausible differences in parameter values.' (Forrester, 1987, p. 108) In such a high-order non-linear system the structure remains constant despite many changes and perturbations at the micro-level.

This suggests an approach to analysis other than the reductionist method of building up a model on the assumption of the restrictive behaviour of its microeconomic elements. By recognising the limitations of reductionism, the 'old' institutionalists have prepared the ground for an approach to economic theory that is more in line with the implications of recent developments in the theory of complex, non-linear systems (Laszlo, 1987; Prigogine and Stengers, 1984; Zeleny, 1987).

Finally, the institutionalist adherence to the evolutionary metaphor has a number of advantages. Evolutionary theory, for instance, emphasizes the concept of irreversibility or the 'arrow of time'.[16] It instates a concept of process rather than comparative statics. It includes disequilibrium as well as equilibrium situations. It embraces diversity and qualitative, as well as quantitative, change. It involves error-making, and not simply optimizing, behaviour.[17] With increasing awareness of the limitations of the mechanistic paradigm in economics it has been argued that the biological analogy, as used by many institutionalists, has a great deal to offer (Georgescu-Roegen, 1971, 1979).

Institutionalism is not yet sufficiently developed to replace orthodoxy. On the other hand, however, the pressures for change are now so strong that orthodox economics is unlikely to emerge unaltered. It is indeed a sign of the times that an orthodox theorist of the stature of Frank Hahn (1991, pp. 48–50) has predicted that in the next hundred years 'the subject will return to its Marshallian affinities to biology', noting that

---

[16] The irreversibility of economic processes has been investigated by a number of writers, notably Nicholas Georgescu-Roegen (1971) and Joan Robinson (1974).

[17] Stochastic error-making has been incorporated into mainstream economics, as in the theory of rational expectations. However, not only is systematic error excluded, but also error is generally treated negatively as a disturbance, rather than positively as a potential source of creativity and change.

evolutionary theories are already beginning to flourish. His successors, he concludes, will not be so preoccupied with a 'grand unifying theory' or so immersed in 'the pleasures of theorems and proof.' What will take their place? Hahn candidly writes: 'the uncertain embrace of history and sociology and biology.' Such would be a victory of the 'old' institutionalism, perhaps in everything but name. With the current impasse in neoclassical general equilibrium theory, the recent theoretical developments and debates in biology, and rapid institutional and structural change in the real world, the present context would seem, in some respects, to be more fertile than that of the early decades of the twentieth century for the development of the 'old' institutionalist theory.

REFERENCES

Agassi, J. (1975) 'Institutional Individualism', *British Journal of Sociology*. 26, pp. 144–55.

Alchian, A. A. and Demsetz, H. (1972) 'Production, Information Costs, and Economic Organization', *American Economic Review*. 62(4), December, pp. 777–95. Reprinted in Putterman (1986).

Aoki, M., Gustafsson, B. and Williamson, O. E. (eds) (1990) *The Firm as a Nexus of Treaties* (London: Sage).

Arrow, K. J. (1974) *The Limits of Organization* (New York: Norton).

Axelrod, R. M. (1986) 'An Evolutionary Approach to Norms', *American Political Science Review*, 80(4), December, pp. 1095–111.

Boettke, P. (1989) 'Evolution and Economics: Austrians as Institutionalists', *Research in the History of Economic Thought and Methodology*, Vol. 6, pp. 73–89.

Buchanan, J. M. (1991) 'Economics in the Post-Socialist Century', *The Economic Journal*, 101(1), January, pp. 15–21.

Buchanan, J. M. *et al.* (eds) (1980) *Toward a Theory of the Rent-Seeking Society* (College Station: Texas A&M University Press).

Cheung, S. N. S. (1983) 'The Contractual Nature of the Firm', *Journal of Law and Economics*, 26(2), April, pp. 1–21.

Clark, N. G. and Juma, C. (1987) *Long-Run Economics: An Evolutionary Approach to Economic Growth* (London: Pinter).

Coase, R. H. (1937) 'The Nature of the Firm', *Economica*, 4(4), November, pp. 386–405. Reprinted in Putterman (1986).

Coase, R. H. (1960) 'The Problem of Social Cost', *Journal of Law and Economics*, 3, pp. 1–44.

Commons, J. R. (1924) *Legal Foundations of Capitalism* (New York: Macmillan).

Commons, J. R. (1934) *Institutional Economics – Its Place in Political Economy* (New York: Macmillan). Reprinted 1990 with a new introduction by M. Rutherford (New Brunswick: Transaction Publishers).

Commons, J. R. (1950) *The Economics of Collective Action* (New York: Macmillan).

Coricelli, F. and Dosi, G. (1988) 'Coordination and Order in Economic Change and the Interpretative Power of Economic Theory', in Dosi *et al* (1988, pp. 124–47).

Dopfer, K. (ed.) (1976) *Economics in the Future* (London: Macmillan).

Dopfer, K. (1988) 'Classical Mechanics With an Ethical Dimension: Professor Tinbergen's Economics', *Journal of Economic Issues*, 22(3), September, pp. 675–706.

24 *G. M. Hodgson*

Dosi, G. (1988a) 'Institutions and Markets in a Dynamic World', *The Manchester School*. 56(2), June, pp. 119–46.

Dosi, G. (1988b) 'The Sources, Procedures, and Microeconomic Effects of Innovation', *Journal of Economic Literature*. 26(3), September, pp. 1120–71. Reprinted in Freeman (1990a).

Dosi, G., Freeman, C., Nelson, R., Silverberg, G. and Soete, L. (eds) (1988) *Technical Change and Economic Theory* (London: Pinter).

Dow, G. K. (1987) 'The Function of Authority in Transaction Cost Economics', *Journal of Economic Behavior and Organization*. 8(1), March, pp. 13–38.

Dugger, W. M. (1983) 'The Transaction Cost Analysis of Oliver E. Williamson: Towards a New Synthesis?', *Journal of Economic Issues*. 16(1), March, pp. 75–106.

Eggertsson, T. (1990) *Economic Behavior and Institutions* (Cambridge: Cambridge University Press).

Eldredge, N. and Gould, S. J. (1972) 'Punctuated Equilibria: An Alternative to Phyletic Gradualism', in T. J. M. Schopf (ed.) (1972) *Models in Paleobiology* (San Francisco: Freeman, Cooper and Co.), pp. 82–115.

Eldredge, N. and Gould, S. J. (1977) 'Punctuated Equilibria: The Tempo and Mode of Evolution Reconsidered', *Paleobiology*, 3, pp. 115–51.

Elster, J. (1982), 'Marxism, Functionalism and Game Theory', *Theory and Society*, 11(4), pp. 453–82.

Elster, J. (1989) 'Social Norms and Economic Theory', *Journal of Economic Perspectives*. 3(4), Fall, pp. 99–117.

Field, A. J. (1979) 'On the Explanation of Rules Using Rational Choice Models', *Journal of Economic Issues*, 13(1), March, pp. 49–72.

Field, A.J. (1981) 'The Problem with Neoclassical Institutional Economics: A Critique with Special Reference to the North/Thomas Model of Pre-1500 Europe', *Explorations in Economic History*. 18(2), April, pp. 174–98.

Field, A. J. (1984) 'Microeconomics, Norms and Rationality', *Economic Development and Cultural Change*. 32(4), July, pp. 683– 711.

Forrester, J. W. (1987) 'Nonlinearity in High-Order Models of Social Systems', *European Journal of Operational Research*. 30(2), June, pp. 104–9.

Foster, J. (1987) *Evolutionary Macroeconomics* (London: George Allen and Unwin).

Francis, A., Turk, J., and Willman, P. (eds) (1983) *Power, Efficiency and Institutions: A Critical Appraisal of the 'Markets and Hierarchies' Paradigm* (London: Heinemann).

Freeman, C. (ed.) (1990a) *The Economics of Innovation* (Aldershot: Edward Elgar).

Furubotn, E. G. and Pejovich, S. (1972) 'Property Rights and Economic Theory: A Survey of Recent Literature', *Journal of Economic Literature*, 10(4), December, pp. 1137–62.

Furubotn, E. G. and Pejovich, S. (eds) (1974) *The Economics of Property Rights* (Cambridge, MA: Ballinger).

Galbraith, J. K. (1958) *The Affluent Society* (London: Hamilton).

Galbraith, J. K. (1969) *The New Industrial State* (Hammondsworth: Penguin).

Georgescu-Roegen, N. (1971) *The Entropy Law and the Economic Process* (Cambridge, MA: Harvard University Press).

Georgescu-Roegen, N. (1979) 'Methods in Economic Science', *Journal of Economic Issues*, 13(2), June, pp. 317–28.

Giddens, A. (1984) *The Constitution of Society: Outline of the Theory of Structuration* (Cambridge: Polity Press).

Gleick, J. (1988) *Chaos: Making a New Science* (London: Heinemann).

Gordon, W. and Adams, J. (1989) *Economics as a Social Science: An Evolutionary Approach* (Riverdale, Maryland: Riverdale).

Gustafsson, B. (ed.) (1991) *Power and Economic Institutions: Reinterpretations in Economic History* (Aldershot: Edward Elgar).

Hahn, F. H. (1991) 'The Next Hundred Years', *The Economic Journal*, 101(1), January, pp. 47–50.

Institutional economics   **25**

Hamilton, W. H. (1963) 'Institution', in E. R. A. Seligman and A. Johnson (eds) *Encyclopaedia of the Social Sciences*. Vol. 7, pp. 84–89.

Hanusch, H. (ed.) (1988) *Evolutionary Economics: Applications of Schumpeter's Ideas* (Cambridge: Cambridge University Press).

Hayek, F. A. (1982) *Law, Legislation and Liberty*. 3-volume combined edn. (London: Routledge and Kegan Paul).

Hayek, F. A. (1988) *The Fatal Conceit: The Errors of Socialism, Collected Works of F. A. Hayek*. Vol. 1 (London: Routledge).

Hodgson, G. M. (1988) *Economics and Institutions: A Manifesto for a Modern Institutional Economics* (Cambridge and Philadelphia: Polity Press and University of Pennsylvania Press).

Hodgson, G. M. (1989) 'Institutional Economic Theory: The Old Versus the New', *Review of Political Economy*, 1(3), November, pp. 249–69. Reprinted in Hodgson (1991a).

Hodgson, G. M. (1991a) *After Marx and Sraffa* (Basingstoke: Macmillan).

Hodgson, G. M. (1991b) 'Economic Evolution: Intervention Contra Pangloss', *Journal of Economic Issues*, 25(2), June, pp. 519–33.

Hodgson, G. M. (1991c) 'Socio-Political Disruption and Economic Development', in G. M. Hodgson and E. Screpanti (eds) (1991) *Rethinking Economics: Markets, Technology and Growth* (Aldershot: Edward Elgar).

Hodgson, G. M. (1992). 'Marx, Engels and Economic Evolution', *International Journal of Social Economics*. (forthcoming).

Hodgson, G. M. (1993) *Economics and Evolution* (Cambridge: Polity Press) forthcoming.

Holton, R. J. (1985) *The Transition from Feudalism to Capitalism* (Basingstoke: Macmillan).

Ingrao, B. and Israel, G. (1990) *The Invisible Hand: Economic Equilibrium in the History of Science* (Cambridge, MA: MIT Press).

Jensen, M. C. and Meckling, W. H. (1976) 'Theory of the Firm: Managerial Behavior, Agency Costs and Ownership Structure', *Journal of Financial Economics*, 3(4), October, pp. 305–60. Reprinted in Putterman (1986).

Kaldor, N. (1972) 'The Irrelevance of Equilibrium Economics', *The Economic Journal*, 82(4), December, pp. 1237–55. Reprinted in N. Kaldor (1978) *Further Essays on Economic Theory: (Collected Economic Essays Vol. 5)* (London: Duckworth).

Kapp, K. W. (1976) 'The Nature and Significance of Institutional Economics', *Kyklos*. 29, pp. 209–32. Reprinted in Samuels (1988, Vol. 1).

Lachmann, L. M. (1969) 'Methodological Individualism and the Market Economy', in E. Streissler, (ed.) (1969) *Roads to Freedom: Essays in Honour of Friedrich A. von Havek* (London: Routledge and Kegan Paul), pp. 89–103. Reprinted in L. M. Lachmann (1977) *Capital, Expectations and the Market Process* (Kansas City: Sheed Andrews and McMeel).

Langlois, R. N. (ed.) (1986) *Economics as a Process: Essays in the New Institutional Economics* (Cambridge: Cambridge University Press).

Langlois, R. N. (1989) 'What Was Wrong With the Old Institutional Economics (and What is Still Wrong With the New)?', *Review of Political Economy*, 1(3), November, pp. 270–98..

Laszlo, E. (1987) *Evolution: The Grand Synthesis* (Boston, MA: New Science Library – Shambhala).

Lawson, A. (1985) 'Uncertainty and Economic Analysis', *The Economic Journal*, 95(4), December, pp. 909–27.

Lawson, A. (1987) 'The Relative/Absolute Nature of Knowledge and Economic Analysis', *The Economic Journal*, 97(4), December, pp. 951–70.

Leathers, C. G. (1989) 'New and Old Institutionalists on Legal Rules: Hayek and Commons', *Review of Political Economy*. 1(3), November, pp. 361–80.

Leathers, C. G. (1990) 'Veblen and Hayek on Instincts and Evolution', *Journal of the History of Economic Thought*, 12(2), June, pp. 162–78.

26 *G. M. Hodgson*

Lowry, S. T. (1976) 'Bargain and Contract Theory in Law and Economics', *Journal of Economic Issues*. 10(1), March, pp. 1–22. Reprinted in Tool and Samuels (1989c).

Lukes, S. (1973) *Individualism* (Oxford: Basil Blackwell).

March, J. G. and Olsen, J. P. (1984) 'The New Institutionalism: Organizational Factors in Political Life', *American Political Science Review*, 78(3), September, pp. 734–49.

Marx, K. (1973) *Grundrisse: Foundations of the Critique of Political Economy*, translated by M. Nicolaus (Harmondsworth: Penguin).

Mayhew, A. (1989) 'Contrasting Origins of the Two Institutionalisms: The Social Science Context', *Review of Political Economy*, 1(3), November, pp. 319–33.

Menger, C. (1963) *Problems of Economics and Sociology*, translated by F. J. Nock from the German edition of 1883 with an introduction by Louis Schneider. (Urbana, IL: University of Illinois Press).

Mirowski, P. (1981) 'Is There a Mathematical Neoinstitutional Economics?', *Journal of Economic Issues*, 15(3), pp. 593–613. Reprinted in Samuels (1988, Vol. 2).

Mirowski, P. (1989) *More Heat Than Light: Economics as Social Physics, Physics as Nature's Economics* (Cambridge: Cambridge University Press).

Mises, L. von (1949) *Human Action: A Treatise on Economics* (London: William Hodge).

Mitchell, W. C. (1950) *The Backward Art of Spending Money and Other Essays* (New York: Augustus Kelley).

Moe, T. M. (1984) 'The New Economics of Organization', *American Journal of Political Science*, 28(4), pp. 739–77.

Mokyr, J. (1990) *The Lever of Riches: Technological Creativity and Economic Progress* (Oxford: Oxford University Press).

Mokyr, J. (1991) 'Evolutionary Biology, Technical Change, and Economic History', *Bulletin of Economic Research*, 43(2), pp. 127–49.

Myrdal, G (1939) *Monetary Equilibrium* (London: Hodge).

Myrdal, G. (1944) *An American Dilemma: The Negro Problem and Modern Democracy* (New York: Harper and Row).

Myrdal, G. (1957) *Economic Theory and Underdeveloped Regions* (London: Duckworth).

Myrdal, G. (1958) *Value in Social Theory* (New York: Harper).

Nelson, R. R. and Winter, S. G. (1982) *An Evolutionary Theory of Economic Change* (Cambridge MA: Harvard University Press).

Niskanen, W. A. (1971) *Bureaucracy and Representative Government* (Chicago: Aldine-Atherton).

Nitecki, M. H. (ed.) (1988) *Evolutionary Progress* (Chicago: University of Chicago Press).

North, D. C. (1981) *Structure and Change in Economic History* (New York: Norton).

North, D. C. (1990) *Institutions, Institutional Change and Economic Performance* (Cambridge: Cambridge University Press).

North, D. C. and Thomas, R. (1973) *The Rise of the Western World* (Cambridge: Cambridge University Press).

Nozick, R. (1977) 'On Austrian Methodology', *Synthese*, 36, pp. 353–92.

Olson, M., Jr (1965) *The Logic of Collective Action* (Cambridge, MA: Harvard University Press).

Olson, M., Jr. (1982) *The Rise and Decline of Nations* (New Haven: Yale University Press).

Polanyi, K. (1944) *The Great Transformation* (New York: Rinehart).

Popper, K. R. (1945) *The Open Society and its Enemies*, 2 vols (London: Routledge and Kegan Paul).

Popper, K. R. (1960) *The Poverty of Historicism* (London: Routledge and Kegan Paul).

Posner, R. (1973) *Economic Analysis of Law* (Boston: Little, Brown).

Prigogine, I. and Stengers, I. (1984) *Order Out of Chaos: Man's New Dialogue With Nature* (London: Heinemann).

Prisching, M. (1989) 'Evolution and Design of Social Institutions in Austrian Theory', *Journal of Economic Studies*, 16(2), pp. 47–62.

Putterman, L. (ed.) (1986) *The Economic Nature of the Firm: A Reader* (Cambridge: Cambridge University Press).

Radzicki, M. J. (1990) 'Institutional Dynamics, Deterministic Chaos, and Self-Organizing Systems', *Journal of Economic Issues*, 24(1), March, pp. 57–102.

Robinson, J. (1974) *History versus Equilibrium* (London: Thames Papers in Political Economy).

Rowe, N. (1989) *Rules and Institutions* (Hemel Hempstead: Philip Allan).

Rutherford, M. C. (1989a) 'Some Issues in the Comparison of Austrian and Institutional Economics', *Research in the History of Economic Thought and Methodology*, Vol. 6, pp. 159–71.

Rutherford, M. C. (1989b) 'What is Wrong With the New Institutional Economics (And What is Still Wrong With the Old)?', *Review of Political Economy*, 1(3), November, pp. 299–318.

Samuels, W. J. (1977) 'Technology *Vis-à-Vis* Institutions in the JEI: A Suggested Interpretation', *Journal of Economic Issues*, 11(4), December, pp. 871–95. Reprinted in Samuels (1988, Vol. 3).

Samuels, W. J. (ed.) (1988) *Institutional Economics*. 3 vols (Aldershot: Edward Elgar).

Samuels, W. J. (1989b) 'Austrian and Institutional Economics: Some Common Elements', *Research in the History of Economic Thought and Methodology*, Vol. 6, pp. 53–71.

Samuels, W. J., Hodgson, G. M. and Tool, M. R. (eds) (forthcoming) *Handbook of Institutional and Evolutionary Economics* (Aldershot: Edward Elgar).

Schotter, A. (1981) *The Economic Theory of Social Institutions* (Cambridge: Cambridge University Press).

Schotter, A. (1990) *Free Market Economics: A Critical Appraisal*, 2nd edn. (Oxford: Basil Blackwell).

Schumpeter, J. A. (1934) *The Theory of Economic Development*. translated by R. Opic from the German edition of 1912 (Cambridge, MA: Harvard University Press).

Schumpeter, J. A. (1954). *History of Economic Analysis*. New York: Oxford University Press.

Schumpeter, J. A. (1976) *Capitalism, Socialism and Democracy*, 5th edn. (London: George Allen and Unwin).

Simon, H. A. (1957) *Models of Man: Social and Rational* (New York: Wiley).

Simon, H. A. (1959) 'Theories of Decision-Making in Economic and Behavioral Sciences', *American Economic Review*, 49(2), June, pp. 253–83.

Smith, V. L. (1982) 'Microeconomic Systems as an Experimental Science', *American Economic Review*, 72(5), December, pp. 923–55.

Sowell, T. (1967) 'The "Evolutionary" Economics of Thorstein Veblen', *Oxford Economic Papers* 19(2), July, pp. 177–98.

Sugden, R. (1986) *The Economics of Rights, Co-operation and Welfare* (Oxford: Basil Blackwell).

Sugden, R. (1989) 'Spontaneous Order', *Journal of Economic Perspectives*, 3(4), Fall, pp. 85–97.

Thomas, B. (1991). 'Alfred Marshall on Economic Biology, *Review of Political Economy*, Vol. 3, No. 1, January, pp. 1–14.

Tool, M. R. and Samuels, W. J. (eds) (1989a) *The Methodology of Economic Thought*, 2nd edn. (New Brunswick: Transaction).

Tool, M. R. and Samuels, W. J. (eds) (1989b) *The Economy as a System of Power*, 2nd edn. (New Brunswick: Transaction).

Tool, M. R. and Samuels, W. J. (eds) (1989c) *State, Society and Corporate Power*, 2nd edn. (New Brunswick: Transaction).

Udéhn, L. (1987) *Methodological Individualism: A Critical Appraisal* (Uppsala: Uppsala University Reprographics Centre).

Ullmann-Margalit, E. (1977) *The Emergence of Norms* (Oxford: Oxford University Press).

Vanberg, V. (1986) 'Spontaneous Market Order and Social Rules: A Critique of F. A.

28 *G. M. Hodgson*

Hayek's Theory of Cultural Evolution', *Economics and Philosophy*, 2, June, pp. 75–100.

Vanberg, V. (1989) 'Carl Menger's Evolutionary and John R. Commons' Collective Action Approach to Institutions: A Comparison', *Review of Political Economy*. 1(3), November, pp. 334–60.

Veblen, T. B. (1899) *The Theory of the Leisure Class: An Economic Study of Institutions* (New York: Macmillan).

Veblen, T. B. (1919) *The Place of Science in Modern Civilisation and Other Essays* (New York: Huebsch). Reprinted 1990 with a new introduction by W. J. Samuels (New Brunswick: Transaction Publishers).

Veblen, T. B. (1934) *Essays on Our Changing Order*, ed. L. Ardzrooni (New York: The Viking Press).

Waddington, C. H. (1957) *The Strategy of the Genes* (London: George Allen and Unwin)

Waller, Jr, W. J. (1988) 'Habit in Economic Analysis', *Journal of Economic Issues*, 22(1), March, pp. 113–26.

Ward, B. (1972) *What's Wrong With Economics?* (London: Macmillan).

Weber, M. (1930) *The Protestant Ethic and the Spirit of Capitalism* (London: Allen and Unwin).

Weber, M. (1947) *The Theory of Social and Economic Organization* (New York: Free Press).

Williamson, O. E. (1975) *Markets and Hierarchies: Analysis and Anti-Trust Implications: A Study in the Economics of Internal Organization* (New York: Free Press).

Williamson, O. E. (1985) *The Economic Institutions of Capitalism: Firms. Markets, Relational Contracting* (London: Macmillan).

Wynarczyk, P. (1992) 'Comparing Alleged Incommensurables: Institutional and Austrian Economics as Rivals and Possible Complements?', *Review of Political Economy*, 4(1), January, pp. 18–36.

Young, A. A. (1928) 'Increasing Returns and Economic Progress', *The Economic Journal*, 38(4), December, pp. 527–42.

Zeleny, M. (1987) 'Autopoiesis', in M. G. Singh (ed.) (1987) *Systems and Control Encyclopedia. Theory, Technology, Applications* (Oxford: Pergamon Press), pp. 393–400.

The Judge Institute of Management Studies
University of Cambridge
Mill Lane
Cambridge CB2 1RX, U.K.

Part II
Institutions and Modern Economics

[5]

Jei JOURNAL OF ECONOMIC ISSUES
Vol. XIII   No. 1   March 1979

On the Explanation of Rules
Using Rational Choice Models

Alexander James Field

Methodological debates in economics have a reputation for sterility based on their pleasant contribution to casual conversation and their apparent lack of any visible impact on the actual practice of the discipline.[1] This reputation naturally discourages the thoughtful individual from making an additional contribution to the literature in this area. Such discouragement, however, can be counterbalanced by the general belief that the proper approach to important but difficult problems is not to ignore them, and by the specific conviction, which must in turn be justified, that one has something of importance to say on these matters. Needless to say, the author holds the former belief. In particular, it can be argued that economists, as a profession, have not adequately confronted the methodological issues associated with the analysis or explanation of that category of phenomena known as institutional or rule structures.

At the risk of some violence to the historical record, one can group economists into three categories according to the methodological position they have taken regarding institutional structures. The first, associated with the names of John R. Commons, Richard T. Ely, and most of the founders of the American Economic Association, was that institutions

The author is Assistant Professor of Economics, Stanford University, Stanford, California. He would like to thank Victor Goldberg, Hajime Miyazaki, Douglass North, Richard Sutch, Gavin Wright, Oliver Williamson, and several anonymous referees for comments, both critical and positive, on earlier versions.

50   Alexander James Field

had to be understood on a case-by-case basis, in detail: Historical understanding or immersion in the current laws and customs organizing the
process under investigation was essential if meaningful analyses or policy
recommendations were to be developed. The second methodological
position, associated with the development of the neoclassical synthesis,
especially after World War II,[2] essentially granted the institutionalists
(advocates of position 1) their point and then read them out of the
profession by interpreting the analysis of institutions as beyond the scope
of economic inquiry.[3] This was reflected in the eventual classification by
many libraries of books by Commons and others under the subject head-
ing of sociology, as opposed to economics.[4] The third position, which has
attracted an increasing number of devotees, especially in the last decade,
attempts to bridge the gap between the former two by accepting the argument that economists have a responsibility to investigate not only the
consequences but also the origins or causes of institutional variation. But
advocates of this third position (and here they differ from the pioneers
of institutional economics) maintain that variation and change in institutional structures can be explained using the same type of economic
models whereby price and quantity vectors are explained.[5] Thus, whereas
positions 1 and 2 conflict with regard to the appropriate scope of economic inquiry, positions 1 and 3 are in agreement. But the latter positions
differ on the appropriate methodology of institutional analysis and, more
basically, on the issue of whether a general theory of institutions is possible.

This essay is intended as a qualified defense of position 1, that associated with an older generation of institutionalist economists. It consists
essentially of a qualified critique of position 3, especially that variant of
it which claims that, with more effort, the category of rule structures
could eventually be made totally endogenous. One way to develop this
critique is to argue that there is an important difference between analysis
and explanation, that economists have not adequately recognized this
distinction in recent years, and that some advocates of position 3 have
at times claimed explanation whereas, in fact, only the weaker claim of
analysis is justified.

Analysis and Explanation

In methodological discussions, the concept of explanation has come
to have several meanings. Here, the use of the term is restricted to that
definition associated with the writings of Aristotle and J. S. Mill: to make
clear the cause or reason of, or to account for.[6] Using the term in this

sense necessarily involves the assertion of a causal relationship. Although causality is a concept suspect in some epistemological circles, it continues nevertheless to surface because of the nihilism which its denial entails.[7] Because of the controversies surrounding the concepts of explanation and causality, economists generally have been reluctant to describe their activities as explanation. They have preferred the weaker term *analysis,* as in partial equilibrium analysis, general equilibrium analysis, or micro-economic analysis. To analyze a phenomenon is to determine its essential features by resolving it into its elements or constituent parts. The claim that we have explained a phenomenon, then, appears to be far stronger than the claim that we have analyzed it.

To help understand this distinction, consider a general equilibrium model. Such a model works backward from observed endogenous vari-ables (prices and quantities) and examines their mutual determination, given a set of exogenous variables (preferences, technologies, and initial endowments) and the behavioral principle of maximization.[8] Is such a model an explanation of the endogenous variables? Only in the sense that it implies that a different set of exogenous variables might have led to different price and quantity vectors and in the sense that, given the exogenous parameters of the model, the only solution is the price and quantity vectors observed.[9] Thus, only if the solution to the system is *unique* can it lay claim to being not only an analysis, but also an explana-tion of the endogenous variables (the price-quantity vectors) under con-sideration.[10] If the solution is not unique, then the model does not qualify as an explanation, because it fails to indicate why one or another possible equilibrium was not attained.

Simple prudence probably explains why neoclassical economists have tended to prefer the term *analysis* to *explanation*; it is a weaker claim. Problems have developed, however, as economists have moved into new areas where they have often, in an effort to attract attention to the power of their analytical framework, claimed to have explained, whereas they have only analyzed. This is particularly evident among advocates of position 3. It is not sufficient that the initial conditions of a model be consistent with the outcome to be explained. They must also be incon-sistent with other outcomes not observed. Another way of saying this is that the exogenous variables must be necessary and sufficient conditions for the phenomena one is trying to explain. If the logic of an economic model is such that the initial conditions, coupled with the behavioral proposition, can imply the phenomenon one is trying to explain as well as another set of possible phenomena, then the model is not sufficiently restrictive to qualify as an explanation.

52   Alexander James Field

The simplest and most obvious example of such failed explanation is the "theory" of oligopoly. Economists can analyze an existing cartel by pointing to the benefits which participating companies receive as the result of restricting output and raising prices. But economists can equally well analyze the absence of a cartel by pointing to the benefits individual members would obtain by violating such an agreement. In neither case does such simple analysis qualify as explanation, because the initial conditions of the model and the behavioral principle (maximization of profit) can, in both cases, be similar or identical. Common sense tells us that if a model can account for both the existence of a phenomenon and its absence, it does not qualify as an explanation of either.

The problems with the theory of oligopoly exemplify a more general set of problems involving the explanation of the institutional or rule structures, both formal (legal) and informal, which organize social and economic interaction. Until relatively recently, most neoclassical theory, having been developed by proponents of position 2, has taken institutional or rule structures as given (as outside the purview of economic analysis) and has attempted to analyze the determination of prices and quantities by modeling short-term maximizing behavior within the constraints implied by these structures and the prevailing technologies, preferences, and initial endowments. In the past several years, however, a number of economists (advocates of position 3) have attempted to explain the choice of institutional structure as resulting from some logically prior process of short-term maximization, given technologies, initial endowments, and preferences.[11] This effort is an attempt to make endogenous the variation in rule structures which had previously been viewed as exogenous and thus beyond the scope of economic analysis. According to models of this sort, differences in institutional structures reflect differences in relative factor endowments (such as land/labor ratios), and changes over time in these structures reflect, for example, changes in such endowments or in the technologies and preferences which characterize the system.[12]

A survey of the literature written by advocates of position 3, at least its macrosocial variant, unfortunately leads to the conclusion that whereas economists have in some sense been able to analyze institutional structures using economic theory, they have not come any closer to explaining them than they have cartels.[13] One is led to ask whether this is due to the inadequacies of the investigations or rather to an unresolved problem in the underlying theory itself. The working hypothesis of this essay is the latter: These economic or, as they are sometimes called, rational choice models are not and perhaps cannot be sufficiently restrictive to qualify as explanations of prevailing rule structures. In under-

standing the logic of this argument, the prudence of neoclassical economists in avoiding the claim of explanation will become evident. Indeed,
it is a very strong claim.

The Definition of Economics

Let us begin with the proposition that all stable social and economic
activity must be organized by a system of rules (formal or informal).
Without positing the existence of such rules, one is left with no explanation of why the interplay of purely selfish agents does not degenerate
into a Hobbesian war of all against all. This problem has been recognized
by most critics of microeconomic theory and has recently been elo-
quently restated by Roberto Unger in the first chapters of his book
Knowledge and Politics.[14] The solution proposed by the developers of
neoclassical theory is embodied in position 2, that is, a categorical distinction is made between the modeling of short-term self-interested behavior
within rules and the rules themselves.[15] As argued above, neoclassical
economists have taken the implicit and explicit position that the description and analysis of these rules or institutional structures are beyond the
purview of economic theory; they thus are the responsibility of sociologists, political scientists, or legal scholars. This position contrasts with
that of the pioneers of institutional economics, particularly Commons
and his students, who did concern themselves with these tasks, although
they did not attempt to construct a general theory of institutions.

The methodological compromise embodied in position 2, in which the
legitimacy of institutionalist endeavor was granted in a backhanded
fashion by its exclusion from the range of serious economic inquiry, has
resulted in an intellectual division of labor and a clear differentiation of
economic analysis from other disciplines in the social sciences on not one,
but two, dimensions: by subject matter and by methodological approach.
The first type of differentiation has a long and distinguished patrimony
stretching back to Adam Smith. According to this definition, economics
deals with a specific set of empirical topics: the production, distribution,
and exchange of goods and services. In recent years, nevertheless, economists increasingly have tended to deal with these using analytical and
evaluative techniques specific to the discipline. In turn, the training of
neoclassical economists, particularly in microeconomic analysis, has
predisposed them to concentrate on those phenomena (variation across
time and space) which can be attributed to economic forces. To say that
an outcome is explained by or attributable to an economic force, as
opposed to a political or social force, is to say that it results from the
decisions not of any one individual or group, but from the interaction of

54   Alexander James Field

the decisions of many agents, none of whom has any appreciable impact
on the outcome.

For example, the rise of protectionist sentiment on the European
peninsula in the late nineteenth century can be attributed in part to the
decline in the world prices of foodstuffs, an economic force, in that no
individual or identifiable group of individuals can be held responsible
for that decline.[16] In contrast, the adjustments incident upon the recent
worldwide rise in the price of oil have been caused by political forces,
since the decisions of an identifiable group of agents, the OPEC countries, led to that rise. Situations in which economic forces predominate,
then, are situations in which competitive markets operate; oligopoly or
monopoly, in turn, implies the generation of political forces.

The terms *political* and *economic* are used here in a different and more
precise manner than is usual, a procedure which is essential if the traditional and largely empty conclusion that the adjectives can be used interchangeably is to be avoided.[17] To complete this set of definitions, let us
tentatively define a social force as one which, like an economic force,
cannot be attributed to the decisions of any one individual or group, but
unlike an economic force, cannot be explained as resulting from the
aggregation of the decisions of many maximizing individuals.[18] Social
forces permit economic forces to operate, condition the pattern of political activity within a society, and are equivalent to institutional structures
or rules. The basic question here is whether social forces (institutional
structures or rules), such as those which might permit the members of a
cartel to trust each other and cooperate, can necessarily be explained as
resulting from economic forces, that is, the aggregation of the decisions
of participating economic agents.

The neoclassical economist's predisposition to concentrate on phenomena caused by or attributable to economic forces has created several
problems. Insofar as economics is the study of how resources are allo-
cated to satisfy wants among individuals and over time (the modern subject matter definition), and insofar as it is not to be culture bound, it
cannot restrict itself to behavior largely determined by economic or
market forces, since many economies assign and have assigned such
decisions to identifiable individuals or administrative bureaucracies. Similarly, explicit and implicit rules (social forces) affect the ways in which
markets operate. Nonetheless, insofar as its methodology gives economics
a claim to being a particular discipline within the social sciences, its
comparative advantage lies in an understanding of those outcomes largely
determined by economic or market forces, as defined above. The fundamental social implication of economic theory is that social outcomes (the

price of wheat in the nineteenth century, for example) can be explained as resulting from the aggregation of the decisions of individual agents, subject to the constraints which available technologies, endowments, and preferences imply.

This analytical insight is an important alternative to historical explanations which concentrate on the decisions of one or a few men (political forces), or on the independent role of "emergent properties" or transcendent factors such as culture, ideology, or social structure (social forces). But even the most fervent proponents of laissez-faire should recognize that there must be some rules and/or enforcement mechanism for providing elementary guarantees against the use of force and fraud, for without these the interplay of short-term maximizing agents would degenerate into a Hobbesian war of all against all in which exchange, let alone production, would be impossible. The existence of markets presupposes stable institutional structures and the social order incident upon them.

The framework of neoclassical microeconomic analysis, then, implies an instability in its practice, an instability based on the lack of a precise *a priori* specification of the division between the modeling of short-term maximizing behavior within rules and the rules themselves, which according to position 2 must be taken as exogenous. That division is an analytical abstraction which must be justified on the basis of the phenomena being studied and the purposes of the investigation. The development of position 3 may be understood as resulting from the fact that the training of economists gives them a vested interest in making the former category as large as possible, larger perhaps than is reasonably justifiable given the purposes of the investigation. Some recent work on institutional structure tries to carry this process to its conclusion; it attempts to eliminate rule structures as an exogenous category by explaining them as resulting from some prior process of short-term maximization. Unfortunately, such attempts invariably flounder on the necessity of adducing something about the time frame in which the agents are operating, which is equivalent to adducing a set of rules for making rules. This does not eliminate the category of rules as something separable and not derivable from maximizing behavior.[19]

The General Problem

One general problem for economists is that variation in what they consider their core subject matter (the production, distribution, and exchange of goods and services) is partially attributable to political and

social forces. If it were true that economic forces determined the nature
of these forces, that is, if the aggregation of decisions based on maximizing behavior subject to the constraints of technologies, initial endowments, and preferences determined unique coalitions and patterns of
cooperation, then there would be no problem: Social and political forces
would simply be derivatives of logically prior economic forces. Indeed,
that appears to be the hope and objective of some of the new institutionalists.[20] Unfortunately, attempts to achieve such explanation have not
succeeded for the same reasons that games of more than two persons
do not have determinate solutions or, to use an example already mentioned, that we have no good overall theory of oligopoly. To the extent
that political and social forces are important, the economist is faced with
a real dilemma, for he is generally not well prepared to model cooperation and activity in groups.

Some advocates of position 3 have attempted to turn models based on
the aggregation of the choices of short-term maximizing agents to the
task of explaining collective action and have rapidly reached an impasse.
The initial impulse, after all, has likely been to try and minimize the
empirical importance of political and social forces. This impulse originates in three related factors: an assertion about the state of the world,
a theoretical argument, and a vested interest. The assertion is that collective activity (and the political forces which it permits) is relatively unimportant in the explanation of the variation with which the economist
must deal. This assertion is reinforced by the theoretical argument that
the choice to cooperate and participate in collective activity is in many
cases not rational from the standpoint of the individual, since the expected benefits associated with, for example, participation in a political
struggle are often very small. Even in a situation in which one might
stand to benefit substantially if an organizational drive were successful,
the probability that one's own actions will influence the outcome is so
small that it pays to let others do the work.[21] Thus, it is argued, attempts
to organize unions will usually be hampered by those who try to get a
free ride, and producer cartels will usually have a tendency toward disintegration. Finally, many economists recognize that the analytical tools
used in assessing the activity organized in markets will be much less
useful in analyzing situations in which collective activity predominates;
thus there is a vested interest in minimizing the importance of such
activity.

But the fact remains that unions do exist, cartels do persist, families
somehow endure, and nation states do not always degenerate into civil
war. When the explanatory importance of such collective decisions units

cannot be minimized, or when the formation of such units is the object of explanation itself, one impulse has been to try and retain rational choice models by transplanting them from environments in which individual agents are the key decision makers to those in which collectivities are the locus of decision making.[22] The motivation is understandable: Only in this fashion can the economist's comparative analytical advantage be maintained. So long as the decisions of a collectivity have no appreciable effect on the outcomes, the advantage is maintained, but since the ability to exercise effects on outcomes is often one of the motivations for the formation of collective decision-making units, this is not always the case.

Given existing patterns of cooperation, it may not be unreasonable to assume that collectivities maximize over the interests of their members.[23] There are, however, two conceptually distinct phenomena to be explained: the initial decisions to participate in collective cooperative activity (thus the formation of such collective units) and the behavior of these collectivities once formed. The problems in modeling the former are by far the more serious and, interestingly, are formally analogous to the difficulties in explaining outcomes when the number of interacting collectivities is small enough to constitute a game theoretic or political situation, as is the case with the oligopoly problem. The prediction that individuals will participate in goal-oriented collective activity when it is in their interest to do so—when the net benefits are positive—conflicts with the free rider argument, which implies that, assuming self-interested short-term maximizing agents, such association would almost never occur. Because of the externalities involved in the benefits achievable through association, the expected benefits attributable to the act of participation will almost always be less than the actual costs for the individual. The decision to vote, according to this argument, is irrational, since the costs in terms of time are not trivial, and the probabilities of influencing the outcome are so infinitesimally small.

Thus, the aggregation of choices based on self-interest can be used *ex post* to account either for cooperation or for its absence. And in accounting for both, it explains neither. Whether one is talking about constitution formation or marginal changes in the patterns of cooperation or institutional structures, this conflict between the fact that cooperative solutions are often Pareto efficient and the fact that the free rider problem creates incentives for rule violation and coalition disintegration will not disappear.[24]

In a world in which agents do not cooperate, it makes no sense to cooperate. But we do observe cooperation. People engage in what, from

a game theoretic standpoint, we might call contingent strategies of generalized reciprocity. In certain situations they operate within a group
according to the categorical imperative and expect that, in the long run,
benefits and costs will balance out. The time horizon not only of the
agent, but also of those with whom cooperation is being considered, is
crucial in determining what is rational and what is not. The success of
a long-run strategy is contingent on others pursuing it as well. But how
are these strategies orchestrated to mutual advantage? John Locke suggested the answer was to be found in man's inherent reasonableness,
while later economists (Adam Smith, for example) attributed it to a
natural identity of interests. Both solutions imply an exogenous specification, in one form or another, of rules for making rules. Neither solution
is derivable using rational choice models. Although economists can
analyze cooperative behavior using economic theory, they have not as
yet been successful in explaining it.[25]

The implications of these arguments are important. Research motivated implicitly or explicitly by the belief that a sufficient application of
a priori theorizing will produce an internally consistent theory of the
origin, persistence, and change of institutions or rules is misguided.[26] If
past experience is any guide, any model of stable economic and social
activity will have to assume some basic structure of rules governing
interactions, some structure not ultimately reducible to the individual
interests of the agents involved, that is, not ultimately explainable as
resulting from the aggregation of their choices. This is not to say that
men and women are not self-interested; that remains a useful analytical
abstraction. But people pursue their interests within constraints determined not only by the output and input prices they face, but also by
definite structures of rules, structures which are not ultimately reducible
to the aggregation of some logically prior round of choices based on
short-term maximization.

Prices and Rules

Prices and rules constrain short-term maximizing behavior, and it is
useful to consider the different ways they do so and their reactions to
changes in the underlying parameters of the system. In a general equilibrium system, budget constraints are determined not only by initial
endowments of productive resources, but also by factor prices, which
result from the interaction of economywide supply functions and the
demands derived from the demands for final products. The prices of

final goods constrain the amount of goods and services which can be purchased, given income. Their prices are similarly and simultaneously determined as the result of the interaction of many agents' decisions (and preferences).

Rules also constrain behavior. Indeed, without rules, organized markets and prices could not exist. But rules respond very differently than prices to changes in the system. Prices are supposed to be flexible, responsive to changes in the parameters of the economic system. Rules are not; they embody reciprocal expectations of predictability, and expectations, for better or worse, are based on past experience. That is why rules are usually treated as exogenous. Games in which the rules change every play are not stable, because rules which change continuously are not rules. A rule which has changed since the last play, and is expected to change before the next, will not produce the same outcomes as a rule, formally identical, which has prevailed since the start of the game. This accounts for the reluctance to change rules and for their resistance, at times, to massive changes in technologies, preferences, or factor endowments. This is not to say that revolutions do not sometimes succeed, with far-reaching implications for the legal structure, but the conservative principle often prevails.[27] Because the effectiveness of rules rests on the expectation that they will persist, there is an understandable reluctance to tamper with these expectations by frequently changing the rules. *Ex post,* one can rationalize either the change of a rule or its persistence as reflecting a short-term social cost-benefit calculation, but as pointed out earlier, the ability to rationalize either explains neither. There is no *a priori* reason, then, for expecting that environments characterized by similar factor endowments and technologies should not be organized by different rules, or for expecting that widely divergent environments might not be organized by essentially similar rules.

It does not follow that the entire corpus of microeconomic theory should be jettisoned. Rather, such theory should be used in those cases where the abstractions embodied in it reasonably apply. Competitive markets, in which agents are price takers and respond to economic forces not directly attributable to the actions of any one agent, are one such sphere. But the assumption of short-term profit or utility maximization, for example, is not a basic law of human behavior. Rather, it results from a particular complex of rules governing interactions producing the abstraction we call the market economy. Given that these rules prevail, we may appeal to the assumption of short-term maximizing behavior to help explain the price and output combinations observed. But the behavioral assumption of short-term profit maximization cannot, in turn, be used to explain the existence of rules which sanction and make possible (but also constrain) such behavior in the first place.

That is not to deny that men and women attempt and have attempted throughout history to preserve and advance themselves. Those who do not act consciously to avoid pain and danger may not survive long. But there are many time frames within which agents may pursue their interest. Extremely short-term strategies if pursued by many may lead to a break-down of production and exchange and to reductions in overall output. Long-term strategies may prove unsustainable, but cannot be rejected out of hand as naïve. It is in leading agents from shorter to longer term strategies, in a sense, that great politicians pursue their vocation. Rules, whether embodied in constitutions, laws, or informal understandings, provide the framework for that progression.

For analytical purposes, we might think of society as a matrix of points, representing short-term maximizing individuals, over which rests a series of transparent overlays, similar to those found in anatomy texts. These overlays represent the expectational bonds which tie agents together in relations of loyalty and power and permit them to pursue their inter-ests within longer time frames and within the contexts, for example, of families, ethnic and religious groups, unions, political parties, classes, age cohorts, friendships, or nation states. The variety and patterns of these overlays differ markedly in different societies and change over time, although they also have strong tendencies toward stability. These bonds place additional constraints on the short-term maximizing decisions which agents make. They represent, from a game theoretic standpoint, the rules which coordinate longer term strategies. The patterns of these bonds, however, do not correspond on a one-to-one basis with variations or changes in factor endowments, such as land/labor or capital/labor ratios, technologies, or preferences. To a certain extent, their develop-ment may have to be approached on a case-by-case basis, and once established, they may have an existence and dynamic of their own. This leaves unanswered the question of what does determine their pattern.

These bonds are, simultaneously, a means of restraining conflict, the determinants of patterns of conflict, and the result of conflict itself. In order effectively to use microeconomic analysis, economists must draw an analytical distinction between that which is exogenous and that which is endogenous in the system. Unlike technologies, whose variation or change is sometimes regarded as endogenous and sometimes as exogenous in economic theory, the rules of exchange, production, and distribution, because of their nature, cannot be treated as totally endogenous in such models. They represent nontechnical and nonresource constraints, variations in which, in the opinion of the analyst, cannot ultimately be reduced to the aggregation of the short-term maximizing decisions of self-interested agents. Nor are rules simply preferences. Preferences are defined over leisure and goods and services intended for final consumption, whereas rules are means or instrumentalities for facilitating the exchange and production of those goods and services.

Some Historical and Cross-Disciplinary Perspectives

Commons and others believed that formal institutional rule structures should be treated as exogenous and, moreover, subject to social control, which explains the importance they attached to the study of such structures. The methodological dispute which divides advocates of position 1 and position 3, and proponents of position 3 from some of their associates in other social sciences, can in a sense be reduced to a difference of opinion about the extent of social activity which should be regarded as governed by identifiable rules or reciprocal expectations (which make possible the pursuit of self-interest in longer time horizons) and the extent to which short-term self-interested behavior should be viewed as the norm. A cynical economist who believes the maxim that all's fair in love and war is the guiding principle of social interaction still must explain why POWs expect to be treated according to the Geneva Convention and why lovers expect at least minimal standards of "decent" behavior from those with whom they are involved.[28] Social scientists differ over the sources of the rules which produce these expectations and over the degree of independent explanatory importance which should be attached to them. Although the actual significance of these rules in restraining short-term self-interested behavior cannot be observed directly, it is, in principle, an empirical and not a theoretical question. In their role as social scientists, it is incumbent upon economists to make assumptions which abstract reasonably from reality. The previous discussion should indicate that the extreme position that rules which permit moves from shorter to longer time frames are explainable as resulting from short-term maximizing behavior must be rejected. This is not to say that abiding by the rules necessarily runs counter to one's self-interest; rather, it is a contingent strategy, and the existence of conceptually autonomous rules is what coordinates these strategies and permits their success. To the extent that we observe an ordered social life, to the extent that we observe exchange and production, we observe situations in which customs and rules exercise quasi-autonomous influences over those whose activities they constrain.

Commons recognized this in defining an institution as collective activity in control of individual action, but he added optimistically that such control could liberate and expand individual activity.[29] Although the pursuit of narrowly defined individual interest is a major element in the explanation of many social outcomes, it is not the only determinant for the simple reason that society would not long survive if it were. As Kenneth Arrow observed several years ago, "purely selfish behavior of individuals is really incompatible with any kind of settled economic life."[30] Oliver Williamson recognized the same problem when, in *Markets and Hierarchies,* he considered the implications of economic agents acting with guile.[31] Forty years ago, Talcott Parsons characterized the major weakness of what he called economic or utilitarian models of social action as their failure to solve the problems of order. There was no inherent explanation for why the system did not degenerate into a war of all against all or, in other words, why extremely short-term strategies did not prevail. The solution to this problem, which Parsons saw emerging in the works of Alfred Marshall, Vilfredo Pareto, Emile Durkheim, and Max Weber, was an emphasis on the role of shared values in legitimizing political authority and providing a mechanism of social integration.[32]

Systems of shared values are the equivalent, for our purposes, of the existence of rules governing interactions. Yet, neither the shared value systems nor the rules are explanations; they are merely descriptions of the ways in which collective activity is organized and sustained in associations. This may be as far as we can and should go using purely *a priori* reasoning. In fact, this is what general equilibrium theorists usually have done in taking the institutional structure as given. The historic methodological compromise embodied in position 2 also recognized this, although it was left to others to do the describing. In his *History of Economic Analysis,* Joseph Schumpeter, who viewed Walrasian economics as the most significant analytical development in the history of economics, defined sociological individualism as "the view that the self-governing individual constitutes the ultimate unit in the social sciences, and that all social phenomena resolve themselves into decisions and actions of individuals that need not or cannot be analyzed in terms of superindividual factors."[33]

Schumpeter added in the next sentence that this view was, of course, untenable. The reasons for that should now be clear. Although one can point to many cases in which rules or institutional structures do respond to change in, for example, technologies or factor endowments, one can equally well point to cases in which this does not happen, in which the institutional fabric appears to have an autonomous dynamic. *Ex post,* either outcome can be rationalized as representing the results of rational choice processes. A similar problem exists in the derivation of the overall institutional structure. Posit a state of asocial individuals. Knowledge of technologies, endowment ratios, and preferences, combined with the behavioral assumption that agents maximize short-term interest, does not restrict the set of rules or coalitions which might develop to organize the activity of these agents to a unique set. As a result, such models fail to explain prevailing rule structures. James Buchanan's models of constitution formation suffer from this defect.[34]

Positive and Normative Interaction

Accepting for the moment that the extreme position should be rejected, we are still left with the question of what represents a reasonable abstraction. If rules (laws, customs, reciprocal expectations, shared value systems, or whatever we wish to call elements of the institutional structure) determine the pattern of time frames within which maximization occurs, what is the appropriate pattern to assume? Unfortunately, the issue is not a purely academic one; there is an interaction between our models of the world and the state of the world in the next period. In other words, our descriptions of what is (or was) may not be neutral acts, but may affect what happens tomorrow. Pareto once observed that the utility or disutility of an idea bore little relation to its truth content.[35] For example, a teacher, parent, or preacher trying to teach a child why he or she should not steal may object to a positive model of the world which asserts that people adopt extremely short-term strategies and will lie or steal when they can get away with it. This objection may be heard despite the fact that the proposition might appear to be empirically justifiable, based on the extrapolation of past frequencies, for the validity of that teaching is precisely contingent on the falsity of that proposition in the future, that is, on the widespread acceptance of longer term strategies.[36]

Adopting a model in which rules exercise a greater or lesser degree of constraint than is evidenced by past experience may be a self-fulfilling act; widespread dissemination of such positive models may produce a situation in which future time horizons correspond to those embodied in the model. In that sense, models which maintain that all rules are at base derivable from short-term self-interested maximizing behavior can be subversive of established rules. Although Adam Smith did not adopt the extreme position described above, it is no coincidence that his *positive* models of social interaction were used as an attack on the elaborate role of law and custom in regulating economic activity in eighteenth-century England. This point underlines the responsibility which economists (and other social scientists) have to abstract reasonably from the phenomena under investigation.

The latent instability in microeconomic theory results from the absence of any means based on first principles of determining what the assumed pattern of time frames should be.[37] Some deny on *a priori* grounds the constraining influence of customs or law by pointing to the forces of individual interests which constantly threaten to break them down. This type of argument, if carried to its logical conclusion, can be used to attack the constraining influence of *all* laws, including the fundamental bases of political legitimacy which tie a society together and make market exchange and production possible. This type of argument is not sustainable. Individual interest does create a tendency toward disintegration of rules or cooperative structures, but individual interest can equally well be viewed as responsible for their creation. The effect of an actual rule in constraining behavior, then, cannot be discovered using purely *a priori* reasoning, any more than *a priori* reasoning will tell us when a cartel will develop and when it will disintegrate.

A case can be made for the proposition that, as a matter of public policy, the unrestricted pursuit of short-term individual self-interest should not be encouraged. This runs counter to the prejudices of those economists who view such behavior not only as a reasonable abstraction from fact, but also as a prescriptive ideal. The conflict emerges when the prescription of family, school, church, and courts, namely, obey rules because they are rules (and because everyone, including the individual, will be worse off if everyone disobeys them), is juxtaposed to what appears to be the prescription of the marketplace: Violate rules if one can benefit from so doing and get away with it. Actually, the rules of the marketplace are more complex; maximization is constrained both, by rules and by prices. Most economists (advocates of positions 1 or 2) recognize this conflict and restrict the range of their application of microeconomic models accordingly. The "laws" of the market cannot and should not be expected to explain the rules without which such markets could not operate.

Induction versus Deduction

Natural scientists have tended to interpret their endeavor as the inductive search for general laws. In contrast, the tradition of *a priorism* in economics has led to the view that the discipline consists of the deductive manipulation of assumptions derived from introspection or from empirical generalization so casual that it was not, in principle, subject to empirical verification.[38] We have argued that, when applied to rule structures, such *a priori* theorizing leads to an impasse because it does not yield sufficiently restrictive predictions. We argue further that this is not because the theory is in the early stages of its development; rather, it is inherent in the phenomenon itself. The simple failure to develop a workable theory of oligopoly is confirmation.

The issue of the appropriate balance between primarily inductive and primarily deductive approaches to the analysis of economic phenomena is not a new one. In 1848 Mill published the first edition of *Principles of Political Economy*. In it he discussed the relative influences of competition and custom and argued that it was only when competition prevailed that political economy had any pretentions to the character of a science. Only then could one speak of the "laws" of supply and demand, or of rent, profit, and wages.[39] Mill implied that economists had to resist, in their desire to be scientists, the urge to assume that competition prevailed when it did not. The founders of the American Economic Association took at least that part of Mill's message to heart and organized a set of standing committees ranked in the following order: Labor, Transportation, Trade, Finance, Local Government, Exchange, and, at the very end, General Questions of Economic Theory, and Statistics.[40] There is, of course, a substantial divergence between the positions represented in the formation of the AEA ,and those revealed in its chief publication today. In light of the arguments raised here, it is worth reconsidering whether the present-day balance is appropriate, given the problems at hand.[41]

Recent controversies confirm that this issue is not dead. In September 1976 John Dunlop delivered an address in Geneva to the International Industrial Relations Association. He questioned the relevance to policy makers of most of the work in labor economics in the past fifteen years. His attack was not restricted to the microeconomic work based on human capital theory; he also questioned the relevance of the macroeconomic investigations of the unemployment-inflation trade-off (the Philips curve). He argued that he "knew of no occasion [in recent years] in which either the simple concept of a Philips curve or a more sophisticated model of wage determination [had] ever been used to discuss or to resolve a public policy issue."[42] Dunlop attributed this, in part, to the atrophying in the United States of "a great academic tradition which cultivated a detailed knowledge of all the major institutions of the industrial relations system." He specifically mentioned Commons, George Rogers Taylor, and a number of other economists who held what has been referred to here as position 1.[43]

This attack was considered so unprecedented that five labor economists were invited to respond in the October 1977 issue of the *Industrial and Labor Relations Review*, the journal which published the text of Dunlop's remarks in April. Considering the nature of the charges, the responses are remarkable for their weakness. Albert Rees, in an otherwise measured reply, resorted to warning aspiring labor economists that they had best not listen to Dunlop if they expected to receive summer salaries or consultants' fees in the future.[44] Ronald Ehrenberg, Daniel Hamermesh, and George Johnson argued that it was "unfair . . . to expect that those who have the requisite quantitative skills to be successful modern economists will also have time to learn about all the institutions associated with each topic they research. In some areas . . . the institutions are so complex that the effort required to gain anything approaching complete knowledge of the institution is sufficient to preclude the analysis of the economics of the institution by most economists."[45]

Such a statement says a great deal about the current state of economics. There is no question that quantitative and statistical techniques are a useful complement to knowledge of the topic one is investigating. But they are not, nor were they ever intended to be, a substitute for such knowledge. No one has ever claimed that good research does not require hard work. This is not to say that economists are not justified, in the pursuit of an intellectual division of labor, in relying occasionally on secondary materials. Nor is it to suggest that all institutional detail need be incorporated in an economic model. The decision of what to omit is often as essential as the choice of what is included. But such choices should, in principle, be made on the basis of knowledge, not ignorance. Dunlop's critique is not and should not be directed against the practice of abstraction. The point is that this abstraction should be reasonable.

The degree of justifiable abstraction will depend on the purposes for which the model is being constructed. But the bottom line for most of this research must be the extent to which it is helpful in informing our understanding of or policy decisions regarding the phenomena under study. Dunlop suggests with some justification that the report card for at least this subdiscipline of modern economics is not very favorable. Part of the problem may be due to the insensitivity and lack of training of government bureaucrats, but part of it is certainly due to the nature of the output which economists have been producing.

Conclusion

John R. Commons was a pioneer in labor economics as well as in the general area of institutional economics discussed here. The issues Dunlop raises in discussing Commons complement those raised here. If we are serious about our research, we may have to abandon the neoclassical economists' traditional disdain for the particular. An important range of phenomena, such as cooperation, cartels, and more generally the rules which organize economic activity, may have to be approached on a case-by-case basis. That this involves hard work and the redevelopment of historical, institutional, and legal sensitivities cannot be denied. It does not mean that the progress made in diffusing knowledge of statistical and analytical techniques need be abandoned. It is not an argument for a total return to the particularism of the German historical school, nor is it directed against the use of abstraction in economic theory. It is, rather, a call for a reasonable approach to the modeling of phenomena upon whose importance, at least, economists can now agree.

If advocates of position 3 have made their peace with Commons on the appropriate scope of economic inquiry, it is time that peace be made as well on the issue of method. The best theoretical work has always been that which combines a detailed knowledge of the subject under investigation with the ability to abstract and interrelate its essential features. The challenge of achieving an appropriate balance between realism and generality is indeed one which requires considerable and sustained efforts on the part of economists. But the hope that rule structures can, in principle, be made totally endogenous using economic models, thus avoiding the sort of research which Commons and his students undertook, is a chimera. That type of research has been and will continue to be essential as an empirical foundation for evaluating the realism of the assumptions built into economic models as well as the realism of the stylized facts which the new institutional economists view as their object of explanation. When this is more generally accepted by the profession, we may be able effectively to address the challenge.

Notes

1. See Albert Ando's Introduction to Albert Ando, Franklin M. Fisher, and Herbert A. Simon, *Essays on the Structure of Social Science Models* (Cambridge, Mass.: The MIT Press, 1963), p. 1
2. By the neoclassical synthesis I mean the tradition of Marshallian partial

and Walrasian general equilibrium analysis as embodied in modern microeconomics texts. See, for example, J. M. Henderson and R. E. Quandt, *Microeconomic Theory: A Mathematical Approach*, 2nd ed. (New York: McGraw-Hill, 1971). One might describe this synthesis as combining the enthusiastic revival of Ricardian methodology with an equally enthusiastic rejection of Ricardian economics.

3. Samuelson wrote: "In the general equilibrium analysis of, let us say, Walras, the content of the historical discipline of theoretical economics is practically exhausted. The things which are taken as data for that system happen to be matters which economists have traditionally chosen not to consider within their province. Among these data may be considered tastes, technology, the governmental and institutional framework, and many others." Paul A. Samuelson, *Foundations of Economic Analysis* (New York: Atheneum, 1970), p. 8. The use of the adjective "traditionally" is of note. It clearly did not apply to the tradition of institutionalist economics (advocates of position 1), still remarkably strong at the time Samuelson was writing.

4. This is the case, for example, at Harvard's Widener Library.

5. Douglass C. North and Robert Paul Thomas, in *The Rise of the Western World* (Cambridge: the University Press, 1973), illustrate this approach in its purest form. Ronald Coase's work is something of an anomaly within this framework. He argued that, in the absence of transaction costs, changes in the structure of property rights, while affecting distribution, would not affect, at least in the small, the structure of output. (In a general equilibrium sense, however, such changes could affect output by shifting incomes between individuals with different tastes.) If one believes that transaction costs are relatively unimportant, then Coase's argument is a justification for not spending much time studying institutions. Alternatively, if one believes they are important, then such costs appear to be the key to understanding institutional change and variation. Coase's article can be used in support of both positions. See Ronald Coase, "The Problem of Social Cost," *Journal of Law and Economics* 3 (October 1960): 1–44.

6. John Stuart Mill, *A System of Logic, Ratiocinative and Inductive*, in two vols. (London: Longmans, 1961).

7. See Barrington Moore, Jr., *Reflections on the Causes of Human Misery and Upon Certain Proposals to Eliminate Them* (Boston: Beacon Press, 1973), p. 6

8. See Kenneth J. Arrow and Frank H. Hahn, *General Competitive Analysis* (San Francisco: Holden Day, 1971), chapters 1–2.

9. See Samuelson, *Foundations*, pp. 9–10.

10. Or if we have expanded the model through some historical (dynamic) or probabilistic mechanism to account for why this equilibrium, and not some other, was attained.

11. Economists have displayed a reluctance to rationalize institutional change as reflecting exogenous preference change. Changes in technologies or endowments have proved to be the mechanisms of choice.

12. An extreme example, again, is North and Thomas: "This book explains . . . the rise of the Western World. . . . The development of an efficient

economic organization in Western Europe accounts for the rise of the West. . . . We shall describe the parameter shifts which induce the institutional change" (*Western World*, p. 1). But similar models are implicit in Steven Cheung's model of sharecropping, or James Buchanan's model of constitution formation. See Steven Cheung, *The Theory of Share Tenancy* (Chicago: University of Chicago Press, 1969); and James Buchanan, *Between Anarchy and Leviathan* (Chicago: University of Chicago Press, 1975).

13. Continuing the use of North and Thomas as an example, see Alexander J. Field, "*The Rise of the Western World*: A Methodological Critique," mimeographed, Stanford University, July 1977. For the microeconomic variant, see Lance Davis and Douglass C. North, *Institutional Change and American Economic Growth* (Cambridge: the University Press, 1971).

14. Roberto M. Unger, *Knowledge and Politics* (New York: The Free Press, 1975), especially chapters 1–3.

15. Rules as in "the rules of the game." This is not necessarily the same as a behavioral rule, which is used as a criterion for determining individual action. Such behavioral rules (of thumb) may be used, however, to achieve compliance with rules governing interpersonal relations.

16. See Charles G. Kindleberger, "Group Behavior and International Trade," *Journal of Political Economy* 59 (February 1951): 30–48.

17. This was a common position among New Left critics of neoclassical economics in the late 1960s. Such critics frequently titled works "The Political Economy of (such and such)," the implication being that all economics was political. Although there is some truth in this assertion, these critics used the term in a very different sense than had the classical economists. The latter used the term *economy* in the sense of parsimony, not in the sense of "The Economy." Economics was to be a guide to the legislator, enabling him to encourage the greatest happiness for the greatest number with a minimum (but nonzero) set of legislative guidelines. See Elie Halévy, *The Growth of Philosophic Radicalism* (Boston: Beacon Press, 1955).

18. The definition is tentative because it does, in effect, deny what proponents of position 3 are claiming: It denies that rule structures (social forces) can, in principle, be explained as the result of a logically prior round of short-run maximization.

19. Whether this represents an explanatory failure depends on the ambitions of the investigator. It is a failure if the long-run objective is the elimination of the ad hoc appeal to rules for making rules, and if the implicit standard of theory evaluation is the avoidance of such ad hoc explanations. This is not to say that some ad hoc explanations are not better than others. But the superiority of one to another must be justified on the basis of the purpose of the investigation. One must be careful about defending a new model on the grounds that it is a way station on the road to the total elimination of rule categories as something exogenous and not, in turn, explained as the result of short-term maximization, if that goal is in principle not attainable.

Mordecai Kurz, for example, has adduced the concept of a "supergame"

70   Alexander James Field

(that is, one which is repeated) in order to obtain results in his discussion of what he calls altruistic equilibrium. See Mordecai Kurz, "Altruistic Equilibrium," in *Economic Progress, Private Values and Public Policy, Essays in Honor of William Fellner,* edited by Bela Belassa and Richard Nelson (Amsterdam: North Holland, 1977), p. 188. This assumes away the question of why some games are repeated while others are not, which, in a sense, is the question we keep coming back to in this essay.

20. See once again, North and Thomas, *Western World,* at least for the pre-1500 period. Contrast this aproach with that evidenced in J. R. T. Hughes, "Transference and Development of Institutional Constraints Upon Economic Activity," in *Research in Economic History,* vol. 1, edited by Paul Uselding (Greenwich: JAI Press, 1976), pp. 45–68.

21. This argument is spelled out in Mancur Olson, *The Logic of Collective Action: Public Goods and the Theory of Games* (Cambridge, Mass.: Harvard University Press, 1965). See especially p. 12.

22. For example, in microeconomic theory firms or households rather than individuals are often treated as the key decision makers, even when theories of the internal operations of the firm or household were not specified. Organizational theory and the "new home economics" are attempts to deal with this apparent discrepancy.

23. Although the literature on problems of social choice suggests that preferences will not be aggregated effortlessly within such decision units. See Kenneth J. Arrow, *Social Choice and Individual Values* (New York: Wiley, 1951).

24. Pareto efficient in the sense that the same output can be produced using fewer resources or, alternately, that equivalent inputs yield larger total output. On constitutions, see Buchanan, *Anarchy and Leviathan.*

25. Some economists have made tentative steps toward greater realism by questioning the reasonableness of such assumptions as perfect certainty, perfect information, and costless transactions. Of course, such assumptions are unreasonable. But the criticism here is different: Even if we are willing to grant these assumptions, the resulting models can account either for the existence of the phenomena or their absence and as a result can explain neither. Radical *a priorists* (see note 38) such as Milton Friedman or Lionel Robbins reject the proposition that the unreasonableness of assumptions is a legitimate ground for criticizing a model. Prediction or explanation, they argue, is the only real test. This author disagrees with that position. For the sake of argument, nevertheless, it is worth pointing out that these models continue to fail when evaluated according to that latter test. The critique, then, is based on the methodological standard accepted by radical *a priorists* themselves.

26. Despite printed protestations to the contrary, much of Gordon Tullock's work belongs in this category. See Richard McKenzie and Gordon Tullock, *The New World of Economics* (Homewood: Irwin, 1975), especially chapter 5. Page 50 includes a protestation to the contrary.

27. The French Revolution and the subsequent diffusion of the Napoleonic Code symbolize the shift from a society based on estates or *Stände* to one

On the Explanation of Rules 71

based on the formal equality of all citizens before the law. Edmund Burke argued, in reaction to this revolution, that "it is with infinite caution that any man ought to venture upon pulling down an edifice which has answered in any tolerable degree for ages the common purposes of society." See his *Reflections on the Revolution in France* (New York: Liberal Arts Press, 1955), pp. 69–70.

28. Diplomatic historians, for example, attribute the absence of major wars in the forty years following the Congress of Vienna to the willingness of the major European powers to adhere to an "international code of behavior." See Charles Breunig, *The Age of Revolution and Reaction* (New York: Norton, 1977), p. 53. But the problem is a more general one. Some economists are openly skeptical of proposed business codes of ethics, arguing that they would simply be violated and could not eliminate the abuses (bribery, corruption) at which they are directed. There is even the hint that such abuses should really not be viewed as abuses since, as Mozart said, they all do it. This position is equivalent to the argument that we should repeal the laws against murder because the history of such legislation is ample proof of its inability to eliminate this abuse. This is a nihilistic position with regard to the possibility of improving wealth and welfare through rule changes. It is interesting in this light to reexamine the works of Jeremy Bentham, the intellectual father of Utilitarianism. In his later years Bentham argued that if the unrestricted pursuit of individual self-interest led to outcomes which a majority of members of a group did not like, they should rewrite the rules so that individual greed might lead to desirable collective activity. Note that Smith's invisible hand was in Bentham quite visible: It belonged to the jurist. See Halévy, *Philosophic Radicalism;* and J. B. Brebner, "Laissez Faire and State Intervention in Nineteenth Century Britain," *Journal of Economic History* 8 (Supplement 1948) : 59–73.

29. John R. Commons, *The Economics of Collective Action* (Madison: University of Wisconsin Press, 1970), pp. 34–35.

30. Kenneth Arrow, "Social Responsibility and Economic Efficiency," *Public Policy* 21 (Summer 1973) : 303–10.

31. Oliver E. Williamson, *Markets and Hierarchies: Analysis and Antitrust Implications: A Study of the Economics of Internal Organizations* (New York: The Free Press, 1975), p. 9. Williamson defines *opportunism* as "a lack of candor or honesty in transactions, to include self-interest seeking with guile." Williamson argues that such behavior poses little risk so long as markets are competitive and large number of exchanges take place. That solution is not satisfactory when one is dealing with the determination of the rules which make that competition and exchange possible in the first place.

32. See Talcott Parsons, *The Structure of Social Action* (New York: The Free Press, 1968). Parsons, a central figure in the development of American sociology, did his graduate work in economics and was thus familiar with both the power and limitations of microeconomic analysis.

33. Joseph A. Schumpeter, *History of Economic Analysis* (New York: Oxford University Press, 1954), p. 888. Sociobiology appears to be the

most recent attempt to contravene Schumpeter's conclusion. See Jack Hirshleifer, "Economics from a Biological Viewpoint," *Journal of Law and Economics* 20 (April 1977): 1–52.

34. Buchanan, *Anarchy and Leviathan.*
35. Vilfredo Pareto, *Sociological Writings,* edited by S. E. Finer (New York: Praeger, 1966), p. 14.
36. Validity in the sense that not stealing is a less viable strategy when all others are stealing.
37. By latent instability I mean the ever-present temptation to move phenomena from the rule category to the category of endogenous variables explained as the result of the aggregation of the choices of self-interested agents.
38. See Mark Blaug, *Economic Theory in Retrospect* (London: Heinemann, 1968), p. 666; Lionel Robbins, *An Essay on the Nature and Significance of Economic Science* (London: Macmillan, 1932); and Milton Friedman, "The Methodology of Positive Economics," in *Essays in Positive Economics* (Chicago: University of Chicago Press, 1935), pp. 3–43.
39. John Stuart Mill, *Principles of Political Economy, with some of their Applications to Social Philosophy,* edited by W. J. Ashley (Clifton: Augustus M. Kelley, 1973), p. 242.
40. "Report of Organization of the American Economic Association," *Publications of the American Economic Association,* vol. 1, no. 1 (Baltimore: John Murphy, 1887), p. 38.
41. I say again because the AEA was founded, to a large extent, in reaction to methodological Ricardianism (the extreme deductive approach), which, rightly or wrongly, U.S. economists viewed as infusing English political economy. Macroeconomics, the study of the behavior of economic aggregates, at least until fairly recently, has not been based on choice-theoretic foundations.
42. John T. Dunlop, "Policy Decisions and Research in Economics and Industrial Relations," *Industrial and Labor Relations Review* 30 (April 1977): 276–77.
43. Ibid., p. 279.
44. Albert Rees, "Policy Decisions and Research in Economics and Industrial Relations: An Exchange of Views: Comment," *Industrial and Labor Relations Review* 31 (October 1977): 4.
45. Ronald G. Ehrenberg, Daniel S. Hamermesh, and George E. Johnson, "Policy Decisions and Research in Economics and Industrial Relations: An Exchange of Views: Comment," *Industrial and Labor Relations Review* 31 (October 1977): 10.

[6]

Excerpt from Philip Mirowski (ed.), *The Reconstruction of Economic Theory*, 241–63.

7 INSTITUTIONS AS A SOLUTION CONCEPT IN A GAME THEORY CONTEXT

Philip Mirowski

... he believed that human beings, when it had been clearly explained to them what were their vital needs and necessities, would not only altruistically but selfishly become honest and reasonable: they would sacrifice what might be short term advantages for long term ends. What he never saw was that in politics as in other forms of human activity, human beings are for the most part interested in struggle, in manoeuvrings for power, in risks and even unpleasantnesses; and that these are often in direct opposition to what might reasonably be seen as their long term ends....

This was one reason why he could so often make rings around his opponents by reasoning: he believed in it; while they, although they said they did, ultimately did not. Yet what they felt instinctively, and might have answered [him] by, was traditionally unspoken. They could not say to him in effect—Look, in your reasoning you leave out of account something about human nature: you leave out the fact that human beings with part of themselves like turmoil and something to grumble at and perhaps even failure to feel comfortable in: your economic perfect blueprint will not work simply because people will not want it to.

Mosley, 1983, pp. 68–69

242   THE RECONSTRUCTION OF ECONOMIC THEORY

Confounding the Critics

In the history of neoclassical economic theory, there have been two major
categories of rejoinders to critics of the theory: one, that the critics did not
adequately understand the structure of the theory, and thus mistook for
essential what was merely convenient; or two, that the criticism was old hat,
and had been rendered harmless by recent (and technically abstruse) innovations with which the critic was unacquainted.[1] The freedom of passage
between these defenses has proven to be the bane of not only those opposed
to neoclassicism, but also of those who have felt the need for reform and
reformulation of economic theory from within. It has fostered the impression that, with enough ingenuity, any arbitrary phenomenon can be incorporated within the ambit of conventional neoclassical theory, therefore
rendering any particular change in "assumptions" as innocuous as any
other, and thus rendering them all equally arbitrary.

Nowhere has this impasse been more evident than in the confrontations
between the various partisans of an "institutional" economics and the adherents of neoclassical economic theory. The early institutionalists, such as
Thorstein Veblen, John R. Commons, and Wesley Clair Mitchell, mounted
a scathing attack on neoclassical value theory in the first three decades of the
century, ridiculing the "hedonistic conception of man [as] that of a lighten-
ing calculator of pleasures and pains, who oscillates like a homogeneous
globule of desire of happiness under the impulse of stimuli that shift him
about the area but leave him intact."[2] The unifying principles of this movement were: (a) an assertion that neoclassical economists were the advocates
of a spurious scientism which insisted upon imitating physics without understanding the implications of such mimesis; (b) an expression of an alternative to the above conception of society based upon a study of the working
rules that structured collective action and going concerns, such as the corporation, the trade union, the bank and the state; (c) in conjunction with the
construction of theories that took as their province the explanation of the
evaluation of the working rules and then attendant institutions. The institutionalists' writings on the vagaries of behavior, such as Veblen's book on
"conspicious consumption", were intended to show that theories based on
individual psychologies were built upon shifting sands; and that, as Commons wrote, "cooperation does not arise from a presupposed harmony of
interests, as the older economists believed. It arises from the necessity of
creating a new harmony of interests" (Commons, 1934, p. 6).

The initial rebuttal to the institutionalists adopted the first tactic. To cite
just one prominent example, Paul Samuelson insisted that nothing substan-

tial would be lost if economists relinquished utility (Wong, 1978), and that institutions were effectively included in the assumptions of neoclassical economic theory (Samuelson, 1965, p. 8). When fully interpreted, this assertion meant that the study of institutions was *separable* from neoclassical economic theory, to the point of being independent of any particular institutional framework (Mirowski, 1981). Economics could cut itself free of the inessential institutional considerations, and preserve its core as the study of rational allocation of scarce means in a thoroughly abstract frame. Veblen and Commons were drummed out of the economists' camp, and exiled to the provinces of Sociology or Anthropology.

With the passage of time, this first rebuttal has fallen into disuse, and the second option has gained favor. Among a certain subset of theorists, it has become acceptable to admit that conventional neoclassical theory is "mechanistic", in the sense that it slavishly imitates certain theoretical structures and procedures in physics, and that this might be undesirable in certain respects. In most cases, this admission is accompanied by an assertion that this flaw has been remedied by the development of new techniques in the theory of games, to such an extent that there is a "new mathematical institutional economics" which has incorporated the concerns of the earlier critics (Johansen, 1983; Schotter, 1981, 1983; Schotter and Schwödiauer, 1980; Shubik, 1975, 1976).

It is a curious fact that the language of the critique of neoclassical theory of the game theorists is so close to that of the earlier institutionalists as to be almost indistinguishable. For example: "The neoclassical agents are bores who merely calculate optimal activities at fixed parametric prices.... No syndicates or coalitions are formed, no cheating or lying is done, no threats are made.... The economy has no money, no government, no legal system, no property rights, no banks ..." (Schotter, 1981, p. 150). "The general equilibrium model is: (1) basically noninstitutional. (2) It makes use of few differentiated actors. (3) It is essentially static. No explanation of price formation is given. (4) There is no essential role for money. (5) It is non-strategic" (Shubik, 1976, p. 323). However, similarities in languages can be misleading. How justified is the claim that institutionalist concerns have been absorbed by game theorists?

For the purposes of this paper, we shall choose to avoid discussion of the first variant of the neoclassical defense. We shall simply assume that the central concept of neoclassical economic theory is the application of a physical metaphor to the market.[3] This will allow us to concentrate our attention on the second variant: Are recent game theoretic models different in any substantial way from neoclassical theory? Do game theory models capture the concerns that institutionalists believed were ignored in neo-classical economics? How can one judge the various claims made for the superior efficacy of game theory?

Game Theory and Institutional Analysis: Shubik and Schotter

It is a difficult task to discern the wood from the many trees that have passed through the pulper in the cause of game theory. Game theory burst upon the scene in 1944 with von Neumann and Morgenstern's book. The solutions of games were claimed to be isomorphic to "orders of society," "standards of behavior," "economic organizations"; and yet these models also claimed to be following "the best examples of theoretical physics" (von Neumann and Morgenstern, 1964, pp. 43, ix). Forty years of development have revealed that game theory is not the philosopher's stone its progenitors had claimed: more than half of any competent textbook in game theory is occupied with developing taxonomies of the numerous variants of games—cooperative and noncooperative; constant- or nonconstant-sum; static or sequential; extensive, strategic or characteristic forms; cardinal or noncardinal payoffs; various permutations of information sets and sequences of moves; small and large numbers of players; different conceptions of uncertainty; stationary versus nonstationary payoffs and/or strategies—so that the permutations and their attendant solution concepts have far outstripped any claims for generality or unity.

Doubts about the efficacy of game theory have begun to surface—sometimes during inauspicious occasions, such as Nobel Prize lectures (see, e.g., Simon, 1982, pp. 486–487). In this context, it is noteworthy that its most vocal defenders have chosen to reemphasize the potential of game theory to encompass institutional considerations. We shall therefore concentrate our initial attention on the work of the two most prolific proselytizers for a "new institutional economics": Martin Shubik and Andrew Schotter.

Shubik has built an illustrious career upon the development of game theory in economics, providing many of the basic theorems and results in that literature, as well as writing the best introductory textbook (Shubik, 1982). In this respect, he is particularly well qualified to judge which areas of game theory should be credited with having made substantial contributions and novel innovations, as well as revealing the motivations behind the prosecution of game theoretic research. In a series of journal articles, Shubik has been persistently critical of Walrasian general equilibrium because it

INSTITUTIONS AS SOLUTION CONCEPTS   245

does not explain price formation; it merely *assumes* it. The actors in a Walrasian world have no freedom to make errors or even choices about process, he says; and in this, he sounds very similar to Veblen. More unexpectedly, he is also critical of cooperative game theory: "As an early proponent of the core and of the replication process for studying mass economic behavior, I am completely willing to admit that to a great extent the results on the core have helped to direct attention away from the understanding of the competitive process ..." (Shubik, 1975a, p. 560; see also Shubik, 1982, p. 286). He believes that whole other classes of games tend to be mere repetitions of pregame-theoretic models and add little insight to the corpus; for example, constant-sum games impose conservation rules which hinder the adequate description of process (Shubik, 1975a, p. 557; Shubik, 1972; Mirowski, 1984a).

Where, then, does the advantage of game theoretic techniques lie? Shubik claims that the future belongs to noncooperative nonconstant-sum games. "Noncooperative game theory appears to be particularly useful for the study of mass phenomena in which the communication between individuals must be relatively low and individuals interact with a more or less faceless and anonymous economy, polity or society" (Shubik, 1982, p. 300). Since strategic considerations are linked to a perception of society as consisting of impersonal social forces, and this conception informs Shubik's notion of "institutions", he therefore proselytizes for the appearance of a "new mathematical institutional economics": "... my basic approach to economics is through the construction of mathematical models in which the "rules of the game" derive not only from the economics and technology of the situation, but from the sociological, political and legal structure as well" (Shubik, 1982, p. 10).

Shubik's research programme is not so very different from the seventeenth-century dream of Hobbes, that "in the same way as man, the author of geometrical definitions can, by starting from those arbitrary definitions, construct the whole of geometry, so also, as the author of the laws which rule his city, he can synthetically construct the whole social order in the manner of the geometers" (Halévy, 1972, p. 494). Just as with Hobbes, there is some equivocation in deciding what is *necessary* and what is *adventitious*; we are referring in this case to the notion of social structures "external" to what is identified as the "economy". Shubik has, in places, suggested that institutions are merely ad hoc rules (Shubik, 1975a, p. 558), of which he is providing mathematical descriptions. In other places, he suggests he is actively constructing optimal rules with regard to various problems, such as the treatment of bankruptcy (Shubik, 1975b, p. 526; Dubey and Shubik, 1979). In either event, Shubik's claim to be including "sociological, political and legal structures" is in practice, reduced to the mathematical specification of rules which impinge upon the operation of a market whose basic constituents—tastes, technologies, and endowments—are essentially the same as in the conventional Walrasian models. These rules have a different analytical status than the tastes, technologies, and so forth, because they are not treated as "natural" or fundamental givens, but rather as arbitrary intrusions from outside the sphere of the economy.

The arbitrary character of the rules is only confronted once, to my knowledge, in the Shubik corpus. In (Shubik, 1974, p. 383) he asks the two revealing questions: "Should we assume that the laws and customs are to be modelled as rules of the game which are given and never broken? . . . Why should individuals accept fiat money or the laws and customs of trade in the first place?" Both questions are not answered: they are instead relegated to be outside the competence of the mathematical institutional economist, and by implication, outside of the sphere of the "economic".

It is possible to attempt a summary of Shubik's cannonical institutional model. He distinguishes between "market games", which can be represented by a characteristic function, because the payoff of any subset of players is independent of the activities of the complement (i.e., all other traders); and a "strategic market game", in which the activities of all traders are linked by an explicit price formation mechanism and a distinct monetary system. One valuable insight of Shubik's work has been to show how the neoclassical economists' notion of "externalities" pervades the entire price system through a demonstration that realistic descriptions of the trading process preclude the possibility of treating traders' options and objectives as independent of one another. Nonetheless, he retains the neoclassical predisposition to see prices mainly as the means of conveyance of information. He writes:

> The key aspect of many economic activities that differentiates them from the viewpoint of information processing and coding from say political or societal activities or from abstract games is that a natural metric exists on many of the strategies. In mass markets, for example, for wheat, the information that two million tons were produced last season is probably more useful to most buyers and sellers than is a detailed list of the quantities produced by each individual farmer. (Shubik, 1975a, p. 560)

A strategic market game is modelled as a noncooperative nonconstant sum game. It consists of a list of traders[4] and their endowments, the postulation of a market structure as a set of rules governing the process by which traders may convey information about bids and offers, as well as rules for the clearing of markets, and the utility functions of and strategies available to each player. The specification of market structure may become quite complicated, including the role of a bank, the rules for bankruptcy, and so on (Shubik and Wilson, 1977). Another further assertion of Shubik is that the specification of the generic types of strategies pursued by the traders captures the presence or absence of "trust" in the market. The predominance of historical strategies—i.e., where a player's move is conditional upon the past moves of a set of players—is said to represent a situation of low trust. On the other hand, the acceptance of state strategies, where a player's move depends solely upon the present state of the game, is said to represent a situation of widespread trust. There is a hint, but no more, of an evolutionary argument embedded in this distinction: as markets become more anonymous and threats, by their very nature, become less specific, state strategies slowly displace historical strategies. Shubik explicitly links this development to the spread of the use of money, which he calls "the symbol of trust" (Shubik, 1974, p. 379).

Perhaps the most striking characteristic of Shubik's published work is the relative unpretentiousness of the claims made for its efficacy. He admits that game theory enforces a symmetry upon the personalities of the players which belies any serious intrusion of personal detail, while also abstracting away from social conditioning and role playing; he also admits that game theory requires a fixed and well-defined structure of payoffs. Even more significantly, he explains that "there is as yet no satisfactory blending of game theory with learning theory" (Shubik, 1982, p. 358). The impression conveyed is that game theory is one of many techniques of social analysis, with its own strengths and weaknesses; the matter of choice of analytical technique is left to the individual reader without any explicit discussion. This attitude is encouraged by statements that one should choose the solution concept to fit the preconceived objective: "The [Walrasian] price system may be regarded as stressing decentralization (with efficiency); the core shows the force of countervailing power; the value offers a "fairness" criterion; the bargaining set and kernel suggest how the solution might be delineated by bargaining conditions . . ." (Shubik, 1982, p. 382). One cannot help, however, but receive a different impression from the collected body of his writings. There intermittent claims are made that game theoretic models are necessary prerequisites for the integration of macroeconomic and Walrasian microeconomic theory, and ironically, that Nash equilibrium points of strategic market games frequently include the conventional Walrasian general equilibrium (Dubey and Shubik, 1979, p. 120). It would appear that all the different solution concepts really are subordinate to the one "real" solution, the Walrasian general equilibrium.

Shubik's circumspection contrasts sharply with the claims made by the other prominent mathematical institutional economist, Andrew Schotter. Schotter (1983, p. 692) writes, "game theory is the only tool available today that holds out hope for creating an institutionally realistic and flexible economic theory." Schotter reveals that he is aware that other economists, such as John R. Commons, also have tackled these issues, but feels that such research can be written off as ineffectual without any extended critical discussion, simply because it is not phrased in game theoretic terms.

In certain respects Schotter resembles Shubik: Schotter, also, disparages Walrasian theory for leaning on the *deus ex machina* of the auctioneer rather than directly confronting process (Schotter, 1983, p. 674); and, as well, repudiates cooperative game theory and the solution concept of the core, because after limit theorems that showed the core converged to the Walrasian general equilibrium (Debreu and Scarf, 1963; Aumann, 1964) "what we have left is an economy that is not any richer institutionally than the neoclassical analysis, which merely assumed that this degenerate set of market institutions existed at the outset" (Schotter, 1983, p. 682). Schotter gives voice to what many have said privately: these results stole the thunder from game theory by demonstrating that it added little or nothing to the analytical content of Walrasian general equilibrium (Schotter, 1981, p. 152).

It is here that Schotter begins to diverge from Shubik. Whereas the latter seems to pursue a live-and-let-live policy in the house of neoclassicism, the former is critical of the modern general equilibrium trick of handling time, uncertainty, externalities, and a host of other complications by redefinition and expansion of the commodity space. (A Hershey bar at 6 P.M. on Tuesday on the Boston Common in the rain is different from a Hershey bar at 7 P. M. etc., etc.; and presumably is traded in a separate "market". See chapter 6 in this volume.) "When market institutions fail, as in the case of economies with uncertainty and externalities, the neoclassical economist does not, as he should, try to explain what alternative sets of institutions would be created to take their place" (Schotter, 1981, p. 151). It is the stress on the creation of institutions that Schotter believes sets him apart from Shubik and others. Shubik, as we have observed, has a tendency to define institutions as ad hoc rules which act to constrain or restrict the operation of the market; Schotter, on the other hand, insists that institutions are *solutions* to games (Schotter, 1981, p. 155; Schotter, 1983, p. 689). Initially, the distinction might seem to be excessively subtle: although Shubik will not commit himself on where his "rules" come from, he is not hesitant to suggest bankruptcy rules are a reaction to a perceived market failure, and then examine the spectrum of possible rules to discover which are "optimal." But Schotter insists this conception is wrong because he does not believe institutions are consciously constructed; instead, behavioral regularities "emerge endogenously" or "organically." In his book, he makes a preliminary attempt at developing a taxonomy of different kinds of institutions (Schotter, 1981,

p. 22), but quickly abandons all but one category as not being sufficiently "organic." His rationale is worth quoting in its entirety:

> If the social institutions we are investigating are created by a social planner, their design can be explained by maximizing the value of some objective function existing in the planners mind.... On the other hand, if the form of social organization created is the outcome of a multilateral bargaining process, a bargaining theory would be required. (Schotter, 1981, p. 28)

A number of references to the Austrian school,   and particularly Hayek, are provided in support of this conception of an institution.

Again, appearances suggest an affinity with the earlier institutionalists' stress on the unintended consequences of both conscious choices and evolutionary drift. For this reason, it is all the more important to be clear and precise about how Schotter conceptualizes an institution. In his scenario, institutions do not lead a separate or semiautonomous existence: "Social and economic institutions are informational devices that supplement the informational content of economic systems when competitive prices do not carry sufficient information to totally decentralize and coordinate economic activities" (Schotter, 1981, p. 109). Institutions are stopgaps or *pis aller* which evolve naturally whenever a market is not capable of producing a Pareto optimal outcome. The failure of the market to produce these outcomes is not explored in depth, nor are there any suggestions of the ubiquity or the determinants of the presence or absence of failure; and in this it stands in stark contrast to the work of Shubik. Without any motivation, all market failures are attributed to the existence of prisoner's-dilemma structures, given presumably by "states of nature". The overall picture is of a market that organically heals itself, with health defined as the conventional Walrasian general equilibrium.

Schotter has provided us with a canonical model which can be easily summarized. His model starts by *assuming* "that the only institution existing is the auctioneer-led market institution, whose origin is left unexplained by the model" (Schotter, 1981, p. 120). Schotter's "market" is not Shubik's "market": for all practical purposes it is not strategic; its only glitch is that it does not clear in any short sequence of "gropings" for the correct vector of Pareto-optimal prices, due to the fact that preferences are not strictly convex (Schotter, 1981, p. 124). Traders cannot communicate directly with each other, but must communicate through the "price system" by making *quantity* offers to the auctioneer. It is asserted (Schotter, 1981, p. 125) that this is isomorphic to a supergame played over individual component games which are both stationary and of the form of the prisoner's dilemma. The purported reason the payoff is of prisoner's-dilemma form is that it is assumed that if all

250   THE RECONSTRUCTION OF ECONOMIC THEORY

parties cannot arrive at agreement upon the same aggregate quantity of the commodity both bid upon and offered, *no trades are executed*.

Before we summarize the technical details of the supergame, it will be instructive to examine the structure of one of these component "moves" or subgames. Table 7–1 is a presentation of the situation presented graphically in Schotter (1981, p. 125). Let us restrict our attention to two traders each with endowments of a single commodity. Because utility is not strictly convex, auctioneer-provided equilibrium prices are tangent to utility functions at more than one point: here, for simplicity's sake, let us assume there are only two possible trading points: A, where trader 1 (seller of commodity X) ends up with less of his endowment, and B, where he ends up with more. Because utility is "flat" in this region, both traders end up with the same level of utility whichever quantity is traded at the fixed price. However, if no trade is executed (because the traders could not agree upon relative quantities), they would be stuck with their initial endowments, and their concomitant lower utility levels. It is a curiosity of Schotter's graph that he neglects to discuss the presence or absence of symmetry in the level of utility of the two traders, because as one can readily observe, this game is not of the prisoner's-dilemma format. The problem here is not that the equilibrium point is suboptimal: it is only that there are a *multiplicity of equally desirable equilibria* and that the game does not allow any external coordination to agree upon which of these indifferently acceptable equilibria will be settled upon. If utilities are not comparable and side payments are not allowed, there are only two possibilities as one adds more traders to the market: (1) everyone is psychologically identical up to a scalar multiple, and the number of multiple equivalent equilibria proliferate; or (2) people have different utility functions, and as the number of traders increases, the solution shrinks to a single Walrasian general equilibrium, which the auctioneer effectuates. Schotter seems not to have noticed that this is not an intrinsically noncooperative game, and that only in the most idiosyncratic of special cases of utility functions is there any problem of coordination.

Far from being a niggling criticism, this observation reveals that contrary to his statement in section 4.2 (Schotter, 1981), the "market model" is not isomorphic to the supergame model in chapter 3 (Schotter, 1981), because the latter model is predicated on the Nash equilibrium point solution concept applied to a sequence of generic prisoner's-dilemma games, which the former clearly is not.

Let us assume that Schotter has found a way of recasting his model of the market process so that it is in the form of a prisoner's dilemma. From whence come his claims of "evolution" and "organic developments"? First he must postulate a fixed prisoner's-dilemma situation that is repeatedly played over and over again by an identical set of players. Players are assumed to "learn" from past plays of the game, but this learning is constrained to a very small subset of experience: they are allowed neither threat strategies nor to be different from other players, and cannot "remember" past the last immediate play of the game. Technically, allowable strategies are restricted to a mixed strategy over best responses in which the probabilities attached to each response are updated with a mechanical Bayesian procedure (Schotter, 1981, p. 72). The rule is so constructed that it will eventually converge to a pure-strategy Nash equilibrium point if that strategy is played at some juncture in the game. For Schotter, an institution is any one such Nash equilibrium of a fixed game converged upon after repeated play. He does not claim to have identified the single unique institutional outcome of the situation: there are in general multiple Nash equilibria; all he can guarantee is that the Markov chain of mixed strategies will eventually converge upon one of the equilibrium points, which is an absorbing state.

Table 7–1:   A Trading Subgame

		Trader 2	
		A	B
Trader 1	A	10, 20	3, 6
	B	3, 6	10, 20

One point needs elucidation not received in Schotter's book. The necessity for the single component subgame to be of the form of a prisoner's dilemma derives from the narrow conception of learning implied in the mechanical Bayesian updating rule. The question arises, as it does in all Austrian theory, how the institutional regularity is to be "policed" if it is, in fact, "organic" or "evolutionary". If the game is not of the prisoner's-dilemma form, there is no longer any unique way for a player to "punish" the others for behavior undesirable from his point of view (Schotter, 1981, p. 83). This can be easily observed by again looking at table 7–1. Suppose trader 1 in the last around of play has chosen *A* while trader 2 has chosen *B*. Clearly both of their situations could be improved, but how can trader 1 teach this to trader 2? No message can be sent that would not involve the recall of the pattern of all plays previous to the last, and that is prevented by the Bayesian updating rule, due to the fact that mixed strategies are allowed. In other words, no strategy is explicitly identified as punishment by the structure of the game.

Schotter, like many other latter-day Austrians, shies away from explicitly discussing *learning*, as opposed to the transmission of a discrete and seemingly prepackaged commodity called *knowledge*, because the former suggests a social process, whereas the latter conjures up the grocer's dairy case (Field, 1984). This is done largely by mathematical sleight-of-hand: assuming that everyone's psychology is identical (Schotter, 1981, p. 88), and ruling out what Schotter calls "disguised equilibria," that is, situations where the opponent's choice of strategy cannot be divined from the actual outcome or payoff. In effect, he defines the "problem" to be so straightforward and unambiguous that only one choice can be made: it is not so much learning as it is mechanism. Any discussion of the influence of history is rendered pointless, since only state strategies (in Shubik's terms) are allowed, or indeed, make any sense, given that the situation is so well defined. It should not surprise us, then, that at the end of the narrow corridor through which we are allowed to pass, we arrive at—voilà—a Walrasian general equilibrium (Schotter, 1983, p. 185–186). It is difficult to maintain that this model transcends the passive cooperation of the zombies found in conventional neoclassical general equilibrium. The question posed at the beginning of this section remains: where has game theory gotten us?

The Rules of the Game: Game Theory and Neoclassical Economics

What is a game? It is, as quite correctly perceived by von Neumann, a set of rules, a set of objectives or payoffs, and a ranking of those objectives by the set of players. If all of these sets are *discrete* and well defined, they may be expressed in the format of mathematical formalism; and then further manipulation of the symbols can serve to suggest potential outcomes. However, it is also true, as Wittgenstein wrote in his *Remarks on the Foundations of Mathematics*, "A game, a language, a rule is an institution" (Wittgenstein, 1978, VI 32). The copula "is" in this quote should not be confused with an equals sign, for the relationship is neither commutative nor symmetrical. To say that a game is an institution is not necessarily to say that an institution is a game.

Game theory and neoclassical market theory start from an identical premise: market trades are not adventitious, but possess a regularity and stability which permits them to be causally explained. So what is the constancy postulated by game theory? The first, and least discussed postulate,[5] is the persistence and constancy of the players (Heims, 1980, p. 307). Within a static one-shot game the persistence of the players' identities may be ignored; but with any repetition or learning this condition becomes critical.

INSTITUTIONS AS SOLUTION CONCEPTS 253

The constancy of humans, and therefore the putative constancy of human nature is the key to the translation of any game into mathematical formalism. If humans are not to be treated with all their individual quirks and idiosyncracies (that is, are to be the subject of generalization), then their communication and behavior must be treated symmetrically. If one merely assumes that language is always adequately shared, that the content of a transmitted message is identical to the content received, and that interpretation is not problematic, then the people who are the subject of the analysis must be substantially "the same", no matter what happens.

The second postulate of game theory is the assumed constancy of the rules. As we have observed, this appeared to be the bone of contention between Shubik and Schotter. Shubik seemed content to accept the rules as arbitrarily fixed; Schotter claimed that the rules were solutions to supergames. Examination of Schotter's model revealed that the rules were no more flexible than in Shubik's models; if anything, Schotter mistakes arbitrary psychological rigidities for rule structure. As with the previous postulate, this problem is not apparent in one-shot games, but only attains importance upon repetition. The rules are what exist to be learned by the players, although this is often obscured by mathematically posting the game in strategic form.[6] We shall return to this issue shortly.

The third postulate of game theory is the relative stability of the objectives and the environment. Interestingly enough, this is not an endogenous outcome in game theory, but must be given a priori as part of the mathematical formalism. Many pages have been written about the necessity of expendability of cardinally measurable payoffs, and especially the requirement of cardinal utility, but few have realized that this is merely the tip of the iceberg. A game must have a single-valued objective function which somehow summarizes the jumbled, confused, and sometimes unconsciously contradictory desires and drives of human beings. Further, this index must generally conform to the axiom of Archimedes (Krantz et al., 1971, pp. 25–26), which translates into the requirement that all potential outcomes be comparable before the fact; or more prosaically, every man must have his price. It is of paramount importance that these rankings be stable,[7] for without them, there is no sense in which a game can be "solved".

Now, the most important aspect of these postulates is not their tenuous connection to "reality" (game theorists have been historically thick skinned when it comes to empirical disconfirmation of solutions and/or assumptions), but rather what passes for analysis and explanation. Given the fixed actors with their fixed objectives and the fixed rules, the analyst (and *not the actors*) prereconciles the various sets, insists the prereconciled outcome is the one that will actually obtain, and calls this a "solution". The critical role of the three postulates of constancy becomes evident: without them, there is no preordained reconciliation to be discovered. The process in which the actors take part is irrelevant, because the deck has been stacked in a teleological manner. Insofar as the three postulates are "naturally" given, equilibrium is identified with harmony and natural order, while conflict and disharmony can only be expressed as disequilibrium.

This caricature is crudely drawn, and the game theorists would surely complain (at least there, if not in their published work) that the world is not that simple. I should think they would aver that the distinction between cooperative and noncooperative games was invented precisely to conjure up a more subtle and penetrating analysis of harmony and conflict. I would like to suggest that the promise of game theory to encompass conflict and strategy in a rigorous manner is more than a little illusory, and is rooted in a confusion over the role of the analyst in the solution of games.

The clearest definition of a cooperative game has been provided by Shubik (1981, p. 165): Pareto optimality is taken as an axiom, sidepayments of utility or other payoff unit are permitted outside of the actual structure of the game, and communications and bargaining of an unspecified nature are permitted and presumed to take place (at least virtually, in that the value of each potential coalition must be well defined). Cooperation is not modelled; it is subsumed in the various payoffs to coalitions. In the presence of the three postulates, the players know what the analyst knows, and both the players and the analyst "agree" upon the feasible and desirable outcomes. It is no surprise that early partisans of cooperative games have lately been repudiating their premature enthusiasm: in this scenario, "natural order" is imposed by the analyst.

The distinctive characteristic of noncooperative games is that the players and the analyst no longer "think" the same things: in essence, the analyst would like to impose a solution that the players would not choose as a result of obeying the rules. The conflict is not located among the players as much as it resides in the tension between the rule-governed situation and the Pareto optimum. The analyst, obeying his own self-denying ordinance, resists simply imposing the naturally given optimum (or optima), and then is challenged by the need to provide a description of simple rule-governed stability in the presence of infinite degrees of freedom. The analyst is faced with the prospect of constructing some definition of the rationality that is not transparently a reflection of the natural givens.

This impasse has surfaced whenever someone tries to explain what a Nash equilibrium point means or signifies (Johansen, 1982; Harsanyi, 1982; Shubik, 1981; Friedman, 1977). Mathematically, the Nash EP is the maximum point or points on a compact convex set of the "best replies" of each player's

INSTITUTIONS AS SOLUTION CONCEPTS 255

strategy set. The Nash EP is often motivated by appealing to some lack of knowledge or ability to compare goals among players, but this is not strictly true. Each player knows all the relevant information about the other players, and has the ability to prereconcile the entire process in his own head. The only difference from a cooperative game is that the rules create the potentiality that rationality is indeterminate, in that the interpretation of strategy sets becomes an issue.

It is well known that every finite N-person game has at least one Nash EP if mixed strategies are allowed. This mathematical existence proof does us a disservice, however, once we realize that mixed strategies are only rational if deployed outside of a one-shot static game (Shubik, 1981, p. 155). Therefore, a noncooperative game can in most cases only be seriously discussed if it is repeated; more generally, after Wittgenstein, we can say that no one is capable of following a rule only once. Games, if they are to describe behavior rather than a set of prearranged natural conditions, must be repeated. But it is precisely in repetition that the notion of a fixed strategy set slowly unravels: more and more ad hoc assumptions must be made about how each player interprets the sequences of the other players' moves over time. In general, the solutions to a sequence of noncooperative games will not be the sequence of individual solutions to each of the component games (van Damme, 1981; Friedman, 1977, p. 199). It is in this sense that rationality, as conceived in game theory, is indeterminate.

At this juncture we once again return to the postulates of constancy. Shubik is right to point out that it is a misnomer to call the Nash solution concept "rational expectations", because there is no guarantee that the outcome will meet the *analysts'* criteria of rationality (i.e., Pareto optionality) (Shubik, 1981, p. 153). He suggests it is more appropriate to think of a Nash EP as displaying "consistent expectations," in that conjectures about players' behavior match ex post outcomes. However, the definition of consistency is a function of the time frame over which the Nash equilibrium is defined; once that is realized, it follows directly that all Nash EP require our three postulates of constancy. How else could we possibly "construct" consistency solely from the payoffs of the game, unless the players, the rules, and the objectives where identical through time?

Contrary to the claims often made in the literature on supergames, those models cannot encompass historical change. Works that claim to include change of players over time—(Schotter 1981, pp. 127–139) for example—in fact specify the sequential agent characteristics so that they are functionally identical. In contrast, works, such as that of Friedman (1977), which vary the payoffs over time, do so in such a way that the change can be specified independent of history (i.e., are stationary). If changes in strategy sets are allowed, they are restricted to stationary Bayesian revisions, by their very structure myopic and ahistorical. There is no published work that attempts to change all three postulates simultaneously. This poor showing cannot be excused as a temporary situation contingent upon further mathematical effort and virtuosity. It is a corollary of the neoclassical notion of rationality, which can only augment the psychological abilities of *homo rationalis* in order that all interactions must be virtually prereconciled in their heads, whether or not they actually occur. This conception, of course, is exactly what caused the older institutionalist school to renounce neoclassical economics.

It is easy to be lulled by all the language of "conflict", "retaliation", and "enforcement" into believing that the solvable supergames portray processes. Harsanyi (1982) and Aumann (1981) both define the Nash EP as a self-enforcing equilibrium, but we should now understand this to mean that the solution would persist if the postulates of constancy held and if the analyst imposes an arbitrary set of rules governing how players interpret each other's moves. These requirements wreak havoc with any commonsense notion of this enforcement of rules. Neoclassical economists want to portray a world where there is no active coercion, because rationality polices itself. What causes this goal to elude their grasp is that there is no such thing as a self-justifying rule (Levison, 1978). Quoting Wittgenstein: "However many rules you give me—I give a rule which justifies *my* employment of your rules" (Wittgenstein, 1978, I 113). "The employment of the word 'rule' is interwoven with the employment of the word 'same'" (Wittgenstein, 1978, VII 59). The exercise of rationality, as opposed to the twitches of a zombie or a machine, depends upon active interpretation of whether the rule applies in the particular instance, and on whether to regard anomalies as exceptions or failures to abide by the rule. Rationality is the deployment of judgment as a process, which cannot itself be justified by a rule at the risk of falling into an infinite regress (Field, 1979).[8]

This is nowhere better illustrated than in the proliferation of solution concepts and individual solutions in game theory. As soon as someone proposes a "rational" solution to a particular game someone else generates a counterexample that questions its rationality. For example, Morgenstern and Schwödiauer (1976) criticize the core as being dominated by other imputations if the players are aware of the theory of the core. Or, Johansen (1982, p. 430) points out that if player X knew player Y was experimenting with his options, and had any basis for guessing the pattern of player Y's experiments, then player X would in general choose strategies outside of the Nash equilibrium. van Damme (1981, p. 37) shows that in certain game structures, "a player can punish the other as badly as he wishes and therefore each player can force the other player to steer the system to any state he wishes. So all kinds of behavior (even rather foolish) can appear when one plays according to a history dependent EP." Aumann (1981) reports that the solution points of supergame depend critically upon the discount rate used to calculate the present value of future payoffs; I believe no one has yet indicated how vulnerable these results are to the paradoxes arising out of the Cambridge capital controversy (Harcourt, 1982, pt. V). We have already noted that the Nash EP for a one-shot noncooperative game is not identical to a Nash EP for the same game repeated over and over again.

Game theorists have opened the Pandora's Box marked "rationality," and do not know how to close it again. Walrasian general equilibrium was based upon a direct appropriation of a metaphor from physics, and this meant that the natural givens of the analysis would directly determine the optimal outcome (Mirowski, 1984b). Planets in motion are passive and do not talk back, and neither did the passive Walrasian trader. The natural world is stable and unchanging,[9] which allowed postulations of laws that were independent of their spatial or temporal location. The Walrasian laws were also stationary and static. Then game theorists proposed to discuss bargaining, which led to cooperative games, which begat noncooperative games, which begat discussions of process, which allowed the transactors the freedom to differ in their interpretations of the roles of others and the constancy of the world, all of which is now undermining the older construct of mechanistic rationality. This is not happening because game theorists have willed it so—in fact, much effort is spent demonstrating that special sorts of solutions to special sorts of games converge to Walrasian equilibria. It is happening because game theory exposes the weaknesses of the physical metaphor that all the excessive mathematical formalism served to obscure. Game theory does not, however, suggest what to put in its place. It cannot conceptualize the reduction of a language or of an institution to a game.

Rules are not Homogeneous

The word "institution" has been so far used loosely; the time has arrived to suggest a more precise definition. In view of the criticisms voiced in the previous sections of this paper, it may prove illuminating to conceptualize institutions as consisting of three tiers of rules. In the first tier are the rules most familiar to game theorists: these are rules grounded in stable, persistent, and independent givens of the analysis. These rules are in some sense "policed" by the stability of the environment. A good example of this type of situation is provided by prisoner's-dilemma games describing the overgrazing of a commons or the depletion of a fish species. Insofar as the "payoff" is well defined and not socially defined (i.e., fish caught or animal fed), and the players are fairly homogeneous, Nash equilibria can explain certain regularities in behavior. We could refer to these situations as "natural" rules.

The rules in the second tier are based upon the recognition that human rationality cannot be an algorithm, but must constantly be flexible and prepared for change. These rules are social, consciously constructed, and consciously policed. Into this category would fall property rights, money, religion, the family, and much else that comprises social order. The rules of this class cannot be explained as the outcome of underlying natural forces, because their enforcement mechanisms are not "natural": they possess neither persistence nor independence from the phenomena. We could refer to those situations as *bootstrap* rules.

The third tier of rules derives from the recognition that the first two classes of rules must interact over time. For example, the overgrazing game will be influenced by the institution of money, and any natural regularity of behavior may be destabilized or redefined by the penetration of market relationships: here, the "payoff" itself becomes partly socially defined. The exercise of human rationality itself transforms the environment. The recognition that there may be temporal regularities to the relative dominance or importance of natural rules versus bootstrap rules leads to the metarationality of evolutionary regularities. Unlike the first two classes of rules, evolutionary regularities by their nature cannot be teleological: they reflect interactions of natural rules and bootstrap rules beyond the imagination of any player.

It should be clear from previous comments that most neoclassical economists would insist that a scientific economics would only recognize explanations that linked any given social phenomenon to its natural rules (Mirowski, 1981). Explanation in this framework is satisfied to take as given tastes, technologies, and endowments, and to identify equilibrium with the extremum of some objective function. Why can't all social processes be reduced to their natural rules? To reiterate, this program leads to a logical contradiction. All natural rules must be subject to human interpretation. Natural constraints do not inexorably compel us to do anything, because human reason intervenes. This freedom is what provides us with all the multiform variation that comprises the history of the human race. To put it in Wittgensteinian terms: A rule does not certify its own correct application. To pretend that it does so is to appeal to other rules, and can only lead in a circle. Whether a reason or an activity conforms to a rule in a particular case is a problem in reasoning and interpretation, having to do with judgments about when situations are "the same". We may feel compelled to follow a rule, but the rule itself cannot compel us.

There are also those who believe that the world is only comprised of bootstrap rules. Let us call this opinion *conventionalism*. Why cannot all social phenomena be reduced to bootstrap rules? This position also meets an insuperable logical difficulty: knowledge of this theory of social phenomena tends to undermine its efficacy. To argue that all social regularities are consciously instituted is to argue that the only prerequisite for change is will; a society based upon this premise cannot ultimately enforce or maintain the stability required to define rules. In other words, just as the natural world is intrinsically incapable of defining the totality of social life, so too is the belief that might makes right. Even if the world of language, markets, and culture were ultimately organized by bootstrap rules, these rules would themselves be asserted by some actors to be grounded in natural rules, in order to provide stability and diffuse responsibility.

What then, is the function of the evolutionary regularities? These must be present because bootstrap rules influence natural rules, and vice versa. They are the locus of the understanding of change. The determination that a natural situation is producing regularities in behavior is itself a function of society's conception of science; and, as twentieth-century philosophers of science have come to argue, science consists largely of bootstrap rules. As our understanding of what is natural evolves, it cannot help but change the formal relations of bootstrap rules to natural rules in social life. These changes are not purely erratic: a good example of this is provided by Wesley Clair Mitchell in his "Role of Money in Economic History." He argues that money cannot be cogently explained by the prosaic notion that it made life naturally easier for traders. "When money is introduced into the dealing of men, it enhances their freedom. For example, personal service is commuted into money payment.... Adam Smith's obvious and simple system of natural liberty seems obvious and natural only to the denizens of a money economy" (Mitchell, 1953, p. 200). More significantly, Mitchell proposes that the penetration of the money economy into social life altered the very configurations of rationality, to the extent of encouraging particular conceptions of abstraction, quantification, and thus ultimately, the ontology of modern Western science. Here we have socially constructed rules, slowly transforming the understanding of natural constraints through the rational interpretative structure, finally changing the natural rules themselves.

What has all this to do with game theory and economic theory? It clearly and concisely provides a framework within which to evaluate the claims that there is a new mathematical institutional economics in the offing. Neoclassical economists will only sanction explanation in terms of natural rules. This is a reflection of their perennial search for a natural order, an invisible hand, and so forth. Since bootstrap rules and evolutionary regularities cannot be reduced to natural rules, their project is doomed to failure. One need only compare Schotter's "explanation" of the rise of money as a game theoretic solution to a naturally given problem of transactions costs to Mitchell's broad interpretation of the influence of money on economic life to see this failure.

There are other economists who believe that conscious and deliberate planning will solve all economic ills; they are partisans of the view that the world is nothing but a collection of bootstrap rules. Since neither natural rules nor evolutionary regularities can be reduced to bootstrap rules, this research project is also doomed to undermine itself.

Game theoretic explanations of human institutions fall into one of these two categories. Contrary to Schotter, all phenomenal rules cannot be reduced to their underlying natural rules. Contrary to Shubik, the postulation of rules as boostrap or ad hoc leaves explanations without any firm foundations. A theory of institutions must operate simultaneously on all three levels. The mathematical formalism of game theory is best suited for the discussion of natural rules. It can be used to *describe* bootstrap rules. But it also reveals that notions of rationality and equilibrium are distorted beyond recognition in those models, to the point that neither the existence nor efficacy of those rules can be said to be illuminated by the analysis. Since evolutionary rules are not teleological, they are not suited to game theoretic structures.

In conclusion, game theory is not a substitute for a theory of institutions. It can only be one component of such a theory, a theory committed to the explanation of change as well as of complacency.

Notes

[1] This history of the critique of the concept of the maximization provides a clear example of the peripatetic migration between one defense and the other. For recent examples of the former, the 'straw man' defense, see Boland (1981); for the latter, the insinuation of sour grapes, see Wong (1978).

[2] The quote is from Veblen's "Why is Economics Not an Evolutionary Science?" reprinted in Veblen (1919). The best introduction and summary of the thought of the institutionalists is still chapters 14 and 15 of Mitchell (1950).

[3] Evidence for this statement is provided in Mirowski (1984b), and in chapter 6 of this volume.

[4] Sometimes there is postulated a continuum of traders, i.e., a nonatomic agglomeration, who therefore cannot be subject to a discrete list. This assumption is often used to "prove" that Nash equilibria converge to Walrasian competitive equilibria.

INSTITUTIONS AS SOLUTION CONCEPTS   261

[5] This absence of discussion may provide a counterexample to the common opinion that mathematical models, by their very nature, make assumptions more clear and transparent than common speech. As such it illustrates a thesis developed in this volume, chapter six.

[6] "There is a not completely innocent modelling assumption that any finite game in extensive form can be reduced to a game in strategic form, which is equivalent to the original description of the game from the viewpoint of the application of solution theory" (Shubik, 1981, p. 157).

[7] We say "stable" and not "constant," because of the tradition of probabilistic concepts of utility dating back to the original work of von Neumann & Morgenstern (1964).

[8] Perhaps this explains Schotter's final chapter (1981) with its discussion of sociobiology. One way to short-circuit the infinite regress is to locate "fundamental" rules in our genes.

[9] At least until the twentieth century, when physics left the economists behind.

References

Aumann, R. 1964. Markets With a Continuum of Traders. *Econometrica* 32:39–50.

Aumann, R. 1981. Survey of Repeated Games. In *Essays in Game Theory and Mathematical Economics in Honor of Oskar Morgenstern*. Mannheim: B.I.

Boland, Lawrence. 1981. On the Futility of Criticizing the Neoclassical Maximizing Hypothesis. *American Economic Review* 71:1031–1036.

Commons, John R. 1934. *Institutional Economics*. New York: MacMillan.

van Damme, E. E. 1981. History-Dependent Equilibrium Points in Dynamic Games. In O. Moeschlin and D. Pallaschke (eds.), *Game Theory & Mathematical Economics*. Amsterdam: North Holland.

Debreu, G., and Scarf, H. 1963. A Limit Theorem of the Core of the Economy. *International Economic Review* 4:234–246.

Dubey, Pradeep, and Shubik, Martin. 1979. Bankruptcy and Optimality in a Closed Trading Mass Economy Modelled as a Noncooperative Game. *Journal of Mathematical Economics* 6:115–134.

Dubey, Pradeep, and Shubik, Martin. 1980. A Strategic Market Game with Price and Quantity Strategies. *Zeitschrift Für Nationalökonomie* 40:25–34.

Field, Alex. 1979. On the Explanation of Rules Using Rational Choice Models. *Journal of Economic Issues* 13:49–72.

Field, Alexander. 1984. Microeconomics, Norms and Rationality. *Economic Development and Cultural Change* 32:683–711.

Friedman, James. 1977. *Oligopoly and the Theory of Games*. New York: Elsevier-North Holland.

Halevy, Elie. 1972. *The Growth of Philosophical Radicalism*. London: Faber.

Harcourt, Geoffrey. 1982. *The Social Science Imperialists*. Boston: Routledge Kegan Paul.

Harsanyi, John. 1982. Noncooperative Bargaining Models. In M. Deistler, E. Furst, and G. Schwödiauer (eds.), *Games, Economic Dynamics and Time Series Analysis*. Wein: Physica-Verlag.

Heims, Steve. 1980. *John von Neumann and Norbert Wiener*. Cambridge, MIT Press.

Johansen, Leif. 1982. On the Status of the Nash Type of Noncooperative Equilibrium in Economic Theory. *Scandinavian Journal of Economics* 34:421–441.

Johansen, Leif. 1983. Mechanistic and Organistic analogies in Economics: The Place of Game Theory. *Kyklos* 36:304–307.

Krantz, D., Luce, R., Suppes, P., and Tversky, A. 1971. *Foundations of Measurement.* New York: Academic Press.

Levinson, Arnold. 1978. Wittgenstein and Logical Laws. In K. T. Fann, ed. *Ludwig Wittgenstein: The Man and His Philosophy.* New York: Humanities.

Mirowski, Philip. 1981. Is There a Mathematical Neoinstitutional Economics? *Journal of Economic Issues* 15:593–613.

Mirowski, Philip. 1984a. The Role of Conservation Principles in 20th Century Economic Theory. *Philosophy of the Social Sciences* 14:461–473.

Mirowski, Philip. 1984b. Physics and the Marginalist Revolution. *Cambridge Journal of Economics* 8:361–379.

Mitchell, Wesley Clair. 1950. *The Backward Art of Spending Money.* New York: Kelley.

Mitchell, Wesley Clair. 1953. The Role of Money in Economic History. In F. Lane and J. Riemersma (eds), *Enterprise and Secular Change.* Homewood, IL.: Irwin.

Morgenstern, O., and Schwödiauer, G. 1976. Competition and Collusion in Bilateral Markets. *Zeitscrift Für Nationalökonomie* 36:217–245.

Mosley, Nicholas. 1983. *The Rules of the Game.* London: Fontana.

von Neumann, J., and Morgenstern, O. 1964. *The Theory of Games and Economic Behavior.* 3rd edition. New York: Wiley.

Rosenberg, Alexander. 1979. Can Economic Theory Explain Everything? *Philosophy of the Social Sciences* 9:509–529.

Samuelson, Paul. 1965. *Foundations of Economic Analysis.* New York: Atheneum

Schotter, Andrew. 1981. *The Economic Theory of Social Institutions.* Cambridge: Cambridge University Press.

Schotter, Andrew. 1983. Why Take a Game Theoretical Approach to Economics? *Economie Appliquée* 36:673–695.

Schotter, A., and Schwödiauer, G. 1980. Economics and the Theory of Games: a Survey. *Journal of Economic Literature* 18:479–527.

Shubik, Martin. 1972. Commodity Money, Oligopoly, Credit and Bankruptcy in a General Equilibrium Model. *Western Economic Journal* 11:24–38.

Shubik, Martin. 1974. Money, Trust and Equilibrium Points in Games in Extensive Forms. *Zeitscrift Für Nationalökonomie* 34:365–385.

Shubik, Martin. 1975a. The General Equilibrium Model is Incomplete and Not Adequate for the Reconciliation of Macro and Micro Theory. *Kyklos* 28:545–573.

Shubik, Martin. 1975b. Mathematical Models for a Theory of Money and Financial Institutions. In R. Day and T. Groves (eds.), *Adaptive Economic Models.* New York: Academic Press.

Shubik, Martin. 1976. A General Theory of Money and Financial Institutions. *Economie Appliquée* 29:319.

Shubik, Martin. 1981. Perfect or Robust Noncooperative Equilibrium: A Search for

INSTITUTIONS AS SOLUTION CONCEPTS 263

the Philosopher's Stone? In *Essays in Game Theory and Economics in Honor of Oskar Morgenstern*. Mannheim: B.I.

Shubik, Martin. 1982. *Game Theory in the Social Sciences*. Cambridge: MIT Press.

Shubik, Martin, and Wilson, Charles. 1977. Optimal Bankruptcy Rule in a Trading Economy Using First Money. *Zeitschrift Für Nationalökonomie* 37:337–354.

Simon H. 1982. *Models of Bounded Rationality*. Cambridge: MIT Press.

Veblen, Thorstein. 1919. *The Place of Science in Modern Civilization*. New York: Huebsch.

Wittgenstein, Ludwig. 1978. *Remarks on the Foundations of Mathematics*, rev. ed. Cambridge: MIT Press.

Wong, Stanley. 1978. *The Foundations of Paul Samuelson's Preference Theory*. Boston: Routledge Kegan Paul.

Wright, Crispin. 1980. *Wittgenstein on the Foundations of Mathematics*. London: Duckworth.

[7]

Excerpt from Giovanni Dosi, Christopher Freeman, Richard Nelson, Gerald Silverberg and Luc Soete (eds), *Technical Change and Economic Theory*, 124–47.

6 Coordination and order in economic change and the interpretative power of economic theory

Fabrizio Coricelli

IRS, Milan, and University of Pennsylvania, Philadelphia

Giovanni Dosi

Faculty of Statistics, University of Rome, Rome and SPRU, University of Sussex, Brighton

'I . . . side with Heraclitus in arguing that you could not step twice into the same river, for new waters are ever flowing on to you'. It is the appearance of stability that is illusory; just look a little closer and wait a little longer. We Herclitus types find it difficult to understand what the Ecclesiastes types—who think that 'there is no new thing under the sun'—are talking about, what with the universe expanding, the continents drifting, the arms race racing and the kids growing up. The observed predictive performance of economic models also seems to us to be considerably more consonant with the Heraclitus view than with the alternative [Winter, 1986 p. 428]

Introduction

This chapter discusses the ability of economic theory to interpret dynamic economies, and in particular those undergoing technical change.

In chapter 2 as well as in the contributions to Part V of this book, arguments are presented for an evolutionary approach to economic analysis in which the process of coordination among agents is intertwined with the processes generating change of various sorts. Here we shall address the question of whether such an analysis of dynamic economies can also be undertaken by separating—on theoretical grounds—the *coordination problem* of an economy, typically represented as a stationary system, on the one hand, from the interpretation of *dynamic factors* on the other. That is, can we analyse the problems of static allocation on the safe assumption that they are dynamics-independent? Can we reduce problems of change to exogenously determined changes in the parameters of the general equilibrium model?

A good part of the economic discipline, especially in the post-war period, has essentially explored three theoretical perspectives. First, the General Equilibrium tradition focused upon the *theoretical possibility* of coordination between agents who are uniform in terms of decision procedures (maximization, etc.), but diverse with respect to initial endowments and tastes. The exploration of the existence, determinacy and stability of equilibria under more or less restrictive assumptions (e.g. completeness of contingency markets and information, convexity of production possibility sets, etc.) has been in many respects a fascinating attempt to assess the power of the 'Invisible Hand' in a highly stylized, stationary and perfectly competitive environment defined in terms of some 'fundamentals' of the economy (given technology, given individual preferences and a universal maximizing decision procedure for individual agents).[1]

The other two major analytical perspectives are more directly macro-economic-based. One of these approaches—recently rather out of fashion—focuses upon 'stylized' aggregate regularities (e.g. the patterns of investment, consumption, etc.) and 'explains' them on the grounds of both the 'fundamentals' of the economy and *ad hoc* (in principle, empirically derived) assumptions about context-specific behaviour, adjustment lags, etc. So-called 'neo-Keynesians' basically share this methodology.

Finally, some current macroeconomic analysis (of which possibly the most fashionable is the so-called 'new classical macroeconomics') attempts to 'carry over' to macroeconomics an *implicit* Walrasian equilibrium microfoundation and somehow 'explain' macro variables solely on the basis of a maximizing principle of behaviour and the fundamentals of the economy.

The principle of rationality and the role of the market as coordination mechanism have been extended to the study of dynamic economies. This programme has mainly constructed models of equilibrium dynamics, i.e. models in which equilibrium holds at each point in time, while their (supposedly General Equilibrium) microfoundations are, so to speak, squeezed into single ('representative') agent formalizations.

Of course, theories do, and *must*, abstract and simplify. Indeed, one of the criteria on which the analytical power of various theories can be assessed is the simplicity and degree of generality of their abstractions. However, one must always ask questions such as: how robust are these abstractions? What are the domains of interpretative applicability of the models? For our purposes, the assessment of the analytical results and perspectives of the neo-classical research programme in relation to the understanding of coordination and change in market economies involves two major questions, namely (a) can a model based only on the 'fundamentals' (given technologies and tastes) and on a rationality principle for individual choice reveal to us some fundamental properties of economic processes which hold irrespective of the (history-bound) specification of, for example, particular behavioural rules, institutions, adjustment processes, etc.?; (b) can one incrementally build upon the basic static model and apply it to the analysis of environments characterized by technical change and, more generally, non-stationarity? For an affirmative answer to these questions and in particular to the latter, one should require that, at least under the highly simplified conditions generally assumed by these models, the theory should be able to (i) generate and explain 'order' at the macro level; (ii) handle micro diversity (otherwise one of the major distinctions between micro and macro would disappear); (iii) define an adjustment process leading to the equilibria studied by the models.

We shall argue that, in fact, the project of building dynamic models with economic content and descriptive power by relying solely on the basic principles of rationality and perfect competition through the market process has generally failed. In order to give economic content to equilibrium 'macro' models, we shall argue, one has to sacrifice, in fact, the decentralization of the decision-making processes of economic actors, which is obviously a fundamental premise of the theory.

Conversely, if one sticks to a 'decentralized' representation of diverse actors, it seems hardly possible to retain any robust analytical result on economic coordination whenever one introduces any sort of dynamics, or even relaxes the most demanding assumptions about the perfection of the markets and information sets (needless to say, any innovative environment is *necessarily* characterized by, for example, asymmetric information, non-perfectly competitive markets, etc.). Thus one goes back to a somewhat Schumpeterian dilemma, namely, can one find a sort of division of labour between General Equilibrium theory—meant to explain static allocative processes—and evolutionary theory—meant to deal with dynamic processes? Such a complementarity is implicit in the 'Classical Defence' of equilibrium models and of 'as if' assumptions on literally maximizing agents (see Friedman, 1953, and, for a critical discussion, Winter, 1986). This conjecture has been recently revived by Lucas (1986). According to this view the realm of economic theory (identified with General Equilibrium analysis) is that of steady states or, in any case, regular repetitive environments; adaptive processes, describing dynamic situations, are instead complex, irregular, disturbed by a vast number of factors specific to individual actors, industries, countries. Economic theory—it is claimed—cannot be concerned with these 'noisy' problems. It remains crucial, however, to show that from such a noise the regular stationary equilibria reflecting the rationality of behaviour and expectations of economic actors are selected.

However, we will show, first, that *general equilibrium models with stationary preferences and technologies and with rational expectations do not in general yield simple and regular outcomes. Second, we will show that in general, rational expectations equilibria are not the stationary state of dynamic processes arising from adaptive rules*.

In the sections that follow we shall discuss the attempt to 'explain' the levels and changes of macro variables on the basis of a direct transposition of micro behaviours (maximization) and the fundamentals of the economy We shall then explore the coordination power of the markets (or lack of it) implicit in neo-classical macro models, and the impossibility of deriving, in general, robust results on macro-order simply on the grounds of the rationality principle, endowments and given tastes. On the contrary, complex dynamics and unpredictability of equilibria may well emerge even in simple competitive models. Can neo-classical macro models (of the rational expectation kind) be considered the results of adaptive processes? The section 'Rational expectations equilibria and adaptive processes' will discuss why this is not generally the case. Thus one must investigate the characteristics of individual behaviours and of economic environments which account for a relative order in *both coordination and change*. We shall suggest that some of these characteristics can be found precisely amongst those factors underlying the main difficulties of neo-classical theory in dealing with economic dynamics. Indeed, several features that are sources of theoretical problems for the neo-classical view are instead the main ingredients of a positive theory: diversity, heterogeneity of agents, non-linearities, continuous change, and hence non-stationarities, the role of learning, beliefs, the importance of 'history' and of 'contexts' and, situation-specific behaviours, are all fundamental features of the evolutionary, self-organization approach to economic dynamics.

Aggregation, 'representative agents' and competitive mechanisms

According to a taxonomy proposed by Malinvaud (1981), any attempt to place macroeconomic analysis on a solid microeconomic footing should go through the following three phases: (i) the microeconomic study of agents' decisions and, in addition, the interaction among agents and thus the constraint on individual behaviour of other agents; (ii) the aggregation of behaviours, i.e. the study of the macroeconomic implications of micro-behaviours and the deduction from the micro choices of the laws of macro-economic behaviour; (iii) the comparison of the findings of the theory with empirical data.

It seems to us that the current fashion in macroeconomic theory relies upon the mere direct transposition to the macroeconomic level of the results obtained in the microeconomic analysis of the behaviour of a single agent ('the representative agent'). The phase of 'aggregation' is completely neglected and the study of micro interactions is carried out in a very peculiar way: in fact, as we shall see, very little is left of 'inter-actions'. This approach implies, in terms of empirical testing, that the observation of empirical macro data is assumed to be directly consistent with microbehaviours; in econometric language, macroparameters are taken to be nothing but the reproduction on a larger scale of micro-parameters.[2]

Of course, it is generally acknowledged that the mere knowledge of individual characteristics is of little help in predicting the outcome at the level of the whole system. The interaction among agents introduces a qualitative difference between micro and macro behaviours. In that version of neo-classical macroeconomics which calls itself 'new classical macroeconomics', the solution to this problem has to be found in model-ling this interaction in terms of competitive equilibria. According to Lucas, it is the hypothesis of competitive equilibrium which permits group behaviour to be predicted from knowledge of individual preferences and technology without the addition of any free parameters . . . It is possible, we know, to mimic aggregate outcome of this interaction fairly well in a competitive equilibrium way, in which wages and manhours [Lucas is indeed referring to a competitive equilibrium theory of employment] are generated by the interaction of 'representative' households and firms. [Lucas, 1981, pp. 289–90]

Through a competitive equilibrium model, it is argued, the micro–macro link will be transparent, the aggregate outcome being predicted with precision from the knowledge of individual preferences and technology. As a consequence, there is no need to add any *free parameters* (the famous 'ad hockeries') to the structure of the model based on optimizing behaviour of fully rational agents. This type of model is claimed to be capable of pinning down macroeconomic equilibria which are consistent with both empirical observations and results of Walrasian general equilibrium theory—in particular with welfare theorems.[3]

The central message of such a research programme is that under *laissez faire* a competitive economy, not disturbed by destabilizing policies and/or exogenous shocks, will settle on stationary macro equilibria, resembling static Walrasian equilibria. In this way, not only the normative implications of general equilibrium models would carry over to macroeconomic theory, but the Walrasian approach would acquire an extraordinary descriptive power. What is the theoretical validity of this claim?

First, let us consider the theoretical implications of developing macro-economic models—as is currently done—on the basis of optimizing behaviours of representative agents. Most of the recent developments in macroeconomics rely upon the simple assumption that economic actors are identical. This assumption is also accompanied by the identification of a macro model with a system with only one good. For an approach which claims to have put macroeconomics on steady microeconomic foundations, these are certainly heroic assumptions. By reducing the set of individuals to a 'representative agent' it is implied that aggregate behaviours are just a transposition of micro behaviours: qualitatively they do not differ. In this way the problem of aggregation of individual behaviours is hidden under the rug. It is a sort of paradox that a 'microfounded' approach to micro-economics, instead of shedding light on the complex nature of the link between individual behaviours and aggregate outcomes, has created so-called macro models as oversimplifications of the general equilibrium system (in fact, a general equilibrium model with only one agent and one good!). Moreover the assumption of 'representative agents' appears to lead to theoretical problems[4].

The difficulties arising in the aggregation of individual behaviours have been recognized in the economic literature since the last century, in the partial equilibrium approach to both the theory of consumption and the theory of production.[5]

In a general equilibrium setting the work initiated by Sonnenschein and developed by Debreu and others points out the important result that

> strong restrictions are needed in order to justify the hypothesis that a market demand function has the characteristics of a single-consumer demand function. Only in special cases can an economy be expected to act as an 'idealized consumer'. The utility tells us nothing about market demand unless it is augmented by additional requirements. [Shafer and Sonnenschein, 1982, p. 672][6]

As a consequence we cannot expect aggregate relations, which we have called macro relations (i.e. relations between aggregate variables), to reproduce on a larger scale micro relations. The link between micro and macro behaviour does not entail a simple enlargement of scale but a qualitative change of perspective. In the general competitive equilibrium framework the descriptive and predictive power of the results on individual behaviour for the aggregate outcome is extremely vague. In the textbook by Varian (1984), the Sonnenschein–Debreu theorem is interpreted as an indication that since the utility maximization hypothesis places no restrictions on aggregate demand behaviour and hence any continuous function satisfying Walras's law can be an excess demand function for some economy, practically *any* dynamical system on the price sphere can arise from a Walrasian general equilibrium model of economic behaviour.[7]

The analysis can be pushed further, and it can be shown that in general the price dynamics involved in the tatonnement story can give rise to a whole family of extremely complex and erratic dynamics (Saari, 1983). Even leaving aside the question of dynamics out of equilibria, it can be easily shown that asymmetries among individuals modify the dynamical representation of equilibria over time.[8]

Let us summarize the implications of the discussion so far. In many respects, the General Equilibrium tradition has undertaken the fascinating task of exploring the interdependencies of a decentralized economy through the axiomatization of 'selfish' individual motives and an extremely parsimonious use of ancillary hypotheses (on adjustment processes, institutions, etc.). Under the assumptions of the theory (which, one must admit, are quite restrictive, on information, competition, etc.), one has demonstrated the *possibility* (i.e. the logical consistency) *of coordination* via the 'Invisible Hand' of the market. This is, in the last resort, the meaning of the existence theorems. However, without further (and somewhat *ad hoc* or observation-based) restrictions, the results are not determinate enough to be, so to speak, 'carried over' to a synthetic macro representation which would hold irrespectively of any specific representation of the underlying characteristics of actual agents (in terms of tastes, distribution of endowments, etc.). These properties, together with the quite heavy restrictions that must be introduced in order to obtain stability and determinacy (local uniqueness) of equilibria in an explicit general equilibrium model highlight, in our view, the boundaries of the set of empirical economic phenomena which the neo-classical research programme, at least in its present form, can interpret. Certainly, the set does not include non-stationary environments, but neither does it include relatively orderly sequences of macro states. At the very least, the latter cannot be explained via a 'reduced form' neo-classical macro model without losing the 'interdependencies' of the market, the autonomy of the agents (in terms of beliefs and expectations) and/or the 'parsimoniousness' in auxiliary assumptions (and thus the generality of the models). We shall now discuss these latter issues.

Decentralization and the coordination power of the market mechanism

It may be enlightening to see how the assumption of homogeneity among individuals which underlies the concept of 'representative agents', extends to the characterization of the uniformity of expectations and beliefs.

We shall consider here 'rational expectations' models. In fact, if expectations are non-rational, aggregation problems become even more serious (e.g. for the purposes of a synthetic representative-agent stylization of macro phenomena, identical agents with different rules of expectation formation are different agents: aggregation necessarily involves situation-specific knowledge of the rules, their distribution among agents, etc.). Even in the 'rational' case, as Frydman and Phelps (1983) put it, 'an instantaneous transition to the new rational expectations equilibrium requires a perceived and actual unanimity of beliefs. Such consensus of perceptions cannot generally be achieved by individual agents acting alone in decentralized markets'. To circumvent the problem of forming expectations of other agents' expectations, the Rational Expectations school assumes that every agent forms his expectations on the basis of the equilibrium model and everyone expects that the other agents form their expectations in the same way. This apparently innocuous assumption is in fact very 'totalitarian' and also in marked contrast with the leitmotiv of the neo-classical theory of individual behaviour, whereby 'individual behaviour is not based on the collective consistency of plans, but on the assumption of individual rationality' (Frydman and Phelps, 1983). Assuming an *ex ante* consistency of plans either contradicts the fundamental task of neo-classical microeconomics aimed at demonstrating how market processes, *ex post*, make consistent the independent plans of agents based only on selfish considerations, or makes the theory plainly tautological in the sense that, in order to demonstrate the existence of coordination amongst agents, it assumes it *ex hypothesi*.

It is not far from the truth to say that the current neo-classical approach to the microfoundation of macroeconomics is based on a representation of the economy as a *centralized* system. The assumption of a 'representative agent' together with the rational expectations hypothesis (with homogeneity of expectations) is tantamount to an *ex ante* collective consistency of behaviours in which the market plays no role. In fact, most of the results of the 'new macroeconomics' pointing to the power of *laissez faire* in achieving desirable macroeconomic equilibria derive from an *a priori* exclusion of the analysis of the relationship—and potential conflict—between individual behaviour and aggregate outcomes in a decentralized economy.

Indeterminacy of equilibria: beliefs and behaviour-dependent equilibria

In order to have any 'positive' meaning, that is, in order to have some interpretative power, equilibria have to be at least *locally* unique. If an equilibrium is not locally unique it follows that there are several equilibria arbitrarily close to it. If this is the case it is impossible to carry out any exercise in comparative statics, and thus the dynamic analysis becomes meaningless (loosely speaking, one has a macro model that simply says that 'anything can happen'). For these reasons, a situation characterized by the absence of local uniqueness is usually defined as indeterminacy of equilibria.

The dynamic extensions of equilibrium models to macroeconomic analysis generally suffer from this indeterminacy.[9] As a consequence, preferences, endowments and technology alone may not suffice to determine the allocation of resources in a dynamic economy, even when perfectly competitive markets exist for all goods. In this context the possibility arises of a critical role for the *beliefs* of the agents as well as for an active government policy. Phenomena such as 'sunspot' equilibria or bubbles may be interpreted as a way of selecting particular equilibria from among the large number of competitive equilibria.[10] These equilibria are characterized by the fact that the allocation of resources depends on beliefs, i.e. on factors which are unrelated to the fundamentals of the economy, and that these beliefs will be confirmed by the equilibrium of the system; in other words, expectations of the agents are self-fulfilling. Note that this result is consistent with the assumption of 'rational expectations' and, unlike 'bubbles', it is also compatible with stability of the equilibria. The implication is that beliefs of agents not only are relevant in determining the equilibrium allocations, but also that—when they are stationary—there are no forces causing the system to move necessarily to equilibria reflecting only the fundamentals (as it is the case for 'bubbles' which, by their nature, will eventually explode). It should also be noted that the multiplicity of equilibria in the above sense in a decentralized economy implies the need for every single agent to form expectations not only about the realizations of economic variables, but also about the expectations of other agents. A decentralized economy is therefore caught in the vicious circle of an 'infinite regress' of forecasts about how others forecast the forecast of their forecast, etc., reminding us of the famous 'beauty contest' discussed by Keynes. Consequently, the power of the competitive economy to coordinate agents' behaviour, as described by these neo-classical macro models, in the absence of external intervention, appears to be very weak.

Beliefs matter in determining aggregate outcomes. Moreover, individual forecasting mistakes—or deviations from optimal 'rational' behaviour—matter, regardless of how small they are. Akerlof and Yellen (1985) show that individual behaviours which are only marginally non-maximizing induce a significant effect on macroeconomic outcomes. Small departures from perfectly 'rational' maximizing behaviour which result in only second-order losses to the individual, will nevertheless have first-order effects on real variables.

Complex dynamics and unpredictability in simple competitive models

Of course, the belief-dependency and behaviour-dependency of equilibria challenge the extreme (or 'pure') neo-classical research programme to provide an account of macroeconomic order without invoking empirically based assumptions about behaviour. They do not challenge, *per se*, the theoretical conjecture that neo-classical macroequilibria (no matter how belief-ridden) can provide a justification for the 'Invisible Hand' which pulls together and provides coherence to a dynamic economy. However, the idea that under *laissez faire* a competitive economy, unaffected by exogenous shocks and destabilizing policies, will settle on stationary equilibria resembling the Walrasian equilibrium, is radically challenged by a growing body of literature.[11] Simple economies—simple in that utility and production functions are 'regular'[12] and the economy is populated by 'representative agents'—in which the environment (technology, preferences, endowments) is *stationary* and *deterministic* show in many, far from special, circumstances an extremely complex dynamic behaviour.[13] The complexity of the dynamics is solely the result of the workings of the competitive mechanism, and is not due to friction and disturbances. It has been shown that the motion of the system may present forms of highly irregular dynamic behaviour which is called deterministic *chaos*.[14]

There are several definitions and properties of chaos which cannot be discussed here. One aspect is, however, of greatest interest to us, namely the fact that chaotic systems are extremely sensitive to initial conditions.[15] As a consequence, the behaviour of the model in the future cannot be predicted from a knowledge of its 'fundamentals', nor can it be predicted from a knowledge of its history. The system is thus characterized by a serious problem of unpredictability.[16] Of course, the result is devastating for the assumption of rational expectations, since it implies that the predictive possibilities of agents are necessarily extremely weak and imperfect even if the environment itself is deterministic. Moreover, the fact that in deterministic and very simple models, with stationary preferences and technologies, the 'rational' (perfectly optimizing) behaviour of agents who also have the gift of perfect foresight leads to such complex and erratic dynamics of the economy is a strikingly negative result. This throws serious doubts on its ability to interpret empirical macrodynamics which inevitably reflect the non-stationarity of technology, tastes, etc.. Finally, note that in these models erratic behaviour is an *equilibrium* phenomenon and not the movement of the system out of equilibrium: equilibrium is actually assumed *ex hypothesi*, while attempts to show how agents 'learn' how to get there have generally failed. We shall now turn to this issue.

Rational expectations equilibria and adaptive processes

There have recently been attempts to overcome the difficulties discussed in the two previous sections by suggesting that rational expectations equilibria can be seen as a steady state of adaptive processes. These are ostensibly an attempt to build a bridge between the neo-classical approach and some kind of evolutionary theory (Lucas, 1986). (Note that in this instance 'evolution' only hints at 'adaptation', since there is no 'selection': the economic consequences of 'mistakes' are ruled out.)

However, it can be shown that, in general, rational expectations equilibria *cannot* be seen as stationary states of adaptive processes. To put it differently, dynamic paths determined by adaptive rules do not generally converge to rational expectations equilibria (see Fuchs, 1979). Obviously, examples of models in which adaptive rules and learning processes lead to a convergence to rational expectations steady states may be easily formulated (see also Bray and Kreps, 1987). This convergence, however, is linked to particular structures of the system. A simple example may help in clarifying the point.

Let us take a system in which the rational expectations steady state is not an attractor of the rational expectations dynamics. If rationality of expectations is assumed even outside stationary states, hence assuming instantaneous learning (which is equivalent to neglecting the 'gradualism' of learning processes), the system will not converge to the rational expectations steady state. In this situation, by assuming that expectations outside steady states are formed in an adaptive fashion, the instability property of the steady state can be repaired: the rational expectations steady state becomes stable in the adaptive expectations dynamics. This case is shown in Figure 6.1, which is derived from a slight modification of Lucas's example (Lucas, 1986). Every point on the A-curve is an equilibrium for a given instant t. Any sequence of points $\{q(t)\}$ with $t=0, 1 \ldots \infty$, on the same curve is a rational expectations (or perfect foresight) dynamic equilibrium. Consequently, there is a continuum of dynamic equilibria, each of them indexed to a different initial condition $q(0)$, which the model cannot endogenously determine. We are thus back to the indeterminacy problem

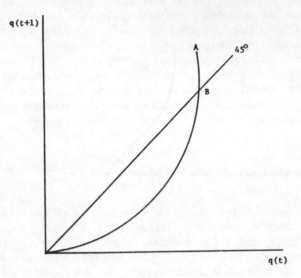

Figure 6.1

discussed earlier. Notice that there are two steady states, the origin and the point B. B is an unstable steady state, but it is the equilibrium point which reflects, so to speak, the 'predictions' of the theory. The locus of equilibrium points described by the curve A is obtained, for instance, from the dynamic solution of an overlapping generations model.[17]

The equilibrium dynamics of the system (see Note 17 for its derivation) is represented by the following equation: $q(t+1)=q(t)^2$. This is obtained by assuming perfect foresight, which allows us to substitute the actual realization to $Eq(t+1)$, that is, the expectation of $q(t+1)$. If we abandon this assumption in favour of an adaptive expectation function we obtain a different dynamic equation. For instance, if the expectation of $q(t+1)$ is based on a weighted average of current and past prices: $Eq(t+1) = q^a(t)$ $q^{1-a}(t-1)$, with $0 < a < 1$, the dynamic equation of the system becomes $q^a(t) \, q^{1-a}(t-1) = q^2(t)$, which is equivalent to $q^{(1-a)/(2-a)}(t-1) = q(t)$. By propagating this equation one period ahead we obtain $q(t+1) = q^{(1-a)/(2-a)}(t)$. This equation gives rise to a curve which is a sort of mirror image of the A-curve, since $(1-a)/(2-a) < 1$. The new dynamics is illustrated in Figure 6.2.

The steady states are obviously the same as before; their dynamic properties are, however, inverted; the steady state B is now locally stable. For every initial condition $q(0)$ in $(0,1]$ the system will converge to B. All the dynamic paths reflect the *adaptive* expectation rule and they all converge to the rational expectations equilibrium B. It should be noted that the relation between adaptive processes and rational expectations equilibria

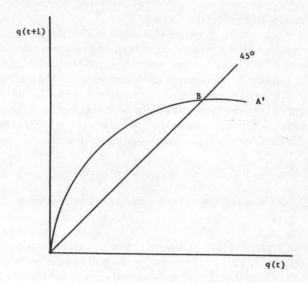

Figure 6.2

depends on the specific structure of the model considered. The same result could have been obtained by changing the functional form of the utility function. For example, with a utility function different from the one underlying the model just discussed we could have achieved a steady state stable in the rational expectations dynamics, but unstable in the adaptive rule dynamics (on these issues see also Grandmont and Laroque, 1986).[18] In such a case the rational expectations equilibrium cannot be seen as a steady state of adaptive processes. In fact the contrary would be true: in a sense, steady *adaptive* expectation dynamics would be the realization of a rational expectation process!

In general, the dynamic properties of the system are determined by the interplay between the structure of the system and the expectation function. However, the latter must be considered as a structural feature of the system: a change in the expectation function is in general indistinguishable from a change in utility or production functions. Borrowing a definition used by Azariadis (1983), a variation in the expectation function is 'observationally equivalent' to a change in preferences or technologies.

To summarize, once it is recognized that learning cannot be dismissed even in a rational expectations framework, it follows that one cannot dispose of a characterization of individual behaviour which is also 'situation-' or 'environment-specific'. However, inclusion of these factors into the theoretical picture makes the rational expectations assumption quite irrelevant: the rationality principle together with the nature of the fundamentals of the economy are *unable to determine the dynamic* processes of the economy, nor, in general, even the asymptotes of out-of-steady-states adaptive processes.

Finally, it is interesting to notice that problems of a somewhat similar nature also emerge in the stricter microeconomic domain whenever one goes beyond the analysis of the properties of equilibria and tries to model the (out-of-equilibrium) adjustment processes which could lead there. A recent, thorough and bold discussion can be found in Hahn (1987): 'whatever the form of learning that takes place on the grounds of the information that markets deliver, adjustment processes, *in general*, cannot be represented independently from history-specific and environment-specific conditions.'

Stabilizing, order-generating mechanisms and the power of macroeconomic theory

Most contemporary accounts of macroeconomics (and thus also of aggregate economic 'order') lead to a curious paradox. They generally start with an act of faith in both the 'Invisible Hand' and in the substantive capabilities of individual agents to process information and 'choose' correctly and freely—constrained only by their endowments—and end up with results that show a very crippled Hand, incapable of orderly coordination even in extremely simple environments. Moreover, note that these results are obtained despite an increasing attribution of rational competence and information processing power to individual agents.[19] Certainly, we believe, the attempt to 'explain' macroeconomics solely on the basis of some kind of 'hyper-rationality' of the agents (Winter, 1986) and the (pre-analytical) fundamentals of the economy (i.e. given technology and tastes) has failed.

There seem to be three ways out. First, one may, so to speak, 'stabilize the models' by working one's way 'backward', from the nature of the results one obtains to the restrictions one needs to impose in order to obtain the results one prefers. Just to give an example: the interpretation of the saddle-point properties of rational expectations macro models is quite instructive.[20] The structural model is characterized by a serious problem of instability: for every initial condition different from the one which puts the system on the unique convergent path, the system will diverge from the steady state. The heuristic strategy generally adopted to solve the problem is then to rule out, *a priori*, the instability of the solution, often justifying the choice on the ground that the world is not unstable. In the last instance one imposes stability to the solution (not to the model, which is highly unstable). One may forecast that, for example, the exploration of the conditions under which models generate chaos may lead towards a somewhat similar methodology: that is, use the results precisely to *assume away* these conditions. Frankly, it seems to us that this intellectual strategy is quite close to that scientific fallacy which epistemologists call '*explenans explenandum*': you assume your theory to be true and use your results to prove that it is true. Certainly, following this route no proper refutation is possible and economics becomes more akin to theology than empirical science.

The second strategy is to rediscover the *ad hocs*—auxiliary assumptions empirical character—plug them into a model which maintains a more or less strict neo-classical ascendancy (micro choices based on standard maximization, tatonnement assumptions about adjustments, etc.), and estimate econometrically using these auxiliary assumptions and 'free parameters' (e.g. expectation formation, etc.). This is, loosely speaking, that 'out-of-fashion' approach to macroeconomics mentioned in the introduction to this chapter, which the Rational Expectation school dismissed as theoretically unfounded.

However, there is a general point: in this kind of macroeconomic analysis, as well as in other domains, the results depend very little either on the 'core' behavioural model, based on individual rationality (in neo-classical sense) or on its implicit microeconomics, and very much on the auxiliary assumptions themselves (Simon, 1986), which, to repeat, are of an empirical nature, although generally introduced with the most casual empiricism.

The third approach is, broadly speaking, an 'evolutionary' and 'institutionalist' one. In a way, it starts with similar considerations, thus acknowledging that various institutions *structure* individual decision-making and collective coordination, but *explicitly* considers these institutions as an essential part of the interpretation of the (varying degrees of) order which one observes at the macro level.

An interesting example of the very simple micro 'rules' which order behaviour is shown by Heiner (1983 and Chapter 7 of this book). According to his view, the main source of unpredictability, and also of irregular, chaotic dynamics (see Heiner, 1986), is to be found in the assumption of perfect rational agents on which the conventional neo-classical approach rests. Introducing a form of 'imperfection' of agents, summarized by their 'competence gap' in correctly detecting environmental signals, he is able to show that previously unpredictable actions become regular and consistent with empirical observation of economic behaviour. Notably, Heiner's analysis applies to environments in which individuals *could* notionally be literal maximizers. As mentioned in Chapter 2 and analysed in Dosi and Egidi (1987), there is a wide class of (empirically very plausible) environments in which agents *cannot* adopt maximizing decision processes due to the environmental uncertainty associated with particular kinds of non-stationarity and/or the complexity of problem-solving tasks. Thus, rather general *rules* of behaviour inevitably emerge. Macro models, of course, should embody as their implicit or explicit microfoundations: (a) generalizations of these rules—whenever they are sufficiently stable—and (b) some theoretical propositions about how individual 'rules' aggregate and/or interact in order to produce the 'macro' (observed) patterns.

In a sense, macroeconomics neo-classical models attribute, at the same too much and too little freedom and power to individual agents: too much because their behaviour is totally unconstrained (apart, of course, from the endowed resources) in judging, computing, deciding; too little because, given their preferences, there is only one 'right' thing to do—all possible opportunities are exploited and it is hard to imagine how non-stationarity in technology, etc., can come about, except via some exogenous input.

Precisely the (observation-based) specification of 'structures', which encompass not only 'outside' institutions such as governments but also institutional aspects permeating individual behaviour, appears to be a promising way of avoiding the typical problems of unpredictability emerging from ahistorical, structure-free models. Social habits, routinized behaviour of firms, and contracts are a few examples of structures which delimit the context of individual behaviour and shape adjustment processes (see, for example, Okun, 1981; Kaldor, 1985).

In many respects, several 'positive' (that is interpretative rather than critical) chapters of this volume represent initial contributions to the understanding of these phenomena. Pushing it almost certainly beyond what the author intended, we place a central theoretical importance on the conjecture that 'There are collective norms . . . that are very important in social action. People just do not maximize on a selfish base every minute. In fact the system would not work if they did. *A consequence of that hypothesis would be the end of organized society as we know it*' (Arrow, 1987, p. 233, our italics). Certainly, continuing this quotation, we also agree that '. . . we do not have a good theory of how these norms come into existence' (ibid.). It remains a major interdisciplinary challenge—to economists as well as organization theorists, sociologists, experimental psychologists, etc. However, we *do* have the *beginnings* of a theory of the *process* through which certain behaviours are selected and become dominant: combinations of learning and competitive selection contribute to these processes, as discussed at greater length in other chapters. Clearly, evolutionary/self-organization models focus precisely on these processes.

History, institutions and order in economic change: can they be explained within the neo-classical microeconomic framework?

One rather commonly held belief is that any alternative to the neo-classical research programme would have to be based on highly specific empirical observations and thus would not be very generalisable beyond its original context. Can the neo-classical approach avoid degenerating in this direction? Our foregoing assessment of the recent developments of neo-classical macro theory shows that it cannot. It is indeed recognized that without an explicit consideration of the specificity of economic behaviour depending on contexts, environments, initial conditions, of learning processes and, we could add, of institutions other than markets, equilibrium models have no economic content or descriptive power. Unfortunately, the lagging belief in the history-free interpretative power of the models sometimes only helps in justifying the most 'cavalier' attitude toward the specification of the structure of the model (for convenience we assume convexity, or infinitely lived agents, or homogenous of degree-one production functions, or risk-neutrality,' etc.), which in turn crucially affects the results.

Certainly, both neo-classically inspired models and that of 'alternative' (e.g. evolutionary/self-organization) models frequently entail a multiplicity of equilibria which may or may not be stable (the former) and a multiplicity of 'evolutionary attractors' and asymptotic states (the latter). What then is the difference in the analytical power between the two, and why should one choose the latter, given that the former derive from a longer established formal tradition.

The first point we want to make is that, equilibrium models *cum* rational agents are simpler, but at the price of a very low economic plausibility of the assumptions.

After all, apples tend to fall down from trees whatever their initial condition, shape, colour, etc. Indeed, it would not be so bad if a theory would allow more than one stationary state for the apples, provided that it specified under what circumstances it went towards either one, but it would certainly be devastating to have a theory that allowed the apples to go in almost any direction.

The story is different for evolutionary/self-organization approaches. There one specifies *economically meaningful processes*, behaviours, initial conditions—in principle, based on observation-related generalizations—and studies the dynamic paths of the system. These paths may often diverge, and there may be a number of asymptotic states (see, for example, Arthur's chapter in this volume). Such a theory would, of course, be highly redundant and unnecessarily cumbersome in all those cases of globally stable equilibria such as falling apples, but it appears to be the more necessary the more 'history matters' and the more the specific features of micro agents matter, too.

The second point is that an evolutionary/self-organization approach can deal more straightforwardly with various sorts of non-stationarities, while 'equilibrium' approaches, as we argued earlier, appear to be ill-suited to the task.

If one believes that a sequential, evolutionary and institutional representation is required in order to account for the values and changes in macrovariables, it is difficult to escape the implication that *its microfoundations, too,* must be in some sense 'evolutionary' and 'institutional', allowing for variety, learning, mistakes, selection and imitation. This, is, of course, one of the main points argued in this book, with particular reference to technology and technical change.

Some conclusions

At a very general level, one tends to observe broad regularities in the values and/or changes of macro variables such as, for example, relatively regular patterns of growth of output per head and capital per head; roughly cyclical, although irregular, movements of employment rates possibly around longer-term trends; relatively steady patterns of income distribution, etc. (for an extensive list of both long-term and cyclical 'stylized facts' drawing on Kaldor and Mitchell, see Simon, 1986). These empirical regularities plausibly hint at some underlying process governing both economic coordination amongst agents (otherwise no regularity whatsoever could be expected to appear) and economic change (for, otherwise, no regularity, however rough, would be likely in the time derivatives). Moreover, there appear to be 'micro' regularities, some of which are investigated in this book, which are related to typical patterns of behaviour of the agents (such as firms, but also recognizable aggregates, such as whole industries or even countries), technologies, the ways they cope or even themselves generate change, their internal structure, and the ways they interact with the external environment. Micro-observations of behavioural rules such as those discussed at length in this book, have, on the one hand, a strong flavour of 'idiosyncrasy', specificity to contexts, periods and institutions. On the other hand, there are phenomena related to quite general features of technologies, competitive environments and organizations, discussed at length in other chapters, which seem to hold, in different forms, across industries and across countries. Overall, the micro picture conveys an impression of marked inter-agent diversity and environmental non-stationarity. Ideally, one would like to find a unified or at least consistent theoretical link between 'macro' and 'micro' phenomena.

In fact, at the 'micro' (or, if one prefers, 'partial equilibrium') level there are two distinct views which compete for the theoretical representation of environments characterized by innovative phenomena. The first view draws quite closely on the way neo-classical economics handles choice, allocation and equilibria in stationary environments.

The other view (call it the evolutionary/self-organization approach), discussed at greater detail in the chapters by Dosi–Orsenigo, Allen, Arthur and Silverberg, takes in many respects an opposite stance and focuses on behavioural diversity, out-of-equilibrium processes, various sorts of externalities, environmental selection and unintentional outcomes of decentralized decision-making. In the former view, order in change comes from the fact that (i) in one and every period the system hits some scarcity constraint; (ii) the environment is 'transparent' enough for the agents to make 'rational' choices; and (iii) there are some processes which, although they have never been specified, ensure the *ex ante* consistency of individual strategies. Conversely, in the evolutionary/self-organization view, relatively ordered patterns of change come from (i) technological and institutional factors which form the basis of expectation formation and orient decision under general conditions of uncertainty and complexity; (ii) selection processes which limit (but do not eliminate) the variety of 'visions' and behaviours of the economic agents; and (iii) the continual generation of new sources of increased efficiency and new product markets.

It is our impression that there is a growing overlap between the stylized phenomena addressed by traditional economic theory—what we called the equilibrium/maximization approach and the emerging evolutionary/ self-organization view. For example, within the former approach, various 'micro' and 'macro' models have demonstrated the relevance of beliefs in terms of attained equilibria; extensive form game models hint at the importance of institutions governing repeated behaviours; explicit accounts of market signalling even in simple set-ups highlight the role of initial conditions; theoretical accounts of externalities yield path-dependent models, etc.

This loose convergence in the underlying phenomena which the models address highlights both analytical complementaries and more radical differences in the frameworks underlying these models. Certainly, we agree with Hahn (1984, p. 140) that the study of asymptotic (equilibrium) states of evolutionary environments is also of theoretical importance. It helps in showing under what circumstances such states are actually the attractor of the evolutionary process. Here possibly rests one of the major complementaries between 'equilibrium' and explicitly 'evolutionary' analyses. However, as we have argued in this chapter, one of the few robust results that can be obtained by relaxing some of the most demanding assumptions of the 'unrestricted' equilibrium/maximization model is precisely the *lack of robustness* of its results (in terms of existence, determinacy, stability, and Pareto-optimality of its equilibria).

Conversely, the emerging evolutionary/self-organization approach takes as its 'building blocks' precisely what to neo-classical theory are 'extensions' or 'exceptions', such as externalities, increasing returns, non-stationarity, different and coexisting priors held by agents, complex strategic interactions without dominant strategies, and fundamental uncertainty. It might even be argued that the evolutionary/self-organization approach *predicates* its empirical adequacy on precisely these conditions.

Of course, one could assume that micro diversity, 'noise', mistakes, etc., cancel out in the aggregate by a sort of law of large numbers. Or one may assume that they simply represent empirical imperfections which nonetheless are in some sense 'ordered' by, or tend towards, a (theoretically) much simpler stationary state. Our position, however, is that detailed, observation-based analyses of behaviour, institutions and economic processes are *unavoidable* ingredients of both micro *and* macro theories of coordination and change, which—as the development of post-war economic theory shows—cannot be short-circuited by invoking a 'more general', history-free theory. This is also one of the *theoretical* justifications for many of the contributions to this book.

Notes

1. It might be worth recalling Arrow's view on the epistemological status of General Equilibrium analysis: 'I *do not* believe in the perfectly competitive view of the world, I think the general equilibrium theory is an imaginatively manipulative theory; one can get results out of it. It serves for many purposes as a good approximation for reasons that one does not fully understand. Therefore it is a useful tool for various micro problems. I think it is essential to remember the fact that in some industries there are increasing returns. But if you look at the economy, so to speak, in the gross these exceptions are very small. That is, all these exceptions are small on the scale of the economy. On the whole, what the existence problem has done was to force us to think a lot more rigorously about what it is. That may be the biggest benefit, rather than the existence theorem itself' (Arrow, 1987, pp. 197–8).
2. The following statement by Lucas describes very neatly the 'neo-classical' view of microfoundations: 'If we consider the question: How will a monkey that has not been fed for a day react to a banana tossed into its cage? I take it we have sufficient previously established knowledge about the behaviour of monkeys to make this prediction with some confidence. Now alter the question to: How will five monkeys that have not been fed for a day react to one banana thrown into their cage? This is an entirely different question' (Lucas, 1981, p. 289).
3. Obviously, the analysis of macroeconomic phenomena has forced a revision of the standard Arrow–Debreu model of general equilibrium; in order to deal with issues such as money, public debt, etc., the model has been modified and the main change has been that to make the general equilibrium model a truly dynamical model. An example of this extension, to which we will often refer in the sequel, is the overlapping generations model originally proposed by Samuelson (1958). This requires the issue of expectations to be tackled and the avenue taken has been that of assuming rational expectations, or perfect foresight in a deterministic world.
4. As far as welfare analysis is concerned, a very interesting work by Dow and Costa Werlang (1985) shows that welfare judgements based on the utility of the representative consumer are misleading. Indeed, they prove that it is possible 'that the representative consumer shows an increase in utility when, in fact, every consumer has been made worse off'.
5. See Antonelli (1886); Nataf (1953); Gorman (1953); Eisenberg (1961).
6. Recent contributions have tried to respond to the extremely negative implications of these results for neo-classical theory. It is interesting to note that the restrictions imposed either on the distribution of income (Hildenbrand) or on the shape of the distribution of preferences (Grandmont) 'cannot be deduced from the general hypothesis of individual rational behaviour alone' (Hildenbrand, 1986). They are indeed based on empirical facts. Obviously this avenue—although interesting for its empirical implications—is not a solution

to the weaknesses of the neo-classical view, based as it is upon a 'deductionist approach' which derives general results dependent only on primitive assumptions about the economy and not on *ad hoc* hypotheses justified in terms of empirical observations. Other attempts to solve the aggregation problem, such as the one by Grandmont (1985), are not applicable to general equilibrium models because they assume that income is independent of prices. Even after some qualifications indicated in recent works (see Balask, 1986), it is true that in a general equilibrium model, in order to satisfy the assumption of a 'representative agent', extremely strong restrictions have to be imposed.

7. Interestingly enough, if we consider a particular adjustment rule—of the form $p(i)=k(i)z(i)[p]$, with i denoting a particular good, p the price and z the excess demand—in order to obtain stability it is necessary to assume conditions ensuring that the aggregate excess demand function is a single consumer function; therefore, it is necessary to assume away differences among consumers or to impose strong restrictions on preferences and income distribution.

8. See Cass, Okono and Zilcha (1979).

9. See Woodford (1984); Kehoe and Levine (1983). This result is due to the fact that a dynamic economy such as the overlapping generations model can be seen as a general equilibrium system with an infinite number of agents and goods.

10. See Azariadis (1981); Cass and Shell (1983). It should be noted that sunspot equilibria arise even in economies in which equilibrium is unique (see Cass and Shell, ibid.).

11. That is, the utility function is continuous, differentiable, strictly quasi-concave, while the production function is continuous and homogeneous of degree one.

12. See, among others Grandmont (1985a); Benhabib and Nishimura (1985); Reichlin (1986).

13. We take just as an example the model by Pietra (1986). Deterministic chaos is obtained in an overlapping generations model with the following utility and production functions: utility function: $C(t+1) - (1/2) L^2(t)$, with $C(t+1)$ and $L(t)$ being respectively future consumption and current supply of labour. Production function (Leontief): $Q(t+1) = \min \{L, K/\alpha\}$, with $\alpha < 1$.

14. Although often used in the economic literature (Benhabib and Day, 1981, 1982; and Day, 1982, 1983), the definition derived from the Li and Yorke (1975) paper, suggesting that the existence of a cycle of period 3 is a signal of chaotic behaviour, may be misleading, since there can be a stable cycle which can make the 'chaotic' set irrelevant (of Lebesgue measure 0). One can thus define chaos as the case in which all cycles are unstable (cf. Grandmont, 1984).

15. For a definition of sensitive dependence on initial conditions, see Collet and Eckmann (1980).

16. The attractor—i.e. the set where trajectories starting from different initial conditions asymptotically end up—peculiar to deterministic chaos has been denoted 'strange attractor'. The dimension of this attractor is smaller than the dimension of the system and is usually noninteger, making the attractors fractals.

17. For example, an overlapping generation model in which people live for two 'periods', consume when they are old and work in their youth—young people maximize the utility function $U(C,l) = C(t+1) - \frac{1}{2}l^2$, where C stands for consumption and l for labour. Technology is given by the trivial constant

return to scale production function $y(t)=l(t)$. The old receive from a central bank a fixed quantity of money, M, at the beginning of each period. The young solve the following maximization problem: max $U(.)$ subject to $p(t+1)C(t+1)=p(t)y(t)$. The first-order condition of this maximization yields the supply of output of the young at time t: $y(t) = p(t)/p(t+1)$. The old obviously try to get rid of all their monetary holdings. Real demand is thus $M/p(t)$. Equilibrium requires equality of demand and supply, or $M/p(t)=p(t)/p(t+1)$. Defining $m(t)=M/p(t)$, we can rewrite the equilibrium condition in terms of real balances, m: $m(t+1)=m^{\zeta}t)$. Substituting q for m we obtain the equation in the text.

18. For instance, it has been shown that replacing rational expectations by an expectation function based on an explicit learning process does not generally stabilize the economy (Fuchs, 1979). As argued by Grandmont and Laroque (1986), 'one should be very cautious when interpreting the stability results one gets from dynamical rational expectation models in which times goes forward. Taking into account the agents learning behaviour on the transition path, as one should, may reverse the stability diagnosis' (p. 139).

19. One of the authors has discussed this issue in Dosi and Egidi (1987); recent and more classic references whose content we broadly share are Simon (1986) and Winter (1986); for a broad discussion see the special issue of the *Journal of Business* where the latter two references appear.

20. Recall that when a steady state is a saddle point its inset (the state of all points converging to it) has zero Lebesgue measure.

References

Akerlof, G. A. and Yellen, J. L. (1985), 'A near-rational model of the business cycle', *Quarterly Journal of Economics*, 100, pp. 803–38.

Antonelli, G. B. (1886), 'Sulla teoria matematica della economia politica', Pisa; English translation in J. S. Chipman *et al.* (eds.) (1971), *Preferences, Utility and Demand*, New York, Harcourt Brace Jovanovich.

Arrow, K. J. (1987), 'Oral history: an interview', in G. R. Feiwel (ed.), *Arrow and the Ascent of Modern Economic Theory*, New York, New York University Press.

Atkinson, A. and Stiglitz, J. (1969), 'A new view of technological change', *Economic Journal*, 79, pp. 573–8.

Azariadis, C. (1981), 'Self-fulfilling prophecies', *Journal of Economic Theory*, 25, pp. 380–96.

Azariadis, C. (1983), 'Intertemporal Macroeconomics: Lecture Notes', University of Pennsylvania, mimeo.

Balasko, Y. (1986), 'The class of aggregate excess demand functions', in W. Hildenbrand and A. Mas-Colell (eds.), *Contributions to Mathematical Economics*, New York, North Holland.

Benhabib, J. and Day, R. H. (1981), 'Rational choice and erratic behaviour', *Review of Economic Studies*, 4, pp. 37–55.

—— (1982), 'A characterization of erratic dynamics in the overlapping generations model', *Journal of Economic Dynamics and Control*, 48, pp. 459–72.

Benhabib, J. and Nishimura, K. (1985), 'Competitive equilibrium cycles', *Journal of Economic Theory*, 35, pp. 284–30.

Bray, M. and Kreps, D. M. (1987), 'Rational learning and rational expectations', in G. R. Feiwel (ed.), *Arrow and the Ascent of Modern Economic Theory*, New York, New York University Press.

Cass, D. and Shell, K. (1983), 'Do sunspots matter?', *Journal of Political Economy*, 91, pp. 193–227.

Cass, D., Okuno, M. and Ziicha, I. (1979), 'The role of money in supporting the Pareto optimality of competitive equilibrium in consumption-loan type models', *Journal of Economic Theory*, 20, pp. 41–80.

Collet, P. and Eckmann, J.P. (1980), *Iterated Maps on the Interval as Dynamic Systems*, Boston, Birkhauser.

Coricelli, F. (1987), 'Adaptive behaviour and rational expectations equilibria: some examples', Milan, Istituto per la Ricerca Sociale, mimeo.

Day, R. H. (1982), 'Irregular growth cycles', *American Economic Review*, 72, pp. 406–414.

—— (1983), 'The emergence of chaos from classical economic growth', *Quarterly Journal of Economics*, 98, pp. 201–212.

Dosi, G. and Egidi, M. (1987), 'Substantive and procedural uncertainty: an exploration on economic behaviour in complex and changing environments', Brighton, University of Sussex, SPRU, DRC Discussion Paper; presented at the Conference on Programmable Automation, Paris, 2–4 April 1987.

Dow, J. and Ribeiro da Costa Werlang, S. (1985), 'The consistency of welfare judgements with a representative consumer', Princeton University, Econometric Research Program Research Memorandum No. 318.

Eisenberg, B. (1961), 'Aggregation of utility functions', *Management Science*, 7, pp. 337–50.

Friedman, M. (1953), *Essays in Positive Economics*, Chicago, University of Chicago Press.

Frydman, R. and Phelps, E. S. (eds.) (1983), *Individual Forecasting and Aggregate Outcomes*, Cambridge, Cambridge University Press.

Fuchs, G. (1979), 'Is error learning behaviour stabilizing?', *Journal of Economic Theory*, 3, pp. 300–17.

Gorman, W. M. (1953), 'Community preference fields', *Econometrica*, 21, pp. 63–80.

Grandmont, J. M. (1984), 'Periodic and aperiodic behaviour in discrete one-dimensional dynamical systems', Stanford University, Economic Series Technical Report No. 446.

—— (1985a), 'On endogenous business cycles', *Econometrica*, 53, pp. 995–1046.

—— (1985b), 'Distributions of preferences and the "law of demand" ', mimeo.

Grandmont, J. M. and Laroque, G. (1986), 'Stability of cycles and expectations', *Journal of Economic Theory*, 40, pp. 138–51.

Hahn, F. (1984) *Equilibrium and Macroeconomics*, Oxford, Basil Blackwell.

Hahn, F. (1987), 'Information dynamics and equilibrium', presented at the Conference of Scottish Economists, mimeo.

Heiner, R. (1983), 'The Origin of predictable behavior', *American Economic Review, 83, pp. 560–95.*

—— (1986), 'The Origin of predictable dynamic behavior', Brigham Young University, mimeo.

Hildenbrand, W. (1986), 'Equilibrium analysis of large economies', Bonn University, Discussion Paper No. 72.

Kaldor, N. (1980), *The Role of Increasing Returns, Technical Progress and Cumulative Causation in the Theory of International Trade*, Paris, ISMEA.

—— (1985), *Economics without Equilibrium*, New York, Sharp.

Kehoe, T. J. and Levine, D. K. (1983), 'Indeterminacy of relative prices in overlapping generations models', MIT Working Paper No. 313.

Leijonhufvud, A. (1981), *Information and Coordination*, Oxford, Oxford University Press.

Li, T. and Yorke, J. A. (1975), 'Period three implies chaos', *American Mathematical Monthly*, 82, pp. 985–92.

Lucas, R. E. Jr (1981), *Studies in Business-Cycle Theory*, Cambridge, Mass., MIT Press.

—— (1986), 'Adaptive behaviour and economic theory', *Journal of Business*, 59, pp. 401–76.

Malinvaud, E. (1981), *Théorie macro-économique*, Paris, Dunod.

Nataf, A. (1953), 'Sur des questions d'agrégation en econométrie', Publications de l'Institut de Statistique de l'Université de Paris, 21, pp. 5–61.

Nelson, R. R. and Winter, S. (1982), *An Evolutionary Theory of Economic Change*, Cambridge, Mass., The Belknap Press of Harvard University Press.

Okun, A. M. (1981), *Prices and Quantities*, Oxford, Basil Blackwell.

Pietra, T. (1986), 'On the dynamic properties of an economy where production takes time: some examples of erratic and strange dynamics', University of Pennsylvania, mimeo.

Reichlin, P. (1986), 'Equilibrium cycles in an overlapping generations economy with production', *Journal of Economic Theory*, 40, pp. 89–102.

Saari, D. G. (1983), 'Dynamical systems and mathematical economics', in H. F. Sonnenschein (ed.), *Models of Economic Dynamics*, Berlin, Springer-Verlag.

Samuelson, P. (1958), 'An exact consumption-loan model of interest with and without the social contrivance of money', *Journal of Political Economy*, 66, pp. 467–82.

Shafer, W. and Sonnenschein, H. (1982), 'Market demand and excess demand functions', in K. J. Arrow and M. D. Intriligator (eds), *Handbook of Mathematical Economics*, vol. II, New York, North Holland.

Simon, H. A. (1986), 'Rationality in psychology and economics', *Journal of Business*, 59, pp. 209–24.

Varian, H. (1984), *Microeconomic Analysis*, 2nd ed., New York, Norton.

Winter, S. G. (1986), 'Adaptive behaviour and economic rationality: comments on Arrow and Lucas', *Journal of Business*, 59, pp. 427–34.

Woodford, M. (1984), 'Indeterminacy of equilibrium in the overlapping generations model: a survey', mimeo.

[8]

DAVID P. ELLERMAN

Myth and metaphor in orthodox economics

End of the pseudo-debate between capitalism and socialism

These are interesting times to think anew about orthodox neoclassical economics. With the collapse of communism, the bipolar economic-political order is breaking down.

Suppose that the proslavery writers had managed to pose "The Slavery Question" as a question of whether slave plantations should be publicly or privately owned. Instead of being privately owned and exploited for private greed (the "Athens model"), shouldn't the slave plantations be publicly owned and operated for the Public Good (the "Sparta model")?

Public ownership of plantations would, however, be inefficient. Publicly owned slaves would be "owned by everyone and thus by no one." Without clear-cut property rights and claims to the residual in the hands of an effective monitor, the slaves would shirk and the plantation assets would be mismanaged. Eventually the public plantations would collapse under the weight of their own inefficiency and would thus prove the superiority of "Athenian" private ownership of slave plantations.

The Great Debate between the public or private ownership of slave plantations would finally be over. Athens and private ownership would win. Pundits would declare "the end of history." So-called abolitionists might speak of a "Third Way" involving self-ownership but the slaves who have been reduced to near-starvation on the public plantations cannot afford some other "experiment." Across the long sweep of human history, the economic system with the greatest longevity and stability is slavery under private ownership. That is the verdict of history. The slaves should forget any half-baked dreams of an untried

The author is President of EOS/Ljubljana, Ljubljana, Yugoslavia.

and untested "Third Way." The public plantations should be straight-away privatized.

This hypothetical Great Debate about slavery has a familiar ring to it. With the end of that pseudo-debate, the ground would be cleared for the recognition that the real question was not whether slaves should be privately or publicly owned, but whether people should always be "self-owning."

Today, the economic systems of the world are based not on owning workers but on hiring, employing, or renting workers. Today's pseudo-debate is over whether workers might be privately employed for private interests or should always be publicly employed for the Public Good. The real question, however, is whether people might be rented at all (by a public or private party) or should always be jointly self-employed in their place of work (see Dahl, 1985, or Ellerman, 1990, for a discussion of an economic democracy with democratic worker-owned companies). Now that the pseudo-debate between capitalism and socialism is over, perhaps the real question can be addressed.

Conventional economics—after over a century of the Great Debate with Marxist socialism—has developed a number of bad habits of mythical and metaphorical thought, particularly when applied to the capitalist firm (i.e., the firm based on the employer–employee relationship). Since the socialist firm is also based on the employment relationship, socialist economics has not been an effective critic.

Neoclassical economic models often seem to have a bare skeleton of applied mathematics (various models of constrained optimization) with an overlay of shifting metaphors that obscure rather than elucidate the underlying reality. The postmodernist philosopher Richard Rorty has argued against the traditional notion of an "underlying reality" in favor of seeing "truth" along with Nietzsche as "a mobile army of metaphors" (1989, p. 17). We shall argue that much of neoclassical economics already is "a mobile army of metaphors," so, by those standards, it may be very near to the "truth."

The liabilities cancellation metaphor

Applied to stocks on the balance sheet

Stocks of property (three apples and five oranges) and flows of property (an apple a day) can be described in physical terms. Given a set of prices, the stocks and flows of property can be reduced to stocks and flows of value. Values are commensurate. One cannot subtract apples from oranges, but one can subtract the value of apples from the value of oranges.

Suppose an individual owns five oranges as an asset and holds a debt or liability of three apples to another person. It would not be meaningful to subtract the liability of three apples from the assets of five oranges and to conclude that the person has "net assets" of two "fruit." The individual does not just own two oranges: he or she owns all five oranges and *also* owes a liability of three apples to another party. The liabilities do not somehow cancel part of the property rights.

Given prices for the apples and oranges, the values can indeed be canceled. If oranges are $1.00 each and apples are $1.30 each, then the net worth is $1.10 (but there are no "net assets"). (See Figure 1.)

Figure 1   Debtor's balance sheet

Assets	Liabilities
5 oranges @ $1 = $5.00	3 apples @ $1.30 = $3.90
	Net worth $5.00 − 3.90 = $1.10

"Liabilities cancellation" is the practice of metaphorically reinterpreting the perfectly valid value cancellation as some type of *property* cancellation so that the debtor is viewed as only owning two "fruit" (see Figure 2).

Figure 2   Incorrect "liabilities cancellation"

Assets	Liabilities
5 oranges	3 apples
	"Net assets" 2 "fruit"

Applied to flows on the income statement:
distributive shares metaphor

The liabilities cancellation metaphor can be applied to property flows as well as to property stocks, for example, to the income statement as well as to the balance sheet (for the physical versions of these accounting statements, see Ellerman, 1982, 1986a). Consider the usual stylized description, $Q = f(K,L)$ of a production opportunity, which means that the workers and managers perform certain human activities described by the labor services, L, which use up the capital services, K, and produce the outputs, Q, during a given time period. If the fixed unit prices of Q, K, and L are respectively P, R, and W, then the net income or profit is $\pi = PQ - RK - WL$. The liabilities cancellation metaphor applied to the income statement yields the "distributive shares" metaphor (Figure 3).

Figure 3   Distributive shares metaphor

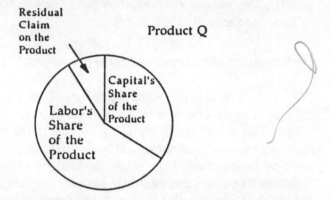

Each input supplier receiving an expense payment is depicted as a co-claimant on a share of the product, with the "residual claimant" claiming any remaining residual. The distributive shares metaphor presents the capitalist firm as some type of partnership. Each input supplier shares in the product, with the residual claimant taking what is left. Attention is directed away from the structure of property rights toward the array of input prices which in part determine the "relative shares" of the product.

The value cancellation used to compute the net income is perfectly legitimate, but the metaphorical extension to a property cancellation is illegitimate. The input suppliers—*qua* input suppliers—do not own a share of the product. The "residual claimant" owns *all* of the product Q, not just some residual share. How can this be consistent with the income to the input suppliers? The point is that the residual claimant also holds *all* the liabilities for the used-up inputs. In addition, the residual claimant also has *all* the discretionary control rights over the work process within the confines of the input supply contracts.

The residual claimant claims not just the residual but a bundle of incommensurate rights and liabilities $(Q, -K, -L)$ consisting of the produced assets Q *and* the liabilities for the used-up inputs symbolized by $-K$ and $-L$. In the modern, nonmetaphorical treatment of property rights, this bundle of property rights and obligations is called the "whole product" (Ellerman, 1982). Technically feasible whole-product vectors are the production vectors used in the modern production set representation of technical opportunities. In the economics literature, a whole-product vector is also called a "production possibility vector" (Arrow and Debreu, 1954, p. 267), an "activity vector" (Arrow and Hahn, 1971, p. 59), a "production" (Debreu, 1959, p. 38), or an "input-output vector" (Quirk and Saposnik, 1968, p. 27).

The metaphor of the firm as a "nexus of contracts"

The latest fashion in the "mobile army of metaphors" is the idea of the firm as "a nexus of contracts" or "a nexus of treaties" (see Aoki et al., 1989). This should not be confused with the trivial truth that the firm lies *in* a nexus of contractual and quasi-contractual relationships with employees, input suppliers, output demanders, and governmental authorities. The idea is that the firm *is* just a nexus of contracts, a relational entity like a weekend flea market that vanishes on weekdays.

> This is the set of contracts theory of the firm. The firm is viewed as nothing more than a set of contracts. One of the contract claims is a residual claim (equity) on the firm's assets and cash flows. [Ross and Westerfield, 1988, p. 14]

It is not easy to imagine the stocks and flows of property in a corporation like General Motors as "nothing more than a set of contracts," but apparently the idea is a wholesale application of the liabilities cancellation metaphor. Like a liquidation bankruptcy carried out at the metaphorical level, the assets and revenues are divvied up between the creditors and suppliers. Even the residual claim—ordinarily pictured as getting what is left after contractual claims are satisfied—is depicted as "[o]ne of the contract claims." Thus, the new-fangled "nexus of contracts" metaphor improves on the old-fashioned distributive shares metaphor by treating the residual claim or equity as another contractual relationship.

An actual nonmetaphorical firm is a legal party that owns 100 percent of the produced outputs, holds 100 percent of the liabilities for the used-up inputs, and has 100 percent of the discretionary control rights over the work process. A legal party that only supplies inputs—such as the workers in a capitalist firm—owns 0 percent of the produced outputs, holds 0 percent of the liabilities for the used-up inputs, and has 0 percent of the discretionary control rights over the work process. Those are the actual institutional facts—not the metaphors. It is not a picture of symmetry; it is total asymmetry.

The fundamental question about production—which is the fundamental question of political economy—is "Who is to be the Firm?" Capital (suppliers of equity capital), the State, or Labor (the people working in the enterprise)?

The distributive shares metaphor obfuscates the question by picturing all the input suppliers in symmetrical roles as contractual claimants on shares of the product. But the noncontractual residual claimant's role still hints that one party is not symmetrical with the others. The nexus of contracts picture mops up that untidy detail by presenting the residual claim as just another contractual claim. Then the fundamental question of "Who is to be the Firm?" has *completely* vanished; the firm is "nothing more than a set of contracts." The "mobile army of metaphors" marches on.

Laissez-faire appropriation

Markets transfer property rights. But in order to be transferred, a property right must first be "born," or initiated, and it will eventually "die," or be terminated. The birth of property rights is called "appropriation," and the death of property rights is the original meaning of "expropriation" (as opposed to the acquired meaning involving eminent domain).

In a production process, new property is created and old property is used up. In the stylized example, the property rights to the outputs Q are created, and the property rights to the input services K and L are terminated. In order to avoid confusion with the acquired sense of "expropriation," we will rephrase the "termination of the rights to K and L" as the "appropriation of the liabilities $-K$ and $-L$." Thus, in the stylized production example, the output assets Q *and* the liabilities $-K$ and $-L$ are *all* appropriated, that is, the whole product $(Q, -K, -L)$ is appropriated.

What is the legal mechanism of appropriation? When a law is broken, the liabilities are assigned by the legal authorities through the court system. But when no law is broken, a "laissez-faire" system of appropriation is the default. One legal party buys or already owns all the (exclusively owned) inputs needed for production, and that party "swallows" or bears those costs when the inputs are consumed in production. Then that party has the legally defensible claim on the produced outputs. Hence that party legally appropriates the whole product of production.

How is the question "Who is to be the Firm?" answered descriptively in a private property market economy? First we must define "firm" so as not to beg the question. Consider a production process that is noninstitutionally described in the usual manner by a production function, $Q = F(K,L)$. Take "firm" to mean the legal party that legally appropriates the whole product $(Q, -K, -L)$ of the production process in the institutional setting of a private property market economy. Then the laissez-faire mechanism of appropriation provides an answer to the descriptive question of "Who is to be the Firm?"—namely, the hiring party.

The fundamental myth about capitalist property rights

The neglect of appropriation

Conventional economics does not even recognize that appropriation takes place in production. The nonrecognition of appropriation in production is one of the remarkable oversights of the field called the "economics of property rights."

Philosophers follow Locke and discuss appropriation as the birth of private property rights in some primordial state where goods were held in common or were unowned. Economists follow suit and discuss the formation of private property rights out of common ownership. For instance, Harold Demsetz (1967) considers how private property in land with fur-bearing animals was established as a result of the growth of the fur trade. John Umbeck (1981) considers how rights to gold deposits were created during the 1848 California gold rush on land recently ceded from Mexico. Yoram Barzel (1989) considers how the common property rights to minerals under the North Sea were privatized. But in Barzel's book (e.g., his chapter 5, "The Formation of Rights"), as elsewhere in the economics of property rights literature, there is no recognition of the appropriation of the outputs and the symmetrical termination of rights to the used-up in inputs in the normal production process. That omission, like "the dog that didn't bark," calls for an explanation.

The fundamental myth

There is a "fundamental myth" accepted by both sides in the Great Debate between capitalism and socialism. The myth can be crudely stated as the belief that "being the firm" is part of the bundle of property rights referred to as "ownership of the means of production." Any legal party that operates as a capitalist firm, such as a conventional company, actually plays two distinct roles:

• the *capital owner role* of owning the means of production (the capital assets such as the equipment and plant) used in the production process; and
• the *residual claimant role* of bearing the costs of the inputs used up in the production process (e.g., the material inputs, the labor costs, and the used-up services of the capital assets) and owning the produced outputs.

The fundamental myth can now be stated in more precise terms. It is the myth that the residual claimant's role is part of the property rights owned in the capital owner's role, that is, part of the "ownership of the means of production." *That* is why "appropriation" does not appear in the conventional treatment of production; the ownership of the (whole) product is taken as part of the "ownership of the means of production."

It is simple to show that the two roles of residual claimant and capital owner can be separated without changing the ownership of the means of production. *Rent out the capital assets.* If the means of production, such as the plant and equipment, are leased out to another legal party, then the lessor retains the ownership of the means of production (the capital owner role) but the lessee renting the assets would then have the residual claimant's role for the production process using those capital assets. The lessee would then bear the costs of the used-up capital services (which are paid for in the lease payments) and the other inputs costs, and that party would own the produced outputs. Thus, the residual claimant's role is *not* part of the ownership of the means of production.

The separation of the two roles has become clear *even* in the Soviet Union. Over a thousand firms in the Soviet Union are organized as "lease firms" wherein the worker collective leases the needed physical assets from the ministry (see Ellerman, 1990). Thus, residual claimancy switches to the workers while the ministry maintains the ideological fetish of "ownership of the means of production."

The "miracle" of incorporation

This "rent out the capital" argument is very easy to understand. But it is astonishing how many economists fail to understand the argument when the capital owner is a corporation. If an individual owns a machine, say, a "widget maker," then that ownership is independent of the residual claimant's role in production using the widget maker. The capital owner could hire in workers to operate the widget maker and to produce widgets—or the widget maker could be hired out to some other party to produce widgets.

Now suppose the same individual incorporates a company and issues all the stock to himself in return for the widget maker. Instead of directly owning the widget maker, he is the sole owner of a corporation that owns the widget maker. Clearly this legal repackaging changes nothing in the argument about separating capital ownership and residual claimancy. The corporation has the capital owner's role and—depending on the direction of the hiring contracts—may or may not have the residual claimant's role in the production process using the widget maker. The corporation (instead of the individual) could hire in workers to use the widget maker to manufacture widgets, or the corporation could lease out the widget maker to some other party. The process of incorporation does not miraculously transsubstantiate the ownership of a capital asset into the ownership of the net production vector produced using the capital asset.

The fundamental myth in economic theory

The fundamental myth in theory of the firm

In the early models of perfectly competitive equilibrium, constant returns to scale in production was assumed. This implied zero economic profits in equilibrium, so from the viewpoint of value theory, it was immaterial who was the firm, that is, who appropriated the whole product vector (since it had zero net value). In 1954, Professors Kenneth Arrow and Gerard Debreu published a paper (Arrow and Debreu, 1954) in which they claimed to show the existence of a competitive equilibrium under the general conditions of nonincreasing returns to scale, that is, decreasing or constant returns to scale. Under decreasing returns to scale, there would be positive economic or pure profits. Hence the Arrow–Debreu model alleges to show the existence of a perfectly competitive equilibrium with *pure profits*. In the following passage, Arrow contrasts the Arrow–Debreu model with the model by McKenzie (1959), which used constant returns to scale:

> The two models differ in their implications for income distribution. The Arrow–Debreu model creates a category of pure profits which are distributed to the owners of the firm; it is not assumed that the owners are necessarily the entrepreneurs or managers. . . .
>
> In the McKenzie model, on the other hand, the firm makes no pure profits (since it operates at constant returns); the equivalent of profits appears in the form of payments for the use of entrepreneurial resources, but there is no residual category of owners who receive profits without rendering either capital or entrepreneurial services. [Arrow 1971, p. 70]

Since the whole-product vectors could have a positive value in the Arrow–Debreu model, the model had to face the question as to how these vectors got assigned to people. The Arrow–Debreu model does not answer the question by postulating "hidden factors" since that would compromise the model in a number of ways (see Ellerman, 1982, ch. 13, or McKenzie, 1981). Arrow explicitly states that "pure profits" are distributed to "the owners of the firm," and that, in contrast, the McKenzie model does not have this "residual category of owners who receive profits without rendering either capital or entrepreneurial services."

The Arrow–Debreu model answers the question by assuming that there is a property right such as the "ownership" of the production sets of technically feasible whole-product vectors. The train of reasoning is that production sets represent the production possibilities of "firms" and "firms" are (mistakenly) identified with specific corporations which, of course, are owned by their shareholders.

In a private enterprise capitalist economy, there is no such property right as the "ownership" of production sets of feasible whole-product vectors. In the Arrow–Debreu model, each consumer-resourceholder is endowed prior to any market exchanges with a certain set of resources and with shares in corporations. However, prior to any market activity, ownership of corporate shares is only an indirect form of ownership of resources such as widget maker machines. It is the subsequent contracts in input markets that will determine whether a corporation, like any other resource owner, successfully exploits a production opportunity by purchasing the requisite inputs.

The Arrow–Debreu model mistakes the whole logic of appropriation. The question of who appropriates the whole product of a production opportunity is not settled by the initial endowment of property rights. It is only settled in the markets for inputs by who hires what or whom. In other words, the determination of who is to be the "firm" (the whole-product appropriator) is not exogenous to the marketplace; it is a *market-endogenous* determination. This adds a degree of freedom to the model that can only be ignored in the special case of universal constant returns to scale when it does not matter (for income determination) who is the firm. This degree of freedom eliminates the possibility of a competitive equilibrium with positive economic profits (e.g., with decreasing returns to scale in some production opportunity). Any profit seeker would bid up the price of the inputs that could be engaged in any opportunity with pure profits.

The symmetry is restored between decreasing and increasing returns. Competitive equilibrium fails under decreasing returns because everyone tries to be the firm (positive profits) just as it fails under increasing returns because no one wants to be the firm (negative profits). Competitive equilibrium can only exist under constant returns where profits are zero. Our point is not that the idealized model is unrealistic; it is that the Arrow–Debreu model (with decreasing returns) does not correctly model an *idealized* competitive private property market economy. The structural modeling error is the assumed "ownership" of production set—which in turn disallows profit-seeking arbitrageurs from bidding on inputs to undertake production. Idealized competitive models should allow all forms of arbitrage (see Ellerman, 1984)—including the "production arbitrage" of buying the inputs and selling the outputs.

The imputation fallacies of capital theory

Broadly speaking, capital has two types of uses: "active" or "passive." Capital is used passively when it is sold or rented out in return for some market price or rental. Capital is used actively when, instead of being evaluated directly on the market, it is used up in production, usually along with other resources. Then the liabilities for the used-up resources and the rights to any produced assets are appropriated. Thus, appropriation is involved in the active use, but not in the passive use, of capital.

One of the basic concepts of capital theory is the notion of the *capitalized value of an asset*. The definition is usually stated in a rather general fashion: owning the asset "yields" a future income stream and the discounted present value of the income stream is the capitalized value of the asset. But there are quite different ways in which "owning an asset" can "yield" an income stream. In particular, there are the "active" and the passive uses of capital. The capitalized value concept is unproblematic in the passive case where the income stream is the stream of net rentals plus the scrap value. The capitalized value of that stream is, under competitive conditions, just the market value of the asset. Bonds and annuities provide similar examples of income streams generated by renting out or loaning out capital assets, that is, by the passive use of capital.

The capitalized value definition is, however, applied to the quite different active case where, instead of hiring out the capital, labor is hired in, a product is produced and sold, and the net proceeds are all imputed to the capital assets. When the discounted profits are included in the "capitalized value *of the capital asset*," then the role of appropriation is overlooked. One might then think that by purchasing the asset or the "means of production," one is thereby purchasing the outputs and the net proceeds—so there is no need to appropriate the outputs.

> When a man buys an investment or capital-asset, he purchases the right to the series of prospective returns, which he expects to obtain from selling its output, after deducting the running expenses of obtaining that output, during the life of the asset. [Keynes 1936, p. 135]

But that is a factually incorrect description of property rights. A man thereby purchases only the asset. Any further return will depend on his contracts. If he rents out the asset and sells the scrap, then he receives only the rental-plus-scrap income stream. If, instead, he hires in labor, bears the costs of the used-up labor and capital services, and claims and sells the outputs, then he receives the net proceeds mentioned by Keynes.

Another example of assigning the whole product to the capital asset is involved in the notions of "marginal efficiency of capital" or "net productivity of capital." The discount rate that discounts all the future returns (including the profits) back to the market cost of the capital asset is sometimes called an *internal rate of return* or *average rate of return over cost.* However, it is also presented as the yield rate *of the capital asset* and then it is called the *marginal efficiency of capital* (Keynes, 1936, p. 135), or the *net productivity of capital* (Samuelson, 1976, p. 600—where Samuelson correctly notes that it is not a marginal concept). This usage presents the profit stream *as if* it were part of the return to owning the capital asset, when in fact it is the return to being the hiring party. Thus, the "net productivity of capital" is actually the net rate of return to the combined role of owning the capital *and* having the contractual role of being the residual claimant.

Samuelson asserts that "capital goods have a 'net' productivity" (1976, p. 661) (while the other factors have only a marginal productivity), as a "technological fact" (1976, p. 600). That is a clear-cut case where the *social* role of capital as the hiring party in capitalist society is presented as a *technological* characteristic of capital goods. It is a capital theoretic version of the fundamental myth. Unfortunately, the Cambridge controversy in capital theory failed to uncover these basic imputation fallacies which have nothing to do with "reswitching and all that."

Labor in conventional economics: uttering the R-word

One of the most astonishing aspects of neoclassical economics is its studied inability meaningfully to differentiate the actions of persons (a.k.a. "labor") from the services of things. When burglaries are committed, it is the alleged burglars—not the burglary tools—that are hauled into court. Burglary tools are nonetheless useful ("productive") for the burglar. But only people can be *responsible.* Things cannot be responsible for anything.

"Responsibility" is the R-word that conventional economists cannot utter (except, of course, metaphorically). For instance, Alfred Marshall (1920, ch. 4 and 5 of Book 6) went to unusual lengths to note a number of peculiarities of labor: (1) workers may not be bought and sold, only rented or hired; (2) the seller must deliver the service himself; (3) labor is perishable; (4) labor owners are often at a bargaining disadvantage; and (5) specialized labor requires long preparation time. Yet none of these "peculiarities" explains why people, not things, are charged in court. Marshall could not find the R-word.

Another example of this studied incapacity is the conventional treatment of the "labor theory of value" in the textbooks. Orthodox economics depicts adherents of the so-called labor theory of value as not understanding that land (and perhaps capital) is "productive" in the sense of being causally efficacious. They "seemed to deny that scarce land and time-intensive processes can also contribute to competitive costs and to true social costs" (Samuelson, 1976, p. 545). Happily, neoclassical economics has discovered that land is useful in producing the harvest, so economics has finally moved beyond the "labor theory." In the "happy consciousness" of neoclassical theory, there is no inkling that some other unmentionable attribute might be involved in addition to causal productivity. "Responsibility" is not a concept of physics. From the viewpoint of physics, human actions are simply causally efficacious services like the services of things. In view of the physics envy of modern economics (see Mirowski, 1989), economists can ignore the R-word and thereby be even more "scientific."

One of the original developers of marginal productivity theory, Friedrich von Wieser, found the R-word. Wieser even admitted in print that, of all the factors of production, only labor is de facto responsible. Thus, the usual imputation of legal responsibility in accordance with de facto responsibility will go back through the instruments solely to the human agents.

> The judge, . . . who, in his narrowly-defined task, is only concerned with the legal imputation, confines himself to the discovery of the legally responsible factor,—that person, in fact, who is threatened with the legal punishment. On him will rightly be laid the whole burden of the consequences, although he could never by himself alone—without instruments and all the other conditions—have committed the crime. The imputation takes for granted physical causality. . . .
>
> If it is the moral imputation that is in question, then certainly no one but the labourer could be named. Land and capital have no merit that they bring forth fruit; they are dead tools in the hand of man; and the man is responsible for the use he makes of them. [Wieser, 1889, pp. 76–79]

These are astonishing remarks. Wieser at last sees the explanation of the old radical slogans, "Only labor is creative" or "Only labor is productive," which the classical radicals could never explain clearly. Since labor is the only responsible factor, capitalist apologetics clearly requires that "responsibility" be metaphorically reinterpreted. Simple causal efficacy must be animistically interpreted as the special type of "responsibility" needed by economic theory:

> In the division of the return from production, we have to deal ...
> similarly,—with an imputation, save that it is from the economic, not the
> judicial point of view. [Wieser, 1889, p. 76]

By defining "economic responsibility" in terms of the animistic version of marginal productivity, Wieser could finally draw the conclusion demanded by his ideological goal: to show that competitive capitalism "economically" imputes the product in accordance with "economic" responsibility. Then neoclassical economists could use words such as "imputation," and even the dreaded R-word—metaphorically.

Metaphors are like lies: one metaphor requires others to round out the picture. The ideological interpretation of marginal productivity theory (pioneered by Friedrich von Wieser and John Bates Clark) uses one metaphor to justify another metaphor. We previously considered the distributive shares metaphor, which pictured each factor as getting a share of the product. The Wieser–Clark interpretation of MP theory metaphorically pictures each factor as being "responsible" for a share of the product. And, lo, under appropriate competitive conditions, the two metaphors match; each factor "gets what it produces." By justifying one metaphor with another metaphor, capitalist apologetics can "slip the surly bonds" of reality and soar freely in the metaphorical void.

It is, however, the actual property relations of capitalist production (i.e., the employer's appropriation of the whole product) that need to be judged, and the notion of responsibility relevant to the structure of legal property rights is the normal nonmetaphorical juridical notion of responsibility that is used every day from "the judicial point of view."

Labor and inalienability

We warm to the modernity of Immanuel Kant's call for "universal suffrage" until we see the jarring footnote, "except, of course, for women, children, and lunatics"—not to mention servants (now called "employees" in our newspeak). The Founding Fathers' proclamation that "All men are created equal" similarly excluded slaves and women. When a society is based on an institutional form of dehumanization, the people born and raised in that society will see it as "natural." It is "hard-wired" into their social perceptions of reality—into their "happy consciousness."

We live in a society based on the renting of human beings, and that is perceived as being totally natural. The recent "alternative" was a society where all workers were rented by the government. That was the choice: capitalism or socialism.

Yet something is amiss. Labor is peculiar. Being the sole responsible factor is only one of labor's peculiarities. This can be illustrated by using the case of the criminous employee as an "intuition pump." Suppose that an entrepreneur hired an employee for general services (no intimations of criminal intent). The entrepreneur similarly hired a van, and the owner of the van was not otherwise involved in the entrepreneur's activities. Eventually the entrepreneur decided to use the factor services he had purchased (man-hours and van-hours) to rob a bank. After being caught, the entrepreneur and the employee were charged with the crime. In court, the employee argued that he was just as innocent as the van owner. Both had sold the services of factors they owned to the entrepreneur. The use the entrepreneur made of these commodities was "his own business."

The judge would, most likely, be unmoved by these arguments. The judge would point out it was plausible that the van owner was not responsible. He had given up and transferred the use of his van to the entrepreneur, so unless the van owner was otherwise personally involved, his absentee ownership of the factor would not give him any responsibility for the results of the enterprise. Absentee ownership of a factor is not itself a source of responsibility.

The judge would point out, however, that the worker could not help but be personally involved in the robbery. Man-hours are a peculiar commodity in comparison with van-hours. The worker cannot "give up and transfer" the use of his own person, as the van owner can the van. Employment contract or not, the worker remained a fully responsible agent, knowingly cooperating with the entrepreneur. The employee and the employer share the de facto responsibility for the results of their joint activity, and the law will impute legal responsibility accordingly. The servant in work becomes the partner in crime.

> All who participate in a crime with a guilty intent are liable to punishment. A master and servant who so participate in a crime are liable criminally, not because they are master and servant, but because they jointly carried out a criminal venture and are both criminous. [Batt, 1967, p. 612]

It should be particularly noted that the worker is *not* de facto responsible for the crime *because* an employment contract that involves a crime is null and void. Quite the opposite. The employee is de facto responsible because the employee, together with the employer, committed the crime (not because of the legal status of the contract). It was his de facto responsibility for the crime that invalidated the contract, not the contractual invalidity that made him de facto responsible.

When the venture being carried out is not criminous, the facts about the nontransferability of de facto responsibility do not change. It is the reaction of the legal system that changes. When no law has been broken, the law does not intervene, so laissez-faire appropriation takes over. When the employee cooperates in the same manner with the employer, that now "counts" as fulfilling the labor contract to "deliver" the labor services to the buyer. The hiring party has then borne the costs of the labor and the other inputs, so the hiring party has the defensible legal claim on all the outputs produced. Thus, the employer receives the legal, or de jure, responsibility for the whole product.

But workers do not suddenly turn into nonresponsible things when their actions are not criminous. The working employer and employees are still de facto responsible for the fruits of their joint labor, that is, for using up the inputs and producing the outputs. Labor is de facto nontransferrable and inalienable. The whole idea of a "labor contract" to buy and sell labor as a commodity—the contract to rent human beings—is fraudulent at its very roots.

Modernity and the Enlightenment Project

None of this is new. It is part of the Enlightenment Project. Consider, for instance, the Enlightenment doctrine of inalienable rights based on the de facto inalienability of a person's capacity for responsible decisions and actions. One source was Martin Luther's Reformation doctrine of the liberty of conscience. It is de facto impossible for a person to alienate his decision-making power to the Church on matters of faith:

> Furthermore, every man is responsible for his own faith, and he must see it for himself that he believes rightly. As little as another can go to hell or heaven for me, so little can he believe or disbelieve for me; and as little as he can open or shut heaven or hell for me, so little can he drive me to faith or unbelief. [Luther 1942, p. 316]

Francis Hutcheson, a teacher of Adam Smith, developed this inalienability argument as a part of the Scottish Enlightenment. Hutcheson is important for another reason. The American Declaration of Independence is one of the high points in the praxis of the inalienable rights tradition. The conventional scholarly view has been that "Jefferson copied Locke" (Becker, 1958, p. 79). But Locke had no serious theory of inalienability, and he in fact condoned a limited voluntary contract for slavery, which he nicely called "Drudgery."

In Garry Wills' important study, *Inventing America*, he reinvented Jeffersonian scholarship concerning the intellectual roots of the Declaration of Independence. Wills convincingly argued that the Lockean influence was more indirect and even to some extent resisted by Jefferson, while Hutcheson's influence was central and pervasive. In particular, "Jefferson took his division of rights into alienable and unalienable from Hutcheson, who made the distinction popular and important" (Wills, 1979, p. 213).

In Hutcheson's *An Inquiry into the Original of Our Ideas of Beauty and Virtue* (1725), he first distinguished between alienable and inalienable rights. The de facto inalienability argument is developed in Hutcheson's influential *A System of Moral Philosophy* (1755). He followed Luther in showing how the "right of private judgment" or "liberty of conscience" was inalienable. He focused on the *factual* nontransferability of private decision-making power. In the case of the criminous employee, the employee ultimately makes the decisions himself in spite of what is commanded by the employer. Short of physical coercion, an individual's faculty of judgment cannot in fact be short-circuited by a secular or religious authority.

> A like natural right every intelligent being has about his own opinions, speculative or practical, to judge according to the evidence that appears to him. This right appears from the very constitution of the rational mind which can assent or dissent solely according to the evidence presented, and naturally desires knowledge. The same considerations show this right to be unalienable: it cannot be subjected to the will of another: tho' where there is a previous judgment formed concerning the superior wisdom of another, or his infallibility, the opinion of this other, to a weak mind, may become sufficient evidence. [Hutcheson, 1755, p. 295]

This inalienable rights doctrine, based on the de facto inalienability of a person's capacity for thought and action, developed into the Enlightenment critique of the contract to sell all of one's labor at once (the voluntary self-enslavement contract) and of the Hobbesian *pactum subjectionis* (see Ellerman, 1986b, 1990). Adam Smith did not follow his teacher, Francis Hutcheson, in this doctrine—and the rest is the intellectual history of modern economic thought.

Postmodern criticism should not give modern economics credit for fulfilling the Enlightenment Project in the social sciences. Quite to the contrary, economics has betrayed the ideals of the Enlightenment in order to better serve an economic system based on renting human beings. Economics has offered up applied mathematics smothered with a thick sauce of myths and metaphors in order to obfuscate the structure of property rights, to justify treating the inalienably responsible actions of persons as the transferable, nonresponsible services of things, and to apologize for the limited *pactum subjectionis* of the workplace, the employment contract.

REFERENCES

Aoki, Masahiko; Gustafsson, Bo; and Williamson, Oliver. *The Firm as a Nexus of Treaties*. London: Sage Publications, 1989.

Arrow, K. J. "The Firm in General Equilibrium Theory." In *The Corporate Economy*, R. Marris and A. Woods, eds. Cambridge, MA: Harvard University Press, 1971.

Arrow, K. J., and Debreu, G. "Existence of an Equilibrium for a Competitive Economy." *Econometrica*, 1954, *22*, 265–290.

Arrow, K. J., and Hahn, F. H. *General Competitive Analysis*. San Francisco: Holden-Day, 1971.

Barzel, Yoram. *Economic Analysis of Property Rights*. New York: Cambridge University Press, 1989.

Batt, Francis. *The Law of Master and Servant*, 5th ed. by G. Webber. London: Pitman, 1967.

Becker, Carl. *The Declaration of Independence*. New York: Vintage Books, 1958.

Dahl, Robert. *Preface to Economic Democracy*. Berkeley: University of California Press, 1985.

Debreu, G. *Theory of Value*. New York: John Wiley, 1959.

Demsetz, Harold. "Toward a Theory of Property Rights." *American Economic Review*, May 1967, *57*, 347–359.

Ellerman, David P. *Economics, Accounting, and Property Theory*. Lexington, MA: D. C. Heath, 1982.

———. "Arbitrage Theory: A Mathematical Introduction." *SIAM Review*, 1984, *26*, 241–261.

———. "Property Appropriation and Economic Theory." In *Reconstruction in Economic Theory*, Philip Mirowski, ed. Boston: Kluwer–Nijhoff, 1986a.

———. "The Employment Contract and Liberal Thought." *Review of Social Economy*, April 1986b, *44*, 13–39.

————. *The Democratic Worker-Owned Firm.* London: Unwin and Hyman, 1990.

Hutcheson, Francis. *An Inquiry into the Original of Our Ideas of Beauty and Virtue.* London: 1725.

————. *A System of Moral Philosophy.* London: 1755.

————. *Collected Works of Francis Hutcheson.* Hildesheim: Georg Olms Verlangsbuchhandlung, 1969.

Keynes, J. M. *The General Theory of Employment, Interest, and Money.* New York: Harcourt, Brace and World, 1936.

Luther, Martin. "Concerning Secular Authority." In *Readings in Political Philosophy,* F. W. Coker, ed. New York: Macmillan, 1942.

Marshall, Alfred. *Principles of Economics.* New York: Macmillan, 1920.

McKenzie, L. "On Equilibrium in Graham's Model of World Trade and Other Competitive Systems." *Econometrica,* April 1954, *22,* 147–161.

————. "On the Existence of a General Equilibrium in a Competitive Market." *Econometrica,* 1959, *27,* 54–71.

————. "The Classical Theorem on Existence of Competitive Equilibrium." *Econometrica,* July 1981, *49*(4), 819–841.

Mirowski, Philip. *More Heat than Light.* New York: Cambridge University Press, 1989.

Quirk, J., and Saposnik, R. *Introduction to General Equilibrium Theory and Welfare Economics.* New York: McGraw-Hill, 1968.

Rorty, Richard. *Contingency, Irony, and Solidarity.* Cambridge, MA: Cambridge University Press, 1989.

Ross, Stephen A., and Westerfield, Randolph W. *Corporate Finance.* St. Louis, MO: Times Mirror/Mosby, 1988.

Samuelson, Paul A. *The Collected Scientific Papers of Paul A. Samuelson, vol. 3,* Robert C. Merton, ed. Cambridge, MA: MIT Press, 1972.

————. *Economics,* 10th ed. New York: McGraw-Hill, 1976.

Umbeck, John. "Might Makes Right: A Theory of the Formation and Initial Distribution of Property Rights." *Economic Inquiry,* 1981, *19*(1), 38–59.

Wieser, Friedrich von. *Natural Value,* trans. C. A. Malloch. New York: G. E. Stechert, 1930. (Originally published in 1889.)

Wills, Garry. *Inventing America.* New York: Vintage Books, 1979.

[9]

PHILIP MIROWSKI

Postmodernism and the social theory of value

While the other contributors to this symposium have focused upon issues of epistemology, canon creation in the history of economic thought, and the metaphors governing our cultural images of ownership and control, I should like to propose that the implications of the cultural changes that travel under the rubric of "postmodernism" could potentially transcend a critique of orthodox economics, to the point of initiating an alternative to the neoclassical theory of value. If it is a hallmark of postmodernism to deny the text has a single fixed and stable referent, then what if the "economy" were treated in a similar manner? And, indeed, what if this reconceptualization went beyond discussions of methodology to actually frame an alternative mathematical formalization of the notion of value?

I have argued elsewhere (Mirowski, 1989, 1990a) that, far from there being a surfeit of theories of value to choose from in the history of economic thought, from the quantitative/analytic point of view there really have only been two: the "substance theory of value," exemplified by such particular instances as the physiocratic corn theory and the classical labor-embodied theory of value; and the "field theory of value," best exemplified by the neoclassical theory of utility. There has also been a third subterranean (and relatively ineffectual) current that denies the existence of the phenomenon of value altogether, exemplified

The author is Carl Koch Professor of Economics and the History and Philosophy of Science at the University of Notre Dame, Notre Dame, Indiana. He would like to thank David Ellerman for helpful comments and discussion, without implicating him in any of the author's own errors; he is also not responsible for any uses to which his own work has been put in this paper. Various audiences have played a part in shaping this outcome, including the Seminar in Institutionalist Economics at the University of Tennessee and the auditors of Economics 785b at Yale University. The literary "dual" to the present mathematical argument may be found in Mirowski, 1990a.

by the writings of Samuel Bailey and William Thornton. The pitfalls and attractions of this radical abjuration of "value" have also been discussed elsewhere (Mirowski, 1991).

The primary reason for such slim pickings can be traced to the Durkheim–Mauss–Douglas thesis (Mirowski, 1988, p. 109), which predicts that the social categories employed to organize our discourse would be reflections of the categories we use to discuss the natural world. The structure of the classical substance and of the neoclassical field theories were both largely projections of mathematical models of the physical world dominant in those respective eras. In other words, the social structures of the economy were invested with the determinacy and lawlike character of things. I would claim that (with very few partial exceptions, such as the American institutionalists) there has *never* been a serious exploration of the logical structure of a thoroughgoing social theory of value. It would be explicitly "social," and perhaps even "postmodern," because it would refrain from grounding any aspect of value either in the "natural" attributes of the commodities (the substance theories), or in the supposed inherent psychological regularities of the individual mind (neoclassical field theory). Instead, it would opt for the third modality of rooting the structure of value in contingent social institutions. As Mary Douglas (1986) has explained, institutions are founded upon analogy and provide the conceptual identity for phenomena. While Douglas most likely did not intend the technical mathematical definition of "identity" (i.e., one of the requirements in abstract algebra for the existence of a group), I do.

I. Four central issues in value theory

The full justification of the quantification of prices is profoundly more complicated than the rather cursory discussion found in Mirowski (1986). There seem to be four somewhat separable issues, each demanding the use of a different mathematical formalism to be expressed properly. The first is the problem of the constitution of the identity of the commodity, which would be the province of *measurement theory*. The second is the problem of conceptualizing trade as an ongoing network of permitted and blocked exchanges of idealized classes of goods between individual human beings. This question would be the province of *graph theory*. The third is the description of the institution of "value" as distinct from, yet predicated upon, the previous two issues. This would largely be a question of *abstract algebra*. The social theory of value would be consolidated by a concatenation of the above devices. Far from being a pipe dream, the way forward has already been indicated by Ellerman (1984, 1988) using the formalism of *directed graphs* under the rubric of "arbitrage theory." Fourth, the irreducibly contingent character of value would be expressed by linking the above formalisms to the structures of *probability theory*, by revealing that probability is itself a special case of arbitrage theory.

It is important at this point to be self-consciously skeptical about this or any other program that imports still more relatively unfamiliar mathematical devices into a situation where the profession is already rife with superfluous and ill-considered abstract mathematical formalisms (Mirowski, 1986, 1991). In orthodox neoclassical economics, there is no serious intellectual justification for this escalation of technique, other than to disguise further its origins in nineteenth-century physics, or to provide a pecking order within the discipline and perhaps to exclude the curious layman. Here the role of mathematics will be different. The formalisms sketched out in these notes are required because it is a historical fact that modern market actors predicate their economic interactions upon prices and quantities expressed as rational numbers. This central fact of markets must have an explanation grounded in the theory of social institutions. But more significantly, mathematics is a superior method of the translation of metaphors between disciplines (Mirowski, 1988, ch. 8); and a major problem of a social theory of value is to reorient the culture away from its failed naturalism. Hence, it will be no accident that most of the formalisms proposed here are *not* generally found in physics.

II. The identity of the commodity

This first problem has almost never been dispassionately entertained in the economics literature, since it has simply been assumed that the categorical identity of any commodity was immediately transparently obvious to everyone and determined by external natural attributes. However, as argued in Mirowski (1986), not all apples are alike; not even all Macintoshes are identical. The very idea that identity is unproblematically determinate violates the purported methodological individualism of neoclassical theory: has anyone ever asked you if you thought all bottled water was "alike"? The question then arises: why would a market system be driven to standardize commodities and make them interchangeable in the social sphere (if not for each individual)?

The way commodities have been measured for purposes of trade has a very strange history (Kula, 1986). Briefly, commodity identities seem to have evolved from definitions tied to individual personalities (e.g., the feudal lord defined a bushel of grain differently for each person), to more relatively impersonal measures, culminating in the metric system in the French Revolution. This history can be seen as one chapter in a progressive attempt socially to constitute the identity of the commodity, and more precisely to remove it from the sphere of the personal and idiosyncratic. Such abstraction from the realm of the personal is an absolute prerequisite to rendering market trade quantitative.

There is no one "correct" way for a society to measure a commodity, and the way its measurement is instituted has important consequences for its subsequent manipulation in various formal mathematical schemes. It may be represented on an interval, ordinal, ratio, or absolute scale (Roberts, 1979); the attribute chosen to ground the measurement may be continuous or discrete; it may be reversible or irreversible. All of these considerations are the subject of a mathematical discipline called *measurement theory* (Roberts, 1979; Osborne, 1978). Measurement theory has appeared in a fringe literature in economics (de Jong, 1967; Luce and Narens, 1987), but almost exclusively in the context of trying to characterize utility; and therefore this literature has seemed somewhat superfluous. Instead, our proposed social theory of value would use it to highlight the difficulty in getting a society to measure something consistently, and to establish that this standardization is an important aspect of the spread of the market, ranging from the imposition of a metric system to the persistent drive down to the present day to standardize commodity identities through mass production, advertising, and the elimination of the craft character of precapitalist production. On a more pragmatic note, measurement theory would also be used to check that equations in the social theory of value are always dimensionally conformable. (This would prevent such travesties as $Y = (K,L)$.) Finally, in a world where, because of their contingent historical character, measurement scales are arbitrarily mixed, such justifications of the formal basis of economics such as that of Gerard Debreu would be barred as simply fallacious:

> Having chosen a unit of measurement for each one of them [the commodities], and a sign convention to distinguish inputs from outputs, one can describe the action of an economic agent by a vector in the commod-

ity space R^1. The fact that the commodity space has the structure of a real vector space is a basic reason for the success of the mathematicization of economic theory. [Debreu, 1984, pp. 267-268]

The point of departure of a social theory of value should be: commodities must be rendered socially "measurable," preferably on some interval scale, in order for trade to be quantified and value to be defined. Because of the heterogeneity of individual perceptions, of scales and of their conventions, commodities do not genuinely span a real vector space at any specific historical nexus. And, in any event, the notion of an independent natural metric in "commodity space" is meaningless. Hence, value cannot be grounded in or deduced from the nature of the commodity itself: it cannot be collapsed to a problem of arbitrarily picking a *numeraire*. Commodities are rendered quantitative in the marketplace as part of the construction of standardized production and marketing, or, in other words, as part and parcel of the fabrication of value.

III. The network of trade

There is a sporadic and underdeveloped literature on the "dual coincidence of wants" and the problems of getting the trading activities of numerous individual actors to mesh. Contrary to the claims of neoclassical theory to base itself on individual behavior and the coordination activities of a market, it has had little to say about this problem (Clower, 1984; Ostroy and Starr, 1974; Eckalbar, 1984). The reason for this neglect is that the enumeration of the permutations of the possible channels of trade is itself another issue that should be formalized prior to the inscription of value theory. The problem of who may deal with whom on a social basis is qualitatively different from the "effective demand" problem of who has the resources to engage in exchange.

In order to guarantee that we don't lose sight of the people in the economy, let us begin by defining a "social traffic" matrix z where the rows $i = 1, \ldots, M$ index the people in our market and the columns $j = 1, \ldots, N$ index the various classes of commodities that have been subjected to the local process of standardization and measurement described in the section above. With the following sign convention, the various entries in this matrix tell us who stands willing and able to trade each commodity. Let

$$z_{ij} = \begin{cases} 1 \text{ if person } i \text{ will sell good } j \text{ in trade;} \\ -1 \text{ if person } i \text{ will buy good } j \text{ in trade;} \\ 0 \text{ if person } i \text{ will not trade good } j. \end{cases}$$

It is well known in the specialist neoclassical literature that certain configurations of the z matrix—namely those where the dual coincidence of wants is frustrated—would stymie exchange, even in the presence of an "equilibrium" vector of Walrasian prices.[1] A simple example is provided by the following three-person, three-good matrix, z^*:

$$z^* = \begin{bmatrix} 1 & -1 & 0 \\ -1 & 0 & 1 \\ 0 & 1 & -1 \end{bmatrix}$$

Here, person 1 would like to sell good one and buy good two, but neither of the other participants can both take good one off his hands and give him something he wants in return, even in any pairwise sequence of exchanges. The existing literature has tried to get around this problem in one of three ways: (a) by simply presuming that everyone starts out with sufficient stocks of all commodities and/or effectively wants everything all the time; (b) by positing the existence of a trade coordinator(s) who stands ready to buy and sell unlimited amounts of a designated set of commodities; or (c) by positing the existence of a commodity that everyone stands ready to buy and sell at all times (making everyone a trade coordinator). I find none of these expedients historically plausible or especially theoretically interesting, especially given that the posited trade coordinator looks a bit too much like the inexplicably benevolent and other-worldly Walrasian auctioneer, and the universally acceptable commodity does not capture all the signifi-

[1] For instance, Eckalbar (1984), and Davidson (1978, ch. 6). Further, since Ostroy and Starr (1974) take prices as given exogenously and all equal to unity, abjuring all discussions of utility, their matrices all qualify as social traffic matrices; therefore, many of their results may be absorbed into the social theory of value with little or no alteration. For instance, they demonstrate that simple coordination requires either (a) the existence of a commodity that everyone is willing to buy and sell and keep appreciable stocks for trading purposes; or (b) the existence of a trade coordinator who is willing to buy or sell unlimited quantities of most goods. Since neither situation occurs "naturally" (or, as they phrase it, decentralization is impossible in a pure barter economy), the moral of their work is that one cannot take a "connected" trading system for granted; rather, institutions must be created in order to guarantee its existence.

cant functions of money. The social traffic matrix does keep us aware
that money can reduce the number of pairwise trades necessary to arrive
at any particular commodity; but it will also serve to demonstrate that
all the problems of market coordination are not therein dissolved, as we
shall witness below in section VI.

Another aspect of the social traffic matrix critical for the subject of
section V below is the existence of "circuits" in the matrices. A "circuit"
would describe the ability to arrange a sequence of trades in a circle in
order to arrive back at exactly the same commodity and person from
whence the sequence originated, without trading the same commodity
twice or "visiting" the same trader more than once. While this may seem
a little strange, it begins to express the ability of a market system to
combine minimized "shoe leather" with minimum restriction upon
permitted trades. Further, it is of paramount mathematical importance
for providing the identity of a trading system, and is a prerequisite for
the definition of value. Without this condition, a system of traders cannot
themselves constitute a stable value index, because in any other case
their trading activities will be thwarted by the existence of culs-de-sac
that terminate sequences of trade.

IV. Money as the abstract algebra of value

A social theory of value would demonstrate that even with the existence
of socially specified commodity identities, and the institution of a
connected social trading network, the problem of value is still not
resolved. For instance, in Ostroy and Starr (1974), there is still no ability
to discuss "price," and the mere introduction of debt undermines all of
their results. In a social theory of value, it would be recognized that a
distinct algebra of value is required that cannot depend for its identity
upon the characteristics of any particular commodity (Mirowski,
1986). Another way of putting this is: why must any particular
bilateral trade have any significant implications for any subsequent
bilateral trade? How can any traders gauge their overall gain or loss?
To put it just a tiny bit more formally, why should it ever be the case
that $p_{ab} \times p_{bc} \times p_{cd} \times p_{de} = p_{ae}$? This question is the province of
abstract algebra.

In a pure barter economy, any arbitrary trade has no significance for
any subsequent trade, mainly because there is no stable natural identity
or benchmark against which all trades may be compared. What is
required is a transpersonal transtemporal index of gain and loss, which

also provides the identity element in the algebra of exchange. Money, by its very nature a social institution, renders the price system an algebraic "field" (Durbin, 1985, ch. 5): namely, the set of {all prices} and two operations, addition (with identity zero) and multiplication (with identity unity, the monetary unit). What this guarantees is that (a) prices of different goods may be added and subtracted—a condition that is *not* guaranteed by their own measurement schemes (see section II)—and (b) trade is treated as if it were a reversible process. This ideal of reversibility provides the benchmark of gain and loss. An analogy could be drawn here with thermodynamics, where ideal reversible processes provide the benchmark for real-world irreversible processes (Ellerman, 1984, p. 246).

Hence, in a very narrowly defined sense, in a social theory of value money *is* value; but precisely because it is socially constituted, its invariance is not guaranteed by any "natural" ground, and must be continually maintained by further social institutions, such as the development of double-entry accounting and financial institutions such as banks. (This sets the social theory of value apart from all previous theories of value, which parlay a skepticism over invariance of the monetary unit into an exile of money from the theory of value. See Mirowski, 1989.) The possibility of mutual gain outside of a zero-sum game in a market economy is to be ultimately attributed to the expansion of the monetary unit, especially through debt creation, which gives rise to irreversible trading schemes through time. However, from the vantage point of the participants, the proximate cause of profit is the attribution of property rights to the proliferation of newly created assets and liabilities in their own balance sheets. This stress on the importance of the legal setting of the algebra of double-entry accounting is derived from Ellerman (1986), although it can be traced back to the work of John R. Commons in the 1930s. What was missing from the older institutionalist tradition, however, was a model that expressed how this expansion of value at the individual level is constrained by the social structures at the level of the market system.

V. Market graphs and the value system

In order to develop the ideas broached in the previous section, we shall draw upon the work of Ellerman (1984, 1988) in formalizing what he calls "market graphs." A *directed graph* $\zeta = \{\zeta_0, \zeta_1, t, h\}$ is a set of ζ_0 nodes numbered $1, \ldots, N$, a set ζ_1 of "arcs" or "arrows" numbered

Figure 1   A path from $j = 1$ to $j = n$

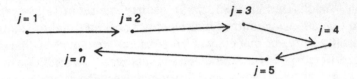

Figure 2   An element of a market graph

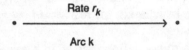

$1, \ldots, L$, and head and tail functions which indicate that arc k is directed from its tail node, $t(j)$, to its head node, $h(j)$ (Wilson, 1985; Roberts, 1978; Rockafellar, 1984). It will be assumed below (for the economic reason that virtual self-exchange has no role in a social theory) that no arc is a loop at a node, that is, $h(j) \neq t(j)$. A path from node $j = 1$ to $j = n$ is a sequence of arcs connected at their heads or tails that reach from node $j = 1$ to node $j = n$ (see Figure 1).

A graph is called "connected" if a path exists between any two nodes. The graph in Figure 1 is connected, as one can see by inspection. A closed circular path where no arc occurs more than once is called a "circuit." Figure 1 does not contain a circuit.

In order to endow graphs with economic significance, we shall associate each generic commodity (already indexed $j = 1, \ldots, N$ as above) with a node, and associate each arc with a possible exchange. In order to discuss the price mechanism, we shall associate each arc $k = 1, \ldots, L$ with a nonzero rational number, r_k, called a "rate." Given any arc k, one unit of the commodity at the tail node can be exchanged for r_k units of the commodity at the head node. At this stage, we have no reason to believe that commodities are intrinsically comparable, so that the r_k values should be regarded as merely notional and speculative (who is doing the speculating will be clarified shortly). (See Figure 2.)

It is the object of this section to show that the introduction of money in conjunction with the presence of other specific social arrangements renders this system of "rates" an algebraic group, or, more specifically, a multiplicative group of the nonzero rational numbers. Moreover, it will only be because of money that each rate will be regarded as reversible: that is, if a path traverses an arc in the opposite direction of the arrow, the rate will be treated as the reciprocal $1/r_k$.

Let us define an ideal situation (i.e., in the presence of money) as one where one can define a composite rate over a path as the product of the relevant rates over the path, $r[\alpha] = \Pi_\alpha\, r_k$. In such a situation, it will be possible to associate a number, p, called a price with each of the nodes/commodities, derived from the set of rates associated with the graph. This triple $\{\zeta, r, p\}$ is what we shall call a "market graph." The important conditions for the existence of such a market graph are that: (1) there are no loops at any node, which means that virtual self-exchange of any commodity is prohibited (this is motivated by the discussion in section II above); (2) the graph ζ must be connected, which means that one can always get to a specific commodity starting at any other (the subject of section III above and some further comments below); and (3) any circuit of exchange that begins and ends at the same commodity results in a composite rate $r[\alpha] = 1$. Under these conditions, Ellerman (1984) proves what he calls the "Cournot–Kirchoff arbitrage theorem" for market graphs:

Cournot–Kirchoff arbitrage theorem: Let $\{\zeta, r, p\}$ be a market graph with $r[\alpha]:\zeta_1 \to T$ taking values in any group T. Then the following conditions are equivalent:

1. There is a price system P derived from the rate system r;
2. The rate system r is path-independent; and
3. The rate system r is arbitrage-free.

This is the fundamental theorem of the social theory of value because it summarizes the conditions under which a market may be considered a *price system* as opposed to a disparate motley of unconnected barter activities. Only when it is always the case that any arbitrary ratio of exchange is consistent with any ratio referring to the same generic commodities but derived from other distinct exchange ratios, can we say that every exchange has calculable implications for every other exchange. This condition is isomorphic to the condition that no arbitrage opportunities are present due to mismatches in the system of prices. Another way of stating this condition is to assert that *value is conserved in the exchange process.*[2]

---

[2] In Mirowski (1989) I asserted that such conservation principles are central to the understanding of the history of Western economic thought. This link to the Cournot–Kirchoff theorem could be considered one more installment in that argument.

Figure 3   An arbitrage-free market graph

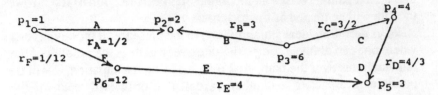

The relationship between the Cournot–Kirchoff theorem and the price system may be rendered more transparent by linking the graph formalism to its matrix representation.[3] Let us define a node–arc incidence matrix S of the graph $\{\zeta_0, \zeta_1, r\}$ as follows:

$$S_{jk} = \begin{cases} r_k & \text{if arc } k \rightarrow \text{node } j; \\ -1 & \text{if arc } k \leftarrow \text{node } j; \\ 0 & \text{otherwise.} \end{cases}$$

The matrix S has dimensions $N \times L$, with the rows representing the nodes/commodities, and the columns representing the arcs/exchange possibilities. If the matrix is descriptive of a market graph meeting all the conditions for the Cournot–Kirchoff theorem, then the rank of S will be equal to $N - 1$. (This is a quick procedure to check for the arbitrage-free condition.) Moreover, let us define a price vector $p = \{p_1, \ldots, p_N\}$ where price p_j is associated with the commodity node indexed j. Then the arbitrage-free system of prices can be solved as follows:

$$pS = p_{j_a} \cdot r_k - p_{j_1} = 0.$$

Of course, the zero price vector is always a trivial solution to this problem, but it should be rejected as the case where a relative price system does not exist. If the product of the price vector and the incidence matrix is nonzero, then those amounts represent the "arbitrage profit" in money terms from making a circuit of exchanges beginning and ending at that particular node.

---

[3] Another advantage of the incidence matrix approach is that it allows the incorporation of certain results from parts of advanced Sraffian analysis without adopting the conventional interpretations of the "standard commodity," etc. (Krause, 1982). For instance, one can show that the Sraffian requirement that the input/output matrix be indecomposable is primarily dictated by the fact that a fully connected incidence matrix is the primary prerequisite of a successful trading system.

Perhaps a numerical example will help demonstrate the intimate relationship between arbitrage theory, directed graphs, and the linear algebra. In Figure 3 we have the graph-theoretic representation of a very simple six-commodity market. The nodes are different commodities numbered from one to six, and labeled with their attached prices. Each arc is labeled with a letter from A to F and with its attendant rate of exchange between the relevant nodes. From inspection, one can see the entire graph consists of a single circuit; also by inspection one can tell it is arbitrage-free since the composition of rates around the entire circuit multiplies to unit, that is:

$$r[\alpha] = (1/2)\ (1/3)\ (3/2)\ (4/3)\ (1/4)\ (12) = 1.$$

The entire structure of the graph can be expressed in its corresponding node–arc incidence matrix:

	A	B	C	D	E	F	
1	−1	0	0	0	0	−1	⇐k
2	1/2	3	0	0	0	0	
3	0	−1	−1	0	0	0	
4	0	0	3/2	−1	0	0	
5	0	0	0	4/3	4	0	
6	0	0	0	0	−1	1/12	
⇑							
j							

Solving for $pS = 0$, we arrive at the price vector,

$$p = [1, 2, 6, 4, 3, 12],$$

which corresponds to the prices attached to each of the nodes.

What sort of economy is described by this formalism? Prices are adjusted through system bids and offers in order to attempt to achieve a system of reversible, arbitrage-free exchange with a positive price vector **p***, which can be found by solving **p*S** = 0. Traders do not engage in this activity out of benevolence, but rather in self-interested (but *not* maximizing!) pursuit of arbitrage profits.

Far from being a simple mechanical calculation, the persistent attempt to reconcile money prices with ratios of commodity quantities and to attain the "arbitrage-free" state is the very core of an institutionalist value theory. This model describes a system that is both "intentional," in the sense that numerous social institutions from the standardized weights and measures to the monetary authority all strive to structure the value unit, and also "unintentional," in that the mathematical structure of the value system falls out of the persistent individual attempts to make arbitrage gains in trade. The arbitrage-free state thus arrived at embodies what classical economists tried to express as the conservation of value in exchange. These conservation principles are built in at the very foundations of double-entry accounting practices; hence, the approach of actual exchange relationships to the accounting system is the very definition of a stable unit of value.

VI. Against equilibrium

Given the almost neurotic concern of orthodox mathematical economics with the physical metaphor of "equilibrium," it may be appropriate here to insist that in no case should the vector **p*** be regarded as an equilibrium price vector in this theory.[4] While absence of further arbitrage opportunities would signal a fully path-independent system within its own terms, real-time approach to that state would inevitably alter the underlying r_k values, and consequently the resulting **p***. The "law of one price" has never made much sense in a dynamic context in orthodox theory, and much the same situation holds here (Bausor, 1986).

It may help to recall who is responsible for the r_k values, which provide the raw material for the Cournot–Kirchoff theorem. From one potential point of view, the r_k is the only psychological term in the entire theory, representing the conjectures of individuals with regards to the exchange ratios they might achieve within the limited ambit of their "social traffic." If this indeed were so, then the full social theory of value would require concatenation of the social traffic matrix with the node–arc incidence matrix, along the lines of the matrix Ω:

$$\Omega = \begin{bmatrix} \overline{z}_1 & S^1 \\ \overline{z}_2 & S^2 \\ \cdot & \\ \cdot & \\ \cdot & \\ \overline{z}_m & S^m \end{bmatrix}$$

[4] Or to address those of mathematical bent directly: there is no sense in trying to turn $pS = 0$ into some sort of difference or differential equation, and then applying Liapunov techniques, nonlinear dynamics, or any other faddish device taken over from physics to it. On this related issue, see Mirowski, 1990b.

where $\bar{z}_i$ represents the ith row of the matrix z, distributed along the diagonal of a square matrix of order $N \times N$ with zeroes on the off-diagonal, and S^m is the node–arc incidence matrix for each individual, indexed $1, \ldots, m$. One could then apply the Cournot–Kirchoff theorem to the matrix Ω, but it should already be apparent that there is little reason to think that the prior conditions of connectivity would hold, given our discussion in section III. It would be prudent, rather, to conclude that one cannot depend upon some mechanical adjustment procedure applied to individual psychologies to succeed in explaining market coordination.

An alternative interpretation of the r_k values is to regard them as the conjectures of various trade coordinators (as identified by their locations in the z matrix) in their relationships with one another. These coordinators would be responsible for enforcing the invariance of price in their locality with regard to the larger public, as well as for forging the connectivity of the market graph (hence the prevalence of "sticky" price behavior among such units). But even in this instance we should not expect to find true invariance. The intrinsic fluidity of the system militates against any strict causal directionality from the r_k values to the reigning prices.

Consequently, the "arbitrage-free" state is never realized in a capitalist system. Its existence would demand a stasis not encouraged within the system, and in any event would imply that globally trade was a zero-sum game, and therefore would rule out the existence of profit generated at the system level. Instead, the various macro determinants of system expansion discussed in section IV persistently perturb trade away from any approximation to the arbitrage-free state and feed back upon the definition of the subsequent state. Thus, prices never "approach" any fixed or deterministic point, and time series of prices will inevitably appear stochastic from the perspective of both the actors and the economic analyst. But does this then imply that the system wanders aimlessly? Why have we bothered with the whole formalism of market graphs, social traffic matrices, and all the rest?

These questions bring us to the "postmodern" character of the social theory of value. Economists seem to think that "models" exist to capture the reality of the situation in which the economic actor finds himself embedded. This unobtrusive postulate of a fixed reality, independent of the interpretative engagement of human beings, has undoubtedly been fostered by the persistent tendency of economists to imitate physicists and their models. The role of our mathematics is different: it is intended to describe the interpretative structures of modern market institutions without implying that these structures are permanent, inevitable, or deterministic. This "model" exists to give an impression of what it is like to "read" the economy without presuming there is a single fixed text to be read, or a single correct interpretation at which we can arrive.

Hence, the function of the mathematics of market graphs is not to describe the prices that actually exist, but to explain why prices are constituted as a field over the rational numbers. The numerical character of prices is an artifact of the way our society has evolved for "reading" the consequences of our actions in the economic sphere: so I have opted to purchase this stereo system? The price system then provides a way for me to "read" the consequences of this action for any other actions I may take. The consequences range from the rather banal (with my salary, I am not able to buy a computer this month, or even next month) to some rather subtle cues. They include:

a.   The effect of my purchase upon the identity of the commodity is disregarded in the process of exchange.
b.   Buying nothing is treated as costing me nothing.
c.   Prices over time and space can be added, but the order in which the items are presented for purchase are not treated as having an impact upon the sum total paid for them.
d.   If it is possible to "return" the item, then the net result should be zero.

The assertion is not that any of these principles are "true"; indeed, for most people in most instances, they are not. The point is rather that in order to read the consequences of our actions, some forms of change have to be ignored, or bracketed, or exiled to the margins of the text. Something must be treated as effectively invariant, even as we know all along it is not. In this sense, the price system should be situated upon the same epistemic level as double-entry bookkeeping (if indeed they are not merely two sides of the same historical phenomenon); the mathematics merely makes this more transparent.

VII. The fundamentally stochastic character of the economy

How is it possible that market actors live a schizophrenic existence of treating value as if it were invariant, and yet are also fully cognizant that they cannot depend upon the invariants? This question leads us into the realm of probability theory and its intimate relationship with the social theory of value.

The biggest source of disruption to value invariants is also the primary economic motivation in a market system: the pursuit of profit. At the aggregate level, there is a trade-off between the expansion of value through debt creation and the breakdown of the value invariant through inflation; the relationship is *socially constructed* and therefore non-mechanical, and thus further social institutions are required to intervene continually to offset one or the other trend. The overriding social problem of all market-oriented societies is to find some means to maintain the working fiction of a monetary invariant through time, so that debt contracts (the ultimate locus of value creation, as indicated above) may be written in terms of the unit at different dates.

This can be thought of as a "homeostatic system": fluctuations in the underlying value unit are unavoidable in a system of private contracts, both because anyone can charge a "time premium," and because the arbitrage-free state is never attained, so everyone is calculating with faulty prices. Nevertheless, if debt creation is kept within certain limits, the system functions as if a value invariant exists. It is important to note that, in this system, any time series of specific prices is inherently and irreducibly stochastic: unlike in neoclassical "efficient markets theory," the fluctuations are not due to external "noise" superimposed upon "fundamentals," but to the internal operation of the value system. Such an alternative metaphor for what the market does may be more attractive in a period that acknowledges that the earlier reconciliation of the image of equilibrium with stochastic ideas has failed (Leroy, 1989).

It is possible to link the social theory of value to the findings of Benoit Mandelbrot (1963a, 1963b) that price distributions do not generally conform to Gaussian stories of the separation of "noise" from signal (Mirowski, 1990b). The task of a social theory of value would then be to reconcile "arbitrage theory"—that is, the conviction that prices can be brought closer to their underlying determinants or coherency conditions—with the knowledge that the underlying determinants are not given by nature, but are constituted by the very process of exchange itself, and therefore are intrinsically stochastic.

The crowning achievement of a social theory of value would be to demonstrate that the very axioms of probability are themselves not innate, but rather are jointly constructed with the value system as part of the operation of markets described above. Following a hint in Eller-man (1984, p. 254), and building from the insights of de Finetti (1974), we can show that the conventional Kolmogorov axioms of probability theory (namely, $0 \leq P(x) \leq 1$; $P(\Omega) = 1$; and $P(x \cup y = P(x) + P(y))$ can be derived from the simple requirement of "coherence" in betting: that is, the "arbitrage-free" condition extended to all monetary wagers. Here "risk" is a socially constructed concept (Douglas, 1985) in the sense that the existence of an arbitrage-free value unit plus the requirement that actors not allow "Dutch books" to be made persistently against them teaches market participants to behave in the aggregate as if the Kolmogorov axioms described the world of uncertainty that they face. Again, this condition is only approached, and never attained, which is why so many neoclassical researchers have "discovered" that individuals in control situations do not "obey" the laws of probability in a von Neumann–Morgenstern framework. In an institutionalist theory of value, probability theory is relegated to the same epistemic level as double-entry bookkeeping: while not "true," it is the pragmatic instrumentality by which market transactors reckon their gains and losses. Thus, the laws of probability are intimately bound up with a money economy, not because people's neurons come hard-wired for the Kolmogorov axioms, but rather because the axioms are simply one more projection of the arbitrage-free conditions in a social theory of value.

REFERENCES

Anderson, Benjamin. *Social Value.* New York: Kelley, 1966 [1911].

Bausor, Randall. "Time and Equilibrium." In *The Reconstruction of Economic Theory,* P. Mirowski, ed. Boston: Kluwer, 1986.

Bergé, Claude, and Ghouli-Houri, A. *Programming, Games and Transportation Networks.* New York: Wiley, 1962.

Clower, Robert. *Money and Markets.* New York: Cambridge University Press, 1984.

Davidson, Paul. *Money and the Real World,* 2d ed. New York: Wiley, 1978.

Debreu, Gerard. "Economic Theory in a Mathematical Mode." *American Economic Review,* 1984, *74,* 267–278.

de Finetti, Bruno. *Theory of Probability.* New York: Wiley, 1974.

de Jong, Frits. *Dimensional Analysis for Economists.* Amsterdam: North Holland, 1967.

Douglas, Mary. *Risk Acceptability According to the Social Sciences.* New York: Russell Sage, 1985.

———. *How Institutions Think.* Syracuse, NY: Syracuse University Press, 1986.

Durbin, John. *Modern Algebra,* 2d ed. New York: Wiley, 1985.

Eckalbar, John. "Money, Barter and Convergence to Competitive Allocation." *Journal of Economic Theory,* 1984, *32,* 201–211.

Ellerman, David. "Arbitrage Theory: A Mathematical Introduction." *SIAM Review,* 1984, *26,* 241–261.

———. "Appropriation and Property Theory." In *The Reconstruction of Economic Theory,* P. Mirowski, ed. Boston: Kluwer, 1986.

582 JOURNAL OF POST KEYNESIAN ECONOMICS

————. "An Arbitrage Interpretation of Classical Optimization." Unpublished manuscript, Tufts University, 1988.

Grossman, I., and Magnus, W. *Groups and Their Graphs*. New York: Mathematics Association of America, 1964.

Heilig, Klaus. "The Dutch Book Argument Reconsidered." *British Journal for the Philosophy of Science*, 1978, *29*, 325–346.

Krause, Ulrich. *Money and Abstract Labour*. London: NLB Verso, 1982.

Kula, Witold. *Measures and Men*. Princeton, NJ: Princeton University Press, 1986.

Leroy, Stephen. "Efficient Capital Markets and Martingales." *Journal of Economic Literature*, 1989, *27*, 1583–1621.

Luce, H., and Narens, L. "Measurement Theory." In *The New Palgrave*, ed. J. Eatwell, et al. London: Macmillan, 1987.

Mandelbrot, Benoit. "New Methods in Statistical Economics." *Journal of Political Economy*, 1963a, *71*, 421–440.

————. "The Variation of Certain Speculative Prices." *Journal of Business*, 1963b, *36*, 394–419.

Mirowski, Philip. "Mathematical Formalism and Economic Explanation." In *The Reconstruction of Economic Theory*, P. Mirowski, ed. Boston: Kluwer, 1986.

————. *Against Mechanism*. Totawa, NJ: Rowman and Littlefield, 1988.

————. *More Heat Than Light: Economics as Social Physics, Physics as Nature's Economics*. New York: Cambridge University Press, 1989.

————. "Learning the Value of a Dollar: Conservation Principles and the Social Theory of Value," *Social Research*, 1990a, *57*, 687–717.

————. "From Mandelbrot to Chaos in Economic Theory." *Southern Economic Journal*, 1990b, pp. 289–307.

————. "The How, the When and the Why of Mathematics in Economics." *Journal of Economic Perspectives*, 1991, forthcoming.

Osborne, D. "On Dimensional Invariance." *Quantity and Quality*, 1978, *12*, 75–89.

Ostroy, J. "Money and General Equilibrium Theory." In *The New Palgrave*, ed. J. Eatwell, et al. London: Macmillan, 1987.

Ostroy, J., and Starr, R. "Money and the Decentralization of Exchange." *Econometrica*, 1974, *42*, 1093–1113.

Roberts, Fred. *Graph Theory and Applications to Problems of Society*. Philadelphia: SIAM, 1978.

————. *Measurement Theory*. Reading, MA: Addison-Wesley, 1979.

Rockafellar, R. T. *Network Flows and Monotropic Optimization*. New York: Wiley, 1984.

Rosen, Joe. "Fundamental Manifestations of Symmetry in Physics." *Foundations of Physics*, 1990, *20*, 283–307.

Schick, Frederick. "Dutch Bookies and Money Pumps." *Journal of Philosophy*, 1986, *83*, 112–119.

Swamy, M., and Thulasiraman, K. *Graphs, Networks and Algorithms*. New York: Wiley, 1981.

Wilson, Robin. *An Introduction to Graph Theory*, 3d ed. Essex: Longman, 1985.

Part III
Rules and Norms

[10]

Microeconomics, Norms, and Rationality*

Alexander James Field
University of Santa Clara

I. Introduction

A divergence of views among microeconomists in general and game theorists in particular regarding the explanatory objectives of microeconomic theory has become apparent in recent years. This divergence concerns, most fundamentally, the question whether institutions, legal or customary rules, or social norms are to be classified among the endogenous as opposed to the exogenous variables in the framework of microeconomic analysis.[1] The majority of economists are probably agnostic or ambivalent on this question, not having confronted, or not having had to confront, the issue in their own work. Many have sidestepped it by treating institutions as immutable or by restricting their analyses to a given rule regime. But rules do vary and change, and among those who are concerned with studying variation in institutions, two diverging views are increasingly identifiable, sometimes coexisting even within the writings of the same author.

The first sees game theory (and microeconomic theory in general) as an analytical device useful for considering the comparative incentive features of (and corresponding outcomes associated with) different institutional regimes, regimes that might be changed in one's capacity as a policymaker or that have varied in fact as the result of differential historical development in different regions. The second position accepts this statement of the objectives of microeconomic theory vis-à-vis institutions for the short run but takes it as the ultimate task of microeconomic and game theory to provide a dynamic theory of the origin, persistence, and change of institutions, using a model that does not make appeal to "ad hoc" exogenously specified rules or norms.

This second position greatly expands the scope of microeconomic analysis and makes work consistent with the first position seem limited by comparison. Whereas the first approach concerns itself only with the consequences of institutional variation, the second addresses causes as well. Theoretical frameworks must nevertheless be judged not only according to what they promise but also according to what they deliver. Work consistent with the second position has not, by and large, delivered what it has promised.[2] This paper investigates some of the reasons why this has been true. In particular, it is argued that if one accepts the second position in its extreme form,[3] the analytical structure of microeconomic theory begins to unravel, in the sense that one is left with no consistent explanation of why the world does not degenerate into a war of all against all.

An implication of this paper is that the contribution microeconomic theory offers to the analysis of institutional variation lies primarily in work consistent with the first position: comparative exercises where rules are varied and the impact on endogenous variables (such as output and prices) is investigated, but where adherence to basic rules in each of the cases compared is taken as given or as accounted for by forces outside the model.[4] The more limited objective of work consistent with this first view, that is, the absence in such work of a general theory of the causes of institutional variation, does not necessarily render it deficient any more than the absence in economic theory of explanations for the origin, persistence, and possible change of individual preferences should necessarily be viewed as a deficiency of such theory. In any social scientific model, defining what is not to be explained is an essential part of delineating what is to be explained.

A common critical approach to microeconomic theory has been to accept the proposition that the theory embodies a methodological individualist approach in an extreme form and then to criticize or reject methodological individualism and thus, derivatively, microeconomic theory.[5] This paper adopts a different strategy and suggests that the problem lies not so much with the "true" structure of the theory, but rather with the perception of its structure.[6] Markets require and presuppose certain fundamental relations of predictability in the actions of economic agents, which can be thought of as the constitutive rules of the market. These rules form part of the description of a market game. Although they may change (for reasons understood imperfectly), they cannot, or at least all of them cannot, usefully be thought of as arising as the result of previous plays of the game in which they did not prevail. The rules of any game—"cooperative" or "noncooperative" (these terms have very specific meanings in game theory)—define both what can be varied in pursuit of one's interest and what cannot. The outcome of a "noncooperative" chess game and the particular sequence of moves leading up to it are not specified in advance; the rules do, however, constrain the movements of various pieces. Similarly, neither the outcome nor the entire sequence of actions in a market game is specified in detail by its rules. Nevertheless, the assumption of privately owned endowments does form part of the description of the game, as do the prohibitions against theft and fraud. In any persisting

Alexander James Field 685

market game, whether interpreted as a cooperative or a noncooperative game, the fundamental legal and customary rules that define it are not subject to bargaining, in the sense that at least a large fraction of individual agents exclude from consideration the option of failing to abide by such rules as part of the range of possibilities open to them for improving their welfare. In other words, these rules confront individuals as one contributor to the constraints they face, constraints also influenced by technologies, endowments, preferences, and the decisions of others. Why agents rule out such possibilities for rule violation is an important question, but such behavior does not necessarily follow from the kind of instrumental means-end calculations assumed to take place within these rules.

It is not material for the purposes of this essay whether these rules are actually perceived as such, nor does this essay take a position on whether these rules or structures have their origin in genetic endowments, as the sociobiologists would have it, or are viewed as culturally or historically given, or represent a particularly human capability voluntarily to recognize imperatives of moral obligation. But the assumption that some system of rules, norms, or structures persists is an analytical necessity if microeconomic theory or game theory is to be undertaken within the empirical context of stable political and social orders. The structure of the logical argument in favor of this proposition might be called, instead of reductio ad absurdum, reductio ad anarchia. It consists, in its barest form, of the following syllogism:

PROPOSITION 1: If one views the world as consisting of self-interested agents unconstrained by rules or norms, or norm-like phenomena, there exists no explanation for why the world does not degenerate into a Hobbesian war of all against all.

PROPOSITION 2: One frequently observes stable social existence.

CONCLUSION: If the behavioral principle of social science models is to be self-interest maximization, and one wishes to model stable social orders, one must posit logically anterior rules or norms that help define the constraints and, thus, the arena within which such maximization takes place.[7]

Not all economists accept this argument. At his most polemical, Gary Becker clearly disagrees:

> . . . economists cannot resist the temptation to hide their own lack of understanding behind allegations of irrational behavior, unnecessary ignorance, folly, ad hoc shifts in values, and the like, which is simply acknowledging defeat under the guise of considered judgment. . . . Naturally, what is tempting to economists nominally committed to the economics approach becomes irresistible to others without a commitment to the scientific study of sociology, psychology or anthropology. With an ingenuity worthy of admiration if put to better use, almost any conceivable behavior is alleged to be dominated by ignorance and irra-

tionality, values and their frequent unexplained shifts, custom and tradition, the compliance somehow induced by social norms or the ego and
the id.[8]

An example suggested by Becker of the type of explanation emanating
from those who lack "a commitment to scientific study" is the claim
that "businessmen talk about the social responsibilities of business
because their attitudes are said to be influenced by public discussions
rather than because such talk is necessary to maximize their profits
given the climate of public interventionism."[9] To the extent that "social responsibility" encompasses adhering to corporate codes of ethics, Becker directly questions the sincerity of statements such as the
following from David Rockefeller in an issue of the *Hofstra Law Review:*

> A moral foundation is imperative in a free society that affords each
> individual the latitude for independent thought and action. Without ethi-
> cal values a free society would become a jungle. . . . Ethical principles
> are the glue that holds a business system of free enterprise together.
> Business runs on mutual trust and confidence that others will live up to
> their word. The marketplace, which is the heart of a human society,
> could not exist without it.[10]

There is no a priori reason to believe that this statement, which
accompanied a call for adherence to corporate codes of ethics, reflects,
as Becker would have it, the individual profit-maximizing strategy.
Adherence to ethical norms may be "reasonable" and socially desirable, but it does not necessarily follow from instrumental means-ends
calculations. Some businessmen and economists view statements such
as Rockefeller's (whether accompanied by adherence or not) as representing appeasement of naive or malevolent reformers, and argue that
the only good defense against such reformers is a good offense in which
the need for corporate codes of ethics is denied: that strategy indeed,
tends increasingly to dominate discussion.[11] Justifying rule violation
(e.g., bribery) on the grounds that it is an "efficient" solution (both the
briber and the bribee are made better off), many businessmen and
professionals neglect or deny responsibility for the corrosive effect of
such behavior in the aggregate on adherence to the Rule of Law.[12] As
will become apparent, it is difficult to counter such conclusions with
arguments that stress only the self-interest of the individuals involved.
Nevertheless, Becker seems to deny on a priori grounds the possibility
that Rockefeller might mean what he says—that there can be such a
thing, as Charles Fried puts it, as a "moral cause."[13]

In addition to questioning the sincerity of businessmen who might
publicly support corporate codes of ethics, Becker comes close to
attacking the scholarly integrity of those who, for example, might at-

tribute compliance to rules as in part the result of adherence to social norms. But in a more restrained passage of the work quoted above Becker identifies the economic approach with three key assumptions: (a) the assumption of maximizing behavior, (b) the assumption that markets exist, and (c) the assumption that individuals have stable preferences over the psycho-physiological states induced by consumption of goods and services, preferences which do not differ substantially across social class or region.[14] The second assumption is the most interesting from the standpoint of this paper. If by assuming that "markets exist" Becker takes as given adherence to the fundamental legal or customary framework within which exchanges take place, then very little separates his position from that advanced here. But what ensures compliance with these rules in his model?[15] As the quoted passage indicates, he is disdainful of any explanation that relies on adherence to norms. Since much of Becker's work appears to involve the application of strictly individualistic cost-benefit calculations to behavior one might otherwise believe to be constrained, at least in part, by rules or norms, there is an obvious tension in Becker's analysis between positions 1 and 2. This tension is observable, as will become apparent, also in the writings of Walras and of some game theorists today.

John Harsanyi, for example, in criticizing the work of Talcott Parsons, argues that "social norms should not be used as basic explanatory variables in analyzing social behavior, but rather should be themselves explained in terms of peoples' individual objectives and interests."[16] A number of game theorists, rising to this challenge and recognizing what is taken for granted in the assumption of a "cooperative" game, now see the task of game theory to be the demonstration of how "cooperative" games are the outcomes of, or are embedded in, "noncooperative" games. Two objections can be raised against this line of attack, insofar as it is designed to produce a theory of social organization that avoids reference to culturally or genetically determined norms. First, even "noncooperative" games contain, as part of their description, certain rules adherence to which is assumed as part of the analysis. Although *additional* cooperation is precluded by the assumption that the game is "noncooperative," the very fact that interaction can be described and perceived as a game is evidence of a rudimentary structure of interaction. Chess is not described by game theorists as a cooperative game; certain moves are, nevertheless, considered to be "illegal." Pocketing one's opponent's rook when it threatens one's queen may dramatically improve one's chances of winning, but is ruled out of discussion in considerations of chess strategy. Second, a common theoretical device in the attempt to derive "cooperative outcomes" from "noncooperative" games has been to assume that the noncooperative game is repeated.[17] Is it not just as ad hoc to assume, without explanation, that a game is repeated, as it is to assume that binding (enforceable) contracts can be entered into while it is being played (one of the key distinguishing features of "cooperative" games)? Yet some game theorists appear to deny this.

If Becker, Harsanyi, and others with similar views are correct, the work of microeconomic theorists for the next couple of decades is cut out. The task must be to show how phenomena previously explained as the result of nonrational behavior or the operation of such ad hoc devices as social norms in fact result from the rational interaction of freely choosing self-interested individuals unconstrained by such norms. If the constraining influence of rules or laws, at least in the short run, is to be granted (and it is hard not to do this) then the choice of these rules or laws as opposed to others is what must be explained as the result of interacting, freely choosing individuals. A great deal of recent work in microeconomic theory has been motivated by such methodological objectives, and this research program is increasingly attractive to a minority in such noneconomic disciplines as political science, sociology, psychology, anthropology, and philosophy.[18]

This paper argues that not only preferences, technologies, and endowments, but also certain additional exogenous variables, need to be taken as given within the framework of microeconomic analysis. Among these are language and the human predisposition (whether genetically, culturally, or individualistically explained) to adhere to law or custom when others do so, even when there are individual incentives to do otherwise. In a limited number of cases involving regulative rules, game theory suggests how the existence of shared language and the possibility of communication could explain why some rather than others of a set of possible norms or rules have emerged. But interagent communication is only part of what distinguishes political order from political chaos and only part of what, in game-theory terms, distinguishes a "cooperative" from a "noncooperative" game. The ability to make binding contracts in a cooperative game is at least equally important in distinguishing it from a noncooperative one. The capability and willingness to make such contracts presuppose agreement on a more fundamental set of rules, and the assumption of interagent communication alone cannot account for why or how the norms or rules making possible such agreements emerge or are selected.

II. Microeconomics, Game Theory, and Norms

Microeconomic theory has traditionally been subdivided into a theory of nonstrategic interaction, the theory of general competitive equilibrium in a market economy first developed in its modern form by Leon Walras, and a theory of strategic interaction,[19] a subset of the theory of games developed initially by John von Neumann and Oskar Morgenstern.[20] In the Walrasian model, no one agent believes that varying the quantity of any output or input individually demanded or supplied will

Alexander James Field 689

affect prices or quantities for the system as a whole. Walras captured this aspect of a market economy by assuming that agents placed their orders after hearing an announced price vector that they could not alter, although no actual trades were to take place until an equilibrium vector was found. Total excess demands and supplies for the economy guided the auctioneer through a sequence of announced price vectors and orders as the system "groped" toward an equilibrium price vector, at which these excess demands and supplies were eliminated. Through the metaphor of the auctioneer and tatônnement, Walras was able both to have prices confront the individual as external and beyond influence and in the aggregate to have them reflect the joint desires and capabilities of the collectivity. The theory of strategic interaction, by contrast, has been concerned with the examination of behavior and outcomes in situations (such as an oligopolistic noncompetitive market) where one agent's actions may directly depend on and in turn influence the actions and payoffs of other agents.

In recent years the competitive/game-theoretic, nonstrategic/strategic-interaction dichotomies have become less distinct as an entirely different (non-Walrasian) approach to competitive equilibrium has developed. This approach stems from the work of Francis Edgeworth and embodies the assumption that final allocations are reached as the result of bargaining over quantities within the context of a cooperative game, that is, a game in which direct communication is possible and players can make "binding" contracts among themselves. Edgeworth originally analyzed a two-person, two-good bargaining game, each player endowed with certain quantities of each good and having preference orderings over them.[21] He demonstrated that there usually exists a set of possible trades that share the attributes (*a*) that each player is not made worse off than in the absence of trade and (*b*) that there are no trades more beneficial to both. This *core* of an exchange economy has been more formally defined as redistributions of the total endowment that no group of agents (or single agent in a two-person game) can improve upon.[22] Edgeworth also showed that if one increases the numbers of the two types of players (with identical endowments and preferences within each type), the core of this exchange economy would shrink to the Walrasian equilibrium (or equilibria, if nonunique).[23] That is, in the unique equilibrium case, the exchanges that take place in the Edgeworth scheme will be identical to those induced by the Walrasian equilibrium price vector.

About the existence both of language and of a normative legal or customary structure in the Edgeworthian story there can be no doubt, because it models a competitive exchange economy as a *cooperative* game.[24] The two most important features which definitionally distinguish "cooperative" from "noncooperative" games are (1) the possibility of interagent communication and (2) the assumption that binding (i.e., enforceable) contracts can be made.[25] As soon as one assumes that one is operating within a "cooperative" game, two of the most fundamental prerequisites of social organization—shared language and the enforceability of agreements where there are incentives to violation—have been taken as givens: their origins, perforce, cannot be elucidated by analysis of the process or outcome of a cooperative game.

Obviously, one also needs a shared language in the Walrasian story. But the status of legal or customary rules in the Walrasian version is more problematic. Werner Hildebrand terms the Walrasian equilibrium concept "noncooperative,"[26] distinguishing it from the "cooperative" core concept, but this does not satisfactorily dispose of the issue. Walras himself was unclear about the analytical status of institutions or rules in his model, although there are passages that unambiguously demonstrate that he assumed four categories of exogenous variables in his system: tastes, technologies, endowments, *and* rules.[27] Logically, this seems the only way to make sense of the apparatus of the auctioneer and the implicit assumption of privately owned endowments. In *Foundations of Economic Analysis,* Paul Samuelson recognizes the importance of this fourth category of exogenous variable,[28] but in several other important expositions institutions get remarkably little emphasis. Bent Hansen, for example, fails to mention institutions or rules in his *Survey of General Equilibrium Systems*:[29] there is no entry in the index for anything even vaguely related to these concepts. Government appears only late in the book, when money is introduced, and then only as the agency that fixes the stock of this commodity. A reader may emerge from such expositions with a less than clear understanding of the importance (or at a minimum, the debate over the importance) of exogenously specified rules, norms, or institutions in determining (along with tastes, technologies, and endowments) a general equilibrium. A similar neglect is evident in Gerard Debreu's *Theory of Value.*[30]

One of the often emphasized advantages of the limited rules associated with a Walrasian competitive economy has been its purported economizing both on rule formation and on transactions costs of exchange. The existence of a universally known price vector avoids the complicated higgling and haggling of an N-person Edgeworth economy or the elaborate and specific rules necessary in a command economy undertaking reallocation of resources by central directive. Moreover, if endowments or technologies change (creating disequilibria in the form of excess demands of supplies), information concerning the needed direction of quantity adjustment is "automatically" communicated to all market participants through variation in the price vector, enabling individuals to coordinate their plans so as to avoid unfilled demands or unsold output.

Alexander James Field 691

An example can illustrate the posited adjustment mechanisms. Suppose an economy to consist of only two regions (agents). In the first instance, each region places demands and offers supplies according to a pattern which corresponds to self-sufficiency. A new transport technology now becomes available, drastically lowering the cost of transportation between the two regions. Markets will no longer clear at the previous price levels, and excess supplies will show up at previously equilibrating input prices and (region-specific) output prices. The auctioneer will grope for a new equilibrium by offering a slightly different set of prices, with lower region-specific output prices for the affected commodities. Given different regional endowments, the adjustment to a new interregional regime of specialization will be automatically coordinated by the change in the equilibrium price vector.

The automaticity of this market adjustment process, however, depends on the auctioneer, on the mutually agreed-on respect for privately owned endowments, and on the fulfillment of promises to supply certain amounts of such endowments at certain prices. The fact that the Walrasian market game involves a solution concept that is in strict game-theoretic terms "noncooperative" does not mean that it is a game played without rules any more than the fact that chess is a "noncooperative" game means that one can ignore its rules in understanding or predicting its sequence of moves.

In discussions of market interaction, where the basic constitutive rules of the market are presupposed, it is not usually necessary to make explicit reference to the concept of rules or norms in explaining why the game ends as it does: one need only appeal to individuals pursuing their own self-interests given the structure of the situation as it is presented to them. But the outcomes "explained" using these models are just as conditional on the basic rules of the game as they are on technologies, preferences, endowments, or the behavioral assumption of utility or profit maximization. There is nothing mystical about the coordination capabilities of a market: those capabilities inhere in its rules.

To what degree, however, can the analytical techniques of game theory be used to explain why certain rule structures prevail rather than others? That is, do observed rules tend to represent "efficient" solutions to problems presented by prevailing resource, preference, and technological environments? A response to this question requires some subtle distinctions. In the case of a limited number of regulative rather than constitutive rules, the answer is affirmative. These rules are regulative in the sense that the posited choice among rules presupposes shared language as well as a prevailing more fundamental set of rules. Insofar as the origins of language or of the more fundamental constitutive rules of a group or society are concerned, the answer is negative, or at least that is the argument of this paper.[31] Section III begins by considering the choice of certain kinds of regulative rules, which correspond to solutions of games of coordination. It concludes with a discussion of the limitations of coordination game models with respect to the explanation of the origin of language. Section IV considers why the explanatory program that, in principle, works for problems of coordination does not work for the explanation of the choice of more fundamental constitutive rules (even assuming shared language).

III. Games of Coordination and Regulative Rules That Solve Them

Suppose a group has a basic shared language but is trying to reach agreement on a set of linguistic symbols to correspond to a set of newly encountered phenomena. The problem of selecting such a set of rules of communication is formally analogous to a problem popularized by Thomas Schelling:[32] Suppose two individuals wish to meet in New York. They do not care where they meet but care greatly that they do in fact meet. Assuming only three possible meeting places in New York, each has to choose one of these as his or her destination. The situation has a payoff matrix corresponding to figure 1.

Any combination of a row choice and column choice can be thought of as a rule organizing the behavior of these two individuals. These rules are regulative, not constitutive, in the sense that the structure of the problem presupposes the existence of a stable civil society (i.e., shared language and agreement on fundamental rules). In this case there are nine possible regulative rules, three of which (the on-diagonal elements of the matrix) are Pareto superior to any of the other six (the off-diagonal elements), in the sense that these rules are associ-

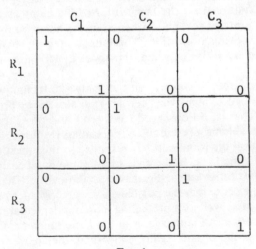

FIG. 1

Alexander James Field   693

ated with payoffs that make both parties better off than they would be under an off-diagonal rule. Once established, any one of these three "efficient" rules presents no incentive to either party to try to create a new rule. There is unfortunately no guarantee that the parties will arrive easily, in the absence of preplay communication, at a rule corresponding to a diagonal element. This is a pure problem of coordination in a game which involves no real conflict of interest. The problem was "solved" (by Schelling) by appeal to a process of socialization undergone by both individuals, which suggested to each of them that the most obvious place to meet (perhaps) was the information booth at Grand Central Station.[33]

Some problems with basically the same formal structure are such questions as what gauge our railroads should have; what side of the road one should drive on; what sublanguages, including computer languages, one should use; where the keys on the typewriter should be located; what system for broadcasting and receiving color television signals should be employed; what our standards of weights and measures should be (metric or otherwise); how large one should make the computer card;[34] what international standard there should be for audio and video cassettes, video discs; and so on. The actual problems of choice among regulative rules are frequently complicated by the fact that they emerge over time, that they do not always involve identical benefits to all parties, and that there is sometimes sunk physical and human capital associated with one or more of the options. But this capital in principle can be included in a social calculus by giving it a definite valuation, at least in terms of current replacement costs, and therefore differs from the invested "capital" that may appear to be associated with the resolution of more fundamental problems, as will become apparent in the next section.

This analysis of rules of coordination seems to offer some support for the proposition that those rule structures that now prevail do so because they are efficient. The prevalence of certain rules rather than others can be explained by reference to their consequences. The rules associated with the three on-diagonal elements in figure 1 are efficient in comparison with those associated with the off-diagonal elements. Suppose in the Schelling problem that the two individuals are not indifferent about which of the three places they meet at: Grand Central Station was in fact preferred to Lincoln Center or the Empire State Building, because the two travelers intended to continue together by train. However, because they had met elsewhere in the past, each could not be sure the other would go to the train station: they were still faced with a dilemma. One can examine this new situation by considering a payoff matrix similar to figure 1, but where the R_2C_2 payoff has been changed to (3, 3).

This is still a *pure game of cooperation*—where the term does not mean that this is necessarily a cooperative game in which communication between the agents is possible and binding contracts can be made, but rather that in any given cell, payoffs to the two agents are equal. (These two uses of similar terms must be carefully distinguished.) Neverthless, as compared with the situation described in figure 1, the R_2C_2 choice is now clearly the optimal rule. Imagine that one observes that a rule yielding the R_2C_2 choice prevails. (Note that one could as well be talking about railway gauges or computer languages as meeting places.) Then, according to a neoclassical institutional economist,[35] who wants to make rule selection and changes endogenous, the explanation for why one observes this rule is that it had been selected *as if* a social maximizer had considered all nine possible rules and had chosen the Pareto-superior one. Recognizing that it is costly to change established patterns, especially if they are embodied in human and physical capital (i.e., the cases of metric conversion, railway gauges, etc.), it does not seem totally unreasonable to hypothesize that in the long run political processes would arise to solve problems of this sort by creating channels of communication and permitting coordination. Indeed, one might define the presence or absence of a political process according to whether or not communication is permitted among the agents. Another way of saying that a political process is likely, in the long run, to solve pure problems of coordination is that the R_2C_2 rule is the one that the agents would quickly arrive at if they were able to communicate.

In the absence of communication, however, there is no automatic mechanism to get one from R_1C_1 or R_3C_3 to R_2C_2. Both parties would obviously prefer to be at the latter point, but may hesitate before abandoning a traditional solution for fear that they will end up in one of the off-diagonal (0, 0) situations. But when the benefits of a new standard, meeting place, or railway gauge exceed those of the current outcome by a margin larger than the cost of conversion, including losses due to equipment or training made unusable by the conversion, then it does not seem totally unreasonable to search for (or indeed create, if one is in a policymaking position) a political process establishing communication and coordination of the move so as to avoid the losses associated with an off-diagonal situation. Solutions to such problems require a somewhat more interventionist auctioneer than Walras described, one who must not only announce price vectors and total orders but also promulgate additional regulative rules, but it is not unreasonable to assume that a political process could solve such problems easily and predictably (especially if compensation can be paid).

The presence or absence of communication is obviously central to the solution of coordination problems, which are problems of establishing conventions. Both the Edgeworth "cooperative" and the Walrasian "noncooperative" versions of the competitive economy also pre-

Alexander James Field 695

suppose the ability of agents to communicate—the former in order that they may negotiate trades, and the latter so that they may understand the meaning of the price vectors *criés au hasard* by Walras's auctioneer. Language is perhaps the most pervasive example of a set of rules organizing interaction (in this case communication) between individuals. To what extent can language itself be viewed as the outcome of a game of coordination in which conventions are established? Consideration of the problem of infinite regress warrants pessimism about such inquiries.

The most serious difficulty with this approach is the lack of explanation for the language that negotiators could use in establishing these conventions. In an amusing but important foreword to David Lewis's book on *Convention*, W. V. O. Quine recollects how he originally conceived of it: "When I was a child I pictured our language as settled and passed down by a board of syndics, seated in grave convention along a table in the style of Rembrandt. The picture remained for a while undisturbed by the question what language the syndics might have used in their deliberations, or by dread of vicious regress."[36]

Quine alludes here to his eventual rejection of the proposition that the rules of language could be understood as if they originated in conventions: as Lewis puts it, Quine concluded that "our use of language conforms to regularities—but no more."[37]

Although one can posit, following Noam Chomsky, that all human beings are born with the genetic capability for mastering the syntax of a language, the rules of any specific language are transmitted culturally from generation to generation as part of the process of socialization: individuals do not rely on a process of negotiation or market interaction to ensure that each new generation in a particular region grows up speaking a similar language. Moreover, historical evidence suggests that linguistic traditions demonstrate remarkable powers of persistence. The explanations for why people in certain wards of Manchester, New Hampshire, or towns in Cape Breton, Nova Scotia, speak French at home rather than English reflect accidents of history and culture rather than rational responses to different resource endowments or technological problems from those faced by their English-speaking neighbors. Although some languages are slightly more flexible in dealing with certain types of communication than others, in general any number of languages can satisfactorily provide a medium of communication, provided all members of the relevant group know them. Whereas it is true that among sets of possible regulative rules designed to solve problems of coordination, efficient ones tend to persist, it is not true that the specific character of a language itself can be explained in the same fashion. A shared basic language is a prerequisite, not an outcome, of the establishment of such conventions.

The rules dealt with in the first part of this section were regulative.

The structure of these problems presupposed the existence of shared language and an otherwise stable, functioning social order. But if the choice among these rule sets can in principle be explained using these techniques, is it not possible that the research program can be extended to explain choice among more fundamental rules and, in the limit, all rule and institutional structures? Doubts have already been raised about the possibility of explaining the origin of language along such lines. Suppose, however, shared language is taken as given. If it were true that political processes arose and operated solely to deal with problems of coordination, then the research program suggested by a neoclassical approach to institutional economics might be quite promising. But to assume that this is true is to assume away most of the important problems of political, economic, and social organization. Coordination problems correspond to games of pure cooperation,[38] and only a limited subset of social rules are designed to solve problems of coordination. As soon as one considers the origin and persistence of rules that provide guarantees against the use of force and fraud, thus providing an environment in which individuals are capable of (and willing voluntarily to enter into) binding contracts, one faces situations where "socially desirable" outcomes are not stable (i.e., there are strong individual incentives to rule violation and thereby rule breakdown). In these cases the explanatory program associated with neoclassical institutional economics runs into obstacles that are probably insurmountable.

IV. Prisoner's Dilemma Rules versus Coordination Rules
The so-called Prisoner's Dilemma has received so much attention that it has almost become a cliché. Cliché or not, the dilemma has not in any way been attenuated by game theorists' familiarity with it. The standard example involves two prisoners[39] (perhaps freedom fighters in a just war) who are faced with the following choices by their captors: if they both confess, they are each sentenced to 5 years in jail; if they both refuse to confess, they are sentenced to 1 year; but if one turns state's evidence and the other does not, the squealer goes free and the other is executed. This creates a payoff matrix in the two-person case which can be represented by figure 2.

What is immediately apparent is that the outcome best for both individuals considered together (the upper left) is not the best for each prisoner considered individually. Moreover, as each prisoner considers the options, he realizes that regardless of what the other decides to do, he will be individually better off choosing the squealer strategy. Unless imbued with very strong norms of solidarity, then, the two prisoners end up in the R_2C_2 situation, in spite of the fact that ex post each prisoner would have been better off individually in two of the remaining outcomes. The problem here is that the presence or absence

Alexander James Field 697

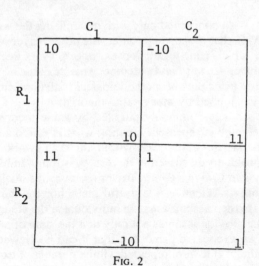

FIG. 2

of preplay communication makes absolutely no difference in the structure of the problem: the temptation to cheat on an agreement apparently makes the game with communication degenerate into exactly the same game that exists without it.

The Prisoner's Dilemma, although it can describe a situation within an established social context, is relevant more generally as a metaphor for the fundamental problem of civil society: How does one escape from the Hobbesian state of nature? Since the fundamental rules which prevent such a war of all against all from developing are among those termed the constitutive rules of society in this paper, it is important to ask whether the emergence of or choice among such rules can be understood as resulting from the actions of freely choosing self-interested individuals unconstrained by such rules. Option 1 can be interpreted as disarming oneself in the expectation that one's opponents will do likewise, trusting others or, in general, letting down one's guard.

There are several ways to "solve" the Prisoner's Dilemma analytically, depending on which outcome one wishes to rationalize. One "solution" is to recognize that self-interest drives each player to a betrayal—because betrayal is the dominant strategy for each player in the single-play case (R_2C_2 is a minimax Nash equilibrium)[40]—throw up one's hands, and conclude on theoretical a priori grounds that a nonbetrayal outcome is impossible. But this is a troubling solution, since one in fact frequently does observe mutual nonbetrayal (R_1C_1 behavior). Another solution is to impose externally a norm of solidarity that permits the agents to reach the upper-left-hand outcome. A solution with equivalent consequences would be to assume that the players are

pure altruists, each concerned only with maximizing the welfare of the
other. Observing that if one keeps quiet, the other player will be better
off no matter which course he chooses, both players keep quiet and
end up with the upper-left-hand outcome. This "explains" nonbetrayal
but violates the principles of methodological individualism as defined
here; thus it is shunned by many game theorists.

Another strategy commonly pursued by game theorists is to assume that the game is repeated, creating what is called a supergame.
One effort in this direction, cast within the framework of some of
the political problems discussed in the essay, is found in Michael Taylor's *Anarchy and Cooperation.*[41] Taylor assumes, as does this paper,
that the Prisoner's Dilemma is a useful metaphor for the Hobbesian
state of war. He then assumes that an individual in the state of nature is
in a supergame: Taylor assumes not only that the state of nature can be
conceived of as a repeated game, but that it can be viewed as a game
repeated infinitely. If it were repeated a finite number of times, a dominant strategy would obviously be to betray on the last play. Since one
could predict the outcome on the last play, the same logic would apply
to the penultimate play, and so on, until one reached the conclusion
that betrayal was the dominant strategy for all plays. In other words,
turning the Prisoner's Dilemma problem into a finitely repeated game
does not change the nature of the dilemma: the dilemma in each iteration of a series is exactly what it would be in an isolated single play
game. Luce and Raiffa recognized this logic but still felt it would be
"reasonable" in the finite-play case to choose strategy 1 in an attempt
to "teach" one's opponent not to defect, responding to defections with
"punishments" in the form of one's own defections. This gets to the
heart of what is meant by "reasonable," but their argument as it stands
is tortuous and ultimately unconvincing, and most subsequent writers,
including Taylor, do not accept it.[42]

By assuming an infinitely repeated game and, at least in chap. 3,
exponential discounting of payoffs, Taylor is able to show that there
exist other pairs of equilibrium strategies (in the sense that once established, neither player has an incentive to deviate) besides the strategy
pair where each player betrays continually.[43] Taylor is not primarily
concerned with the problem of methodological individualism, but
rather with the justification or lack thereof for a coercive state.[44] He
does not limit himself to the case where individuals are assumed to be,
as he puts it, purely egoistic. The central part of his analysis (chap. 3),
however, is conducted under this assumption, including the demonstration that under the aforementioned conditions individuals acting
purely egoistically could attain outcomes other than continuous betrayal.

Can this explanation account for nonbetrayal outcomes and at the
same time preserve the principles of methodological individualism? By

assuming that a state of nature can be represented by an infinitely repeated game, Taylor has already assumed an overall structure of rudimentary nonbetrayal interaction. There is no a priori reason for assuming that a Prisoner's Dilemma game in a state of nature is repeated, let alone infinitely repeated. If one lays down one's guns in pursuit of a nonbetrayal outcome and is annihilated by one's devious opponent, there is no replay. Taylor must implicitly presume some sort of legal or customary structure that prevents his players from exiting prematurely from the series of plays. This seems to be the fundamental difficulty with efforts (by no means limited to Taylor's work) to derive nonbetrayal outcomes as the result of a series of "noncooperative" games and thereby to claim to have explained cooperation without the aid of the ad hoc assumptions associated with a "cooperative" game. The specific game-theoretic meaning of "noncooperative" must always be kept in mind when using this term. "Noncooperative" games are not played without rules.

The Prisoner's Dilemma payoff matrix characterizes a great many situations in which a group (or two people) are jointly better off under a rule organizing their behavior that nevertheless leaves great temptations for rule violations. On some campuses in the United States a bicycle can be left unguarded and unlocked and still be retrieved: on others this is a certain prelude to a visit with one's insurance agent. If members of a group agree not to steal each others' bicycles, they all save the real resources that would othewise be used to purchase locks and chains. But there is a clear incentive (especially if no police force is provided) for each and every individual publicly to support the agreement and privately to appropriate bikes when they need them. If more than a few yield to this temptation, the agreement breaks down, and the upper-left-hand solution (no chains, no thefts) degenerates into the lower-right-hand solution (chains, no thefts).

Much of our legal system has evolved in order to deal with problems of this sort, and although enforcement expenditures generally accompany rules where there are incentives to violation, the maintenance of the nonstealing outcome relies to a great extent on the willingness of a sufficiently large fraction of the population to forgo the temptations of immediate gain. An individual may be willing to do this if he has confidence that a sufficiently large fraction of the rest of the population will act in the same fashion. Similarly, the Internal Revenue Service relies on intimidation and fines to ensure that taxes will be paid, but as their literature points out again and again, the fundamental basis of the system is voluntary compliance. One final example is from the realm of foreign affairs. In 1929, Secretary of State Henry L. Stimson unilaterally closed the joint State Department–War Department Cipher Bureau, explaining that "gentlemen do not read each other's mail," and believing that mutual trust was the best route to world peace.[45] Was Stimson a courageous diplomat or a naive fool? Can a response to this question be made simply on the basis of the analytical structure of the situation?

In a Prisoner's Dilemma situation, even assuming ability to communicate, there can be no presumption that negotiation or a "political process" will get the parties to a nonbetrayal solution. First of all, the socially desirable situation (socially desirable in the bicycle case, if not the Prisoner case) is not Pareto superior. As compared with either of the off-diagonal elements, it makes one party much better off at the expense of another who is made a little worse off. There is absolutely no theoretical presumption based on the behavioral assumption of strict pursuit of self-interest that the political process will succeed in establishing and maintaining an R_1C_1 rule: the social stability resulting from widespread acceptance of norms against theft or physically harming others is always precarious, always subject to disturbance, always subject to the risk that a large number of people in the relevant population will decide to go for short-run gains. Clearly, when all do so and the stability breaks down, they are all worse off. But how does one respond to what one might call the Yossarian argument? In *Catch 22*, an associate begrudges the protagonist his unwillingness to fly combat missions by asking what would happen if everyone felt that way. Yossarian replies that in that case he would "certainly be a damn fool to feel any other way."[46]

The logical and moral problems created by situations of this type would be more amusing were they not so serious. For example, it is commonly argued that one ought to pay taxes because if no one paid, all would suffer. This type of argument by generalization (one should not do *a*, because if all did *a*, it would be disastrous) is however not always valid, as can be seen by substituting "not be an economist" for "pay taxes." The argument that one should not be an economist, because if everyone were an economist we would have nothing to eat, is not a valid argument against joining the profession (although there may be others). Furthermore, the argument in favor of paying taxes is subject to devastating rebuttals, especially if they are used in tandem. First, one can argue that since everyone is going to pay, no one will be the wiser if one cheats. If this argument does not work, one can come back with, "Since no one would be fool enough to pay their taxes, disaster will arrive anyway, and you don't expect me to be a sucker, do you?"[47] Philosophers have wrestled with these normative problems with varying degrees of success, without being able to resolve them. This lack of resolution, in a sense, mirrors the positive indeterminacy of Prisoner's Dilemma outcomes.

Historically, some level of enforcement expenditure (if only to convince those willing to abide by the rule if others do that they will not be suckers) has usually been required to ensure tolerable levels of

Alexander James Field 701

compliance. The problem for the research program set forth by neo-classical institutional economists is that the enforcement costs associated with maintaining a tolerable level of compliance may not be independent of the length of time a rule has been in place, although the functional form relating enforcement costs to rule longevity is not obvious on a priori grounds. In the limit, enforcement costs may drop to zero, and the weight of tradition, through a process understood only imperfectly, may make it simply *unthinkable* for any agent to violate the current practice, in spite of individual incentives to do so.

Suppose one is willing to assume, without explanation, the existence of shared language and of a political process capable of scanning actual and potential organizational blueprints in search of the most "efficient" one. Such a scan could be done on the basis of Benthamite utilitarian principles, with interpersonal comparisons of utility; or it could be done by a Pareto optimizer who respects utility levels associated with some initial resource distributions, or by a Kaldor-Hicks compensator, whether or not he actually pays compensation. Such a political scanner ought in principle to be able to solve regulative problems involving games of coordination. Regardless of which of these (or other) algorithms is used, however, such a program will confront a very serious difficulty when applied to the selection of more fundamental rules. Such rules govern Prisoner's Dilemma—like situations and frequently require expenditures on enforcement to ensure that R_1C_1 behavior does not degenerate into the more stable R_2C_2 outcomes. To the extent that the political scanner does not know these costs, his attempt to select efficient rules will break down, because the true individual payouts associated with various rules under consideration are net of enforcement costs; and without known enforcement costs, one does not know the true payout vector. Deductive logic does not point the way toward knowledge of these costs: a priori theorizing provides no obvious method for assigning probabilities to various levels of enforcement costs. One might be able to assign such probabilities using historical data, but such procedures are inductive and would raise difficulties for those who wish to obtain results using strictly a priori theorizing. What deductive foundation would there be for the persistence of these probabilities?

The cultural or historical conditions that may make it possible to sustain R_1C_1 behavior with relatively low real expenditures on enforcement can be thought of as invested "capital" associated with the existing institutional arrangements. But this "capital" differs from the capital associated, for example, with a narrow-gauge railway in one part of the country, which may have to be torn up and replaced if a different gauge is adopted nationwide. The difference is that one can, given technical or engineering data on the costs of extracting and transforming raw materials, calculate the approximate replacement cost of the

The Economics of Institutions

junked tracks and compare this with what would have to be junked if another gauge were at some time adopted universally. There is no obvious way either analytically or with engineering data to calculate the "replacement" cost of the "capital" associated with the more fundamental rule structures now under consideration. The technology of reconstructing credibility, expectations about future behavior, or more generally, political legitimacy, depends not on predictable physical relationships but on the much less predictable human propensities to forget, to trust, to cooperate. A state of mutual trust is not therefore a commodity, like a locomotive, that can easily be given a market valuation approximating its cost of construction or replacement.

For example, imagine that as the result of institutional innovation or a change in the resource or technological environment, a new organizational option became available—an option which, *if* it could be established as a new rule structure with no increase over current levels of enforcement costs, would be Pareto superior (preferred or tolerated by all parties) to current practice. Is there any presumption that the political process will operate so as to get one to this new position? Conservatives might with good reason suspect that, in reality, a rise in enforcement costs over current levels would be necessary to maintain this newly introduced regime in the context of the disruptions of the changeover, more than wiping out any apparent advantage. Radicals might argue that one could rapidly establish a new "stable order" and move to the level where the original (or even lower) levels of enforcement expenditures were necessary. There is no a priori means of deciding between the conservative and radical arguments; and there is therefore no presumption that the political process would necessarily operate so as to select the most "efficient" rule where elements of conflict exist potentially, because the true payouts associated with the rule depend on knowledge of its enforcement or overhead costs. Such costs may be influenced by longevity of rules; then again they may not: the functional form relating costs to longevity cannot be determined using deductive logic alone.

When considering fundamental constitutive rules, the posited political institution scanner could not be assumed to select "efficient rules," because the true payout vector in these cases could not be known with certainty. This is not necessarily a matter of different attitudes toward risk. Differences between conservatives and radicals, to the extent that they frame their arguments in terms of the good of the collectivity—generally a prerequisite for political discourse—may reflect substantial differences in the perception of uncertain net payoff matrices even in cases where there are no differences in risk preferences. In order to make such a scan theoretically feasible, one would have to assume invariance of "rule abidance willingness" with respect to potential changes in rules. Having made this final assumption, along

Alexander James Field   703

with the assumptions of shared language and a basic political framework, one would find that what began as an attempt to defend the more ambitious second position outlined at the start of this essay, had arrived, through a slow process of attrition, at the first position.

Game theorists sometimes become so enamored of the mechanics of the theory and the single-minded determination of their players to win that they lose sight of what any game-theoretic problem presupposes: the arena in which the players are to compete or cooperate. To give a striking example: von Neumann and Morgenstern demonstrated that it is theoretically possible to develop for the game of chess, as for checkers and other games of perfect information, a theory that would predict what actions a rational opponent interested in winning would undertake given the layout of the board and the next move one makes.[48] But one will not obtain, nor does one expect to obtain from such a theory, an explanation for why knights move in an L-shaped pattern or bishops move diagonally. Similarly, although one can investigate with game theory the dilemmas possibly faced by two prisoners, one should not expect from such a theory an explanation for why escape or insurrection is not part of the strategy space. As has been argued, the arena of any interactive game is partly determined by resources and technologies, but the social norms that pervade the atmosphere are an equally important characteristic of that arena. A Prisoner's Dilemma game where the players are imbued with a strong norm of solidarity may have a different outcome from one where this is lacking The same may be said for a game where the guards share the political objectives of the captives. Even war, on the face of it a complete breakdown of international norms or rules, is in fact conducted according to highly elaborated rules and conventions. Few responsible military personnel maintain that all is fair in war:[49] constraints on acceptable military action are an integral part of most military training.

V. Conclusions

The question whether such concepts as norms can in principle be completely dispensed with (by reducing them to some logically prior round of individual interaction in which appeal to norms or normlike concepts is *not* made) is an important one, too important indeed for economists to remain agnostic about. Some practitioners of microeconomic analysis answer this question unhesitatingly in the affirmative. Many others remain somewhat skeptical, although basically sympathetic: the thought that with further development the techniques of game-theoretical analysis will lead us in this direction is a comforting one.

Economists have frequently been hostile to structuralist explanations, and this essay is not intended as support for an extreme structuralist view of the world, in which agents lack free will and dangle like marionettes on strings connected to structures deeply embedded in history, culture, or genetics. But the legitimacy of the concept itself cannot be gainsaid (although one may, if one desires, view these structures as continually and voluntarily reaffirmed, generation after generation). Their effect at the individual level is to define the range and nature of options treated by the individual as legitimate in considering ways to improve his individual welfare and, residually, those which are not. Those options excluded in principle (murder, theft, kidnapping, blackmail, etc.) clearly constrain individual action. The range of excluded options and thus the severity of these constraints may vary across time and space, but so long as civil society persists, this constraining influence never disappears entirely; and so long as social stability is desired, one will not wish that it do so. In any society not all individuals respect all these exclusions, but a sufficiently large number do to make stable social interactions possible.

If one maintains that norms or rules logically antedate markets (and indeed situations of strategic interaction), then one must pay close attention to the historical, legal, or cultural evolution of the situation under study. Recognizing that norms need to be analyzed in their own right, using extraeconomic and often case-specific methods, one can redefine microeconomic analysis as the analysis of the results of behavior by self-interested agents acting within constraints determined in part by technologies, resources, and the preference of others, but also in part by the systems of rules or norms confronted (in the sense that they constrain the behavior of others) or participated in (in the sense that they influence individual behavior irrespective of others' behavior). Any outcomes predicted or explained by such behavioral models are as conditional on the specified "social restraints" (norms) as they are on the other more commonly specified categories of exogenous variables.

Given shared language and other fundamental rules, the techniques of game theory do provide a framework for understanding how, in the case of a limited set of regulative rules, a political process might select from a group of possible rules or norms those which are most efficient. This technique does not, unfortunately, work for the explanation of the origin of those fundamental rules (or the origin of language). If one defines rational behavior as the selection of appropriate means for the achievement of desired ends, and defines these ends strictly in terms of the interests of the individual who is selecting these ends, one reaches the conclusion that all organized social activity presupposes behavior on the part of individuals that could easily be stigmatized as nonrational, if not irrational, according to this definition. Why, after all, should the individual, so careful about calculating individual gains as affected by variations in what he sees as legitimate options, be so willing to accept a certain range of other options as illegitimate when he has no real guarantee that others will continue to do so? How came he

Alexander James Field 705

to accept these in the first place? This paper has argued that it is impossible to understand such behavior as resulting from rational means–individual end calculations without first assuming a set of logically anterior rules, norms, or excluded options.

Utilitarianism and the methodological individualism frequently associated with it have historically performed yeoman service in calling into question various established institutions and procedures. But its weakness had been the problem of order. This paper has argued that in order to maintain analytically an arena of human choice in which means-end type calculations can legitimately be assumed to prevail, one must assume a complementary range of options that are ruled out of consideration by individuals, in spite of the fact that means-end calculations would suggest to them opportunities for individual gain from doing otherwise. For any historical situation, the delineation of that arena is a tricky but essential business, and it cannot be done on the basis of first principles. The recognition of boundaries beyond which means-end calculations cannot reasonably (and should not) be assumed to prevail is the intellectual price that must be paid for preserving an arena in which they can.

The inscription "Obedience to Law is Liberty" is emblazoned over the Main Street courthouse in Worcester, Massachusetts. This fundamentally conservative sentiment, expressed though it is in terms some would find overbearing, nevertheless embodies a truth about the persistence of all stable social orders: norms established through the process of socialization, perhaps "voluntarily" accepted or affirmed, perhaps building on certain genetic predispositions, provide part of the framework within which individuals pursue their self-interests. Intellectually defensible microeconomic analysis, in its competitive or game-theoretic variant, can be undertaken only if this principle is recognized; the refusal to recognize it leaves one with no satisfactory explanation for why the world does not degenerate into a war of all against all. As a positive statement about the operation of the real world and the tasks of social science, this proposition is straightforward enough. This having been said, it remains true that there are many solutions to problems of order, and this paper has only touched upon the normative problems associated with evaluating, according to a standard yet to be agreed upon, various possible rules and acts.[50]

Notes

* The development of this paper benefited from funds provided by the Institute for Research on Educational Finance and Governance, Stanford University, and research opportunities afforded during a year (1979–80) spent at the Institute for Advanced Study, Princeton, New Jersey. Earlier versions were presented at the Social Science seminar at the Institute in October 1979; at the Conference on Irrationality: Explanation and Understanding held at the

Maison des Sciences de l'Homme in Paris, France, January 7–9, 1980; and at the University of Washington, Seattle, December 1982. I am grateful to participants in these sessions and to two anonymous referees for their comments and reactions.

1. The term "norm" is used here in a restricted sense to refer to legal, cultural, or conventional rules regulating interaction between individuals. Sociologists and anthropologists sometimes use a broader definition, e.g., when they speak of consumption norms. Such behavior-influencing variables influence interactions between persons and things and, following standard economic usage, can more appropriately be termed preferences. Admittedly the distinction is not hard and fast and may be difficult to operationalize, since exhibition of certain consumption behavior may represent willingness to abide by the rules of a group or subgroup. See also n. 27.

2. For a detailed discussion of the promise and achievement of work along these lines by Richard Posner, Douglass North, and Robert Paul Thomas, see Alexander J. Field, "The Problem with Neoclassical Institutional Economics: A Critique with Special Reference to the North-Thomas Model of Pre-1500 Europe," *Explorations in Economic History* 18 (April 1981): 174–98.

3. "Extreme" in the sense that all rules, including the most fundamental, are to be explained in this fashion. Section III of this paper argues that the emergence and persistence of a limited number of regulative rules can be explained *as if* they had been selected as the result of some sort of maximizing process, assuming the existence of shared language and a stable political and social order within which these choices are made.

4. For an example, consider any number of articles in the optimal tax literature, where individuals may vary their supply of inputs in response to tax changes, but compliance rates are assumed invariant to policy changes.

5. The term "methodological individualism" is used here to refer to models (*a*) where individuals are concerned with their own individual interest and (*b*) where the analysis does not introduce concepts that are not or cannot be reduced to the results of the interaction of strictly self-interested individuals. In order to avoid any confusion, models in which utility of others enters own utility functions are excluded as not being consistent with what people generally mean when they speak of methodologically individualist models (see Joseph Schumpeter, *History of Economic Analysis* [New York: Oxford University Press, 1954], p. 888).

6. It is always difficult, without Gallup Polls, to support statements about disciplinary opinion. It is encouraging to find that Martin Hollis and E. J. Nell share this perception: "[Western economists] swear . . . even if they would not always admit to it, a methodological individualism in the attempt to explain human behavior" (Martin Hollis and E. J. Nell, *Rational Economic Man: A Philosophical Critique of Neoclassical Economics* [Cambridge: Cambridge University Press, 1975], p. 1). Examples, in addition to those discussed in the text, include the writings of Gordon Tullock. In *The Social Dilemma: The Economics of War and Revolution* (Blacksburg, Va.: University Publications, 1974), pp. 46, 140, Tullock argues that revolutionaries are motivated solely by a desire for a good job in the new regime. See also Ludwig von Mises, *Human Action* (New Haven, Conn.: Yale University Press, 1949), pp. 42–43, or 143–44. Adam Smith wrote, "It is not from the benevolence of the butcher, the brewer or the baker that we expect our dinner but from their regard to their own interest," but this must be understood in the context of his earlier work, esp. *The Theory of Moral Sentiments* (Adam Smith, *The Wealth of Nations* [1759; New York: Modern Library, 1937], p. 14).

7. Talcott Parsons's *The Structure of Social Action* (New York: McGraw-Hill Book Co., 1937) is still a useful source for this critical argument. See also Emile Durkheim, *Moral Education* (Glencoe, Ill.: Free Press, 1961).

8. Gary Becker, *The Economic Approach to Human Behavior* (Chicago: University of Chicago Press, 1976), pp. 11–13.

9. Ibid., p. 13.

10. David Rockefeller, "Ethics and the Corporation," *Hofstra Law Review* 8 (Fall 1979): 135–39.

11. In an interesting article that embodies some of this spirit, Karl Brunner and William Meckling ("The Perception of Man and the Conception of Government," *Journal of Money, Credit, and Banking* 9 [February 1977]: 70–85) contrast the "resourceful, evaluating, economic man model" (REMM) with sociological, political, and psychological models of man. Their article displays a sympathetic attitude toward political corruption and white collar crime, accusing liberals of a double standard, whereby corporate crime is condemned while street crime is excused as being a product of the environment of poverty. Apparently unimpressed with the argument that the more privileged members of society have a responsibility to set ethical standards by their example, they express amazement that in Sweden some legal procedures affecting those accused of tax evasion are more severe than those for persons accused of street crime (p. 83). One senses in this article a longing for a return to a regime in which there would be de jure one law for the rich and one law for the poor. In such a regime rich people could plead "benefit of wealth" when accused of capital or other crimes, as members of religious orders were, in previous centuries, able to plead benefit of clergy, as evidenced by their literacy. Following this line of argument, incarceration for the wealthy could be argued to represent an inefficient allocation of resources, since the costs of incarceration plus the forgone output of any person with such high marginal productivity would more than counterbalance a deterrent effect, whose value might be questionable in the first place.

12. A good discussion of this tendency can be found in Warren S. Gramm, "Industrial Capitalism and the Breakdown of the Liberal Rule of Law," *Journal of Economic Issues* 7 (December 1973): 577–603. See also Kenneth Boulding, "Ethics and Business: An Economists View," in *Beyond Economics* (Ann Arbor: University of Michigan Press, 1968).

13. Charles Fried ("Moral Causation," *Harvard Law Review* 77 [May 1964]: 1258–70) contrasts moral causation with "physical or purely psychological" causation. When the explanation for an act is that the individual concerned thought the action was *right*, one has an example of moral causation. Becker's position is apparently that the set of acts explicable as results of moral causes is empty; all actions are attributable to what Fried calls "physical or purely psychological causes." See also Charles Fried, "The Cunning of Reason in Moral and Legal Theory," *Journal of Legal Studies* 9 (March 1980): 335–53.

14. Becker, p. 5.

15. Sociobiological arguments are one means of providing such an explanation. Becker is sympathetic to such work, which explains, e.g., altruism toward kin as a trait favored by natural selection: although altruism may reduce the genetic fitness of the actor, it may increase the probability that genes of the altruist shared by kin whose genetic fitness is being increased will persist in the gene pool. Becker points out correctly that such models do not explain altruism directed toward nonrelatives. Denying Edward O. Wilson's statement that altruism by definition reduces genetic fitness, Becker claims that through its

effect on the behavior of others, altruism may serve to increase the fitness of the actor himself. Becker does not explain how altruism in the two-person single play Prisoner's Dilemma increases the genetic fitness of those who practice it (Gary Becker, "Altruism, Egoism and Genetic Fitness: Economics and Sociobiology," *Journal of Economic Literature* 14 [September 1976] reprinted in Becker, pp. 282–94). See also Edward O. Wilson, *On Human Nature* (Cambridge, Mass.: Harvard University Press, 1978).

16. John Harsanyi, "Individualistic and Functionalistic Explanations in the Light of Game Theory: The Example of Social Status," in *Problems in the Philosophy of Science,* ed. I. Lakatos and A. Musgrave (Amsterdam: North-Holland, 1968), p. 321. Harsanyi, however, represents only one tendency among game theorists. Oskar Morgenstern, in contrast, makes it clear that game theoretical analysis presupposes agreement by players on basic rules: "Games are described by specifying possible behavior within the rules of the game. The rules are in each case unambiguous. For example, certain moves are allowed for certain pieces in chess but forbidden for others. The rules are also inviolate. When a social situation is viewed as a game the rules are given by the physical and legal environment within which an individual's actions may take place" ("Game Theory: Theoretical Aspects," *International Encyclopedia of the Social Sciences* [New York: Macmillan Publishing Co., 1968]).

17. A "cooperative outcome," in this context, is one that might result from bargaining within a "cooperative" game but would not normally or automatically arise in a "noncooperative" game. (See n. 24.)

18. See Alexander Rosenberg, "Can Economics Explain Everything?" (*Philosophy of the Social Sciences* 9 [December 1979]: 509–29), for a discussion of this trend.

19. This emphasis on the presence or absence of strategic interaction exludes, obviously, the case of monopoly. Nor is this paper specifically concerned with variants in the competitive model, such as the theory of monopolistic competition.

20. Thomas Schelling (*The Strategy of Conflict* [London: Oxford University Press, 1960], p. 5) distinguishes between games of skill, games of chance, and games of strategy, only the latter involving dependence of individual payoffs on the actions of others. James Henderson and Richard Quandt (*Microeconomic Theory,* 3d ed. [New York: McGraw-Hill Book Co., 1980], p. 213) restrict the theory of games to the analysis of strategic interaction. This has been a common convention. See also A. Schotter and G. Schwödiauer, "Economics and Game Theory: A Survey," *Journal of Economic Literature* 18 (June 1980): 479–527, esp. 484.

21. Francis Y. Edgeworth, *Mathematical Psychics* (London: P. Kegan, 1881).

22. Werner Hildebrand, *Core and Equilibria of a Large Economy* (Princeton, N.J.: Princeton University Press, 1974), p. 123.

23. In an influential paper, Debreu and Scarf have generalized this result to an exchange economy with m types of players and n commodities (Gerard Debreu and Herbert Scarf, "A Limit Theorem on the Core of an Economy," *International Economic Review* 4 [1963]: 235–46).

24. In this paper, the terms "cooperative" and "noncooperative" have frequently been enclosed in quotation marks to emphasize that they are being used in their strict game-theoretic senses. Game-theoretic terminology also creates the danger of a possible confusion between what Luce and Raiffa call a strictly competitive game (i.e., zero sum) and nonstrictly competitive exchange economies. The core of a constant or zero sum game is empty. Exchange

Alexander James Field   709

economies generally have nonempty cores—which is to say mutually beneficial trades are possible. Game theorists' meaning in characterizing certain games as "strictly competitive" is not the same as economists' use of similar terms (e.g., "purely competitive") to describe certain economies: a purely competitive economy in the economists' sense is not a strictly competitive game in the game theorists' sense (see R. Duncan Luce and Howard Raiffa, *Games and Decisions* [New York: John Wiley, 1957], p. 59).

25. Ibid., p. 114.

26. Hildebrand, p. 123.

27. " . . . a fundamental distinction must be drawn in the realm of human phenomena. We have to place in one category those phenomena which are manifestations of the human will, i.e., of human actions in respect to natural forces. This category comprises the relations between persons and things. In another category, we have to place the phenomena that result from the impact of the human will or of human actions on the will or actions of other men. This second category comprises the relations between persons and persons. . . . I call the sum total of the first category *industry,* and the sum total of phenomena of the second category *institutions.* The theory of industry is called *applied science* or *art,* the theory of institutions *moral science* or *ethics"* (Leon Walras, *Elements of Pure Economics,* trans. W. Jaffé [Homewood, Ill.: Richard D. Irwin, 1954], p. 63). Philip Mirowski ("Is There a Mathematical Neo-Institutional Economics?" *Journal of Economic Issues* 15 [September 1981]: 593–613) sees more ambiguity in Walras's treatment of institutions.

28. Paul A. Samuelson, *Foundations of Economic Analysis* (New York: Atheneum Publishers, 1970), p. 8.

29. Bent Hansen, *A Survey of General Equilibrium Systems* (New York: McGraw-Hill Book Co., 1970).

30. Gerard Debreu, *The Theory of Value* (New Haven, Conn.: Yale University Press, 1959), does not mention government in his exposition, although in his chapter on equilibrium he does refer to "private ownership economies" (pp. 78–79).

31. The distinction between constitutive and regulative rules was developed initially by linguistic philosophers and concerned rules about what words meant. The distinction has come to be applied also to rules organizing social interaction and is used here primarily in this latter sense. Constitutive rules are basically rules for making rules, not subject in "normal" times to negotiation or change. They include language and the fundamental organizational basis of society. Regulative rules, on the other hand, may be modified without calling into question the fundamental organizational basis of a group or society (see John Searle, *Speech Acts: An Essay in the Philosophy of Language* [Cambridge: Cambridge University Press, 1969], pp. 33–34). Whereas Searle views all regulative rules as imperative, he views some constitutive rules as imperative and some as definitional. He also views what I call the behavioral assumption that agents want to maximize profits, or win a game, as a constitutive rule of the game.

32. Schelling, p. 56.

33. Schelling does not actually use the word 'socialization,' although he grants that the solution "may depend on imagination more than on logic" and includes "precedent" and "who the parties are and what they know about each other" in his list of potential contributions to a solution (Schelling, p. 57).

34. Herman Hollerith, one of the founders of the Computing Tabulating Recording Company (later IBM), developed in 1886 the punched cards first used in tabulating the 1890 U.S. census. An associate apparently asked him

how large the cards should be and in response he pulled out a one dollar bill. That size remains with us to this day. James Burke (*Connections* [Boston: Little, Brown & Co., 1979], p. 112), argues that the preexistence of dollar bill–sized filing drawers contributed to this decision.

35. For a more detailed discussion of this label, see Alexander J. Field, "The Problem with Neoclassical Institutional Economics"; and "On the Explanation of Rules Using Rational Choice Models," *Journal of Economic Issues* 13 (March 1979): 49–72.

36. W. V. O. Quine, "Foreword," in David Lewis, *Convention: A Philosophical Study* (Cambridge, Mass.: Harvard University Press, 1969), p. xi.

37. Lewis, p. 2. See also W. V. O. Quine, "Truth by Convention," in *Philosophical Essays for A. N. Whitehead,* ed. O. H. Lee (New York: Longman, Inc., 1936).

38. Again, these terminological distinctions are important in the game-theoretical literature. The distinction between cooperative and noncooperative games rests on the assumption of (*a*) the possibility of preplay communication *and* (*b*) the ability to make binding (enforceable) contracts. A "purely cooperative" game can be defined as one in which only communication is required to ensure a move to the Pareto-superior outcome.

39. Luce and Raiffa, p. 95.

40. Note that the Nash equilibrium solution to a "noncooperative" game should not be confused with the Nash bargaining solution to a "cooperative" game.

41. Michael Taylor, *Anarchy and Cooperation* (London: John Wiley, 1976).

42. Luce and Raiffa, p. 101; Taylor, p. 29. This conclusion does not depend on the rate at which payoffs are discounted in the finite play case.

43. If, e.g., each player chooses the following strategy: cooperate until met with defection, then defect for k plays; cooperate again until met with defection, then defect for $k + 1$ plays, and so forth, then neither player has an incentive to alter his strategy, provided certain inequalities involving the discount rate and the individual play payoff matrix are satisfied (Taylor, pp. 31–43).

44. Taylor is interested in getting people out of the state of nature without appeal to the deus ex machina of a coercive state, and he claims to have done so in the central part of his argument without appeal to norms or normlike phenomena: ". . . the payoffs are assumed *not* to reflect two kinds of incentives: on the one hand, those due to internal norms and values . . . and on the other, those due to external coercion . . ." (p. 7); or again, "the treatment of the problem of voluntary cooperation . . . rest[s] solely on assumptions about individuals . . ." (p. 129). Taylor's assumption that the game is infinitely repeated does not follow by any means automatically from the assumption that the players are egoists. What does it follow from? Taylor attempts to justify this critical assumption both by a discourse on what Hobbes really meant in *Leviathan,* chap. 6, and by appeal to empirical reality: "Needless to say it [the case where the game is played only once] is not always like this in the real world" (p. 29). It is hard to accept both Taylor's claim that he has explained voluntary cooperation solely with a priori assumptions about individuals and his justification of the supergame assumption on empirical grounds.

45. David Kalm, "Cryptology Goes Public," *Foreign Affairs* 58 (Fall 1979): 141–59, esp. 142.

46. Joseph Heller, *Catch 22* (New York: Dell, 1955), p. 107.

47. See Davis Lyons, *Forms and Limits of Utilitarianism* (Oxford: Oxford

Alexander James Field   711

University Press, 1965), pp. 1–7; Edna Ulmann-Margalit, *The Emergence of Norms* (Oxford: Clarendon Press, 1960), pp. 56–57.

48. Anatol Rapoport and Albert M. Chammah, *Prisoner's Dilemma: A Study in Conflict and Cooperation* (Ann Arbor: University of Michigan Press, 1965), p. 16; Luce and Raiffa, p. 68.

49. See Michael Walzer, *Just and Unjust Wars: A Moral Argument with Historical Illustrations* (New York: Basic Books, 1979).

50. Lyons (n. 47) is a good introduction. Implicitly, the ethics of a neo-classical institutional economist are the ethics of a rule utilitarian, who believes that "acts are to be regarded as right only if they conform to rules that can be supported on utilitarian grounds" (p. vii). The ethics of an economist such as Tullock, by contrast, are those of an act utilitarian. Charles Fried has argued for a return to what he calls a nonconsequentialist approach to ethics. He wishes to evaluate actions as categorically right or wrong and not to judge them as good or bad according to their consequences, as a utilitarian would. "To propound a categorical norm, to argue that an action is wrong, is to invite inquiry into the kinds of actions intended to be covered, but not an inquiry into the cost of compliance" (Charles Fried, *Right and Wrong* [Cambridge, Mass.: Harvard University Press, 1978], p. 12).

[11]

AN EVOLUTIONARY APPROACH TO NORMS

ROBERT AXELROD
University of Michigan

Norms provide a powerful mechanism for regulating conflict in groups, even when there are more than two people and no central authority. This paper investigates the emergence and stability of behavioral norms in the context of a game played by people of limited rationality. The dynamics of this new norms game are analyzed with a computer simulation based upon the evolutionary principle that strategies shown to be relatively effective will be used more in the future than less effective strategies. The results show the conditions under which norms can evolve and prove stable. One interesting possibility is the employment of metanorms, the willingness to punish someone who did not enforce a norm. Many historical examples of domestic and international norms are used to illustrate the wide variety of mechanisms that can support norms, including metanorms, dominance, internalization, deterrence, social proof, membership in groups, law, and reputation.

An established norm can have tremendous power. This is illustrated by a historical instance of the norm of dueling. In 1804 Aaron Burr challenged Alexander Hamilton to a duel. Hamilton sat down the night before the duel was to take place and wrote down his thoughts. He gave five reasons against accepting the duel: his principles were against shedding blood in a private combat forbidden by law; he had a wife and children; he felt a sense of obligation toward his creditors; he bore no ill against Colonel Burr; and he would hazard much and could gain little. Moreover, he was reluctant to set a bad example by accepting a duel. Yet he did accept, because "the ability to be useful, whether in resisting mischief or effecting good, in those crises of our public affairs which seem likely to happen, would probably be inseparable from a conformity with public prejudice in this particular" (Truman, 1884, pp. 345–48). In other words, the prospect of sanctions imposed by the general public in support of dueling caused Hamilton to risk, and ultimately to lose, his life—a powerful norm indeed, and yet one that has all but disappeared today after centuries of power over life and death.

Today, norms still govern much of our political and social lives. In politics, civil rights and civil liberties are as much protected by informal norms for what is acceptable as they are by the powers of the formal legal system. Leadership is itself subject to the power of norms, as Nixon learned when he violated political norms in trying to cover up Watergate. The operation of Congress is shaped by many norms, including those governing reciprocity (Matthews, 1960) and apprenticeship (Krehbiel, 1985). Across many nations, tolerance of opposition is a fragile norm that has great impact on whether a democracy can survive in a given country (Almond and Verba, 1963; Dahl, 1966). In international political economy, norms are essential for the understanding of the operations of many

American Political Science Review Vol. 80

functional domains such as banking, oil, and foreign aid (Axelrod and Keohane, 1985; Keohane, 1984; Krasner, 1983). Even in the domain of power politics, norms have virtually wiped out colonialism, inhibited the use of chemical warfare, and retarded the spread of nuclear weapons.

Not only are norms important for many central issues in political science, but they are vital to the other social sciences as well. Sociology seeks to understand how different societies work, and clearly norms are important in these processes (e.g., Opp, 1979, 1983). Anthropology frequently deals with the unique features of various peoples by describing in great detail their practices and values, as in the case of feuding (e.g., Black-Michaud, 1975). Psychologists are concerned with how people influence each other and the manner in which an individual becomes socialized into a community (e.g., Darley and Batson, 1973; Sherif, 1936). Economists are becoming interested in the origin and operation of norms as they have come to realize that markets involve a great deal of behavior based on standards that no one individual can determine alone (e.g., Furubotn and Pejovich, 1974; Schotter, 1981).

Large numbers of individuals and even nations often display a great degree of coordinated behavior that serves to regulate conflict. When this coordinated behavior takes place without the intervention of a central authority to police the behavior, we tend to attribute the coordinated behavior and the resulting regulation of conflict to the existence of norms. To make this appeal to norms a useful explanation, we need a good theory of norms. Such a theory should help explain three things: how norms arise, how norms are maintained, and how one norm displaces another.

One of the most important features of norms is that the standing of a norm can change in a surprisingly short time. For example, after many centuries of colonialism, the intolerance of colonial dependence took hold in the relatively short period of just two decades after World War II. Before and after such a transition, the state of affairs seems very stable and perhaps even permanent. For this reason, awareness of a given norm is most intense precisely when it is being challenged. Examples of norms being challenged today include the right to smoke in public without asking permission, the use of gender-laden language, and the prohibition against the use of chemical warfare. Some of these challenges will succeed in establishing new norms, and some will fail altogether. Thus, what is needed is a theory that accounts not only for the norms existing at any point in time, but also for how norms change over time. To clarify these processes, one must first be clear about exactly what is being discussed.

In this next section the evolutionary approach to be used in this paper is explained. Following this, the results of computer simulations of the evolution of norms are presented. The computer simulations are then extended to include a specific mechanism for the enforcement of norms, called *metanorms*. After these formal models are investigated, a wide variety of processes that might help to sustain norms are discussed, along with suggestions about how they too can be modeled. The question of the origin and content of norms is considered, and finally, a summary and conclusion presents the findings of this paper in the broad context of social and political change.

The Evolutionary Approach

Norms have been defined in various ways in the different literatures and even within the same literature. The three most common types of definitions are based upon expectations, values, and behavior.

1986 Evolution of Norms

That these different definitions are used for the same concept reflects how expectations, values, and behavior are often closely linked. Definitions based upon expectations or values are favored by those who study norms as they exist in a given social setting. Such definitions are convenient because interviews can elicit the beliefs and values of the participants, whereas systematically observing their actual behavior is more difficult. Because for many purposes the most important thing is actual behavior, a behavioral definition will be used in this study.

DEFINITION. *A norm exists in a given social setting to the extent that individuals usually act in a certain way and are often punished when seen not to be acting in this way.*

This definition makes the existence of a norm a matter of degree, rather than an all or nothing proposition, which allows one to speak of the growth or decay of a norm. According to this definition, the extent to which a given type of action is a norm depends on just how often the action is taken and just how often someone is punished for not taking it.

To investigate the growth and decay of norms, I have formulated a norms game in which players can choose to defect and to punish those they have seen defecting. The goal of the investigation is to see when cooperation based upon emerging norms will develop. Ultimately, the purpose is to learn what conditions favor the development of norms so that cooperation can be promoted where it might not otherwise exist or be secure.

To see what rational actors would do in a particular setting, a game theory approach can be used. Game theory assumes the players are fully rational and choose the strategy that gives the highest expected utility over time, given their expectations about what the other players will do. Recent work by economists has shown great sophistication in dealing with

problems of defining credible threats and of showing the consequences of requiring actors' expectations about each other to be consistent with the experience that will be generated by the resulting actions (Abreu, Pearce, and Stacchetti, 1985; Friedman, 1971; Kreps and Wilson, 1982; Selten, 1975).

While deductions about what fully rational actors will do are valuable for their own sake, empirical examples of changing norms suggest that real people are more likely to use trial and error behavior than detailed calculations based on accurate beliefs about the future. Therefore, I have chosen not to study the dynamics of norms using an approach that depends on the assumption of rationality.

Instead, I use an evolutionary approach. This approach is based on the principle that what works well for a player is more likely to be used again while what turns out poorly is more likely to be discarded (Axelrod, 1984). As in game theory, the players use their strategies with each other to achieve a payoff based upon their own choice and the choices of others. In an evolutionary approach, however, there is no need to assume a rational calculation to identify the best strategy. Instead, the analysis of what is chosen at any specific time is based upon an operationalization of the idea that effective strategies are more likely to be retained than ineffective strategies. Moreover, the evolutionary approach allows the introduction of new strategies as occasional random mutations of old strategies.

The evolutionary principle itself can be thought of as the consequence of any one of three different mechanisms. It could be that the more effective individuals are more likely to survive and reproduce. This is true in biological systems and in some economic and political systems. A second interpretation is that the players learn by trial and error, keeping effective strategies and altering ones that turn out

American Political Science Review Vol. 80

Figure 1. Norms Game

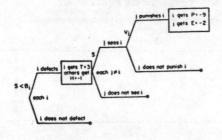

Key:

i, j	individuals
S	probability of a defection being seen by any given individual
B_i	boldness of i
V_j	vengefulness of j
T	player's temptation to defect
H	hurt suffered by others
P	cost of being punished
E	enforcement cost

poorly. A third interpretation, and the one most congenial to the study of norms, is that the players observe each other, and those with poor performance tend to imitate the strategies of those they see doing better. In any case, there is no need to assume that the individual is rational and understands the full strategic implications of the situation.

The evolutionary approach is inherently probabilistic and involves nonlinear effects. For these reasons, it is often impossible to use deductive mathematics to determine the consequences of a given model. Fortunately, computer simulation techniques (e.g., Cyert and March, 1963) provide a rigorous alternative to deductive mathematics. Moreover, simulation can reveal the dynamics of a process, as well as the equilibrium points. By simulating the choices of each member of a population of players and by seeing how the players' strategies change over time, the unfolding of a given evolutionary process can be analyzed to determine its overall implications.

The Norms Game

The norms game is described in Figure 1. It begins when an individual (i) has an opportunity to defect, say by cheating on an exam. This opportunity is accompanied by a known chance of being observed. The chance of being observed, or *seen*, is called S. If S is .5, each of the other players has an even chance of observing a defection if it takes place. If player i does defect, he or she gets a payoff of T (the *temptation* for defecting) equal to 3, and each of the others are *hurt* (H) slightly, getting a payoff of H equal to -1. If the player does not defect, no one gets anything.

So far the game is similar to an n-person Prisoner's Dilemma (see, e.g., G. Hardin, 1968; R. Hardin, 1982; Schelling, 1978). The new feature comes in the next step. If player i does defect, some of the other players may see the defection, and those who do may choose to punish the defector. If the defector is *punished* (P) the payoff is a very painful $P = -9$, but because the act of punishment is typically somewhat costly, the punisher has to pay an *enforcement cost* (E) equal to -2.

The strategy of a player thus has two dimensions. The first dimension of player i's strategy is *boldness* (B_i), which determines when the player will defect. The player will defect whenever the chance of being seen by someone is less than the player's boldness, which is to say, whenever $S < B_i$. The second dimension of a player's strategy is *vengefulness* (V_i), which is the probability that the player will punish someone who is defecting. The greater the player's vengefulness, the more likely he or she will be to punish someone who is spotted defecting.

1986 Evolution of Norms

**Table 1. Example of Payoffs in the Norms Game Attained by a
Player With Boldness Equal to 2/7 and Vengefulness Equal to 4/7**

Event	Payoff per Event	Number of Events	Payoff
Defection	$T = 3$	1	3
Punishment	$P = -9$	1	-9
Hurt by others	$H = -1$	36	-36
Enforcement cost	$E = -2$	9	-18
Score			-60

Simulation of the Norms Game

The simulation of the norms game
determines how the players' strategies
evolve over time. The two dimensions of
a strategy, boldness and vengefulness, are
each allowed to take one of eight levels,
from 0/7 to 7/7. Because the representation of eight levels requires three binary
bits, the representation of a player's
strategy requires a total of six bits, three
for boldness and three for vengefulness.

The simulation itself proceeds in five
steps, as follows:

(1) The strategies for the initial population of 20 players are chosen at random
from the set of all possible strategies.

(2) The score of each player is determined from the player's own choices and
the choices of the other players. Each
individual gets four opportunities to
defect. For each of these opportunities,
the chance of being seen, S, is drawn from
a uniform distribution between 0 and 1.
To see how the scores are attained, let us
focus on an arbitrary player in the initial
population of one of the runs, who will be
called Lee. Lee has a boldness level of 2/7
and vengefulness level of 4/7. The total
payoff Lee achieved was the result of four
different kinds of events, as shown in
Table 1. Lee defected only once because
only one of the four opportunities had a
chance of being seen that was less than
Lee's boldness of 2/7. This defection gave
a temptation payoff of $T = 3$ points.

Unfortunately for Lee, one of the other
players observed the defection and chose
to punish it, leading to a loss for Lee of P
$= -9$ points. In addition the other
players defected a total of 36 times, each
hurting Lee $H = -1$ point. Finally, Lee
observed who was responsible for about
half of these defections and chose to
punish each of them with a probability
determined by his vengefulness of 4/7.
This lead to a punishment of 9 of the
defections at an enforcement cost of $E =$
-2 each, for a further loss of 18 points.
The net result of these four types of events
was a total score of -60 for Lee.

(3) When the scores of all the players
are determined, individuals whose strategies were relatively successful are selected
to have more offspring.[1] The method is to
give an average individual one offspring
and to give two offspring to an individual
who is one standard deviation more
effective than the average. An individual
who is one standard deviation below the
population average will not have his or
her strategy reproduced at all. For convenience, the number of offspring is
adjusted to maintain a constant population of 20. A final step is the introduction
of some mutation so that new strategies
can arise and be tested. This is done by
allowing a 1% chance that each bit of an
individual's new strategy will be altered.
This mutation rate gives a little more than
one mutation per generation in the entire
population.

American Political Science Review Vol. 80

Figure 2. Norms Game Dynamics

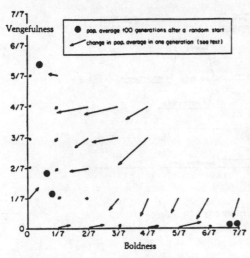

(4) Steps 2 and 3 are repeated for 100 generations to determine how the population evolves.

(5) Steps 1 to 4 are repeated to give five complete runs of the simulation.

The results of the five runs are shown in Figure 2. The five circles indicate the average boldness and vengefulness of a population after 100 generations. Three completely different outcomes appear possible. In one of the runs, there was a moderate level of vengefulness and almost no boldness, indicating the partial establishment of a norm against defection. On two other runs there was little boldness and little vengefulness, and on the remaining two runs, there was a great deal of boldness and almost no vengefulness—the very opposite of a norm against defection. What could be happening?

The way the strategies actually evolve over time is revealed by the change that takes place in a single generation in a population's average boldness and vengefulness. To calculate this, the data are used from all 100 generations of all five runs, giving 500 populations. The populations with similar average boldness and vengefulness are then grouped together, and their average boldness and vengefulness one generation later is measured. The results are indicated by the arrows in Figure 2.

Now the various outcomes begin to fit into a common pattern. All five of the runs begin near the middle of the field, with average boldness and vengefulness levels near one-half. The first thing to happen is a dramatic fall in the boldness level. The reason for the decline is that when there is enough vengefulness in the population, it is very costly to be bold. Once the boldness level falls, the main trend is a lowering of vengefulness. The reason for this is that to be vengeful and punish an observed defection requires paying an enforcement cost without any direct return to the individual. Finally, once the vengefulness level has fallen nearly to zero, the players can be bold with impunity. This results in an increase in boldness, destroying whatever restraint was established in the first stage of the process—a sad but stable state in this norms game.

This result raises the question of just what it takes to get a norm established. Because the problem is that no one has any incentive to punish a defection, the next section explores one of the mechanisms that provides an incentive to be vengeful.

Metanorms

A little-lamented norm of once great strength was the practice of lynching to enforce white rule in the South. A particularly illuminating episode took place in Texas in 1930 after a black man was arrested for attacking a white woman. The mob was impatient, so they burned down the courthouse to kill the prisoner within. A witness said,

> I heard a man right behind me remark of the fire, "Now ain't that a shame?" No sooner had the

1986 Evolution of Norms

Figure 3. Metanorms Game

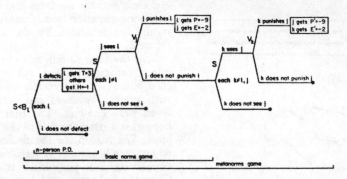

Key:

i, j, k	individuals
S	probability of a defection's being seen by any given individual
B_i	boldness of i
V_j	vengefulness of j
T	temptation to defect
H	hurt suffered by others
P	cost of being punished
E	punisher's enforcement cost
P'	cost of being punished for not punishing a defection
E'	cost of punishing someone for not punishing a defection

words left his mouth than someone knocked him down with a pop bottle. He was hit in the mouth and had several teeth broken. (Cantril, 1941, p. 101)

This is one way to enforce a norm: punish those who do not support it. In other words, be vengeful, not only against the violators of the norm, but also against anyone who refuses to punish the defectors. This amounts to establishing a norm that one must punish those who do not punish a defection. This is what I will call a *metanorm*.

Metanorms are widely used in the systems of denunciation in communist societies. When the authorities accuse someone of doing something wrong, others are called upon to denounce the accused. Not to join in this form of punishment is itself taken as a defection against the group

(Bronfenbrenner, 1970; Meyers and Bradbury, 1968).

As another example, when the Soviet Union supported the suppressionn of the Solidarity movement in Poland, the United States asked its allies to stop supplying components to the Soviet Union for its new gas pipeline. The allies, not wanting to pay the enforcement cost of this punishment, refused. The United States government then undertook the metapunishment of imposing sanctions on foreign companies that defied the sales ban (*New York Times*, January 5 and June 19, 1982).

The formulation of a metanorms game can help in the exploration of the effectiveness of this mechanism. Figure 3 shows how the metanorms game is based upon an extension of the norms game. If

Figure 4. Metanorms Game Dynamics

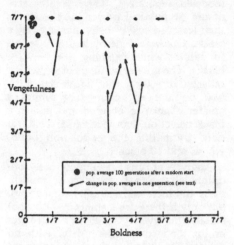

someone defects, and Lee sees but does not punish that defection, then the other players have a chance to see and punish Lee. The model makes the critical assumption that a player's vengefulness against nonpunishment is the same as the player's vengefulness against an original defection.[2] The validity of this assumption will be addressed later, but first let us see what affect it has on the evolution of the process.

A set of five runs was conducted with the metanorms game, each done as before with a population of 20 players and a duration of 100 generations. The results are shown in Figure 4. They are unambiguous. In all five runs a norm against defection was established. The dynamics are clear. The amount of vengefulness quickly increased to very high levels, and this in turn drove down boldness. The logic is also clear. At first there was a moderate amount of vengefulness in the population. This meant that a player had a strong incentive to be vengeful, namely, to escape punishment for not punishing an observed defection. Moreover, when each of the players is vengeful out of self-protection, it does not pay for anyone to

be bold. Thus the entire system is self-policing, and the norm becomes well established.

This result is dependent, however, on the population's starting with a sufficiently high level of vengefulness. Otherwise the norm still collapses. Thus, while the norms game collapses no matter what the initial conditions are, the metanorms game can prevent defections if the initial conditions are favorable enough.

Mechanisms to Support Norms

The simulations of the norms game and the metanorms game have allowed the exploration of some of the important processes in the dynamics of norms. The simulation of the norms game shows that relying on individuals to punish defections may not be enough to maintain a norm. Therefore, the question to be considered now is, What mechanisms can serve to support a norm that is only partially established? The evolutionary approach helps to develop a list of such processes, and in some cases, suggests specific methods for modeling the process by which a norm can be supported.

Metanorms

As the computer simulations show, the existence of a metanorm can be an effective way to get a norm started and to protect it once it is established. By linking vengefulness against nonpunishers with vengefulness against defectors, the metanorm provides a mechanism by which the norm against defection becomes self-policing. The trick, of course, is to link the two kinds of vengefulness. Without this link, the system could unravel. An individual might reduce the metavengeance level while still being vengeful and then later stop being vengeful when others stopped being metavengeful.

The examples cited earlier suggest that

1986 Evolution of Norms

people may well punish those who do not help to enforce a valued norm. The model suggests norms can be supported if people tend to have correlated degrees of vengefulness or anger against someone who violates a particular norm and someone who tolerates such a violation. What the evolutionary approach has done is raise the possibility that metanorms are a mechanism that can help support norms, thus suggesting the interesting empirical question of whether the two types of vengefulness are indeed correlated. My guess is that there is such a correlation. The types of defection we are most angry about are likely to be the ones whose toleration also makes us angry. As of now, however, the possibility of metanorms remains speculative.

Dominance

Another mechanism for supporting a norm is the dominance of one group over another. For example, it is no coincidence that in the South, whites lynched blacks, but blacks did not lynch whites. The whites had two basic advantages: greater economic and political power, and greater numbers.

Simulation of the effects of power and numbers can be readily done with slight extensions of the basic model to allow for the existence of two different groups. The competition between two groups can be modeled by assuming that the defections of a player only hurt the members of the other group and are therefore only punished by members of the other group. Similarly, in the metanorms version of the model, punishments for not punishing a defector would only occur within a group, as illustrated by the pop bottle used by one white against another in the lynching example discussed above. Moreover, in determining strategies for the next generation, the strategies of two groups would be allowed to adapt separately so that whites learn from whites and blacks learn from blacks.

The two advantages of the whites are modeled separately. Their greater economic or political power is reflected in their lessened cost of being punished by a black. This was done by letting $P = -3$ for whites while retaining $P = -9$ for blacks. The greater numbers of whites are reflected directly in the relative size of the two populations, giving the whites a greater chance to observe and punish a black defection than vice versa. This was done by letting the population be 20 whites and 10 blacks.

Analysis of runs based upon these conditions shows that resistance to punishment and increased size can help a group, but only if there are metanorms. Without metanorms, even members of the stronger group tend to be free riders, with no private incentive to bear enforcement costs. This in turn leads to low vengefulness and high boldness in both groups. When metanorms are added, it becomes relatively easier for the strong group to keep the weak group from being bold, while it is not so easy for the weak group to keep the strong one from defecting.

Another form of potential strength is illustrated by the case of a major power interacting with many smaller nations. For example, the U.S. may not only be in a favorable position on a given bilateral interaction but also may have many more bilateral interactions than others. Thus, its behavior has a greater impact on the development of norms than would the behavior of a minor power. When Libya wanted to modify the international norm of the twelve-mile limit of territorial waters to include the entire Gulf of Sidra, the United States fleet deliberately sailed into the Gulf and shot down two Libyan planes sent up to try to change the norm. Clearly the U.S. was not only stronger but had incentives to enforce the old norm based upon its naval interests in other parts of the world.

While the process of frequent interactions by a single strong player has not

American Political Science Review Vol. 80

yet been simulated, it is plausible that such a process would help to establish a norm against defection because the central player would have a greater unilateral incentive to be vengeful against defections.

Norms can also be promoted by the interests of a few major actors, such as the U.S. and the Soviet Union's both working to retard the proliferation of nuclear weapons. Their actions need not be coordinated in detail as long as together they are important enough to others to enforce a norm of the major actors' choice. The logic is somewhat analogous to Olson's "privileged group" in a collective action problem (Olson, 1965, pp. 48–50).

Internalization

Norms frequently become internalized (Scott, 1971). This means that violating an established norm is psychologically painful even if the direct material benefits are positive. This is frequently observed in laboratory experiments where subjects are more equitable than they have to be and explain their behavior by saying things like "you have to live with yourself." In terms of the norms game, this type of internalization means that the temptation to defect, T, is negative rather than positive. If everyone internalizes a given norm this strongly, there is no incentive to defect and the norm remains stable. Obviously families and societies work very hard to internalize a wide variety of norms, especially in the impressionable young. They do so with greater or lesser success depending on many factors, including the degree to which the individual identifies with the group and the degree to which the norm and its sponsors are seen as legitimate.[3]

Clearly, it is rare for everyone in a group to have a norm so strongly internalized that for each the temptation to defect is actually negative. An interesting question for future modeling is, How

many people have to internalize a norm in order for it to remain stable?

The logic of the norms game suggests that lowering the temptation to defect might not be enough. After all, even if most people did not defect, if no one had an incentive to punish the remaining defectors, the norm could still collapse. This point suggests that we look for internalization, not only in the reduced incentive to defect, but also in an increased incentive to punish someone else who does defect.

An increased incentive to punish, through internalization or by some other means, would lead some people to feel a gain from punishing a defector. For them, the payoff from enforcement, E, would actually be positive. Such people are often known as self-righteous busy bodies and often are not very well liked by those who enjoy a defection now and then. Given enough people who enjoy enforcing the norm, the question of its maintenance then becomes whether the chance is high or low that the defection will be seen.

Deterrence

In the norms game and the metanorms game the players do not look ahead. Instead they try a particular strategy, see how it does, compare their payoff with the payoff of others, and switch strategies if they are doing relatively poorly. While trial and error is a sensible way of modeling players of very limited rationality, it does not capture the idea that players may have a great enough understanding of the situation to do some forward-looking calculations as well as backward-looking comparisons with others. In particular, a person may realize that even if punishing a defection is costly now, it might have long-term gains by discouraging other defections later.

A good example is the strong U.S. response to New Zealand's refusal in February 1985 to allow a U.S. destroyer into

1986 Evolution of Norms

Aukland harbor without assurances that it did not carry nuclear weapons. The U.S. government presumably did not care very much about nuclear access to New Zealand ports, but it did care a great deal about deterring the spread of a new norm of "nuclear allergy" among its many allies in other parts of the world (Arkin and Fieldhouse, 1985).

Social Proof

An important principle from social psychology is "social proof," which applies especially to what people decide is correct behavior. As Cialdini (1984, p. 117) explains,

> we view a behavior as more correct in a given situation to the degree that we see others performing it. Whether the question is what to do with an empty popcorn box in a movie theater, how fast to drive on a certain stretch of highway, or how to eat chicken at a dinner party, the actions of those around us will be important in defining the answer.

The actions of those around us serve several functions. First, they provide information about the boldness levels of others, and indirectly about the vengefulness of the population. Hence, we can infer something about whether it pays for us to be bold or not. Second, the actions of others might contain clues about what is the best course of action even if there is no vengefulness. For example, people may be driving slowly on a certain stretch of highway, not because there is a speed trap there, but because the road is poorly paved just ahead. Either way, the actions of others can provide information about how the population has been adapting to a particular environment. If we are new to that environment, this is valuable information about what our own behavior should be (Asch, 1951, 1956; Sherif, 1936). The actions of others provide information about what is proper for us, even if we do not know the reasons. Finally, in many cases, by conforming to the actions of those around us, we fulfill a psychological need to be part of a group.

Our propensity to act on the principle of social proof is a major mechanism in the support of norms. The current model of norms already has a form of this mechanism built in: when a relatively unsuccessful individual seeks a new strategy, that strategy is selected from those being used by the rest of the population. This is a form of social proof, refined by giving weight to the more successful strategies being employed in the population.

In cases where other people differ in important ways, the principle of social proof tends to apply to those who are most like us. This too is easy to build into simulations with more than one group. In the simulation of blacks and whites, the blacks look only to other blacks when selecting a new strategy, and the whites look only to other whites. This makes good sense because a strategy that is very successful for a white might be disastrous if employed by a black.

Membership

Another mechanism for the support of norms is voluntary membership in a group working together for a common end.[4] Contracts, treaties, alliances, and memberships in social groups all carry with them some power to impose obligations upon individuals. The power of the membership works in three ways. First, it directly affects the individual's utility function, making a defection less attractive because to defect against a voluntarily accepted commitment would tend to lower one's self-esteem. Second, group membership allows like-minded people to interact with each other, and this self-selection tends to make it much easier for the members to enforce the norm implicit in the agreement to form or join a group. Finally, the very agreement to form a group helps define what is expected of the participants, thereby clarifying when a defection occurs and when a punishment is called for.

One might suppose it would be easy for a bold individual to join and then exploit a group that had gathered together in the expectation of mutual compliance. Actually, this does not usually happen, in part because the factors just outlined tend to isolate a defector and make it relatively easy for the others to be vengeful—especially with the help of metanorms. Another factor is that, according to recent experimental evidence, cooperators are more likely to stay in a group than are defectors (Orbell, Schwarz-Shea, and Simmons, 1984). This happens because cooperators have a stronger ethical or group-regarding impulse than defectors, a factor that led them to cooperate in the first place.

The metanorms game can be expanded to include the choice of whether to join a group or not.[5] In general, the value to a person of joining a group would depend on how many others joined. Each player would make this choice at the start of the game. Then the interactions concerning defections and punishments would occur as before, with the interactions limited to those who had actually joined. As an example, an alliance for collective security would include a group of nations that had joined for this common purpose. Once a nation had joined, a defection would consist of not supporting the alliance in some collective security task. A defection would hurt the other members of the alliance, and some of them might choose to punish the defector; they might also choose to punish someone who did not punish the defector. Typically, the larger the number of nations joining the group, the greater the benefits of cooperation would be for its members.

In the political sphere, voluntary membership taking the form of a social contract has been a powerful image for the support of democratic forms of governance. In effect, a mythical agreement is used to give legitimacy to a very real set of laws and institutions.

Law

Norms often precede laws but are then supported, maintained, and extended by laws. For example, social norms about smoking in public are now changing. As more and more people turn vengeful against someone who lights up in a confined space, fewer and fewer smokers are so bold as to do so without asking permission. As this norm becomes firmer, there is growing support to formalize it through the promulgation of laws defining where smoking is and is not permitted.[6]

A law supports a norm in several ways. The most obvious is that it supplements private enforcement mechanisms with the strength of the state. Because enforcement can be expensive for the individual, this can be a tremendous asset. In effect, under the law the collective goods problem of enforcement is avoided because selective incentives are given to specialized individuals (inspectors, police, judges, etc.) to find and punish violations.

The law also has a substantial power of its own, quite apart from whether it is or can be enforced. Many people are likely to take seriously the idea that a specific act is mandated by the law, whether it is a requirement to use seat belts or an income tax on capital gains. However, we all know this respect for the law has its limits, and we suspect that many people do not pay all the tax they should. Even when enforcement is possible and is attempted, the strength of the law is limited. In most cases, the law can only work as a supplement (and not a replacement) for informal enforcement of the norm. The failure of Prohibition is a classic example of an attempt to enforce a norm without sufficient social support.

In addition to enforcement and respect, a third advantage of the law is clarity. The law tends to define obligations much

1986 Evolution of Norms

more clearly than does an informal norm. A social norm might say that a landlord should provide safe housing for tenants, but a housing code is more likely to define safety in terms of fire escapes. Over the domain covered by the law, the norm might become quite clear. However, this clarity is gained at the expense of suggesting that conformity with the law is the limit of one's social obligations.

Modeling the power and operation of the law is beyond the scope of this project. However, it should still be emphasized that often law is the formalization of what has already attained strength as a social or political norm. An important example is civil liberties, the very foundation of a democratic system. There are laws and constitutional provisions in support of civil liberties such as freedom of speech, but the legal system can only protect free speech if there is substantial support for it among a population willing to tolerate dissent and willing to protect those who exercise it.

In short, social norms and laws are often mutually supporting. This is true because social norms can become formalized into laws and because laws provide external validation of norms. They are also mutually supporting because they have complementary strengths and weaknesses. Social norms are often best at preventing numerous small defections where the cost of enforcement is low. Laws, on the other hand, often function best to prevent rare but large defections because substantial resources are available for enforcement.

Reputation

An important, and often dominant, reason to respect a norm is that violating it would provide a signal about the type of person you are. For example, if there is a norm dictating that people should dress formally for dinner, and you don't, then others might make some quite general inferences about you.

The importance of dressing formally when the occasion requires is not just that others will punish you for violating the norm (say, by giving you a disapproving look) but also that they will infer things about you and then act in ways you wish they wouldn't. This is an example of the signaling principle: a violation of a norm is not only a bit of behavior having a payoff for the defector and for others; it is also a signal that contains information about the future behavior of the defector in a wide variety of situations.[7]

There are several important implications of the signaling principle for the origin and durability of a norm. A norm is likely to originate in a type of behavior that signals things about individuals that will lead others to reward them. For example, if a certain accent signals good breeding, then others may give better treatment to those who speak that way. Once this happens, more people are likely to try to speak that way. Eventually, people might be punished (e.g., despised) for not having the right accent. Thus, what starts out as a signal about one person's background can become a norm for all.[8]

The signaling principle helps explain how an "is" becomes an "ought." As more and more people use the signal to gain information about others, more and more people will adopt the behavior that leads to being treated well. Gradually the signal will change from indicating a rare person to indicating a common person. On the other hand, the absence of the signal, which originally carried little information, will come to carry substantial information when the signal becomes common. When almost everyone behaves in conformity with a signal, those who don't stand out. These people can now be regarded as violators of a norm—and dealt with accordingly.

Note that there is an important distinction between a convention, which has no

American Political Science Review Vol. 80

direct payoffs one way or the other (such as wearing a tie for men), and a cooperative act, the violation of which leads to injury to others (e.g., queuing for service). A type of behavior with no direct payoffs can become a norm once it develops some signaling value, as is the case when fashion leaders adopt a new style (Veblen, 1899). Once this happens, a violator of this style will be looked down upon. Thus the style will become a norm; individuals will usually follow the style, and those who do not will likely be punished.

The Origin and Content of Norms

Eight mechanisms have now been identified that can serve to support a norm that is already at least partially established. What, however, are the characteristics of the behaviors that arise and then become more and more established as norms? Or to put it another way, just what is the content of behavior that might later turn into a norm?

The answer depends on what types of behavior can appear and spread in a population even when only a few people initially exhibit the behavior. This, in turn, depends on what kind of behavior is likely to be rewarded and punished for its own sake, independently of whether or not it is common behavior.

Two of the supporting mechanisms already considered can serve in this initial role: dominance and reputation. Dominance can work because if only a few very powerful actors want to promote a certain pattern of behavior, their punishments alone can often be sufficient to establish it, even if the others are not vengeful against defections. The implications for the substance of norms are obvious: it is easier to get a norm started if it serves the interests of the powerful few.

In fact, many norms obeyed and even enforced by almost everyone actually serve the powerful. This can happen in forms disguised as equalitarian or in forms that are blatantly hierarchical. An apparently equalitarian norm is that the rich and the poor are equally prohibited from sleeping under bridges at night. A blatantly hierarchical norm is that soldiers shall obey their officers. Both forms are "norms of partiality," to use the term of Ullman-Margalit (1977).

To say that the powerful can start a norm suggests a great deal about the potential substance of such norms. Once started, the strong support the norms because the norms support the strong.

Dominance is not the only mechanism capable of starting a norm. Reputation can do so as well. Consider, for example, the idea of keeping one's promise. In a hypothetical society in which few people kept their promises, you would be happy to deal with someone who did. You would find it in your narrow self-interest to continue dealing with such a person, and this in turn would be rewarding to the promise-keeper. Conversely, you would try to avoid deals with those you knew did not keep their promises. You would, in effect, be vengeful against defectors without having to pay an enforcement cost. Indeed, your enforcement would simply be the result of your acting in your own interests, based upon the reputations of others and your calculation about what was good for yourself.

International regimes depend on just such reputational mechanisms to get norms started (Keohane, 1984). In such cases, countries can be very deliberate about what promises they make and which ones they want to keep when the stakes are high (Axelrod, 1979). Reputational effects can also be based upon the limited rationality of trial and error learning. If a person associates another's response to a particular act (say a refusal to continue dealing as a reaction to the breaking of a promise), then the violator can learn not to break promises.

This learning approach suggests the

1986 Evolution of Norms

importance of being able to link the behavior with the response. Behaviors will be easier to establish as norms if the optimal response of others is prompt and rewarding. Failing a prompt response, learning can also take place if the delayed punishment is explicitly cited as a response to the earlier defection.

Summary and Conclusion

To study the development of norms, the strategic situation has been modeled as an n-person game. In the basic norms game, everyone has two types of choice: the choice to cooperate or defect, which affects everyone, and the choice of whether or not to punish a specific person seen defecting. A player's strategy is described in terms of how these choices will be made. A strategy consists of two parameters: boldness (the largest chance of being seen that will lead to a choice of defection) and vengefulness (the probability of punishing someone observed defecting). To the extent that players are vengeful, but not very bold, a norm can be said to have been established.

To study the dynamics of the process, an evolutionary approach was employed. In this approach, the initial strategies are chosen at random, and the population of players is given opportunities to defect and to punish the defections they observe. The evolutionary approach dictates that strategies proving relatively effective are more likely to be employed in the future while less effective strategies are dropped. Moreover, strategies undergo some random mutation so that new ones are always being introduced into the population.

The computer simulation of this process revealed an interesting dynamic in the norms game. At first, boldness levels fell dramatically due to the vengefulness in the population. Then, gradually, the amount of vengefulness also fell because there was no direct incentive to pay the

enforcement cost of punishing a defection. Once vengeance became rare, the average level of boldness rose again, and the norm completely collapsed. Moreover, the collapse was a stable outcome.

This result led to a search for mechanisms that could sustain a partially established norm. One possibility is the metanorm: the treatment of nonpunishment as if it were another form of defection; that is, a player will be vengeful against someone who observed a defection but did not punish it. Simulation of the evolution of strategies in this metanorms game demonstrated that players had a strong incentive to increase their vengefulness lest they be punished by others, and this in turn led to a decline of boldness. Thus, metanorms can promote and sustain cooperation in a population.

Other mechanisms for the support of norms are also important. These include dominance, internalization, deterrence, social proof, membership, law, and reputation. In some cases, the resulting norms are hierarchical rather than equalitarian, and the cooperation exhibited is coerced rather than freely offered. A good example is the norm of black deference in the old South.

Dominance processes have been simulated by subdividing the population and letting one segment be relatively resistant to the effects of punishment by members of the other segment. Internalization can be investigated by studying the effects of making defection costly rather than rewarding for some of the defectors and by making punishment a pleasure rather than a cost for some of the observers of a defection. A more drastic change in the modeling procedures would be necessary to study some of the other mechanisms in question.

Norms are important in society and, not surprisingly, have been given a great deal of attention in the social sciences, including sociology, anthropology, political science, psychology, and economics.

American Political Science Review Vol. 80

While descriptions of actual norms abound, investigations of the reasons for people to obey or violate a given norm have been much less common. Even among the strategic approaches to norms, relatively little attention has been devoted to understanding the dynamics of norms: how they can get started, how a partial norm can be sustained and become well established, and how one norm can displace another. An evolutionary approach is helpful in studying these dynamics because it can help show how strategies change over time as a function of their relative success in an ever-changing environment of other players who are also changing their own strategies with experience.

A major goal of investigating how cooperative norms in societal settings have been established is a better understanding of how to promote cooperative norms in international settings. This is not as utopian as it might seem because international norms against slavery and colonialism are already strong while international norms are partly effective against racial discrimination, chemical warfare, and the proliferation of nuclear weapons. Because norms sometimes become established surprisingly quickly, there may be some useful cooperative norms that could be hurried along with relatively modest interventions.

Notes

I owe a great deal to Stephanie Forrest, my research assistant, and to those who helped me think about norms: Michael Cohen, Jeffrey Coleman, John Ferejohn, Morris Fiorina, Robert Gilpin, Donald Herzog, John Holland, Melanie Manion, Ann McGuire, Robert Keohane, Robert McCalla, Amy Saldinger, Lynn Sanders, Kim Scheppele, Andrew Sobel, Charles Stein, Laura Stoker, and David Yoon. I am also pleased to thank those who helped support various aspects of this work: the Harry Frank Guggenheim Foundation, the National Science Foundation, the Sloan Foundation, and the Michigan Memorial Phoenix Project.

1. The procedure used is inspired by the genetic algorithm of computer scientist John Holland (1975, 1980).

2. For convenience, it is also assumed that the chance of being seen not punishing is the same as the chance of the original defection being seen. The payoff for metapunishment is $P' = -9$, and the metaenforcement cost is $E' = -2$.

3. Marx goes as far as to say that social norms are merely reflections of the interests of the ruling class, and the other classes are socialized into accepting these norms under "false consciousness."

4. I thank David Yoon and Lynn Sanders for pointing this out to me.

5. I thank David Yoon for formulating this variant of the metanorms game and the application to alliances that follows.

6. The same process of formalizing norms applies to private laws and regulations, as in the case of a business that issues an internal rule about who is responsible for making coffee.

7. For the theory of signaling, see Spence (1974). For a theory of how customs can be sustained by reputations, see Akerlof (1980).

8. Signals can also help to differentiate groups and thereby maintain group boundaries and cohesiveness.

References

Abreu, Dilip, David Pearce, and Ennio Stacchetti. 1985. Optimal Cartel Equilibria with Imperfect Monitoring. Minneapolis: University of Minnesota Institute for Mathematics and its Applications.

Akerlof, George A. 1980. A Theory of Social Custom, of Which Unemployment May Be One Consequence. *Quarterly Journal of Economics*, 94:749–75.

Almond, Gabriel, and Sidney Verba. 1963. *The Civic Culture*. Princeton: Princeton University Press.

Arkin, William, and Richard W. Fieldhouse. 1985. Focus on the Nuclear Infrastructure. *Bulletin of the Atomic Scientists*, 41:11–15.

Asch, Solomon E. 1951. Effects of Group Pressure upon the Modification and Distortion of Judgment. In Harold Guetzkow, ed., *Groups, Leadership and Men*. Pittsburgh: Carnegie Press.

Asch, Solomon E. 1956. Studies of Independence and Conformity: I. A Minority of One Against a Unanimous Majority. *Psychological Monographs*, 41:258–90.

Axelrod, Robert. 1979. The Rational Timing of Surprise. *World Politics*, 31:228–46.

Axelrod, Robert. 1984. *The Evolution of Cooperation*. New York: Basic Books.

Axelrod, Robert, and Robert O. Keohane. 1985. Achieving Cooperation Under Anarchy: Strategies and Institutions. *World Politics*, 38:226–54.

1986 Evolution of Norms

Black-Michaud, Jacob. 1975. *Cohesive Force: Feud in the Mediterranean and the Middle East.* Oxford: Basil Blackwell.

Bronfenbrenner, Urie. 1970. *Two Worlds of Childhood: U.S. and U.S.S.R.* New York: Russell Sage.

Cantril, Hadley. 1941. *The Psychology of Social Movements.* New York: Wiley.

Cialdini, Robert H. 1984. *Influence—How and Why People Agree to Things.* New York: Morrow.

Cyert, Richard M., and James G. March. 1963. *A Behavioral Theory of the Firm.* Englewood Cliffs, NJ: Prentice-Hall.

Dahl, Robert A., ed. 1966. *Political Oppositions in Western Democracies.* New Haven: Yale University Press.

Darley, John M., and C. Daniel Batson. 1973. "From Jerusalem to Jerico": A Study of Situational and Dispositional Variables in Helping Behavior. *Journal of Personality and Social Psychology,* 27:100–108.

Friedman, James W. 1971. A Non-cooperative Equilibrium for Supergames. *Review of Economic Studies,* 38:1–12.

Furubotn, Eirik G., and Svetozar Pejovich, eds. 1974. *The Economics of Property Rights.* Cambridge, MA: Ballinger.

Hardin, Garrett. 1968. The Tragedy of the Commons. *Science,* 162:1243–48.

Hardin, Russell. 1982. *Collective Action.* Baltimore: Johns Hopkins University Press.

Holland, John H. 1975. *Adaptation in Natural and Artificial Systems.* Ann Arbor: University of Michigan Press.

Holland, John H. 1980. Adaptive Algorithms for Discovering and Using General Patterns in Growing Knowledge Bases. *International Journal of Policy Analysis and Information Systems,* 4: 245–68.

Keohane, Robert O. 1984. *After Hegemony: Cooperation and Discord in the World Political Economy.* Princeton: Princeton University Press.

Krasner, Stephen D., ed. 1983. *International Regimes.* Ithaca: Cornell University Press.

Krehbiel, Keith. 1985. Unanimous Consent Agreements: Going Along in the Senate. Working paper no. 568. California Institute of Technology, Social Science Department.

Kreps, David M., and Robert Wilson. 1982.

Sequential Equilibria. *Econometrica,* 50:863–94.

Matthews, Donald R. 1960. *U.S. Senators and Their World.* Chapel Hill: University of North Carolina Press.

Meyers, Samuel M., and William C. Bradbury. 1968. The Political Behavior of Korean and Chinese Prisoners of War in the Korean Conflict: A Historical Analysis. In Samuel M. Meyers and Albert D. Briderman, eds., *Mass Behavior in Battle and Captivity, The Communist Soldier in the Korean War.* Chicago: University of Chicago Press.

Olson, Mancur. 1965. *The Logic of Collective Action.* Cambridge, MA: Harvard University Press.

Opp, Karl-Dieter. 1979. Emergence and Effects of Social Norms—Confrontation of Some Hypotheses of Sociology and Economics. *Kylos,* 32: 775–801.

Opp, Karl-Dieter. 1983. Evolutionary Emergence of Norms. *British Journal of Social Psychology,* 21: 139–49.

Orbell, John M., Peregrine Schwartz-Shea, and Randall T. Simmons. 1984. Do Cooperators Exit More Readily than Defectors? *American Political Science Review,* 78:163–78.

Schelling, Thomas. 1978. *Micromotives and Macrobehavior.* New York: W. W. Norton.

Schotter, Andrew. 1981. *Economic Theory of Social Institutions.* Cambridge: Cambridge University Press.

Scott, John F. 1971. *Internalization of Norms.* Englewood Cliffs, NJ: Prentice-Hall.

Selten, R. 1975. Reexamination of the Perfectness Concept for Equilibrium Points in Extensive Games. *International Journal of Game Theory,* 4:25–55.

Sherif, Muzafer. 1936. *The Psychology of Social Norms.* New York: Harper and Brothers.

Spence, A. Michael. 1974. *Market Signalling.* Cambridge, MA: Harvard University Press.

Truman, Ben C. 1884. *Field of Honor: A Complete and Comprehensive History of Dueling in All Countries.* New York: Fords, Howard and Hilbert.

Ullmann-Margalit, Edna. 1977. *The Emergence of Norms.* Oxford: Oxford University Press.

Veblen, Thorstein. 1899. *The Theory of the Leisure Class.* New York: Macmillan.

Robert Axelrod is Professor of Political Science, University of Michigan, Ann Arbor, MI 48109.

[12]

Rules and Choice in Economics and Sociology

by

VIKTOR VANBERG*

Center for Study of Public Choice
Department of Economics George Mason University

> It is not irrelevant to... consider briefly the role which
> abstract rules play in the coordination not only of the actions
> of many different persons but also in the mutual adjustment
> of the successive decisions of a single individual or organiza-
> tion. ...Many of these rules will be "customs" of the social
> group in which we have grown up and only some will be
> individual "habits" which we have accidentally or deliber-
> ately acquired. But they all serve to abbreviate the list of
> circumstances which we need to take into account in the
> particular instances, singling out certain classes of facts as
> alone determining the general kind of action which we
> should take. At the same time, this means that we systemati-
> cally disregard certain facts which... it is rational to neglect
> because they are accidental partial information which does
> not alter the probability that, if we could know and digest all
> the facts, the balance of advantage would be in favour of
> following the rule (F. A. HAYEK 1964, p. 11).

I. Introduction

The relation between economics and sociology as contemporary academic disciplines is somewhat difficult to characterize for the simple reason that there is no
paradigmatically unified economics and much less so a paradigmatically unified
sociology. Though, judged from textbooks, major journals and professional
meetings, standard neoclassical economics apparantly is the dominant perspective in economics, there exist today a variety of theoretical approaches which
distance themselves more or less from the neoclassical mainstream. For sociology, it is not even possible to identify a mainstream theory. Now that functionalism and neo-marxism have both lost their temporary prominent positions,
sociology has disintegrated, at least on the level of theory, into an amorphous set
of numerous perspectives with no indication of theoretical convergence in sight.

Under such conditions a comparative study of economics and sociology must
either go into considerable detail, or it has to be deliberately selective. In this

---

* I am indebted to James M. Buchanan, Hartmut Kliemt, and Michael Baurmann for
helpful comments and suggestions on earlier drafts.

paper I will opt for the second alternative and try to identify certain aspects that seem to be largely characteristic for the two disciplines, despite their internal heterogeneity. Rather than trying to give a comprehensive account of the current profiles of the two disciplines, I will focus on the relation between two theoretical notions that are commonly considered to reflect a fundamental difference between a sociological and an economic perspective, both broadly conceived: The notion of norm- or rule-guided behavior on the one side, and that of rational, self-interested choice on the other or, in short, the "homo sociologicus" vs. the "homo oeconomicus" notion[1].

An essential part of the traditional and ongoing tension between sociology and economics apparently has its roots in their different emphasis on social norms and individual choice respectively, a difference that is ironically captured in Duesenberry's aphorism that "economics is all about how people make choices; sociology is all about why they don't have any choices to make." Though a deliberate caricature, Duesenberry's statement captures an important aspect of the observed conflict between the economic and the sociological perspective: Sociologists typically accuse economics for inappropriately emphasizing *choice* while ignoring the relevance of genuinely *rule- or norm-guided behavior*, and economists tend to criticize sociology for its preoccupation with norms and rules while ignoring the relevance of *choice*[2].

The purpose of this paper is to argue that the "choice without rules vs. rules without choice"-conflict is not as inescapable as it is often perceived, and that a more appropriate and fruitful approach ought to systematically reconcile the notion of rule- or norm-guided behavior with the notion of rational choice[3]. The crucial issue in this context is, of course, the definition and theoretical interpretation of the notion of *rule- or norm-guided* behavior, in particular the possibility of consistently incorporating such a notion into a rational choice framework. The discussion in this paper will be largely devoted to this issue. Section II specifies the explanatory problem that is raised by the notion of genuine rule-following. Sections III and IV analyze the place that this notion may find within the sociological, normative approach and within the economic, rational choice perspective respectively. Section V proposes an explanation of rule-guided

---

[1] J. S. COLEMAN 1987, p. 133: "Use of the concept of social norms is one of the stigmata of the sociologist. ... Especially for theories based on rational choice, invoking a norm to explain behavior constitutes an almost diametrically opposed approach. The rational choice theorist sees action as the result of choice ... ; the social-norm theorist sees behavior as the result of conformity to norms." – For similar statements see S. LINDENBERG 1983, p. 466 ("... economics is based on 'expedient choice' and sociology is based on 'moral obligation'"), R. BOUDON 1980, pp. 195 ff., or K. D. OPP 1986, who contrasts the sociological *normative paradigm* with the *rational choice model* of economics.

[2] A related issue is discussed, though with a somewhat different focus, in M. GRANOVET-TER 1985.

[3] A similar argument is made by K. D. OPP (1986, p. 15), though Opp's and my own line of reasoning are somewhat different.

behavior within an extended rational choice framework. Sections VI and VII discuss some distinctions that are relevant to the issue, namely the distinction between "personal rules" and "social rules", and the distinction between "constitutional interests" on the one side and "compliance-" or "action-interests" on the other. Section VIII will conclude the paper.

II. Compliance with Rules and Rule-guided Behavior

It is important to understand the sense in which providing an explanatory account for *rule-following behavior* is different from explaining why a person complies with a rule in particular instances. A social norm or rule is a prescript for how generally to act in certain types of situations. When a person is observed generally to comply with certain rules in recurrent choice situations, this may be attributed to the fact that on each and every single occasion rule-compliance is measured against the particular situational reward structure, the maximizing choice. What is referred to here as *genuine rule-following* is different from such regularity in case by case choices. Though it is certainly possible to understand many instances of observed rule-compliance as a rational adaption to the specific constraints present in particular choice situations, it will be claimed here that observed rule-compliance cannot in general be explained in terms of rational case by case choices. It seems to be somewhat doubtful whether a tolerable level of rule-conforming behavior could ever be achieved if the rules that constitute a society's moral and institutional order would only be obeyed in those instances where the particular situational constraints render rule-compliance in fact the utility-maximizing choice. At least beyond the narrow confines of very small face-to-face groups, a viable social order seems not even conceivable if rule compliance were exclusively or primarily a matter of rational *case by case adjustment*[4]. It seems to allow for a more appropriate understanding of the foundations of social order if we assume that people's compliance with rules and norms is not only a matter of case by case adjustments but also reflects, what one may call, *genuinely rule-following behavior* in the sense of a disposition to abide by rules *relatively independently* of the specifics of the particular situational constraints[5]. In any event, the present paper starts from the presumption that *genuine rule-following* is indeed a real phenomenon rather than a mere theoretical fiction, and it supposes that the issue of how this phenomenon can be best understood is *a*, if not *the*, crucial issue in the enduring conflict between a sociological and an economic perspective.

[4] H. KLIEMT (1987, p. 23) characterizes a central argument of Herbert Hart's legal philosophy as implying "that the existence of a legal order could not be explained if individuals would rely on case to case calculations of the comparative advantages of alternative actions".

[5] The issues that are implied in the phrase "relatively independently" will be discussed in more detail later in this paper.

III. The Sociological Model of Norm-guided Behavior

In particular, though not only, in the Durkheim-Parsons-tradition sociology has tied itself to the methodological postulate that a satisfactory theoretical solution to the "Hobbesian problem of social order" can, in principle, not be provided from an individualistic-utilitarian perspective. An explanation of norm-guided social conduct in terms of rational, self-interested choice-behavior has thus been programmatically excluded from sociology's explanatory repertoire. It is far from being clear, however, what *alternative* explanatory account has been advanced, if any. Indeed, as has been often critically observed, the assumption that peoples' behavior is guided by social norms and rules tends to be treated as an axiom from which sociological analysis starts and not as an observation that is in need of being explained[6].

It is of particular interest in the present context that the Durkheimian-Parsonian quarrel with utilitarian individualism is in part over the very same issue that is the subject of this paper, namely the role of genuine rule-guided behavior as opposed to situational, case by case adaptation. As Parsons explains in his affirmative review of Durkheim's approach, the central principle in the utilitarian scheme is "the explanation of conduct in terms of the rational pursuit of the wants or desires of individuals" (Parsons 1968, p. 344). In pursuit of their ends men are assumed to "act rationally, choosing, within the limitations of the situation, the most efficient means" (ibid., pp. 90f.). In this view the prototype of mutually advantageous, peaceful cooperation is the economic exchange relationship, and an implicit assumption is "that it is mutual advantage derived by the parties from various exchanges which constitutes the principal binding, cohesive force in the system" (ibid., p. 311). It is precisely this assumption, Parsons argues, that was the principal target of Durkheim's attack on Spencer and on the tradition of economic individualism in general. Durkheim accused Spencer and the other individualists of omitting the fact that the contractual relations and transactions on which they focus are embedded in a preexisting normative framework, that these transactions "are actually entered into in accordance with a body of binding rules" that exists prior to the particular transactions and independently of "immediate individual interests" (ibid., pp. 311, 315)[7].

---

[6] On this issue and for further references cf. e. g. K.-D. Opp 1986, in particular pp. 5f., and J.S. Coleman, 1987, p. 134. – As an aside: It results from such a perspective that the sociologist's interest has been typically in the "why do people deviate" rather than in the "why do people comply" question, an analytical focus that is quite irritating to rational choice theorists to whom the omnipresence of "temptations to cheat on the rules" appears to be a quite obvious feature of social life.

[7] T. PARSONS 1968, p. 314: "This vast complex of action in the pursuit of individual interests takes place within the framework of a body of rules, independent of the immediate individual motives of the contracting parties. This fact the individualists have either not recognized at all, or have not done justice to." – See also PARSONS 1960, p. 119: "As is well

The Durkheim-Parsons criticism of utilitarian individualism – that it "takes as its fundamental basis the rational unit act and treats it atomistically" (ibid., p. 316) and that it is unable "to account for the element of normative order in society" (ibid., p. 346) – can be read, at least in some parts, as an objection against a theoretical perspective that, by focussing on the particular situational reward structure, tends to ignore the significance of genuine rule-guided behavior for social cooperation[8]. One may well agree with such an objection even if one strongly disagrees with the conclusion about the proper nature of sociological theory that Durkheim and Parsons arrived at[9]. Their own interpretation of the "normative element" in social cooperation stresses the role of *socialization* as a process in which, through (positive and negative) sanctions imposed by their social environment, individuals come to abide by norms. This is, as Parsons emphasizes, meant to imply more than just the notion that individuals in pursuit of their interest are constrained by externally imposed sanctions, a notion that would not seem to require departing from a utilitarian framework. The crucial notion that actually marks the dissociation from utilitarianism is, so Parsons, the concept of *internalization*, according to which a persons' willingness to abide by norms becomes independent of external sanctions and, instead, becomes part of a person's character[10].

The concept of "internalization" has an obvious affinity to the notion of a

---

known, Durkheim's emphasis is on the *institution* of contract, which at one point he characterizes as consisting in the "noncontractual elements" of contract. These are not items agreed upon by contracting parties in the particular situation, but are norms established in the society, norms which underlie and are independent of any particular contract." – For a detailed discussion of Durkheim's notion of the "noncontractual elements of contract" see K. F. RÖHL 1978.

[8] A distinction similar to that between the two levels of dispositional and situational rule-compliance appears in Parsons' early essay on "Ultimate Values in Sociological Theory" (1934/35, p. 299) where a distinction is made between two "modes in which institutional norms become enforced on individual actions," namely: "(F)irst, by the inherent moral authority of the norm itself... Second, there is the appeal to interest. That is, conformity to the norm may, apart from any moral attitude, be in the given concrete situation a means to the realization of the actor's private ends."

[9] For a critical analysis of these conclusions cf. V. VANBERG 1975, pp. 147 ff.

[10] PARSONS (1968, pp. 387 f.) argues that Durkheim superseded the "utilitarian dilemma" (moral duty vs. individual desires) when he viewed the issue of morality no longer as "a question of... desires *against* external constraining factors, but the constraining factors actually enter into the concrete ends and values, in part determining them. And since normative rules... become an integral part of the individual's system of values in action, it ceases to be strange to think of them as also desired. ...The most fundamental criticism of utilitarianism is that it has had a wrong conception of the concrete human personality. ...(T)he norm to which his action is oriented is no longer exterior... It becomes, in the Freudian sense, 'introjected' to form a constitutive element of the individual personality itself." – Cf. also Parsons 1960, p. 143: "Durkheim could not abandon the doctrine of the independence of institutional norms from the 'individual'. ...(T)o abandon it would have meant reverting to the utilitarian position. Hence the only solution was the conception of the interpenetration of personality and social system, the conception that it must be true, in

persons' *disposition* to abide by rules relatively independently of the specifics of the particular situational constraints, a notion that was invoked in our earlier (Sect. II) explanation on the contrast between rule-following behavior and situational rule compliance. I will return later to the issue of how the sociological concept of internalization relates to the interpretation of rule-following behavior that is to be suggested in this paper. At this point, it should only be mentioned that the internalization concept, as commonly understood, seems to suffer from a fundamental ambiguity: On the one hand, internalization is typically seen as the outcome of a process in which individuals are affected by sanctions, that is, by the reward structure they face in their relevant environment. In other terms: they are assumed to respond to incentives. On the other hand, for the state of "internalization" itself the typical assumption seems to be that rule-compliance is unconditional and unaffected by external incentives, or, at least, there is no systemic account for how peoples' responsiveness to incentives operates on the dispositional trait that the concept of "internalization" refers to. By invoking at the same time, through the concept of sanctions, that people respond to incentives and, through the notion of internalization, that their rule-compliance is unresponsive to incentives, the sociologist's interpretation of rule-following behavior seems to be based on two incompatible conceptions[11].

IV. The Economic Model of Rational Choice

The essence of the economic model of rational choice apparently lies in the assumption that in any given situation an actor chooses among potential alternative courses of action the one that he expects to serve his interests best, given his preferences and his perception of the relevant situational constraints. From this perspective it seems to be natural to interpret human behavior as a continuous sequence of singular choices. Conceptually, each particular act is viewed as a discrete event, an explanation of which is provided if one can show that it is the actor's maximizing choice, given the relevant constraints he faces in the particular choice situation. Such an interpretation of human behavior as a sequence of situational choices is clearly in contrast to the sociological, normative model that emphasizes the rule-following nature of social behavior.

Even if one acknowledges that the notion of rational choice can be, and typically is, interpreted quite broadly as including not only deliberate choices but "implicit" choices as well, a rational choice perspective still seems to leave little systematic room for the concept of genuinely rule-following behavior[12]. There

some sense, that values and norms were part of the 'individual consciousness', and were, at the same time, analytically independent of 'the individual'."

[11] S. LINDENBERG (1983, p. 451) makes a similar argument on what he calls *"the sociologist's dilemma"*.

[12] Herbert A. Simon's critique of the traditional assumption of rational, maximizing

             Viktor Vanberg

appears to be a fundamental tension between the notion of *choice* and that of *rule-following*, at least to the extent that the latter invokes the idea of a kind of *pre-programmed* behavior, for which, in some sense, the *very absence of choice* seems to be constitutive.

To be sure, that social rules do have an impact on peoples' behavior is not simply ignored in economics. In fact, there is an increasing interest in an economic analysis of rules and institutions. Yet, such analysis typically tends to discuss the rules-issue in terms of situational, case by case choices and thus to distract attention from the element of genuine rule-following that is our specific concern in this paper. Rules are typically looked at as choice-constraining factors basically in the same way as conventional income and price constraints[13]. If this perspective is applied as a model of case by case, situational choices, it would seem to suggest that rule-compliance extends only so far as the particular situational incentive-structure "dictates" a rule-conforming choice. A rule-compliant act under circumstances where rule-violation would be the maximizing choice is a "square circle" to such a perspective, it is something that it simply rules out. And consequently it would seem to be necessarily incompatible with the notion of genuinely rule-following behavior, a notion that implies that particular acts of rule-compliance may very well not be maximizing. According to the model of case by case, situational choices, rule-following behavior should be observed only to the extent that over a sequence of recurrent choice situations the relevant incentive structure is stable enough so that rule compliance is in each and every case the preferable alternative[14]. As mentioned earlier, however, it seems doubtful whether a viable social order could be sustained if rule-compliance were exclusively a matter of case by case adjustment. A functioning social order apparently is dependent on a kind of rule-compliance that is not limited to those instances where the particular situational constraints actually make rule-following the maximizing choice. Rather it appears to be always

---

choice (SIMON 1957, p. 241: "Broadly stated, the task is to replace the global rationality of economic man with a kind of rational behavior that is compatible with the access to information and the computational capacities that are actually possessed by organisms, including man, in the kinds of environment in which such organisms exist.") is of obvious relevance to the present issue though it was not explicitly stated in terms of the contrast of case-by-case maximization vs. rule-following behavior. – The latter aspect is addressed by NELSON and WINTER (1982, pp. 65 ff.) in their discussion of the maximization assumption.

[13] The notion of "rules as constraints" is often used in a rather fuzzy and ambiguous way. For the sake of clarity it should be understood that it is, of course, not a rule "per se" that imposes constraints on anybody's behavior. A social rule, in the strict sense, is a prescriptive statement on how one should behave in certain types of situations, and the statement *as such* does not constrain anything. A rule becomes an effective constraint by some kind of motivating force or "enforcement", in the broadest sense, whatever its source and nature may be.

[14] S. LINDENBERG (1983, p. 454) refers to this type of situation when he assumes that "the reward structure of the repeated choice situations is stable enough that the same alternative has the highest expected utility throughout the series of repetitions."

based, to some extent, on what I refer to here as *genuine rule-following*, that is, a disposition in general to abide by certain rules without choosing in each and every situation anew whether or not to obey. As Hayek (1973, p. 11) asserts, man is in fact "as much a rule-following animal as a purpose-seeking one."

Neither the sociological nor the economic perspective provide a theoretical framework that consistently integrates both, the notion of choice and that of rule-following. In other terms, neither the sociologial nor the economic perspective provide a theoretical conception that would allow us systematically to account for both features of human behavior, its responsiveness to incentives *and* its rule-following nature[15]. The sociological perspective does not simply ignore that people respond to incentives – after all, the concept of *sanctions* is one of its core notions. But this is not systematically integrated with the notion of rule-following and role-playing that dominates the sociological approach. Correspondingly, the economic model of rational choice is not unaware of the role of rules and of rule-guided behavior. But, again, its explanatory focus on particular, situational choices does not seem to allow for a consistent account of genuine rule-following behavior[16].

To the extent that both features, responsiveness and rule-following, are characteristic of human behavior, we would want to base our social theory on a model of man that consistently reconciles the notion of choice with the notion of rule-following[17]. Given a choice between the sociologial and the economic models of man, it seems to me that the latter lends itself more readily than the

---

[15] K. D. Opp (1986, p. 15) arrives at a similar conclusion: "Während also Soziologen normalerweise davon ausgehen, daß Normen sozusagen blind befolgt werden, wird in der Ökonomie genau die entgegengesetzte Annahme getroffen: In jeder Situation hat das Individuum eine Wahl zwischen Alternativen. ...Vermutlich ist keine der alternativen Hypothesen richtig."

[16] To the extent that the issue is addressed in economics, it tends to be so in a mere ad hoc fashion. W. H. Meckling, for instance, in his defense of the economic model of man concedes that, from a "positive standpoint, it is... important to recognize the impact of tradition, custom, mores, and taboos on human behavior" (1976, pp. 552 f.), but he does not explain how the economic model is supposed to systematically account for this phenomenon. Another type of ad hoc account is reflected in the following statement by G. Tullock and R. B. McKenzie (1985, p. 143): "The cost of cheating is, first, the fact that the cheater's conscience may bother him. If Pete has been ethically endoctrinated... then there is some positive cost to him for violating that ethical principle." – This kind of argument sounds somewhat more systematic but it consists in fact in little more than an ad hoc specification of the relevant "utility- function", a strategy that is not uncommon in economic discussions on the norms and rules issue.

[17] H. Kliemt (1987, pp. 13 f.) pursues a very similar argument: "In explaining social reality we have to combine in one behavioral model two human dispositions simultaneously: that of acting according to some rules and that of choosing according to the exigencies of the moment." Such a 'combined model' would, Kliemt (ibid., p. 14) argues, resolve "the old controversy between so-called social and so-called economic man as basic concepts of social theory." – Kliemt's ideas about how such a reconciliation might be achieved (cf. also Kliemt 1984, in particular pp. 32 ff. and 40 ff.) are somewhat different from, though not incompatible with, the approach that is advocated in the present paper.

154 *Viktor Vanberg*

former to the kind of the theoretical modifications that are necessary for such a reconciliation. In the remainder of this paper I will argue that the economic perspective can be consistently extended so as to allow for a systematic incorporation of the notion of rule-following behavior into a rational choice framework.

V. The Rationality of Rule-following

As mentioned earlier, a behavioral regularity may emerge because the relevant incentive structure remains sufficiently stable over a sequence of recurrent choice situations, making rule-compliance in each particular choice situation the maximizing choice. In contrast to such de facto regularities genuine rule-following behavior reflects the fact that the actor does not choose on a case by case basis but is predisposed or preprogrammed to act in a certain way in certain *types* of situations. To argue that the actor does not choose on a case by case basis is, to be sure, not the same as arguing that his behavior is not based on choice at all. The contradiction between the notion of choice and the apparent absence of choice in rule-following behavior can be resolved by distinguishing between *different levels* at which behavioral choices can be made. Analoguous to the distinction between *in-period* and *constitutional* choices in the realm of collective or group decisionmaking[18], we may – when analyzing individual behavior – distinguish between *personal* in-period or situational choices on the one hand and *personal* constitutional choices on the other.

Rule-following behavior is, necessarily, relatively unresponsive to variations in particular situational circumstances. The very point in following a rule is in not "calculating" each case individually. In this sense, rule-following means the very absence, to some extent, of choice on the in-period, situational level. This is quite compatible, however, with choice and calculation at the "constitutional" level. We can view an individual's adoption of a behavioral rule as a personal constitutional choice among potential alternative general patterns of behavior. To adopt a rule in this sense is rational if it is perceived as a more advantageous strategy compared to potential alternatives, where attempting to maximize on a case by case basis can be viewed as *one* alternative. Such comparative "calculation" of the expected benefits of alternative rules and of case by case maximization need not be a deliberate act. The central notion is that practices are adopted *because* they are advantageous to the actor, whether such adoption occurs explicitly and consciously or implicitly and habitually. Rule-following by necessity implies that on particular occasions the person will miss out on opportunities where, given the particular situational circumstances, rule-violation

---

[18] J. M. BUCHANAN 1987, p. 248.

would be his maximizing choice. To miss out on such opportunities is rational, however, if rule-following is on balance advantageous[19].

The tendency to adopt rules, to behave in a pre-programmed way rather than on the basis of case-by-case adjustments, is inherent in human nature as it is, for that matter, to the nature of living organisms in general (Heiner 1983). There are basically three ways by which the fact that following certain rules is advantageous (compared to case by case adaptation) may be translated into effective behavioral dispositions: Through natural selection and genetic evolution, through unreflected, habitual learning on part of the individual, and through deliberate and conscious choice to adopt a rule[20].

Our concern in this paper will be with *learnt* rule-following behavior and deliberate adoption of rules rather than with innate behavioral regularities. As far as the latter are concerned there is an obvious answer to the question of how individuals come to follow them. They follow these rules simply because they are part of their biological nature. We shall here ignore the issue of how the socially relevant innate regularities of human behavior may be explained as the outcome of evolutionary selection, an issue to which sociobiology has contributed important insights. Assuming a *given* genetic nature of man our interest is in understanding the forces that account for learned rule-following behavior. We want to explore the reasons why rational, self-seeking beings come to adopt rules, that is, come to have their behavior preprogrammed.

In general it can be argued that adopting a rule for how to behave in certain types of situations is rational if rule-following can be expected to result in larger overall payoffs (over a relevant period of time) than case by case adjustment. For rule-following to allow for larger payoffs, it would seem that the kinds of action that the rule requires have to meet one (or both) of the following conditions: They generate – within the relevant environment – *in general* consequences that are sufficiently beneficial to the actor. Or, they generate beneficial consequences because of the very reason that they are carried out regularly[21]. There are (at least) three principal reasons why one or both of these conditions may be met. These reasons have to do with,

---

[19] The situation is analogous to the one J.M. BUCHANAN (1987, p. 248) describes for the choice of collective decision rules: "In this framework, an individual may rationally prefer a rule that will, on particular occasions, operate to produce results that are opposed to his own interests. The individual will do so if he predicts that, on balance over the whole sequence of "plays", his own interests will be more effectively served..."

[20] Drawing a distinction between genetic evolution and individual learning allows, to be sure, for the two types of processes to interact, in particular in that the genetical structure of instincts may determine what can be learned and how the learning occurs (GOULD and MARLER 1987).

[21] I adopt this useful distinction from Michael Baurmann who used it in his written comment on an earlier draft of this article.

Viktor Vanberg

first, decision making costs, second, with the risk of mistakes, and, third, with the precommitment problem. Though, in any particular case, it might be difficult to isolate one from the others, it is useful briefly to discuss each of these reasons separately.

Rule-following reduces decision making costs as compared to case by case choices. This apparent fact plays a central role in Arnold Gehlen's anthropological theory of institutions. Gehlen's theory rests on the fundamental idea that *institutions* are a *cultural* analogue to, and substitute for, natural *instincts*. Compared to non-human animals, human behavior is much less preprogrammed by instincts. It is much more variable or "plastic", adaptable to varying environments. This openness or plasticity of behavior enables humans to adjust to an extraordinary variety of living conditions, but it also creates its own problems. It causes uncertainty concerning other persons' behavior and it imposes the burden of being permanently required to make decisions about how to act. Institutions in the sense of socially shared behavioral routines serve, so Gehlen's argument, as a remedy for both problems[22]. They make other persons behavior more predictable and they offer relief from being permanently pressured to choose among potential alternative courses of action[23]. With regard to the second aspect, the one that is of particular interest in the present context, Gehlen argues that the relief provided by institutions and their behavioral routines is *productive* in that it releases energies that would otherwise be absorbed in the process of case by case decision making[24].

[22] A. GEHLEN 1961, p. 68: "Die Institutionen wie Recht, Ehe, Eigentum usw. erscheinen dann als haltgebende und gestaltbestimmende Stabilisierungen von Antriebskräften, die isoliert gedacht als plastisch und richtungslabil erscheinen... Solche Institutionen bedeuten dann für den einzelnen eine Entlastung von Grundentscheidungen und eine eingewohnte Sicherheit der maßgeblichen Orientierungen, so daß das Verhalten reflexionsfrei und stetig, auch in der Gegenseitigkeit gleichförmig erfolgen kann. Man muß daher das institutionell eingeregelte Verhalten (Fühlen, Denken, Werten usw.) als eine Wiederherstellung der verlorenen tierischen Instinktsicherung auf sehr viel höherer Ebene auffassen."

[23] A. GEHLEN 1964, p. 23: "Anthropologisch ist das Thema der Bildung von Gewohnheiten von großer Bedeutung, schon weil alle Institutionen als Systeme verteilter Gewohnheiten gelebt werden. Gewohnheiten... sind... nicht notwendig unbewußt, ihre Pointe ist vielmehr die Entlastung vom Aufwand improvisierter Motivbildung... (E)in solches praktisches Gewohnheitsverhalten (steht) beim Menschen an der Stelle, wo wir beim Tier die Instinktreaktion finden." – Ibid., p. 43: "Die allen Institutionen wesenseigene Entlastungsfunktion von der subjektiven Motivation und von dauernden Improvisationen fallweise zu vertretender Entschlüsse ist eine der großartigsten Kultureigenschaften... Wenn Institutionen... in Verfall geraten, ... fällt diese Verhaltenssicherheit dahin, man wird mit Entscheidungszumutungen gerade da überlastet, wo alles selbstverständlich sein sollte: 'too much discriminative strain' – zu viel Unterscheidungs- und Entscheidungsdruck ist eine gute amerikanische Formel."

[24] A. GEHLEN 1964, p. 43: "(D)ie Habitualisierung des Verhaltens (ist) selbst produktiv, da sie die Entlastungschance für höhere, kombinationsreiche Motivationen herstellt und diese damit geradezu ermöglicht." – See also GEHLEN 1973, p. 97: "Diese Entlastung wirkt sich produktiv aus, denn die wohltätige Fraglosigkeit, die dann entsteht, wenn der

Following a rule rather than adjusting to the particular circumstances of each individual choice situation may involve a trade-off: The savings in decision making costs may have to be paid for by a decreased overall "quality" of choice-outcomes. However, and this is the second source of potential benefits from rule-following, it is also possible that rule-following improves the overall quality of choice-outcomes compared to case by case choices. Such an improvement is possible if the risk of "mistakes" or "errors" is sufficiently high in a case by case choice setting, a risk that may be due to such factors as limited capacity of collecting and processing relevant information[25]. This argument is central to Ronald Heiner's attempt to provide a systematic "alternative to traditional optimization theory" (1983, p. 560), an alternative that accounts for various of the persistent critiques on the rationality postulate of economics[26]. Heiner's suggestion for an alternative to standard maximization theory rests on the conjecture that "rule-governed" behavior – in all its varieties, human and nonhuman (instincts, habits, routines, rules of thumb, customs, norms) – can be viewed as an adaptive response to environmental complexities and uncertainties which make it difficult for an individual in recurrent choice situations to select the most preferred alternative[27]. Under conditions where an agent's competence

Einzelne innen und außen von einem Regelgefüge getragen wird, macht geistige Energien nach oben hin frei."

[25] There is an obvious interrelation between this aspect and the decision making cost aspect discussed before. F. A. HAYEK (1967, p. 90) refers to both of these aspects when he argues: "We all know of course that in fact we have learned to act according to rules in order to give our successive action some coherence, that we adopt general rules for our lives not only to save us the trouble of reconsidering certain questions every time they arise, but mainly because only thus can we produce something like a rational whole." – As Hayek (cf. e.g. ibid., p. 88) has pointed out, these kinds of considerations have been central to David Hume's moral philosophy. An interesting contribution in this context is M. J. COSTA (1984) where Hume's response to the question "Why be just?" is characterized as follows (ibid. pp. 472f.): "Hume is asking us to consider the plight of the knave, the person who attempts to make each action decision on the basis of calculating the costs/ benefits of that particular action... How could one possibly perform the kind of careful calculation that would be needed for each such decision situation? General rules or guidelines have to be consulted as matter of practical necessity... Many errors can be saved by having a disposition to do the just thing. The person who has such a disposition does not typically even consider a cost/benefit analysis on the effects of acting unjustly. It may be that the failure to take up the analysis will result in missed opportunities, but the chances are that the cost of such missed opportunities will be much less than the costs resulting from miscalculation of costs/benefits done on an individual case basis or by following some other form of general rules."

[26] HEINER 1988, p. 1: "Conceptional choice theory assumes agents perfectly respond to information in the sense of always making decisions that maximize expected utility based on their observed information. Opposing this view has been the persistent criticism that 'real world' agents have severe limitations in their ability to process information, which thereby prevents them from perfectly using information without error."

[27] HEINER 1983, p. 561: "I believe there is a viable alternative to standard models – one that directly comes to grips with the persistent critiques of economic theory... In particular, I believe that observed regularities of behavior can be fruitfully understood as 'be-

158   *Viktor Vanberg*

in processing the relevant information does not match the difficulty in selecting
the most preferred alternatives, rule-following may generate a pattern of outcomes superior to those resulting from attempted case by case maximization.
Rule-following will be an overall superior strategy if the protection against
erroneous decisions outweighs the disadvantage of missing out on potential
preferred exceptions[28].

A third reason why rule-following may allow for a preferable pattern of
outcomes has been referred to above as the *precommitment problem*. This label
is used here to subsume all cases where, in one way or another, the consistency of
choices over time is the very precondition for certain desirable outcomes to be
realized. That is, the relevant benefits result *because* an agent *as a rule* behaves in
certain ways in certain types of situations – or because he is *known* to behave in
such consistent ways. The fact that one is less likely to become a target for
blackmail attempts if one is known not to give in to blackmailers is an example of
this principle. Examples of a different kind are those situations for which
"Ulysses and the Sirens" has become a parable, situations that are the subject of
the theory of *self-management*[29].

VI. Personal Rules and Social Rules

For obvious reasons, adopting a rule makes sense only where recurrent rather
than individual decision problems are concerned. *Rules* can be viewed as providing standard solutions to *recurrent choice problems*. Accordingly, one may
differentiate among kinds of rules in terms of systematic differences in the types
of problems to which they are related. In the present context it is useful to reflect
on a very fundamental distinction, namely that between *personal* and *social*

havioral rules' that arise because of uncertainty in distinguishing preferred from less-
preferred behavior. Such uncertainty requires behavior to be governed by mechanisms
that restrict the flexibility to choose potential actions... Thus, it is in the limits to
maximizing that we will find the origin of predictable behavior."

[28] HEINER 1983, p. 585: "Uncertainty exists because agents cannot decipher all of the
complexity of the decision problems they face, which literally prevents them from selecting
most preferred alternatives. Consequently, the flexibility of behavior to react to information is constrained to smaller behavioral repertoires that can be reliably administered.
Numerous deviations from the resulting behavior patterns are actually superior in certain
situations, but they are still ignored because of uncertainty about when to deviate from
these regularities."

[29] Cf. TH. SCHELLING 1983; see also R. A. FRANK 1987. – T. COWEN (1987) has pointed to
an interesting parallel between contributions on the issue of dynamic consistency of plans
in microeconomics (STROTZ 1955/56) and in macroeconomics (KYDLAND and PRESCOTT
1977) that both concern situations where, in the absence of precommitment or self-
constraint, decisions (consumer choices on the one side and policy decisions on the other)
result in a suboptimal overall outcome though they are individually and separately maximizing.

rules, a distinction that pertains to the *rationale* of rules. The rationale for *personal rules* is "personal" in that the rule-following person himself is the principal and direct beneficiary of his rule-following. The payoffs a person realizes from following a personal rule are essentially independent from other persons' behavior. In particular, these payoffs are not contingent on whether the respective rule is simultaneously followed by others in the relevant community. By his own rule-following, the individual does not (or does so only incidentally) produce benefits to other persons. Individual habits or routines, like getting up at certain times in the morning or regularly riding an exercise bike half an hour per day, fall into this category.

By contrast, the rationale for *social* rules is "social" in that an actor's rule-obedience generates direct benefits to others, while benefits to himself result only indirectly, mediated through the responses of others. The rule-follower may benefit as others in the relevant community respond to his behavior, or benefits may be contingent on the generality of rule-following over all persons in the group, both his own and others. By following a rule like "keeping promises" a person generates direct benefits to others and it is only *indirectly*, through others' reciprocating responses, that following such a rule can be advantageous to the actor himself. For rules like "driving on the right side of the road", it is not his own rule-following *per se* that is advantageous to a person but the combination of his own and other persons' simultaneous rule-following. While *personal* rules can be viewed as providing solutions to recurrent choice problems an individual faces in organizing his own private life, *social* rules can be viewed as providing solutions to recurrent *interaction problems*, i.e. to choice-problems individuals jointly face in organizing their social interactions, one with another.

The distinction between personal and social rules should not be understood as separating two mutually exclusive categories. A rule a person adopts primarily for organizing his private life, e.g. not to mow his lawn on Sundays, may at the same time serve a social function, and, conversely, a rule which primarily serves a social coordination purpose, e.g. to worship god on Sundays, may at the same time serve the purpose of organizing a person's private life. In addition, the distinction between personal and social rules is not a simple matter of fact but may be subject to social interpretation and redefinition. It is the presence or absence of "relevant" external effects from certain activities that will determine whether or not a rule concerning those activities takes on a more private or social character, and persons' perceptions of what "relevant" externalities are can and do change over time and vary across communities.

The distinction between personal rules and social rules allows us to separate three explanatory problems that an "economics of rules" should explore. First, there is the question of why and under what circumstances it may be rational/advantageous for an individual to constrain his own behavior by a personal rule. There is, second, the question of why and under what conditions it can be rational/advantageous for separate individuals of an interacting group to agree jointly on submitting to the constraints of social rules. And there is the third question of why and under what conditions it may be rational/advantageous to an individual to follow a social rule. To answer the first question is to provide a rationale for personal rules. To answer the second question is to provide a rationale for social rules. And, an important aspect of answering the third question can be seen in providing a rationale for *morality*, understood as a person's disposition to follow moral rules[30].

It is instructive to note that even for personal rules a compliance problem may exist. An individual's interest in adopting a rule does not necessarily secure compliance with the rule, a fact of life that everybody experiences who tries to break a "bad" habit and that provides a potential source of income to people like psychiatrists. In order to make himself actually follow a rule that he wants to adopt, an individual may have to restructure deliberately the circumstances that will affect his in-period choices[31].

The differences between "agreeing" to a rule and complying with a rule is, as will be discussed later, of particular significance where *social* rules are concerned. Yet, it is noteworthy that this issue does not only arise for social rules but may be present with personal rules as well[32]. To explain why an individual may want to adopt a personal rule X is not necessarily the same as explaining why he actually lives up to the rule. There are – in the sense explained above – two choice levels that are to be separated here: Choices to adopt or not to adopt rules for one's own behavior, and choices to comply or not to comply with self-chosen rules in particular situations. *A fortiori*, to explain why an individual would want to see a social rule Y being adopted in his community is not the same as explaining why he would want to adopt rule Y as a maxim for his own behavior or why he would want to comply with the rule in particular choice situations. Where social rules are concerned, a third choice-level is, in a sense, added to the "compliance-level" and the "personal-constitutional level" that can be separated with regard to personal rules. At this third level, the "social-constitutional level", a person can be said – actually or fictiously – to "choose" rules for a group or a community of which he is a part. The reasons for which a person may prefer a certain rule on the "social-constitutional level" are typically different from the reasons for which he would want to adopt the rule as a maxim for his own

---

[30] The third question can actually be subdivided into two issues, namely the issue of compliance in particular situations and the issue of genuine rule-following. For the present discussion only the second issue is of relevance.

[31] For these types of issues the above mentioned theory of *self-management* or *self-command* (e. g. SCHELLING 1984) is of obvious relevance.

[32] The systematic reason for the need of "enforcement" even of preferred personal rules is, as H. KLIEMT (1987, p. 5) states, that "in a present situation the decision maker can causally influence incentives of future decision situations but he cannot now control his future decision itself."

behavior and they are different from the reasons for his rule-compliance in particular cases[33].

VII. *Social Rules: Constitutional Interests and Compliance Interests*

The distinction between personal rules and social rules is helpful in separating two critically different kinds of rule-interests that a person may have, namely the interest in adopting a certain rule for his own behavior and the interest in seeing a certain rule implemented in a social community within which he operates. The two kinds of interests may be distinguished as (individual) *dispositional interest* and (social) *constitutional interest*. To argue that a person has an interest in adopting a personal rule by definition implies that he has a *dispositional interest* in complying with the rule. There remains, of course, the question of whether, in particular situations, he will actually comply or not comply with the rule, that is, whether he will live up or not live up to his dispositional interests. For instance, a person may want to adopt the rule of doing thirty minutes exercise every day, but the situational incentives on particular days may keep him from doing what his dispositional interests would require him to do.

There is a totally new dimension added to the issue of rule-interests vs. compliance-interests when social rules are concerned, namely the dimension that has been referred to above as "constitutional interests". It is crucial to realize that a person's *constitutional interest* in a certain social rule and his *dispositional interest* in adopting this rule for himself are, in principle, completely independent from each other. That a person may have a constitutional interest in seeing a certain rule practiced in his community means that he prefers to live in a social environment where this rule is observed rather than in one where this is not the case. This *constitutional* interest does not per se imply that the person must have a *dispositional* interest in adopting the rule for himself. Whether he has or does not have such a dispositional interest will depend on certain factual conditions, in particular the constraints he is facing, conditions that do or do not render it in his interest to adopt the rule for himself. There is nothing logically inconsistent about a thief preferring to live in a community of honest people or about a tax-evader preferring to live in a community where taxes are generally paid.

If a person's constitutional and dispositional interests, as defined, should

---

[33] The three levels of choice involving rules can be illustrated by a single example, alcohol consumption. A person may adopt a personal rule that dictates abstinence; he may pre-program his behavior to incorporate a disposition to turn down offers of drinks; and he may try to effect a change in future incentives, e. g. by publicly anouncing his intentions. When a drink is offered, however, this person faces a compliance choice concerning adherence to or violation of the previously selected personal rule. The same person may or may not agree on a proposal that would impose a social rule of prohibition on all members of the community, himself included.

coincide, the question can still be asked whether or not he will in particular situations comply with the rule. For instance, somebody may have a constitutional interest in a rule prohibiting adultery and he may have, at the same time, a dispositional interest in adopting the rule for himself, because he senses that in abiding to the rule he will fare better overall. He may nevertheless fail in particular situations to live up to such a dispositional interest.

In what follows I will simply contrast *constitutional interests* and *compliance-* or *action-interests* without always specifying whether the latter terms refer to a person's dispositional interests or to his rule-compliance in particular situations. The emphasis will be primarily on the fact that a person's constitutional interests in living in a social environment with certain rule-characteristics should be carefully distinguished from his dispositional interest in adopting certain rules as personal maxims[34].

The issue of constitutional interests has some apparent resemblance to what, at least in part, the *functionalist* perspective in sociology and anthropology is about. In reflecting on potential constitutional interests of persons in a social community, we may provide a *rationale* for certain rules, and providing a rationale for rules is exactly what functionalism is about. The problem with functionalism, the issue of its collectivistic tendencies set aside, is not its focus on the rationale for rules and institutions. The problem lies in the "functionalist fallacy" of supposing that by identifying the "benefits" that a rule provides to a group or community we answer the question of why the rule is practiced in the group.

Clearly to distinguish between constitutional interests and compliance interests allows one to avoid the functionalist fallacy without giving up theorizing about the rationale for social rules. The distinction between these two kinds of interests seems to be typically implied when "individual and group interests", "private and common interests", or similarly labelled interests are contrasted. These terminologies tend to be misleading, though, in suggesting either that there are different subjects experiencing these interests, the "individual" and the "group", or by implying that these are *conflicting* interests within one person. In contrast to these terminologies the distinction between constitutional and compliance interests is supposed to emphasize that the relevant difference in interests is about *different kinds of choices* rather than about conflicting preferences with regard to the same kind of choice. An actor's constitutional interests determine what he would prefer if he were to participate in choosing the *constitution*, in the broadest sense, for his respective social community. A person's compliance interests are his preferences over potential alternative courses of action, given the constraints that he faces – including the rules of his social environment and the ways these rules are enforced, formally or informally.

In order for a generally – in the limit: by all participants – preferred constitu-

---

[34] The issue of "constitutional interests vs. compliance interests" is discussed in more detail in V. VANBERG and J. M. BUCHANAN 1987.

tional order to be operative, a tolerable correspondence between constitutional interests and compliance interests is required. There are basically two ways in which such a correspondence may be brought about, two ways which are complementary rather than mutually exclusive[35]. The one is based on individuals' rational capacity purposefully to implement their constitutional interests, their capacity to diagnose the constitutional problems that they face and to change the choice-environment so as to make mutually preferred behavior individually rational[36]. The other solution to the "correspondence problem" is of an "invisible hand" nature. It results from the fact that, under certain conditions, the constraints that make it rational for individuals to comply with constitutionally preferred rules are, at least to some extent, "naturally" or unintentionally produced as a byproduct of actions that persons choose in pursuit of their direct action interests, without any regard to their constitutional interests. This solution has been emphasized by the "spontaneous order tradition" in social theory, the most prominent contemporary representative of which is F. A. Hayek. The constitutional-constructivist solution, emphasizing the potential for deliberately implemented constitutional reform, is emphasized in J. M. Buchanan's work in the area of constitutional economics.

VIII. Calculating Homo Sociologicus

In terms of the preceding analysis the central issue of this paper, namely that of explaining genuine rule-following behavior, can now be stated in a (hopefully) somewhat more precise way. It can be advantageous for a person to adopt a disposition generally to comply with a social rule even if there are situations where, considered in terms of case by case optimization, deviation would be the maximizing choice. A person can be expected to adopt such a disposition if rule-following is experienced as, or expected to be, an overall advantageous behavioral strategy. For the disposition to be adopted, the person need not be actually aware of its advantage. In other terms, the "calculation" of the costs and benefits from following a particular rule is not necessarily a conscious act. This "calculation" can be done by "nature" in an evolutionary process, it can be an unreflected process of habitual learning, and it may be a deliberate rational act.

When sociologists invoke the notion of "internalization of norms", what they typically have in mind is a process of unreflected, habitual learning. If inter-

---

[35] This issue is discussed in more detail in V. VANBERG and J. M. BUCHANAN 1987.

[36] That this notion might be an element in T. Parsons' "voluntaristic theory of action" seems to be indicated, though not unambiguously, by the following statement (PARSONS 1968, p. 76): "The logical starting point for analysis of the role of normative elements in human action is the fact of experience that men not only respond to stimuli but in some sense try to conform their action to patterns which are, by the actor and other members of the same collectivity, deemed desirable."

                                    Viktor Vanberg

preted in this way, the concept of internalization can be very well incorporated into the theoretical framework suggested in this paper. To be sure, such incorporation would require giving up certain assumptions that tend to be part of the sociological notion of internalization, in particular the assumption that through internalization compliance with social rules becomes unconditional and a "motive of its own"[37]. From the perspective that is suggested here, the kind of genuine rule-following that we are concerned with is based on a disposition that individuals cannot be expected to acquire if their – direct or indirect – experience does not tell them that general rule-compliance will be overall advantageous, and that they will not preserve if their experience systematically changes. In other words, such a disposition – we may call it *morality* – is always in some sense conditional[38].

Whether or not individuals have reasons to learn that general rule-compliance or morality is an advantageous behavioral pattern or disposition will crucially depend on characteristics of the environment within which they act[39]. A person can be expected systematically to discriminate among social settings in which general rule-compliance is or is not experienced as an advantageous strategy, and he can be expected to respond to changes in his environment that systematically affect the relative payoffs from genuine rule-following as compared to case by case optimization. Although genuine rule-following by necessity is to some extent unresponsive to environmental variation (perfect responsiveness is, for obvious reasons, inconsistent with the very notion of rule-following), it certainly does not mean total unresponsiveness. Morality is a matter of an individual's adaptation to relevant characteristics of his environment, even if this adaptation is on a more general dispositional level rather than on the level of single choices in particular situations.

Throughout the discussion in the previous sections no systematic reference has been made to what we call *conscience*, something that is generally considered a most crucial aspect of "morality". It does not seem, however, that accounting for this phenomenon would require any major revisions in the theoretical framework that has been suggested here. A few remarks on this issue may be made by way of concluding this paper.

The psychic reactions that we commonly call a "good conscience" or a "bad conscience" apparently are learned concomitantly to the process in which the disposition generally to abide by certain rules is acquired. Once such a disposition is learned or acquired by a person, rule-compliance and rule-violation are no

---

[37] Cf. e.g. R. König's (1965, p. 58) interpretation of Durkheim's thoughts: "Im Gewissen gibt es aber keine... Polarität von Individuum und Kollektiv, sondern einzig Komplementarität der persönlichen Motivationsstruktur und der einer Gesellschaft oder einer Gruppe gemeinsamen Normen durch 'Internalisierung'."

[38] For a more detailed discussion of *morality* from the perspective described here cf. V. Vanberg 1988.

[39] For an interesting contribution on this issue cf. U. Witt 1986.

longer emotionally neutral events. An act of rule-violation typically causes a feeling of uneasiness (Hayek 1967, pp. 79 f.), a fact that tends to make a person's moral dispostion less responsive to changes in the environmental incentive-structure than it would otherwise be. But still, it does not make a person totally unresponsive to such changes. As *learned* responses, the emotional reactions to which the notion of conscience refers are themselves *conditional* and they can be expected to become *unlearned* if a person experiences – directly or indirectly – that rule-violations are typically not "punished". In other words, the internal sanctions of conscience cannot be considered an autonomous, independent source of rule-enforcement. It is a source that ultimately derives from, and ultimately remains, dependent on the kind of environmental reward-structure that a person experiences. In the absence of appropriate environmental responses to his behavior an individual can hardly be expected to develop a conscience. And, if relevant environmental characteristics change, his conscience cannot be expected to remain unaffected.

Summary

The subject of this paper is the relation between two theoretical notions that are commonly considered to reflect a fundamental difference between a sociological and an economic perspective: The notion of norm- or rule-guided behavior on the one side, and that of rational, self-interested choice on the other or, in short, the "homo sociologicus" vs. the "homo economicus" notion. Rather than discussing the two notions as alternative approaches, it is argued here that they can be and ought to be consistently integrated into one behavioral model.

Zusammenfassung

Gegenstand dieses Beitrages ist das Verhältnis zwischen zwei theoretischen Vorstellungen, die allgemein als Ausdruck des grundlegenden Unterschiedes zwischen einer soziologischen und einer ökonomischen Sichtweise betrachtet werden: Die Annahme normen- oder regelgeleiteten Verhaltens einerseits und die Annahme rationalen Handelns andererseits, oder kürzer, das Modell des "homo sociologicus" und das des "homo oeconomicus". Die beiden Vorstellungen werden hier nicht als alternative theoretische Ansätze diskutiert. Es wird vielmehr argumentiert, daß sich beide Annahmen konsistent in ein Verhaltensmodell integrieren lassen und integriert werden sollten.

References

BOUDON, RAYMOND, 1980: *Die Logik des gesellschaftlichen Handelns*, Neuwied und Darmstadt: Luchterhand.
BUCHANAN, JAMES M., 1987: "The Constitution of Economic Policy", *The American Economic Review*, Vol. 77, 243–250.

COLEMAN, JAMES S., 1987: "Norms as Social Capital", in: G. RADNITZKY and P. BERN-HOLZ, eds., *Economic Imperialism – The Economic Approach Applied Outside the Field of Economics*, New York: Paragon House Publishers, 133–155.

COSTA, MICHAEL J., 1984: "Why be Just? Hume's Response in the *Inquiry*", *The Southern Journal of Philosophy*, Vol. 22, 469–479.

COWEN, TYLER: *Dynamic Inconsistency and the Theory of Consumer Choice*, mimeographed (University of California, Irvine).

GAUTHIER, DAVID, 1987: *Morality, Rational Choice, and Semantic Representation: A Reply to my Critics*, mimeographed, University of Pittsburgh.

FRANK, ROBERT H., 1987: "If *Homo Economicus* Could Choose His Own Utility Function, Would He Want One with a Conscience", *The American Economic Review*, vol. 77, 593–604.

GEHLEN, ARNOLD, 1961: *Anthropologische Forschung*, Reinbek bei Hamburg: Rowohlt.

GEHLEN, ARNOLD, 1964: *Urmensch und Spätkultur,* 2. Aufl., Frankfurt: Athenaum Verlag.

GOULD, JAMES L. and PETER MARLER, 1987: "Learning by Instinct", *Scientific American*, Vol. 256, No. 1, 74–85.

GRANOVETTER, MARK, 1985: "Economic Action and Social Structure: The Problem of Embeddedness", *American Journal of Sociology*, Vol. 91, 481–510.

GRAY, JOHN, 1987: "The Economic Approach to Human Behavior: Its Prospects and Limitations, in: G. RADNITZKY and P. BERNHOLZ, op. cit., 33–49.

HARMAN, GILBERT, 1986: *Moral Agent and Impartial Spectator*, The Lindley Lecture, University of Kansas, Department of Philosophy.

HAYEK, FRIEDRICH A., 1964: "Kinds of Order in Society", *New Individualist Review*, Vol. 3, No. 2, 3–12.

HAYEK, FRIEDRICH A.,, 1967: "Notes on the Evolution of Systems of Rules of Conduct", in: Idem, *Studies in Philosophy, Politics and Economics*, Chicago: The University of Chicago Press, 66–81.

HAYEK, FRIEDRICH A., 1973: *Law, Legislation and Liberty*, Vol. 1, *Rules and Order*, London: Routledge & Kegan Paul.

HEINER, RONALD A., 1983: "The Origin of Predictable Behavior", *American Economic Review*, Vol. 73, 560–595.

HEINER, RONALD A., 1988: "The Necessity of Imperfect Decisions", forthcoming in *Journal of Economic Behavior & Organization*, February Issue.

KLIEMT, HARTMUT, 1984: "Nicht-explanative Funktionen eines 'Homo oeconomicus' und Beschränkungen seiner explanativen Rolle", in: M.J. HOLLER, ed., *Homo oeconomicus II*, München.

KLIEMT, HARTMUT, 1987: *The Reason of Rules and the Rule of Reason*, mimeographed.

KÖNIG, RENÉ, 1965: "Einleitung", in: E. DURKHEIM, *Die Regeln der soziologischen Methode*, Neuwied and Berlin: Luchterhand, 21–82.

KYDLAND, FINN and PRESCOTT, EDWARD, 1977: "Rules Rather than Discretion: The Inconsistency of Optimal Plans", *Journal of Political Economy*, vol. 85, 473–492.

LINDENBERG, SIEGWART, 1983: "Utility and Morality", *Kyklos*, Vol. 36, 450–468.

McPHERSON, MICHAEL S., 1984: "Limits on Self-Seeking – The Role of Morality in Economic Life", in: DAVID C. COLANDER, ed., *Neoclassical Political Economy*, Cambridge, Mass.: Ballinger, 71–85.

MECKLING, WILLIAM R. 1976: "Values and the Choice of the Model of the Individual in the Social Sciences", *Schweizerische Zeitschrift für Volkswirtschaft und Statistik*, Vol. 112, 545–559.

MENGER, CARL, 1985: *Investigations into the Method of the Social Sciences with Special Reference to Economics*, New York and London: New York University Press.

NELSON, RICHARD R. and SIDNEY G. WINTER, 1982: *An Evolutionary Theory of Economic Change*, Cambridge, Mass.: Harvard University Press.

OPP, KARL-DIETER, 1986: "Das Modell des Homo Sociologicus. Eine Explikation und eine Konfrontierung mit dem utilitaristischen Verhaltensmodell", *Analyse & Kritik*, Vol. 8, 1–27.

PARSONS, TALCOTT, 1934/35: "The Place of Ultimate Values in Sociological Theory", *The International Journal of Ethics*, Vol. 45, 282–316.

PARSONS, TALCOTT, 1960: "Durkheim's contribution to the Theory of Integration of Social Systems", in: K. H. WOLFF, ed., *Essays on Sociology and Philosophy by Emile Durkheim et al.*, New York: Harper & Row, 118–153.

PARSONS, TALCOTT, 1968: *The Structure of Social Action*, 2 vols.; New York: Free Press.

RÖHL, KLAUS F., 1978: "Über außervertragliche Voraussetzungen des Vertrages", in: F. KAULBACH and W. KRAWIETZ, eds., *Recht und Gesellschaft – Festschrift für Helmut Schelsky zum 65. Geburtstag*. Berlin: Duncker & Humblot, 435–480.

SCHELLING, THOMAS C., 1984: *Choice and Consequence*, Cambridge, Mass., and London: Harvard University Press.

SIMON, HERBERT A., 1957: "A Behavioral Model of Rational Choice", in: Idem, *Models of Man*, New York, 241–260.

STROTZ, ROBERT, 1955/56: "Myopia and Inconsistency in Dynamic Utility Maximization", *Review of Economic Studies*, vol. 23, 165–180.

TULLOCK, G. and R. B. McKENZIE, 1985: *The New World of Economics*, Fourth Edition, Homewood, Ill.: Richard D. Irwin.

VANBERG, VIKTOR, 1975: *Die zwei Soziologien*, Tübingen: Mohr.

VANBERG, VIKTOR, 1988: *Morality and Economics – De Moribus Est Disputandum*, New Brunswick, N.J.: Transaction Books (Social Philosophy and Policy Center, Original Paper Series).

VANBERG, VIKTOR, and JAMES M. BUCHANAN, 1987: *Rational Choice and Moral Order*, Center for Study of Public Choice, mimeographed.

WITT, ULRICH, 1986: "Evolution and Stability of Cooperation without Enforceable Contracts", *Kyklos*, Vol. 39, 245–266.

[13]

Journal of Economic Perspectives— Volume 3, Number 4— Fall 1989—Pages 99–117

Social Norms and Economic Theory

Jon Elster

O ne of the most persistent cleavages in the social sciences is the opposition between two lines of thought conveniently associated with Adam Smith and Emile Durkheim, between *homo economicus* and *homo sociologicus*. Of these, the former is supposed to be guided by instrumental rationality, while the behavior of the latter is dictated by social norms. The former is "pulled" by the prospect of future rewards, whereas the latter is "pushed" from behind by quasi-inertial forces (Gambetta, 1987). The former adapts to changing circumstances, always on the lookout for improvements. The latter is insensitive to circumstances, sticking to the prescribed behavior even if new and apparently better options become available. The former is easily caricatured as a self-contained, asocial atom, and the latter as the mindless plaything of social forces. In this paper I characterize this contrast more fully, and discuss attempts by economists to reduce norm-oriented action to some type of optimizing behavior.[1]

Rational action is concerned with outcomes. Rationality says: If you want to achieve *Y*, do *X*. By contrast, I define social norms by the feature that they are *not outcome-oriented*. The simplest social norms are of the type: Do *X*, or: Don't do *X*. More complex norms say: If you do *Y*, then do *X*, or: If others do *Y*, then do *X*. More complex norms still might say: Do *X* if it would be good if everyone did *X*. Rationality is essentially conditional and future-oriented. Social norms are either unconditional or, if conditional, are not future-oriented. For norms to be *social*, they must be shared by other people and partly sustained by their approval and disap-

---

[1]A fuller account of norms, with applications to collective action and bargaining problems, is found in Elster (1989).

■ *Jon Elster is Professor of Political Science and Philosophy at the University of Chicago, Chicago, Illinois, and Research Director at the Institute for Social Research, Oslo, Norway.*

proval. They are also sustained by the feelings of embarrassment, anxiety, guilt and shame that a person suffers at the prospect of violating them. A person obeying a norm may also be propelled by positive emotions, like anger and indignation. Djilas (1958, p. 107) refers to the feeling of a person enacting the norms of vengeance in Montenegro as "the wildest, sweetest kind of drunkenness." Social norms have a grip on the mind that is due to the strong emotions they can trigger.

This initial statement somewhat exaggerates the mechanical, unreflective character of norm-guided behavior. Social norms offer considerable scope for skill, choice, interpretation and manipulation. For that reason, rational actors often deploy norms to achieve their ends. Yet there are limits to the flexibility of norms, otherwise there would be nothing to manipulate.

Social norms must be distinguished from a number of other, related phenomena. First, social norms differ from moral norms. Some moral norms, like those derived from utilitarian ethics, are consequentialist. Secondly, social norms differ from legal norms. Legal norms are enforced by specialists who do so out of self-interest: they will lose their job if they don't. By contrast, social norms are enforced by members of the general community, and not always out of self-interest (see below). Thirdly, social norms are more than the convention equilibria described in Robert Sugden's accompanying article. As Sugden explains, the evolution of a convention equilibrium is guided by whether the conventions lead to a substantively better outcome. I argue below, however, that many social norms do not benefit anyone. Fourthly, social norms differ from private norms, the self-imposed rules that people construct to overcome weakness of will (Ainslie 1982, 1984, 1986). Private norms, like social norms, are non-outcome-oriented and sustained by feelings of anxiety and guilt. They are not, however, sustained by the approval and disapproval of others since they are not, or not necessarily, shared with others. Finally, norm-guided behavior must be distinguished from habits and compulsive neuroses. Unlike social norms, habits are private. Unlike private norms, their violation does not generate self-blame or guilt. Unlike neuroses and private norms, habits are not compulsive. Unlike social norms, compulsive neuroses are highly idiosyncratic. Yet what in one culture looks like a compulsive neurosis may, in another society, be an established social norm (Fenichel 1945, p. 586). Compulsive revenge behavior could be an example (Djilas, 1958).

To fix our ideas, let me give some examples of social norms.

Consumption norms regulate manners of dress, manners of table and the like. As shown by Proust's masterful account of life in the Guermantes circle, conformity with such norms can be vitally important to people, in spite of the fact that nothing of substance seems to be at stake. Pierre Bourdieu (1979) has extended the notion of consumption norms to cover cultural behavior: which syntax, vocabulary and pronunciation do you adopt? which movies do you see? which books do you read? which sports do you practice? what kind of furniture do you buy?

Norms against behavior "contrary to nature" include rules against incest, cannibalism, homosexuality and sodomy. The rule against cannibalism allows, however, for exceptions in case of *force majeure* (Edgerton, 1985, p. 51). The point obtains quite generally: Whenever there is a norm, there are often a set of adjunct norms defining legitimate exceptions. Often, these are less explicit than the main norm, and rely heavily on judgment and discretion.

Norms regulating the use of money often become legal, like the law against buying and selling votes. Often, however, they remain informal, like the norm against buying into a bus queue or the norm against asking one's neighbor to mow one's lawn for money. I discuss both of these cases later.

Norms of reciprocity enjoin us to return favors done to us by others (Gouldner, 1960). Gift-giving is often regulated by these norms. There may not be an unconditional norm of giving Christmas presents to a first cousin, but once the cousin begins to give me a gift I am under an obligation to return it.

Norms of retribution enjoin us to return harms done to us by others. Rules regulating revenge are often highly elaborate (Hasluck, 1954; Boehm, 1984; Miller, forthcoming). Nevertheless, revenge often seems to be contrary to self-interest: "Who sees not that vengeance, from the force alone of passion, may be so eagerly pursued as to make us knowingly neglect every consideration of ease, interest, or safety?" (Hume, 1751, Appendix II).

Work norms. The workplace is a hotbed for norm-guided action. There is a social norm against living off other people and a corresponding normative pressure to earn one's income from work (Elster, 1988). At the workplace one often finds informal norms among the workers that regulate their work effort. Typically, these set lower as well as upper limits on what is perceived as a proper effort: neither a chiseler nor a ratebuster be (Roethlisberger and Dickson, 1939, p. 522). Akerlof (1980) argues that employed workers have a "code of honor" that forbids them to train new workers who are hired to do the same job for lower wages.[2]

Norms of cooperation. There are many outcome-oriented maxims of cooperation. A utilitarian, for instance, would cooperate if and only if his contribution increases the average utility of the members in the group. There are also, however, non-outcome-oriented norms of cooperation. One is what one may call "everyday Kantianism:" cooperate if and only if it would be better for all if all cooperated than if nobody did. Another is a "norm of fairness:" cooperate if and only if most other people cooperate. Among the phenomena based on norms of cooperation one may cite voting (Barry, 1979) and tax compliance (Laurin, 1986).

Norms of distribution regulate what is seen as a fair allocation of income or other goods. In democratic societies, the norm of equality is especially strong. As Tocqueville (1969, p. 505) wrote: "the passion for equality seeps into every corner of the human heart, expands and fills the whole. It is no use telling them that by this blind surrender to an exclusive passion they are compromising their dearest interests; they are deaf." People may be willing to take a loss rather than accept a distribution they find unfair (Kahneman, Knetsch and Thaler, 1986). The solution concept for cooperative bargaining proposed by Kalai and Smorodinsky (1975) embodies a norm of fair distribution (McDonald and Solow, 1981, pp. 905–6).

---

[2]This was written before the introduction of two-tiered wage systems in several American airlines.

Drawing on these examples, I shall consider a number of arguments that have been made to the effect that social norms are "nothing but" instruments of individual, collective or genetic optimization. First, however, I want to make two brief remarks.

To accept social norms as a motivational mechanism is not to violate methodological individualism. True, many sociologists who have stressed the importance of social norms have also advocated methodological holism (e.g. Durkheim, 1958), but there is no logical connection between these views. Social norms, as I understand them here, are emotional and behavioral propensities of individuals.

To accept social norms as a motivational mechanism is not to deny the importance of rational choice. One eclectic view is that some actions are rational, others are norm-guided. A more general and more adequate formulation would be that actions typically are influenced both by rationality and by norms. Sometimes, the outcome is a compromise between what the norm prescribes and what rationality dictates. The subjects in the experiment of Kahneman, Knetsch and Thaler (1986) who rejected very unfair distributions, preferring to take nothing rather than to be exploited by others, did accept mildly skewed distributions. At other times, rationality acts as a constraint on social norms. Many people vote out of civic duty, except when the costs become very high. Conversely, social norms can act as a constraint on rationality. Cutthroat competitiveness in the market can go together with strict adherence to norms of honesty (Coleman, 1982).

Are Norms Rationalizations of Self-Interest?

Is it true, as argued by early generations of anthropologists and sociologists, that norms are in the saddle and people merely their supports? Or is it true, as argued by more recent generations, that rules and norms are just the raw material for strategic manipulation or, perhaps, for unconscious rationalization?

Sometimes, people will invoke a social norm to rationalize self-interest. Suppose my wife and I are having a dinner party for eight, and that four persons have already been invited. We discuss whether to invite a particular couple for the last two places, and find ourselves in disagreement, for somewhat murky reasons. I like the woman of the couple, and my wife doesn't like it that I like her. But we don't want to state these reasons. (Perhaps there is a social norm against doing so.) Instead we appeal to social norms. I invoke the norm of reciprocity, saying, "Since they had us over for dinner, it is our turn to invite them now." My wife invokes another norm: "Since we have already invited two single men, we must invite two women, to create a balance."

In wage negotiations, sheer bargaining power counts for much. Appeals to accepted social norms can also have some efficacy, however. There is a norm of fair division of the surplus between capital and labor. Employers will appeal to this norm when the firm does badly, workers when it does well. There is a norm of equal pay for equal work. Workers will appeal to this norm when they earn less than workers in similar firms, but not when they earn more. The norm of preservation of status, or wage differences, can also be exploited for bargaining purposes.

Social psychologists have studied norms of distribution to see whether there is any correlation between who subscribes to a norm and who benefits from it. Some findings point to the existence of a "norm of modesty:" high achievers prefer the norm of absolute equality of rewards, whereas low achievers prefer the norm of equity, or reward proportionally to achievement (Mikula, 1972; Kahn, Lamm and Nelson, 1977; Yaari and Bar-Hillel, 1988). More robust, however, are the findings which suggest that people prefer the distributive norms which favor them (Deutsch, 1985, Ch. 11; Messick and Sentis, 1983). This corresponds to a pattern frequently observed in wage discussions. Low-income groups invoke a norm of equality, whereas high-income groups advocate pay according to productivity.

Conditional norms lend themselves easily to manipulation. There is, for instance, a general norm that whoever first proposes that something be done has a special responsibility for making sure that it is carried out. This can prevent the proposal from ever being made, even if all would benefit from it. A couple may share the desire to have a child and yet neither may want to be the first to lance the idea, fearing that he or she would then get special child-caring responsibility.[3] The member of a seminar who suggests a possible topic for discussion is often saddled with the task of introducing it. The person in a courtship who first proposes a date is at a disadvantage (Waller, 1937). The fine art of inducing others to make the first move, and of resisting such inducements, provides instances of instrumentally rational exploitation of a social norm.

Some have said that this is all there is to norms: they are tools of manipulation, used to dress up self-interest in more acceptable garb. But this cannot be true. Some norms, like the norm of vengeance, obviously override self-interest. In fact, the cynical view of norms is self-defeating. "Unless rules were considered important and were taken seriously and followed, it would make no sense to manipulate them for personal benefit. If many people did not believe that rules were legitimate and compelling, how could anyone use these rules for personal advantage?" (Edgerton, 1985, p. 3). Or again, "if the justice arguments are such transparent frauds, why are they advanced in the first place and why are they given serious attention?" (Zajac, 1985, p. 120). If some people successfully exploit norms for self-interested purposes, it can only be because others are willing to let norms take precedence over self-interest. Moreover, even those who appeal to the norm usually believe in it, or else the appeal might not have much power (Veyne, 1976).

The would-be manipulator of norms is also constrained by the need—in fact, the social norm—to be consistent. Even if the norm has no grip on his mind, he must act as if it had. Having invoked the norm of reciprocity on one occasion, I cannot just dismiss it when my wife appeals to it another time. An employer may successfully appeal to the workers and get them to share the burdens in a bad year. The cost he pays is that in a good year he may also have to share the benefits. By making the earlier appeal, he committed himself to the norm of a fair division of the surplus (Mitchell, 1986, p. 69). The Swedish metal workers in the 1930s successfully invoked a

---

[3] I am indebted to Ottar Brox for this example.

norm of equality to bring about parity of wages with workers in the construction industry. Later, when they found themselves in a stronger bargaining position, their previous appeal to equality forced them to pull their punches (Swenson, 1989, p. 60). Finally, the manipulator is constrained by the fact that the repertoire of norms on which he can draw is, after all, limited. Even if unconstrained by earlier appeals to norms, there may not be any norm available that coincides neatly with his self-interest.

When I say that manipulation of social norms presupposes that they have some kind of grip on the mind since otherwise there would be nothing to manipulate, I am not suggesting that society is made up of two sorts of people: those who believe in the norms and those who manipulate the believers. Rather, I believe that most norms are shared by most people—manipulators as well as manipulated. Rather than manipulation in a direct sense, we are dealing here with an amalgam of belief, deception and self-deception. At any given time we believe in many different norms, which may have contradictory implications for the situation at hand. A norm that happens to coincide with narrowly defined self-interest easily acquires special salience. If there is no norm handy to rationalize self-interest, or if I have invoked a different norm in the recent past, or if there is another norm which overrides it, I may have to act against my self-interest. My self-image as someone who is bound by the norms of society does not allow me to pick and choose indiscriminately from the large menu of norms to justify my actions, since I have to justify them to myself no less than to others. At the very least, norms are soft constraints on action. The existence of norms of revenge shows that sometimes they are much more than that.

Are Norms Followed Out of Self-Interest?

When people obey norms, they often have a particular outcome in mind: they want to avoid the disapproval—ranging from raised eyebrows to social ostracism—of other people. Suppose I face the choice between taking revenge for the murder of my cousin and not doing anything. The cost of revenge is that I might in turn be the target of a counter-vengeance. At worst, the cost of not doing anything is that my family and friends desert me, leaving me out on my own, defenselessly exposed to predators. At best, I will lose their esteem and my ability to act as an autonomous agent among them. A cost-benefit analysis is likely to tell me that revenge (or exile) is the rational choice. More generally, norm-guided behavior is supported by the threat of social sanctions that make it rational to obey the norms. Akerlof (1976) argues, along these lines, that in India it is rational to adhere to the caste system, even assuming that "tastes" are neutral.

In response to this argument, we can first observe that norms do not need external sanctions to be effective. When norms are internalized, they are followed even when violation would be unobserved and not exposed to sanctions. Shame or anticipation of it is a sufficient internal sanction. I don't pick my nose when I can be observed by people on a train passing by, even if I am confident that they are all perfect strangers whom I shall never see again and who have no power to impose sanctions on me. I don't throw litter in the park, even when there is nobody around to observe me. If punishment was merely the price tag attached to crime, nobody would feel shame when caught. People have an internal gyroscope that keeps them adhering steadily to norms, independently of the current reactions of others.

A second answer to the claim that people obey norms because of the sanctions attached to violations of norms emerges if we ask why people would sanction others for violating norms. What's in it for them? One reply could be that if they do not express their disapproval of the violation, they will themselves be the target of disapproval by third parties. When there is a norm to do X, there is usually a "meta-norm" (Axelrod, 1986) to sanction people who fail to do X, perhaps even a norm to sanction people who fail to sanction people who fail to do X. As long as the cost of expressing disapproval is less than the cost of receiving disapproval for not expressing it, it is in one's rational self-interest to express it. Now, expressing disapproval is always costly, whatever the target behavior. At the very least it requires energy and attention that might have been used for other purposes. One may alienate or provoke the target individual, at some cost or risk to oneself. Opportunities for mutually beneficial transactions are lost when one is forbidden to deal with an ostracized person. By contrast, when one moves upwards in the chain of actions, beginning with the original violation, the cost of receiving disapproval falls rapidly to zero. People do not usually frown upon others when they fail to sanction people who fail to sanction people who fail to sanction people who fail to sanction a norm violation.[4] Consequently, some sanctions must be performed for other motives than the fear of being sanctioned.

Do Norms Exist to Promote Self-Interest?

I believe that for many economists an instinctive reaction to the claim that people are motivated by irrational norms would be that on closer inspection the norms will turn out to be disguised, ultrasubtle expressions or vehicles of self-interest. Gary Becker (1976, pp. 5, 14) argues, for example, that the "combined assumptions of maximizing behavior, market equilibrium and stable preferences, used relentlessly and unflinchingly ... provides a valuable unified framework for understanding *all* human behavior." This view suggests that norms exist because they promote self-interest, over and above the avoidance of sanctions.

Some social norms can be individually useful, such as the norm against drinking or overeating. Moreover, people who have imposed private norms on their own

---

[4]The argument in Akerlof (1976, p. 610) seems to rest on the assumption that sanctions can go on forever, without losing any of their force. Anyone who violates any rule of caste, including anyone who fails to enforce the rules, automatically becomes an outcaste. Abreu (1988) offers a formal analysis built on a similar assumption. I know too little about the caste system to assess the validity of the assumption in this case, but I am confident that it is false in the cases about which I have some knowledge. Sanctions tend to run out of steam at two or three removes from the original violation.

behavior may join each other for mutual sanctioning, each in effect asking the others to punish him if he deviates, while being prepared to punish them if they do not punish him. Alcoholics Anonymous provide the best-known example (Kurtz, 1979, p. 215): "Each recovering alcoholic member of Alcoholics Anonymous is kept constantly aware, at every meeting, that he has *both* something to give *and* something to receive from his fellow alcoholics." Most norms, however, are not social contracts of this kind.

It might also be argued that social norms are individually useful in that they help people to economize on decision costs. A simple mechanical decision rule may, on the whole and in the long run, have better consequences for the individual than fine-tuned search for the optimal decision. This argument, however, confuses social norms and habits. Habits certainly are useful in the respect just mentioned, but they are not enforced by other people, nor does their violation give rise to feelings of guilt or anxiety.

A further argument for the view that it is individually rational to follow norms is that they lend credibility to threats that otherwise would not be believable. They help, as it were, to solve the problem of time inconsistency. Vendettas are not guided by the prospect of future gain but triggered by an earlier offense. Although the propensity to take revenge is not guided by consequences, it can have good consequences. If other people believe that I invariably take revenge for an offense, even at great risk to myself, they will take care not to offend me. If they believe that I will react to offense only when it is in my interest to react, they need not be as careful. From the rational point of view, a threat is not credible unless it will be in the interest of the threatener to carry it out when the time comes. The threat to kill oneself, for instance, is not rationally credible. Threats backed by a code of honor are very effective, since they will be executed even if it is in the interest of the threatener not to do so.

This observation, while true, does not amount to an explanation of the norm of vengeance. When a person guided by a code of honor has a quarrel with one who is exclusively motivated by rational considerations, the first will often have his way. But in a quarrel between two persons guided by the code, both may do worse than if they had agreed to let the legal system resolve their conflict. (Mafiosi seem to do better for themselves in the United States than in Sicily.) Since we are talking about codes of honor that are shared social norms, the latter case is the typical one. The rationality of following the code then reduces to the desire to avoid sanctions, discussed above.

In any case, one cannot rationally decide to behave irrationally, even when one knows it would be in one's interest to do so. To paraphrase Max Weber, a social norm is not like a taxi from which one can disembark at will. Followers of a social norm abide by it even when it is not in their interest to do so. In a given situation, following the norm may be useful, but that is not to say that it is always useful to follow it. Moreover, there is no presumption that its occasional usefulness can explain why it exists.

The distinction between the usefulness of norms and their rationality can also be brought out by considering Akerlof's explanation of why workers refuse to train new workers who are hired at lower wages. In an analysis of wage rigidity, Assar Lindbeck and Dennis Snower (1986) argue that the explanation is to be sought in the self-interest of the employed workers. By keeping potential entrants out, they can capture a greater deal of the benefits of monopoly power. The weapons at their disposal for keeping the unemployed at bay include the following:

> First, by being unfriendly and uncooperative to the entrants, the insiders are able to make the entrants' work more unpleasant than it otherwise would have been and thereby raise the wage at which the latter are willing to work. In practice, outsiders are commonly wary of underbidding the insiders. This behavior pattern is often given an *ad hoc* sociological explanation: 'social mores' keep outsiders from 'stealing' the jobs from their employed comrades. Our line of argument, however, suggests that these mores may be traced to the entrants' anticipation of hostile insider reaction and that this reaction may follow from optimisation behavior of insiders. Second, insiders are usually responsible for training the entrants and thereby influence their productivity. Thus insiders may be able to raise their wage demands by threatening to conduct the firm's training programs inefficiently or even to disrupt them... In sum, to raise his wage, an insider may find it worthwhile to threaten to become a thoroughly disagreeable creature.

The insider may, to be sure, make this threat, *but is it credible*? If an outsider *is* hired, would it then still be in the insider's interest to be unfriendly and uncooperative? Since Lindbeck and Snower (1988, p. 171) believe that "harassment activities are disagreeable to the harassers," they ought also to assume that outsiders will recognize this fact and, in consequence, will not be deterred by fear of harassment. I believe Akerlof is right in arguing that it takes something like a social norm to sustain this behavior. While useful, the ostracism is not rational.

Do Norms Exist to Promote Common Interests?

Among economists, those who do not subscribe to the individual rationality of norms will mostly argue for their collective rationality, claiming that social norms have collectively good consequences for those who live by them and that, moreover, these consequences explain why the norms exist. Most writers on the topic probably use the term "socially useful" to mean that a society with the norm is at least as good for almost everybody and substantially better for many than a society in which the norm is lacking, perhaps with an implied clause that no other norm could bring further Pareto-improvements.

Among those who have argued for the collective optimality of norms, Kenneth Arrow (1971, p. 22) is perhaps the most articulate and explicit:

> It is a mistake to limit collective action to state action... I want to [call] attention to a less visible form of social action: norms of social behavior,

including ethical and moral codes. I suggest as one possible interpretation that they are reactions of society to compensate for market failure. It is useful for individuals to have some trust in each other's word. In the absence of trust, it would become very costly to arrange for alternative sanctions and guarantees, and many opportunities for mutually beneficial cooperation would have to be foregone. Banfield has argued that the lack of trust is indeed one of the causes of economic underdevelopment.

It is difficult to conceive of buying trust in any direct way (though it can happen indirectly, e.g. a trusted employee will be paid more as being more valuable); indeed, there seems to be some inconsistency in the very concept. Non-market action might take the form of a mutual agreement. But the arrangement of these agreements and especially their continued extension to new individuals entering the social fabric can be costly. As an alternative, society may proceed by internalization of these norms to the achievement of the desired agreement on an unconscious level.

There is a whole set of customs and norms which might be similarly interpreted as agreements to improve the efficiency of the economic system (in the broad sense of satisfaction of individual values) by providing commodities to which the price system is inapplicable.[5]

I shall adduce three arguments against this view. First, not all norms are Pareto-improvements. Some norms make everybody *worse* off, or, at the very least, they do not make almost everybody better off. Secondly, some norms that would make everybody better off are not in fact observed. Thirdly, even if a norm does make everbody better off, this does not explain why it exists, unless we are also shown the feedback mechanism that specifies how the good consequences of the norm contribute to its maintenance.

To support the first argument I shall consider a number of norms that do not appear to be socially useful in the sense defined. The social sciences being what they are, no conclusive proof can be given, but I hope the overall impact of the counterexamples will be persuasive.

Consumption norms do not appear to have any useful consequences. If anything, norms of etiquette seem to make everybody worse off, by requiring wasteful invest-ments in pointless behaviors. Let me, nevertheless, mention three possible arguments for the social usefulness of these norms, together with corresponding objections.

First, there is the argument that norms of etiquette serve the useful function of confirming one's identity or membership in a social group. Since the notion of social identity is elusive, the argument is hard to evaluate, but one weakness is that it does not explain why these rules are as complicated as they often are. To signal or confirm one's membership in a group one sign should be sufficient, like wearing a badge or a

---

[5]See also Ullmann-Margalit (1977), p. 60.

tie. Instead, there is often vast redundancy. The manner of speaking of an Oxford-educated person differs from standard English in many more ways than what is required to single him out as an Oxford graduate.

Secondly, there is the argument that the complexity of the rules serves an additional function, that of keeping outsiders out and upstarts down (Bourdieu, 1979). It is easy to imitate one particular behavior, but hard to learn a thousand subtly different rules. But that argument flounders on the fact that working-class life is no less norm-regulated than that of the upper classes. Whereas many middle-class persons would like to pass themselves off as members of the upper class, few try to pass themselves off as workers.

Thirdly, one might combine the first and the second position, and argue that norms simultaneously serve functions of inclusion and exclusion. Evans-Pritchard's (1940, p. 120) classical argument about the Nuer can help us here. "A man of one tribe sees the people of another tribe as an undifferentiated group to whom he has an undifferentiated pattern of behavior, while he sees himself as a member of a segment of his own group." Fine-tuned distinction and gamesmanship within a group is consistent with "negative solidarity" towards outsiders. This view is more plausible, but it does not really point to social benefits of norm following. It is not clear why the working-class as a whole would benefit from the fact that it contains an infinite variety of local subcultures, all of them recognizably working-class and yet subtly different from each other in ways that only insiders can understand. Nor is it clear that the local varieties provide collective benefits to members of the subculture. One might say, perhaps, that norms are useful in limiting the number of potential interaction partners to a small and manageable subset, thus making for greater focus and consistency in social life. A community of norms would then be a bit like a convention equilibrium, since it is important that one's partners limit *their* partners by the same device. This explanation, however, fails to account for the emotional tonality of norms and for their capacity to induce self-destructive behavior.

Consider, as a second example, the social norms against behavior "contrary to nature." Some of these norms like those against cannibalism and incest, are good candidates for collectively beneficial norms. Everybody benefits from a norm that forces people to look elsewhere than to other people for food.[6] Norms against incest may well be optimal from a number of perspectives: individual, collective or genetic. Norms against sodomy, by contrast, involve only harmful restrictions of freedom and no benefits. They make everybody worse off. Norms against homosexuality might also, under conditions of overpopulation, make everybody worse off.

Many social norms against various uses of money do not appear to be collectively rational either. Consider the norm against walking up to a person in a bus queue and asking to buy his place. Nobody would be harmed by this action. Other people in the queue would not lose their place. The person asked to sell his place is free to refuse. If

[6]Note that the norm cannot be justified by individual "Tit for Tat" rationality: if I eat someone I have no reason to fear that he may eat me on a later occasion.

the forbidden practice were allowed, some would certainly gain: the norm does not create a Pareto-improvement. Yet I cannot assert that it makes everybody worse off, since some individuals could lose from its abolition. That question can only be answered in a general-equilibrium model which, to my knowledge, does not exist.

The norm that prevents us from accepting or making offers to mow other people's lawn for money seems more promising. Consider a suburban community where all houses have small lawns of the same size.[7] Suppose a houseowner is willing to pay his neighbor's son ten dollars to mow his lawn, but not more. He would rather spend half an hour mowing the lawn himself than pay eleven dollars to have someone else do it. Imagine now that the same person is offered twenty dollars to mow the lawn of another neighbor. It is easy to imagine that he would refuse, probably with some indignation. But why is mowing one lawn worth $10 or less, while mowing an identical lawn is worth $20 or more?

Thaler (1980) has suggested, as one possible explanation, that people evaluate losses and gains foregone differently. (Credit card companies exploit this difference when they insist that stores advertise cash discounts rather than credit card surcharges.) The houseowner is more affected by the out-of-pocket expenses that he would incur by paying someone to mow his lawn, than by the loss of a windfall income. But this cannot be the full story, because it does not explain why the houseowner should be indignant at the proposal. Part of the explanation must be that he doesn't think of himself as the kind of person who mows other people's lawns for money. It *isn't done*, to use a revealing phrase that often accompanies social norms.

One may argue that the norm serves an ulterior purpose. Social relations among neighbors would be disturbed if wealth differences were too blatantly displayed, and if some treated others as salaried employees. An unintended consequence of many monetary deals among neighbors could be the loss of the spontaneous self-help behavior that is a main benefit from living in a community. By preventing deals, the norm preserves the community.

The norm could also have a more disreputable aspect, however. The norm against flaunting one's wealth may just be a special case of a higher-order norm: *Don't stick your neck out.* "Don't think you are better than us, and above all don't behave in ways that make us think that you think you are better than us" (Sandemose, 1936). This norm, which prevails in many small communities, can have very bad consequences. It can discourage the gifted from using their talents, and may lead to their being branded as witches if nevertheless they go ahead and use them (Thomas, 1973, p. 643–44). By preserving the community, the norm stifles progress.

It is plausible that norms of reciprocity do, on the whole, have good consequences. Even in this case, however, there are counterexamples, since these norms can become the object of strategic manipulation. An extreme example of such ambiguous altruism is found in Colin Turnbull's description of gift and sacrifice in this society

---

[7] I am indebted to Amos Tversky for suggesting this to me as an example of social norms.

among the miserable Ik of Uganda:

These are not expressions of the foolish belief that altruism is both possible and desirable: they are weapons, sharp and aggressive, which can be put to divers uses. But the purpose for which the gift is designed can be thwarted by the non-acceptance of it, and much Icien ingenuity goes into thwarting the would-be thwarter. The object, of course, is to build up a whole series of obligations so that in times of crisis you have a number of debts you can recall, and with luck one of them may be repaid. To this end, in the circumstances of Ik life, considerable sacrifice would be justified, to the very limits of the minimal survival level. But a sacrifice that can be rejected is useless, and so you have the odd phenomenon of these otherwise singularly self-interested people going out of their way to 'help' each other. In point of fact they are helping themselves and their help may very well be resented in the extreme, but it is done in such a way that it cannot be refused, for it has already been given. Someone, quite unasked, may hoe another's field in his absence, or rebuild his stockade, or join in the building of a house that could easily be done by the man and his wife alone. At one time I have seen so many men thatching a roof that the whole roof was in serious danger of collapsing, and the protests of the owner were of no avail. The work done was a debt incurred. It was another good reason for being wary of one's neighbors. Lokeléa always made himself unpopular by accepting such help and by paying for it on the spot with food (which the cunning old fox knew they could not resist), which immediately negated the debt.[8]

Similarly, I may try to benefit from the conditional norm that if I give something to a friend for Christmas, he has an obligation to reciprocate. Suppose the friend is wealthy and that there is a norm that wealthier people should give more in absolute terms (although allowed to give less in relative terms). I can then exploit the situation to my advantage by making the initial gift.

Norms of retribution are often said to serve the social function of resolving conflicts and reducing the level of violence below what it would otherwise have been. There will be fewer quarrels in societies regulated by codes of honor, since everybody knows that they can have disastrous consequences (Boehm, 1984, p. 88). But it is not clear that this is a good thing. One could probably get rid of almost all criminal behavior if all crimes carried the death penalty, but the costs of creating this terror regime would be prohibitive. Also, it is not clear that there is less violence in a vendetta-ridden society than in an unregulated state of nature. In the state of nature, people are supposed to be rational. Hence there would be less violence because people

---

[8]Turnbull (1972), p. 146. These strategies are universally employed. As I was completing this paper, I came across a passage in a crime novel (Engel, 1986, p. 155) making the same point: "I decided to make a fast getaway. I had done Pete a favour and it didn't pay to let him thank me for doing it. It was more negotiable the other way. I heard him calling after me but I kept going."

would not harm others just to get even. Also, codes of honor generate quarrels, because honor is attained by brinkmanship and demonstrated willingness to run the risk of initiating a feud (Boehm, 1984, p. 146). On the other hand, the state of nature could be more violent, since people need not fear that others might retaliate just to get even. The net effect is anybody's guess, since the state of nature is not really a well-defined notion.

Consider next Akerlof's analysis of the norm against two-tiered wage systems. This norm does not seem to benefit the employed workers, while harming both employers and the unemployed who have a common interest in such systems. If the employed workers have good reasons to think that the new workers would drive their wages down, the code of honor makes good collective sense, at least with respect to the short-run interests of the local group of workers. Society as a whole might, however, suffer because of the unemployment generated by the practice. In that case, codes of honor would embody solutions to local collective action problems while also creating a higher-order problem.

Somewhat similar arguments apply to the norm against rate-busting. It has been argued that this norm is due to sheer conformism (Jones, 1984) or to envy (Schoeck, 1987, pp. 31, 310). The obvious alternative explanation is that the norm is a collectively optimal response to the constant pressure of management to change piece-rates. Workers often express the view that any increase in effort will induce management to reduce rates. It remains to be shown, however, that this argument is more than rationalization of envy. In the words of one notorious rate-buster: "There are three classes of men: (1) Those who can and will; (2) those who can't and are envious; (3) those who can and won't—they're nuts!" (Dalton, 1948, p. 74). The third category, presumably, are moved by solidarity and norms of justice.

The question cannot be treated separately from the behavior of management. On the one hand, management has a clear incentive to make it clear that they will never cut rates as a result of increased efforts. "Changes in piece rates at the Western Electric Company ... are not based upon the earnings of the worker. The company's policy is that piece rates will not be changed unless there is a change in the manufacturing process" (Roethlisberger and Dickson, 1939, p. 534).

On the other hand, how can management make this promise credible? They cannot commit themselves to never introducing new methods of production, nor easily prove that a new method is not just a subterfuge for changing rates. A knowledgeable engineer wrote, "I was visiting the Western Electric Company, which had a reputation of never cutting a piece rate. It never did; if some manufacturing process was found to pay more than seemed right for the class of labor employed on it—if, in other words, the rate-setters had misjudged—that particular part was referred to the engineers for redesign, and then a new rate was set for the new part" (Mills, 1946, p. 9, cited after Roy, 1952). Knowing that management has the capability of taking actions of this kind, workers have good reasons to be skeptical.

Three conclusions emerge. First, both management and workers would benefit if a way was found to distinguish "good" from "bad" changes in the piece rates. Second, the worker collective as a whole may well benefit from the norm against rate-busting, given that management cannot credibly commit itself to maintain rates. Third, however, the norm may work against the interest of society as a whole, including the working-class as a whole, if the loss of productivity caused by the norm is sufficiently serious.[9] Even granting that the norm represents the successful solution of a collective action problem within the enterprise, it might create a new problem among enterprises.

At the very least, I believe these examples demonstrate that the social usefulness of social norms cannot be taken for granted. In fact, I think I have shown more than that. Even though each of my claims about non-optimality could be contested and the facts be represented and explained in different ways, I believe that the cumulative impact of the claims is very difficult to refute.

A second strategy for attacking the claim that social norms spring from collective rationality is to imagine some socially useful norms that do not, in fact, exist. If public transportation was widely chosen over private driving, the roads would be less congested and everyone would spend so much less time commuting that the loss of comfort would be offset. Yet there is no social norm to use public transportation in crowded cities. In many developing countries private insurance motives create an incentive to have large families, although the aggregate effect is overpopulation and pressure on resources. Yet there is no social norm against having many children. Japan has apparently imposed the norm "Buy Japanese," but other countries have been less successful. The small Italian village described by Edward Banfield (1958) would certainly have benefited from a social norm against corruption. Instead it had what appears to have been a norm against public-spirited behavior. Nobody would frequent a person stupid enough not to violate the law when he would get away with it. Criminals could benefit from a minimum of solidarity among themselves. A book about the Brooklyn wiseguys suggests, however, that as soon as you're in trouble, you're forgotten: there is no honesty among thieves (Pileggi, 1986). The reader is encouraged to think of other examples.

A third strategy is to criticize the explanatory impact of the collective benefits of social norms. In the absence of a mechanism linking the benefits to the emergence or perpetuation of the norm we cannot know if they obtain by accident. Social scientists should be suspicious of theories of society that deny the possibility of accidental benefits. Moreover, and perhaps more importantly, the beneficial or optimal nature of the norm is often controversial. It is only a slight exaggeration to say that any economist worth his salt could tell a story—produce a model, that is, resting on various simplifying assumptions—which proves the individual or collective benefits derived from the norm. The very ease with which such "just-so stories" can be told suggests that we should be skeptical about them. We would be much more confident about the benefits if a mechanism could be demonstrated.

There are not many plausible candidates for a feedback mechanism. Individual reinforcement could not work here, since the benefits are collective rather than

[9]As participant-observer in a machine shop Roy (1952) found substantial losses due to deliberately suboptimal efforts.

individual. Chance variation and social selection might seem a better alternative.[10] On this account, social norms arise by accident. Societies which happen to have useful norms thrive, flourish and expand; those which do not disappear or imitate the norms of their more successful competitors. Whether the successful societies proceed by military conquest or economic competition, the end result is the same. The argument is popular, but weak. The norms of the strong are not as a rule taken over by the weak, nor do the weak always disappear in competition with the strong. Greece was conquered by Rome, but Rome assimilated more Greek norms than the other way around. When China was conquered by the barbarians, the latter ended up assimilating and defending the culture they had conquered. Today, few developing countries are taking over the norms and work habits that were a precondition for Western economic growth, nor is there any sign of these countries going out of existence.

These arguments do not add up to a strong claim that the social usefulness of norms is irrelevant for their explanation. I find it as hard as the next man to believe that the existence of norms of reciprocity and cooperation has *nothing* to do with the fact that without them civilization as we know it would not exist. Yet it is at least a useful intellectual exercise to take the more austere view, and to entertain the idea that civilization owes its existence to a fortunate coincidence. On this view, social norms spring from psychological propensities and dispositions that, taken separately, cannot be presumed to be useful, yet happen to interact in such a way that useful effects are produced.

Do Norms Exist to Promote Genetic Fitness?

The final argument against the autonomy of norms is that they owe their existence to their contribution to genetic fitness. I do not know of explicit statements of this view. Several writers have, however, taken this position on the closely related issue of the emotions of guilt and shame that sustain norm-guided behavior (Trivers, 1971; Hirschleifer, 1987; Frank, 1988). Chagnon (1988) argues that revenge can be explained as fitness-maximizing behavior, but he does not explicitly consider norms of revenge. I know too little about evolutionary biology to evaluate these claims. I would like, nevertheless, to record my skepticism and make a few general remarks, largely inspired by Kitcher (1985).

Evolutionary explanations do not take the narrow form "Feature X exists because it maximizes the genetic fitness of the organism." Rather, their general form is "X exists because it is part of a package solution that at some time maximized the genetic fitness of the organism." The latter form allows for two facts that the former excludes. First, there is the omnipresent phenomenon of *pleiotropy*. A tendency to conform to a social norm might detract from genetic fitness and yet be retained by natural selection if it is the by-product of a gene whose main product is highly

[10] Faia (1986) has a good discussion of the (severely limited) range of cases in which social selection arguments make good sense.

beneficial. Secondly, the general form allows for time lags. A social norm may be maladaptive today and yet have been adaptive at the stage in history when the human genome evolved and, for practical purposes, was fixed.

When I said that norms might owe their existence to "psychological propensities and dispositions", a natural reply would be to say that these in turn must be explicable in terms of genetic fitness. Let me concede the point, provided that the explanation is allowed to take this general form. Advocates of evolutionary explanations, however, usually have the narrower form in mind. I am not saying that in doing so they are always wrong, only that they cannot take it for granted that an explanation of the narrow form always exists. What is true, is that a plausible story of the narrow form can almost always be told. Again, however, the very ease with which just-so stories are forthcoming should make us wary of them.

Let me summarize the discussion in a diagram:

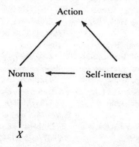

I believe that both norms and self-interest enter into the proximate explanations of action. To some extent, the selection of the norm to which one subscribes can also be explained by self-interest. Even if the belief in the norm is sincere, the choice of one norm among the many that could be relevant may be an unconscious act dictated by self-interest. Or one might follow the norm out of fear of the sanctions that would be triggered by violation. But I do not believe that self-interest provides the full explanation for adherence to norms. There must be some further explanation, X, of why norms exist. I have discussed various candidates for X, and found them wanting. I have no positive account of my own to offer. In particular, I have no suggestion as to how norms emerge and disappear. I suggest, however, that a good research strategy might be to investigate the role of emotions in maintaining social norms. Also, the often-ignored phenomena of envy and honor might repay further study. Finally, the psychological theory of conformism should be brought to bear on the subject.

■ *I am grateful to the editors of this journal for comments on an earlier draft of this paper.*

References

Abreu, D., "On the Theory of Informally Repeated Games with Discounting," *Econometrica*, 1988, *56*, 383–396.

Ainslie, G., "A Behavioral Economic Approach to the Defense Mechanisms: Freud's Energy Theory Revisited," *Social Science Information*, 1982, *21*, 735–79.

Ainslie, G., "Behavioral Economics II: Motivated Involuntary Behavior," *Social Science Information*, 1984, *23*, 247–74.

Ainslie, G., "Beyond Microeconomics." In Elster, J., ed., *The Multiple Self*. Cambridge: Cambridge University Press, 1986, pp. 133–76.

Akerlof, G., "The Economics of Caste and of the Rat Race and Other Woeful Tales," *Quarterly Journal of Economics*, 1976, *90*, 599–617.

Akerlof, G., "A Theory of Social Custom, of Which Unemployment May be One Consequence," *Quarterly Journal of Economics*, 1980, *94*, 749–75.

Arrow, K., "Political and Economic Evaluation of Social Effects and Externalities." In Intriligator, M., ed., *Frontiers of Quantitative Economics*. Amsterdam: North-Holland, 1971, pp. 3–25.

Axelrod, R., "An Evolutionary Approach to Norms," *American Political Science Review*, 1986, *80*, 1095–1111.

Banfield, E. G., *The Moral Basis of a Backward Society*. New York: The Free Press, 1958.

Barry, B., *Sociologists, Economists and Democracy*, 2nd Edition. Chicago: University of Chicago Press, 1979.

Becker, G., *The Economic Approach to Human Behavior*. Chicago: University of Chicago Press, 1976.

Bochm, C., *Blood Revenge: The Anthropology of Feuding in Montenegro and Other Tribal Societies*. University of Kansas Press, 1984.

Bourdieu, P., *La Distinction*. Paris: Editions de Minuit, 1970.

Chagnon, N., "Life Histories, Blood Revenge, and Warfare in a Tribal Population," *Science*, 1988, *239*, 985–92.

Coleman, J. S., "Systems of Trust," *Angewandte Sozialforschung*, 1982, *10*, 277–300.

Dalton, M., "The Industrial 'Rate-Buster:' A Characterization," *Applied Anthropology*, Winter 1948, 5–18.

Deutsch, M., *Distributive Justice*. New Haven: Yale University Press, 1985.

Djilas, M., *Land Without Justice*. London: Methuen, 1958.

Durkheim, E., *The Rules of Sociological Method*. Glencoe, Ill.: The Free Press, 1958.

Edgerton, R., *Rules, Exceptions and the Social Order*. Berkeley: University of California Press, 1985.

Elster, J., "Is There (Or Should There Be) A Right to Work?" In Guttman, A., ed., *Democracy and the Welfare State*. Princeton: Princeton University Press, 1988, pp. 53–78.

Elster, J., *The Cement of Society*. Cambridge: Cambridge University Press, 1989.

Engel, H., *A City Called July*. New York: Penguin Books, 1986.

Evans-Pritchard, E., *The Nuer*. Oxford: Oxford University Press, 1940.

Faia, M. A., *Dynamic Functionalism*. Cambridge: Cambridge University Press, 1986.

Fenichel, O., *The Psychoanalytic Theory of Neurosis*. New York: Norton, 1945.

Frank, R. K., *Passions within Reason*. New York: Norton, 1988.

Gambetta, D., *Did They Jump or Were They Pushed?* Cambridge: Cambridge University Press, 1987.

Gouldner, A., "The Norm of Reciprocity," *American Sociological Review*, 1960, *25*, 161–78.

Hasluck, M., *The Unwritten Law in Albania*. Cambridge: Cambridge University Press, 1954.

Hirschleifer, J., "On the Emotions as Guarantors of Threats and Promises." In Dupre, J., ed., *The Latest on the Best*. Cambridge: MIT Press, 1987, pp. 307–26.

Hume, D., *An Enquiry Concerning the Principles of Morals*, 1751.

Jones, S. F., *The Economics of Conformism*. Oxford: Blackwell, 1984.

Kahn, A., H. Lamm, and R. Nelson, "Preferences for an Equal or Equitable Allocator," *Journal of Personality and Social Psychology*, 1977, *35*, 837–44.

Kahneman, D., J. Knetsch, and R. Thaler, "Fairness and the Assumptions of Economics," *Journal of Business*, 1986, *59*, S285–S300.

Kitcher, P., *Vaulting Ambition*. Cambridge: MIT Press, 1985.

Kurtz, E., *Not-God: A History of Alcoholics Anonymous*. Center City, Minnesota: Hazelden Educational Services, 1979.

Laurin, U., *Pa Heder och Samvete*. Stockholm: Norstedts, 1986.

Lindbeck, A., and D. J. Snower, "Wage Rigidity, Union Activity and Unemployment." In Beckerman, W., ed., *Wage Rigidity and Unemployment*. London: Duckworth, 1986, pp. 97–126.

Lindbeck, A., and D. J. Snower, "Cooperation, Harassment and Involuntary Unemployment," *American Economic Review*, 1988, *78*, 167–88.

McDonald, I. M., and R. Solow, "Wage Bargaining and Employment," *American Economic Review*, 1981, *71*, 896–908.

Messick, D. M., and K. Sentis, "Fairness, Preference and Fairness Biases." In Messick, D. M., and K. Cook, eds., *Equity Theory*. New York: Praeger, 1983, pp. 61–94.

Mikula, G., "Gewinnaufteilung in Dyaden bei variiertem Leistungsverhaltnis," *Zeitschrift für Sozialpsychologie*, 1972, *3*, 126–33.

Miller, W., *Bloodtaking and Peacemaking: Society and the Disputing Process in Medieval Iceland*. Chicago: University of Chicago Press, forthcoming.

Mills, J., *The Engineer in Society*. New York: Nostrand, 1946.

Mitchell, D. J., "Explanations of Wage Inflexibility." In Beckerman, W., ed., *Wage Rigidity and Unemployment*. London: Duckworth, 1986, pp. 43–76.

Pileggi, N., *Wiseguy*. New York: Pocket Books, 1986.

Roethlisberger, F. J., and Dickson, W. J., *Management and the Worker*. Cambridge: Harvard University Press, 1939.

Roy, D., "Quota Restriction and Goldbricking in a Machine Shop," *American Journal of Sociology*, 1952, *67*, 427–42.

Sandemose, A., *A Fugitive Crosses His Track*. New York: Knopf, 1936.

Schoeck, H., *Envy*. Indianapolis: Liberty Press, 1987.

Swenson, P., *Fair Shares*. Ithaca: Cornell University Press, 1989.

Thaler, R., "Towards a Positive Theory of Consumer Behavior," *Journal of Economic Behavior and Organization*, 1980, *1*, 39–60.

Thomas, K., *Religion and the Decline of Magic*. Harmondsworth: Penguin, 1973.

Tocqueville, A. de, *Democracy in America*. New York: Anchor Books, 1969.

Trivers, R. E., "The Evolution of Reciprocal Altruism," *Quarterly Review of Biology*, 1971, *46*, 35–57.

Turnbull, C., *The Mountain People*. New York: Simon and Schuster, 1972.

Tversky, A., and Kahneman, D., "The Psychology of Choice and the Framing of Preferences," *Science*, 1981, *211*, 4353–58.

Ullmann-Margalit, E., *The Emergence of Norms*. Oxford: Oxford University Press, 1977.

Veyne, P., *Le Pain et le Cirque*. Paris: Editions du Seuil, 1976.

Waller, W., "The Rating and Dating Complex," *American Sociological Review*, 1937, *2*, 727–34.

Yaari, M., and Bar-Hillel, M., "Judgments of Justice," unpublished manuscript, 1988.

Zajac, E. P., "Perceived Economic Justice: The Example of Public Utility Regulation." In Young, H. P., ed., *Cost Allocation*. Amsterdam: North Holland, 1985, pp. 119–53.

[14]

A Mechanism for Social Selection and Successful Altruism

Herbert A. Simon

Within the framework of neo-Darwinism, with its focus on fitness, it has been hard to account for altruism, behavior that reduces the fitness of the altruist but increases average fitness in society. Many population biologists argue that, except for altruism to close relatives, human behavior that appears to be altruistic amounts to reciprocal altruism, behavior undertaken with an expectation of reciprocation, hence incurring no net cost to fitness. Herein is proposed a simple and robust mechanism, based on human docility and bounded rationality, that can account for the evolutionary success of genuinely altruistic behavior. Because docility—receptivity to social influence—contributes greatly to fitness in the human species, it will be positively selected. As a consequence, society can impose a "tax" on the gross benefits gained by individuals from docility by inducing docile individuals to engage in altruistic behaviors. Limits on rationality in the face of environmental complexity prevent the individual from avoiding this "tax." An upper bound is imposed on altruism by the condition that there must remain a net fitness advantage for docile behavior after the cost to the individual of altruism has been deducted.

IT IS OF NO LITTLE MOMENT FOR THE HUMAN FUTURE WHETH-er people are necessarily and consistently selfish, as is sometimes argued in population genetics and economics, or whether there is a significant place for altruism in the scheme of human behavior. Do centrally important institutions like business and government depend entirely on motivating participants through their selfish interests in order to operate successfully? Is reciprocal altruism (actually a form of self interest) the only kind that can survive?

In recent years there have been many attempts to derive theoretical answers to these questions from the first principles of natural selection (1). Most of the answers give a central, almost exclusive, role to self-interest, and, apart from altruism to close kin, leave little room for genuine, as distinct from reciprocal, altruism.

The proposal in this paper can be read as an "even if" argument. Even if we accept the genes of individual persons as the controlling sites for natural selection—the assumption most antagonistic to altruism—a mechanism can be described that selects for altruistic behavior well beyond altruism to close kin and beyond support from expected reciprocity or social enforcement. The mechanism will select for behavior that reduces the fitness of the altruist while increasing average fitness in the society.

The argument does not deny the existence of social mechanisms for transmitting behavior traits; in fact, socially learned behavior is central to the theory. Nor is it concerned with the many forms of behavior usually called "altruistic" that are unrelated to biological fitness. The argument shows that even though altruistic behavior, strictly defined, is penalized, altruism can still be positively selected.

Essentially, the theory accounts for altruism on the basis of the human tendency (here called docility) to learn from others (more accurately, the tendency to accept social influence)—which is itself a product of natural selection. Because of the limits of human rationality, fitness can be enhanced by docility that induces individuals often to adopt culturally transmitted behaviors without independent evaluation of their contribution to personal fitness.

Altruism

By altruism I mean behavior that increases, on average, the reproductive fitness of others at the expense of the fitness of the altruist. Fitness simply means expected number of progeny. An exchange in which both parties are compensated for what they initially cede does not count as altruism but as enlightened self-interest (sometimes called soft or reciprocal altruism). Still, the boundaries are tricky, as we shall see.

Notice that "altruism" and "selfishness" in genetics bear no close resemblance to these terms in everyday language. Presumably, Don Juan was fitter than Croesus or Caesar. From a genetic standpoint, the amassing of wealth or power does not count at all toward fitness, only the amassing of progeny. By the same token, liberality with wealth or willingness to cede power do not constitute genetic altruism. Altruism means forgoing progeny.

We could debate at some length whether, either at the present time or earlier in the history of our species, wealth and power have or had any strong connection with genetic fitness. If the connection is weak, then the evolutionary argument that people are essentially selfish in the everyday sense of that word—that is, striving only for economic gain, power, or both—is correspondingly weakened. Under those circumstances, there could be any amount of altruism, in the usual sense of that term, without any behavior that would qualify as altruistic in a genetic sense.

In this article, I am concerned with fitness, altruism, and selfishness only in the genetic meanings of those terms. In the concluding section I will return briefly to desire for wealth and power as human motives. In any event, our goal is not to establish how much or how little altruism, in either sense, there is in human behavior, but rather to show that altruism on a substantial scale is not inconsistent with the strictest neo-Darwinian assumptions.

The author is professor of computer science and psychology, Department of Psychology, Carnegie-Mellon University, Pittsburgh, PA 15213.

The Neo-Darwinian Analysis

The acceptance by many modern geneticists of the axiom that the basic unit of selection is the "selfish gene" quickly led to the production of population models that left little room for the survivability of altruistic behavior (2). If altruism incurred any cost in fitness, that is, in reduced potential or reproduction, then it could not compete against selfishness.

To be sure, it was recognized that altruism was viable under several specific (and rather narrow) conditions. First, altruism toward close relatives could increase fitness through the genes shared with those relatives. But the closest relatives (except identical twins) have only half their genes in common, and this fraction drops by a factor of two with each step of distance in the relationship. Consanguinity can account for altruism only toward close kin (3).

The second qualification is that, if several mixed societies (trait groups) contain varying fractions of altruists and non-altruists, then (i) the groups with the larger fractions of altruists may outbreed the groups with smaller fractions, (ii) as a result, the fraction of altruists in the entire population may increase for some time, (iii) even though the fraction of altruists in each separate group will necessarily decrease (4).

Of course, if the groups inbreed, then, in the long run, as the least altruistic (and least successful) groups became extinct or nearly so, the number of altruists in the entire population would begin to decrease, and altruism would ultimately become extinct. If, however, the population members periodically mixed thoroughly for purposes of reproduction, then the fraction of altruists in the total could continue to increase indefinitely.

All of these results can be formalized with relatively simple mathematical models. I will borrow heavily from these mathematical formulations, but my assumptions will be different from those in the model just described (5).

In addition to the models mentioned above, several explicit theories analyze the co-evolution of culturally transmitted and genetically transmitted traits. Among the most prominent of these are the theories of Cavalli-Sforza and Feldman, Lumsden and Wilson, and Boyd and Richerson (6–8). I will discuss them after I have presented my own model.

A Simple Model of Altruism

Consider a population consisting of n individuals, of two types, A and S, in proportions p and $1 - p$, respectively. The individuals of type A are altruistic, while those of type S are selfish. Each A expresses a behavior that contributes b offspring to members of the population (including himself), the recipients being chosen at random. The cost of this altruistic behavior is that each A has c fewer children than he or she otherwise would have. The average number of offspring, F_A, and F_S, of each A and S will be: $F_A = X - c + bp$, and $F_S = X + bp$, where X is the number of offspring in the absence of altruistic behaviors, the same for both types of individuals. All individuals, including altruists, can serve as recipients to the np altruists, and selfish S individuals incur no cost of altruism. Since c is positive, selfish individuals always have more offspring than altruistic ones. To the degree that the behaviors are heritable, selfish individuals will therefore be found with greater relative frequency in each succeeding generation.

Notice that the total contribution of each altruist to the population is b, assumed independent of the size of the population. Under an alternative assumption, which does not affect our main conclusions, each altruist contributes b to the fitness of each member of the population, thereby making the total contribution of the altruist bn,

where n is the size of the population. In this latter case, the contribution is a "public good"—its consumption by one member does not decrease the amount available to others. (An attractive garden visible to passersby is an example.)

As was mentioned earlier, if there are a number of groups instead of one, and if the groups are segregated during most of their life cycle but intermingle thoroughly while reproducing, then altruists may have greater net fitness than non-altruists and may grow in numbers at the expense of the latter. Systems with this property are called "structured demes," and mathematical models of them are examined in considerable detail by Wilson (4).

Social Learning and Altruism

With only a single change of assumption, which I will now motivate, my simple model can be converted into one in which altruists are fitter than selfish individuals even within a single, self-contained population that is not a structured deme. In this system, altruism will not only survive, but will gradually permeate the entire population (9).

The human species is notable, although not unique among animals, in requiring for survival many years of nurture by adults. In most human societies, the survival and fitness even of adults depends on the assistance, or at least forbearance, of other adults. Leaving aside active hostility from others, even access to food and shelter cannot be ensured in most societies without the consent of others.

The human species also has a notable ability to learn, and especially to learn from other people, particularly with the help of language. We will use the term "social learning" to refer to learning from others in the society.

Social learning makes two major contributions to an individual's fitness. First, it provides knowledge and skills that are useful in all of life's activities, in particular, in transactions with the environment. Second, goals, values, and attitudes transmitted through social learning, and exhibited in the speech or behavior of the learner, often secure supportive responses from others. For brevity, we will call the knowledge and skills of the first kind "skills," and those of the second kind "proper behaviors."

Learning of both kinds obviously contributes to fitness. We will use the term "docile" (in its dictionary meaning of "disposed to be taught") to describe persons who are adept at social learning, who accept well the instruction society provides them. Individuals differ in degree of docility, and these differences may derive partly from genetic differences. There are differences in intelligence (cognitive ability to absorb what is taught) and in motivation (propensity to accept or reject instruction, advice, persuasion, or commands).

Docile persons tend to learn and believe what they perceive others in the society want them to learn and believe. Thus the content of what is learned will not be fully screened for its contribution to personal fitness. This tendency derives from the difficulty—often an impossibility—for individuals to evaluate beliefs for their potential positive or negative contribution to fitness. For example, many of us believe that less cholesterol would be beneficial to our health without reviewing (or even being competent to review) the medical evidence. Hundreds of millions of people believe that behaving in a socially acceptable way will enhance the probability of enjoying blissful immortality.

Belief in large numbers of facts and propositions that we have not had the opportunity or ability to evaluate independently is basic to the human condition, a simple corollary of the boundedness of human rationality in the face of a complex world. We avoid most hot stoves without ever having touched them. Most of our skills and knowledge, we learned from others (or from books); we did not discover or invent them. The contribution of docility to fitness is enormous.

Guilt and shame, although perhaps genetically independent of docility, also serve most people as strong motivators for accepting social norms. Guilt is particularly important because it can operate independently of the detection of nonconformity.

In analogy with earlier simple models, I assume a population made up of two kinds of people: those who are docile, D, and those who are not, S. We assume that both kinds of people are identical in fitness, except that docile people, because of the skills and proper behaviors they have acquired, produce an average d more offspring than the others. Thus, $F_D = X + d$, while $F_S = X$. Clearly, docile people will increase in relative number in the society.

Now if the society coexists in its environment with other societies, we may also compare the relative rates of growth of these societies. As in the models of qualified altruism that we have already examined, there may be certain altruistic behaviors that, although costly to the fitness of the individual who exhibits them, have more than a compensating advantage for other individuals in the society.

A society that instilled such behaviors in its docile members would grow more rapidly than one that did not; hence such behaviors would become, by evolution at the social level, a part of the repertory of proper behaviors of successful societies. Societies that did not develop such a repertory would be less fit than those that did, and would ultimately disappear. But could the altruism ultimately survive within the more successful societies?

To answer this question, I add altruism acquired by social learning to the model and see how docile-altruistic individuals fare relative to selfish ones. I will now simply call docile-altruistic individuals "altruistic," F_A, as in the previous models: $F_A = X + d - c + b(c)p$ and $F_S = X + b(c)p$. Again, p is the percentage of altruists in the population; X is the number of offspring in the absence of altruistic behaviors; d is the gross increase in A's offspring due to A's docility; c is the net cost to A, in offspring, of altruistic behavior acquired through the docility mechanism; $b(c)$, which replaces the b of the previous model, is the number of offspring contributed to the population of A's altruistic behavior. I express this number as a function of c, because the amount of altruism exacted from A, and its corresponding contribution of fitness to others, depend on the society's definition of proper behavior, itself subject to cultural evolution.

Under these assumptions, an individual who is docile, enjoying the advantage (d) of that docility, will consequently also accept the society's instructions to be altruistic as part of proper behavior. Because of bounded rationality, the docile individual will often be unable to distinguish socially prescribed behavior that contributes to fitness from altruistic behavior. In fact, docility will reduce the inclination to evaluate independently the contributions of behavior to fitness. Moreover, guilt and shame will tend to enforce even behavior that is perceived as altruistic. Hence the docile individual will necessarily also incur the cost, c, of altruism.

Now unlike the previous model, in this case, because $F_A - F_S = d - c$, the fitness of altruists will actually exceed the fitness of selfish individuals as long as d exceeds c, that is, as long as the demands for altruism that society imposes on docile individuals are not excessive compared with the advantageous knowledge and skills acquired through docility. If this condition is satisfied, the proportion of altruists will increase.

Suppose there are decreasing marginal returns from altruism, so that $d^2b/dc^2 < 0$. In the short run (that is, for fixed p), it will be optimal for the society to fix c at the level where $db/dc = 1$, but the long-run optimal strategy will be to demand less altruism initially so as to increase the absolute number of docile individuals as rapidly as possible, that is, to set $p(db/dc) = 1$. For small p, this implies that

db/dc will be large, hence that c will be small or even zero [if $(dc/dc)_0 < (1/p)$]. As p grows, social demands on the altruists can be increased correspondingly—the greater the fraction of altruists in the society, the more altruistic it can be.

In this scheme of things, altruism is a relative matter, for only a subset of the altruist's behaviors reduce fitness. Moreover, the altruist is rewarded, in advance, by the "gift" of docility; altruism is simply a by-product of docility. Docile persons are more than compensated for their altruism by the knowledge and skills they acquire, and moreover not all proper behaviors are sacrificial. (Learning to drive in the right lane is a proper behavior, but not sacrificial.) The term "altruism" applies only to the sacrificial subset of the behaviors engendered by docility.

If docility were something the individual deliberately chose, one might even rename the accompanying altruism "enlightened selfishness." But docility (at least its genetic component) is bestowed, not chosen, and with the bestowal goes the propensity to adopt proper behaviors, including altruistic ones. By virtue of bounded rationality, the docile person cannot acquire the personally advantageous learning that provides the increment, d, of fitness without acquiring also the altruistic behaviors that cost the decrement, c.

Three final observations: first, altruism includes the effort individuals spend to induce and enforce learning and proper behavior in others. The docility mechanism will work only if there are providers of skills and knowledge as well as recipients. But nurturing and enforcing behaviors will be learned as an essential component of the proper behaviors of altruism. In enforcement are included carrots as well as sticks—praising and nurturing others who exhibit proper behavior, as well as frowning on, shunning, or otherwise punishing those who do not.

Second, the fitness advantage of altruists would be decreased if individuals could feign proper behavior without detection. (They would be motivated to do so only when they knew the behavior was altruistic.) There are probably severe limits, however, as to how far deception will be successful (10).

Third, the effectiveness of the docility mechanism would be impaired if individuals could discriminate perfectly proper behaviors that were "for their own good" from those that were altruistic. But people can discriminate only very imperfectly between beneficial and altruistic proper behaviors.

Moreover, much of the value of docility to the individual is lost if great effort is expended evaluating each bit of social influence before accepting it. Acceptance without full evaluation is an integral part of the docility mechanism, and of the mechanisms of guilt and shame.

Comparison with Alternative Models

I return now to the models of Cavalli-Sforza and Feldman, Lumsden and Wilson, and Boyd and Richerson and compare their mechanisms for altruism with the docility mechanism.

Cavalli-Sforza and Feldman (6, footnote 6), examining the interaction between cultural and genetic transmission of traits (6, pp. 102–107 and pp. 133–143), show that a selectively disadvantageous trait can spread to a whole population, where by a disadvantageous trait they mean "a maladaptive social custom (for example, one creating some degree of danger to life that is not compensated for by other advantages in Darwinian fitness) or a custom decreasing fertility . . . , or an infectious disease" (6, p. 106).

They do not consider, however, traits that, while maladaptive to individuals, confer net benefits on the population (altruistic behaviors); nor do they explain why negative selection of maladaptive social customs does not remove them, either by positive selection of those individuals who reject them, or by selection or social norms, or both. Many sociobiologists would therefore regard their model as incomplete, holding constant things that evolutionary forces would change in the long run. The mechanism I have proposed avoids both of these difficulties.

Lumsden and Wilson provide no mechanism for altruism other than altruism toward close kin and reciprocal or "soft" altruism (11).

Boyd and Richerson (8, chap. 7, footnote 6) introduce a mechanism that produces altruism by "conformist transmission," which is, essentially, preferential selection of the behaviors individuals encounter most frequently. Conformist transmission has something in common with the docility mechanism, but differs from it in several crucial respects.

Degree of conformism, in the initial version of the Boyd and Richerson model (8, pp. 206–213) depends solely on frequency of exposure, without individual differences between conformers and defectors. If such differences are introduced for traits that are individually disadvantageous, there will be negative selection of conformers and positive selection of rejecters until the traits disappear.

The authors recognize this difficulty (8, p. 213) and introduce the possibility of individuals rejecting individual culturally transmitted traits. They then show that for rather special circumstances (involving migration among groups living in varying environments) conformist transmission (hence altruism) could be stably maintained.

But the docility mechanism I have proposed accounts for altruism even in a homogeneous environment, and does not depend on the frequency with which a trait is encountered. Finally, it is considerably simpler and more robust than conformist transmission, depending only on a couple of system parameters.

This review of these alternative theories of altruism shows that altruism based on docility provides a simpler mechanism, valid under a wider range of conditions, than the others.

Implications for Economics and Politics

The existence of heritable docility, and the consequent possibility for a society to cultivate and exploit altruism, has very strong implications for social theory, including economics, and the theories of political institutions and other organizations. I will mention just a few such implications as examples.

First, goals like gaining wealth and power might become very strong motivations even if they made no direct contribution to genetic fitness. If it were advantageous to the success of a society for people to seek wealth or power, then these could be taught and rewarded as proper behaviors. The dangers of early assassination (and consequent deficit of offspring) to those who exercise power could be absorbed in the term c, among the costs of altruism. In particular, the desire for glory becomes, in this framework, an understandable human motive.

Motives like wealth, power, and glory would be difficult to sustain if associated with major costs to fitness. They are readily sustained if they are both useful to the society and nearly neutral for individual fitness. Power motives might have net value to the society by providing leaders who enhance the society's ability to organize to exploit resources or defend against enemies. Wealth-amassing motives might be useful if they created more wealth than was drawn off by those who strove for gain.

Consider next an example from politics. It has been difficult to explain what self interest leads many people to go to the polls on election day. Any single vote is unlikely to change an election outcome, so it should seem pointless to a rational person to exert effort to vote. Even a small opportunity cost of casting a ballot is too much. But a society that includes voting among the proper behaviors can, at a minute cost to the fitness of altruists, secure their participation in elections.

Many other troublesome issues of public goods can be explained in the same way—contributions to charity and volunteer work being important examples. Of course other motives may also help to cause these behaviors. People may volunteer in order to make useful acquaintances. There are many possibilities, but no reason to rule out altruism as an important motivation.

Finally, many people exhibit loyalties to organizations and organization goals that seem wholly disproportionate to the material rewards they receive from the organization or its success (12). In particular, few people (including top executives) receive rewards from business firms that are proportional to the profits. Yet executives and other employees seem often to make decisions in terms of their expected effects on the firm's profitability. And empirical evidence suggests little difference in the relative efficiencies of profit-making and non-profit firms in the same industry (for example, health care, water supplies, education) (13). With profits or without, people often identify with organization goals and organizational survival.

All these topics deserve a more thorough treatment than they are given here. Mentioning them suggests what a wealth of possible behaviors opens up when we admit docility as a major mechanism of social transmission.

As a final caution, I repeat that what I have called altruism, a partial sacrifice of genetic fitness, may be very different from the forgoing of wealth and power that is called altruism in common discourse. Nothing in the model predicts that we will not see people attending to their economic interests in most of their everyday behavior; or for that matter, that we will not see them giving away a large part of the wealth they have taken great pains to amass.

In our century, we have watched two great nations, the Peoples' Republic of China and the Soviet Union, strive to create a "new man," only to end up by acknowledging that the "old man" —perhaps we should say the "old person"—self-interested and concerned with his or her economic welfare or the welfare of family, clan, ethnic group, or province, was still alive and well. It will be important to reexamine this striking historical experience, not in terms of oversimple models of the "selfish gene," but in a framework that acknowledges that altruism, either as defined socially or as defined genetically, is wholly compatible with natural selection and is an important determinant of human behavior.

REFERENCES AND NOTES

1. G. C. Williams, *Adaptation and Natural Selection: a Critique of Some Current Evolutionary Thought* (Princeton Univ. Press, Princeton, 1966); R. D. Alexander, *Annu. Rev. Ecol. Syst.* 5, 325 (1974).
2. R. Dawkins, *The Selfish Gene* (Oxford Univ. Press, Oxford, 1976).
3. W. D. Hamilton, *J. Theor. Biol.* 7, 1 (1964).
4. D. S. Wilson, *The Natural Selection of Populations and Communities* (The Benjamin-Cummings Press, Menlo Park, CA, 1980).
5. The reader who wants to pursue the mathematics further will find Wilson's book (4, footnote 4, pp. 23–32) indispensable.
6. L. L. Cavalli-Sforza, M. W. Feldman, *Cultural Transmission and Evolution* (Princeton Univ. Press, Princeton, NJ, 1981).
7. C. Lumsden and E. O. Wilson, *Genes, Mind, and Culture* (Harvard Univ. Press, Cambridge, MA, 1981).
8. R. Boyd and P. J. Richerson, *Culture and the Evolutionary Process* (Univ. of Chicago Press, Chicago, IL, 1985).
9. The docility mechanism described in this section was introduced less formally by H. A. Simon, *Reason in Human Affairs* (Stanford Univ. Press, Stanford, CA, 1983).
10. This issue has been examined by R. H. Frank, *Passions Within Reason* (Norton, New York, NY, 1988).
11. C. J. Lumsden and E. O. Wilson, *Promethean Fire* (Harvard Univ. Press, Cambridge, MA, 1983), pp. 30–32.
12. H. A. Simon, *Administrative Behavior* (Macmillan, New York, ed. 3, 1976).
13. B. A. Weisbrod, *Science* 244, 541 (1989).
14. I am very grateful to a number of geneticists and others who have contributed to my education on this subject by reading and commenting upon earlier drafts of this paper, including D. T. Campbell, J. F. Crow, R. C. Lewontin, D. S. Wilson, and E. O. Wilson. Supported by the Personnel and Training Programs, Psychological Sciences Division, Office of Naval Research, under contract N00014-86-K-0768.

Part IV
Institutions, Knowledge and Uncertainty

[15]

An institutional perspective on information

Geoffrey Newman

Recent research in economics has produced two theories of unusual promise: an economic theory of information[1] and an economic theory of institutions.[2] Both developments are important because they fundamentally challenge the types of assumptions traditionally used in models of economic decision-making and resource allocation: that all agents are fully informed about their decision-making environment, that information can be produced and disseminated costlessly, and that the characteristics of individual economic behaviour are largely independent of the characteristics of the institutional structure of a given economic society. The fundamental proposition in the economic theory of information is that questions concerning optimal resource allocation in any economic society cannot be divorced from questions concerning the extent to which economic agents know relevant features of their decision-making environment and the extent to which they wish to alter the existing informational basis of their decisions. Correspondingly, the fundamental methodological proposition in the economic theory of institutions is that questions concerning optimal resource allocation cannot be divorced from questions concerning the 'incentive structure' of a given economic society, the specific constellation of institutions and property rights which gives rise to such, and the attempts by economic agents to reform their institutional environment in their own best interest.

The methodological similarity of these two propositions deserves attention since it would seem to imply that any fully extended model of optimal resource allocation should make reference to both informational and institutional features of a given economic setting. Such an integrated model has yet to be constructed.[3] The object here, however, is to put forward an even stronger claim: that such a model must make reference to both these features. In particular, it is the central thesis of this article that the informational and institutional characteristics of any given society are interdependent, and thus cannot be separated. It is therefore implied

Geoffrey Newman is sessional lecturer at Simon Fraser University, at Burnaby, B.C. (Canada). He has been a Canada Council fellowship holder and has published some articles in the fields of his interests: economic theory and the methodology of the social sciences.

both that the important questions in the theory of information cannot find a satisfactory answer without reference to properties of institutional environments and that the important questions in the theory of institutions cannot find a satisfactory answer without reference to properties of informational environments. Here we are concerned primarily with the former implication—defining an explicit institutional foundation for information theory.

The traditional economics of information and its problems

It is only very recently that anything approaching a reasonable body of theory in the economics of information has begun to surface The dominant tendency throughout the history of modern economic theory, especially Neoclassical economic theory, has been to treat informational conditions as phenomena to be assumed rather than formally explained within models of resource allocation.[4] The two standard assumptions in this tradition are: (a) that all economic agents are informed at least to the extent that all relevant variables of their decision-making environment are known with a definite probability, the ideal case being one in which the probabilities are unity—'perfect knowledge';[5] and (b) that all such information is available instantaneously and costlessly. As the assumption of 'perfect knowledge' has been used most extensively, the only economic analysis which really results from this approach is a comparison of resource allocation outcomes produced under perfect knowledge with those produced under any state of imperfect knowledge.[6] This comparison is, however, questionable: since imperfect knowledge is regarded as a 'distortion' from the outset, and it becomes hard to avoid the conclusion that resource allocation is improved if the distortion is not present.[7] Demsetz (1969) has rightly criticized this comparison of idealized perfect situations with real imperfect ones as an embodiment of the 'nirvana approach' to economic theorizing since the only meaningful type of comparison is between two real imperfect situations.[8] The more general criticism however is that the approach simply does not explain informational phenomena.

The principal modern attempt to overcome such explanatory problems derives from the view that information is a marketable commodity and like any other can be analysed by way of the Neoclassical principles of supply and demand (Arrow, 1962; Boulding, 1966). Information is thus analysed in the context of a traditional equilibrium theory where the chief tasks are to explain the quantities and prices which will mutually satisfy suppliers and demanders of information. Moreover, if the information market were perfect, then the quantities so produced could be regarded as 'optimal'. The early developments of this approach are interesting because they represent a shift in concern from the optimality of the economic system as a whole, given predetermined informational assumptions, to the optimality of the information market *per se*. They are also interesting because the analysis of information as a marketable commodity is largely suggested as a mere analogy to the analysis of other more traditional items as marketable commodities. And it was immediately recognized that the analogy was far from perfect (Arrow, 1962).

The Neoclassical framework requires information to be unambiguously measurable in quantitative terms, yet except in the narrowest possible view of information, it is simply not clear what such a measure might be.[9] Furthermore, the central questions concerning information are not those about its sheer quantity but its quality (or truth-value), and finding a measure for this dimension is just as difficult.[10] The peculiar properties of information as a commodity arise even more fundamentally in the characteristics of the supply of and demand for information. As Arrow (1962) points out, information typically violates three classical properties of privately supplied goods: (a) since producers of information cannot normally charge for further uses of information once disseminated the returns on information supply are not fully appropriable; (b) since further users of information are able to employ or transmit information received at a lower cost than the original supplier, information is subject to increasing returns in use; and (c) information is not an infinitely divisible commodity. These difficulties in the supply of information, especially (a), lead to the well-known proposition that information, as an imperfect private good, will be underproduced relative to what would obtain if it were a perfect private good.[11] This comparison may be regarded as the modern version of the 'nirvana approach'.

The demand side of the information market is no easier. There are similar problems of indivisibility and undervaluation of information, and as Arrow further states: '. . . there is a fundamental paradox in the determination of the demand for information; its value to the purchaser is not known until he has the information, but then he has in effect acquired it without cost.'—Arrow, 1962, p. 616. The general thrust of this paradox is evident: in order to make specific judgements on the resource allocation properties of the information market, we are also required to make some judgement about the very *informational* basis of decisions in this market.[12] If we assume that demanders of information are fully informed about conditions in the information market and that their demands for information are a manifestation only of uncertainty in all other markets, then analysis of the traditional type is tractable, but the original assumption of full information is question-begging. If, by contrast, we do not make this stringent assumption, then the total demand for information is indeterminate unless we specify the demand for information in the information market in particular. This requires another independent market or another arbitrary assumption and so on in the fashion of a classical infinite regress.

The problems noted here are clearly serious for those theorists who wish to use the Neoclassical supply/demand paridigm for the analysis of informational phenomena. They lead to severe doubts concerning the optimality of the information market in itself[13] and more generally to the view that '. . . when knowledge production is introduced into . . . an economy then neither for the simple competitive mechanism nor for any simple modification of it is the optimality of equilibrium preserved, and even the existence of equilibrium is doubtful.'—Marshack *et al.*, 1967, p. 9. This is not however to underestimate the influence of the simple Neoclassical analysis. On one hand, it has led to the emergence of an interesting body of research on the micro-foundations of informational search behaviour. This has added invaluable insights into, among other things, the pressing economic problems of inflation and unemployment (Phelps, 1970). On the other hand, it has permitted a healthy scepticism to emerge about the possibilities of using the equilibrium properties of the Neoclassical framework to analyse market behaviour in general. What is central to both approaches, moreover, is the specification of an environment where information is neither costlessly nor instantaneously available.

Briefly, the former development may be regarded as a characteristically Neoclassical attempt to explain fully supply and demand outcomes in the information market by reference to the rational choices of individuals, subject to posited constraints.[14] The major output of this research has been a microeconomic theory of the demand for information, a theory of the willingness of an individual to engage in costly information search to maximize profits or wages. This leads to the familiar condition for 'optimal' search behaviour: that an individual continue search (demand information) to the point where the marginal gain from searching equals the marginal time and money costs of searching. While propositions of this type allow a reasonable completion of the Neoclassical explanation, it is important to note none the less that they must assume away the fundamental problem in the demand for information—that demanders may not have information on the costs and benefits of information search. Further, the approach tends to perpetuate the view that informational phenomena can be handled in the context of an equilibrium theory. Doubts about the viability of equilibrium theories in a world of imperfect and costly information are central to the latter development. Two of the most prominent ideas follow from the modern interpretation (Leijonhufvud, 1968; Shackle, 1973) of Keynes' *General Theory* (1936): (a) that in a world of imperfect and costly information, the properties of a Neoclassical general equilibrium cannot be preserved and must give way to an analysis of general disequilibrium (Clower, 1965; Barro and Grossman, 1971); and (b) that the principal characteristic of a world of imperfect knowledge is that the future is unknowable, so that economic choices involving the future cannot have a rational or equilibrium-determined foundation.[15]

We note that none of the research discussed here gives a significant place to institutional aspects of informational phenomena. Arrow (1962) mentions peripherally that problems of information provision may, to a degree, be problems of legal adjustment but little else is said within the Neoclassical analysis. The theory of optimal information search, in particular, is developed quite independently of any institutional context. These matters are dealt with in the following two sections. Furthermore, within the neo-Keynesian analysis of general disequilibrium, little is said of the role institutions might play in a world of uncertainty.[16] We shall discuss this issue later (page 474).

The traditional Neoclassical view of institutions

While traditional Neoclassical information theory has been developed independently of a theory of institutional structure, there is none the less a rather naïve institutional assumption which permeates Neoclassical analysis in general. This is simply that the institutional structure of an economy is a fixed parameter in the analysis of resource allocation problems. This assumption has been rationalized either in terms of the long-run view that the institutional structure has already adapted to its long-run optimum position and that analysis proceeds given this optimum,[17] or in terms of the short-run view that the period which is being considered by analysis is too short to permit of any institutional change whatsoever.[18] While both views lead to the same result, the essential difference between them may be understood in terms of the potential benefits and costs to individuals of changing the institutional structure. In the long-run view, the costs of institutional reform tend to zero, but since the economy is already at an institutional optimum, so do the benefits and institutional reform drops out of the economic problem altogether. This is consistent with the postulates of classical individualist social theory: that in long-run social equilibrium, the institutional structure does not (and cannot) constrain the decisions of individual economic agents. In the short-run view, by contrast, the benefits of institutional change may be very large (since we need not be at an optimum) but the costs approach infinity, so that the institutional structure becomes an essential constraint on economic behaviour.

Taking the long-run view as representative of most Neoclassical analysis and applying it to informational phenomena, a weak institutional theory of information may be constructed. Its properties are straightforward. Since the institutional structure is fixed at an optimum, changes in the characteristics of resource allocation in the information market cannot logically follow from institutional changes. Further, since this institutional structure does not constrain or influence resource allocation decisions, equilibrium demands for or supplies of information (including information search) cannot be regarded as a direct manifestation of the institutional properties of the economy in question. This particular institutional theory of information is *prima facie* not very illuminating. Clearly the major task of such a theoretical framework must be to sketch the route between short-run constraint and long-run equilibrium where, in particular, the costs of institutional reform need not be infinite and the benefits of institutional reform need not be zero. In such an environment, the possibility of institutional reform is central and any analysis must necessarily explain the possible impacts of realized institutional reforms on the characteristics of optimal resource allocation.

This important explanatory scheme was not worked out in the context of traditional Neoclassical theory.[19] (We deal with some recent attempts in the following section.) More attention perhaps was directed at the general question of what the basic institutional requirements must be for such fundamental things as the formation and perpetuation of economic markets and the over-all co-ordination of decentralized decision-making and exchange. The specific question of establishing institutions 'to co-ordinate' is prominent here and it leads to the widely espoused view (Arrow, 1974; Hayek, 1945; Koopmans, 1957) that decentralized decision-making co-ordinated by 'a price system' is the most efficient institutional organization of an economy. Interestingly, the view rests on the demonstration that such an arrangement has superior 'informational properties'. In particular, Hayek argues that in so far as prices are a consolidation of relevant behavioural data for the whole economy and in so far as they can be transmitted efficiently (and simultaneously) to all economic agents,[20] an individual need only know his own personal circumstances (i.e. tastes, technology, budget) in order to make economic decisions. This is understood to be less information than would be required under any non-price co-ordinated scheme.[21]

The view is important since it suggests generally that the amount of information which individuals need in order even to make economic decisions—their minimum demand for information—may vary with the institutional organization of the economy. This proposition will prove important to the analysis undertaken later. What was perhaps more important to Hayek at the time when he put forward the argument, however, was to show that institutional alternatives to a price-co-ordinated market economy (e.g. a centralized socialist state) could not be made to work on informational grounds. Centralized planning requires the transfer of the informational needs of all agents to some small body which, according to Hayek, would either be too costly in economic terms or too much information would be lost in the process.[22] If Hayek is correct, we then have a further institutional proposition of interest: that there may be severe constraints on the types of institutional arrangement which even marginally satisfy the informational requirements of a co-ordinated economic society.

Information and institutional structure: the property rights perspective

Since the Neoclassical perspective on the institutional features of an economy casts little light on resource allocation problems when institutions change, we way regard the recent theory of property rights[23] as an attempt to solve this problem. The seminal analysis of information in this context is that of Demsetz (1969) whose ideas provide the basis for the arguments which follow.

The essence of the property rights approach to resource allocation problems may be summarized in two simple propositions: (a) that the types of purportedly general resource allocation results produced by traditional (static) Neoclassical economic theory are in fact very special outcomes, depending crucially on the characteristics of the property rights structure assumed for the analysis,[24] and (b) that in the Neoclassical time-setting between very short-run and very long-run institutional rigidity, the chief questions lying behind any analysis of resource allocation outcomes are those concerning feasible property rights reforms and their potential effects on resource allocation. As applied to the analysis of resource allocation problems in the information market in particular, the implications of this viewpoint are striking. First, such resource allocation problems can often be regarded independently as problems of institutional or legal adjustment. Second, and especially with respect to information policy, efforts to resolve such problems can often be more appropriately directed at the institutional superstructure of the information market than at the latter itself.[25]

Consider in this light the traditional problem that the information market must imperfectly allocate resources since information has unconventional properties as a commodity: non-appropriability, increasing returns in use and indivisibility. Consider, in particular, appropriability, where the purported problem is that if returns to information provision are not fully appropriable, there will be an under-supply of information relative to what would obtain if returns were fully appropriable. The degree of this under-supply will furthermore depend on the precise degree to which these returns are appropriable. It is important to note that the explanatory part of this Neoclassical proposition is not really that which concerns information supply; it is that which concerns appropriability. In particular, the substance of this explanation rests on a theory of why returns to information provision cannot be made fully appropriable or, at least, a theory of why the degree of appropriability cannot be changed. This in turn requires a potential justification for the complete (or nearly complete) rigidity of those contractual arrangements and property rights specifications involving information supply. As the theory of property rights has stressed, however, just as there is *a priori* no reason to assume anything about the rigidity of institutional arrangements, there is *a priori* no reason to assume anything about the appropriability characteristics of information supply. If individuals are in a position to supply information but are faced with unsatisfactory supply conditions, they will—depending upon the costs and benefits of institutional reform—attempt to modify these conditions. They will attempt through the legal system to redefine and extend the conditions pertaining to the ownership and use of information. The extent to which individuals do this will then determine the degree of appropriability of the returns to information provision and thus their incentives to supply information.[26]

The supply of information in any economy therefore depends crucially on determining the degree of appropriability of returns to information provision. This in turn depends on the extent to which individuals are induced to reform existing property rights structures so as to increase appropriability. Moreover, under-supply of information is only a problem in the information market *per se* if the property rights structure is (or is assumed to be) unchangeable. Otherwise, the major problem is one of institutional reform, and the chief question is not why there might be difficulties in inducing individuals to supply information at a given level of appropriability but why there might be difficulties in inducing individuals to undertake reforms affecting appropriability. These same arguments would seem to apply equally well to the other problems of increasing returns in use and indivisibility.[27]

The argument has been conducted in principle; a further task must then be to explain the precise conditions under which individuals will actually undertake institutional reforms affecting information supply. While it is not appropriate to undertake a detailed analysis of this issue here and though in general any successful analysis of institutional reform must involve a full specification of the costs and benefits of that reform, two further points must still be made. The first is simply that it would be especially convenient if the costs and benefits of institutional reform could be viewed as given parameters in the analysis of resource allocation problems involving institutional change. This would provide a concrete starting-point to determine the likelihood of reform undertakings as well as their magnitude. Unfortunately, it is probably not possible to determine this parameter. In so far as the costs and benefits of reform can be regarded as items registered in a market for reform (Breton and Breton, 1969) which are thus manifested in some set of prices for the activity in question, it becomes simply impossible within any sort of Neoclassical general equilibrium framework to view these items as given. The (relative) prices associated with reform must depend on all other prices through supply/demand equilibration. This argument has a serious implication: that the analysis of the allocation of resources to reform must be undertaken simultaneously with the analysis of all other resource allocation problems.[28]

Accepting the idea of a market for reform, there is a second point to be made: that there is no guarantee that this market would be a perfect one by Neo-classical standards. In fact, it can be convincingly argued that since the returns to reform are not fully appropriable, there may very well be under-investment in reform.[29] The interesting feature of this argument is not only that it can explain an under-supply of information by way of an under-supply of reform but also that it is identical to the argument concerning the under-supply of information. Here, a consistent application of the property rights perspective would suggest an analysis of alternative institutional settings for the market for reform. The basic problem is reforming 'reform institutions' so as to induce increased investment in reform through increased appropriability.[30] This is not as paradoxical as it sounds; the problem simply occurs in two stages. If it proves economically feasible to move to a setting where more of the returns on reform can be appropriated then more reform in general will be induced, and presumably part of this will flow to the information market if changes are created there also. If such a move is not economically feasible, then the basic problem remains. The fixed supply of reform will constrain institutional change in the information market and any attempts to circumvent this will require the use of non-market instruments.

These arguments emphasize the close interdependence between the resource allocation properties of the information market and the characteristics of institutional reform in general. The resource allocation properties of the information market depend not only on the institutional structure of that market but also on the extent to which its structure is amenable to reform. In turn this depends upon the over-all supply of reform which itself is influenced by the (broader) institutional characteristics of a market for reform.

Information and institutional structure: the supply of institutional information

In the previous section we have demonstrated the link between information and institutional structure from the perspective of the economic incentives generated by alternative institutional or property rights arrangements. This link, however, forms only one part of the institutional foundations of information theory. A second concern is the extent to which institutional structures themselves supply information for decision-making. This question has received little attention[31] yet it is absolutely fundamental to the analysis of information supplied in markets. First, if institutions supply information—henceforth denoted 'institutional information',[32] then the resource allocation properties of market-supplied information must depend on the quantity and quality of institutional information. Second, and more specifically, if institutions supply information which at least in some respects plays the same role in decision-making as market-supplied information, then institutional information may in fact substitute for market-supplied information in decision-making. As will become evident below, these arguments are central to our general view of the role of institutional information in economic decision-making: individuals are seen as making rational choices between institutional information and market-supplied information, the market supply being relied upon only if the quantity and quality of institutional information is insufficient for their purposes. In the extreme case institutional information may simply replace market-supplied information.[33]

To obtain some idea of the possible role played by institutional information in economic decision-making and to clarify its basic characteristics, it is appropriate to consider a number of places in economic theory where the concept has been

implied but not formally explicated. We stress that, in referring to the role of institutional structures in providing information, we take a broad sociological view
of these structures, including any social contract or convention which limits individuals' expectations of possible social interaction—whether or not they relate to
economic exchange alone or can be enforced by legal sanctions. In general, it
is by placing limits on spontaneous social behaviour that institutional structures
supply information, providing individuals with guidance to 'acceptable' behavioural decisions or constraints on their ability to undertake 'unacceptable'
decisions.[34]

Rees' (1966) analysis of informal information networks in the labour market
is set out in the following terms:

> Most employers have a strong preference for using informal information networks. . . .
> Employee referrals—the most important informal channel—usually provide good
> screening for employers who are satisfied with the present workforce. Present employees
> tend to refer people like themselves, and they may feel that their own reputation is affected
> by the quality of the referral. . . . informal sources have important benefits to the applicant.
> He can obtain much more information from a friend who does the kind of work in which
> he is interested than from an advertisement in the paper or a counselor at an employment
> agency, and he places more trust in it.—Rees, 1966, p. 562.

What Rees clearly identifies here is a structure of social interaction and, in
particular, a definite institutional structure which plays a most important role in
transferring information between individuals in the labour market. Furthermore the
quality (or trustworthiness) of the information transferred is seen to depend on the
institutional role occupied by the supplier of information. The institutional bias of
Rees' analysis is noteworthy but so is his insistence that such informal channels do
not involve market exchange and 'are usually costless to the employee' (p. 562).
Much of this spirit is also conveyed in sociological research on the diffusion of
inventions[35] and in Shubik's comment that the popular saying that 'it is not what
you know but who you know' is 'reasonable in a world where the gathering and
evaluation of information is costly'—Shubik, 1967, p. 773.

A more obvious use of the concept of institutional information can be found
in the now fairly common reference to the use of 'rules of thumb' in economic
decision-making (Baumol and Quandt, 1964). In particular, it has often been noted
in empirical studies that firms do not use classical profit-maximizing rules for their
production decisions.[36] Instead, they use a number of simple historical rules (on
prices, on profits) picked up from experience within their industry, informal
associations with long-standing producers, and so on. A more contemporary use
of such a rule of thumb is found in the modern theory of economic policy:
Friedman's advocacy of a simple rule of money supply expansion in lieu of policies
based on knowledge of critical feedback relationships in the economy (Friedman,
1969; Sargent and Wallace, 1965).

Perhaps the most interesting and fundamental use of the concept of institutional information, however, is Keynes' (1936, 1937) analysis of decision-making under future uncertainty. Here Keynes seems to suggest that, since knowledge of future economic outcomes is impossible, it is only institutionally established rules of thumb (or expectations) which can be relied upon for decision-making. The most important of Keynes' guides to practical action under future uncertainty is as follows:

Knowing that our own individual judgement is worthless, we endeavour to fall back on the judgement of the rest of the world, which is perhaps better informed. That is, we endeavour to conform with the behaviour of the majority or average. The psychology of a society of individuals each of whom is endeavouring to copy the others leads to what we may strictly term a conventional judgement.—Keynes, 1937, p. 214.

Despite Keynes' psychological bias, the explicitly institutional content of this statement is evident and the characteristics which Keynes sees in 'conventional judgements' are precisely those which we wish to impute to institutional information.[37]

While these examples from traditional economic theory convey a number of the important features of institutional information, further work must be done in order to make the concept truly operational. All we wish to stress here is that institutional information is in principle different from the type of market-supplied information normally analysed. Its provision is not directly related to the economic gains of individuals; it is not supplied in formal markets, and consequently, it does not have a (positive) price. Furthermore, the acceptance of institutional information in economic decision-making need not involve an explicit search for some 'true state of affairs' but may often follow simply from the sociological constraints and behavioural expectations of a particular institutional arrangement.[38]

The special significance of the concept of institutional information lies in the possibility that it may often be substituted for market-supplied information in economic decision-making.[39] There are a number of reasons why this might obtain:

(i) institutional information is normally cheaper than market-supplied information (i.e. costless), even if of lower quality, (ii) in given circumstances, there may not be any higher quality information available in the market or obtainable by search, (iii) there may be social costs involved for individuals who apply 'unconventional judgements',[40] and (iv) institutional prescriptions on behaviour normally specify behaviour directly; information in the market usually provides estimates of the parameters of a decision-problem which can only be transformed into behaviour if the *costs of rational calculation* (Anspach, 1966) are borne.

It follows from (i) and (ii), however, that the extent to which institutional information may be substituted for market-supplied information depends on quality. Since the use of institutional information need not involve a costly search for some 'true state of affairs', one could initially assume that institutional information must be of unambiguously lower quality than market-supplied information. Keynes, however, points to a situation where the future is unknowable through any informational channel so that the quality of market-supplied information would appear to be no better than that of institutional information (even if the latter is devoid of all quality). In fact, if we accept Keynes' view that mass acceptance of conventional judgements may lead to self-fulfilling outcomes,[41] then the quality of institutional information may actually be higher. Rees (1966) notes that information passed on by non-market, informal channels may be regarded by its recipient as more trustworthy (even if it is not), which complicates the issue still further.[42] These matters aside, there is one simple proposition concerning the quality of institutional information which we can state unambiguously: that its perceived quality depends directly on the stability of the institutional structure of an economy over time. If the institutional structure is stable over long periods, institutional information will appear to be of high quality and thus of consistent value in decision-making. If the institutional structure is characterized by a 'capricious instability' (Shackle, 1973, p. 225) or is subject to the 'forces of disillusion' (Keynes, 1937, p. 214), then institutional information will appear to be relatively worthless as a guide to decision-making.[43]

The methodological significance of institutional information

The importance of the concept of institutional information may easily be appreciated by considering its injection into a simple Neoclassical environment which contains only market-supplied information. Its methodological significance becomes even clearer, however, if we contrast such a Neoclassical environment with the other extreme where the only available information is institutional information. A central argument here is that neither of these extreme environments satisfactorily explains informational phenomena. The appropriate matrix of a decision-making environment for information theory must contain both institutional and market-supplied information.

To understand the nature of an environment which contains only institutional information, it is probably not necessary to look beyond a number of popular 'holistic' social theories—for example, those of Marx, Kuhn (1970) and Galbraith (1958, 1967). In all these theories, the dominant idea is that the institutional (or economic) structure of a given society sets such severe constraints that individuals cannot effectively make decisions. In fact, in non-revolutionary times, the only behavioural option open is to follow institutionally dictated rules as transmitted through a paridigm, a class, or, in general, the socially and economically powerful. No real private demands for, or supplies of information are present; all information is institutional in character. Furthermore, the only technical problem in such a society is to guarantee the existence of a mechanism by which these institutionally dictated rules can be effectively transmitted to and enforced upon all members.

The characterization of societies along these lines is easily seen to be problematic. As a matter of fact, none of these social theories make it clear how institutionally dictated rules are to be successfully transmitted and enforced. It may simply be a function of economic control and socialization, but even so, it would still be necessary to explain why such control or socialization efforts cannot fail or why individuals might not rationally find alternative information supply channels.[44] More important, however, are the well-known problems of explaining institutional change within these theories (Agassi, 1960). While the very characterization of holistic societies would seem to preclude successful reforms by individuals from the outset, an even greater problem is simply that if individuals can use only the existing institutional information of a (decaying) society to reform that society, then holistic social change would appear to be impossible on these grounds alone.[45] The problem, of course, is that holistic institutional change requires information which is somehow independent of that transmitted by the existing institutional structure. Without independent information—such as that obtainable through private exchange—the essential 'novelty' of institutional change cannot be dealt with. Much the same conclusion, interestingly enough, may be drawn from a proposition advanced earlier: that in times of great institutional instability, institutional information will be of sufficiently low quality to appear worthless as a guide to decision-making in any case.

The problem of analysing institutional change within an environment which contains only institutional information has two important implications. First, it suggests that at least part of the analysis of large-scale social reform must involve some notion of an 'institutional information failure'. In particular, a change in the consciousness of a Marxist worker, or the identification of an anomaly by the paradigm-bound scientist would seem to imply both: (a) that the institutional structure has failed to transmit appropriate information to at least some set of individuals, and (b) that at least some set of individuals has established alternative information supply channels. These informational matters clearly cannot be buried under an all-embracing dialectical process. Second, this explanatory problem would seem to sharpen the methodological need for a framework which incorporates both institutional information and market-supplied information; one which contains institutional information alone can only produce an incomplete theory of institutional change. Yet, as has been argued earlier, a framework which contains market-supplied information alone can also only produce an incomplete theory of information.

A general framework

In this section, we assemble the institutional features of information discussed above into a general framework. While it is evident that certain of these features might best be analysed quite independently of the framework of Neoclassical equilibrium theory, this simple paradigm will none the less remain our present point of reference. The analysis which follows may then be regarded either as a way of generalizing Neoclassical information theory to incorporate various institutional, non-market and dynamic aspects of informational phenomena or as a way of solving problems in the Neoclassical framework by making its institutional foundations explicit. In either case, the central distinguishing feature of the proposed framework is that it contains both market-supplied information (MSI) and institutional information (II) and thus constitutes a methodological advance over those which contain only one or the other. The exposition is largely non-technical; a detailed mathematical exposition, originally prepared, has been omitted here.

Three simple assumptions identify the Neoclassical perspective on information and institutional structure:
1. There exists no (relevant) II; all (relevant) information is MSI.
2. The institutional structure of the economy is fixed.
3. The demand for and the supply of MSI depend upon its price.

Under these assumptions, and the further assumption that well-defined and conventionally-sloped demand and supply curves for information exist (see page 467 et seq.), a stable equilibrium price for MSI is determined. This equilibrium price will consistently prevail unless there is some exogenous change in the parameters behind the supply and demand functions. We note furthermore that even if we generalized 3 so that the demand for, and supply of, MSI depended upon the institutional structure of the economy, in addition to price, the potential impacts of institutional changes on market outcomes are nullified by 2.

Our proposed framework modifies this set of assumptions as follows:
1'. There exists both (relevant) II and MSI.
2'. The institutional structure of the economy can potentially be changed.
3'. The demand for and the supply of MSI depend upon *both* the price of MSI and the institutional structure of the economy.
4'. The supply of II depends upon the institutional structure of the economy.

Under these assumptions, the price of MSI can no longer be determined independently of institutional structure, since it directly determines the supply of, and demand for, information, and must therefore directly determine the equilibrium price of MSI. Further, since any change in institutional structure must normally change the relative supplies of MSI and II and the over-all demand for information, it must also change the equilibrium price of MSI.[46]

More specifically, we assume that the total supply of information in any economy consists of the sum of the quantities of MSI and II. These two types of supplies are distinguished in the terms set out earlier (p. 476).[47] The MSI component is specified in the spirit of the theory of property rights (see page 471 et seq.) as depending upon both the price of MSI and the institutional structure of the economy. Here different institutional (property rights) structures imply, for example, different degrees of appropriability of the returns to information provision and thus different economic incentives to supply information. The II component is also seen to depend upon the characteristics of institutional structure. Different institutional structures provide, in differing degrees, 'rules of thumb' or conventions for decision-making on present (and potential future) economic activities. II however does not depend upon prices since it is not supplied in formal markets.[48]

The total supply of information as defined here neglects important quality considerations. It is therefore necessary to recast the supplies of MSI and II in quality-adjusted terms. Referring to these quality-adjusted supplies as 'effective supplies', we assume that the quality of MSI is always fixed (for convenience, at unity) but that the quality of II varies directly with the stability of the institutional structure of the economy over time (see page 477).[49] Clearly as the institutional structure changes more and more quickly (becomes more and more unstable), the quality of II falls and the effective supply of II falls relative to the (fixed-quality) supply of MSI. On the other hand, both the quality and the effective supply of II are maximized when the institutional structure of the economy is perfectly stable (i.e. fixed).

Turning now to the demand side, it would be characteristic of Neoclassical demand theory to regard the total demand for information as depending upon: (a) the price of MSI and the (relative) qualities of MSI and II and perhaps (b) some (objectively measured) difference between the average stock of information at present held in the economy and 'full information'. We reject both of these specifications; the former in the light of obvious problems in the determination of the value of information (see page 468), the latter as reflecting the unsatisfactory features of the 'nirvana approach' to information theory (see above). Instead we make a very simple (and indeed Neoclassical) assumption following Hayek (1945): that individuals have a minimum total demand for information which is just sufficient for economic decision-making to take place in the society in question.[50] This minimum total demand is seen to depend upon the institutional organization of the economy but not upon price or quality considerations. Furthermore, by ruling out price and quality-induced demands, we also assume that the over-all demand for information in any economy is equal to this (institutionally determined) minimum.[51]

The static analysis: fixed institutional structure

To understand how the above institutional features interact to determine the equilibrium price of MSI, it is convenient to examine a situation where the institutional structure of the economy is perfectly stable (i.e. fixed). This is the system we would obtain if we used Neoclassical assumption 2, rather than 2', in our modified framework. The fixity of the institutional structure implies the threefold fixity of: (a) the over-all demand for information; (b) the quality of II (at a maximum); and (c) the effective supply of II.

The fixed over-all demand for information is especially important here. Clearly individuals must satisfy this over-all demand by some combination of MSI and II. Thus far, we have not determined the separate demands for these two varieties of information, so this combination cannot yet be determined. This problem can be overcome, however, simply by recognizing that, if II can be costlessly obtained (and disposed of) by economic agents, economic rationality dictates that individuals will always demand the effective supply of II. As such, the demand for MSI becomes a 'residual demand' (the difference between the fixed over-all demand for information and the fixed effective supply of II) and the equilibrium price of MSI is determined simply as the supply-price of MSI which will equate the supply of MSI to this residual demand. Under this logic, the extent to which individuals will be forced to satisfy their informational requirements through the market thus depends upon the extent to which the effective supply of II is (or is not) sufficient to meet their over-all demand for information. In short, the larger (or smaller) the extent to which over-all demand can be satisfied through II, the smaller (or larger) the pressure on the information market and the lower (or higher) the equilibrium price of MSI.

In any given institutional setting, the equilibrium price which actually comes to prevail will, of course, depend upon the specific way in which the institutional structure affects the demands for and supplies of information. Different institutional structures, moreover, will normally entail different supplies and demands and thus different equilibrium prices for MSI. It is important to recognize that such differences in the equilibrium price of MSI in general reflect differences in the 'informational efficiency' of alternative institutional structures. Consider, for example, an institutional structure which is 'informationally efficient' in all three senses that: (a) it requires that individuals have a very small amount of information to make economic decisions; (b) it provides very strong market incentives to supply information; and (c) it provides a large effective supply of II.

Since such a structure is typified by a very high supply of both MSI and II and a very low demand for information over-all, the price of MSI must be very low. In the extreme case, the price of MSI would be zero if the supply of II was by itself sufficient to meet the (small) over-all demand for information. Now consider an institutional structure which is inefficient in at least one of the above senses. Since any inefficiency must entail, in relative terms, either a higher demand for information or a lower supply of information, the equilibrium price of MSI must now be higher. An institutional structure which is grossly inefficient in all three senses will normally produce a very high price for MSI.

The dynamic analysis: institutional reform

What is crucial to the above analysis is the very special Neoclassical assumption of a fixed institutional structure. A more interesting and general analysis must then permit institutional changes and explain the impacts of these changes on the resource allocation properties of the information market. There are three fundamental items which require explanation in this connexion: (a) the basis for institutional change; (b) the magnitude of the institutional change; and (c) the rate at which the institutional change proceeds over time. The determination of the last item is most important. First, in so far as the time-rate of institutional change determines the time-path of changes in the supply of and demand for information, it determines the time-path of changes in the equilibrium price of MSI. Second, in so far as it is a proxy for the 'stability' of an institutional structure over time, it determines the quality, and thus the effective supply, of II (see page 477).

An interesting way to approach the question of the basis of institutional reform within this framework is to assume that individuals hold (exogenous) expectations regarding the time-rates of change of three key macroeconomic variables: the general price level, real output and labour's share in real output. These expected values are compared with the actual time-rates of change of the variables in question. The differences between these expected and actual values are then seen to lead to a gap between i^*, the institutional structure individuals anticipate would lead to the fulfilment of their expectations, and i, the existing institutional structure. The basis for institutional change is thus simply that at least some expectations are not realized under the prevailing institutional structure (i.e. $i \neq i^*$). The magnitude of the institutional change required is the size of the gap between i and i^*. Furthermore, the problem of determining the time-rate of change of the institutional structure becomes the problem of determining how quickly this gap will be filled. Our principal task here is to determine the characteristics of the adjustment path of i to i^* and to do this, we make explicit the characteristics of a market for institutional reform which generates this path.[52]

Thus, following Breton and Breton (1969), let us assume the existence of well-defined demand and supply functions for institutional reform. It is noted that these demands and supplies are not defined in terms of quantities of reform independent of time but as quantities of reform per unit time. We are therefore concerned with the demand for, and supply of, particular time-rates of institutional change (i.e. speeds of institutional adjustment). The demand for reform is seen to depend positively on the size of the gap between i and i^* and negatively on the price of reform. The negative relationship is rationalized on the grounds that the lower the speed of adjustment demanded, the longer individuals will have to wait in order to realize the benefits of institutional change and thus the higher price they are willing to pay to avoid these opportunity costs. We posit further that there is no demand for institutional reform if the existing institutional structure is optimal (i.e. $i = i^*$).

The supply of reform is seen to depend positively on the price of reform on the grounds that its marginal cost rises the more rapidly a supply of reform effort is required from individuals and the more rapidly this reform has to be implemented.[53] Equilibrium in this market then requires that the time-rate of institutional change demanded equal the time-rate of institutional change supplied. If the gap between i and i^* is assumed to be fixed at the onset of institutional change, this condition determines the equilibrium price of reform and the equilibrium time-rate of change of the institutional structure simultaneously. The equilibrium time-rate in turn determines the quality of II and the initial adjustments in both the institutional structure and the price of MSI.

The addition of a reform market equilibrium condition to our framework thus allows us to make our explanatory structure richer. We are no longer asking the simple question of whether there exists some price of MSI which will be consistent with information market equilibrium at a point in time. We are now asking the more complex question of whether there exists some time-path of the prices of both MSI and reform which will be consistent with continuing equilibrium in both the information market and the market for reform over time. Moreover, the explicit specification of a market for reform allows us to isolate clearly the conditions under which the Neoclassical assumption of a fixed institutional structure (i.e. a time-rate of institutional change of zero) will hold. These conditions may be understood especially well if we regard the supply function for reform posited immediately above as an intermediate or long-run supply function and recognize the existence of a very short-run supply function where the supply of reform is zero (at all prices of reform). As such, the relevant conditions are either that the demand for reform equals zero or that the supply of reform equals zero. The former corresponds to the Neoclassical long-run view (i.e. $i = i^*$); the latter corresponds to the Neoclassical short-run view (see page 470 et seq.).[54]

While we are not concerned here with developing the formal dynamics of this framework, certain elementary dynamic implications of this analysis should still be noted. These are perhaps most simply brought out by seeing the implied adjustment process in a number of separate stages. Thus, consider an economy which is in long-run equilibrium (where the institutional structure is optimally adjusted) and which at a point in time undergoes an exogenous, once-for-all expectational change. This will lead to a gap between i and i^* which must be filled. Individuals will seek institutional changes and their demands for, and supplies of, reform will determine an initial reform market equilibrium. The positive time-rate of institutional change associated with this equilibrium will have three different impacts. Let us presume that the first impact is only upon individuals' perceptions of the quality of II.[55] As the institutional structure is now seen to be more unstable, the quality of II falls from its long-run equilibrium quality. This lowers the effective supply of II so that, in equilibrium, more information must be supplied by the market. This additional supply can only be induced if the price of MSI rises at this stage of the analysis.

A second impact stage may be defined when the institutional changes implied by a positive time-rate of institutional change actually take effect on the supplies of, and demands for, information. It is evident that the more these changes imply an increased demand for information over-all or a reduced supply of either or both MSI and II, the higher the price of MSI will rise, and continue to rise at this stage of the analysis too. But this impact is not clear-cut; the price or MSI may potentially fall here. A third impact stage may be defined when these initial institutional adjustments towards i^* feed back to modify the original reform market equilibrium. Clearly, as the economy starts moving towards i^*, the gap between i and i^* closes, the demand for reform decreases, and both the price of reform and the time-rate of institutional change fall to a new lower level. The new lower time-rate produces another round of effects analogous to those outlined above—only with less impact since the adjustment pace has now slowed. It is evident that the process described ultimately converges towards a new long-run optimum; i will approach i^* at an ever slower rate. In long-run equilibrium, $i^* = i$ once again, the time-rate of institutional change is zero once again, and the quality of II returns to its original maximum value. Moreover, when $i = i^*$, the demand for reform equals zero and thus the price of reform equals zero. With the institutional structure now fixed at the new optimum, the static framework presented earlier may be employed unambiguously once again. The price of MSI is determined by an unchanged quality of II and a changed institutional structure.

Conclusion

The above framework represents one very simple way of capturing the important links between information and institutional structure. We have refrained from making sophisticated expectational assumptions in our analysis,[56] we have not made explicit the role of adjustments in actual time-rates of change of prices, real income and labour's share in the dynamic process,[57] and we have not developed a concrete set of micro-foundations for our model. These omissions could easily be corrected—but that would be hardly consistent with our purpose. Our purpose has simply been to show that the analysis of informational phenomena cannot be separated from the analysis of institutional phenomena. To this end, we have demonstrated how the explanatory and predictive structure of simple Neoclassical models of information must remain logically incomplete without a detailed specification of the characteristics of the institutional structure associated with any given informational environment.

Of central importance in our analysis is the concept of 'institutional information'. It is responsible not only for the evident non-market and dynamic properties of our framework but also for the explication of a key substitution relationship between II and MSI in economic decision-making. This substitution relationship is of especial interest precisely because it permits a wide variety of purportedly non-rational decision-making behaviour (e.g. in the traditional Neoclassical theories of the firm and of the consumer) to be explained as the outcome of the eminently rational choice between II and MSI. Since, under this view, it becomes informationally efficient for individuals to largely forego all the traditional Neoclassical principles of rational choice (i.e. profit-maximizing calculation, rational search and the reliance on MSI) when there is a large amount of high-quality II available for decision-making, a basic problem of consistency is revealed in the traditional Neoclassical framework. This stems from the fact that the informational efficiency of rational calculation is likely to be the smallest (and the informational efficiency of using conventional judgements and rules of thumb the greatest) when, as the Neoclassical view further posits, the institutional structure of the economy is perfectly stable (fixed). In this respect, the relevance of rational calculation for decision-making is most clearly defined within an environment where the institutional structure is unstable and changing and, thus, where the quality and the effective supply of II are low. The traditional Neoclassical conjunction of rational choice principles with a statically fixed institutional structure must therefore be called into question. In general, if we wish to preserve the relevance of rational calculation in our traditional models of consumer and producer behaviour, then we must give up the assumption of a statically fixed institutional structure. Correspondingly, if we wish to preserve the assumption of a statically fixed institutional structure, then we must accept the potential irrelevance of rational calculation.

This view is seen to be of some importance when set beside Shackle's (1973) notion that rational choice and economic dynamics are inconsistent. On the most sceptical plane, our view could be seen to reinforce Shackle's by arguing not only that rational choice is inconsistent with economic change and instability but also that it is largely irrelevant in a static, unchanging economic universe. However, this is not our objective. As I have argued elsewhere (Newman, 1974), Shackle's argument is unsatisfactory: rationality and economic dynamics are consistent if we give up the assumption that 'perfect knowledge' is a precondition for rational choice. As such, our central argument becomes quite the opposite of Shackle's: (a) that rational economic choice is consistent with both imperfect knowledge and economic dynamics, an essential touchstone of rationality under imperfect knowledge being the (second-order) rational choice between II and MSI; and (b) that rational economic choice is potentially only relevant (i.e. non-trivial) in a dynamic and institutionally changing economic setting. These arguments of course have other fundamental implications: for the appropriate characterization of rational decision-making under uncertainty, for the analysis of the informational conditions underlying institutional reform and, more generally, for the appreciation of the complex links between information, rationality and dynamics. Such matters must ultimately prove crucial to our understanding of both informational and institutional phenomena, and economic phenomena in general.

486   Geoffrey Newman

Notes

[1] For a reasonable modern survey of developments in this area, see Hirshliefer (1972). A brief methodological survey may be found on pages 470–1.

[2] With the exception of Roberts and Holdren (1972), most of this literature is concerned with the somewhat restricted area of 'property rights' (Furubotn and Pejovich, 1972, 1974; Manne, 1975). As Furubotn and Pejovich (1972, p. 1139) make clear, the chief focus of this research is legal contracts involving economic exchange. While we will use the terms 'institutional structure' and 'property rights structure' more or less interchangeably throughout the paper, we recognize that a general concept of institutional structure includes a great number of social conventions which are not necessarily associated with economic exchange or enforced by legal sanctions.

[3] Some important attempts to provide such an integrated model are Demsetz (1969), Hurwicz (1973) and Roberts and Holdren (1972). For an early assessment of the importance of such a model, see Boulding (1966).

[4] We refer to the wide variety of Neoclassical models based on Hicks (1946) and Samuelson (1947).

[5] For the accepted modern treatment of cases where the probabilities are less than unity, see Borch (1968).

[6] This has its parallel in the traditional comparison of resource allocation outcomes produced under perfect competition with those produced under any imperfectly competitive market organization.

[7] The only interesting policy questions which arise here then concern the size of the distortion, the welfare costs involved, and its potential removability. Moreover, as the actual world being explained by the model is clearly one of imperfect knowledge, there is one simple policy prescription: remove the distortion and approach the ideal. It is easily seen however that this prescription may be problematic if the elimination of the informational distortion creates other more serious distortions (Lipsey and Lancaster, 1956; Buchanan and Stubblebine, 1962). For a modern expression of the 'distortion' viewpoint, see Johnson (1972).

[8] The more fundamental point is that any model of ideal behaviour in ideal circumstances can serve as a standard of comparison for behaviour in non-ideal circumstances if and only if decision-makers still behave ideally. In general, there is no reason to expect this to be the case: non-ideal informational conditions may change behavioural dispositions. For a justification of the use of such 'ideal models', see Friedman (1953, p. 3–43); for a criticism, see Boland (1970). On the relation of these issues to the rationality of economic agents, see Tisdell (1975).

[9] The attempt to establish objective quantity units for information has become synonymous with the attempt to define the 'bits' of information in a 'message' (Theil, 1967, Chap. 1). The problems of this approach are, first, that the 'bits' may vary with the problems the decision-maker faces, i.e. his concept of 'relevant information' may change with the problems he faces. Second, even if the approach could be applied to simple factual propositions about the world, it is not clear how it could be applied to universal theories if such theories were viewed as other than just simple aggregates of empirical facts (Agassi, 1966).

[10] For the importance of the quality dimension, see Lamberton (1971, p. 10). The essential problem here is that the commitment to any general measure of quality (or truth-value) must also imply a commitment to a philosophy of science. This will only prove satisfactory if all decision-makers in fact interpret their informational environment in terms of this philosophy of science. A technical problem still emerges even if one was prepared to regard information of different qualities as different commodities: since an unrestricted view of the quality dimension should permit an infinity of different qualities of information, there would then be an infinity of different commodities and the traditional properties of Neoclassical markets normally hold in the case of a finite number of commodities.

[11] For the early basis of this viewpoint, which is fundamental to the theory of public goods, see Samuelson (1954).

[12] For example, a decision-maker needs, to know the price of information as registered in the information market as well as prices registered in all other markets. Another interpretation of this point involves the theory of job-search: an individual needs to know not only the going vacancies and their remuneration but also the channels through which he can procure such employment information.

[13] This state of affairs is usually taken to imply that government should subsidize the information industry or provide information on its own. See Arrow (1962) and the criticism of Demsetz (1969).

Notes (*continued*)

[14] The seminal paper here is that of Stigler (1961) although most of the advanced research dates from Phelps (1970) and concentrates on the labour market. We should also note the work of Theil (1967) and Marshak (1971) on developing the microfoundations of a 'statistical' theory of information.

[15] For a critical appraisal of this view, see Newman (1974).

[16] In essence the Neo-Keynesian view may be regarded as a very specific theory of the failure of one central market institution—the price mechanism. As such, it neither suggests a positive theory of institutions nor does it specify a theory of the failure of institutions other than the price mechanism.

[17] This theory has not been explicitly stated but is implied by the nature of the analysis. For example, see Bator (1957). As can be noted, there is a great similarity between the way institutional structure has been treated in long-run Neoclassical analysis and the way 'income distribution' has been treated in this analysis.

[18] The most obvious example of this view is found in the traditional short-run Keynesian models of income and employment which assume wage rigidity. The explicit assumption is that the analysis applies to a period shorter than that of the shortest institutional wage bargain. It is stressed that the basic foundations for this type of analysis (which dates from Hicks (1937)) are very much Neoclassical in spirit; the only thing which makes the analysis Keynesian is the introduction of short-run institutional rigidities.

[19] This programme, however, has been of long-standing concern to many followers of the Marshallian tradition of economic analysis. For a recent appreciation, see Friedman (1970).

[20] The problem of efficient (and simultaneous) transmission of price signals is central to the neo-Keynesian position reviewed earlier (see pages 467 et seq.).

[21] It should be noted that Hayek developed this argument assuming the 'independence' of individual decision-making. If preferences of individuals over states of the economy were 'interdependent', then individuals would require information in addition to price information and information on their own personal circumstances. For example, an individual whose consumption behaviour depended upon the quantities consumed by other individuals would have to know these other quantities for his decision-making. Interdependence not only weakens Hayek's argument as such but also it raises the question of whether institutions could be efficiently designed to either co-ordinate non-price information of decision-making relevance or turn it into information which is manifested in prices. The co-ordination of non-price information is a common role for social institutions in general to take.

[22] For a brief survey of these traditional arguments, see Hurwicz (1973, p. 5).

[23] As we have suggested in note 2, the theory of property rights is a special part of a more general economic theory of institutions. For the property rights literature, see Furubotn and Pejovich (1972, 1974) and Manne (1975).

[24] As Furubotn and Pejovich (1974, p. 1) state: '. . . individuals respond to economic incentives, and the pattern of incentives present at any time is influenced by the prevailing property rights structure.'

[25] We refer to the argument that government should use some economic policy—some tax-subsidy programme, some policy of providing information itself (Arrow, 1962)—to remove the problems rather than some institutional policy designed to alter incentives. Standard Neoclassical analysis neglects the potential efficiency of the latter policy.

[26] We are not claiming here that there exists some set of contractual arrangements which could make the returns to information perfectly appropriable, or even if there was, that they would ever be undertaken. The point is that the degree of appropriability may often be changeable within quite wide limits.

[27] See Demsetz (1969) for fuller details and examples.

[28] It thus becomes important in the analysis of institutional reform (or institutional rigidity) to distinguish between reforms which would not be undertaken at the prevailing set of relative prices and those which would not be undertaken at any and all sets of relative prices.

[29] The 'public good' properties of reform have been noted by Olson (1965). The underinvestment argument of course suggests the desirability of collectivizing reform effort. This in turn creates the problem that individuals may attempt to 'free ride' on the action of the collective by distorting their preferences so as to undervalue reform.

[30] We follow Breton and Breton (1969) in regarding the market for institutional reform as a macro-market which is not explicitly split up

Notes (*continued*)

into sectors (e.g. a market for informational reform). As such, we regard 'reform institutions' as a rather broad class of social institutions which are not specific to any particular type of market activity (e.g. the legislative process).

[31] The chief exception is Roberts and Holdren (1972, p. 111).

[32] We distinguish carefully our concept of 'institutional information' from information supplied, for example, by government institutions. The latter normally comes into play only if there is some market failure—inadequate supply and no market inducements. 'Institutional information', as we define it, is not supplied by governments and normally coexists with market-supplied information.

[33] Throughout the following analysis, we regard rational search activity as a vital part of market activity. Therefore a fundamental part of this analysis is examining the conditions under which institutional information may substitute for rational search activity.

[34] See Roberts and Holdren (1972, p. 111 et seq.); also Smelser (1963, p. 27).

[35] See Arrow (1969, p. 31).

[36] The two most important early studies are those of Hall and Hitch (1939) and Lester (1946). For a general survey of the critical issues involved, see Machlup (1967).

[37] For the more general features of Keynes' viewpoint, see Keynes (1936, Chap. 13). For a discussion of 'conventional judgements', see Shackle (1973, p. 224).

[38] One may rationalize the costlessness of institutional information in two ways: either the externalities associated with its provision are too costly to remove or, in so far as institutional information is a debt incurred by past generations, it places no burden on its present users. With reference to the latter, we might suggest a dynamic process here in which 'new' information is initially provided in markets and then becomes increasingly institutionalized with the passage of time.

[39] We admit that the substitution between market-supplied information and institutional information is not the only type of behaviour which might occur under uncertainty. Clearly individuals may try to reduce the *total* amount of information they need either by attempting to control relevant variables in their decision-making environment (i.e. gain monopoly power) or by producing and consuming items which are more uncertainty-proof.

[40] As Keynes (1936, p. 157) states: 'Worldly wisdom teaches us that it is better for reputation to fail conventionally than to succeed unconventionally.'

[41] As Keynes (1936, p. 203) states: 'Any level of interest which is accepted with sufficient conviction as likely to be durable will be durable. . . .'

[42] This sort of view of the trustworthiness of information is consistent with the problems of evaluating information before it is received (see page 468). In Rees' case, economic agents really have no direct or objective criteria for evaluating the information they are to receive. Therefore they turn to indirect sociological criteria: how much they trust the supplier of information.

[43] For interesting discussions on this point, see Gellner (1964, Chap. 3) and Malmgren (1968, p. 321).

[44] All three theories provide the foundations for such an explanation however. Galbraith stresses control of media and potency of advertising; Marx stresses 'economic necessity', and Kuhn would seem to stress the reward-cost structure confronting the scientist in times of 'normal science'.

[45] For the general and most complete arguments for the impossibility of holistic social change, see Popper (1945).

[46] In all of the following analysis, we assume the existence of some general measure of 'institutional structure'. This is a difficult measure to construct even in principle, although we should note Roberts' (1973) attempt to measure institutions in terms of a number of their dominant characteristics.

[47] It is noted that the assumption that MSI and II can be directly summed does not imply that MSI and II cover mutually exclusive economic phenomena. There may be information from both channels on the same phenomena, except they differ in type. An interesting way to characterize this difference is to regard II as 'background' or 'historical' knowledge and MSI as 'new' knowledge. This is an application of the view that MSI is systematically institutionalized over time.

[48] In any economy, it would be possible to construct a complete matrix of informational 'coverage' depending upon whether either or both of II and MSI were available on the set of present (or potential future) activities of the economy. To concentrate on the explicit substitution relationships between II and MSI, we make

Notes (*continued*)

the assumption here that both types of information are available on these activities. Also, since we wish to keep the analysis simple, we use the term 'institutional structure of the economy' to represent a number of potentially heterogeneous items. In the specification of the supply of II, it represents the broadest possible conception of the institutional structure of the economy; in the specification of the supply of MSI, it represents the institutional structure underlying the information market in particular. It is then convenient to introduce the general assumption that the institutional structure of the information market is perfectly representative of the institutional structure of the aggregate economy. This assumption will be employed consistently throughout the analysis.

[49] We define the 'effective supply' of either type of information simply as the quantity of that information multiplied by its quality. Since we assume that that quality of MSI is fixed at unity, it is evident that there is no difference between the quantity of MSI and its effective supply; the quality adjustment really only affects II. As the quality of II falls, for example, more and more (quantity) units of II are required for equivalence with a (quantity) unit of MSI. We should note furthermore that while the assumption that the quality of MSI is always at least as great as that of II is intuitively appealing here, it may be unfounded (see page 477) and it is unnecessary to this analysis in any case.

[50] This idea of a minimum threshold for decision-making is also suggested by Roberts and Holdren (1972, p. 73).

[51] This assumption is, of course, a very special one. The problem is not that the introduction of price or quality-induced demands would be inconsistent with the structure of this framework. They are simply difficult to introduce in the light of problems discussed earlier (page 468). In any case, this particular demand specification allows a clear appreciation of the institutional features we are attempting to isolate.

[52] The general approach employed here follows Friedman (1970, p. 223 et seq.). In choosing this 'macro-economy' approach to institutional change, we clearly conceal those inducements for institutional reform which arise directly from within the information market itself. These will prove important in considering the impact of institutional changes

on the supply of MSI (as property rights theorists would stress), although they will have little effect on the over-all demand for information or the supply of II. Our assumption that the institutional conditions in the information market are perfectly representative of the institutional conditions prevailing in the aggregate economy is an attempt to remove this problem for the expository purposes at hand. As will become evident, this permits us to use the same gap between i and i^* and, most important, the same equilibrium time-rate of institutional change, for the information market as for the aggregate economy.

[53] As noted on page 474, we could make the supply of reform depend upon the institutional structure of the market for reform, since different institutional structures may permit individuals to appropriate more (or less) of the returns to reform activity. We refrain from doing this here in order to keep our dynamic analysis simple.

[54] The major difference between the views is thus revealed in their respective implications for the price of reform. In the long-run view, the price of reform tends to zero; in the short-run view, it tends to infinity. We note furthermore that to ensure that the above conditions absolutely hold, it is necessary to make the technical assumption that the supply of reform is zero when the time-rate of institutional change is zero (i.e. the supply function for reform passes through the origin).

[55] The formal interpretation of this first impact stage is as one where the time-period is too short to permit the realization of institutional changes (since in the very short-run, the supply of reform is zero) but where the mere perception of planned reforms is sufficient to induce individuals to discount the quality of II.

[56] For example, rather than treating i^* as a fixed parameter in the analysis, we could make it 'adaptively' or 'progressively' dependent upon past realized institutional changes.

[57] In particular, what we have left implicit in all our analysis is the ultimate feedback of changes in informational and institutional conditions to expected and actual values (and changes) of prices, real output and labour's share. We have simply assumed the equilibration of expected and actual values of these variables when $i^* = i$. Clearly an explicit macroeconomic model of the economy must be

Notes (*continued*)

tied to our structure and the problem becomes one of examining the conditions necessary to generate simultaneous dynamic equilibria in the information market, the market for reform and the macroeconomy itself. If such simultaneous equilibration is out of reach, then the analysis becomes that of general dynamic disequilibrium and the relevant features of the recent neo-Keynesian programme (Clower, 1965; Leijonhufvud, 1968) may be entered explicitly into this structure.

References

AGASSI, J. 1960. Methodological Individualism. *British Journal of Sociology*, Vol. 11, No. 3, September, p. 244–70.

——. 1966. Sensationalism. *Mind*, Vol. 66, No. 9, January, p. 1–24.

ANSPACH, R. 1966. The General Incompatibility of Traditional Consumer Equilibrium with Economic Rationality—An Exploratory Analysis. *Oxford Economic Papers*, Vol. 18, No. 1, March, p. 71–82. (New series.)

ARROW, K. J. 1962. Economic Welfare and the Allocation of Resources for Invention. In: National Bureau of Economic Research, *The Rate and Direction of Inventive Activity: Economic and Social Factors*, p. 609–25. Princeton, Princeton University Press. x+635.

——. 1969. Classificatory Notes on the Production and Transmission of Technological Knowledge. *American Economic Review*, Vol. 59, No. 2, May, p. 29–33.

——. 1971. *Essays in the Theory of Risk-Bearing*. Chicago, Ill., Markham. vii+278 p.

——. 1974. Limited Knowledge and Economic Analysis. *American Economic Review*, Vol. 64, No. 1, March, p. 1–10.

BARRO, R. J.; GROSSMAN, H. I. 1971. A General Disequilibrium Model of Income and Employment. *American Economic Review*, Vol. 61, No. 1, March, p. 82–93.

BATOR, F. M. 1957. The Simple Analytics of Welfare Maximization. *American Economic Review*, Vol. 47, No. 1, March, p. 22–59.

BAUMOL, W. J.; QUANDT, R. A. 1964. Rules of Thumb and Optimally-Imperfect Decisions. *American Economic Review*, Vol. 54, No. 1, March, p. 23–46.

BOLAND, L. A. 1970. Conventionalism and Economic Theory. *Philosophy of Science*, Vol. 37, No. 2, June, p. 239–48.

BORCH, K. H. 1968. *The Economics of Uncertainty*. Princeton, N.J., Princeton University Press. vii+227 p.

BOULDING, K. E. 1966. The Economics of Knowledge and the Knowledge of Economics. *American Economic Review*, Vol. 56, No. 2, May, p. 1–13.

BRETON, A.; BRETON, R. 1969. An Economic Theory of Social Movements. *American Economic Review*, Vol. 59, No. 2, May, p. 198–205.

BUCHANAN, J. M.; STUBBLEBINE, W. C. 1962. Externality. *Economica*, Vol. 29, No. 4, November, p. 371–84. (New series.)

CLOWER, R. W. 1965. The Keynesian Counter-Revolution: A Critical Re-appraisal. In: F. H. Hahn and F. P. R. Brechling (eds.), *The Theory of Interest Rates*, p. 103–25. London, Macmillan, xv+364 p. (Proceedings of a conference held by the International Economic Association.)

DEMSETZ, H. 1967. Toward a Theory of Property Rights. *American Economic Review*, Vol. 57, No. 2, May, p. 347–59.

——. 1969. Information and Efficiency: Another Viewpoint. *Journal of Law and Economics*, Vol. 12, No. 1, April, p. 1–22.

FRIEDMAN, M. 1953. *Essays in Positive Economics*. Chicago, Ill., University of Chicago Press. 328 p.

——. 1969. *The Optimum Quantity of Money and Other Essays*. Chicago, Ill., Aldine. vi+296 p.

——. 1970. A Theoretical Framework for Monetary Analysis. *Journal of Political Economy*, Vol. 78, No. 2, March/April, p. 193–238.

FURUBOTN, E. G.; PEJOVICH, S. 1972. Property Rights and Economic Theory: A Survey of the Recent Literature. *Journal of Economic Literature*, Vol. 10, No. 4, December, p. 1137–62.

FURUBOTN, E. G.; PEJOVICH, S. (eds.). 1974. *The Economics of Property Rights*. Cambridge, Mass., Ballinger. xvi+367 p.

GALBRAITH, J. K. 1958. *The Affluent Society*. Boston, Mass., Houghton-Mifflin. xii+368 p.

——. 1967. *The New Industrial State*. Boston, Mass., Houghton-Mifflin. xiv+427 p.

GELLNER, E. 1964. *Thought and Change*. London, Weidenfield & Nicholson. 224 p.

References (*continued*)

HALL, R. L.; HITCH, C. J. 1939. Price Theory and Business Behaviour. *Oxford Economic Papers*, Vol. 2, No. 1, May, p. 12–45.

HAYEK, F. A. von. 1945. The Use of Knowledge in Society. *American Economic Review*, Vol. 35, No. 4, September, p. 519–30.

HICKS, J. R. 1937. Mr. Keynes and the Classics: A Suggested Interpretation. *Econometrica*, Vol. 5, No. 2, April, p. 147–59.

——. 1946. *Value and Capital: An Enquiry into Some Fundamental Principles of Economic Theory*. 2nd ed. Oxford, Clarendon Press. xi+340 p.

HIRSCHLIEFER, J. 1972. Where are We in the Theory of Information?. *American Economic Review*, Vol. 62, No. 2, May, p. 31–9.

HURWICZ, L. 1973. The Design of Mechanisms for Resource Allocation. *American Economic Review*, Vol. 63, No. 2, May, p. 1–30.

JOHNSON, H. G. 1972. Uncertainty and Probability in International Economics. In: C. F. Carter and J. L. Ford (eds.), *Uncertainty and Expectations in Economics: Essays in Honour of G. L. S. Shackle*, p. 148–59. Oxford, Basil Blackwell. ix+299 p.

KEYNES, J. M. 1936. *The General Theory of Employment, Interest and Money*, New York, N.Y., Harcourt Brace. xii+403 p.

——. 1937. The General Theory of Employment. *Quarterly Journal of Economics*, Vol. 51, No. 3, February, p. 209–23.

KOOPMANS, T. C. 1957. *Three Essays on the State of Economic Science*. New York, N.Y., McGraw-Hill. 231 p.

KUHN, T. S. 1970. *The Structure of Scientific Revolutions*. 2nd. ed. Chicago, Ill., University of Chicago Press. 210 p.

LAMBERTON, D. M. (ed.). 1971. *The Economics of Information and Knowledge*. Harmondsworth, Midd., Penguin. 384 p.

LEIJONHUFVUD, A. 1968. *On Keynesian Economics and the Economics of Keynes: A Study in Monetary Theory*. New York, N.Y., Oxford University Press. xiv+431 p.

LESTER, R. A. 1946. Shortcomings of Marginal Analysis for Wage-Employment Problems. *American Economic Review*, Vol. 36, No. 1, March, p. 63–82.

LIPSEY, R. G.; LANCASTER K. 1956. The General Theory of Second Best. *Review of Economic Studies*, Vol. 24, No. 1, p. 11–32.

MACHLUP, F. 1967. Theories of the Firm: Marginalist, Behavioural, Managerial. *American Economic Review*, Vol. 57, No. 1, March, p. 1–33.

MALMGREN, H. B. 1968. Information and Period

Analysis in Economic Decisions. In: J. N. Wolfe (ed.), *Value Capital and Growth: Papers in Honour of Sir John Hicks*, p. 319–27. Edinburgh, Edinburgh University Press.

MANNE, H. G. (ed.). 1975. *The Economics of Legal Relationships: Readings in the Theory of Property Rights*. St. Paul, Minn., West Publishing Co. x+660 p.

MARSHAK, J. 1971. Economics of Information Systems. *Journal of the American Statistical Association*, Vol. 66, No. 333, March, p. 192–219. (Invited Papers Section.)

MARSHAK, T.; GLENNAN, T. K.; SUMMERS, R. 1967. *Strategy for R and D: Studies in the Microeconomics of Development*, New York, N.Y., Springer-Verlag.

NEWMAN, G. 1974. Review of G. L. S. Shackle, Epistemics and Economics: A Critique of Economic Doctrines. *Philosophy of the Social Sciences*, Vol. 4, No. 4, Winter, p. 409–12.

OLSON, M. 1965. *The Logic of Collective Action: Public Goods and the Theory of Groups*. Cambridge, Mass., Harvard University Press. x+176 p.

PHELPS, E. *et al.* 1970. *The Microfoundations of Employment and Inflation Theory*. New York, N.Y., Norton. 434 p.

POPPER, K. R. 1945. *The Open Society and its Enemies*. Vol. 2. London, Routledge & Kegan Paul. 420 p.

REES, A. 1966. Information Networks in the Labour Market. *American Economic Review*, Vol. 56, No. 2, May, p. 559–66.

ROBERTS, B. 1973. An Extension of Optimality Criteria: An Axiomatic Approach to Institutional Choice. *Journal of Political Economy*, Vol. 81, No. 2, March/April, p. 386–400.

ROBERTS, B.; HOLDREN, R. 1972. *Theory of the Social Process: An Economic Analysis*. Ames, Iowa, Iowa State University Press. 259 p.

SAMUELSON, P. A. 1947. *Foundations of Economic Analysis*. Cambridge, Mass., Harvard University Press. xii+447 p.

——. 1954. The Pure Theory of Public Expenditure. *Review of Economics and Statistics*, Vol. 36, No. 4, November, p. 387–9.

SARGENT, T. J.; WALLACE, N. 1975. *Rational Expectations and the Theory of Economic Policy*. Minneapolis, Minn., Federal Reserve Bank of Minneapolis. 10 p. (Studies in Monetary Economics, 2.)

SHACKLE, G. L. S. 1973. *Epistemics and Economics: A Critique of Economic Doctrines*. Cambridge, Cambridge University Press. xiv+482 p.

492   *Geoffrey Newman*

References (*continued*)

SHUBIK, M. 1967. Information, Rationality, and Free Choice in a Future Democratic Society, *Daedelus*, Vol. 96, No. 3, Summer, p. 771–8.

SMELSER, N. J. 1963. *The Sociology of Economic Life*. Englewood Cliffs, N.J., Prentice-Hall. viii + 120 p.

SPENGLER, J. J. 1953. Sociological Value Theory, Economic Analysis and Economic Policy. *American Economic Review*, Vol. 43, No. 2, May, p. 340–9.

STIGLER, G. J. 1961. The Economics of Information. *Journal of Political Economy*, Vol. 69, No. 3, June, p. 213–25.

THEIL, H. 1967. *Economics and Information Theory*. Chicago, Ill., Rand McNally. xxii + 488 p.

TISDELL, C. 1975. Concepts of Rationality in Economics. *Philosophy of the Social Sciences*, Vol. 5, No. 3, Autumn, p. 259–72.

[16]

JOURNAL OF ECONOMIC ISSUES
Vol. XIII   No. 4   December 1979

Knowledge and the Role of
Institutions in Economic Theory

Lawrence A. Boland

"Though economic analysis and general
reasoning are of wide application, yet
every country has its own problems; and
every change in social conditions is likely
to require a new development of economic
doctrines."

Alfred Marshall

For many years there has been a dispute between the proponents of two
different methodological views. These can be characterized as anti- and
proneoclassical. The former maintains that since a neoclassical market
economy can be viewed as being merely one particular form of institutional setting, neoclassical economics is merely a special case of institutionalism (for example, Clarence Ayres, John Gambs, and Gunnar
Myrdal). The latter declares that since one can explain any institutional
setting and its evolution as merely the consequences of the logic of choice
(that is, of optimization facing given constraints), our understanding of
institutions is merely another example of neoclassical analysis (for example, James Buchanan, Gordon Tullock, and Douglass North).

The author is Professor of Economics and Commerce, Simon Fraser University,
Burnaby, British Columbia, Canada. He wishes to thank Ludwig Lachmann for his
kind and encouraging remarks on an earlier draft and his friends Donna Wilson and
Richard Schwindt for their valuable editorial assistance.

958   Lawrence A. Boland

Although it is possible for both to coexist, it is not possible for both to be the superior methodological viewpoint. Thus, this dispute continues. It will be argued here that since the neoclassical conception of an institution (that is, a short-run constraint) is inherently static, all attempts to promote and defend the proneoclassical view will necessarily result in methodological failures.

The primary concern of some proponents of the antineoclassical view has been to show that the opposing view is simply false. In particular, they have seen that their opponents presume that neoclassical choice theory can be made dynamic.[1] Some go as far as to argue explicitly that this presumption is completely unfounded.[2] The question of dynamics is even alleged to be the Achilles' heel of neoclassical theory.

So much has recently been made of this criticism that those institutionalists among the antineoclassical group have turned their attention from a study of the nature of institutions to the study of the evolutionary aspects of any economy. So far, the institutionalists' critical program of study— now called "evolutionary economics"—has failed to convince neoclassical economists to drop their "paradigm." To the contrary, many neoclassical theorists believe that the evolution of an economy's institutional setting can be explained *within* the neoclassical paradigm.[3] However, it would be misleading to suggest that this is only a methodological dispute over the ability to "explain within." Underlying this question is a more fundamental theoretical issue concerning the nature and role of institutions.

I will argue that unless the dynamic nature of institutions is properly explained, no explanation (neoclassical or institutional) of evolutionary economics can ever succeed. In particular, the neoclassical view of the nature and role of institutions either is inherently incapable of dealing with the questions of dynamics or is outright inconsistent.

Here I will argue that the essence of the methodological dispute lies not in the depths of sterile philosophy, but in the apparent contradictory roles played by institutions in economic theory. On one hand (in neoclassical theory), institutions are tacit or given static *constraints* which ultimately define various equilibrium positions.[4] On the other hand (in economic policy analysis), institutions are explicitly dynamic or active *instruments* used either to facilitate or to prevent change.[5] It will be shown that the appearance of contradiction can easily be overcome with an explicit recognition of the relationship between institutions and knowledge.

In the first section, I will present the neoclassical view of institutions, namely, that institutions are merely some of the constraints facing the optimizer. Specific attention will be given to the Marshallian method of dealing with the dynamics of constraints. In the second, I will summarize my previous criticism of the adequacy of any neoclassical program for dealing with questions of dynamics. In the next section, I will present a theory of the nature and role of institutions designed to overcome the inadequacy of the neoclassical paradigm. It will be based on an explicit recognition of the relevant epistemological questions involved as well as the instrumental aspects of institutions. In the final section, I will explain the essential relationships among time, knowledge, and institutions.

The Neoclassical View of Institutions

Within neoclassical theory, all *endogenous* variables are explained as the logical consequences of rational (and self-interested) choice, whereby one's choice may be limited by the rational choices of others through any activity in the market. This form of rational choice usually involves maximization (or minimization) of some objective function while facing some *given* constraints. The nature of the constraints facing any *individual's* choice may or may not be explained as a matter of his or others' past or irreversible decisions. Those constraints which are not considered a matter of choice cannot be *explained* in neoclassical theory. Operative constraints which limit individuals' choices (for example, anything which is naturally given or beyond control, such as the availability of resources, technology, and so forth) are by definition the *exogenous* variables of neoclassical theory.[6] Also by definition, any fixed or exogenous variable can be seen to play a determining role (that is, in the determination of the values of the endogenous variables) *only if* changes in that variable necessarily result in changes in the endogenous variables.[7]

Neoclassical theory, of course, recognizes many exogenous variables, including institutional or socially determined constraints (such as legal limits and property rights).[8] Given any (neoclassical) model of the economy, if there are many exogenous variables involved in the explanation of one or more endogenous variables, then formally there are many possible causal explanations for observed changes in the endogenous variables. The explanations formally differ only to the extent to which changes in different exogenous variables are recognized as the causes.

In these terms one can identify many types of neoclassical explanations; they are distinguishable in terms of the method used in each to deal with the multiplicity of "causes." At one extreme, we find the approach which follows Léon Walras and W. S. Jevons by being concerned only with the logical and mathematical adequacy of the neoclassical model.[9] At the other extreme is Alfred Marshall's approach, which is the foundation for all neoclassical theories of institutions.

When there are many possible causes, (causal) explanation becomes a very difficult methodological problem. Solving this problem was the central purpose of Marshall's *Principles of Economics*.[10] His solution was based on an explicit recognition of "the element of time" and its relationship with what he called the "Principle of Continuity." The latter presumes that anything that can be varied in a given amount of time must yield to the "Principle of Substitution," that is, can be explained as a matter of optimizing choice. His solution is built on two assumptions. First, he assumes away changes in all variables which are impossible to control (such as weather) or for which there is not enough time for them to be changed (such as cultural traditions). Such variables cannot be explained with his Principle of Substitution, hence they are unexplained givens or exogenous variables. Note well, however, such "exogeneity" may depend on the amount of time under consideration. The second assumption is that it is possible to rank order the changeability of variables such that those that can be changed more quickly are explained before those that are more rigid. Specifically, his method of periods depends on an assumption about dynamics, namely, about the rate at which the givens could be expected to change.[11] The rigidity of capital stock relative to the variability of labor is the hypothetical basis for the distinction between the long and short period.

Although many variables are to be objects of choice in Marshall's long period, that period is not without some givens. He specifically noted that "there are very gradual . . . movements of long-run equilibrium prices caused by the gradual growth of knowledge, of population and of financial capital, and the changing conditions of demand and supply" as well as changing social conditions "from one generation to another."[12] There is nothing in Marshall's *method* which prevents any neoclassical economist from attempting to explain intergenerational changes in such variables as (long-run) prices or the (long-run) distribution of resources.[13] But, if the changes in the long-run variables are to be explained as the results of changes in institutions (as elements of the "social conditions"), the question is begged as to whether changes in the institutions are themselves the result of additional applications of Marshall's Principle of Substitution, that is, have the existing institutions been chosen in the way that other endogenous variables are chosen (as an object of optimization)? In other words, by including social conditions among the *endogenous* variables (among the objects of choice), neoclassical economists are merely modifying Marshall's long period concept without changing his neoclassical method. Whereas institutions (as social conditions) are among the exogenous givens in Marshall's long period, they are considered endogenous variables in the modified long period analysis. In this manner, the modified long run forms the starting point for the neoclassical view of institutions.

In all neoclassical analyses of endogenous institutions, the prevailing institutional constraints are viewed as the outcomes of attempts to minimize costs or maximize benefits for those individuals or groups who are in the position to alter the institutions in the modified long run. Once the institutional arrangement (or environment) has been established, it becomes the set of ruling constraints on individual choices—at least in the "short run." In the terms of the logic of choice, institutions are like capital, which by definition is fixed in the short run and is the basis for the cost functions facing the decision maker. In the modified long run, when equilibrium has been reached, the optimum institutional constraints as well as the optimum amount of capital must have been chosen. The ultimate modified long-run equilibrium values of all endogenous variables, including the institutional constraints, are logically determined (for any given set of behavior assumptions) by the values of the *recognized* exogenous variables (which cannot be the result of optimization either because they are difficult to change or their changes are beyond control).[14]

As implied early in Marshall's book, every explanation requires the recognition of something exogenous.[15] Since Marshall's long-run explanation (of prices) assumes that institutions (as "social conditions") are exogenously given, any approach which makes them endogenous requires the recognition of something else as an exogenous variable. For example, the primary exogenous variable in Douglass North's neoclassical theory of institutional change is what he calls "ideology." In particular, the evolution of institutions is to be explained as the result of "a fundamental change in ideological perspective."[16] North adds that he sees "no way to account for this transformation without the systematic study of the sociology of knowledge."[17] Although I can agree with this courageous statement, it would create methodological problems for the proneoclassical view, to which I now turn.

A Critique of Neoclassical Theories of Institutional Change

Marshall cannot be blamed for the traditional tendency among neoclassical economists to take institutions for granted. In his theory of market prices, he did allow for the role of changing social conditions (including institutions) in the explanation of the history of an economy, that is, of the intergenerational changes of long-run prices and allocations. However, it must be recognized that in order to explain the dynamics of prices or allocations, one must explain *why* the social conditions have changed. This is because when changes in social conditions are considered exogeous (in the Marshallian long run), they are thereby deemed unexplainable within the economic model. However, if the only reason the endogenous variables (such as long-run prices) change is *because* social conditions changed, then the *changes* in the long-run endogenous variables remain unexplained.[18] It would seem, then, that for an adequate explanation of long-run prices, the evolution of institutional constraints (on short-run optimization) must be explained. In other words, the recent concern for institutions among neoclassical economists is not merely idle curiosity (or neoclassical "imperialism"); it is a fundamental methodological requirement for a complete explanation of the dynamics of long-run prices and allocations.

There are two methodological aspects of neoclassical theories of the evolution of institutions which deserve critical examination.[19] First, every neoclassical analysis presumes that (subject to constraints) individuals always get what they want, that is, all individual decision makers are successful. Although such a presumption may seem plausible in most neoclassical analyses, it should be recognized that it implies that the individual decision maker's knowledge is always correct.[20] As I have discussed in detail elsewhere, this presumption is very questionable on epistemological grounds.[21] Moreover, it involves a very static (since it is timeless) concept of knowledge, one which begs the question as to why there should ever be a change in *long-run* variables. This methodological problem, I argue, can be overcome by explicitly recognizing the role of the decision maker's knowledge and by recognizing that changes are usually the result of systematic failures due to reliance on false knowledge, rather than systematic successes based on necessarily true knowledge.

Second, if the ultimate basis for any explanation of the changes of the institutional constraints is *outside* the neoclassical analysis, then the pro-neoclassical view cannot be sustained. As noted before (to avoid circularity), every explanation of any set of variables requires the recognition of one or more exogenous variables. It should be obvious, then, that without a change in at least one exogenous variable (for example, in an ideological perspective in North's theory), the long-run neoclassical economy is static, since there is no reason for a change in the endogenous variables (such as institutional constraints) once the optimum values of the institutional "constraints" have been successfully established. If, for example, the optimizing changes in the endogenous constraint variables are to be explained as the result of changes in the exogenous ideology variable, then by definition of exogenous (not explained *within*), that change in ideology must be explained *outside* the neoclassical analysis of institutions—an exogenous ideology cannot be an object of optimizing choice. But even worse, if one wishes to make ideology an endogenous variable in a neoclassical model, then another new exogenous variable must be invented. Of course, having to invent a stream of new exogenous variables as the neoclassical program progresses merely means that one is marching down the long road of the infinite regress.

These methodological considerations reveal, I think, the inherent poverty of every neoclassical program for explaining the *evolution* of the organizational structure (institutions) of an economy as the dynamic consequences of constrained optimization. Specifically, these considerations call into question the adequacy of the decision maker's knowledge by questioning the presumed success of the intended optimization. They also question the neoclassical view of the nature of institutions which, for methodological reasons, views them as *static constraints* facing the short-run optimizer.

A Simple Theory of Social Institutions

Although I can agree with the view (of North and others) that the evolution of institutions can be explained, I cannot agree that a neoclassical program by itself is methodologically sufficient. An adequate explanation of dynamics must recognize all limitations on successful decision making as well as the essential role of knowledge. More important, an adequate explanation of the evolution of institutions must be based on a theory which explicitly gives institutions a broader role than is allowed by seeing them as only static constraints on the choices of any individual decision maker. I will outline a theory of institutions which will form a basis for an adequate explanation of institutional dynamics. Although my theory will not necessitate giving up the fundamental assumption of rational decision making, it will show all neoclassical theories of institutional *change* are very special cases.

To begin, I would like to note that the critical issues of the adequacy of the knowledge available to a decision maker and the methodological role of institutions are not independent. The reason is simple. One of the roles that institutions play is to create knowledge and information for the individual decision maker. In particular, institutions provide social knowledge which may be needed for *interaction* with other individual decision makers.[22] Thus, the following theory of institutions emphasizes the primary role of institutions, which is to institutionalize social knowledge. However, for an adequate dynamic theory, I will avoid the presumption of successful decision making; thus, in particular, I will not assume that the social knowledge is correct, even though it may be durable. But I go too fast. Let me proceed very deliberately by putting my theory in the form of explicit propositions.

> Proposition 1: All sociological acts are based on expectations of expectations. Specifically, all interactive decision making involves the actor's knowledge of the other individuals' knowledge.[23]

The significance of this proposition lies primarily in the conceivable alternatives, such as the actor's direct questioning of the other individuals.[24]

> Proposition 2: All social problems result from conflicts over expectations (or knowledge), which in turn result from the lack of acceptable limits on the range of expectations (at either source).

The significance of this proposition is dependent on the first and would mean little without it. Since most of our everyday experience involves previously *solved* social problems, it would be fairly difficult to give a pure description of any social problem apart from its assumed solution. Thus, I turn directly to solved social problems.

It should be clear that, based on the second proposition, all solutions to social problems involve the limits on expectations. There are basically two different ways of limiting expectations: (1) narrowing the range of possible options (with prohibitions, taboos, and so forth), and (2) increasing the likelihood of particular possible options (with norms, standards, guides, conventions, and so forth).

This brings me to my third, fourth, and fifth propositions.

> Proposition 3. All social institutions exist to solve social problems.

> Proposition 4: All social institutions can be divided into two categories: the *consensus institution,* which exists as a socially accepted solution to a specific problem (or set of problems), and the *concrete institution,* which exists to solve a social problem resulting from relying on consensus institutions (common agreements) to solve problems.

> Proposition 5: All concrete institutions are attempts to manifest the extent of a society's learning, that is, they are a society's social knowledge.

As a corollary of the fifth proposition, I note:

> Proposition 5a: The sole job for a concrete institution is to represent a given particular consensus institution (or system of institutions).

There are many examples of concrete institutions; the American Constitution is the most obvious, and legal contracts are the most common. Consensus institutions are much less obvious, but one can identify all "unwritten laws" and "gentlemen's agreements" as common examples.[25]

Propositions 1, 2, and 3 form a static theory of institutions. That is, one can explain the existence of an institution by explaining the problem for which the institution was intended to be (or accepted as) a solution.[26] Such problems, of course, include those discussed by North and others. One can also explain the continuance of the institutions by explaining the current problem for which the members of the society *think* the institution is a solution. In both cases the individual members may be mistaken, either in terms of the competence of the solution (as it may not do the job) or in terms of the realities of the problems (it may be a false problem or an impossible one to solve).

The addition of Propositions 4, 5, and 5a allows for a dynamic theory of institutions.[27] The theory formed views institutions as social conventions which can be influenced by individual members of the society,[28] but which also extend (in terms of time or space) beyond the individuals and thereby can influence the individuals either as constraints or as instruments of change. This theory can best be understood in terms of a sequence of events or steps. *Step 1:* A society faces a problem for which there is at least one conceivable solution. *Step 2:* A consensus is formed around one particular solution, thereby establishing a consensus institution. The establishment of the consensus may depend on a political process.[29] *Step 3:* Step 2 has inherent methodological difficulties because a consensus institution is limited in terms of space and time. In particular, the solution will be limited to the members that form the consensus both in terms of their life-span and their number. For example, in this semester's seminar, everyone may know what to expect of one another in terms of operating rules, but next semester (or in any other seminar at the same time) there will be a new set of students who may not know what to expect. Thus, every semester a new consensus will have to be reached. The fact that there is no carry-over from one period (or place) to another is in effect another social problem for which some form of *durability* is the only solution. *Step 4:* The society establishes a concrete institution to represent the consensus of Step 2; however, the durability or concreteness of the institution is merely another consensus institution.[30] *Step 5:* In the future, the succeeding consensus is formed partly as a result of the existing concrete institutions and partly as a result of the existing social problems, and so forth.[31] Some societies may wish to prevent any further changes; others may design their institutions so that they can be easily altered in order to be able to adapt to changing circumstances. Whether a concrete institution actually possesses the intended durability is an important question of dynamics, but the form of concreteness is still only a consensus institution. In other words, concrete institutions continue to exist only because we allow them to exist. As individuals, we can choose to ignore them or persuade others to ignore them. There may be certain social or personal costs involved in such a stance, but it clearly is an option open to every member of a society.

Clearly, with this theory the question of social change becomes very delicate because of the seemingly indeterminate nature of the structural relationship between problems and solutions at both static and dynamic levels. The structural relationship at issue is an instance of "circular causation." Simultaneously, the prior existence of an institutionalized solution is used in the teaching (or socializing) of new members of a society as evidence of the importance of certain social problems, but the existence of the solution is in turn justified on the basis of the prior existence of the social problem. Such a symbiotic relationship might lead to a very static society if the "elders" are skilled at socializing. It also raises certain difficulties with regard to the concept of a change in "social conditions," including the existing institutions. My presentation of a hypothetical sequence which would lead to a concrete institution presumed the existence of a consensus institution before the creation of the concrete institution. But, given the symbiotic relationship, can the consensus institution be changed *without* a change in the concrete institution?

This methodological problem for the explanation of social change is usually avoided, but not solved, in one of two ways. The first is to view all concrete institutions (such as the laws that constrain individual choices) as the *only real* institutions. Although this view has the advantage of being clear-cut and more appealing to common sense, it also has the methodological disadvantage of leading its proponents to view all matters of social change as matters of *only* power politics. But more important, this view of institutions is inherently static. Once the institutions have been established, there can be no real institutional change, hence changes in other endogenous variables cannot be explained within the given institutional structure.[32]

The second way to avoid the problem is to say that consensus institutions (which underlie any concrete institutions) are the *only real* institutions. Moreover, there may be more than one way to represent a consensus institution; thus, changes in concrete institutions do not imply changes in consensus institutions (or social conditions). This alternative has the advantage of avoiding collectivist dogma, but the disadvantage of viewing all social change entirely as a matter of persuasion (such as "Madison Avenue" advertising techniques). Of course, with this view, changes in social conditions are very slow whenever communication is very controlled (for example, "one should not talk about such things"). But there is a more serious methodological problem. It is virtually impossible to know when a consensus institution has changed, and thus an operational explanation of social change becomes impossible. Any theory (such as Marshall's) which explains long-run changes in prices as the consequences of changes in social conditions (consensus institutions) is inherently untestable!

Neoclassical theories of institutional change can be seen to be variants of the theory represented by Propositions 1 through 5a. But being basically concerned with the individual decision maker, every neoclassical theory would have to view real changes as those in consensus institutions; however, such changes may (have to) be brought about by changes in concrete institutions. It should be clear that most modern societies provide specific institutions which make (orderly) changes or the creation of other institutions possible. Legislative bodies of most Western democracies are an example. In fact, the changeability of any institution is a problem for which the rigidity of other institutions provides the solution.[33]

The critical issue with any neoclassical variant, as noted earlier, is whether a chosen concrete institution is, in fact, a successful representation of a given consensus institution (whether it adequately represents the given ideology). Kenneth Arrow's (im)possibility theorem might easily be seen as an argument against the possibility of (complete) success in every social situation. Specifically, one cannot guarantee a successful social decision mechanism (a concrete institution) which will always represent the society's welfare function (a consensus institution).

Similarly, there is the critical issue of the adequacy of the solution over which the consensus is formed: Does the given ideology, for example, solve the social problems that exist? People may *think* the market system can solve all social problems, but that does not mean that it can. It is only a theory, the truth of which is neither proven nor provable. For example, Arrow has also argued that one essential ingredient for social interaction (which includes doing business in the market as well as within the firm) is simple trust, and the existence of a market for trust would be a virtual contradiction.[34]

Time, Knowledge, and Successful Institutions

The neoclassical program for explaining the evolution of an economy's institutions is quite compatible with my simple theory of the epistemological role of institutions. However, once one recognizes that neoclassical programs (Marshallian or otherwise) presume successful decision making and, hence, for continuing success over time, that every individual must possess correct knowledge (which includes accurate representations of relevant consensus institutions), it becomes clear that a neoclassical theory is a special case of my version of institutionalism. That is, in my theory, when the consensus institutions do solve the relevant social problems *and* concrete institutions do succeed in accurately representing those solutions, then (and only then) are my theory and a neoclassical theory of institutional change completely compatible.

Neoclassical theories are incompatible with mine whenever any individual's knowledge is not correct (not true). But, incompatibility is not the important issue here. As has been argued elsewhere,[35] the existence of false knowledge is an essential ingredient in any dynamic theory of economic decision making. If all knowledge were true (including knowledge about the future), then there would be no reason for (disequilibrium) change without changes in one or more exogenous givens. If one is going to explain change, the source of the change cannot be exogenous. Thus, it has been argued, dynamic theories must recognize false knowledge (and explain why it might be false). Furthermore, a theory of dynamic behavior must specify the *systematic* way each individual responds to the discovery that his knowledge is false.[36]

I have extended this dynamic issue of false knowledge to the question of institutions. I have argued that institutions provide essential knowledge to individual decision makers. If that institutional knowledge is false, there is another reason for change. The only difference between institutional knowledge and knowledge in general is that the former (like capital) takes longer to change. In other words, institutional knowledge may be durable, but this may create problems. Even though an institution may successfully represent social knowledge that is true for one period of time, its durability may extend to a period for which it is false. Thus, since institutional knowledge is durable, it is likely to be false. Moreover, the existence of false institutional knowledge is a reason for change, and, because change takes time, false knowledge is a continuing reason why the success assumption of neoclassical explanations is often unrealistic.

Douglass North's ultimate argument in favor of the proneoclassical view is that to "abandon neoclassical theory is to abandon economics as a science."[37] This pitifully weak argument is rather misplaced, even though it is the same excuse given by Marshall.[38] Those of us who argue for the recognition of false knowledge and inadequate institutions do so not because we think (as North fears) that neoclassical theory should be abandoned, but because we think neoclassical analysis should be kept in perspective, that is, it should be recognized as a *very* special case.

Notes

1. Douglass C. North, "Structure and Performance: The Task of Economic History," *Journal of Economic Literature* 16 (September 1978): 963–78.
2. G. L. S. Shackle, *Epistemics and Economics* (Cambridge: the University Press, 1972); Joan Robinson, "History versus Equilibrium," *Thames Papers in Political Economy* (Autumn 1974); and John R. Hicks, "Some Questions of Time in Economics," in *Evolution, Welfare and Time in Economics*, edited by Anthony M. Tang, Fred M. Westfield, and James S. Worley (Toronto: D. C. Heath, 1976), pp. 135–51.
3. See, for example, James M. Buchanan and Gordon Tullock, *The Calculus of Consent* (Ann Arbor: University of Michigan Press, 1962).
4. See, for example, Lawrence A. Boland, "Uninformative Economic Models," *Atlantic Economic Journal* 3 (November 1975): 27–32.
5. Both aspects of institutions are explicitly recognized in Lance E. Davis and Douglass C. North, *Institutional Change and American Economic Growth* (Cambridge: the University Press, 1971). Following Buchanan and Tullock, Davis and North distinguish between the *institutional environment,* which includes the "legal ground rules" that constrain on-going political and economic business, and the *institutional arrangement,* which provides a workable mechanism either for operating *within* the ground rules or for changing them. Although in some explanations one or both of these institutional constraints is considered endogenous, North, in "Structure and Performance," laments that the "failure of economists to appreciate the transitory character of the assumed constraints and to understand the source and direction of these changing constraints is a fundamental handicap to further development of economic theory" (p. 963).
6. Exogeneity is defined as the purported intrinsic property of certain variables of a model *within which they cannot be explained* (that is, they are not influenced by changes in endogenous or other exogenous variables of the model).
7. For a more detailed discussion of the methodological role of exogeneity and the requirements of determinant explanations, see Boland, "Uninformative Economic Models."

8. The constraints facing any *individual's* choice include some "endogenous givens" which are determined in concert with the rational choices of other individuals; for example, the givens of consumer theory include market determined prices. In this sense, some of *any* individual's *constraints* are explained as the consequences of (the equilibrium or concert of) *all* individuals' choices. Moreover, any constraint the establishment of which requires the (implicit) participation of many individuals is in some sense an institution. For this reason, some economists might consider a system of all market determined prices to be an institution whose function is to provide the decision maker with a "summary of information about the production possibilities, resource availabilities and preferences of all other decision makers" (Tjalling C. Koopmans, *Three Essays on the State of Economic Science* [New York: McGraw-Hill, 1957], p. 53). However, the view that a price system is a social institution is true (if at all) *only* in long-run equilibrium, the attainment of which may take an unrealistic amount of time. More important, it would be very misleading to focus on prices as the *only* institutional constraint. The tendency to do so persists because many neoclassical economists rely on the *normative* view that price should be the only institutional constraint. As a matter of positive economics, dealing with real-time phenomena—which must exist in the short run— there are other institutions which constrain individual choices (see Coase's theorem). Whether or not the existing institutions can be explained away by assuming there are no incentives to change them, because they are optimum, is the moot point this article discusses.

9. Consequently, in terms of the logic of solvability, it does not matter whether a formal constraint is socially given or is a parameter of nature (available resources).

10. Alfred Marshall, *Principles of Economics,* 8th ed. (London: Macmillan, 1920), preface to first edition.

11. Everyone, of course, knows about Marshall's short and long periods. He said they correspond, respectively, to periods of a "few months" and "several years." However, he stressed that "short" and "long" were not absolute concepts, but depend on what variables were recognized to be influenced by the Principle of Substitution and what givens were to be impounded in *ceteris paribus.*

12. Marshall, *Principles,* p. 379.

13. To avoid circularity, it must be remembered that there still have to be some givens which do not endogenously change within or with the generation.

14. For the given values of the exogenous variables, if the current choices of values for the endogenous variables are such that there exist incentives for changes in any endogenous variables, then the (modified long-run) equilibrium has not been reached.

15. Marshall, *Principles,* Book I, chapter 3.

16. North, "Structure and Performance," p. 974.

17. Ibid.

18. See, further, Lawrence A. Boland, "Time in Economics vs. Economics in Time: The 'Hayek Problem,' " *Canadian Journal of Economics* 11 (May

1978): 240–62. For the technical distinction between explanation and description, see Boland, "Uninformative Economic Models."

19. As distinguished from empirical aspects, such as the truth of the assumptions about the relative variability of the givens used to distinguish the short run from the long run.

20. Otherwise, *how* the required true knowledge was acquired must be explained as well. See Friedrich Hayek, "Economics and Knowledge," *Economica* 4 N.S. (February 1937): 33–54.

21. Specifically, since there is no inductive logic, there is no way to guarantee that the knowledge which is essential for successful decision making is *always* true. See, further, Lawrence A. Boland, "A Critique of Friedman's Critics," *Journal of Economic Literature* 17 (June 1979): 500–19; and Lawrence A. Boland and Geoffrey Newman, "On the Role of Knowledge in Economic Theory," *Australian Economic Papers* 18 (June 1979): 71–80.

22. The equilibrium price system is one instance of such a social institution; other institutions include the laws governing trade and advertising practices and tax laws. The extent to which the social knowledge provided (such as norms, guidelines, and legal limits) is *necessary* is directly related to the power of the institution.

23. Such a situation was recognized by Plato in his dialogue "Laches." It is observed at the beginning that "some laugh at the very notion of consulting others, and when they are asked will not say what they think. They guess at the wishes of the person who asks them, and answer according to his, and not according to their own, opinion."

24. Clearly, it does not attempt to be relevant for the explanation of observed behavior of a hermit or anyone else who opts out of a society (although it would apply to a group that opts out). In other words, it does not attempt to apply to any asocial situation.

25. In recent correspondence, Ludwig Lachmann noted to me that in his *Legacy of Max Weber* (London: Heinemann, 1970) he offered a similar theory of social institutions. His illustration of the differences between consensus and concrete institutions is the difference between "the market" and the stock exchange.

26. Of course, not all solutions are invented or designed; some may be "discovered."

27. More technically, these propositions form what has been called "institutional-individualism." See Joseph Agassi, "Institutional individualism," *British Journal of Sociology* 26 (June 1975): 144–55. If all institutions were considered to be *essentially* consensus types, it would lead to the view which Agassi called "psychologistic-individualism." If all institutions were viewed as *essentially* concrete, it would lead to the view called "holism" (sometimes called "collectivism").

28. *How* the institutions can be influenced depends on the institutions designed to deal with that problem (such as election rules).

29. In the modern urban world, a consensus is virtually impossible to achieve. One can easily see that the institutions of political parties and platforms are a solution to the problem of forming a consensus. Specifically, a plat-

972   Lawrence A. Boland

form ties together a set of problems for each of which a consensus for a particular solution cannot be obtained. In order to construct a consensus, every party member agrees to support all planks in the platform, even though he or she may not be interested in every plank.

30. Durability is the essential ingredient for a truly dynamic model, even if the durability is not exogenous.

31. In other words, when *Step 4* has been reached, the succeeding generations are taught how to solve *their* social problems by teaching them about the existing (concrete) institutions. Of course, the process involves, to a great extent, teaching them what their problems "are." Note that concreteness may present other social problems, which in turn are solved by a higher level of concrete institutions (for example, an ombudsman).

32. This view's static nature, combined with its emphasis on power politics, leads its proponents to make political mistakes. For example, its proponents often oppose the establishment of an undesirable (concrete) institution because they fear the rigidity of its concreteness when it can usually be shown that a concrete institution (such as written rules) is easier to change than a consensus institution (unwritten rules). Similarly, when in power, its proponents waste much time or many resources on superficial changes, that is, on those which change (concrete) appearances without altering the underlying consensus.

33. It should be noted that those institutions whose role is to provide information (such as norms, guidelines, and legal limits) are effective only to the extent that they are stable. Thus, the changeability of such institutions compromises their knowledge role. See, further, Geoffrey Newman, "An Institutional Perspective on Information," *International Social Science Journal* 28 (Fall 1976): 466–92.

34. See Kenneth J. Arrow, *Limits of Organization* (New York: Norton, 1974).

35. See Hicks, "Some Questions"; Hayek, "Economics and Knowledge"; and Boland, "Time in Economics."

36. Stochastic theories, their popularity notwithstanding, do not *explain* response variations but only cover up the failure systematically to explain them accurately. See, further, Lawrence A. Boland, "Model Specification and Stochasticism in Economic Methodology," *South African Journal of Economics* 45 (June 1977): 182–89.

37. North, "Structure and Performance," p. 974.

38. Marshall, *Principles*, p. 379n.

[17]

The Origin of Predictable Behavior

By RONALD A. HEINER*

Despite vigorous counterargument by its proponents, optimization theory has been persistently attacked as an acceptable explanation of behavior. In one form or another, these attacks repeat the oldest critique of economics; namely, the ability of agents to maximize successfully. Over the years, this critique has taken various forms which include information processing limitations in computing optima from known preference or utility information, unreliable probability information about complex environmental contingencies, and the absence of a well-defined set of alternatives or consequences, especially in an evolving world that may produce situations that never before existed.

These complaints are not new to economics. Indeed, they have been present during the very intellectual sifting process that produced neoclassical optimization and general equilibrium theory. Thus, if we are to further elaborate this critique of conventional theory, the basic issue is whether there is anything new that is worthy of attention by someone well versed in standard tools and concepts. Are we simply advancing more refined or cleverly argued versions of older critiques, or extensions of them to areas not previously emphasized?

Such arguments would still represent an attack on the basic rationality postulate of economics (that agents are able to maximize), but without providing a clear alternative to traditional optimization theory. However plausible these arguments might be, ultimately they must be set aside by someone desiring a theoretical understanding of behavior, unless they lead to another modeling structure whose analytical ability can be explored and compared with existing optimization theory.

Another argument focuses on the desire to understand the "real" dynamic processes that actually generate observed behavior. In contrast, optimization is thought of as a surrogate theory based on false assumptions about agents' capacity to maximize. Thus, it can be defended only in terms of empirical testability, without really illuminating the underlying processes determining behavior.

Nevertheless, even if this view was fully accepted, it is unlikely by itself to cause a major shift away from conventional thinking. The reason is that evolutionary processes have long ago been interpreted as one of the key mechanisms tending to produce optimizing behavior; or conversely, optimizing models will predict the behavior patterns that will survive in an evolutionary process tending to select relatively superior performance.[1] The latter interpretation is in fact one of the dominant justifications for standard models against the criticism of unrealistic assumptions (i.e., the surviving agents of a selection process will behave "as if" they are able to maximize).[2]

*Department of Economics, Brigham Young University, Provo, UT 84602. I am indebted to Axel Leijonhufvud for constant encouragement about applications to economics, and for numerous stylistic suggestions. Harold Miller helped familiarize me with a broad range of issues across the sociobiological, psychological, and behavioral science literatures. James Buchanan provided stimulating discussion about conceptual issues. I have also benefited from the advice and criticism of Armen Alchian, Ron Batchelder, Bruce Brown, Robert Clower, Daniel Friedman, Jack Hirshleifer, Kai Jeanski, Randy Johnson, Edward Leamer, Stephen Littlechild, John McCall, James McDonald, Richard Nelson, Gerald O'Driscoll, Dennis Packard, Clayne Pope, Lionello Punzo, Ezio Tarantelli, and Sidney Winter. Needless to say, these colleagues are not responsible for inadequacy in the conceptual framework or scope of ideas presented.

[1] See in particular Armen Alchian's well-known 1950 paper, and also Sidney Winter, 1964, 1971; Jack Hirshleifer, 1977; Richard Nelson and Winter, 1974.

[2] A still used reference on the "as if" point of view is Milton Friedman's 1953 paper. Some recent journal illustrations are Benjamin Klein and Keith Leffler, 1981, p. 634; Richard Posner, 1980, p. 5; Hirshleifer, 1977, p. 50; Nelson, 1981, p. 1059. The ultimate extension of this view is to claim not that agents are able to maximize (select most preferred actions), but rather that any ob-

In spite of the above conclusions, I believe there is a viable alternative to standard models—one that directly comes to grips with the persistent critiques of economic theory and which broadens our analytical horizon to encompass a much wider range of phenomena.

In particular, I believe that observed regularities of behavior can be fruitfully understood as "behavioral rules" that arise because of uncertainty in distinguishing preferred from less-preferred behavior. Such uncertainty requires behavior to be governed by mechanisms that restrict the flexibility to choose potential actions, or which produce a selective alertness to information that might prompt particular actions to be chosen. These mechanisms simplify behavior to less-complex patterns, which are easier for an observer to recognize and predict. In the special case of no uncertainty, the behavior of perfectly informed, fully optimizing agents responding with complete flexibility to every perturbation in their environment would not produce easily recognizable patterns, but rather would be extremely difficult to predict. Thus, it is in the limits to maximizing that we will find the origin of predictable behavior.

If the view taken here is correct, it means that predictable features of behavior do not arise from optimizing with no uncertainty in choosing most preferred behavior; and furthermore, evolutionary selection processes will in general not produce approximations to optimizing behavior. Rather, predictable behavior will evolve only to the extent that uncertainty prevents agents from successfully maximizing.

In the following, I sketch the line of thought and the observations which have led me to this conclusion, and briefly outline the elements of a modeling structure that can be applied to a wide range of topics. A number of applications are presented to illustrate the range of issues unified by the analysis, which

is far broader than the reader is likely to anticipate without explicit examples.

I. Problems with the Methodological Arguments for Optimization

Optimizing with full ability to select most preferred behavior is rarely justified as an empirically realistic assumption. Rather, it is usually defended on methodological grounds as the appropriate theoretical framework for analyzing behavior. The chief defense is empirical fruitfulness in generating unfalsified predictions.

We might criticize this testability criteria with modern philosophy of science arguments.[3] Nevertheless, a long list of confirmed predictions would be persuasive evidence in favor of a theory. Yet, it is just here that we have a problem. Suppose we really asked to see the list of clearly implied, unambiguous predictions that have been derived from our basic optimization models.

The answer to this query, one that would be admitted by many practitioners in the field, is that at best we have developed a very short list. All sorts of behavior is consistent with or plausibly suggested by optimization models, yet still not predicted by them. For example, optimization models have never been able to imply the Law of Demand (buying less of a commodity when its price rises), which is probably the oldest and simplest behavioral regularity in economics. Of course, we can use the theory to argue it is unlikely that a negative income effect will outweigh the pure substitution effect, especially for goods that absorb a small fraction of a person's income.[4] The acceptance of this view is heavily influenced by our belief in the

---

[3] See for example, B. Caldwell, 1982; also Karl Popper, 1969; Imer Lakatos and Alice Musgrave, 1970.

[4] I was told in a graduate price-theory class by Armen Alchian that the only clear implication of consumer theory is that with more income, a consumer will buy more of at least something. Harold Demsetz, when informed of this story, responded by saying, "well then just define holding cash balances as saving, and we have no testable implications, just one mass of tautologies." See also the opening remarks of Kenneth Arrow, 1982, p. 1; and the closing remarks of Vernon Smith, 1982, p. 952.

---

served behavior is consistent with the maximization of some function. This latter formulation is probably incapable of either theoretical or empirical disproof (see Lawrence Boland, 1981).

empirical validity of the Law of Demand. Yet, regardless of how cleverly we interpret a Slutsky equation, no clear prediction is implied.

We could pursue a number of other examples, all of which suggest that conventional models have never really been fruitful in generating testable implications.[5] For this reason, I believe allegiance to these models is not grounded in the claim of empirical fruitfulness, despite the usual rhetoric that this is the case. Rather, it is based on a deeper methodological issue about the effect of dropping the basic rationality assumption.[6]

Think of this issue in the following terms. Standard choice theory tries to explain behavior by matching the "competence" of an agent with the "difficulty" in selecting most preferred alternatives. It assumes for the purpose of theoretical explanation that there is no gap between an agent's competence and the difficulty of the decision problem to be

solved (hereafter called a "*C-D* gap").[7] On the other hand, the presence of a *C-D* gap will introduce uncertainty in selecting most preferred alternatives, which will tend to produce errors and surprises. Such mistakes are by their nature unpredictable and erratic. Yet, it is only the systematic elements of behavior that we can hope to scientifically explain and predict. Thus, in order to theoretically isolate the systematic tendencies in behavior, we must exclude a *C-D* gap, no matter how implausible or unrealistic this might be.[8]

This perspective has been a dominant factor in loyalty to traditional optimizing concepts. Nevertheless, I believe it is mistaken, and that essentially the opposite view is true. To see why, think of the above argument as an empirical hypothesis about the effect of "irrationality"; namely, that the additional uncertainty from a larger *C-D* gap will generate more errors and surprises, thus producing more irregularity and noise in behavior. There are numerous complicating factors about how to test this hypothesis, especially how to measure a person's *C-D* gap. We can avoid these problems by broadening our horizon to consider an interspecie comparison between humans and other animals. Here it is clear without detailed argument that the average *C-D* gap of other animals is larger than that of humans.[9] Yet when we observe nonhuman species, the overwhelming qualitative impression is not one of greater irregularity, but instead of greater rigidity and inflexibility of behavior. Pattern is not more

[5]Some other examples are: second Law of Demand, short- and long-run supply dynamics, risk aversion, time preference, self-interest, liquidity preference, expectation lag and adjustment structures, price-taking behavior, oligopoly strategic patterns, relative price vs. quantity elasticities, relative income-consumption elasticities, etc. The so-called "laws of supply and demand" have probably been the most empirically useful tools in economics (both in formulating simple hypotheses about market responses to parameter changes, and in providing the basic structural equation system used in modern econometric model building). Yet, these simple laws are not derivable from basic optimization concepts, and thus empirical analysis derived from them does not confirm these concepts.

[6]Without going into any details, I would also like to mention a large literature in behavioral psychology about the *matching law* (Richard Herrnstein, 1961, 1964, 1970), which has cast doubt on the validity of traditional maximization theory to explain behavior under certain reinforcement schedules. See P. de Villiers, 1977, for a summary of earlier experimental results, and for more recent experiments with human subjects, see C. M. Bradshaw, E. Szabadi, and R. Bevan, 1976; William Buskist and Harold Miller, 1981. For recent articles about the validity of maximization, see Herrnstein and Gene Heyman, 1979; Heyman and R. Duncan Luce, 1979; Howard Rachlin, John Kagel and R. C. Battalio, 1980; D. Prelec, 1982; and for recent experiments in which matching has dominated maximizing behavior, see Herrnstein and William Vaughan, 1980; Vaughan, 1981; John Mazur, 1981.

[7]Posing the problem in terms of a gap in an agent's decision competence relative to the difficulty of a decision problem was suggested to me by Axel Leijonhufvud.

[8]For a recent example of this view, see Jack Hirshleifer's 1980 price theory text, p. 9. A similar argument is used to justify "rational expectations" equilibria. See, for example, Robert Lucas, 1981, pp. 125, 223–24; and Robert Cooter, 1982b, p. 232.

[9]For analysis of cognative differences between humans and animals, and the evolution of intelligence, see M. Konner 1982, David Premack, 1983; P. Rozin, 1976; Carl Sagan, 1977; Harry Jerison, 1973; R. Masterton, William Hodos, and Jerison, 1976.

difficult but rather easier to notice in animals than in humans.

This qualitative difference between humans and other animals is obviously not new to us; it having long ago been given the capsulized description of "instinct." Still, I do not believe that we have recognized the significance of this general pattern for evaluating and constructing theoretical models of behavior. This pattern is telling us that it is not the absence of a C-D gap, but rather its presence which conditions regularity in behavior.

Why should this be the case? Think of an omiscient agent with literally no uncertainty in identifying the most preferred action under any conceivable condition, regardless of the complexity of the environment which he encounters. Intuitively, such an agent would benefit from maximum flexibility to use all potential information or to adjust to all environmental conditions, no matter how rare or subtle those conditions might be. But what if there is uncertainty because agents are unable to decipher all of the complexity of the environment (i.e., there is uncertainty due to a C-D gap)? Will allowing complete flexibility still benefit the agents? For example, if we could somehow "loosen up" the behavior of an organism without affecting its perceptual abilities, would it compete more effectively for food or mating partners than before?

I believe the general answer to this question is negative: that when genuine uncertainty exists, allowing greater flexibility to react to more information or administer a more complex repertoire of actions will not necessarily enhance an agent's performance. Even if we confine our attention to human behavior, we can find evidence for this proposition, especially in highly competitive situations with noticable elements of complexity relative to human information processing and other perceptual abilities.

For example, in sequential replication games of the basic prisoner's dilemma (see Robert Axelrod, 1980a), round robin competition identified the simplest strategy (the tit for tat strategy) as dominant over all of the others (submitted by persons in economics, mathematics, psychology, political science, and sociology).[10] Moreover, the worst performance came from the strategy that specified the most "sophisticated" learning and probability adjustment process to guide its behavior.[11] Another example is the publishing history on strategies to win at blackjack. Earlier books emphasized sophisticated card-counting, bet-variation methods (see especially Edward Thorpe's book, *Beat the Dealer*). However, while no one has challenged the mathematical validity of these earlier more complex methods, their actual use resulted in worse performance by most persons attempting to use them (which generated sizable unexpected profits to the casinos).[12] As a result, later books have steadily evolved toward more rigidly structured methods (for example, two recent books are *No Need to Count* and *Winning Casino Blackjack for the Non-Counter*).[13]

Consider also Rubic's cube. There are over 43 trillion possible initial positions from which to unscramble the cube. Minimizing the number of moves to solve the cube would

[10] For a description of the tournament and its results, see Axelrod, 1980a. The top strategies were all variants of the simple tit for tat strategy, but none were able to beat the basic strategy (in particular, see pp. 8 and 18). When a second round of the tournament was run, tit for tat still won even though numerous more complex strategies were submitted (see Axelrod, 1980b). For recent analytical analysis on this issue, see David Kreps et al., 1982.

[11] Axelrod describes the worst of the submitted strategies in the first round:

This rule has a probability of cooperating, P, which is initially 30% and is updated every 10 moves. P is adjusted if the other player seems random, very cooperative, or very uncooperative. P is also adjusted after move 130 if the rule has a lower score than the other player. Unfortunately, the complex process of adjustment frequently left the probability of cooperation in the 30% to 70% range, and therefore the rule appeared random to many other players. [1980a, p. 24]

[12] For example, see Richard Canfield, 1979, pp. 19, 37–38, 144–47, 150.

[13] Some of the major books in order of publication are: Thorpe, 1962; Lawrence Revere, 1969; John Archer, 1973; Ian Anderson, 1975; Virginia Graham and C. I. Tulcea, 1978; Canfield, 1979; Leon Dubey, 1980; Avery Cardoza, 1981. See Canfield's book, especially pp. 11–12, 16–19, 37–38, 60–61, 62–65. See also Dubey, pp. 11–12, 17–19, 64, 165–66, 168, 172.

require an extremely complex pattern of adjustment from one particular scrambled position to another. Yet, if mistakes are made in trying to select a short cut, the cube will remain unscrambled indefinitely. Consequently, cube experts have developed rigidly structured solving procedures that employ a small repertoire of solving patterns to unscramble the cube. These procedures follow a predetermined hierarchical sequence that is largely independent of the initial scrambled position.[14] However, they almost always require a much longer sequence of moves than the minimum number needed to unscramble the cube. Thus, they are not an approximation to the enormously complex behavior that would be exhibited by an omniscient agent who could immediately select the shortest sequence for each scrambled position. Note also that the information needed to behave in this fashion (present in the initially scrambled patterns on the face of the cube) is costless to observe and instantly available; one need only look at the cube while unscrambling it.

Finally, consider the research of Herbert Simon over a number of years,[15] which has shown that decision makers in a variety of contexts (including both individual and organizational behavior) systematically restrict the use and acquisition of information compared to that potentially available. For example, Simon's idea of "satisficing" represents a feedback mechanism between an internal target variable (called the "aspiration level") and the scope of information evaluated to implement that target. Over time, the feedback process will both guide and discipline the use of information and the resulting behavioral complexity that will evolve within a person or organization. Other learning,

cognitive processes, and decision algorithms can be similarly interpreted.

The above examples suggest that allowing flexibility to react to information or to select actions will not necessarily improve performance if there is uncertainty about how to use that information or about when to select particular actions. Thus, an agent's overall performance may actually be improved by restricting flexibility to use information or to choose particular actions.

II. How Uncertainty Generates Flexibility Constrained Behavior

The argument to this point has suggested that uncertainty due to a *C-D* gap may generate flexibility constrained behavior. The next step is to characterize more precisely how such uncertainty might produce this result. To do so, a simple "reliability condition" is developed that specifies when to allow or prohibit flexibility to select potential actions or to use information that might prompt particular actions to be chosen.

Two major classes of variables determine the uncertainty resulting from a *C-D* gap. The first are environmental variables (denoted by e) which determine the complexity of the decision problem to be solved by an agent (including the complexity of environmental situations potentially encountered; the relative likelihood of these situations; and the stability of the relationships that determine possible situations and their relative likelihood). The second are perceptual variables (denoted by p) which characterize an agent's competence in deciphering relationships between its behavior and the environment.[16] Thus, the p and e variables determine the "gap" between competence and difficulty (the *C-D* gap) which produces

---

[14]In following a typical set of instructions, one selects a side of the cube and begins by placing either its corner or its edge pieces in their proper positions; next, one places in sequence the pieces in the middle section; finally, one repositions the pieces on the remaining, opposite side of the cube (see Czes Kosniowski, 1981). Other similar procedures include D. Taylor, 1980; James Nourse, 1980; Patrick Bussert, 1981; B. W. Barlow, 1981.

[15]For example, Simon, 1955, 1959, 1969, 1976, 1978, 1979a; A. Newell and Simon, 1972.

[16]In economics, the p variables might describe mistaken perceptions about what is more preferred, information processing errors, unreliable probability information, etc.; while the e variables describe the complexity and volatility of both present and future exchange, legal, and political conditions. In biology, p might refer to the sensory and cognitive mechanisms of an organism, and e to the structure and stability of ecological relationships involving competition for food or mating partners.

uncertainty about how to use information in selecting potential actions. In general, there is greater uncertainty as either an agent's perceptual abilities become less reliable or the environment becomes more complex.

These relationships are formally represented as a vector-valued function, $U = u(\vec{p}, \vec{e})$, which describes the structure of uncertainty from a *C-D* gap characterized by **p** and **e**. The signs above **p** and **e** signify that uncertainty is negatively related to an agent's perceptual abilities, and positively related to the complexity and instability of the environment.

Now consider a conceptual experiment about an agent initially limited to a fixed repertoire of actions, and ask whether allowing flexibility to select an additional action will improve the agent's performance. Under certain conditions, the new action will be more preferred than the other actions in the agent's repertoire (the "right" time to select the action), but otherwise it will be less preferred than one of those actions (the "wrong" time to select the action). Depending on the likelihood of different situations produced by the environment, the probabilities of the right or wrong time to select the action are written $\pi(e)$ and $1 - \pi(e)$, respectively.

Because of uncertainty, the agent will not necessarily select the new action when it is the right time to do so. The conditional probability of selecting the action when it is actually the right time is written $r(U)$, where the likelihood of so doing depends on the structure of uncertainty, $U = u(p, e)$. When this happens, the resulting gain in performance (compared to staying within the initial repertoire) is written $g(e)$, which depends on how the environment affects the consequences from different actions. Similarly, the conditional probability of selecting the new action when it is actually the wrong time is written $w(U)$, with consequent loss in performance of $l(e)$.

In the special case of no uncertainty, the new action would always be selected at the right time and never at the wrong time, so that $r = 1$ and $w = 0$. In general, however, the presence of uncertainty will imply $r < 1$ and $w > 0$.

We can intuitively measure the *reliability* of selecting a new action by the ratio r/w, which represents the chance of "correctly" selecting the action at the right time relative to the chance of "mistakenly" selecting it at the wrong time.[17] Greater uncertainty will both reduce the chance of correct selections and increase the chance of mistaken selections, thus causing the ratio r/w to drop (i.e., greater uncertainty reduces the reliability of selecting the new action).

Note also that $r(U)$ and $w(U)$ are not assumed to be known to an agent. The reason is that uncertainty produces mistakes about distinguishing the right from the wrong conditions to select an action, which distinction is necessary to determine the conditional probabilities of choosing an action under these two sets of conditions. For the same reason, the probability of the right situation to select an action, $\pi(e)$, may also be unknown to an agent. Thus, it is not assumed that an agent can tell whether a mistake has been made; nor are we necessarily dealing with situations where an agent consciously decides when to select an action. Rather, the more general issue is whether some process —conscious or not—will cause (or prevent) an "alertness" or "sensitivity" to information that might prompt selection of an action. For example, when will a person develop an alertness to potential information about whether to choose a particular action, or whether to modify a previous behavior pattern; or when will instinctive mechanisms in an organism precondition a sensitivity to certain environmental stimuli, while simultaneously blocking alertness to other potential stimuli.

---

[17] The probabilities r and w can also be interpreted using Type 1 and Type 2 errors used in statistical hypothesis testing. Let the null hypothesis represent the right situation to select an action (when it is more preferred); while the alternate hypothesis represents the wrong situation for selecting it. Thus, intuitively, Type 1 errors represent *excluded benefits* from failing to respond under the right conditions, while Type 2 errors refer to *included mistakes* from still responding under the wrong conditions. If we let t_1 and t_2 denote the respective probabilities of these errors, they characterize r and w by $r = 1 - t_1$, and $w = t_2$. Thus, r equals one minus the chance excluded benefits, and w equals the change in included mistakes.

Now, with the above components, we can formulate an answer to the question posed earlier: *when is the selection of a new action sufficiently reliable for an agent to benefit from allowing flexibility to select that action.*

To answer this question we must determine whether the gains $g(e)$ from selecting the action under the right conditions (when it is actually more preferred) will cumulate faster than the losses $l(e)$ from selecting it under the wrong conditions (when it is actually less preferred). Thus, combine the above elements in the following way. Right conditions occur with probability $\pi(e)$, which are correctly recognized with probability $r(U)$; so that the expected gain from allowing flexibility to select another action is $g(e)r(U)\pi(e)$. Similarly, the expected loss conditional on allowing the action to be selected is $l(e)w(U)(1 - \pi(e))$. Accordingly, gains will cumulate faster than losses if $g(e)r(U)\pi(e) > l(e)w(U)(1 - \pi(e))$. Hence, simple rearrangement yields the following *Reliability Condition*:

$$\frac{r(U)}{w(U)} > \frac{l(e)}{g(e)} \cdot \frac{1 - \pi(e)}{\pi(e)}.$$

The left-hand side of the inequality is a *reliability ratio*, $r(U)/w(U)$, which measures the probability of "correctly" responding under the right circumstances relative to the probability of "mistakenly" responding under the wrong circumstances. The right-hand side of the inequality represents a minimum lower bound or *tolerance limit* (hereafter denoted simply by $T(e) = l(e)/g(e) \times (1 - \pi(e))/\pi(e))$, which a reliability ratio must satisfy. That is, $T(e)$ determines how likely the chance of selecting an action under the right conditions must be compared to the chance of selecting it under the wrong conditions before allowing flexibility to select that action will improve performance.

We can intuitively interpret the ratio $r(U)/w(U)$ as the "actual" reliability of selecting an action, in comparison to the minimum "required" reliability specified by the tolerance limit, $T(e)$. The components of the Reliability Condition summarize a potentially complex set of relationships between

an agent's repertoire and the structure of the environment.[18] Nevertheless, these relationships boil down to a conceptually simple answer about when to allow flexibility to select an additional action: *do so if the actual reliability in selecting the action exceeds the minimum required reliability necessary to improve performance.* Stated in its simplest notational form, this answer amounts to the condition, $r/w > T$.

The question which motivated this answer was phrased in terms of adding a new action to an agent's repertoire. However, once the Reliability Condition has been obtained we can also apply it to a range of further issues about when to allow or ignore particular actions. For example, it can be applied to dropping actions from a repertoire; namely, retain only those actions which satisfy $r/w > T$ compared to ignoring them.

We can also think of the Reliability Condition as solving a "decision" problem in which an agent determines what information he will allow to influence his behavior; or alternatively, as a "design" problem in engineering the appropriate information sensitivity of an agent. For each possible action, the Reliability Condition must be satisfied before allowing potential information to

---

[18]Both the agent's repertoire and the environment may contain a large number of possibilities, and the consequences from selecting an action may vary with different environmental situations. This will also complicate how to measure an agent's performance. Regardless of how performance is measured (for example, it may involve some kind of average over actions and/or environmental conditions), $g(e)$ and $l(e)$ still represent the gain or loss in performance from correct or mistaken selections, respectively; and $r(U)$, $w(U)$ still represent the conditional probabilities of these correct or mistaken selections. The probabilities $r(U)$ and $w(U)$ also result from a complex set of relationships that determine the source and likelihood of particular errors that interact to generate these probabilities. In addition, $l(e)$ and $g(e)$ may depend on an agent's internal components, such as the morphological attributes of an animal.

The objective of this paper is to develop only the bare essential modeling elements needed for a simple analytical solution, whose structure is invariant to the above-mentioned complications. In particular, the basic form of the Reliability Condition will remain the same. Much greater detail about the analytical structure, including extensive applications to economics and other fields, is now in progress.

prompt its selection. Those actions that can be guided with sufficient reliability are permitted; those that cannot are eliminated. In this way, an agent's outward behavior is determined by his response pattern to potential information.[19]

III. Four General Implications

Now that we have the Reliability Condition, its implications in four basic areas are briefly discussed.

A. Uncertainty Generates Rules Which are Adapted Only to Likely or Recurrent Situations

Note a simple but important feature of the tolerance limit. For any given l/g ratio, the likelihood of wrong to right conditions, $(1-\pi)/\pi$, increases for smaller π; so that T also rises as the probability of right circumstances π decreases (see Figure 1). Thus, *an agent must be more reliable in selecting an action if the right situations for exhibiting it are less likely. Moreover, the required reliability quickly accelerates to infinity as the likelihood of right situations drops to zero.* Thus, for a given structure of uncertainty, $\mathbf{U} = u(\mathbf{p}, \mathbf{e})$, which determines the reliability of selecting a particular action (i.e., which determines the ratio $r(\mathbf{U})/w(\mathbf{U})$), the Reliability Condition will be violated for sufficiently small but positive, $\pi(\mathbf{e}) > 0$.

This intuitively means that to satisfy the Reliability Condition, an agent must ignore actions which are appropriate for only "rare" or "unusual" situations. Conversely, an agent's repertoire must be limited to actions which are adapted only to relatively likely or "recurrent" situations. Thus, a general characteristic of such a repertoire is that it ex-

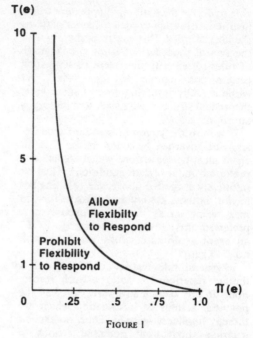

FIGURE 1

The curve shows how the tolerance limit $T(e)$ changes for a constant $l(e)/g(e)$ ratio (in this case $l/g = 1$) as the probability of right conditions π varies. Note how quickly T begins to rise as π drops below .25. The curve represents a boundary of minimum reliability that must be satisfied (i.e., $r/w > T$) before responding to information will enhance an agent's performance.

cludes actions which will in fact enhance performance under certain conditions, even though those conditions occur with positive probability, $\pi(e) > 0$. We thus have a formal characterization of the pervasive association of both human and animal behavior with various connotations of "rule-governed" behavior, such as instinct, habits, routines, rules of thumb, administrative procedures, customs, norms, and so forth. All of these phrases refer to some type of rigidity or inflexibility in adjusting to different situations as a universal qualitative feature of behavior.

Therefore, since behavior patterns which satisfy the Reliability Condition must have this property, we will call them *behavioral rules* or simply *rules*. Note that we have been

---

[19]The relationship between information sensitivity and output complexity is also recognized in cybernetics; see Norbert Weiner, 1948, and W. Ashby, 1956. A reference in organizational behavior that refers to this is Barry Staw, Lana Sanderlands and Jane Dutton: "...a fundamental principle of cybernetics..., the number of output discriminations of a system (i.e., its behavioral repertoire) is limited by the variety of information inherent in its input" (1981, p. 517).

able to derive the basic rigidity feature which justifies attributing to such behavior patterns the idea of rules. This contrasts sharply with the typical procedure of using the language of rules (often with the intent of suggesting certain connotations to the reader), yet without really justifying from a more basic theoretical structure why such terminology is appropriate.

If we use the jargon of standard economics, rule-governed behavior means that an agent must ignore actions which are actually preferred under certain conditions. Thus, as intuitively suggested above, the resulting behavior patterns are *not* an approximation to maximizing so as to always choose most preferred alternatives (i.e., behaving "as if" an agent could successfully maximize with no C-D gap).

In general, rules restrict behavior to only a limited repertoire of actions. Such restrictions do not assume an awareness of all the potential actions or information which are thereby implicitly ignored. Thus, no explicit decision about what potential actions to ignore is necessarily involved.

An agent need only be capable of determining when to select particular actions from a limited range of allowable alternatives. To do so does not require an ability to understand why the resulting behavior patterns evolved. This is obviously the case for animals, where we do not expect them to have an "intellectual awareness" of why they are programmed to exhibit certain behavior patterns. Yet even for humans, the general characteristic will be an inability to articulate a full understanding of why particular behavior patterns have arisen. This is implied even though human behavior is much more flexible than that of other species, and even though conscious mental processes are involved in most human behavior patterns.[20]

As a simple example involving human behavior, consider the solving methods for Rubic's cube mentioned above in Section I.

------

[20] For related comments about the legitimacy of standard psychotherapy practices, see Donald Campbell's 1975 presidential address to the American Psychological Association.

The environment represents all of the different scrambled positions or "situations" which might eventuate on the face of the cube, of which there are over 43 trillion. If each situation is produced by a simple random draw from the set of possible situations, the probability π of the right situation (the appropriate scrambled position) arising for any particular solving sequence is extremely low. Assuming the $1/g$ ratio (resulting from unscrambling the cube in greater or lesser time, or number of moves) is not close to zero, the required reliability for selecting each of these sequences will also be very high. Without this ability, the repertoire of solving patterns must be severely restricted in order to satisfy the Reliability Condition, and structured so that their use is largely independent of particular scrambled positions (i.e., they are adapted only to the recurrent features of the environment).

B. *Selection Processes do not Simulate Optimizing Behavior*

Up to this point we have thought of performance simply in terms of an agent's "preferences" about the consequences of particular actions. Now generalize its meaning to represent any factor that determines whether behavior will continue or persist in the environment encountered by an agent. This might involve a preference evaluation, competition for profits or investment capital, or possibly biological determinants of physical survival or reproductive probability. Whatever the interpretation, we can apply the Reliability Condition to determine when allowing flexibility to use potential information or to select actions will improve rather than worsen performance.

Now suppose the actual process generating behavior is an evolutionary process that tends to select relatively superior performance at any point of time. From what has already been derived, this implies that such selection processes will tend to produce rule-governed behavior that is not an approximation to always selecting actions that maximize performance. Thus, in general, evolutionary processes will *not* generate simulations to optimizing behavior. Rather, they will tend to produce rules that systematically restrict the flexibility of behavior compared to that which would be exhibited by a full optimizer in the absence of uncertainty.

As mentioned earlier, this implication directly contradicts one of the dominant justifications for assuming agents are able to optimize. Predictable behavior is not an "as if" simulation to optimizing, but rather will evolve only to the extent that agent's are unable to maximize because of uncertainty.

Generalizing the meaning of performance also implies that we are not necessarily dealing with traditional economic agents, such as consumer, firm, worker, investor, etc. Rather, we can think of an agent as any system of interacting components. For example, a system might refer to biological entities such as individual organisms, species, ecological systems, or possibly to subsystems within organisms studied in physiology or molecular biology. Still other examples might be computers or other artificial cybernetic mechanisms.

Whatever the interpretation, the Reliability Condition characterizes when to allow flexibility to use information or select actions applicable to that interpretation. For example, we might apply it to the following situations: when is it the right time to unscramble Rubic's cube by starting from a middle section rather than from one of its outer sections; when is it the right time to purchase more of a particular commodity rather than other commodities; when is it the right time to search for additional price or quality information about potential future purchasing decisions; when is it the right time for an animal to deviate from its usual foraging strategies for food; when is it the right time to cooperate by helping other individuals (i.e., when is it the right time to be "altruistic" rather than "selfish"); [21] when is it the right time to modify genetic information to perpetuate traits acquired in the lifetime of a

particular organism (i.e., when is it the right time to use "Lamarkian" genetic transmission); [22] or more generally, when is it the right time to use feedback from the environment to modify behavior (i.e., when is it the right time to "learn")?

C. *Weak Selection Processes May Allow Dysfunctional Behavior to Persist*

The preceding discussion implicitly assumed that selection processes would quickly eliminate relatively inferior performers. If this is actually the case, the Reliability Condition implies the evolution of behavioral rules that appropriately structure and limit the flexibility of behavior. The empirical examples that helped motivate the formal analysis also involved behavior produced in highly competitive conditions (i.e., biological competition for survival between nonhuman agents; strategies to win at blackjack, or in prisoner's dilemma games, or in Rubic's cube contests; organizations competing in exchange environments for profits or investment capital, etc.).

On the other hand, what if there is something about the environment that only sluggishly weeds out worse performers, or which only infrequently produces situations that severely punish vulnerable behavior. This possibility is fundamentally important when genuine uncertainty exists, because there is no magical element (empirically or in theory) to guarantee that only appropriately structured behavior will evolve. Indeed, the core assumption is literally the absence of ability to decifer all of the complexity of the environment; especially one whose very structure itself evolves over time.

Thus, consider an evolving world produced through a mixture of selective processes. These processes will have varying degrees of severity in reacting to differential performance between competing agents. Such a world will be a continual mixture of appropriately and inappropriately structured behavior. In some cases, weak selection processes may allow relatively dysfunctional

[21] Hirshleifer uses "recognition coefficients" (which represent particular examples of the $r(U)$ and $w(U)$ probabilities) to determine the reliability of helping strategies in identifying other agents with altruistic traits (1982, pp. 26–29). See also W. D. Hamilton, 1964; John Maynard Smith, 1964; Robert Trivers, 1971.

[22] On the "irreversibility" of genetic translation, see Jacques Monod, 1972, pp. 104–17.

behavior to persist: possibly with worse average performance than other agents; or with slowly dwindling performance over time; or with vulnerable performance that awaits only the next infrequent but severe test to challenge its further persistence in the environment.

This is clearly a different view from trying to comprehend the world as continually tending toward optimizing behavior. Indeed, we may be able to explain major features about the structure, occurrence, and error patterns of dysfunctional behavior. Only one class of possibilities is mentioned here, and briefly reconsidered at the conclusion of this paper. In particular, we can analyze the pattern of vulnerable behavior arising from political institutions, especially in the form of dysfunctional complexity in trying to manipulate the outcomes resulting from exchange competition. Specific instances of this issue have had a long history in economics about the scope of government regulation, and the debate over discretionary vs. rigid monetary policy.[23]

D. *Greater Uncertainty will Cause Rule-Governed Behavior to be More Predictable*

What is the effect of *greater* uncertainty on rule-governed behavior? In general, greater uncertainty (from either less reliable perceptual abilities or a more unpredictable environment) will both reduce the chance of recognizing the right situation to select an action, and increase the chance of not recognizing the wrong situation for selecting it. That is, greater uncertainty will both reduce $r(U)$ and increase $w(U)$, so that the reliability ratios, $r(U)/w(U)$, of particular actions will drop.

As these ratios drop, some of them may no longer exceed their respective tolerance limits, resulting in violations of the Reliability Condition. More violations will occur as uncertainty becomes more pervasive. Thus, greater uncertainty will cause behavioral rules to be more restrictive in eliminating particular actions or response patterns to potential information. This will further constrain behavior to simpler, less sophisticated patterns which are easier for an observer to recognize and predict. Therefore, *greater uncertainty will cause rule-governed behavior to exhibit increasingly predictable regularities, so that uncertainty becomes the basic source of predictable behavior.*

This is the most important implication of my analysis, one that has far-reaching implications across a diverse range of fields. It also has important implications for how we have been trying to model behavior. It implies that genuine uncertainty, far from being unanalyzable or irrelevant to understanding behavior, is the very source of the empirical regularities that we have sought to explain by excluding such uncertainty.[24] This means that the conceptual basis for most of our existing models is seriously flawed.

A major symptom of this has been the dominant tendency to model more complex decision problems by implicitly upgrading the competence of the agent to handle that complexity (so that traditional optimizing concepts can be used). For example, the number of decision alternatives or competing agents is increased, or complex probabilistic contingencies are introduced, or repercussions from future events are permitted, etc. Over the years this has resulted in the characterization of increasingly sophisticated,

---

[23]Another area involves differences in productivity between U.S. and Japanese industrial firms, because of differential ability either to manage a complex internal use of inputs, or to adjust to volatile external marketing conditions ("just in time" rather than "just in case" inventory management; greater employee discretion in production line monitoring; longer promotion, investment, and $R \& D$ planning horizons; etc.) See William Abernathy, Kim Clark, and A. Kantrow, 1981; Y. Mondon, 1981; Y. Sugimori, K. Kusunoki, and S. Cho, 1977; R. Clark, 1979; Anthony Athos and Richard Pascale, 1981; William Ouchi, 1981.

[24]The various authors that have emphasized the importance of uncertainty (for example, Frank Knight, 1921; the Australian view typified by F. A. Hayek, 1967, and Israel Kirzner, 1973; the subjectivist views of G. L. S. Shackle, 1969, 1972; etc.) have given the impression that genuine uncertainty and its effects cannot be represented with formal modeling tools. The approach suggested here is quite different: to harness the determinants of uncertainty in a modeling structure that characterizes regularity in behavior. Closely related ideas have also been recently analyzed by Richard Bookstaber and Joseph Langsam, 1983.

"optimal" behavior strategies, with little fruit in understanding observed behavior.

This trend is typified by recent Bayesian models of optimal risk behavior, which are synonymous with sophisticated continually updated response to new information. Some examples are optimal "search" models that specify various sequential strategies for job search, price or quality information, etc.[25] Yet, they bypass the issue that overides everything else: when to permit any search given the uncertainty in detecting whether the positive gains from efficient search strategies will outweigh the required search costs; especially when a diverse range of search opportunities might eventuate, and the timing of these future opportunities is also unknown.

IV. Explaining Predictable Behavior: Framework and Illustration

The reliability theory briefly outlined above can be applied to the full spectrum of cases produced by different structures of uncertainty. It thus represents a general framework for analyzing behavior under all of these possibilities. On the other hand, standard choice theory analyzes the special case where there is no uncertainty due to a C-D gap.[26]

The narrowness of standard optimizing concepts is evidenced in the dominant tend-

ency (even after years of extensive experience with conventional models) to steer away from incorporating genuine uncertainty into the analysis of behavior.[27] In contrast, the Reliability Condition directly harnesses the determinants of uncertainty to characterize regularity in behavior. This amounts to a reversal of the explanation assumed in standard economics, which places these determinants in the residual "error term" between observed behavior and the more systematic patterns claimed to result from optimization.

Thus, the idea of uncertainty as the source of predictable behavior is both a generalization and a major shift away from the explanatory framework of existing models, one that may be of importance to a number of fields. The following statements briefly summarize the major differences between the new framework (the economics of genuine uncertainty) and that of traditional optimization theory:

1) The basic theoretical objective is to understand the behavioral implications of genuine uncertainty, rather than the implications of maximizing for a given set of preferences or expectations. Genuine uncertainty results from a gap in an agent's decision competence relative to the difficulty in selecting more preferred alternatives, so that error and surprise cannot be avoided.

2) A wide range of factors contribute to uncertainty. In economics, these include cognitive limitations in processing given information or in interpreting potential information from the environment; vulnerable perceptions about preferences or expectations taken as given in traditional choice models; unreliable probability or expected utility information taken as given in standard risk-behavior theory. In addition, uncertainty may involve the ability to infer from past experience what was misunderstood that led to previous error; or the abil-

---

[25]See, for example, David Blackwell and M. A. Girshick, 1979; Thomas Ferguson, 1967; Peter Diamond and Michael Rothschild, 1978; Stephen Lippman and John McCall, 1979; Hirshleifer and John Riley, 1979.

[26]This conclusion also applies to the more recent models of behavior under uncertainty, which assume agents can infer reliable probabilities of future situations; and also recognize all possible events that might eventuate, or possible actions that might be useful to select. Such ability to comprehend the future is much more difficult than avoiding computational mistakes in a static world of known utility information over a fixed set of options. Consequently, these models are not moving closer but rather further away from dealing with genuine uncertainty due to a C-D gap. The reason is that in order to apply traditional optimizing concepts, the competence of the agent has been implicitly upgraded to handle the extra complexity resulting from an unpredictable future. On this issue, see the closing remarks of John Hey, 1979, pp. 232–34.

[27]For example, a recent statement by Lucas flatly concludes: "In situations of risk, the hypothesis of rational behavior on the part of agents will have usable content, so that behavior may be explainable in terms of economic theory.... In cases of uncertainty, economic reasoning will be of little value" (1981, p. 224; see also p. 223).

ity to identify potential actions which might be selected, or contingencies that might affect the consequences of future behavior.[28]

3) Optimizing with no uncertainty in choosing more preferred alternatives does not tend to produce systematic and stable regularity in behavior. Rather, it tends to destroy such regularity as successively more information can be reliably interpreted in guiding more complex behavior. This does not mean that formal optimization tools cannot be used, but rather that understanding how uncertainty affects behavior will systematically redirect the formulation of models and the questions to which they would be applied.

4) Predictable regularities of behavior are the manifestation of behavioral rules that represent patterns of behavior for which deviations exist that are preferred under certain conditions, but which are nevertheless ignored because of uncertainty in reliably interpreting potential information about when to deviate.

5) Intrinsic to behavioral rules is the ignoring or lack of alertness to potential information, the reaction to which would direct behavior into more complex deviations from such rules; even though such information may be costless to observe. Conversely, it is the alertness or sensitivity to information that determines the patterns and complexity of rules manifested in behavior. The Reliability Condition is a simple but general characterization of when greater flexibility to administer more complex behavior or to use more information will improve rather than worsen performance.

6) Behavioral rules not only involve outward symptoms of information sensitivity, but also internal mechanisms that generate such sensitivity. Thus, research in fields such as psychology, biology, and engineering has

direct bearing on the structure of such rules. In contrast, traditional economic models have largely ignored research in these and other fields.

To help see the range of issues unified by the above analytical framework, a few illustrations are briefly presented.

A. *The Consistency of Rule-Governed Behavior*

Traditional choice theory has tended to equate normative rationality with logical consistency of behavior, as described by various transitivity, intertemporal consistency, probability assessment, and other assumed conditions. For example, Jacques Drèze provides the following evaluation of the risk behavior axioms of standard expected utility theory:

> ... a consistent decision-maker is assumed always to be able to compare (transitively) the attractiveness of acts, or hypothetical acts and of consequences as well as the likelihood of events. These requirements are minimal, in the sense that no consistency of behaviour may be expected if any one of them is violated; *but they are very strong, in the sense that all kinds of comparisons are assumed possible, many of which may be quite remote from the range of experience of the decision-maker.* This is also the reason why the axioms have more normative appeal than descriptive realism; few people would insist on maintaining, consciously, choices that violate them, but their spontaneous behaviour may frequently fail to display such rigorous consistency.
>
> [1974, p. 11, emphasis added]

Drèze is quick to acknowledge and discount the descriptive validity of the expected utility axioms, but like many others he still feels secure in their normative validity in characterizing truly rational behavior under uncertainty.[29] Nevertheless, one might ask what

---

[28] The latter determinants have recently been described as particular types of uncertainty, such as parametric versus structural knowledge by Richard Langlois (1983) and "extended" uncertainty by Bookstaber and Langsam. They are extensions of the "unlistability problem" introduced by Shackle (1972). Whatever terminology or type of uncertainty is involved, we can characterize regularity in behavior depending on how each type of uncertainty affects the reliability of using information or selecting potential actions.

[29] See, for example, John von Neumann and Oskar Morgenstern, 1944, pp. 17–30; L. J. Savage, 1954, pp. 6–7, 19–21, 56–68, 82–84; Friedman and Savage, 1948.

would be the implication of a logically correct set of axioms (or a decision algorithm for search and learning behavior) *if obeying those axioms (or using the algorithm) would require the use and sensitive response to unreliable information* (for example, information remote from the range of experience of a decision maker)? To the extent this is the case, rule-governed behavior will ignore such axioms (or a decision algorithm) regardless of the logical properties violated in disobeying them.[30] Similar issues apply to traditional microeconomic theory. For example, what if preferences are less reliable for commodity bundles remote to a consumer's normal purchasing experience? Must we avoid this likely possibility in assuming fully connected preferences? Or is the violation of this assumption itself a major source of price-response regularities of consumers?

B. *Social Institutions Evolve Because of Uncertainty*

Neoclassical decision and general equilibrium models are typically without any explicit institutional structure, and have thus tended to direct attention away from questions about the evolution of particular forms of market organization and other social institutions.[31] In contrast, the Reliability Condition naturally suggests the systematic importance of such institutions to determine the scope and complexity of exchange relationships, and other social interactions involving cultural norms, customs, and aggressive behavior.

In this regard, it is noteworthy that Schotter's recent book on the theory of institutions defines them in a manner immediately implied by the Reliability Condition: "A social institution is a regularity in social behavior that...specifies behavior in specific recurrent situations, and is either self-policed or policed by some external authority" (p. 11).

Thus, evolved institutions are social rule-mechanisms for dealing with recurrent situations faced by agents in different societies. That is, institutions are regularities in the interaction between agents that arise because of uncertainty in deciphering the complex interdependencies created by these interactions.[32] I will return to this topic in Section V below, which considers the evolution of legal and exchange institutions.

A persistent theme in human literature illustrates a closely related issue that has been largely ignored by traditional choice theory; namely, the attempt of individuals to constrain or bind the flexibility of their actions.[33] A famous example in *The Odyssey* describes Ulysses trying to prevent himself from responding to the allurement of certain sirens: "...but you must bind me hard and fast, so that I cannot stir from the spot where

---

[30] See Paul Slovic and Amos Tversky, 1974, Slovic and Sarah Lichtenstein, 1983; Dirk Wendt, 1975; D. Conrath, 1973; Detlof Winterfeldt, 1980; and for systematic empirical evidence see Daniel Kahneman and Tversky, 1979, 1981, 1982; Ward Edwards, 1962; William Fellner, 1961; R. M. Hogarth, 1975. Some recent attempts to modify standard expected utility theory by dropping the "independence" or "substitution" axiom include Mark Machina, 1982 (equivalence relationships to global risk-aversion axioms); Graham Loomes and Robert Sugden, 1982, 1983 (regret theory); and S. H. Chew and K. R. MacCrimmon, 1979a, b; Peter Fishburn, 1981; R. Weber, 1982 (*alpha*-utility theory).

[31] See the following diverse range of analytical perspectives, including Alchian, 1950; James Buchanan, 1975, 1977; Buchanan and H. G. Brennan, 1981; Ronald Coase, 1937; Carl Dahlman, 1980; Demsetz, 1967; Hayek, 1967, 1973; Menger, 1871, 1883; Nelson and Sidney Winter, 1982; Andrew Schotter, 1981; Joseph Schumpeter, 1942; Oliver Williamson, 1975, 1979, 1981.

[32] Consider a person within a complex interdependent society, where uncertainty in deciphering these interdependencies quickly increases as they widen beyond his immediate experience. The Reliability Condition implies that his behavior will quickly become insensitive to nonlocal social contingencies. If among such contingencies are effects on other individuals, this implies a relatively sensitive or "self-interested" motivation toward a person's own self (and family), and away from alertness or "sympathy" toward other persons. This implication underlies the ideas Adam Smith developed in the *Theory of Moral Sentiments*, published prior to the *Wealth of Nations*. See Coase (1976) for a number of passages from the *Theory of Moral Sentiments*; for example, Smith, 1969, pp. 321–23, 347–48, 109–10.

[33] See John Elster, 1979; R. H. Strotz, 1955; and N. Howard, 1971. Another classic moral dilemma of great literature poses the protagonist in a situation with abnormally convincing information that "right circumstances" are at hand to engage in behavior precluded by social or religious norms.

you shall stand me...and if I beg you to release me, you must tighten and add to my bonds."

C. *Uncertainty and the Reliability of Expectations*

Both past and present economic models are crucially dependent on how they incorporate expectations in guiding behavior. Economists have been aware that beliefs about the future are often mistaken, and thus have been uneasy in both formulating and applying their models.[34] More recently, "rational expectations" models have attempted to resolve these problems by assuming that expectations correctly identify the mean and variance of stochastic variables that affect future environmental contingencies.[35] A key motivation for such models is to predict how "optimal" behavior will respond to changes in the structure of the environment, especially changes influenced by government policy. Yet, from a broader perspective, it is clear that most species that have evolved in nature exhibit relatively programmed behavior patterns that are highly insensitive to environmental changes, even if such rigidity results in their extinction. At best, such models could apply more broadly only by continually introducing specializing assumptions about the type of expectation "rationality" guiding the behavior of particular species.

Thus, in all of our existing models, either we are analyzing the maximizing response to possibly wrong expectations, or we avoid this issue by assuming expectations are reliable. In order to make progress in analyzing the role of expectations, we must understand how their use and formation are affected by genuine uncertainty in comprehending the future. For example, how reliable are agents' abilities to formulate beliefs about the future; and given the vulnerability of such beliefs, when will agents sensitively react to them, or when will they be alert to information that might prompt them to revise them?

D. *The Pattern of Behavioral Complexity Evidenced in Nature*

My departure from standard choice theory was suggested by the general pattern of animals having a larger C-D gap than humans, yet regularity in their behavior is much more noticeable than for humans. The Reliability Condition implies a simple formal characterization of this overall pattern. Suppose we start with a given combination of the p and e variables, and consider a conceptual experiment where the e variables are held fixed, but the perceptual abilities of an agent are successively reduced compared to their initial effectiveness. This will increase the uncertainty in administering the initial behavioral repertoire, thus reducing the reliability ratios of particular actions. As already discussed, greater uncertainty will in general require a more inflexible structure of rules; that is, some of the actions in the initial repertoire must be excluded because their selection no longer satisfies the Reliability Condition.

Now apply this result to us as human observers watching other species with less reliable cognitive equipment than ourselves. We should notice a systematic pattern of greater rigidity and inflexibility in nonhuman species compared to our own behavior. This implication is testable to the extent that the effectiveness of different species' cognitive abilities can be independently measured from simply watching outward behavior (for example, relative brain to body mass). In addition, if we compare across a number of species, there should emerge a general pattern that correlates greater rigidity in behavior with less effective cognitive equipment.[36]

These implications characterize a pervasive qualitative pattern, one that is systematically evidenced in the comparative study of different species. Yet, they were obtained in a very simple way from the Reliability Condition. This is a significant indication that we are on the right track in understanding be-

---

[34]See John Hicks, 1935; Richard Muth, 1961; Axel Leijonhufvud, 1968, pp. 366–85, Rudiger Dornbusch and Stanley Fischer, 1978, pp. 270–75, 283–86.
[35]See for example, Thomas Sargent, 1979, and Lucas, 1981.

[36]For analysis of some of the more rigid, "forced" behavior movements of simple organisms, and other major instinctive patterns, see Roger Brown and Richard Herrnstein, 1975, pp. 23–31.

VOL. 73 NO. 4   HEINER: ORIGIN OF PREDICTABLE BEHAVIOR   575

havior, especially in developing a modeling structure that naturally suggests the very consideration of such questions.

E. *Explaining Instinctive Behavior*

The currently accepted explanation of instinctive rigidities is that they accomplish some function which is useful or adaptive most of the time for the natural environments in which they are exhibited.[37] But as already discussed, this feature is itself implied by the Reliability Condition; namely, that rule-governed behavior will ignore adjustment to unlikely contingencies, thus limiting response patterns to only the more probable or recurrent features of the environment. A number of implications concerning ecological structure, niches, extinction, etc., can also be derived (rather than simply described or assumed) from the analysis.

Explanation of specific behavioral rigidities can be obtained by using the Reliability Condition, $r/w > T$, with explicit variables and assumptions about an organism's perceptual components (p) in terms of the sensory (s) and cognitive (c) attributes of particular organisms. In addition, we can introduce morphological (m) attributes of organisms, along with the environmental variables (e) which determine the structure of the environment. By understanding how these variables (denoted $z = (s, c, m, e)$) affect the reliability and tolerance limit components of the model, particular rule structures can be derived and compared with observed behavior of different organisms (including humans).

F. *Brief Application to Imprinting*

Consider very briefly the phenomenon of *imprinting*.[38] Suppose that responding to a particular pattern in the environment is crucial to an organism's survival (for example, following its parents). Suppose also that without highly developed cognitive mechanisms, if the organism did not initially know the particular pattern, then it could not reliably distinguish that pattern from a number of similar patterns (i.e., a newly born organism could not reliably distinguish its parents from similar adults); but given a specific *reference pattern* to "lock onto," it can reliably distinguish it from other similar patterns. However, if the wrong pattern is locked onto, the organism's survival would be severely jeopardized.

In particular, the probability of right circumstances π to lock onto a pattern is often a function of time since an organism's birth (for example, $\pi(t)$ is the chance of seeing only an organism's parents at time t since birth). Recalling that the required reliability (i.e., the tolerance limit T) will quickly increase as π drops to zero, we can derive the following two-stage behavioral process: stage one is a pattern-locking mechanism that reacts to whatever pattern first appears after the mechanism is initiated; while stage two is a resistance mechanism that severely constrains stage one to only certain sensitive periods for which the required reliability is very low (i.e., $\pi(t)$ is close to 1.0).

It can further be shown that the implied sensitive periods will be highly predictable across particular organisms of a species. In addition, comparative regularities across species in relatively sensitive learning periods can be derived. For example, we can characterize less rigidly patterned sensitivity phases in the development of human children in acquiring language, and the display of other cognitive skills.[39]

G. *Punctuated Dynamics for Scientific Inquiry*

The work of Thomas Kuhn (1962) (see also Popper, 1969; Lakatos and Musgrave,

---

[37]The classic reference on instinct is Nino Tinbergen, 1951 (for example, pp. 151–84, especially 156–57 and 152–53). Other references include John Alcock, 1979, pp. 57–76, 87–102; Brown and Herrnstein, 1975, pp. 31–59; William Keeton, 1980, pp. 490–512, especially 503, 494, 496, 498; Eric Pianka, 1978, pp. 82–86, 152–53.

[38]See Alcock, 1979, pp. 67–73; Keeton, 1980, pp. 498–500; Konrad Lorenz, 1981, pp. 259, 275–87; David McFarland, 1982, pp. 303–05; W. R. Hess, 1973.

[39]See for example, Alcock, 1979, pp. 73–79; E. Mavis Hetherington and Ross Park, 1979; R. Grinder, 1962; Lawrence Kohlberg, 1966, 1969; N. Chomsky, 1972; J. Piaget, 1947, 1952. For related material from ethology, see Lorenz, 1981.

1970) has emphasized a systematic pattern of resistance in the behavior of scientists to quick and sensitive reaction to new ideas and theories. Yet, when sufficient anomalies and awkwardly interpreted evidence about a previous theory build up, a major shift in ideas (a "scientific revolution") will relatively quickly occur. This is an illustration of dynamic properties discussed below in Section VI. The Reliability Condition also implies other features in the behavior of scientists, such as: (a) resistance to accepting or using several competing theories unless there also exist easy to decipher (and reliable) criteria of when to switch between them; (b) similar resistance to incorporating new concepts or variables into accepted theories unless reliable criteria on how to use them are available (consider an economist's reaction to incorporating sociological variables into economic models); (c) differences in accepting and rewarding (salary, promotion, etc.) theoretical vs. empirical research in different fields depending on the reliability of observable data studied in those fields (for example, see Leijonhufvud's 1973 parody about "Life Among the Econ").[40]

H. Uncertainty and Consensus in Social Judgments

Finally, in the area of ethics and social policy, consider the theory of justice advanced by John Rawls (1971). Underlying his whole analysis is the recognition that if individuals have reliable information about their own future circumstances (will they be smart or resourceful, or have special educational opportunities, or own highly valued property, etc.), they will respond to such information in the way they view social policies and institutions that would affect their particular situations.[41] This will produce a wide diversity of opinions about how

to formulate and apply normative principles. Hence, in order to produce a highly uniform consensus or *regularity* in social judgments, Rawls introduced a pervasive uncertainty into the conceptual problem in the form of a "veil of ignorance." Such a procedure virtually eliminates reliable information (even in probabilistic form) about any particular individual's specific future circumstances that might eventuate depending on what principles are mutually agreed to by the whole group.[42] With a sufficient structure of uncertainty, individual judgments might be constrained to possibly a single, universally accepted principle of justice to guide social policy.

The important point is that the source of such a universal consensus, as well as the other behavior patterns discussed above, is uncertainty in using potential information about when to deviate from these regularities.

V. Application to Economic Modeling

In this section, the Reliability Condition is briefly applied to a few modeling issues in standard economics.

A. Reluctance to Insure Against Rare Disasters

Extensive empirical studies have shown that people are reluctant to insure themselves against large but rare disasters, in a manner that directly contradicts expected utility theory (see Howard Kunreuther et al., 1978). A recent statement by Kenneth Arrow summarizes the dilemma posed for standard "uncertainty" theory:

> A striking real life situation has given grounds for doubt about the validity of the expected utility hypothesis. Since 1969, the U.S. government has offered flood insurance at rates which are well below their actuarial value... Under the usual hypothesis of risk aversion, any

---

[40]Edward Leamer's work (1978) illustrates another issue about the reliability of model testing and formulation, which can be viewed as methodological rule-mechanisms to restrict "specification searches" used to claim empirical support for a theory. See Thomas Cooley and Stephen LeRoy (1981) for an application of Leamer's methodology to evaluating previous work on the demand for money.

[41]See Rawls, 1971, pp. 18–19, 137–38, 140, 149.

[42]See Rawls, 1971, pp. 150, 154–55. Notice in these passages how Rawls believes that a crucial feature of the veil of ignorance is the inability to formulate reliable probability information about the impact of social contingencies on particular individuals.

individual should certainly be willing to undertake a favorable bet.... Yet, until the government increased the pressure by various incentives, very few took out this insurance.... The main distinguishing characteristic of those who took out flood insurance was acquaintance with others who took out insurance. This might be taken as an explanation in terms of information costs, but the information seems so easy to acquire and the stakes so large that this hypothesis hardly seems tenable.

[1981, p. 2]

In contrast, the above analysis immediately suggests that even costless information will be ignored if the behavior resulting from its use will not satisfy the Reliability Condition, (recall that solving procedures for Rubic's cube systematically ignore costless information available simply by looking at the cube while unscrambling it). The real issue is why are agents reluctant to engage in behavior that might be prompted by such information.

Consider a brief sketch of the insurance behavior phenomenon. As the probability, p, of a disaster goes to zero, the number of such extremely rare but conceivable events grows indefinitely large. Given any positive setup costs of insuring against each of these possibilities, the total insurance cost will eventually exceed a person's (finite) wealth. Thus, it is clearly not appropriate to insure against all of them. (What do we call someone who is constantly trying to protect against rare but serious sickness; and what would happen to total output net of the demand for medical services if everyone exhibited this propensity?)

The above argument implies that the probability of the right time to insure, π, is bounded by the ratio of a person's wealth to total insurance cost; so that π approaches zero as p approaches zero. Thus, the required reliability will steeply rise for sufficiently rare disasters (i.e., the tolerance limit T will begin to accelerate toward infinity as p approaches zero—see Figure 1).[43] Note also

that rare events are precisely those which are remote to a person's normal experience, so that uncertainty in detecting which rare disasters to insure against increases as p approaches zero. Such greater uncertainty will reduce the reliability of insurance decisions (i.e., reduce the ration r/w) as disasters become increasingly remote to a person's normal experience.

As a result of the above factors, the required reliability of when to insure increases sharply just when the actual reliability is dropping. Thus, at some point as p approaches zero, the Reliability Condition will be violated (i.e., T will rise above the falling r/w ratio). This implies people will switch from typically buying to typically ignoring insurance options, which is just the pattern documented in Kunreuther's 1978 study.

We can also show that after a person switches to ignoring insurance, he will be very reluctantly convinced to insure by any information source, *except those local to his normal experience* (for example, a neighbor, a relative, or an "acquaintance" as suggested in the above quotation). Note further that ignoring insurance does not necessarily mean a person consciously decides to ignore all the various potential insurance options—either those obtainable by contacting an insurance agent, or many other ones for which no market insurance is available.

This is a simple example of a more general implication: agents will only become alert or sensitive to information about options whose selection is reliable; or conversely, they will fail to become aware of information about options whose selection is unreliable. Another example of selective alertness to information is the use (or disuse) of marginal cost information to make production decisions, discussed next.

---

[43] Consider also very briefly the behavior of the l/g ratio of the tolerance limit. The loss l will be a negative function of the expected value of the disaster losses (denoted $E(p)$) relative to the expected value of the insurance costs (denoted $C(p)$); that is, l is a negative function of $E(p)/C(p) = v(p)$, denoted $l(v(p))$. Similarly, g is a positive function of $v(p)$, denoted $g(v(p))$. Now think of a sequence of actuarially fair or "pure" insurance options for which $v(p) \equiv 1$. If the estimated $v(p)$ is close to zero, then the l/g ratio will not deviate substantially from $l(1)/g(1)$. When this result is coupled with a steeply rising $(1 - \pi(p))/\pi(p)$ ratio as $p \to 0$, we have the same acceleration implied for $T(p) \equiv l(1)/g(1) \times (1 - \pi(p))/\pi(p)$.

B. *Spontaneous Alertness to Marginal Cost Information in Simple Production Environments*

A memorable episode in the history of economics was the marginalist controversy about whether businessmen use marginal cost calculations to guide their production decisions. The debate prompted Alchian to write "Uncertainty, Evolution, and Economic Theory" (1950). This was the article that first explicitly justified optimization theory as an explanatory tool to predict the outcome of selection processes (i.e., selection processes will produce simulations to optimizing behavior, which claim is contradicted by the above analysis). Regardless of how one views this debate, it is clear that businessmen typically do not use or are even aware of the kinds of marginal calculations discussed in standard production theory (this lack of awareness is itself an empirical regularity). But what would happen in a relatively simple production environment in which such information could be readily monitored and used with little uncertainty in directing production decisions?

The Reliability Condition implies the spontaneous development (without any special training in economic theory) of alertness and sensitive reaction to marginal cost information for sufficiently simple production environments. This will not be the usual situation, but are there cases that would naturally fit this hypothesis? An example is summarized in the following passage from Hirshleifer's price theory text:

> Electricity is typically generated by companies that operate a number of separate producing plants, with a transmission network providing connections to consumers as well as ties among the generating plants...the operating problem at any moment of time is to assign output most economically among the generating plants....
> Fred M. Westfield investigated the operating practices of a leading American electric utility. He discovered that this company employs a dispatcher to actually "assign the load" from mo-

ment to moment among the different plants. The dispatcher is guided by a Station-Loading Sliderule that shows what the economist would regard as the Marginal Cost function of each plant. By mechanically manipulating his Sliderule, the dispatcher automatically equates Marginal Cost for all plants in operation in such as way as to meet the total generation requirement....
> The company's method of division of output, and the Sliderule itself, were developed by engineers lacking the slightest acquaintance with economic theory. The company's engineers thus independently "discovered" Marginal Cost analysis....   [1980, pp. 286–87]

The engineers did not discover marginal cost analysis, but rather developed a way of reacting to what we as economists would call marginal cost information. Nevertheless, the development of a Station-Loading Sliderule is confirming evidence for the hypothesis of spontaneous sensitivity to marginal cost information in simple production environments. On the other hand, within standard price theory, it can only represent an isolated special case that illustrates a clearly noticeable use of such information.

C. *Uncertainty Implies "Corridor" Dynamics for Macroeconomic Shocks*

A major issue in macroeconomic theory has a direct parallel with the insurance behavior phenomenon discussed above. Instead of deciding whether to insure against various natural disasters, think of a repertoire of activities to prepare for the negative effects of macroeconomic "shocks"; or more generally, anything that produces a coordination failure in an economic system.

When will an economic system evolve so as to "self-insure" against these potential sources of unemployment and other symptoms of coordination failure? Costly shock-preparation activities are beneficial if they are appropriately timed to mitigate the effects of a shock, but otherwise there is a loss from the reduction in output otherwise attainable.

Now suppose, analogous to the insurance case, that there are different types of shocks, some more severe than others; where larger shocks are possible but less and less likely to happen. In addition, the reliability of detecting when and how to prepare for large shocks decreases as their determinants and repercussions are more remote to agents' normal experience.

In a similar manner to that discussed for the insurance case, we can derive that the economy's structure will evolve so as to prepare for and react quickly to small shocks. However, outside of a certain zone or "corridor" around its long-run growth path, it will only very sluggishly react to sufficiently large, infrequent shocks. This is essentially the "corridor hypothesis" for macroeconomic systems recently advanced by Leijonhufvud (1981, pp. 103–29).

In this paper, I have not gone into the specific microprocesses involved (individual agent behavior, intra- and intermarket structures, transmission mechanisms, etc.). Nevertheless, even without adding more specific assumptions we can still derive this general qualitative feature as a necessary consequence of uncertainty. Standard economic theory has been unable to do so, as summarized by Leijonhufvud:

> ...general equilibrium theorists have at their command an impressive array of proven techniques for modelling systems that "always work well". Keynesian economists have experience with modelling systems that "never work". But, as yet, no one has the recipe for modelling systems that function pretty well most of the time but sometimes work very badly to coordinate economic activities.   [1981, p. 103]

D. *A Clear Prediction of the Law of Demand*

Suppose consumers do not have well-defined preference relations, but instead must deal with uncertainty in trying to detect when to buy more or less of particular commodities. Myriad "internal" perceptual and "external" environmental factors come together to determine the relative value of particular commodities. In a prospective sense, there is no reliable information to compare all the margins of choice to calculate the most preferred response for each future situation. Rather, consumers must try to react appropriately to various influences that might prompt them to purchase more of particular commodities.

Now suppose the price of a commodity x rises. In order to benefit from continued purchases, the actual value of successive units of the commodity must exceed the now higher opportunity cost implied from the price increase. The likelihood of this situation arising is less than before, given the same structure of motivational influences affecting the value of x. Thus, the probability π of the right situation to buy more x is smaller. For the same reason, even when the right situation arises, the average excess of actual value over the higher price of x (denoted g) is less than before. In addition, the average loss from purchasing more x at the wrong time (denoted l) is now higher than before the price of x went up. Each of these factors will increase the required reliability for purchasing x (i.e., the tolerance limit for purchasing x, $T = (l/g)(1 - \pi)/\pi$, will rise).

Given that T has risen, *how is the consumer to change his behavior to be more reliable in purchasing* x? A general answer is suggested in an extensive literature in behavioral psychology about signal detection experiments.[44] The earliest experiments were similar to hearing tests where a person tries to detect the presence of a signal amid background noise (over a sequence of trials where the signal's occurrence is randomly distributed). A variety of other detection skills have been tested, which involve pattern recognition situations and various information processing and other cognative skills. All of the experiments exhibit a key feature: a person can increase the reliability of his detection behavior only by being more cautious in detecting the signals. That is, greater reliability requires a person to reduce the probabil-

---

[44] See David Green and John Swets, 1974; James Egan, 1975. A brief appendix on the signal detection experiments (plus some further material on reliability principles suggested by these experiments) is available on request from the author.

ity of reacting regardless of whether the signal is present or not. Note that reliability in these experiments is measured by the r/w ratio used in the Reliability Condition (and reported in graphical form with ROC curves).[45]

Now apply this principle to detecting when to buy more of a commodity x. A person can be more reliable in purchasing x only by reducing the probability that potential influences will successively prompt him into purchasing (whether they be internal promptings, advertising, behavior of other consumers, or whatever).

Thus, we have a simple two-step syllogism: *a higher price requires purchasing behavior to be more reliable, which can be achieved only by reducing the probability of purchase.* This implication is essentially the law of demand for consumer behavior, yet without any qualification for income effects; nor must we use complicated Slutsky derivations, or other technical maximizing conditions. To some of us, the logic involved might even seem "too simple" compared to our intellectual investment in n-dimensional consumer theory. Nevertheless, in its simplicity is a clear, unambiguous implication of the Law of Demand, which we have never been able to derive with traditional optimizing methods.[46]

E. *Evolution of Property Rights, Trading, and Market Structure*

Let me sketch a scenario about the evolution of an exchange system. Suppose initially

that the reliable range of flexibility of agents' behavioral rules is more than sufficient to handle the complexity of the social environment (say in the primitive beginnings of human society). As a result, agent interactions evolve into more complex relationships in which the consequences from each agent's individual behavior depend on the actions of more and more other agents. In addition, the behavior of these other agents will become increasingly remote to the local experience of each agent as the network of social interdependencies broadens. Consequently, uncertainty in determining the consequences from selecting particular actions will successively increase for each agent in the society.

At some point, the evolution of more complex social interdependence will stop, unless social structures also evolve that reduce the scope of nonlocal information that individual agents must know to reliably forecast the consequences of their own behavior. (In more precise terms, the scope of information over which agents can reliably interpret successively narrows as the social environment becomes more complex.)

In general, further evolution toward social interdependence will require institutions that permit agents to know about successively smaller fractions of the larger social environment. That is, *institutions must evolve which enable each agent in the society to know less and less about the behavior of other agents and about the complex interdependencies generated by their interaction.*

One of the basic ways of accomplishing this is to divide up the decision authority to use resources so that only particular agents (or small groups of agents) have the right to control their use. With such a right-to-control institution, individual agents no longer have to know how other agents might use their "privately owned" resources. A whole range of factors that are within an agent's local experience can now be used to determine the consequences of particular use decisions. Two of the more important possibilities are decisions about whether to consume or delay the use of a resource, and about whether to transfer the right-to-control resources to other agents. Obtaining the right to control itself becomes valuable, given that

[45] ROC stands for "receiver operating characteristic"; see Green and Swets, pp. 31–34.

[46] The Reliability Condition also implies a number of other key empirical regularities that are not derivable from basic maximization theory (see fn. 5 above). Another implication is that behavior will be relatively sensitive to information that defines an agent's local frame of reference within the environment. This will produce "framing effects" studied by Kahneman and Tversky, and a number of other anomalies now widely recognized in the risk-behavior literature (see fn. 30 above). Still other examples include the "excessive reaction" of securities and futures markets to "current information"; the "tendency to ignore prior information" used in Bayesian probabilities; and the "insensitivity of judgments to sample size"; even by "professionally trained" econometricians (see Arrow, 1981, pp. 3–7).

only local information is now required to control the use of a resource.

In more basic terms, the question is whether agents will be willing to cooperate with each other through increasingly complex interdependencies that have the potential—if properly coordinated—to increase average output per agent. As the society becomes more complex, agents will cooperate only in ways that enable them to use increasingly local information to detect whether they will individually benefit. That is, they will exhibit a "propensity to cooperate" only in situations where increasingly local experience indicates a benefit—even if such restriction cuts off a whole range of benefits that might result from more subtly interconnected forms of cooperation. A major way of satisfying this restrictive criteria is to cooperate only in situations where agents immediately reciprocate the cooperative actions of each other, such that each perceives a net benefit based on his own self-evaluation of the forsaken and received items.

This form of reciprocation enables agents to decide based on immediately local experience about the results from cooperating. Thus, their tendency to cooperate in such situations will be relatively great compared to myriad other possibilities that would require the reliable use of more nonlocal information to avoid mistakes. (In more precise terms, we can show that the probability of agents cooperating in such situations will be much higher than for other forms of cooperation.) This limited tendency to cooperate can itself be regarded as a behavioral regularity, one that Adam Smith recognized as the "propensity to truck or barter." Notice also that such a propensity depends on a structure of property rights that enables agents' self-evaluations to determine the use of resources without knowing the behavior of other agents.

The above discussion is only a brief illustration of a large number of implications about legal and market institutions. These institutions will evolve so as to provide predictable opportunity for mutual reciprocation situations; and so as to reduce the scope and complexity of information that must be reliably interpreted for agents to benefit from

these situations. For example, a few implications include: a restriction to more centralized market organization and to financial instruments that enable agents to avoid knowing the particular circumstances, attributes, and identity of potential reciprocators and the items reciprocated; a severe restriction of futures markets and auction markets to certain strategic locations within a larger network of inventory markets structured so as to reduce price fluctuations;[47] and ownership structures that enable agents to avoid detecting whether continued reciprocation will be maintained, especially when this is necessary for particular reciprocators to realize longer term benefits or to prevent certain losses.[48] The essential factor in all of these institutional regularities is uncertainty in deciphering the complexity of the social environment.[49]

Finally, let me mention another key feature about the possibility of coordination failures. A complex cooperative system must somehow limit the occurrence of serious coordination failures. Nevertheless, its very complexity can evolve only to the extent that it enables agents to benefit without deciphering more than a tiny fraction of its overall structure. As a result, a complex system can-

---

[47]A few modern references on the above topics are: Alchian, 1969, 1977; Robert Clower, 1967; Clower and Leijonhufvud, 1975; Robert Jones, 1976; Seiichi Kawasaki et al., 1982; Lester Telser, 1981.

[48]The reliability model can be used both to predict the likelihood of opportunistic behavior (discontinuing reciprocation), and how the likelihood of such behavior affects the required reliability of various kinds of contractual arrangements. In many cases, the only solution is to structure ownership of assets in a way that eliminates having to detect when to engage in certain contracts. This will produce a stable regularity in contractual and market ownership patterns, which are also studied under the rubric of "transaction costs" (see Williamson, 1975, 1979, 1981, 1983; Benjamin Klein et al., 1978; also Alchian and Demsetz, 1972; Coase, 1937, 1960; Demsetz, 1969, 1967; Dahlman, 1980).

[49]Standard choice theory concentrates exclusively on the potential gains from trade (via Edgeworth exchange boxes, etc.), rather than on the effect of uncertainties created in trying to realize that potential. Consequently, we now have an elaborate general equilibrium theory of exchange which is devoid of the very institutional regularities necessary for complex exchange economies to evolve in the first place (see the epilogue of Vernon Smith, 1982, p. 952).

not prevent coordination failures that would require agents to understand a sizeable fraction of its complexity in order to avert them.

VI. Switching and Punctuation Dynamics

Recall the notation introduced above in Section IV, Part E, where $z = (s, c, m, e)$ represents an agent's sensory (s), cognitive (c), and morphological (m) components (hereafter denoted by $y = (s, c, m)$), along with the environmental variables e. Using these variables, we can analyze how uncertainty affects the dynamic response of behavioral rules, and how agents' internal components interact with each other and with the environment to generate evolutionary change in themselves and in the surrounding environment. Two key dynamic properties are conditioned by the transition point between satisfying or violating the Reliability Condition (i.e., the point at which $r/w = T$).

First: Changes in the environmental variables e may shift the reliability ratio r/w or the tolerance limit T of an action; causing them to "cross over" each other from their initial positions (i.e., shift r/w from below T to above it, or vice versa). If this happens, rule-governed behavior will switch from allowing to severely restricting that action. Thus, a relatively sudden "switching" between different behavior patterns may occur.

Second: If the reliability ratio of an action is initially bounded below its tolerance limit, then behavioral rules will prohibit that action. Now consider a small change in a particular component, $y^0 \in y$, which would shift r/w and T for such an action closer together, but not enough for them to cross over each other. So long as this is the case, there will be no change in an agent's behavior that might improve or worsen his performance, because the Reliability Condition for selecting that action is still violated. Suppose, however, that movement in some of the *other* z variables besides y^0 (which might include the e variables) shift r/w and T sufficiently for them to cross over each other.

At the point of transition, greater reliability from changes in y^0 will now allow selecting the action to improve an agent's performance; which may initiate evolutionary adjustment of y^0 in the appropriate direction. This means that the y attributes may exhibit relatively sudden increases or decreases in the speed of evolutionary change. Thus, evolutionary adjustment in the y attributes may be "punctuated" with a variety of sudden changes, especially as a large number of such attributes interact through an agent's behavioral rules, or the environment is itself influenced by the actions of other agents.

It is significant that a simple "crossover" mechanism will generate irregular dynamic movement in the outward behavior or internal attributes of an agent, and suggests an alternative to the recent attempts to account for such effects via catastrophe theory.[50] A recursive use of the Reliability Condition can also generate systematic hysteresis effects, in which the crossover point depends on the past history and direction of a variable's movement.[51]

A few examples to illustrate the above two dynamic properties are the following:

1) A number of implications characterize sudden switching of animal behavior between different actions, such as aggressive behavior in either attacking or retreating, or territorial behavior in either attack or defense strategies. A common example in economics involves switching between buying and selling strategies in financial markets, resulting in sudden movement in stock prices. In general, a wide range of behavior in economics is governed by such switching and hysteresis effects and has been obscured by the use of traditional optimization theory.

2) A specific economic illustration of the crossover mechanism is the "corridor hypothesis" for macroeconomic systems discussed above in Section V. Another example

---

[50] See E. C. Zeeman, 1977; Rene Thòm, 1975; David Berlinski, 1975; Hector Sussman, 1975.

[51] Consider very briefly a two-stage use of the Reliability Condition. First, $r/w = T$ is used to characterize a transition point between different behavior patterns. Second, introduce uncertainty about an agent trying to detect unstable shifts in this transition point. An agent may fail to switch once the transition point is reached, or he might mistakenly switch too early. A second application of the Reliability Condition implies that an agent will delay switching until he rarely switches too early; so that the observed switching point will shift depending on the action selected before the switch occurred.

is a structure of expectation "stages" during inflations (ranging from initially "sluggish" to eventually "explosive" expectation adjustment), which contrasts with recent rational expectations modeling.[52]

3) Growing evidence supports the "punctuation hypothesis" recently advanced in evolutionary biology, which claims that irregular bursts in the pace of evolutionary change have produced speciation and macroevolution of dramatic morphological changes (see Stephen Gould and Niles Eldredge, 1977; Steven Stanley, 1979).

4) An example of the latter which has been of considerable interest is the dramatic expansion of the cerebrum responsible for the higher thought processes of humans. Of all the various y attributes, the cerebrum most directly tends to prompt increasingly sophisticated behavior patterns. Right situations for selecting particular actions within a behavioral repertoire will become increasingly rare as the complexity of that repertoire increases.[53] This will cause a steeply rising acceleration in the required reliability for selecting these actions. Thus, if the second dynamic property above ever triggers rapid expansion of the cerebrum, then its sudden leveling off at a larger size is also implied. This dynamic pattern has been of interest and puzzlement in the biology literature.[54]

VII. Hierarchical Structure and Evolution of Reliable Complexity

We can also characterize how uncertainty may generate hierarchical structures of increasingly flexible rules. Such rule-hierarchies have far reaching applications, some of which are briefly discussed in the following remarks:

1) For example, consider a system of components that interact with each other at level v, while these interactions comprise a larger system that interacts within a surrounding environment at level $v + 1$. For simplicity, the relationship between a system and its subcomponents is functionally written, $s_{v+1}(s_v)$, where s_{v+1} denotes the system and s_v denotes its subcomponents. Thus, we have a recursive structure of rule-governed systems, $s_{v+1}(s_v)$, where each element of s_v is itself a system of components at the next lower level $v - 1$, denoted $s_v(s_{v-1})$.

2) Now, suppose that more simply structured subcomponents decrease the reliability of a system in administering more complex interactions with its environment. For example, such components might be more vulnerable in distinguishing nonlocal phenomena. For any given level of subcomponent structure, viable performance requires a minimum degree of behavioral rigidity. Thus no system composed of similarly structured components can allow greater flexibility without hindering its viability. Consequently, the only way more sophisticated behavior could arise from such systems is for a number of them to evolve into the subcomponents of a still larger system. Since the components of the larger system are recursively built up from smaller subsystems, additional structure may be permitted which enables them to reliably guide more complex behavior of a larger system. When this is possible, the behavior of the larger system can be less rigidly constrained than its component subsystems.

3) Recent discoveries in microbiology dramatically illustrate this implication. They show how molecular mechanisms direct the embryological unfolding of living systems. The essential feature of all of these mechanisms are large molecular structures (containing hundreds or thousands of atoms) that interact with each other literally by recognizing each other's shape. That is, they interact with noncovalent bonds which are very much weaker than the covalent bonds (i.e., the merging of electron clouds) of physical chemistry. Thus, stable bonding requires a relatively large surface closely matched to

[52] The explosive stage could refer to the final phase of a hyperinflation in which agent's expectations so quickly adjust that trying to counteract this reaction by further money supply acceleration will drive real balances toward zero.

[53] As an agent's behavior becomes more complex, each additional action must compete against more and more other actions. Thus, the likelihood of an additional action being more preferred than other actions is conditional on the behavioral complexity of an agent; and in general will decrease as the complexity of his repertoire increases.

[54] See, for example, Edward Wilson, 1975, pp. 547–50; Jerison, 1973, pp. 402–43; D. Pilbean, 1972.

584   THE AMERICAN ECONOMIC REVIEW   SEPTEMBER 1983

the shape of another molecule (which large surfaces require many atoms within each molecule).[55] Molecular shape enables the precise calibration of "stereo-specific" bonding, which permits a much more complex structure of interaction possibilities than otherwise possible with the more rigid constraints of physical chemistry. Moreover, the precise recognition properties of stereo-specific bonding enables the reliable direction of complicated molecular mechanisms, as evidenced in the biochemistry of cell regulation and embryological processes.[56] The significance of this is summarized by Nobel Prize biochemist Jacques Monod:[57]

> [Stereo-specific bonding gave] molecular evolution a practically limitless field for exploration and experiment, [which] enabled it to elaborate the huge network of cybernetic interconnections which makes each organism an autonomous functional unit, whose performances appear to transcend the laws of chemistry if not to ignore them altogether.   [1972, p. 78]

4) If the recursive structure, $s_{v+1}(s_v)$, is continued to higher or lower levels ($v+2$, $v+3,\dots$; or $v-1, v-2,\dots$) we obtain a hierarchical structure of increasingly sophisticated systems, where later stages are governed by successively more flexible rules. Such hierarchical structures represent a basic way systems conditioned by uncertainty can evolve into allowing successively more sophisticated behavior without hindering their viability in the process.

This pattern of hierarchical development is systematically evidenced in nature at a number of intertwining levels. For example, there are the invariable behavior patterns of atoms, which are composed of successively more basic subatomic particles; and which are themselves components of larger cosmological systems whose behavior is also synonymous with highly predictable laws.[58] Above this level, there is another hierarchy of organic molecules (discussed above) that eventually form components in living cells. Such cells in turn are subcomponents of still larger organs and tissues that permit relatively more flexible behavior of yet another hierarchy of increasingly sophisticated living organisms. Finally, there is the subtle, usually difficult to predict, behavior of humans and their social institutions. Looking back on this structure, the particular course of its evolution may be extremely improbable. Nevertheless, what did evolve has been through a hierarchical process from very predictable to relatively much less predictable phenomena.

5) Hierarchical structures may also have systematic importance in the design of cognitive and related (natural and artificial) learning processes.[59] For example, there may be

---

[58] The body of this paper has only briefly alluded to the physical sciences. At issue is whether the invariable regularities exhibited by natural phenomena can be regarded as "rule-mechanisms" to cope with extreme uncertainty in avoiding destabilizing interactions between the components of a system that might disintegrate its structure? More generally, what patterns of component interaction are viable in the sense of generating their own continuation, or the continuation of larger interactive patterns between components which are themselves systems? Many topics in the physical sciences could be discussed, but only three topics are mentioned here. First, we can analyze uncertainty in producing stable macrostructures to characterize relationships between the "particles" of matter and the "forces" that interconnect them. Second, we can consider uncertainty in maintaining the structural stability of tightly compacted systems to characterize symmetry properties, and other statistical regularities studied in quantum mechanics. Third, we can analyze the effects of violating the general relativity postulate of modern physics, especially about uncertainties in dealing with complex interdependencies permitted without the constraint of generally covariant interactions. On these three topics see respectively: P. C. W. Davies, 1979; J. P. Elliot and P. G. Dawber, 1979; Enrico Cantore, 1969; Albert Einstein, 1952, 1956.

Underlying these regularities is a persistent theme about the unity of science, as suggested in the following remark by Einstein: "The most incomprehensible thing about the universe is why it is so comprehensible." (See also the closing remarks of Kuhn's 1962 essay, p. 173.) The answer may lie in how extreme uncertainty affects the structure of self-continuing physical systems.

[59] See Simon, 1969, 1979a; Newell and Simon, 1972; J. R. Anderson, 1980; G. T. Miller et al., 1960.

---

[55] See J. Monod, 1972, pp. 45–46.

[56] See J. Monod, 1972, chs. 4–7.

[57] For a recent more technical overview of the subject, see James Watson, 1976.

resistance to knowledge not built up in recursive stages. For example, explicitly hierarchical methods have evolved in the above-mentioned strategy books on playing black-jack, and more recently on how to solve Rubik's cube.[60]

6) It has also been argued by Kohlberg, with extensive supporting experimentation, that the moral development of children as they mature into adults follows a highly patterned hierarchical structure of six stages. The first stage is guided by "blind obedience to rules and authority...," which proceeds though intermediate steps to stage six, which is "guided by self-chosen ethical principles."[61] A pattern of successively more complex moral judgments is clearly suggested in this hierarchy.

7) The viability of an evolving system, (for example an ecological system of organisms, or an exchange system of competing agents), which originates truly novel change (whose interactive possibilities are largely unrelated to the system's past history) may be quite sensitive to uncertainty in avoiding disruptive novelty. If this is the case, the very processes which generate and select such novelty will themselves be organized in a hierarchical structure of increasingly flexible rule-mechanisms. An important illustration is the structure of relationships that connect the rigidly patterned molecular design of DNA to the more visible interactions comprising natural selection.[62]

Other implications characterize the diversity and pace of novel change that can be reliably controlled by an evolving system. For example, a more rapid average pace is permitted as the reliability of selective processes increases. These implications underly the major differences in the qualitative nature and average speed of cultural compared to biological evolution.

VIII. Conclusion

I have argued that uncertainty is the basic source of predictable behavior, and also the main conditioning factor of evolutionary processes through which such behavior evolves. Uncertainty exists because agents cannot decipher all of the complexity of the decision problems they face, which literally prevents them from selecting most preferred alternatives. Consequently, the flexibility of behavior to react to information is constrained to smaller behavioral repertoires that can be reliably administered. Numerous deviations from the resulting behavior patterns are actually superior in certain situations, but they are still ignored because of uncertainty about when to deviate from these regularities.

In contrast, standard economics analyzes the special case of no uncertainty in selecting most preferred options. This way of understanding behavior forces the determinants of uncertainty into the residual "error term" between observed behavior and the more systematic patterns claimed to result from optimization. I am thus suggesting a reversal of the explanation assumed in standard economics: the factors that standard theory places in the error term are in fact what is producing behavioral regularities, while optimizing will tend to produce sophisticated deviations from these patterns. Hence, the

---

[60]A good example of a hierarchical method is Kosniowski, 1981, especially in contrast to David Singmaster, 1979 (called the "definitive treatise" by *Scientific American*), which follows a complex, cyclical development of ideas that switches back and forth between different parts of the book. Singmaster's book is also several times longer than later books (cited above in fn. 14), both in terms of number of words and notational density.

[61]See Kohlberg, 1976, pp. 30 and 32; and 1963, 1969.

[62]Consider the extreme uncertainty of tiny molecular structures directing the construction of living systems. Maurice Wilkin's 1953 paper (which accompanied Watson and Cricks' original paper in *Nature*) begins: "While the biological properties of deoxypentose nucleic acid suggest a molecular structure containing great complexity, X-ray diffraction studies described here show the basic molecular configuration has great simplicity" (p. 738). The Reliability Condition implies the opposite

presumption; namely, that precisely because DNA is the ultimate source of larger biological systems, whose complexity cannot be reliably manipulated from any interaction local to its tiny structure, its internal design must be both rigidly patterned and engineered to replicate virtually without guidance from its local chemical environment.

observed regularities that economics has tried to explain on the basis of optimization would disappear if agents could actually maximize.

Another basic conclusion is that appropriately structured behavioral rules will not necessarily arise. Rather, they will evolve to the extent that selection processes quickly eliminate poorly administered behavior. This will more likely occur when agents are involved in highly competitive interactions that themselves indirectly result from scarcity. However, if weak selection processes are present, relatively vulnerable or dysfunctional behavior may evolve.

One area of major normative significance is the development of human social institutions; in particular, political institutions that have the opportunity to influence the outcomes generated by exchange competition. This is especially important if human agents are able to foresee numerous potential cases where the cooperative results of exchange institutions could be improved, but without being able to reliably administer the additional complexity necessary to realize those improvements.

Think of this issue in terms of the Reliability Condition. People may be able to identify government actions where situations exist in which a society will benefit (i.e., the probability of right circumstances π for selecting these actions is positive). Nevertheless, they may be unable to administer these actions with sufficient reliability to benefit the society by adding them to the government's repertoire of authorized activities (i.e., $r/w < T$ even though $\pi > 0$). If this is the case, the society will benefit by appropriately limiting the scope and complexity of government behavior.

But how is such limitation to arise? It is here that we enter the area of "constitutionalism," defined broadly as the design of rule-mechanisms to restrict the flexibility of government to react to whatever influences might prompt it to engage in vulnerable activities. The writings of seventeenth- and eighteenth-century political philosophers and statesmen were primarily concerned with these issues. Out of their efforts came a number of features incorporated in

the United States Constitution, such as the separation of powers mechanism.[63]

On a wider scale, the history of civilization can be organized around a theme of groping for social rule-mechanisms.[64] Nevertheless, the understanding of such mechanisms is only in its rudimentary beginnings; and in the last hundred years, the general trend has been away from these topics—especially for analysts trained in mainstream economic theory.[65] The reason is that mainstream theories have systematically directed attention away from the study of processes that limit flexibility to choose potentially preferred actions. A refocusing of research on such processes—with the appropriate analytical framework to guide us—may have practical consequences for the viability of existing institutions.

[63] The basic source materials on these issues are the Federalist Papers by Hamilton and Jefferson (for example, numbers 10, 47, 48, 51). For a modern reference, see Martin Diamond, 1981.

[64] The often seemingly bizarre practices of religion and cultural ritual may also represent the design technologies of social rules crucial to the coordination and intensification of social bonds. For some interesting readings about ritual, symbolism, and comparative religion, see William Lessa and Evon Vogt, 1979, and M. Gluckman, 1962.

[65] Notable exceptions to this general trend are the writings of Buchanan and Hayek (see fn. 31 above).

REFERENCES

Abernathy, William J., *The Productivity Dilemma*: *Roadblock to Innovation in the Automobile Industry*, Baltimore: Johns Hopkins University Press, 1978.

_____, **Clark, Kim and Kantrow, A.**, "The New Industrial Competition," *Harvard Business Review*, September-October 1981, *59*, 68–81.

Alchian, Armen A., "Uncertainty, Evolution and Economic Theory," *Journal of Political Economy*, June 1950, *58*, 211–21.

_____, "Information Costs, Pricing and Resource Unemployment," *Western Economic Journal*, June 1969, *7*, 109–28.

_____, "Why Money?," *Journal of Money,*

Credit, and Banking, February 1977, *9*, 133–40.

_____ and Demsetz, Harold, "Production, Information Costs, and Economic Efficiency," *American Economic Review*, December 1972, *62*, 777–95.

Alcock, John, *Animal Behavior: An Evolutionary Approach*, Sunderland: Sinauer Associates, 1979.

Aldrich, R., *Organization and Environments*, Englewood Cliffs: Prentice-Hall, 1979.

Alexander, Richard, *Darwinism and Public Affairs*, Seattle: University of Washington Press, 1979.

_____ and Borgin, G., "Group Selection, Altruism, and the Levels of Organization of Life," *Annual Review of Ecology and Systematics*, September 1978, *9*, 449–75.

Anderson, Ian, *Turning the Tables on Las Vegas*, New York: Harper & Row, 1975.

Anderson, J. R., *Cognitive Psychology and Its Implications*, San Francisco: W. H. Freeman, 1980.

Archer, John, *The Archer Method of Winning at 21*, Hollywood: Wilshire Book Company, 1973.

Arrow, Kenneth J., "Risk Perception in Psychology and Economics," *Economic Inquiry*, January 1981, *20*, 1–9.

_____, "Vertical Integration and Communication," *Bell Journal of Economics*, Spring 1975, *6*, 173–83.

Ashby, W., *An Introduction to Cybernetics*, New York: Wiley, 1956.

Athos, Anthony G. and Pascale, Richard T., *The Art of Japanese Management*, New York: Simon & Schuster, 1981.

Axelrod, Robert, (1980a) "Effective Choice in the Prisoner's Dilemma," *Journal of Conflict Resolution*, March 1980, *24*, 3–25.

_____, (1980b) "More Effective Choice in the Prisoner's Dilemma," *Journal of Conflict Resolution*, September 1980, *24*, 379–403.

Barlow, B. W., *The Cube: A Short and Easy Solution*, Salt Lake City: Hawkes Publishing, 1981.

Berlinski, David, "Mathematical Models of the World," *Synthese*, August 1975, *31*, 211–27.

Black, M. R. and Taylor, H., *Unscrambling the Cube*, Burbank: Zephyr Engineering Design, 1980.

Blackwell, David and Girshick, M. A., *Theory of Games and Statistical Decisions*, New York: Dover, 1979.

Bookstaber, Richard and Langsam, Joseph, "Coarse Behavior and Extended Uncertainty," Working Paper 83–1, Graduate School of Management, Brigham Young University, 1983.

Boland, Lawrence, A., "On the Futility of Criticizing the Neoclassical Maximization Hypothesis," *American Economic Review*, December 1981, *71*, 1031–36.

Bradshaw, C. M., Szabadi, E. and Bevan, R., "Behavior of Humans in Variable-Interval Schedules of Reinforcement," *Journal of the Experimental Analysis of Behavior*, September 1976, *26*, 135–41.

Brown, Roger and Herrnstein Richard, *Psychology*, Boston: Little-Brown, 1975.

Buchanan, James M., *Freedom in Constitutional Contract*, College Station: Texas A&M University Press, 1977.

_____, *The Limits of Liberty: Between Anarchy and the Leviathan*, Chicago: University of Chicago Press, 1975.

_____ and Brennan H. G., *Monopoly in Money and Inflation*, London: Institute for Economic Affairs, 1981.

Buskist, William F. and Miller, Harold L., Jr., "Concurrent Operant Performance in Humans: Matching When Food is the Reinforcer," *Psychological Record*, January 1981, *31*, 95–100.

Bussert, Patrick, *You Can Do the Cube*, New York: Puffin Books, 1981.

Cagan, Phillip, "The Monetary Dynamics of Hyperinflation," in M. Friedman, ed., *Studies in the Quantity Theory of Money*, Chicago: University of Chicago Press, 1956.

Caldwell, B., *Beyond Positivism: Economic Methodology In the Twentieth Century*, London: Allen & Unwin, 1982.

Campbell, Donald C., "On the Conflicts Between Biological and Social Evolution and Between Psychology and Moral Tradition," *American Psychologist*, December 1975, *30*, 1103–26.

_____, "Downward Causation in Hierarchically Organized Biological Systems," in F. J. Ayala and T. Dobzhausky, eds., *Studies in the Philosophy of Biology*, New York: Macmillan, 1974.

Canfield, Richard A., *Blackjack: Your Way to Riches*, Secaucus: Lyle Stuart, Inc., 1979.

Cantore, Enrico, *Atomic Order: An Introduction to the Philosophy of Microphysics*, Cambridge: MIT Press, 1969.

Cardoza, Avery D., *Winning Casino Blackjack for the Noncounter*, Santa Cruz: Cardoza School of Blackjack, 1981.

Carter, C. F. and Williams, B. R., *Industry and Technical Progress: Factors Governing the Speed of Application of Science*, New York: Oxford University, 1957.

Cavelli-Sforza, L., and Feldman, Marcus, *Cultural Transmission & Evolution: A Quantitative Approach*, Princeton: Princeton University, 1981.

Chandler, Alfred D., *Strategy and Structure: Chapters in the History of Industrial Enterprise*, Cambridge: MIT Press, 1962.

_____, *The Visible Hand: The Managerial Revolution in American Business*, Cambridge: Belknap Press, 1977.

Cheung, Steven, "Transactions Costs, Risk Aversion, and the Choice of Contractual Arrangements," *Journal of Law and Economics*, April 1969, *12*, 23–42.

Chew, S. H. and MacCrimmon, K. R., (1979a) "Alpha-Nu Choice Theory: A Generalization of Expected Utility Theory," Working Paper No. 669, University of British Columbia, 1979.

_____ and _____, (1979b) "Alpha Utility Theory, Lottery Composition, and the Allais Paradox," Working Paper No. 686, University of British Columbia, 1979.

Chomsky, N., *Language and Mind*, New York: Harcourt, Brace & Jovanovich, 1972.

Clark, R., *The Japanese Company*, New Haven: Yale University Press, 1979.

Clower, Robert W., "The Keynesian Counterrevolution: A Theoretical Appraisal," in F. Hahn and F. Brechling eds., *The Theory of Interest Rates*, London: Macmillan, 1965.

_____, "A Reconsideration of the Microfoundations of Monetary Theory," *Western Economic Journal*, December 1967, *6*, 1–8.

_____ and Leijonhufvud, Axel, "The Coordination of Economic Activities: A Keynesian Perspective," *American Economic Review Proceedings*, May 1975, *65*, 182–88.

Coase, Ronald H., "The Nature of the Firm," *Economica*, November 1937, *4*, 386–405.

_____, "The Problem of Social Cost," *Journal of Law and Economics*, October 1960, *3*, 1–44.

_____, "Adam Smith's View of Man," *Journal of Political Economy*, October 1976, *19*, 529–46.

Cohen, Michael D. and Axelrod, Robert, "Coping with Complexity: The Adaptive Value of Changing Utility," *American Economic Review*, forthcoming.

Conner, M., *The Tangled Wing: Biological Constraints on the Human Spirit*, New York: Basic Books, 1982.

Conrath, D., "From Statistical Decision Theory to Practice: Some Problems with the Transition," *Management Science*, April 1973, *19*, 873–94.

Cooley, Thomas F. and LeRoy, Stephen F., "Identification and Estimation of Money Demand," *American Economic Review*, December 1981, *71*, 825–44.

Cooter, Robert, (1982a) "The Cost of Coase," *Journal of Legal Studies*, January 1982, *11*, 1–34.

_____, Marks, Stephen and Mnookin, Robert, (1982b) "Bargaining in the Shadow of the Law: A Testable Model of Strategic Behavior," *Journal of Legal Studies*, June 1982, *11*, 225–52.

Dahlman, Carl, *The Open Field System and Beyond*, Cambridge: Cambridge University Press, 1980.

Davies, P. C. W., *The Forces of Nature*, Cambridge: Cambridge University Press, 1979.

Demsetz, Harold, "Information and Efficiency: Another Viewpoint," *Journal of Law and Economics*, April 1969, *12*, 1–22.

_____, "Toward a Theory of Property Rights," *American Economic Review Proceedings*, May 1967, *57*, 347–59.

de Villiers, P., "Choice in Concurrent Schedules and a Quantitative Formulation of the Law of Effect," in W. K. Honig and J. E. R. Standdon, eds., *Handbook of Operant Behavior*, Englewood Cliffs: Prentice-Hall, 1977, 233–87.

Diamond, Martin, *The Founding of the Democratic Republic*, Itasca: Peacock, 1981.

Diamond, Peter and Rothschild, Michael, *Uncertainty in Economics*, New York: Academic Press, 1978.

Dornbusch, Rudiger and Fischer, Stanley, *Macro-Economics*, New York: McGraw-Hill, 1978.

Drèze, Jacques H., "Axiomatic Theories of Choice, Cardinal Utility, and Subjective Probability," a review in his *Allocation Under Uncertainty: Equilibrium and Optimality*, New York: Wiley, 1974, 1–23; reprinted in P. Diamond and M. Rothschild, eds., *Uncertainty in Economics*, New York: Academic Press, 1978, 37–57.

Dubey, Leon B., Jr., *No Need to Count: A Practical Approach to Casino Blackjack*, San Diego: A.S. Barnes & Co., 1980.

Edwards, Ward, "Subjective Probabilities Inferred from Decisions," *Psychological Review*, March 1962, *69*, 109–35.

Egan, James P., *Signal Detection Theory and ROC Analysis*, New York: Academic Press, 1975.

Einstein, Albert, *The Meaning of Relativity: Including the Relativistic Theory of the Non-Symmetric Field*, Princeton: Princeton University Press, 1956.

_____, *The Principle of Relativity*, New York: Dover, 1952.

Elliot, J. P. and Dawber, P. G., *Symmetry in Physics*, Vols. 1; 2, London: Macmillan, 1979.

Elster, John, *Ulyssess and the Sirens*, Cambridge: Cambridge University Press, 1979.

Fellner, William, "Distortion of Subjective Probabilities as a Reaction to Uncertainty," *Quarterly Journal of Economics*, November 1961, *75*, 670–90.

Ferguson, Thomas S., *Mathematical Statistics: A Decision Theoretic Approach*, New York: Academic Press, 1967.

Fishburn, Peter C., "Transitive Measurable Utility," Discussion Paper No. 224, Bell Laboratories, 1981.

Fischer, Stanley, "Long Term Contracts, Rational Expectations, and the Optimal Money Supply Rule," *Journal of Political Economy*, February 1977, *85*, 191–206.

Friedman, Milton, "The Methodology of Positive Economics," in his *Essays in Positive Economics*, 1953; reprinted in W. Breit and H. M. Hochman, eds., *Readings in Microeconomics*, New York: Holt, Rinehart & Winston, 1968, 23–47.

_____, *A Program for Monetary Stability*, New York: Fordham University Press, 1969.

_____ and Savage, L. J., "The Utility Analysis of Choices Involving Risks," *Journal of Political Economy*, August 1948, *56*, 279–304.

Gibson, J., "The Theory of Affordances," in R. E. Shaw and J. Bransford, eds., *Perceiving, Acting, and Knowing*, Hillsdale: Lawrence Erlbaum Assoc., 1977.

Gluckman, M., *Essays on the Ritual of Social Relations*, Manchester: Manchester University Press, 1962.

Gould, Stephen J. and Eldredge, Niles, "Punctuated Equilibria: The Tempo and Mode of Evolution Reconsidered," *Paleobiology*, January 1977, *3*, 115–51.

Graham, Virginia L. and Tulcea, C. Ionescu, *A Book on Casino Gambling*, New York: Pocket Books, 1978.

Green, David M. and Swets, John A., *Signal Detection Theory and Psychophysics*, New York: Robert Kriegur, 1974.

Grinder, R., "Parental Childrearing Practices, Conscience, and Resistance to Temptation of Sixth-Grade Children," *Child Development*, December 1962, *33*, 802–20.

Hahn, Frank, *On the Notion of Equilibrium in Economics*, Cambridge: Cambridge University Press, 1973.

Hamilton, W. D., "The Genetical Evolution of Social Behavior," *Journal of Theoretical Biology*, 1964, *7*, 1–17.

Hayek, F. A., *Studies in Philosophy, Politics, and Economics*, Chicago: University of Chicago Press, 1967.

_____, *Law, Legislation, and Liberty*, Chicago: University of Chicago Press, 1973.

Heiner, Ronald A., "A Theory of Predictable Behavior: Application to Insurance Behavior Anomolies," Department of Economics, Brigham Young University, February 1982.

Heisenberg, Werner, *The Physical Principles of the Quantum Theory*, New York: Dover, 1949.

Herrnstein, Richard J., "On the Law of Effect," *Journal of the Experimental Analysis of Behavior*, November 1970, *13*, 243–66.

_____, "Relative and Absolute Strength of Response as a Function of Frequency of Reinforcement," *Journal of the Experimental Analysis of Behavior*, 1961, *4*, 267–72.

_____, "Secondary Reinforcement and Rate of Primary Reinforcement," *Journal of the Experimental Analysis of Behavior*, January 1964, *7*, 74–91.

_____ and Heyman, Gene M., "Is Matching Compatible with Maximization in Concurrent Variable Interval, Variable Ratio?," *Journal of the Experimental Analysis of Behavior*, March 1979, *31*, 209–23.

_____ and Vaughan, W., "Melioration and Behavioral Allocation," in J. E. R. Staddon, ed., *Limits to Action: The Allocation of Individual Behavior*, New York: Academic Press, 1980, 143–76.

Hess, W. R., *Imprinting: Early Experience and the Developmental Psychobiology of Attachment*, New York: Van Nostrand 1973.

Hetherington, E. Mavis and Park, Ross D., *Child Psychology: A Contemporary Viewpoint*, 2d ed., New York: McGraw-Hill, 1979.

Hey, John D., *Uncertainty in Microeconomics*, New York: New York University Press, 1979.

Heyman, Gene M. and Luce, R. Duncan, "Operant Matching is not a Logical Consequence of Maximizing Reinforcement Rate," *Animal Learning and Behavior*, May 1979, *7*, 133–40.

Hicks, John, "A Suggestion for Simplifying the Theory of Money," *Economica*, February 1935, *2*, 1–19.

Hirshleifer, Jack, "Evolutionary Models in Economics and the Law: Cooperation Versus Conflict Strategies," *Research in Law and Economics*, 1982, *4*, 1–60.

_____, "Economics from a Biological Viewpoint," *Journal of Law and Economics*, April 1977, *20*, 1–54.

_____, *Price Theory and Applications*, 2d ed., Englewood Cliffs: Prentice-Hall, 1980.

_____ and Riley, John, "The Analytics of Uncertainty and Information," *Journal of Economic Literature*, December 1979, *17*, 1375– 421.

Hoffman, Eric and Spitzer, Mathew, "The Coase Theorem: Some Experimental Tests," *Journal of Law and Economics*, April 1982, *25*, 73–98.

Hogarth, R. M., "Cognitive Processes and the Assessment of Subjective Probability Distributions," *Journal of the American Statistical Association*, June 1975, *70*, 271–94.

Holmes, Warren G. and Sherman, Paul W., "Kin Selection in Animals," *American Scientist*, January-February 1983, *7*, 46–56.

Howard, N., *Paradoxes of Rationality*, Cambridge: MIT Press, 1971.

Jerison, Harry, *Evolution of the Brain and Intelligence*, New York: Academic Press, 1973.

Jones, Robert, "On the Origin and Development of Media of Exchange," *Journal of Political Economy*, August 1976, *84*, 757–76.

Judson, Horace F., *The Eighth Day of Creation*, New York: Simon & Schuster, 1979.

Kahneman, Daniel and Tversky, Amos, "Prospect Theory: An Analysis of Decision Under Risk," *Econometrica*, March 1979, *47*, 263–91.

_____ and _____, "The Framing of Decisions and the Psychology of Choice," *Science Magazine*, January 30, 1981, *211*, 453–58.

_____ and _____, "The Psychology of Preferences," *Scientific American*, January 1982, *246*, 160–73.

Kawasaki, Seiichi, McMillan, John and Zimmerman, Klaus F., "Disequilibrium Dynamics: An Empirical Study," *American Economic Review*, December 1982, *72*, 992–1004.

Keeney, Ralph L. and Raiffa, Howard, *Decisions with Multiple Objectives: Preference and Value Tradeoffs*, New York: Wiley, 1976.

Keeton, William, *Biological Science*, 3d ed., New York: Norton, 1980.

Kirzner, Israel M., *Competition and Entrepreneurship*, Chicago: University of Chicago Press, 1973.

Klein, Benjamin, Crawford, Robert and Alchian, Armen, "Vertical Integration, Appropriable Rents, and the Competitive Contracting Process," *Journal of Law and Economics*, October 1978, *21*, 297–326.

_____ and Leffler, Keith, "The Role of Market Performance in Assuring Contractual Performance," *Journal of Political*

Economy, October 1981, *89*, 810–34.

Knight, Frank, *Risk, Uncertainty and Profit*, Boston: Houghton Mifflin, 1921.

Kohlberg, Lawrence, "Stage and Sequence: The Cognitive-Developmental Approach to Socialization," in D. A. Goshn, ed., *Handbook of Socialization Theory and Research*, New York: Rand McNally, 1969, 347–480.

——, "The Development of Children's Orientation Toward Moral Order: Sequence in the Development of Moral Thought," *Vita Humana*, January 1963, *3*, 11–33.

——, "The Domain and Development of Moral Judgment: A Theory and Method of Assessment," in his et al., eds., *Assessing Moral Judgment States: A Manual*, New York: Humanities Press, 1976, 14–45.

——, "Cognitive Stages and Preschool Education," *Human Development*, January 1966, *9*, 5–17.

——, "Justice as Reversibility," in P. Laslett and J. Fishkin, eds., *Philosophy, Politics, and Society*, New Haven: Yale University Press, 1979.

Konner, M., *The Tangled Wing: Biological Constraints on the Human Spirit*, New York: Basic Books, 1982.

Kosniowski, Czes, *Conquer that Cube*, Cambridge: Cambridge University Press, 1981.

Kreps, David et al., "Rational Cooperation in the Finitely Repeated Prisoner's Dilemma," *Journal of Economic Theory*, August 1982, *27*, 245–52.

Kuhn, Thomas, *The Structure of Scientific Revolutions*, Chicago: University of Chicago Press, 1962.

Kunreuther, Howard et al., *Disaster Insurance Protection*, New York: Wiley, 1978.

Kydland, Finn E. and Prescott, Edward C., "Rules Rather Than Discretion: The Inconsistency of Optimal Plans," *Journal of Political Economy*, June 1977, *85*, 473–91.

Lakatos, Imer and Musgrave, Alice, *Criticism and the Growth of Knowledge*, Cambridge: Cambridge University Press, 1970.

Langlois, Richard, "Internal Organization in a Dynamic Context: Some Theoretical Considerations," Economic Research Report No. 83–04, C. V. Starr Center for Applied Economics, New York University, January 1983.

Leamer, Edward, "'Explaining Your Results' As Access Biased Memory," *Journal of the American Statistical Association*, March 1975, *70*, 88–93.

——, *Specification Searches: Ad-Hoc Inference With Nonexperimental Data*, New York: Wiley, 1978.

Leblebici, Huseyin and Salanik, Gerald R., "Effects of Environmental Uncertainty on Information and Decision Processes in Banks," *Administrative Science Quarterly*, December 1981, *26*, 578–96.

—— and ——, "Stability in Interorganizational Exchange: Rulemaking Processes of the Chicago Board of Trade," *Administrative Science Quarterly*, June 1982, *27*, 227–42.

Leibenstein, Harvey, "Allocative Efficiency vs. X-Efficiency," *American Economic Review*, June 1966, *56*, 392–415.

Leijonhufvud, Axel, *On Keynesian Economics and the Economics of Keynes*, New York: Oxford University Press, 1968.

——, *Information and Coordination*, New York: Oxford University Press, 1981.

——, "Life Among the Econ," *Western Economic Journal*, September 1973, *11*, 327–37.

Lessa, William and Vogt, Evon, *Reader in Comparative Religion: An Anthropological Approach*, New York: Harper & Row, 1979.

Levins, Richard, *Evolution in Changing Environments*, Princeton: Princeton University Press, 1968.

Lippman, Stephen and McCall, John, "The Economics of Job Search: A Survey," *Economic Inquiry*, June 1979, *14*, 155–89.

Loomes, Graham and Sugden, Robert "Regret Theory: An Alternative Theory of Rational Choice Under Uncertainty," Department of Economics Working Paper, University of Newcastle-upon-Tyne, 1982.

—— and ——, "A Rationale for Preference Reversal," *American Economic Review*, June 1983, *73*, 428–32.

Lorenz, Konrad, *The Foundations of Ethology*, New York: Springer-Verlag, 1981.

Lucas, Robert E., Jr., "An Equilibrium Model of the Business Cycle," *Journal of Political Economy*, December 1975, *83*, 1113–44.

——, "Expectations and the Neutrality of Money," *Journal of Economic Theory*, April

1972, *4*, 103–24.

——, "Rules, Discretion, and the Role of the Economics Advisor," in S. Fischer, ed., *Rational Expectations and Economic Policy*, Chicago: University of Chicago Press, 1980, 199–210.

——, *Studies in Business Cycle Theory*, Cambridge: MIT Press, 1981.

Lumsden, Charles J. and Wilson, Edward O., *Genes, Mind, & Culture: The Coevolutionary Process*, Cambridge: Harvard University Press, 1981.

McFarland, David, *The Oxford Companion to Animal Behavior*, New York: Oxford University Press, 1982.

Machina, Mark, "Expected Utility Analysis Without the Independence Axiom," *Econometrica*, March 1982, *50*, 277–323.

March, James G., "Bounded Rationality, Ambiguity, and the Engineering of Choice," *Bell Journal of Economics*, Autumn 1978, *9*, 587–608.

Masterton, R., Hodos, William and Jerison, Harry, *Evolution, Brain, and Behavior: Persistent Problems*, New York: Wiley, 1976.

Maynard Smith, John, "Group Selection and Kin Selection," *Nature*, March 14, 1964, *201*, 1145–47.

Mayr, Ernst, *Populations, Species, and Evolution*, Cambridge: Belknap, 1970.

—— and Provine, W., *The Evolutionary Synthesis: Perspectives on the Unification of Biology*, Cambridge: Harvard University Press, 1980.

Mazur, John E., "Optimization Theory Fails to Predict Performance of Pigeons in a Two-Response Situation," *Science*, September 1981, *214*, 823–5.

Menger, Carl, *Principles of Economics*, (1871), trans. by James Dingwall and Bert F. Hozelitz, eds., New York: New York University Press, 1981.

——, *Problems In Economics and Sociology*, (1883), trans. by F. J. Nock, Urbana: University of Illinois Press, 1963.

Michaels, C. F. and Carello, C., *Direct Perception*, Englewood Cliffs: Prentice-Hall, 1981.

Miller, G. T., Galanter, E. and Pribram, K. H., *Plans and the Structure of Behavior*, New York: Holt, 1960.

Miller, James G., *Living Systems*, New York:

McGraw-Hill, 1978.

Mondon, Y., "What Makes the Toyota Production System Really Tick," *Industrial Engineering Magazine*, January 1981, *17*, 37–46.

Monod, Jacques, *Chance and Necessity*, New York: Random House (Vintage Books), 1972.

Montgomery, Viscount, *A History of Warfare*, Cleveland: World Publishing, 1968.

Montross, L., *War Through the Ages*, New York: Harper & Brothers, 1960.

Muth, Richard, "Rational Expectations and the Theory of Price Movements," *Econometrica*, July 1961, *29*, 315–35.

Nelson, Richard, "Research on Productivity Growth and Productivity Differences: Dead Ends and New Departures," *Journal of Economic Literature*, September 1981, *19*, 1029–64.

—— and Winter, Sidney, *An Evolutionary Theory of Economic Capabilities and Behavior*, Cambridge: Harvard University Press, 1982.

—— and ——, "Neoclassical Versus Evolutionary Theories of Economic Growth," *Economic Journal*, December 1974, *84*, 886–905.

Newell, A. and Simon, Herbert, *Human Problem Solving*, Englewood Cliffs: Prentice-Hall, 1972.

Nourse, James G., *The Simple Solution to Rubik's Cube*, New York: Bantam Books, 1980.

Okun, Arthur M., "Inflation: Its Mechanics and Welfare Cost," *Brookings Papers on Economic Activity*, 2: 1975, 351–401.

——, *Prices and Quantities: A Macroeconomic Analysis*, Washington: The Brookings Institution, 1981.

Ouchi, William, *Theory Z*, New York: Avon Publishers, 1981.

Pauli, Wolfgang, *Theory of Relativity*, New York: Dover, 1981.

Phelps, Edmond, "Okun's Micro-Macro System: A Review Article," *Journal of Economic Literature*, September 1981, *19*, 1065–73.

Piaget, J., *The Psychology of Intelligence*, London: Routledge & Kegan Paul, 1947.

——, *The Origins of Intelligence*, New York: International Universities Press,

1952.

Pianka, Eric R., *Evolutionary Ecology*, 2d ed., New York: Harper & Row, 1978.

Pilbean, D., *The Ascent of Man: An Introduction to Human Evolution*, New York: Macmillan, 1972.

Popper, Karl, *Conjectures and Refutations: The Growth of Scientific Knowledge*, 3d ed., rev., London: Routledge & Kegan Paul, 1969.

_____, *The Logic of Scientific Discovery*, New York: Basic Books, 1959.

Posner, Richard, *Economic Analysis of Law*, 2d ed., Boston: Little-Brown, 1977.

_____, "A Theory of Primative Society, With Special Reference to Primative Law," *Journal of Law and Economics*, April 1980, *23*, 1–54.

Prelec, D., "Matching, Maximizing, and the Hyperbolic Reinforcement Feedback Function," *Psychological Review*, March 1982, *89*, 189–230.

Premack, David, *The Mind of an Ape*, New York: Norton, 1983.

Priest, George L., "The Common Law Process and the Selection of Efficient Rules," *Journal of Legal Studies*, January 1977, *6*, 65–83.

Rachlin, Howard, Kagel, John H. and Battalio, R. C., "Substitutability in Time Allocation," *Psychological Review*, July 1980, *87*, 355–74.

Rawls, John, *A Theory of Justice*, Cambridge: Harvard University Press, 1971.

Revere, Lawrence, *Playing Blackjack as a Business*, Secaucus: Lyle Stuart, Inc., 1969.

Roughgarden, Jeffrey D., "Reasons and Rules in Choice: A Framework for Analysis," Department of Engineering Economics Systems, Stanford University, December 1982.

Rowan, B., "Organizational Structure and the Institutional Environment: The Case of Public Schools," *Administrative Science Quarterly*, June 1982, *27*, 259–79.

Rozin, P., "The Evolution of Intelligence and Access to the Cognative Unconscious," in J. A. Spague and A. N. Epstein, eds., *Progress in Psychobiology and Physiological Psychology*, Vol. 6, New York: Academic Press, 1976, 245–80.

Sagan, Carl, *The Dragons of Eden*, New York: Random House, 1977.

Samuelson, Paul A., *Foundations of Economic Analysis*, Cambridge: Harvard University Press, 1947.

Sargent, Thomas J., *Macroeconomic Theory*, New York: Academic Press, 1979.

_____, (1976a) "A Classical Macroeconometric Model for the United States," *Journal of Political Economy*, March-April 1976, *84*, 207–37.

_____, (1976b) "The Observational Equivalence of Natural and Unnatural Rate Theories of Macroeconomics," *Journal of Political Economy*, May-June 1976, *84*, 631–40.

_____ and Wallace, Neil, "'Rational' Expectations, the Optimal Monetary Instrument, and the Optimal Money Supply Rule," *Journal of Political Economy*, April 1975, *83*, 241–54.

Savage, L. J., *The Foundations of Statistics*, New York: Wiley, 1954.

Schelling, Thomas C., *Micromotives and Macrobehavior*, New York: W. W. Norton, 1978.

Schotter, Andrew, *The Economic Theory of Social Institutions*, New York: Cambridge University Press, 1981.

Schumpeter, Joseph, *Capitalism, Socialism, and Democracy*, New York: Harper & Brothers, 1942; Harper Colophon Edition, 1976.

Seligman, Martin E. P., "On the Generality of the Laws of Learning," *Psychological Review*, September 1970, 77, 406–18.

Shackle, G. L. S., *Decision, Order, and Time in Human Affairs*, 2d ed., Cambridge: Cambridge University Press, 1969.

_____, *Epistemics and Economics: A Critique of Economic Doctrines*, Cambridge: Cambridge University Press, 1972.

Simon, A. and Sikossy, L., *Representation and Meaning: Experiments With Information Processing Systems*, Englewood Cliffs: Prentice-Hall, 1972.

Simon, Herbert, "A Behavioral Theory of Rational Choice," *Quarterly Journal of Economics*, February 1955, *69*, 99–118.

_____, *Administrative Behavior: A Study of Decision-Making Processes in Administrative Organization*, 2d ed., New York: Macmillan, 1959.

_____, *The Sciences of the Artificial*, Cambridge: MIT Press, 1969.

_____, "From Substantive to Procedural Rationality," in S. Latsis, ed., *Method and Appraisal in Economics*, Cambridge: Cambridge University Press, 1976, 129–48.

_____, *The New Science of Management Decision*, Englewood Cliffs: Prentice-Hall, 1977.

_____, "On How to Decide What to Do," *Bell Journal of Economics*, Autumn 1978, 9, 494–507.

_____, (1979a) *Models of Thought*, New Haven: Yale University Press, 1979.

_____, (1979b) "Rational Decision Making in Business Organizations," *American Economic Review*, September 1979, 69, 493–513.

Singmaster, David *Notes on Rubik's Magic Cube*, Hillside: Enslow, 1979.

_____ and Frey, Alexander H., Jr., *Handbook of Cubic Math*, Hillside: Enslow, 1982.

Slovic, Paul and Tversky, Amos, "Who Accepts Savage's Axiom," *Behavioral Science*, November 1974, 19, 368–73.

_____ and Lichtenstein, Sarah, "Preference Reversals: A Broader Perspective," *American Economic Review*, September 1983, 73, 596–605.

Smith, Adam, *The Theory of Moral Sentiments*, (1759), New Rochelle: Arlington House, 1969.

Smith, Vernon L., "Microeconomic Systems as an Experimental Science," *American Economic Review*, December 1982, 72, 923–55.

Sowell, Thomas, *Knowledge and Decisions*, New York: Basic Books, 1980.

Stanley, Steven M., *Macroevolution: Pattern and Process*, San Francisco: W. H. Freeman, 1979.

Staw, Barry, Sanderlands, Lana and Dutton, Jane, "Threat Rigidity Effects in Organizational Behavior: A Multilevel Analysis," *Administrative Science Quarterly*, December 1981, 26, 501–24.

Stigler, George, J., "The Economics of Information," *Journal of Political Economy*, June 1961, 69, 213–25.

Strotz, R. H., "Myopia and Inconsistency in Dynamic Utility Maximization," *Review of Economic Studies*, November 1955, 23, 165–80.

Sugimori, Y., Kusunoki, K. and Cho, S., "Toyota Production System and Kanban System: Materialization of 'Just in Time' Production and 'Respect for Human' System," *International Journal of Production Research*, December 1977, 15, 553–64.

Sussman, Hector J., "Catastrophe Theory," *Synthese*, August 1975, 31, 229–70.

Taylor, D., *Mastering Rubik's Cube*, New York: Holt, Rinehart & Winston, 1980.

Telser, Lester, "Why Are There Organized Futures Markets?," *Journal of Law and Economics*, April 1981, 24, 1–22.

Thòm, Rene, *Structural Stability and Morphogenesis*, Reading: W. A. Benjamin, 1975.

Thorpe, Edward, O., *Beat the Dealer: A Winning Strategy for the Game of Twenty-One*, New York: Vintage Books, 1962.

Tinbergen, Nino, *The Study of Instinct*, London: Oxford University Press, 1951.

Toates, Fredric, *Animal Behavior: A Systems Approach*, New York: Wiley, 1980.

Tobin, James, "Are New Classical Models Plausible Enough to Guide Policy?," *Journal of Money, Credit and Banking*, November 1980, 12, 788–99.

Trivers, Robert L., "The Evolution of Reciprocal Altruism," *Quarterly Review of Biology*, March 1971, 46, 35–58.

Tversky, Amos, "Intransitivity of Preferences," *Psychological Review*, January 1969, 76, 31–48.

Ullman-Margalitt, Edna, *The Emergence of Norms*, New York: Oxford University Press, 1978.

Varian, Hal R., "Catastrophe Theory and the Business Cycle," *Economic Inquiry*, January 1979, 17, 14–28.

Vaughan, William, "Melioration, Matching, and Maximization," *Journal of the Experimental Analysis of Behavior*, September 1981, 36, 141–49.

von Neumann, John and Morgenstern, Oskar, *Theory of Games and Economic Behavior*, Princeton: Princeton University Press, 1944.

Watson, James, D., *Molecular Biology of the Gene*, 3d ed., Menlo Park: W. A. Benjamin, 1976.

Weber, R., "The Allais Paradox, Dutch Auctions, and Alpha-Utility Theory," J. L. Kellogg Graduate School of Management Working Paper, Northwestern University, 1982.

Weiner, Norbert, *Cybernetics*, Cambridge: MIT Press, 1948.

Weintraub, E. Roy, "The Microfoundations of Macroeconomics: A Critical Survey," *Journal of Economic Literature*, March 1977, *15*, 1–23.

Wendt, Dirk, "Some Criticism of Stochastic Models Generally Used in Decision Making Experiments," *Theory and Decision*, May 1975, *6*, 197–212.

White, Andrew D., *Fiat Money Inflation in France*, New York: D. Appleton-Century, 1933; Los Angeles: Pamphleteers, Inc., 1945.

Wilkins, Maurice, "Molecular Structure of Deoxypentos Nucleic Acids," *Nature*, April 1953, *171*, 738–40.

Williamson, Oliver E., *Markets and Hierarchies: Analysis and Antitrust Implications*, New York: The Free Press, 1975.

_____, "Transactions-Cost Economics: The Governance of Contractual Relations," *Journal of Law and Economics*, October 1979, *22*, 233–61.

_____, "The Modern Corporation: Origins, Evolution, Attributes," *Journal of Economic Literature*, December 1981, *19*, 1537–68.

_____, "Credible Commitments: Using Hostages to Support Exchange," *American Economic Review*, September 1983, *73*, 519–40.

Wilson, Edward O., *On Human Nature*, Cambridge: Harvard, 1978.

_____, *Sociobiology: The New Synthesis*, Cambridge: Belknap, 1975.

Winter, Sidney G., "Economic 'Natural Selection' and the Theory of the Firm," *Yale Economic Essays*, May 1964, *4*, 225–72.

_____, "Satisficing, Selection, and the Innovating Remnant," *Quarterly Journal of Economics*, May 1971, *85*, 237–62.

_____, "Optimization and Evolution," in R. H. Day and R. Groves, eds., *Adaptive Economic Models*, New York: Academic Press, 1975.

Winterfeldt, Detlof, "Additivity and Expected Utility in Risky Multi-Attribute Preferences," *Journal of Mathematical Psychology*, February 1980, *21*, 66–82.

Zeeman, E. C., *Catastrophy Theory*, New York: Addison-Wesley, 1977.

Part V
Markets and Firms as Institutions

[18]

THE FIRM AS A SOCIAL INSTITUTION: THE FAILURE OF THE CONTRACTARIAN VIEWPOINT

Hans G. NUTZINGER*

I. THE FIRM IN ECONOMIC THEORY

The economic theory of the firm has for a long time been pre-occupied with the market behavior of the firm while at the same time largely neglecting its internal organization. Not only the traditional marginalist approach in this field, but usually even the more recent managerial and behavioral theories treat the firm implicitly as one single maximizing or satisfiying individual reacting to changed market conditions.[1]) The rationale behind this apparently simplistic view is a specific assumption about the conflict resolution between different individuals and groups with different claims and expectations within the firm: it is implicitly or explicitly assumed that the ultimate decision-making power lies in the hands of one or a few individuals 'at the top' of the firm. This means that the firm is viewed as a 'vertical' or 'hierarchical'[2]) organization where authority, subordination and command instead of contractual arrangements prevail. Of course, this hierarchical viewpoint needs some more specification and leaves many problems unsolved; but it seems basically in accordance with everyday experience.

A remarkable attack at this point of view has been made by Armen Alchian and Harold Demsetz in a well-known and frequently quoted article (1972). According to them, there is no essential difference between ordinary market exchange and the organization of production within the firm. The relationship between employer and employee is considered a usual market relation. Consequently, Alchian and Demsetz deny any specific element of power and authority within the firm. They argue that no authoritarian control or subordination is involved in the wage contract. For them the distinguishing mark of the enterprise »is the *centralized contractual agent in a team productive process* — not some superior authoritarian directive or disciplinary power« (p. 778).

---

*) Alfred Weber Institute, University of Heidelberg. — This research has been financed by the Deutsche Forschungsgemeinschaft. I wish to thank Dr Felix Fitz Roy (Heidelberg) for valuable discussion and assistance throughout this work, and Professors Branko Horvat (Beograd), Oliver E. Williamson (Philadelphia) and Egon Sohmen (Heidelberg) for their helpful comments on an earlier version.

[1]) See, for instance, Machlup (1967).

[2]) We use the notion of hierarchy here only in an informal way to indicate an unequal distribution of decision-making power.

218   *HANS G. NUTZINGER*

More specifically, Alchian and Demsetz characterize the classical
capitalist firm »as a contractual structure with: 1) joint input production; 2) several input owners; 3) one party who is common to all the
contracts of the joint inputs; 4) who has rights to renegotiate any
input's contract independently of contracts with other input owners;
5) who holds the residual claim; and 6) who has the right to sell his
central contractual residual status« (p. 794). This characterization *at
the end* of Alchian and Demsetz's article emphasizes, though in a biased
way, the fundamental role of the employer as the central agent of
production. Nevertheless, they maintain their rejection of any authority
in the firm and in the wage contract: »No authoritarian control is involved; the arrangement is simply a contractual structure subject to
continuous renegotiation« (p. 794).

Before we go into a detailed critique of their propositions, we
sketch the prevailing more or less idealized notion of the firm as a
hierarchical organization. Without deep economic reasoning, there appears at first glance a remarkable discrepancy between the formal
principles of social organization and the real conditions of work in
Western societies. At least formally, the political system is determined
by different voting procedures and competition among political parties,
whereby every citizen has theoretically the same influence. In a similar
manner, the relations between the participants on the markets are
characterized by free contractual arrangements: every party — the
large corporation as well as the little consumer — has the same legal
rights. We do not have to mention the unequal distribution of income,
wealth and pover that introduces in practice strong elements of authority and asymmetry into this picture of equal rights on the marketplace.
But there is at least no a priori reason why one party should be always
'on the losing side'.

The discrepancy enters by looking at the firm where most individuals spend most of their time. Here, instead of political democracy
and market coordination, hierarchical forms of decision-making and
of organization seem to prevail. One could go even further to take the
substitution of democratic decision-making and market *coordination* by
entrepreneurial and managerial prerogatives as well as workers' *subordination* as a definition of the modern capitalist firm. As Ronald
Coase put it in his by now classic essay on the nature of the firm, »if
a workman moves from departmen Y to department X, he does not
go because of a change in relative prices, but because he is ordered to
do so ... It can, I think, be assumed that the distinguishing mark of
the firm is the supersession of the price mechanism.«[3] This mutual
exclusiveness of market coordination *between* firms and command subordination *within* firms is also emphasized by Marx. He
sees the contradiction between market 'anarchy' among the capitalists
and workers' subordination under their authority as the distinguishing
mark of the capitalist mode of production. For the workers, the social
character of their production appears »in the form of strictly regulating authority and of a social mechanism organized as a complete

---

[3] Coase (1937), 333—4.

hierarchy« whereas »the bearers of this authority, the capitalists, who meet each other only as commodity owners, are governed by the most complete anarchy«; for them, the social connection of production is only manifested *ex post* through the operation of market exchange.[4]) Moreover, Marx sees this authority as strict vertical hierarchy of different levels, directed by the »command« of the capitalist at the top, and the work organization in the factory system appears as an army of »industrial soldiers«.[5])

Of course, this picture of a complete vertical organization is, at least nowadays, all too idealized: a short look into management literature or, for that matter, only into some daily newspaper, will show this. Today's employers would be more than happy if their critic's assertion of their authority were true for themselves. But even if we mitigate this authoritarian picture by introducing unions, legal restrictions and different forms of limited participation[6]), we still have to explain if and why non-market allocation prevails within the firm, in contrast to Alchian's and Demsetz's belief.

The natural starting point for an analysis of this question will be the deeper investigation of the specific kinds of contracts involved in the legal and social organization of the firm. After analyzing the characteristics of those contracts, we have to explain the economic and social conditions that give rise to their specific — apparently authoritarian — features, even under idealized perfect competition.[7])

II. THE EMPLOYMENT CONTRACT

Alchian and Demsetz raise serious objections against the notion of power and authority as being involved in the employment contract: »To speak of managing, directing or assigning workers to various tasks is a deceptive way of noting that the employer is continually involved in renegotiation of contracts on terms that must be acceptable to both parties« (p. 777). They see no difference between the employer's »presumed power to manage and assign workers to various tasks« and »one little consumer's power to manage and assign his grocer to various tasks«, namely »the task of obtaining whatever the customer can induce the grocer to provide at a price acceptable to both parties«. The only difference they are willing to accept between the two cases is »a *team use* of inputs and a centralized position of some party in the contractual arrangements of all other inputs« as a specific feature of the firm. This fact — and »not some superior authoritarian directive or disciplinary power« (p. 778) constitutes for them the distinguishing mark of the enterprise.

---

[4]) Marx (1894), 888.
[5]) Marx and Engels (1848), 469.
[6]) Those forms of limited participation which are designed to *maintain* the basic hierarchy in the firm by weakening some of its features are, following Pateman (1970, p. 69), better termed »pseudo-participation«.
[7]) One could, however, include additional requirements relating to technology and information into an idealized notion of perfect competition so as to describe the whole problem in terms of »market failure«. But this approach would go beyond the traditional notion of perfect competition in economic theory.

                              HANS G. NUTZINGER

Alchian and Demsetz seem not to be aware that their characterization of production is much closer to the earlier putting-out system
than to the firm.[7a]) This is even more surprising as they themselves mention the transition to the following factory system.[8]) They fail, however, to note the *qualitative change* in the labor contracts involved in
this transition and recognize only one minor advantage of the factory
system in this respect, namely »a reduction in the cost of negotiating
(forming) contracts« (p. 784). But remembering the above mentioned
definitions of the firm, provided by Alchian and Demsetz, we see easily
that their market analogies in production hold to some degree for the
putting-out system. There is a central agent of production with whom
all contracts are made — the putter-outer —, and we have team production in the sense of interdependent and not always separable operations. As Williamson *et al* (1975, p. 255) observe, »it is not the nonseparability by itself that occasions the problem« since most task are
separable simply by introducing buffer inventories. And even with
technologically nonseparable tasks — e. g. Alchian and Demsetz's example of two men loading jointly freight into a truck[9]) — the arising
metering problems do not *per se* call for a central monitor as they
seem to believe; under the putting-out system these problems were
solved simply by the contracting teams themselves.[10]) The imputation
of each member's share in effort and reward had usually been carried
out by the immediate producer and his family; the putter-outer received
the joint output of the whole family and paid for it, leaving the internal
distribution to the other cooperating party.

The »monitor« under the putting-out system faced the problem
of coordinating the results of the different contracting parties and of
metering these results, i.e. the outputs, not the inputs involved. We
would not deny strong power relations even in this case (remember
only the factual assymetry in this exchange relation through the putter-
outer's ownership in part of the means of production and his privileged
access to the markets), but the view of the putting-out system as a
centralized market relationship seems not to be as inadequate as in
the case of the subsequent factory system.

In order to grasp the specific difference between both systems
— overlooked by Alchian and Demsetz —, a short look into history may
be useful. Alfred Marshall's illustrative description of the development
within the British textile industry seems worth quoting at some length:

»At the time of the French revolution there was not a very great
deal of capital invested in machinery whether driven by water
or by steam power; the factories were not large, and there were
not many of them. *But nearly all the textile work of the country
was then done on a system of contracts.* The industry was controlled by a comparatively small number of undertakers who set

[7a]) In fact, they are describing the system of *'inside contracting'*.
[8]) Alchian and Demesetz (1972), 784.
[9]) Alchian and Demsetz (1972), 779.
[10]) Even without family relationships there are only transactional problems caused by
nonseparability as convincingly argued by Williamson *et al* (1975), 255—260.

themselves to find out what it was most advantageous to buy and to sell, and what things it was most profitable to have made. They then let out contracts for selling these things to a great number of people scattered over the country. The undertakers generally supplied the raw material, and sometimes even the simple implements that were used; those who took the contract executed it by the labour of themselves and their families, and sometimes but not always by that of a few assistants.«[11])

Marshall's description of the English textile industry *at that time* comes very close to the idealized picture of *modern* industrial production as constructed by Alchian and Demsetz. In clear contrast to them, Marshall was anxious to emphasize the qualitative changes that took place thereafter. He saw the development towards the factory mainly determined by technical progress, but also acknowledged implicitly the reduction of transaction costs[12]) by gathering people into factories where they lost the control over their work and got suvervised by their employer. For Marshall, one of the most distinguishing marks of the new system is what Alchian and Demsetz try to define away: the notion of managing, directing and superintending of workers by their employers in the place of the former contractual exchange relations.

»As time went on, the progress of mechanical invention caused the workers to be gathered more and more into small factories in the neighborhood of water power; and, when steam came to be substituted for water power into larger factories in great towns. *Thus the great undertakers who bore the risks of manufacturing, without directly managing and superintending, began to give way to wealthy employers, who conducted the whole business of manufacturing on a large scale* ... Thus at length general attention was called to the great change in the organization of industry which had long been going on; and it was seen that *the system of small businesses controlled by the workers themselves was being displaced by the scystem of large businesses controlled by the specialized ability of capitalist undertakers.* The change would have worked itself out even if there had been no factories ... The new organization of industry added vastly to the efficiency of production; for it went far towards securing that each man's labour should be devoted to just the highest kind of work he was capable of performing well, and that his work should be ably directed and supplied with the best meachanical and other assistance that the wealth and knowledge of the age could afford.«[13])

[11]) Marshall (1920), 618 (emphasis added).

[12]) This point is well illustrated by Williamson *et al* (1975) who use Adam Smith's pin-making example to demonstrate that the whole process could have been organized by a system of contracts and conclude: »Transaction costs militate against such an organization of tasks, however« (op. cit., 255).

[13]) Marshall (1920a), 618; emphasis added. We should note that this technological argument for the factory system, shared more or less by all classical writers, even including Marx, has recently been seriously questioned by Marglin (1975). He finds that »the transformation of the independent producer to a wage laborer took place *before* machinery became expensive« (p. 27).

The remarkable[14]) similarity to Marx's extensive description of the process[15]) will be clear for any reader of the first volume of *Das Kapital*. Even more striking is their coincidence in relating this process to basic changes of the labor contract compared with the putting-out system. Like Marx, Marshall sees the evolution of a mass of free wage-workers:

> »The new movement, both in its earlier and later forms, has tended constantly to relax the bonds that used to bind nearly everyone to live in the parish in which he was born; and *it developed free markets for labour*, which invited people to come and take their chance of finding employment. *And in consequence of this change the causes that determine the value of labour began to take a new character. Up to the eighteenth century manufacturing labour had been hired, as a rule, retail; though a large and fluid labour class, which could be hired wholesale, had played a considerable part in the industrial history of particular places* on the Continent and in England febore then. *In that century the rule was reversed*, at least for England ...«[16])

This distinction between *labor* as the worker's productive activity and *labor-power* as the commodity which the free wage-worker has to sell on the market is central for Marx's critique of political economy and his sharp confrontation of the commodity owners's equality in the circulation sphere and the basic inequality within the sphere of production, namely workers' subordination under the capitalist's command. As argued elsewhere it is only in this context in which the notions of labor values and of exploitation by Marx become understandable.[17]) Since we are not interested in a (re-) interpretation of Marxian economics we do not go further into these questions and we note only that this distinction between labor and labor-power can be used as a fruitful starting point for an explanation of the labor exchange and the nature of capitalist production as has been done by Gintis (1975).

The notion of labor-power or labor-capacity[18]) gives a clear hint to the alteration of the labor contract due to the transition from the putting-out system to the modern industrial enterprise. The worker now has to supply on the market not a specific product but his productive capacity. The concrete use of this capacity is not determined by the labor contract but is at the employer's disposal within the contractual and legal limits. Precisely for this reason, the notion of authority and subordination becomes crucial for the understanding of the wage contract. To quote again Ronald Coase: »It is important to note the character of the contract into which a factor enters that is employed within a firm. The contract is one whereby the factor, for a certain

---

[14]) This is especially remarkable in comparison with the very infrequent and unfavorable quotations of Marx by Marshall in his *Principles*.
[15]) See above all the chapters on industrial organization, machinery and big industriy, and on »primitive accumulation« in Marx (1867).
[16]) Marshall (1920a), 619 (emphasis added).
[17]) See Nutzinger and Wolfstetter (1974), Gesamteinleitung: Nutzinger (1974), sections II. 2 and II. 3.
[18]) The latter even more illuminating term (»Arbeitsvermögen«) has been used by Marx in his hitherto untranslated *Resultate des unmittelbaren Produktions-prozesses* (Results of the Immediate Process of Production), published in 1933.

remuneration (which may be fixed or fluctuating), agrees to obey the directions *within certain limits*. The essence of the contract is that it should only state the limits of the power of the entrepreneur. Within these limits, he can therefore direct the other factors of production.«[19])

In fact, it is this peculiar feature of the wage contract that con-situtes the distinguishing mark from other economic and legal relations in Western societies and in comparison with preceding forms of social organization. This contract comprises a *general* agreement »to obey the directions« of the entrepreneur or his delegate within the contractual and legal limits. The ordinary contract on the other hand, specifies the object to be dealt with in more or less detail. One should, however, take care not to exaggerate this esentially legal distinction as telling the whole story. Therefore, we analyze in the next section some legal and institutional complications which sould be taken into account; after that we deal with the even more important economic objections against this abstract characterization of the wage contract.

III. SOME LEGAL AND INSTITUTIONAL CONSIDERATIONS

The employment contract implying a general willingness of the worker to obey his employer's directions may be considered as an extreme example of a more general phenomenon. First we must note that even ordinary contracts and market exchange — apart from the most simple examples usually provided by textbooks — cannot be completely specified in advance. Very frequently, neither the commodity to be sold nor its market value — the return or 'payment' to be provided by the seller — are predetermined in every respect. And even it they were, we had a high probability of the nonfulfilment of some detail of a very detailed contract, but hardly a precise and comprehensive specification of the consequences of some nonfulfilment. In practice, market exchange is very often not a simple equation of the form »x apples equal y dollars« but a highly complicated relationship involving the comparison of two different vectors whose components are not completely specified. This means in turn that even ordinary contracts imply some secondary obligations and the need for a certain degree of loyalty and trust. As Alan Fox (1974) has convincingly demonstrated, the idealized »economic exchange« with predetermined and well-defined properties of the commodities involved and without any reference to the personal characteristics of buyers and sellers is only the limiting case of a broader *social exchange*. This social exchange includes both personal relationships and some general obligations and expectations for the respective parties.

Pure economic theory considers this limiting case as the fundamental paradigm of exchange. Moreover, for perfectly competitive markets the absence of any personal or social relations is a *conditio sine qua non*.[20]) What might be a permissible abstraction for ordinary market exchange becomes highly doubtful in the labor exchange. Yet,

[19]) Coase (1937), 336—7.
[20]) Cf. Arrow and Hahn (1971), especially p. 23.

224
HANS G. NUTZINGER

general equilibrium theory treats labor markets not differently in any degree from other idealized exchange relationships.[21]) But the labor services that households are supposed to offer to the firms are not clearly determined in advance. They imply even under perfect competition necessarily some personal relationships, namely the willingness to »obey the directions« of *one* employer and not of some other. If we assume — as general equilibrium theory does — that labor services are specified the same way as other commodities, we come back to some idealized putting-out system, but not to the factory system or any reasonable abstraction of the firm.

Another way of looking at labor exchange in general equilibrium theory would be the assumption of a peculiar form of voluntary slavery: workers neither sell their own output (as in the case of craftsmen or in the putting-out system) nor their labor-power (as in the factory system). They are assumed to *sell themselves* to a firm — or introducing future markets — to a series of different firms.[22]) This holds since all labor supply decisions under general equilibrium are telescoped into the present. With respect to labor markets, we have to *reverse* the assumption of *impersonal exchange* stated clearly by Arrow and Hahn (1971) by introducing a few alterations and negations: The decision to supply *labor-power, even* in a perfectly competitive economy, is *in fact* a decision to supply so-and-so much *labor-power* to such-and-such *entrepreneurs*, and *not* simply to exchange so-and-so much of the good for other goods.[23])

As we indicated above, one possible objection against the peculiarity of the employment contract could be the complexity of many so-called ordinary contracts that imply also some general obligations and some personal relationships. We could look at long-term contracts such as apartment renting, raising of credits or life insurance. Especially in the first example we have some personal relationship (with the house-owner or his delegate) and some far-reaching secondary obligations that can be partly fixed even unilaterally by the owner (e. g. rules of the house). But the extent of non-specified secondary obligations is considerably smaller than in the wage contract; similarly, the power of one party (hirer, lender, insurance company) to specify unilaterally those general rules is decisively weaker. Finally, long-term contracts tend to be shifted more and more into the category of ordinary contracts by legislation confining the one-sided authority of the hirer, lender or insurer. So it seems to us that, despite some similarities, the specific features of the employment contract remain serious enough as to constitute an important distinction to other long-term agreements.[24])

---

[21]) Cf. Arrow an dahn (1971), 75—6.
[22]) We could look at the *sale* of labor-power also as a *renting* of the laborer. David Ellerman (1974a) goes even further to denote the wage contract as »temporary servitude«. By introducing a specific form of production arbitrage — markets for becoming the central hiring party — he shows the impossibility of general equilibrium with positive profits in a static context without uncertainty (1974. b).
[23]) For the original assertion, see Arrow and Hahn (1971), 23. The italics mark the alterations. — I owe this quotation to Gintis (1975, 24) who also emphasizes the distinction between personal and impersonal exchange.
[24]) The notion of »long-term contract« is here not related to the legal specification but to the expectation of a continued cooperation between both of the contracting parties. See also the discussion of this question at the end of this section.

Another kind of borderline cases should not be overlooked. There are lots of examples in reality where the employment contract, due to social legislation, appears even as *improvement*, if we compare it with the factual dependence of some 'independent' producers. We need only to remember the conditions of many freelance writers and artists who are, in effect, employed by publishers and agencies without enjoying the protection of modern labor law. In a similar way, many small firms delivering their products to big corporations and mail-order houses (very often to a single one) are just as dependent from the other contracting party as if they were integrated into these firms.

One last institutional point has to be considered. When comparing the employment contract with other long-term agreements we do not claim that the *time span* of the employment contract is its distinguishing mark. We quite agree with Alchian and Demsetz (1972) when they state: »Long-term contracts are not the essence of the organization we call a firm« (p. 777). Indeed, most often wage-contracts are not long-term in the sense of involving legally a fixed and far-reaching time space. Usually their duration is only *undetermined:* wage-contracts are open-ended and subject to a notice of one of both parties that becomes valid after a relatively *short* period.[25]) And it would be seriously misleading to take Coase's 'general agreement' or Marshall's 'wholesale hiring' as meaning primarily or essentially a long space of time. *It is the large degree of indeterminateness in the wage contract which leads to a longer duration than in many (not all) other contracts, and not the long duration which leads to its indeterminateness.*

Since the validity of the employment contract is unspecified rather than long-term, the whole question becomes a matter of empiric investigation. Here, we have even more reason to accept Alchian and Demsetz's assertion than they would seem to believe themselves. As many reports indicate, the factual duration of wage contracts in occupations with low job satisfaction is suprisingly short. Thus, Porter *et al* (1975, 278) report high turnover rates for assembly line workers, occasionally »over *100 percent* in a single year«. Indeed, an average duration of half a year is very short compared with many other contracts, e. g. subscriptions, renting, borrowing and lending, insurance and several other contracts. In this example, it is precisely a specific characteristic of the employment relation — that the employee has little or no control over his work — which causes the short, and not the long, duration of the wage contract.[25a])

All these apparently 'authoritarian' features of the employer-employee-relationship take place within market economies. Hence the question arises for the economist: Do we have to relate these features to some market deficiencies, or do we have to go deeper in our analysis? In order to meet this question, we first analyze the effects of exit and entry upon the employment contract.

---

[25]) But even most other 'long-term contracts' are subject to a notice of one party, e.g. in house renting and many insurance contracts. So, Alchian and Demsetz's criticism of this notion is not very specific.
[25a]) One must note, however, that assembly lines are not the predominant form of industrial production.

HANS G. NUTZINGER

IV. EXIT, ENTRY AND HIERARCHY

IV. 1. Leaving the firm

The most common objection to the authoritarian view of the firm and of the employment contract as developed above is the possibility of leaving a hierarchical organization. Indeed, the most effective limit to the employer's authority from an economist's viewpoint are not the legal and contractual restrictions mentioned above. Why should the free wage-worker not simply leave the firm if he dislikes its hierarchy and his own subordination under the aims of the firm, instead of appealing to the courts or hiring a lawyer for better contractual protection? And why should the employer refuse to change the wage-contract if he wants to keep his employee from quitting? Undoubtedly, the possibility to leave the firm is one of the *certain limits* to the employer's authority in the employment relation. But we strongly dispute the picture painted by Alchian and Demsetz that we would have only the same »presumed power« as the little consumer's influence on his grocer to supply the goods he wants to buy. The notion of power and authority does not dissolve into pure fancy or into the same kind mutual dependency inherent in all contracts — simply by leaving the firm.

Alchian and Demsetz themselves give a clear hint for the refutation of their simplistic view of the hierarchy problem. They emphasize »Coase's penetrating insight ... to make more of the fact that markets do not operate costlessly and to rely on the costs of using markets to *form* contracts as his basic explanation for the firm«, and they agree »that, *ceteris paribus*, the higher the cost of transacting across markets the greater the comparative advantage of organizing resources within the firm (1972, 783). But precisely the notion of transaction costs becomes central for the firm as a social institution involving a specific authority relation.

Coase's »penetrating insight« can also be supported by historical evidence: The fundamental cause for the modern enterprise to become the dominant form of production was not its technological superiority. Even under the putting-out system we had a 'minute division of labor' in the sense of Adam Smith.[26] The metering problem put forth by Alchian and Demsetz were not essential for the rise of the firm. As has been observed by Marglin (1971, 6—20), the example of a *pin-factory* given by Adam Smith explains only the advantages of the division of labor in *pin-making, not the factory itself*. While, on principle, each of the activities involved in pin manufacture (wire straightening, cutting, pointing, grinding etc.) »could be performed by and independent specialist and work passed from station to station *by contract, ... transaction costs* militate against such an organization of task, however« (Williamson *et al*, 1975, 255).

These costs did not only give rise to the modern enterprise, they also exercized an important influence on its internal structure. This

---

[26] For this, see Marglin (1971, 15) who asks: »Why, then, did the division of labor under the putting-out system entail specialization as well as separation of tasks? In my view the reason lies in the fact that without specialization the capitalist had no essential role to play in the process.«

THE FIRM AS A SOCIAL INSTITUTION

has been emphasized by Arrow (1974) who defines organizations, similar to Coase's notion of the firm, as »means of achieving the benefits of collective action in situations in which the *price system fails*«[27]). This failure is intimately linked, at least in the case of an enterprise, with the transaction costs of market organization, especially with the costs of forming and enforcing contracts. But essentially the same holds for the individual within the organization: Leaving the firm does not only mean terminating one contract but a whole system of formal and informal relations. The individual loses many of 'the benefits of collective action'.

In this situation, lots of transaction costs arise. First, the need for finding a new occupation in another enterprise leads to search and information costs, not only in terms of money. The costs of leaving imply the loss of informal relations with fellow workers, the claims and respect acquired during the occupation and the need for building-up new social relations at the next workplace. Very often, also other areas are involved: new housing, new schooling, new neighborhood relatioships, and so on. In a way very similar to the firm that can be thought of as a concentration of a highly complex system of specific agreements in a reduced set of generalized contracts involving direct authority relationships, the single can view the employment contract as a concentration of various arrangements into a reduced hierarchical system of contracts, governed by the wage contract. Most other formal and informal arrangements can, at least to some extent, be derived from the former.[28])

The consequences of these transaction costs for the worker are obvious: »The employee is always free to leave, but since the costs of leaving are always present and frequently nontrivial, the employment relation creates an expectation of continued participation«.[29]) As argued above, these costs comprise much more than what would have been imagined at a first glance. The further effect of this long-run expectation mentioned above by Arrow is a certain attitude of loyalty and trust in the organization. This, in turn, weakens the influence exercized by the external market even further. So we can approve of Arrow's illustrative description of the consequences: »Within the scope of the wage contract, the relation between employer and employee is no longer a market relation but an authority relation. Of course, the scope of this authority will usually be limited by the freedom with which one can leave the job. But since there is normally some cost to the exercise of this freedom, the scope of this authority is not trivial«. These consequences of transaction costs are in clear contrast to the pure contractarian viewpont empasized by Alchian and Demsetz (1972).

---

[27]) Arrow (1974), 33; emphasis added.

[28]) If one likes systems theory one could follow Luhman (1971) to denote this case as an example of *Komplexitätsreduktion* (reduction of complexity).

[29]) Arrow (1974), 64. The transaction costs of workers' replacement arising to the firm are less important since this is a *routinized activity* for the enterprise.

228

HANS G. NUTZINGER

IV. 2. Founding participatory firms

We did not exhaust the question of leaving the firm and will take it up again in the next subsection; before that we should discus a connected problem: the possibility of new entry. The denial of a *specific* authority element in the firm could be based on an *argumentum e contrario:* If there were a specific element of authority and power in the firm, why did these presumably hierarchical enterprises not become superseded by 'democratic' organizations? Then the reasoning goes on to the assertion that there is either no such particular authority relation or, if there is one, it must have been optimized by the market process. According to the second version, the degree of power and subordination is determined so as to find a delicate balance between efficiency — presumably due to the internal hierarchy — and the extent of workers' participation sufficient to satisfy some non--monetary wants. In its simplest form, a trade-off between payment and participation could be imagined whereby lower payment is the implicit cost of less hierarchy.

Alchian and Demsetz deny the notion of a *specific* power relation at all. So they have no room for the above-mentioned optimizing considerations. They are, however, anxious to stress the underlying *argumentum e contrario.* So they assume »that general sharing in the residual results in losses from enhanced shirking by residual-sharing employees. If this were not so, profit sharing with employees should have occured more frequently in Western societies where such organizations are neither banned nor preferred politically« (p. 787). Since we are not bound to deny the notion of authority we can easily extend their argument as saying that general *participation* results in losses. The simple reason for this extension is the close connection between participation *in earnings* and participation *in decisions* which we observe in several Western countries.[30]) So we can take this assertion to describe a trade-off between »pay« and »say«. In this view, competition is assumed to effect »precisely the optimal level of alienation« (Dolan, 1971).

As a very quick look into modern management and organization literature will show,[31]) this reasoning is far too simple to provide much understanding of the firm. In addition, there are lots of purely economic considerations which contradict this naive view. One important point overlooked by the adherents of the 'trade-off view' is the interdependence between the social organization of production and the development of technology. After the factory system had been established mainly because of reduced transaction costs without great technological change *at the beginning*, the further technological progress has been adopted to the needs of *this* hierarchical system as to facilitate supervision and to monopolize technical knowledge in the hands of the employers. Marglin (1971) and Braverman (1974) give a lot of striking examples for this process. Catherine Stone's (1974) in-

---

[30]) See the numerous examples in Vanek (1975), part II.
[31]) For this see FitzRoy (1977) and FitzRoy and Dutzinger (1975) with numerous references to literature.

vestigation of the development of job structures in U.S. steel industry shows the further development *within* the steel mill system as a *replacement of contract relations* between employers and more or less independent steel workers selling their *output* to the central agent of production, *by direct authority relationships* involving the immediate instruction of less qualified steel workers after some technological change had been introduced.[32]) In our view this demonstrates the dynamic implications of a certain social organization of production — in the firm — for the way how competition influences technological change.

Though this argument contains some critique of traditional economic theory — especially of its implicit assumption of 'technological neutrality'[33]), there are also a lot of 'neoclassical' reasons for our assertion of a specific technological development. First, the strong separation of tasks in the firm, combined with a *long-run* specialization of workers' activities, raised the central monitor's indispensability for the whole process, and hence his »marginal product« in and for that organization. The often lifelong repetition of a few simple operations did seriously dequalify the factory worker as already observed by Adam Smith in a wellknown passage[34]); this in turn — neoclassically speaking — lowered their marginal productivities, i.e. their marginal contribution to the value of the *firm*. In addition, the specific division of labor in the factory system gave the employer — the only central agent of production — a monopoly of information over the operation of the firm.[35]) So, even specialized workers could not expect to become the central agent of another competing firm after leaving the enterprise.

New entry of former employees into the market was seriously hindered by this fact, and this again strengthened the employer's power over his workers. Finally, in a social environment basically determined by hierarchical firms, leaving one enterprise was not very likely to arise because of the expectations of a lesser degree of authority within other firms. This contributed both to the formation of primarily monetary motivations of the workers and to a reduced desirability for the workers to quit their job. The latter reduced the threat of leaving the firm — and hence the workers' bargaining power —, while the former contributed to a partial integration between the aims of the employers and of their employees. This monetary link of both parties' motivations became then the object of scientific management as developed by Taylor and others[36]). Both these factors strongly supported the maintainance of the authority relations in the work contract.

It might be a simple matter of terminology whether one would choose to view these forces as market deficiencies or not. *In the sense*

---

[32]) This can be viewed as an example of the general *Babbage principle* (1832) connecting labor division and machinery with workers' dequalification. As Ioanides has observed in his excellent survey (1975), Marshall, in his *Industry and Trade* (1920b), was one of the few economists who took notice of this principle.
[33]) For a critique of this assumption see especially Gintis (1975).
[34]) Smith (1937), 734—5.
[35]) A good discussion of this aspect is provided by FitzRoy (1973).
[36]) See Braverman (1974), chapters 4 and 5.

                              HANS G. NUTZINGER

of traditional economic theory, which presupposes a vertical orga-
nization of the firm, they are not. But one should not forget the market imperfections in the usual sense. One important case analyzed
convincingly by Doeringer and Piore (1971) is the formation of 'internal
labor markets' within the corporation. Historically, even more important were certain imperfections on the capital markets, which we shall
analyze in more detail.

Here again, Alchian and Demsetz give a hidden hint for the failure
of the cooperative movement to succeed against the factory system in
the nineteenth century. They mention »the inability to capitalize the
investmtent value as 'take home' property *wealth* of the members of
the socialist firm« (p. 787), and indeed this peculiarity was detrimental
for most nineteenth century cooperatives. Apart from shifting self-
-financed investment projects to those with shorter life compared with
external financing or with the investment behavior of a traditional ca
pitalist firm, this effect tended furthermore to dissolve solidarity among
the members.[37]) The desire to share the yields from self-financed investment with as few members as possible and in any case not with
new members who did not contribute to the investment foregone by
a sacrifice of former current earnings resulted in obvious reactions:
rejection of new members and dismissal of old members (or at least
failure to replace them). So, the cooperative firm did either wither
away with its founding members or it degenerated into a traditional
capitalist firm by hiring wage-workers in the place of retired members.
Especially at that time self-financing — at least to a considerable degree — was unavoidable as capital markets were not very well developed and the opportunities of obtaining external funds were seriously
limited. These problems were even more serious for cooperative firms
that faced additional difficulties, from prejudice and open hostility in
the banking institutions and from unresolved problems of liability.[38])

Up to now, a particular obstacle against the founding of worker-
managed firms in a capitalist environment stems from the fact that
workers usually can only provide their human capital, and scarcely
material capital or money. The latter can easily be mortgaged, the former not. Apart from simple prejudices and some specific (but only
transactional) problems of estimating the expected present value of
the founding members' future incomes, a particular difficulty arises
from the uncertain marketability of this 'security'. In contrast to material wealth or money that can be taken away from the borrower if
he does not meet his obligations it is hardly possible to force an
individual to provide his human capital on the (job) market: how
can you force him to earn future income or, more precisely, to earn
more income in the future than necessary for his subsistence[39]), especially since slavery, feudalism and debtor's prison are abolished? Of

---

[37]) For and extended discussion of the connected theoretical problems see Vanek
(1973), Vanek (1975, article 28), and Nutzinger (1975).
[38]) Also the personal feeling of responsability among cooperative workers was sometimes seemingly underdeveloped. So, Drèze (1975, 3—7) reports complaints of Walras when he was
Director of the Caisse d'Escompte des Associations Populaires: »Unfortunately these cooperatives insisted on low selling prices and high wages, and showed little concern for their capital,
still less for the capital they borrowed. None of them succeeeded or paid back its loans.«
[39]) Remember that subsistence income (in the legal sense) cannot be seized.

course, an insurance system, combined with borrowing on human capital, could provide a solution, as there is a considerable average likelihood that men will earn more than their legal subsistence. We would, however, have to expect that the transaction (above all, insurance) costs are nontrivial and tend to disfavor those contracts in comparison with traditional credit arrangements.

IV. 3. Bargaining power in the Alchian-Demsetz model

We take up again the question of leaving the firm; in the model of Alchian and Demsetz this is the *only* measure an employee can take against the employer. Possibilities of <u>*collective*</u> action, such as strikes, are in practice the most powerful weapon for ordinary workers; but this is beyond the individual relation between the 'monitor' and the employee presupposed by Alchian and Demsetz. On the individualistic level, there is some additional bargaining power for experts and skilled workers in discretionary work rules, arising from their scarcity and the monitor's inability to control completely their activities.[40]

But apart from that, there is a basic inequality in the employment contract. The employer does not have to fire a worker but has a large scale of different instruments at his disposal: admonition, denial of promotion, demotion to another job or department, provision or refusal of certain amenities; granting further training and education (or not!), threat of firing, up to the dismissal itself. What has the oridinary employee to oppose? Apart from moral suasion and court appeals — two very indirect instruments — his only instrument is: leaving the firm. But this is not the adequate weapon against every measure the employer can take. So, if we want to construct a market analogy at all, it is the case of option fixing: either accepting or leaving the »market« — i.e., the firm.

As already mentioned, leaving a grocer and leaving a firm are quite different in terms of the transaction costs involved. But here we have another type of transaction costs meeting the difference between the »costs« of tolerating a certain measure and the costs of leaving the firm.[41] As a consequence of the inequality of weapons in the employment relationship, this difference is not subject to bargaining, but only to the employer himself. Only in the limiting case where both kinds of costs are equal, does this particular form of transaction costs disappear. Again, we have to relate these costs of transaction (bargaining) to the notion of power.

Since Alchian and Demsetz apparently like market analogies, we follow them and use a few other examples from the sphere of exchange

---

[40] They can, for instance, work strictly by rules in a perfunctory way. — For an analysis of the problems involved in those 'ideosyncratic' job structures, see Williamson *et al* (1975).

[41] Whenever this difference is negative the worker is not likely to terminate his labor contract in response to a particular decision made by his employer. One must, however, note that the »costs of tolerating an order« are highly subject to the employee's personal evaluation; they tend to be higher with higher degrees of information, education and qualification. This again increases the bargaining power of the skilled workers beyond the possibility of leaving the firm (cf. footnote 40 above).

232
HANS G. NUTZINGER

in order to illustrate the weakness of their initial propositions.[42])
Identifying the employment contract with other exchange relationships
comes very close to disputing the case of traditional monopoly. There
the consumer is always free to leave the market and to buy another
— distinct — commodity if he is not willing to accept the monopolist's
terms of sale. But no one (to the best of my knowledge) has argued
that there is no such thing as a monopoly at all.

A similar analogy holds with respect to the proposition that *not*
the *actual leaving* but the *threat of leaving* constitutes the essential
bargaining power of the employee since he would lose any influence
on the organization after quitting it. As a possible defense of Alchian
and Demsetz's notion of the employment contract as an (implicit)
system of continual renegotiation[43]) one could say that the employer
always considers the probability that his employee will leave the firm
in reaction to a particular decision he takes. So, any order he gives
his employee may be viewed as an implicit agreement between both.
If the subjective evaluation by the employer proves to be wrong he
will either be 'fired by his employee'[44]) or has to revoke his order;
again, the notion of authority would tend to vanish.

Against this line of defense there are apparently legal objections:
the standards for implicit contracts must be very high if one does not
want to justify everything. By using this construction Reverend Samuel
Seabury (1861) succeeded in reducing the obviously non-contractarian
institution of antebellum slavery to an ordinary contract. He simply
applied an extensive interpretation of implicit agreements.[45]) Also, the
idea of looking at the wage contract as a system of continual (implicit) renegotiation in order to reduce it to an ordinary contractual
relation is not new at all: Alchian and Demsetz seem to have made
independently the same mistake as Commons (1924)[45a]) fifty years ago,
since they use the same construction without mentioning him. The
mistake of this attempt will become clear by another market analogy
related to the threat of new entry into monopolistic markets.

In a way similar to the entrepreneur in the case above, the monopolist must look at the possibility of new entry if the price he charges

---

[42]) Interestingly enough, Alchian and Demsetz, in the later sections of their article
modify the starting propositions when they come to the details of productive organization.
So they characterize the monitor not only as that party which renegotiates but also »hires,
fires, changes, promotes« (p. 786). Indeed, the monitoring functions they attribute to the employer exceed the role of a simple Walrasian *auctioneer* and hence are in clear contrast to
their market view of the firm.

[43]) Alchian and Demsetz (1972), 777, 794.

[44]) If work contracts were ordinary settlements we would have to look at a worker
leaving the firm as 'firing his employer'. This in turn illustrates the inadequate view provided
by Alchian and Demsetz: worker's withdrawal from the firm makes him unemployed but doesn't
change the central agency position of the entrepreneur. But only this would allow the phrase
of firing the employer'.

[45]) Seabury made a remarkable attempt to distinguish American slavery as a system
of implicit contracts offered to the slave's newborn children from mere kidnapping. The content
of these implicit contracts was, of course, providing the means of subsistence during childhood and expecting the reward (slave labor) later on. For Seabury, fugitive slaves escaping
to the North were not 'voting by feet' but simply unwilling to fulfil their part of the
'implicit contract'. — I owe this knowledge to J. Philmore (1975) who does not only accept
Nozicik's (1975, 331) approval of voluntary slavery but goes even further to claim that it is
the necessary consequence of libertarianism.

[45a]) J.R. Commons, in his *Legal Foundation of Capitalism* (1924), argued that the
labor contract »is a continuing implied *renewal* of contracts at every minute and hour, based
on the continuance of what is deemed, on the employer's side, to be satisfactory service, and,
on the laborer's side, what is deemed to be satisfactory conditions and compensation« (p.
285). — I owe this quotation to Fox (1974), 189, who uses it in a quite different way: to
illustrate the employer's superiority in the employment relation.

becomes to high. If he demands excessive prices so as to attract new firms into this market he would either lose his monopoly position (i.e. he would be 'fired as a monopolist') or he must cancel his price increase *before* a new competitor enters the branch. The possibility of new entry plays here much the same role as the threat of leaving: both *limit the power of the* 'monopolist' without removing the 'monopoly' iself. We can rather take the extent of the existing barriers to new competition (Bain, 1956) as a measure of market monopoly power, and, accordingly, can look at the improbability of workers' withdrawal from the firm in response to a particular order as an index of the enterpreneur's decision-making monopoly power.

V. Some concluding remarks

In using market analogies we do not want to claim a basic identity of market exchange and production — far from it. We only tried to demonstrate that those comparisons can be used in the opposite direction: to show that there *is* authority and power as a basic feature of the firm even if we relate it to market exchange. One only has to apply the appropriate examples. But, since the contractarian viewpoint of Alchian and Demsetz appears so appealing to economists, some general remarks are necessary. The one-sided emphasis of traditional economic theory on exchange relations has highly influenced the way economists are accustomed to look at all problems they face. True, this particular view leads to an improved understanding of many issues that seem, at the first glance, not to be related to economics, such as marriage, crime and even politics.[46]) It would be counterproductive to refuse that point of view from the outset, as some Marxists seem to be inclined.[47]) On the other hand, economists tend to overlook the limits to this approach and take one feature of the picture for the whole painting.

Without any doubt, one can look formally at the firm from a purely contractarian viewpoint. But, as we have attempted to show, this way of looking at the firm is seriously misleading in many respects. It contradicts the historical evolution of the firm and leaves out the *essential feature of this institution:* the firm as *a displacement of numerous ordinary agreements by a reduced set of highly undeterminate contracts involving an authority relationskih between employer and employee in order to reduce the transaction costs in production.* Yet, Alchian's and Demsetz's view contains an important grain of truth, often neglected by the adherents of a purely hierarchical view of the firm: the market system does not stop at the entrance of the factory but intervenes in different ways into the internal structure of the firm. But one must note that this general assertion holds also in the opposite direction. Free market exchange and political democracy are influenced by the hierarchical division of labor in the sphere of production.

The basic bias of Alchian and Demsetz's approach is their far too extensive notion of market, exchange and contract in analyzing the

---

[46]) See e.g, Becker (1964), Becker and Landes (1974).
[47]) This is one troublesome point in Gints' otherwise illuminating paper (1975).

234
                              HANS G. NUTZINGER

firm. Looking at the firm as a specialized market comes close to considering the courts as markets for crime. Denoting the wage contract
as a system of continual renegotiations comes close to analyzing the
gift relationship as an exchange under uncertainty.[48]) To deny a specific element of power in the firm is not very far from the assertion
that *marriage* is not »different in the slightest degree from ordinary
market contracting between any two people« since each of both partners can »punish« the other »by withholding future business or by
seeking redress in the courts for any failure to honor [the] exchange
agreement«[49]). The particular problem with this deformation of concepts
is not the complete faultiness of this position but its deceptive half-
-truth.

In order to comprehend the specific operation of the firm one
has to emphasize the characteristic difference between market exchange and internal organization, and not to overstress the similarities.
Further insight can be gained by relating the firm to market failure
(Williamson, 1971) and to the problems arising from uncertainty
Knight, 1921).[50]) The process of »internalization« of economic relations
in the enterprise has to be analyzed as the »substitution of internal
organization for market exchange«[51]), and not as a switching from one
form of marketing to another one. Of course, Alchian and Demsetz
are free to define away the crucial distinction between both forms
of economic organization by their peculiar terminology. The costs of
this procedure are, however, an inadequate understanding of the firm
as a social institution. This is a high price to pay for a doubtful
abstraction.

(Rad primljen aprila 1976.)

REFERENCES

Alchian, Armen A. and Demsetz, Harold: »Production, Information Costs
     and Economic Organization«, *Am. Ec. Rev.*, 1972, Vol. 52, 777—795.
Arrow, Kenneth J.: *The Limits of Organization.* New York: Norton, 1974.
Arrow, Kenneth J. and Hahn, Frank: *General Competitive Analysis.* San Fran-
     cisco: Holden-Day, 1971.
Babbage ,Charles (1832): *On the Economy of Machinery and Manufactures.*
     London; reprinted New York, 1963.
Bain, Joe S.: *Barriers to New Competition.* Cambridge, Mass., Harvard Uni-
     versity Press, 1956.
Becker, Gary S.: *Human Capital.* New York: National Bureau of Economic
     Research 1964.

---

[48]) This was a striking experience at an economic seminar in Switzerland where Serge-
-Christoph Kolm (1975) presented a paper on the gift — return gift relation. Allmost all participants largely independent from their political preferences were inclined to redefine the
gift relationship in the way indicated above. The main objection against this procedure is
the fact that not the expectations about the exchange value of the return gift are the leading
force in this relation but the donators' idea about the use-value of the gift for the other
party.
[49]) Alchian and Demsetz (1972), 777.
[50]) This viewpoint leads to an understanding of the *functional* aspects of hierarchy in
the sense of a gradated system of responsabilities and competence; see my forthcoming paper
on the effects of uncertainty on the internal structure of the firm.
[51]) Williamson (1971), 112. — For an interesting discussion of some similarities see
Hirschman (1970) who analyzes the effects of exit, voice and loyalty as responses to decline in
firms, organizations and states.

Becker, Gary S. and Landes, W. M. (eds.): *Essays in the Economics of Crime and Punishment.* New York — London: Columbia University Press, 1974.

Braverman, Harry: *Labor and Monopoly Capital.* The Degradation of Work in the Twentieth Centry. New York — London: Monthly Review Press, 1974.

Coase, Ronald H.: »The Nature of the Firm«, *Economica,* 1937: Vol. 4, 386—405; reprinted in: *Readings in Price Theory,* ed. by G. J. Stigler and K. E. Boulding, Chicago: Irwin, 1952, 331—351.

Commons, J. R.: *Legal Foundations of Capitalism.* New York: Macmillan, 1924.

Drèze, Jacques: »Some Theory of Labour-Management and Participation«, *CORE Discussion Paper 7520,* October 1975, to appear in *Econometrica.*

Doeringer, Peter B. and Piore, Michael J.: *Internal Labor Markets and Manpower Analysis.* Lexington Mass., Heath, 1971.

Dolan, Edwin G.: »Alienation, Freedom and Economic Organization«, *Journal of Political Economy,* 1971, Vol. 79, 1085.

Ellerman, David: *The Case for Self-Management.* A general statement prepared for the First National Conference on Workers' Self-management held at MIT on January 12—13, 1974.

Ellerman, David: *Some Property Theoretic Aspects of Orthodox Economic Theory,* Research Paper, June 1974, Boston, Department of Economics, Boston University.

FitzRoy, Felix R.: »Economic Organization and Human Capital«, *Discussion Paper 32,* April 1973, Heidelberg, Department of Economics, University of Heidelberg.

FitzRoy, Felix R.: *A General Equilibrium Theory of Entrepreneurial Activity and Profit,* Unpublished manuscript, Heidelberg 1975.

FitzRoy, Felix, R.: »Alienation, Freedom, and Economic Organization«, to appear in: E. Nell (ed.): *Growth, Profits and Property: Essays in the Revival of Political Economy.* Cambridge, Cambridge University Press, 1977.

FitzRoy, Felix R. and Nutzinger, Hans G.: »Entfremdung, Selbstbestimmung und Wirtschaftsdemokratie: eine kritische Übersicht«, in: J. Vanek: *Marktwirtschaft und Arbeiterselbstverwaltung.* Frankfurt/M. — New York, Campus, 1975, 165—223.

Fox, Alan: *Beyond Contract: Work, Power and Trust Relations.* London, Faber and Faber, 1974.

Gintis, Herbert: *The Nature of the Labor Exchange and the Theory of Capitalist Production,* Research Paper, March 1975, Amherst, Mass., University of Massachusetts.

Hirschman, Albert O.: *Exit, Voice, and Loyalty.* Responses to Decline in Firms, Organizations, and States. Cambridge, Mass., Harvard University Press, 1970.

Ioannides, Yannis M.: *Exploration in the Theory of the Firm: Understanding the Production Function,* Research Paper, May 1975, Providence, R. I., Department of Economics, Brown University.

Knight, Frank H. (1921): *Risk, Uncertainty and Profit.* Houghton Mifflin Co.; reprinted Chicago and London ,University of Chicago Press, 1971.

Kolm, Serge-Christophe: *General Reciprocity.* Paper presented to the 2nd Interlaken Seminar on Analysis and Ideology, May 1975.

Luhmann, Nikolaus and Habermas, Jürgen: *Theorie der Gesellschaft oder Sozialtechnologie.* Frankfurt/M., Suhrkamp. 1971.

Machlup, Fritz: »Theories of the Firm: Marginalist, Behavioral, Managerial«, *Am. Ec. Rev.,* 1967. Vol. 57, 1—33.

Marglin, Stephen: »What Do Bosses Do? The Origins and Functions of Hierarchy in Capitalist Production«, Discussion Paper 222, November 1971, Cambridge, Mass.: Harvard Institute of Economic Research; reprinted in *Review of Radical Political Economics,* Vol. 6 (Summer 1974).

Marshall, Alfred: *Principles of Economics.* 8th edition. London: Macmillan; 1920a reprinted 1966 (Papermac 16).

Marschall, Alfred: *Industry and Trade.* London, Macmillan, 1920b.

236   *HANS G. NUTZINGER*

Marx, Karl: *Das Kapital.* Vol. 3 (1894); reprinted in *Marx Engels Werke,*
     Vol. 25, Berlin, Dietz, 1964. English translation: *Capital,* Vol. 3, Moscow,
     Foreign Languages Publishing House, 1961.
Marx, Karl: *Resultate des ummittelbaren Produktionsprozesses.* Moscow:
     Marx-Engels Institute, 1933.
Marx, Karl: *Introduction to the Critique of Political Economy.* Chicago: Kerr;
     1904, reprinted in: D. Horowitz (ed.): *Marx and Modern Economics.*
     London, MacGibbon & Kee, 1968, 21—48.
Marx, Karl and Engels, Friedrich: *Manifest der Kommunistischen Partei,*
     (1848), reprinted in *Marx Engels Werke,* Vol. 4, 459—493.
Nozick, Robert: Anarchy, State, and Utopia. New York: Basic Books, 1974.
Nutzinger, Hans G.: »Investment and Financing in a Labor-Managed Firm and
     Its Social Implications«, *Economic Analysis and Workers' Management,*
     1975, Vol. 9, 181—201.
Nutzinger, Hans G.: *Die Stellung des Betriebes in der sozialistischen Wirt-
     schaft.* Frankfurt/M. — New York: Herder & Herder, 1974.
Nutzinger, Hans G. and Wolfstetter, Elmar: *Die Marxsche Theorie und ihre
     Kritik.* 2 vols. Frankfurt/M. — New York: Herder & Herder, 1974.
Pateman, Carole: *Participation and Democratic Theory.* Cambridge: Cambride
     University Press, 1970.
Philmore, J.: *A Libertarian Plea for Slavery.* Unpublished manuscript, Boston,
     1975.
Porter, Lyman W., Lawler III, Edward E. and Hackman, J. Richard: *Behavior
     in Organizations.* New York *et al:* McGraw-Hill, 1975.
Seabury, Samuel (1861): *American Slavery Justified by the Law of Nature,*
     reprinted Miami, Mnemosyne Press, 1969.
Smith Adam: *The Wealth of Nations.* (Cannan Edition). New York: Random
     House, 1937.
Stone, Katherine: »The Origins of Job Structures in the Steel Industry«, *Re-
     view of Radical Political Economics,* Vol. 6 (Summer 1974), 113—173.
Vanek, Jaroslav: »Some Fundamental Considerations on Financing and the
     Form of Ownership Under Labor Management«, in: H.C. Bos (ed.):
     Economic Structure and Development. Amsterdam: North Holland,
     1973.
Vanek, Jaroslav (ed.): *Selfmanagement: Economic Liberation of Man.* Har-
     mondsworth: Penguin, 1975.
Walras, Léon: *Les associations populaires de consommation, de la production
     et de crédit.* Paris: E. Dentu 1865.
Williamson, Oliver E., Wachter, Michael L. and Harris, Jeffrey E.: »Under-
     standing the employment relation: the analysis of idiosyncratic exchan-
     ge«, *Bell Journal of Economics,* Spring 1975, Vol. 6, No. 1, 250—278.
Williamson, Oliver E.: »The Vertical Integration of Production: Market Fai-
     lure Considerations«, *Am. Ec. Rev.,* 1971. Vol. 61, 112—123.

[19]

The Manchester School Vol LVI No. 2   June 1988
0025–2034 $2.50   00–00

INSTITUTIONS AND MARKETS IN A DYNAMIC WORLD*

by
GIOVANNI DOSI†
DEAST, Venice and
SPRU, University of Sussex

I INTRODUCTION

This article concerns the role of institutions and policies and their relationship with market processes in open economies characterized by various forms of technological change.

The approach which is most familiar to the contemporary economic discipline essentially consists of a process of reduction of institutional and policy issues to exceptions, anomalies and particular cases of a general framework centred around the equilibrium conditions of the economic system postulated by the theory. The impact of policies and institutions is evaluated on the grounds of a yardstick—the equilibrium which the economy would achieve if left to itself—under very special and sometimes rather awkward hypotheses, whose properties, nonetheless, are such as to yield "optimal" outcomes. In this well worked-out and widely-accepted strategy, any normative issue, phenomenon or behaviour is compared with that fundamental yardstick and, *by difference*, one also defines the role and impact of policies. Thus, the economist commonly uses concepts like "externalities", "market failures", "limited information", "imperfect markets", etc., to categorize the most common "sub-optimal" features of the empirical world as compared with the theoretical model. In a very peculiar overlapping of positive and normative judgements, these "imperfections" of the real world also delimit the domain of institutional intervention, which—it is claimed— should make the world more similar to the theory. Generally, the economics profession likewise treats in a similar fashion the problems related to technological and economic change, assessing, for example, the degree of "market failure" associated with technological uncertainty, the "market imperfection" stemming from property rights on innovation, etc.

*Manuscript received 12.7.85; final version received 10.4.87.

†Useful comments on previous drafts by H. Ergas, L. Orsenigo and S. Winter, the participants at the Special Session on Industrial Policies of the 7th World Congress of Political Science (Paris, 14–20 July, 1985) and two anonymous referees are gratefully acknowledged.

This research has been undertaken at the Science Policy Research Unit (SPRU) of the University of Sussex as part of the research programme of the Designated Research Centre funded by the Economic and Social Research Council (ESRC). Since December 1987, the author has held a post at the University of Rome "La Sapienza".

119

The leap from the core theoretical model on which welfare conclusions are generally based to the properties of actual economic systems is a tremendous one: yet, the correspondence between the fundamental hypotheses of the model (on behaviours, technology, interactions between the agents, etc.) and the "stylized facts" of the world is often treated rather casually, and sometimes with the irritation that discussions on methodological issues provoke among the practitioners of the discipline.[1] Yet, in the history of the economic discipline this has not always been so.

Two to three centuries ago, when political economy was emerging as an autonomous discipline, more or less contemporary to the emergence of a "market society"[2] and of a capitalist mode of production, one of the intellectual concerns was the status, function and social implications of the free pursuit of private interests and their relationship with other forms of social coordination. Adam Smith's Invisible Hand related to a fundamental conjecture on the mechanisms of impersonal coordination occurring in decentralized markets. Yet, it was clear among classical writers that strictly non-economic variables and institutions established particular rules of interaction and "meta-codes" of behaviours which were necessary conditions for a satisfactory collective outcome of individual self-seeking attitudes, in terms of collective welfare and dynamic performance of the economy.[3] However, those background conditions which allow the consistency of individual behaviours and their dynamic progressiveness (in a sense, the factors accounting for the "moral" and political constitution of relatively efficient market societies) generally remained a concern of political thinkers, philosophers, sociologists and anthropologists (from the Scottish social thinkers to Hegel and Tocqueville and, later, Weber, Polanyi and Luhmann) but steadily disappeared from the explicit attention of economics.

---

[1] Notably, the "Founding Fathers" of modern General Equilibrium Analysis are generally well aware of the gap between the core theory and the interpretation of empirical economic phenomena. However, one finds much less caution amongst the "normal scientists"—in a Kuhian sense—of the discipline: compare, for example, Hahn (1984) with a random sample of articles in the main economic journals.

[2] *Cf.* Polanyi (1944) and (1971). See also Hirschman (1982).

[3] *Cf.*, for example, Adam Smith's *Theory of Moral Sentiments* (1976) and the discussion in Cropsey (1957). (For fascinating analyses of the "economic anthropology" of the modern economy, see Dumont, 1977, and Hirschman, 1977.) Other challenging (and very different) analyses of the functions and characteristics of the economic domain within the general social fabric are the classic work of de Tocqueville (1969) and, by contemporary authors, Luhmann (1975) and Hirsch (1976). These are only few examples of several ambitious attempts of modern social sciences to answer two fundamental questions which have puzzled Western thought at least since the eighteenth century, namely (a) under what conditions is the free pursuit of private interests consistent with the orderly reproduction of society and what kinds of social organization does it produce; and conversely (b) what are the forms of social organization and norms which allow an orderly expansion of the economy? However, contemporary economic discipline has been conspicuously absent from the debate. (For one of the few cases of dialogue between economics and other social disciplines on these challenges, see the review by Hahn of the cited work of Hirsch, in Hahn, 1984.)

In tune with some insights of early political economists and drawing from a few more recent contributions, we are going to suggest a framework of analysis of institutions which is in its essence *non-reductionist*. The heuristics of this second class of approaches we are thinking of are based on four fundamental hypotheses, namely (a) behaviours (and their outcomes) cannot adequately be represented by the simple and universal rationality of the *homo oeconomicus* postulated by the prevailing economic theory; (b) markets and economic processes occurring within them are themselves institutional set-ups specific to historical periods, cultures, countries, etc.; (c) there are particular combinations between *lato sensu* institutions and market processes which efficiently "match" in terms of some (but most likely not all) performance yardsticks; (d) non-market variables (including, of course, policies in the strict sense) are a permanent feature of the *constitution* of the economic system and an essential part of the ways the economic machine is "tuned" and evolves.[4]

Innovation, change, transformation represent almost a crucial experiment for the relative adequacy of the "reductionist" and "non-reductionist" approaches. For example, is the prevailing frame of economic thought capable of accounting for the process of technological innovation? Can we elaborate non-trivial propositions, on both positive and normative levels, regarding the role and effect of policies in relation to economic change? What accounts for the fact that different countries show systematically different capabilities of innovating and economically exploiting the innovations?

By way of an introduction, consider two rather well-known examples against which the achievements and limitations of the "reductionist" and "non-reductionist" approaches can be assessed.

To illustrate, consider one of the most famous explanations of the differences in the growth record of developed economies, namely the so-called "growth accounting exercises".[5] For this purpose, one uses all the variables strictly consistent with the "proper" economic model (the primary endowments of each economy and their change through time), some variables which in the theoretical model would be considered "imperfections" (economies of scale, etc.) and some spurious variables which can be squeezed into economies with some considerable unease (the "endowment of education", etc.). Here, one can see the reductionist programme at its best: paraphrasing Kindleberger, one tries to account for the degree to which the higher efficiency of the "endowment" École Politechnique in France compensates for the lower throughput of French coal mines, or the ways the Italian

---

[4]These issues are discussed at greater length, with different perspectives, in Nelson and Winter (1982); Boyer and Mistral (1983); and Dosi and Orsenigo (1985).
[5]*Cf.* Denison (1967). For a discussion of the same example within an analysis of economic methodology, *cf.* Salvati (1985).

entrepreneurship compensates for the lower endowments of "capital" or "civil service competence"....[6] Yet, one is left with a large unexplained residual, sometimes called "technical change". In actual fact, the questions one begins with remain mostly unanswered: why the disappointing British economic performance or the impressive Japanese growth? Why did Italy not become another Japan? Is the U.S. technological and economic performance getting weaker? And so on.

The second example, even more fundamental and nearer to the concerns of this paper, concerns technical change. It is well recognized in the economic literature that the very existence of innovation *requires* a "market failure" in the static allocative sense: in decentralized markets, the incentive to innovate needs some kind of asymmetric information and super-normal profits.

Certainly, in the history of economic thought, there are "heretic" attempts to investigate the phenomena of innovation and change as central features of modern economic systems—notably Schumpeter (1961) and (1975)—and in contemporary economics—Nelson and Winter (1982).

However, in a curious paradox, most policy analyses remain based on a theoretical yardstick—the efficiency properties of decentralized processes of allocation under very special and generally stationary conditions—which seems strikingly inappropriate for dealing with innately dynamic phenomena such as technical change over time and across countries.[7]

In what follows here, we will suggest some propositions on the relationship between technical change and market processes (Section II) and explore the role of policies and institutions in both closed and open economies under all those circumstances when change and transformation are permanent and fundamental features of the system (Section III).

II Seven Propositions on Technical Change, Markets and Institutions

Proposition 1

Building on the works on technical change, among others, of Freeman (1974); Nelson and Winter (1977); Nelson (1982); and Rosenberg (1976), we have tried to show elsewhere that the process of technological change is an activity characterized by partly tacit knowledge and highly selective heuristics. Technical progress generally proceeds along rather precise "trajectories", linked by major discontinuities associated with the emergence of new "technological paradigms".[8] Whenever new paradigms emerge, the material

---

[6]*Cf.* Salvati (1985).

[7]See, for example, standard industrial economics textbooks. A similar observation is discussed in Silva (1984).

[8]*Cf.* Dosi (1984) and Dosi and Orsenigo (1985) for a more analytical discussion of this and the following points.

technology, the relevant tasks which are meant to be fulfilled, the heuristics ("where to go" and "where not to go"), the required knowledge skills and equipment, the relevant dimensions of "progress", all contextually change. *Technology, far from being a free good, involves a fundamental learning aspect, characterized*—following Nelson and Winter (1982)—*by varying degrees of cumulativeness, opportunity, appropriability.* This is our first proposition. Both appropriability and cumulativeness of technical change are affected by the degrees of *tacitness* and the degrees of *formal understanding* of each technology (see Nelson and Winter, 1982). The more a technology is tacit (i.e., it involves idiosyncratic capabilities—e.g., the experience-based skills of designing particular machines for particular conditions of use, etc.), the higher the difficulty in transmitting it in the form of blueprints or even to imitate it without a painstaking process of informal learning. (For a discussion of the underlying theory of production, see Winter, 1982.) An implication is that, at any point in time, different companies and countries are likely to be characterized by different technical coefficients and product technologies. These differences do not essentially relate to different factor combinations along a single production function, but to proper technological gaps/leads in relation to a given trajectory of technological progress. In another work,[9] we discuss some empirical evidence on the subject: even within the group of OECD countries, the general case is (i) relatively wide international gaps in labour productivity and innovative capabilities, and (ii) the absence of any significant relationship between these gaps and international differences in the capital/output ratios. This is to say that differences in input coefficients generally represent different techniques which can often be unequivocally ranked irrespective of relative prices. The process of development is strictly associated with the inter- and intra-national diffusion of "superior" techniques (see Nelson, 1968). Thus, at each point in time, there are, in general, one or very few "best practice" techniques of production which correspond to the "technological frontier". Relatedly, the description of the production structure in the short term, by means of fixed coefficients, is a reasonable approximation to the *irreversibility properties* of evolutionary economic processes that occur in real time.

Proposition 2

A fundamental implication of such a view of technology and technical change is that there are *widespread asymmetries in the technological capabilities, input efficiencies and product performances between firms and between countries;* these asymmetries correspond to *equally uneven patterns of economic signals facing the economic agents.* This is our second proposition. The asymmetries in capabilities are a direct consequence of the cumulative idiosyncratic and

---

[9]See Dosi, Pavitt and Soete (1988).

partly appropriable nature of technological advances. The more cumulative are technological advances at firm-level, the higher the likelihood of "success breeding success" (*cf.* Nelson and Winter, 1982, for a formalization). Moreover, the higher the opportunity for technological progress, *ceteris paribus*, the higher the possibility of relatively bigger "technological gaps" between successful innovators and laggard firms. In general, the evolution over time of these asymmetries will depend on the relative rates of innovation and of diffusion and, thus, on the degrees of innovative opportunity, cumulativeness and appropriability which characterizes any one particular technology. Notably, the standard textbook case of industries composed of technologically identical firms is the limiting case in which innovation stops and thus evolutionary dynamics ceases to be relevant.

These features of technical change also determine the nature of the economic signals that firms face, so that, for example, a high technological opportunity, associated with a high degree of appropriability of technological innovation may well perform as a powerful incentive to innovate (related to high expected profitabilities and market shares) for a company which is on or near the technological frontier, being at the same time a powerful *negative* signal (an entry barrier) for a company with relatively lower technological capability.

Proposition 3

In a world characterized by technical change and transformation, the behaviours of the agents are most adequately represented by routines, strategies, meta-rules, search processes (see the seminal work of Nelson and Winter, 1982). That is to say that in an environment which is complex, changing and uncertain, firms do not and cannot adopt maximizing behaviours (and, in many circumstances, might not find it dynamically efficient to try to do so, even if they could).[10] This is our third proposition.

Moreover, behaviours cannot be entirely deduced from the sole knowledge of a generic self-seeking goal of the agent and of the economic structure (taken to include the asymmetries in technological capabilities, the nature of the technology, the patterns of economic signals, etc.).

A specific but very important case concerns the nature of the adjustment processes each firm undertakes in a changing environment. As an illustration, take a firm producing any one particular product. The "signals" that the firm receives, in an extreme synthesis, are of three kinds, namely (i) the technological opportunities (and expected economic benefits) associated with technical change in that and other products; (ii) the rate of growth of demand in that and other products; (iii) the changes in costs, prices, quantities, profitabilities in its markets (and also other markets). These signals loosely

---

[10]*Cf.* Nelson and Winter (1982); Heiner (1983); Dosi (1984); Dosi and Orsenigo (1985).

correspond to three notional adjustment strategies. The first one relates to innovation/imitation/technological upgrading. Let us call it "Schumpeterian adjustment". The second one relates to the search of the most promising growth opportunities. Call it "growth adjustment". The third one refers to price/quantity changes on the basis of an *unchanged* technology. Let us— improperly—call it "Ricardian" or "classical" adjustment.

Clearly, most firms will choose varying combinations of all three adjustment processes. However, the fundamental point is that we have here "open-exit" alternatives (that is, alternatives subject to discretionary decisions) whose outcome cannot be deduced from either the knowledge of the state-of-the-world and/or of an unchanging rationality principle.

Notably, a maximization approach would not lead us very far in explaining the choices. Even *if* we knew that the considered firm will choose the option which maximizes the integral of the expected discounted profits, for a *given* time horizon, the analytical content of such a statement would be practically nil: the indeterminacy about the ways technological and market expectations are formed, and about the time horizon and the intertemporal preferences, is another way of describing our theoretical ignorance. A more fruitful approach, in our view, considers the behavioural regularities (the "routines" and "meta-routines", *à la* Nelson–Winter) in relation to (i) the nature of the signals and (ii) the technological assets firms possess (in terms of technological capabilities, knowledge, expertise, etc.) which—among other things—determine different capabilities of "seeing" and reacting to any given set of signals. Clearly, the structure of the industry and the nature of the technology constrains the set of feasible behavioural rules: for example, investment and R&D commitments will be constrained by the ability to finance them; the adjustments in prices/quantities/market shares will be constrained by minimum profitability requirements, etc. However, the crucial point is that, within these structural and technological constraints, there are varying spaces for *discretionary choices*, related to the propensities to accumulate, to take risks, to trade-off present profits for market shares, to commit more or less resources to innovative search, to search in some directions and not in others, etc.[11]

This applies to both intertemporal comparisons within the same country or, even more so, to inter-country comparisons. In a purely anecdotal way, the reader is invited to think of the specific *weltanschauung* which informed

---

[11]On these points, see Metcalfe (1985, p. 4), who discusses the "differences in the capacity and willingness of the firm to expand market share and accumulate productive capacity with respect to current products and processes". The analysis of these strategic choices is—as known—also the domain of game-theoretical approaches to oligopolistic interactions. Our view is that they certainly highlight some important features of strategic interdependencies; however, they are subject to the same objections to the "maximization" representation of behaviours, mentioned above: simply they move the problem one step backward (how are the "rules of the games" established? How are expectations formed?, etc.). For some comments, see Dosi, Orsenigo and Silverberg (1986).

the strategies of the entrepreneurship in some of the most successful late-coming industrializers, such as Germany in the last century (Veblen, 1915) and Japan in this one (Johnson, 1982). Even if the nature of the economic context might go a long way towards the explanation of such performances, it does not exhaust it. More institutional explanations (in the broad sociological sense, including established behaviours and fundamental cultural traits) are required in order to account for the relative emphasis in the most successful countries upon processes of "growth adjustment" and "Schumpeterian adjustments" as compared to simple short-term allocative efficiency. If this is so, one must relate to this socio-institutional level of analysis any proper investigation of statements—which are part of the conventional wisdom of practical economists—such as "... the trouble with British industry is that it is led by accountants, while German firms are led by engineers...", etc. Or, one certainly realizes by reading a work like Dore's *British Factory, Japanese Factory*[12] that the difference in economic performances stemming from different institutional contexts is much greater than, and irreducible to, the set of economic signals markets deliver. Another related example—almost entirely neglected among economists, with the outstanding exception of Hirschman (1970)—is the economic importance of loyalty:[13] to trivialize, it is intuitive that such commonplace notions as Japanese mechanisms of loyalty to the company and to the state, the Italian sole loyalty to their families and lack of collective loyalties, or, at a more general level, the general perception of the "moral boundaries" in behaviours toward competitors, customers, suppliers, government officials, etc., must have a profound influence on the adjustment processes the economic agents undertake.

Evidence of this "institutional constitution of markets" emerges indirectly also from the highly simplified context of so-called "experimental markets": even under quasi-laboratory conditions, "the institutional organisation of a market has been an important treatment variable. The mechanics of how buyers and sellers get together can substantially influence market performance. That is, *for the same underlying incentives*, the market performance is affected by a change of institutions".[14] There is no reason to believe that this does not *a fortiori* apply to the much more complex real markets. In general, these phenomena hint at suggestions present among the early analyses of "market societies", from Locke, Ferguson and Smith to Hegel, about the "moral" and "ethical" preconditions of modern economies. An interpretation of the different ethical constitutions or, at least, a taxonomy is still to come. Yet, we see here a first fundamental role of non-market institutions (including strictly political ones) in that they are instrumental in *shaping and selecting* the fundamental rules of behaviour and interactions of

---

[12]*Cf.* Dore (1973). We owe this observation to M. Salvati.
[13]On the issue, see also Pizzorno (1985).
[14]Plott (1982, p. 1489), our emphasis.

Institutions and Markets in a Dynamic World   127

the economic agents: policies, implicit social rules, dominant forms of organizing the links within and between the various groups of economic agents (e.g., between firms and banks, between management and workers, etc.), levels and forms of industrial conflict, have a paramount importance in determining the relative mix and the direction of microeconomic adjustment processes, for any *given* set of economic signals and structural conditions.[15]

The importance of this point also from a normative perspective should be clear: it might not be enough to influence the patterns of signals if microeconomic strategies are biased in directions conflicting with the policy objectives (e.g., if the fundamental strategic rules of private agents are heavily biased against "Schumpeterian adjustments", public incentives might not be very effective in promoting a sufficient rate of innovation: see also below).

Proposition 4

Another (and related) aspect of the role of non-market variables in economic performance and technological dynamism refers to the *patterns and organization* of *externalities and the unintentional outcomes of market processes.* In economic theory, externalities are generally considered a fastidious source of non-convexity while strongly counter-intentional outcomes disturb the rationality assumptions of the theory. However, *untraded interdependencies* between sectors, technologies, firms have a primary importance in the process of technological change (see, among others, Freeman, 1974; Rosenberg, 1976 and 1982; Dosi, Pavitt and Soete, 1988). For example, knowledge and expertise about continuous chemical processes may allow technological innovations in food processing even when the latter do not involve any chemical inputs; "arms-length" relationships between producers and users of industrial equipment are often a fundamental element in the innovative process even if sometimes no economic transaction is involved; the production of bicycles originally drew technological knowledge from the production of shotguns, even though neither product is an output or an input in the other activity. Technological complementarities, untraded technological interdependencies and information flows which do

[15]Notably, somewhat similar conclusions can be reached through the exploration of the properties of markets still characterized by maximizing agents, who, however, have only limited information about the outcomes of different courses of action: then, it can be shown, the institutional architecture of the system shapes choices, outcomes and economic performances (see Sah and Stiglitz, 1985). Moreover, even in the unlikely world of rational expectations, one can show the necessity both of "social norms (in particular business practices) imposing some restrictions and coherence on the individual decisions and [of] information generated by institutions external to the market" (Frydman, 1982, p. 662).
A fortiori, institutions which shape behaviours, patterns of interactions and expectation formation are *required* in the more complex environments—characterized by technical change, multi-level decision processes, etc.—discussed here. (On the relationship between expectation formation, behaviours and institutional specializations of the economic agents, see also Kaldor, 1972.)

not entirely correspond to the flows of commodities, all represent a structured set of technological externalities which is in a *collective asset* of groups of firms/industries within countries/regions and/or tends to be internalized within individual companies (see, for example, Teece, 1982). In other words, technological bottlenecks and opportunities, experiences and skills embodied in people and organizations, capabilities and "memories" overflowing from one economic activity to another, etc., tend to organize *context conditions* which (i) are country-specific, region-specific or even company-specific; (ii) are a fundamental ingredient in the innovative process; and, (iii) as such, determine different opportunities/stimuli/constraints to the innovation process for any given set of strictly economic signals. This is our fourth proposition.

These untraded interdependencies and context conditions are, to different degrees, the *unintentional outcome* of decentralized (but irreversible) processes of environmental organization (one obvious example is the "Silicon Valley") and/or the result of explicit strategies of public and private institutions (in this sense one can interpret, for example, the strategies of vertical and horizontal integration of electrical oligopolies into microelectronics technologies or the efforts of various governments to create "science parks", etc.).

Proposition 5

We mentioned above our hypothesis that technical change is organized by "technological paradigms". It is useful to distinguish between that "normal" technical progress which proceeds along the trajectories defined by an established paradigm and those "extraordinary" technological advances which relate to the emergence of radically new paradigms. As regards the latter, we try to show elsewhere (Dosi, 1984, and Dosi and Orsenigo, 1985) that market processes are generally rather weak in directing the emergence and selection of these radical technological discontinuities. When the process of innovation is highly exploratory, its direct responsiveness to economic signals is looser and—especially in this century—the linkages with strictly scientific knowledge are greater.

Then, institutional factors play a direct role, providing the necessary conditions for new scientific developments and performing as *ex ante* selectors of the explored technological paradigms from within a much wider set of potential ones. One can cite, for example, the cases of semiconductors and computer technologies and the influence of both military/space agencies and big electrical corporations in the early days of the development of these new technological paradigms.[16] Somewhat similar cases can be found in the early developments of synthetic chemistry (especially in Germany). In a

---

[16]On these points, *cf.* Dosi (1984).

Institutions and Markets in a Dynamic World   129

less apparent way, strictly non-economic stimuli and "selectors" act in the present development of new technologies, such as bioengineering or new materials.

In general, the features of the process of search and selection of new technological paradigms is such that the *institutional and scientific contexts and public policies are fundamental insofar as they affect* (a) *the bridging mechanisms between pure science and technological developments*; (b) *the criteria and capabilities of search by the economic agents*; and (c) *the constraints, incentives and uncertainty facing would-be innovators*. This is our fifth proposition.

Its counterpart on an international level is that when new technologies emerge, the relative success of the various countries depends on the successful matching between (a) one country's scientific context and technological capabilities (*cf.* Propositions 2 and 4 above); (b) the nature of its "bridging institutions"; (c) its strictly economic conditions (relative prices, nature and size of the markets, availability/scarcity of raw materials, etc.); (d) the nature of the dominant rules of behaviour, strategies, forms of organization of the economic actors (*cf.* Proposition 3 above).

Clearly, all these sets of variables are, to different degrees, affected by public policies, either directly (e.g., procurement policies or R&D subsidies which obviously influence the economic signals facing individual firms), or indirectly (e.g., through the influence of the education system upon scientific and technological capabilities, etc.).

In particular, as regards the "normal" functioning of markets and industries and the "normal" technological activities (as opposed to the extraordinary ones related to the emergence of new technological paradigms), it must be noticed that each sector embodies a different balance between institutions and markets. This appears to be true in two senses.

First, there is a technology- and country-specificity of the balance between what is coordinated and organized through the visible hand of corporate structures and what is left to the invisible hand of the markets (for discussions on the issue, *cf.* Marris and Mueller, 1980; Williamson, 1979 and 1981; Chandler, 1966 and 1977; and Teece, 1982).

Second, there is an analogous differentiation in the balance between public institutions and private organization in the process of innovation (*cf.* Nelson, 1984). For example, some sectors rely on an endogenous process of technological advances (e.g., several manufacturing sectors) while others depend heavily on public sources of innovation (e.g., agriculture).[17]

If anything, one could suggest the following empirical generalization: other things being equal, the higher the role of the *visible* hand of oligopolistic organizations, the lower the requirement for strictly public institutions in the

---

[17]For sectoral analyses of the sources and uses of innovations, see Scherer (1982) and Pavitt (1984).

processes of economic coordination and technological advance and, *vice versa*, the nearer one activity is to the economist's model of "pure competition", the higher also appears to be its need for strictly institutional organization of its "externalities" and technological advances. Agriculture is a case in point: historically a significant part of its technological advances, in the U.S.A., Europe and, also, in the Third World, has been provided by government-sponsored research (*cf.* Nelson, 1984) and even its price–quantity adjustments have been increasingly regulated, both in the U.S.A. and in Europe, by institutional intervention. Conversely, oligopoly-dominated manufacturing produces a good part of its "normal" technological advances endogenously and, apart from major crises, seems to coordinate rather well its price/quantity adjustments.

Proposition 6

We have so far focused on the relationship between *lato sensu* institutional factors, economic processes and technological change without much attention to the consequences induced by the very fact that all economies are, more or less, open economies: they trade with each other and, by doing so, undergo changes in the economic signals each of them faces. One of the few conclusions on which the economic profession agrees is that, under conditions of non-increasing returns, absence of externalities and for given rates of macroeconomic activity, the patterns of allocation stemming from international trade are generally efficient. In other words, there are generally gains from trade for all partners based on "comparative advantages". Let us call this *allocative* (or "Ricardian") *efficiency*, to mean the likely outcome of short-term adjustment processes (essentially linked to relative prices and relative profitabilities) on the grounds of *given* technologies and *given* levels of macroeconomic activity. However, the fundamental question concerns the effect that such a pattern of allocation has upon technological dynamism and upon long-term macroeconomic rates of activity. Let us call the performance criterion related to the former, *Schumpeterian efficiency*, and that related to the latter, *growth efficiency*. Now, the crucial point is that there is nothing in the mechanisms leading to Ricardian efficiency which guarantees also the fulfilment of the other two criteria of efficiency.

The reasons for possible trade-offs amongst these different efficiency criteria is a consequence of the features of technological change mentioned above (for a more detailed discussion, see Dosi, Pavitt and Soete, 1988), namely (a) the cumulative, (partly) appropriable and local nature of technological advances (Atkinson and Stiglitz, 1969; David, 1975; and Arthur, 1985); (b) the widespread existence of static and dynamic economies of scale; (c) the influence that technological gaps between firms and between countries have upon the economic signals faced by the economic agents; (d) the importance of country-specific and area-specific untraded interdependencies.

As discussed by Kaldor (1980), if different commodities or sectors possess significant differences in their "dynamic potential" (in terms of economies of scale, technical progress, possibilities of Smithian division of labour, learning-by-doing, etc.), then specializations which are efficient in terms of the comparison of a given set of input coefficients may not be so in terms of a longer-term assessment of the notional patterns of technological dynamism related to these specializations. This is more than a special case related to infant industries: it is the general condition of an economic system whereby *technological opportunities vary across products and across sectors.* More precisely, within each technology and each sector the technological capabilities and learning processes of each firm and each country are generally associated with the actual process of production in that same activity. Thus, the mechanisms regarding international specialization have a dynamic effect in that they also *select* the areas where technical skills will be accumulated, (possibly) innovation undertaken, economies of scale reaped, etc. However, the potential for these effects is widely different between technologies and sectors. This is another aspect of the irreversibility features of economic processes: present allocative choices influence the direction and rate of the future evolution of technological coefficients. Whenever we abandon the idea of technology as a set of blueprints and we conceive technical progress as a *joint production* with manufacturing itself, then it is possible to imagine an economic system which is dynamically better off (in terms of productivity, innovativeness, etc.) if it always operates in disequilibrium *vis-à-vis* "Ricardian" conditions of allocative efficiency. On the grounds of the foregoing propositions on the nature of technology, it is possible to establish when a trade-off between "allocative efficiency" and "Schumpeterian efficiency" can emerge. "Ricardian" patterns of specialization (with their properties of allocative efficiency) are determined, for each country, by the relative size of the sector-specific technology gaps (or leads).[18] Whenever the gap is higher in the most dynamic technologies (i.e., those characterized by the highest technological opportunities), then allocative efficiency directly conflicts with dynamic efficiency. This is our sixth proposition.

Since this point has important analytical and normative implications, related to the long-term consequences of the patterns of allocation stemming from decentralized market processes, let us consider it in some detail.

By way of an introduction, the reader is invited to think of the case of increasing returns and indivisibilities; as known in the economic literature,[19] multiple equilibria are likely to emerge, without the possibility—for the analyst and *a fortiori* for the economic agents—to establish which one will be selected. As thoroughly discussed in Arthur (1985), increasing returns

---

[18]*Cf.* Dosi, Pavitt and Soete (1988).
[19]See, for example, Arrow and Hahn (1971); Katz and Shapiro (1983); Arthur (1985).

generally show the properties of (i) non-predictability of equilibria; (ii) non-ergodicity (the past is not "forgotten" by the future and strong hysteresis effects emerge); and (iii) potential inefficiency (a particular equilibrium, or, dynamically, a particular path might be "inferior" in terms of any welfare measure but still the system may be "locked" in it).

Somewhat similarly, trade analyses show that, with non-convexities, decentralized processes of allocation may not lead to mutual gains from trade (see, for example, Krugman 1984; Markusen and Melvin, 1984; and Helpman and Krugman, 1985).

Now, generalize these results by considering the fact that (a) technical change always represents a form of increasing returns over time, and (b) most often, technological advances are associated with the actual process of production (see above) and, thus, cannot be treated parametrically (e.g., as exogenous shocks which switch the value of equilibria of time t to those of time $(t + 1)$). One is bound to account for an interaction between decisions of production at time t and technical coefficients at time $(t + 1)$, conceptually similar to the interaction between technical coefficients and levels of production of static analyses of increasing returns. The fundamental point is that, with increasing returns, the market cannot signal to the agents the unintentional outcome of their collective behaviour (think—as the clearest example—of economies of scale external to the firm and internal to the industry). Even more so, markets *cannot* signal the (at least partly) *uncertain, unintentional* and *future* technological advances made possible/fostered/hindered by the present decentralized allocative decisions of a relatively high number of independent profit-motivated agents.[20] *A fortiori* Arthur's conclusions on non-predictability, inflexibility, non-ergodicity and potential inefficiency apply to this case, too.

As an illustration,[21] consider the case of two countries which—before trade—produce, under conditions of non-decreasing returns, two commodities, characterized by different future opportunities of learning and technical progress. As argued earlier, suppose that learning occurs only (or primarily) together with the actual process of production. Now, allow trade to take place. The resulting patterns of specialization, as trade theory predicts, will generally entail a better allocation of resources and, thus, "gains from trade". However, one of the two countries may well be "locked" into an activity where the scope of technical progress is relatively limited. Under such circumstances, in order to have gains from trade in the long term the relative gain stemming from a better allocation of resources must exceed the

---

[20]This independence concerns, of course, decision-making. However, the point is that each agent contributes to creating an "externality" for the whole of them.

[21]At the time of the second revision of this work, a paper by P. Dasgupta and J. Stiglitz on "Exercises in Learning-by-Doing", which shows some similarity with the example that follows, was presented at the Conference on Innovation Diffusion, Venice, 17–21 March, 1986.

productivity increases which would have been obtained by producing also (or more of) a commodity characterized by a higher technological opportunity. Conversely, for the other country the gains from a better "Ricardian" allocation of resources will sum up with the gains from relatively higher technical progress in the commodity in which it is specialized. Thus, the other country will always enjoy gains-from-trade, both in the short and the long term.

If one considers a sufficiently long time span, thus allowing for a significant technical progress to take place, it is plausible that the once-for-all gains in resource allocation coming from the decentralized search of minimum-cost opportunities of production may well fall short of the cumulative gains in productivity which would have been obtained over time with "sub-optimal" allocations (in a static sense) biased in favour of activities characterized by higher technological opportunities (for a similar point, see Pasinetti, 1981).

As an historical illustration, it is not necessary to think of developing countries: it is even possible that the technological leadership in "old" technological paradigms (and, thus, a strong "comparative advantage" in the related commodities) may be a hindrance to a quick allocation of resources to new ones. One could think, as examples, of the relative British delay in electro-mechanical technologies, as compared with Germany and the U.S.A., at the turn of the century, or the European delay in electronics technologies, as compared to Japan, in the post-war period.

As a related empirical generalization, we suggest that the *likelihood of such trade-offs between allocative and Schumpeterian efficiencies is proportional to the distance of each country from the technological frontier* in the newest and most promising technologies, where a high rate of innovation, idiosyncratic processes of learning and appropriation tend to prevent any easy endogenous process of international technological diffusion.[22]

Proposition 7

A somewhat similar argument applies to the possibility of trade-offs between allocative and growth efficiencies. Generally, the analysis of the outcome of the notional transition from autarky to trade is undertaken by focusing upon the adjustments in relative prices and relative quantities on the assumption of unchanged rates of macroeconomic activity.

This condition of *constancy* of the aggregate level of macroeconomic activity before and after trade, is already stated from the start by Ricardo[23]

---

[22]For an analysis also of the forces that, on the contrary, tend to induce technological diffusion and convergence between countries, *cf.* Dosi, Pavitt and Soete (1988). See also Perez (1983) and Metcalfe and Soete (1984).

[23]*Cf.* Ricardo (1951, p. 129).

and it is maintained by modern classical reappraisals *à la* Sraffa–Steedman, whereby the analysis is undertaken in terms of steady-growth paths. This applies—even more so—to neoclassical trade theories, whereby the hypothesis of full-employment of all factors of production is possibly the *core* assumption of the model.

The easiest way to see this condition at work is to imagine that each trading nation operates at full employment rates of activity. In this case, whenever all the other assumptions hold, we can see the full operation of the theorem of comparative advantage: each trading partner "gains from trade" since it can get from abroad more commodities of a certain kind than it would otherwise be able to manufacture domestically without foregoing any amount of consumption of the commodities in which that country is specialized.

Modern economic systems, however, do not often present full employment rates of activity. In these cases the *macroeconomic* efficiency of specialization based on comparative advantages depends on the income intensity (and, dynamically, on income elasticities) of the various commodities in world income. As a first approximation, let us suppose that:

(a) price elasticities, in the generality of the traded commodities for the corresponding world industry as a whole, are relatively low;[24]

(b) commodities present a relatively wide range of income elasticities which are *commodity-specific* and *country-specific*.

Let us also add that, in general, price-related substitution in consumption is limited and the patterns of demand are essentially related to income levels, long-run trends in income distribution and institutional and social factors (more on this point is in Pasinetti, 1981).

Now, under conditions of non-decreasing returns, there is no straightforward way in which markets can relate the varying future growth-efficiencies of the various commodities to relative-profitability signals for the microeconomic agents. In other words, microeconomic units may well find it relatively profitable to produce commodities which a decreasing number of people on the world market wants to buy. The reader may think, as extreme examples, of the dynamic outcomes of patterns of comparative advantages in "inferior" commodities (say, jute, mechanical typewriters or black and white TVs) as compared to income-dynamic ones (say, synthetic fibres, word processors, or colour TVs).

A limited price-induced substitution between commodities and a relatively stable evolution in the baskets of consumption may well imply painful trade-offs between microeconomic mechanisms leading to Ricardian efficiency and those patterns of production which could yield comparatively

[24]This statement must not be confused with price elasticities for individual countries which might well be higher. In other words, relatively small price changes may induce significant changes in the international competitiveness of individual countries even when the overall world demand for the corresponding commodity shows a very low price elasticity. There is, however, an essential "beggar-my-neighbour" element in this process.

higher rates of macroeconomic activity compatible with the foreign balance constraint (via higher foreign-trade multipliers).[25]

This is our seventh proposition.

Possible trade-offs between allocative, Schumpeterian and growth efficiencies have nothing to do with exceptional cases of "infant industry" conditions, but are structurally at the core of the signalling and allocative mechanisms of our economic system.[26]

Remarkably, markets may well work efficiently, deliver all the information they can and even discount contingencies for future states of the world to which probabilities can notionally be attached (although, empirically, these markets rarely exist). What markets *cannot* do is to deliver information about or discount the possibility of future states of the world whose occurrence is itself an "externality" resulting unintentionally from the interaction of present decisions of behaviourally unrelated agents. As we saw, this is precisely one of the characteristics of these particular "increasing returns" over time which are associated with technological learning. In this respect, conflicts between short-term allocative efficiency and Schumpeterian efficiency, as defined earlier, could emerge even if markets were complete (in a neoclassical sense: if all contingencies about future *states of nature* could be discounted).[27]

Somewhat similarly, the possibility of conflict between allocative efficiency and growth efficiency is not associated with any "market imperfection". On the contrary, it is due to the fact that, lacking both generalized substitution in consumption with respect to prices and homotheticity of the patterns of demand in income—as we believe to be the

---

[25] Again, for a more thorough discussion along these lines, we must refer to Dosi, Pavitt and Soete (1988). There, and in Cimoli, Dosi and Soete (1986), we formalize a two-country model with "Ricardian" processes of inter-commodity specialization and "Keynesian adjustments" in the rates of macroeconomic activity under a foreign balance constraint, showing also that, *ceteris paribus*, the rates of growth of any one economy consistent with the foreign accounts will be higher, the higher the income intensity (i.e., dynamically, the income elasticity) of the commodities in which that country is specialized. Under certain conditions, this property is approximated by the Kaldor–Thirlwall foreign trade multiplier, whereby the rate of growth of each economy is determined by the world income elasticity of its exports compared to the domestic income elasticity of its imports (see Thirlwall, 1980).

[26] A way of restating Propositions 6 and 7 which is possibly more familiar to the economist is by saying that the *general case*, in our view, is the non-convexity of production- and consumption-possibility sets (more rigorously, their *non-existence*, except perhaps in the very small). In general, the conclusions we draw from Propositions 6 and 7 are consistent with and broadly similar to the analyses of international competitiveness of Cohen *et al.* (1984) and of Mistral (1982).

[27] It is conceivable, if implausible, to discount states of nature such as "tomorrow it will rain". This is clearly very different from the possibility of trading guesses about states of the world which, in turn, depend on one's own expectations on what all the others are doing, let alone all the problems related to the indivisibilities and public-good features of technological knowledge (Keynes's "beauty contest" parable somewhat resembles this set of "market failures" related to interdependencies between expectations, behaviours and states-of-the-world; see also Schelling, 1978).

general case—there is no general way in which markets can transform "information" about long-term trends in income elasticities of the various commodities into economic incentives for competitive producers who tend to treat the states of the world parametrically.

Incidentally, one might notice that both these sources of conflict between static (allocative) efficiency and the two criteria of dynamic efficiency hint at the possible advantages of oligopoly as compared to free competition. In world oligopolistic markets the "dynamic externalities" associated with technical learning-through-production can be (partly) appropriated by individual firms. Thus, current allocative decisions may take account, to different degrees, of their effects upon future technological advances. Similarly, for oligopolistic agents the slope of and the movements over time in demand schedules matter and so present patterns of allocation may account for different expected income elasticities of demand. To give an example, a few European electrical companies (such as Philips and Siemens) decided in the early 'seventies to increase their involvement in microelectronics, despite heavy losses (i.e., despite "allocative inefficiency" and "comparative disadvantage"). Amongst the motivations, there were the expected very high rates of growth of the market and the technological capabilities which could have been acquired and would perform as an "internalized externality" for technologically-related productions. One could not expect the same behaviour from competitive producers.

The trade-offs that we have discussed between allocative efficiency, growth efficiency and technological dynamism may clearly be one of the determinants of the emergence of vicious and virtuous circles in national patterns of growth. Notably, this conclusion is similar to those which are well established in development theory. However, its determinants do not bear any direct relationship with phenomena specific to developing countries (such as several kinds of supposed "market failures"). For our purposes here, developed and developing countries could be placed on some kind of continuum, according to their distance from the technological frontiers and to the differences between their patterns of production and the long-term patterns of world demand.

Whenever any one country happens to present its highest technological lead (or the lowest technological gap) in new technological paradigms, then its pattern of intersectoral profitability signals points in the directions of activities which generally also present the highest demand growth and the highest potential of future product- and process-innovations. Conversely, countries well behind the technological frontiers may be "dynamically penalized" by their present patterns of intersectoral allocative efficiency. This property, in our view, contributes to explain the relative stability of the "pecking order" between countries in terms of technological innovativeness and international competitiveness and also the relatively ordered ways in which this "pecking order" changes in the long term. The interaction between present economic signals, patterns of specializations and dynamics of the sectoral technology gaps provides the basis for cumulative processes. Significantly, major changes in the international competitiveness of each economy are often associated with the emergence of new technological paradigms. This occurrence reshapes the patterns of technological advantages/disadvantages between countries, often demands different organizational and institutional set-ups and sometimes presents a unique opportunity for the emergence of new technological and economic leaders.

More generally, we may restate the foregoing argument in the following way. Markets characterized by decentralized decision-making fulfil two fundamental functions. First, they provide a mechanism of coordination between individual economic decisions and, in doing so, they reallocate resources in ways, which—under the conditions specified by the theory— have efficiency properties of varying degrees. Second, whenever we allow technological progress to take place (with its features of search, uncertainty, etc.), markets provide an incentive to innovate through the possibility of private appropriation of some economic benefit stemming from technical progress itself. Relatedly, they provide a selection environment for the innovations. It is remarkable that as soon as these second functions of markets are considered in the theoretical picture, their efficiency properties become more blurred and complicated to assess, even in a closed economy context: allocative efficiency in a static sense may conflict with dynamic efficiency in terms of incentives to technological progress. It is not the purpose of this work to analyse in depth these "Schumpeterian trade-offs", which are discussed by Nelson (1981) and Nelson and Winter (1982). Overlapping with, and adding to, the "Schumpeterian trade-offs" of the closed economy case, there is—we argued here—the possibility of a statics *vs.* dynamics trade-off originating from the patterns of economic signals in the international market. In a way, the open economy case induces a *structural distortion* upon that pattern of signals which would have been generated in autarky conditions. In doing so, they may either overrule upon the domestic "Schumpeterian trade-offs" or amplify them. The substantive hypothesis, we suggested, is that this depends on the relative distance of each country *vis-à-vis* the technological frontiers in those technological paradigms showing the highest opportunities of innovation and demand growth.

III ECONOMIC AND TECHNOLOGICAL DYNAMISM: THE ROLE OF
INSTITUTIONS AND POLICIES

The seven propositions discussed above jointly highlight a picture of the process of coordination of economic activities and generation of technological advances whereby institutions (both "micro" institutions, e.g., complex corporate structures embodying specific capabilities, rules of behaviours "rationalities", modes of institutional organization of market interactions, etc.; and "macro" institutions, such as strictly public agencies) enter as a set of crucial factors irreducible to simple economic mechanisms. On the contrary, *lato sensu* institutional factors appear to shape the *constitution of behavioural rules, learning processes, patterns of environmental selection, context conditions* under which economic mechanisms operate—in general, and *a fortiori* with reference to technological change. To put it another way, there appears to be *no* meaningful possibility of (a) separating the strictly economic variables from their institutional context and then assessing the former in relation to their performance outcome, neglecting the latter; (b) assuming that strictly economic variables overdetermine their institutional contexts to such an extent that the latter tend to converge to a unique pattern; (c) simply reducing all extra economic elements to either interferences or exceptional corrections to a supposedly "optimally-performing", self-contained and well-tuned economic machine. That is to say that, if the propositions suggested above are correct, then also any assessment of the role of policies based on the "reductionist" approach is bound to be, at best, incomplete.[28]

In these circumstances, complex normative issues emerge in relation to the definition and assessment of the efficiency of various combinations between institutional set-ups, nature of the technologies and economic processes. Here, we are simply going to suggest some conjectures and methodological remarks.

First, let us start from a classification of the variables upon which policies may act—in general and with particular reference to technological progress. On the grounds of the foregoing discussion they can be categorized as:

(a) the capability of the scientific/technological system of providing major innovative advances and of organizing the technological *context conditions* (ranging from infrastructure to the ways the different varieties of externalities are organized);

(b) the *capabilities of the economic agents,* in terms of the technology they embody, the effectiveness and speed with which they search for new technological and organizational advances, etc.;

(c) the patterns of *signals* (which, as we saw, depend also on inter-firm and inter-national technological asymmetries, and, in turn, shape the boundaries

---

[28]Remarkably, somewhat similar conclusions can be implicitly reached by the exploration of the properties and heuristic limitations of general equilibrium models with externalities, indivisibilities, limited and/or market dependent information (*cf.,* for example, Hahn, 1984 and 1985; Kornai, 1971; and Stiglitz, 1984). The institutional "architecture" of the system must be accounted for as one of the determinants of the performance of the system (Stiglitz, 1984). Once we recognize that (a) externalities, uncertainty, increasing returns, etc. are *general* and *permanent* features of economies characterized by change in general and technical change in particular, and (b) institutions are necessary to explain economic performance at any time and the relative order of economic change over time, then, in our view, not much is left to interpretative powers of the "reductionist" research programme.

of the set of possible microeconomic responses that are economically feasible for agents which—irrespective of their precise strategies—have profitability among their behavioural considerations);

(d) the *forms of organization* within and between markets (e.g., the relationship between financial structures and industry, the forms of industrial relations, the varying balance between cooperation and competition, the degree and forms of corporate internalization of transactions, etc.);

(e) the incentives/stimuli/constraints facing the agents in their adjustment and innovative processes (e.g., the degree of private appropriability of the benefits of innovating, the intensity of competitive threats, the cost and profitability of innovation, etc.).

These categories, we suggest, allow a taxonomy of policies according to their implications in terms of the corresponding groups of variables. Our general conjectures are that (i) all major Western countries indeed present relatively high degrees of intervention—whether consciously conceived as industrial policies or not—that affect all the above variables; (ii) probably, if one simply considers the impact of various forms of financial transfer and public procurement, no striking difference is likely to be detected between most OECD countries (possibly with a relatively lower importance in Japan); and (iii) what primarily differentiates the various countries are the instruments, the institutional arrangements and the philosophy of intervention. As an illustration, consider the case of Japanese policies, especially in relation to electronics technologies. Interestingly, Japan appears to have acted comprehensively upon all the variables categorized in our taxonomy above. A heavy discretionary intervention upon the structure of signals (by means of formal and informal protection against imports and foreign investments and through an investment policy of financial institutions consistent with growth and Schumpeterian efficiencies) recreated the "vacuum environment" that is generally enjoyed only by the technological leader(s). However, this was matched by a pattern of fierce oligopolistic rivalry between Japanese companies and a heavy export orientation which fostered technological dynamism and prevented any exploitation of protection simply in terms of collusive monopolistic pricing.

It is tempting to compare this Japanese experience with others, much less successful, such as the European ones, which heavily relied upon one single instrument, financial transfers (especially R&D subsidies and transfers on capital account), leaving to the endogenous working of the international market both the determination of the patterns of signals and the response capabilities of individual firms. Certainly, there are country-specific features of the Japanese example which are hardly transferable. However, that case, in its striking outcome, points at a general possibility of reshaping the patterns of "comparative advantages" as they emerge from the endogenous evolution of the international markets.

There is a general point here. Historically, a successful catching-up effort in terms of per capita income and wages has always been accompanied by technological catching-up in the new and most dynamic technological paradigms, irrespective of the initial patterns of comparative advantages, specializations and market-generated signals.

Second, from a normative point of view, the foregoing discussion highlights the general role that policies and/or institutions play in technological change. The innovative process *necessarily* embodies a complex and differentiated mixture of private appropriation and public-good aspects (see Nelson, 1981 and 1984) and involves an unavoidable "market failure", to use the language familiar to economists. Thus, the normative counterpart of this phenomenon does not regard *if* but *how* and *to what degree* policies should affect the innovative activities. Moreover, the existence of possible trade-offs between "static" efficiency, on the one hand, and growth/"Schumpeterian" efficiencies, on the other, sometimes amplified by the ways technological gaps feed back on market signals in the international market, implies that policies affecting also economic signals may be required—on whatever welfare criterion is chosen (e.g., income growth, innovativeness, employment, etc.)—in a much wider set of cases than those prescribed by traditional "infant industry" arguments.

Our conjecture is that, *ceteris paribus*, the structural need for policies affecting *also* the patterns of economic signals (including relative prices and relative profitabilities) as they emerge from the international market will be greater, the higher the distance of any one country from the technological frontier. Conversely, endogenous market mechanisms tend to behave in a "virtuous" manner for those countries that happen to be on the frontier, especially in the newest/most promising technologies. This is broadly confirmed by historical experience: unconditional free trade often happened to be advocated and fully exploited only by the leading countries.

Third, as regards the time-profile of technological developments, a fundamental divide can be traced between policies related to the *emergence* of new technological paradigms and policies apt to sustain technological activities along relatively established paths. In the former case, policies should (i) provide a satisfactory flow of scientific advances; (ii) establish "bridging institutions" between scientific developments and their economic exploitation; (iii) develop conducive financial structures to support the trial-and-error procedures generally involved in the search for new technological paradigms; and (iv) act as "focusing devices"[29] in the process of selection of the directions of technological development. As regards "normal" technical progress, important policy tasks appear to be the maintenance of a relatively fluid supply of techno-scientific advances, coupled with "balanced" conditions of private appropriability of the benefits of innovating.

[29]*Cf.* Rosenberg (1976).

Conversely, countries well below the technological frontier may find it necessary also to act directly upon both the capability levels of the domestic companies and *against* the appropriability features of the related technologies insofar as they perform as an *entry barrier* for laggard companies/countries.

Fourth, there is a fundamental policy dimension which relates to context conditions, the organization of externalities and infrastructures. These are likely to be particularly important in the process of transition between different technological regimes (different clusters of technological paradigms), whereby the new set-ups involve new patterns of intersectoral flows of commodities and information, new common infrastructures (think of the role of motorways in relation to the automotive industries or the role of telecommunications in relation to electronics), and a different set of untraded interdependencies between companies and sectors.

Fifth, public policies, whether intentionally or not, affect the fundamental "rationalities" of the agents, the ways their expectations and objectives are formed. By means of an illustration, one may think of the role of military spending. In addition to obvious effects upon the composition of demand and the pattern of economic signals, another indirect, but equally important, implication regards the way it is likely to shape the strategies and the managerial outlooks: almost certainly, public agencies tend to be perceived as a "guarantee of last resort",[30] while the skills of detecting and influencing procurement authorities are likely to become dominant upon the capabilities of understanding and anticipating market trends in competitive environments. Clearly, this is only one—possibly the most straightforward— example of a set of influences that the political structures exert upon the *behavioural constitution* of market processes.[31]

IV   SOME CONCLUSIONS

In a world characterized by technical change (both "continuous" change along defined technological trajectories and "discontinuous" ones related to the emergence of new technological paradigms), technological lags and leads shape the patterns of intersectoral and interproduct profitability signals and, thus, also the patterns of microeconomic allocation. The latter, however, may affect the long-term macroeconomic dynamism of each country, in terms of both rates of growth of income consistent with the foreign balance constraint and of technological innovativeness. In the last resort, this happens because the effects of a multiplicity of signals (related to profitability, long-term demand growth and technological opportunities) upon microeconomic

---

[30]We owe this observation to a discussion with H. Minsky.
[31]Another important example, analysed by Zysman (1983), concerns the effects of country-specific institutional organizations of the financial markets upon the allocation of resources and the industrial attitudes toward risk, growth, innovation, etc.

processes of adjustments are likely to be *asymmetric*. Whenever trade-offs between different notions of efficiency arise, "sub-optimal" or "perverse" macroeconomic outcomes may emerge. Since the *future* pattern of technological advantages/disadvantages is also related to the *present* allocative patterns, we can see at work here dynamic processes which Kaldor calls of "circular causation": economic signals related to intersectoral profitabilities—which lead in a straightforward manner to "comparative advantages" and relative specializations—certainly control and check the allocative efficiency of the various productive employments, but may also play a more ambiguous or even perverse role in relation to long-term macroeconomic trends.

The ("vicious" or "virtuous") circular processes we have discussed concern the very nature of allocative mechanisms, insofar as the economy is characterized by technical change showing varying degrees of sector-specific opportunity, cumulativeness, appropriability, dynamic technological externalities and local and idiosyncratic learning.

This defines also a fundamental domain for policies.

Moreover, we argued, institutional factors—including, of course, policies—are part of the very *constitution* of economic processes, i.e., the ways economic activities are organized and coordinated, technical change is generated and used, the dominant behavioural regularities emerge, etc. This is another fundamental domain for policies.

A detailed understanding of, and intervention upon, patterns of signals, rules of allocative responses and forms of institutional organization of the "economic machine" are particularly important in those phases of transition from a technological regime (based on old technological paradigms) to a new one. These historical periods define a new set of opportunities and threats for each country: the patterns of international generation and diffusion of technologies become more fluid as do, consequently, the international trade flows and the relative levels of per capita income.

The contemporary economy—we believe—is undergoing such a change, in the transition toward an electronics-based technological regime. In the process, comparative advantages become the self-fulfilling prophecy of a successful set of institutional actions and private strategies: *ex post*, technological and economic success makes "optimal" from the point of view of the economist what *ex ante* is a political dream.

One decade after the Second World War, no economist would have suggested that electronics was one of the Japanese comparative advantages. Now it certainly is. If one would have taken the relative allocative efficiency of the different industrial sectors thirty years ago as the ground for normative prescriptions, Japan would still probably be exporting silk ties. In a sense, the use of comparative-advantage criteria as the final and sole ground for normative prescriptions is a luxury that only countries on the technological frontier can afford: *rebus sic stantibus*, it will not take long before Japanese

Institutions and Markets in a Dynamic World   143

economists will learn and preach Ricardo or even Heckscher–Ohlin while it may well be that the Americans and the Europeans will rediscover Hamilton, List and Ferrier.

REFERENCES

Arrow, K. and Hahn, F. (1971). *General Competitive Analysis*, San Francisco, Ca., Holden-Day.

Arthur, W. B. (1985). "Competing Technologies and Lock-in by Historical Events: The Dynamics of Allocation Under Increasing Returns", *Stanford University, CEPR, Discussion Paper.*

Atkinson, A. B. and Stiglitz, J. (1969). "A New View of Technological Change", *Economic Journal*, Vol. 79, No. 3, pp. 573–578.

Boyer, R. and Mistral, J. (1983). *Accumulation, Inflation, Crises* (2nd Edition), Paris, Presses Universitaires de France.

Chandler, A. D. (1966). *Strategy and Structure*, New York, Anchor Books.

Chandler, A. D. (1977). *The Visible Hand. The Managerial Revolution in American Business*, Cambridge, Mass., The Belknap Press.

Cimoli, M., Dosi, G. and Soete, L. (1986). "Technology Gaps, Institutional Differences and Patterns of Trade: A North–South Model, *SPRU, University of Sussex, DRC Discussion Paper.*

Cohen, S., Teece, D., Tyson, L. and Zysman, J. (1984). "Competitiveness", *University of California at Berkeley, BRIE Working Paper.*

Cropsey, J. (1957). *Policy and the Economy. An Interpretation of the Principles of Adam Smith*, The Hague, M. Nijhoff.

Dalton, G. (Ed.) (1971). *Primitive, Archaic and Modern Economies*, Boston, Ma., Beacon Press.

David, P. (1975). *Technical Change, Innovation and Economic Growth*, Cambridge, Cambridge University Press.

Denison, E. F. (1967). *Why Growth Rates Differ*, Washington, D.C., Brookings Institution.

Dore, R. (1973). *British Factory—Japanese Factory*, London, Allen and Unwin.

Dosi, G. (1984). *Technical Change and Industrial Transformation*, London, Macmillan.

Dosi, G. and Orsenigo, L. (1985). "Market Processes, Rules and Institutions in Technical Change and Economic Dynamics", presented at the Conference on "The Impact of Technology, Labour Processes and Financial Structures on Economic Progress and Stability", St. Louis, Missouri, May 1985, forthcoming in H. Minsky and P. Ferri (eds.), *Innovation, Financial Structures and Growth Stability*, New York, Sharp, 1988.

Dosi, G., Orsenigo, L. and Silverberg, G. (1986). "Innovation, Diversity and Diffusion: A Self-Organisation Model", *SPRU, University of Sussex, DRC Discussion Paper.*

Dosi, G., Pavitt, K. and Soete, L. (1988). *The Economics of Technical Change and International Trade*, Brighton, Wheatsheaf, forthcoming.

Dumont, L. (1977). *Homo Aequalis. Genèse et Épanouissement de l'Idéologie Économique*, Paris, Gallimard.

Freeman, C. (1982). *The Economics of Industrial Innovations* (Second Edition), London, Francis Pinter.

Frydman, R. (1982). "Toward an Understanding of Market Processes", *American Economic Review*, Vol. 72, No. 4, pp. 652–668.

Gibbons, M., Gummett, P. and Udgaonkar, B. M. (Eds.) (1984). *Science and Technology Policy in the 1980's and Beyond*, London, Longmans.

Hahn, F. (1984). *Equilibrium and Macroeconomics*, Oxford, Basil Blackwell.
Hahn, F. (1985). "On Equilibrium with Market-Dependent Information" in *Money, Growth and Stability*, Oxford, Basil Blackwell.
Heiner, R. A. (1983). "The Origin of Predictable Behavior", *American Economic Review*, Vol. 73, No. 4, pp. 560–595.
Helpman, E. and Krugman, P. (1985). *Market Structure and Foreign Trade*, Cambridge, Mass., MIT Press.
Hirsch, F. (1976). *Social Limits to Growth*, Cambridge, Mass., Harvard University Press.
Hirschman, A. (1970). *Exit, Voice and Loyalty*, Cambridge, Mass., Harvard University Press.
Hirschman, A. (1977). *The Passion and the Interests*, Princeton, N.J., Princeton University Press.
Hirschman, A. (1982). "Rival Interpretations of Market Society: Civilising, Destructive or Feeble?", *Journal of Economic Literature*, Vol. 20, No. 4, pp. 1463–1484.
Johnson, C. A. (1982). *MITI and the Japanese Miracle: The Growth of Industrial Policies, 1925–1975*, Stanford, Ca., Stanford University Press.
Kaldor, N. (1972). "The Irrelevance of Equilibrium Economics", *Economic Journal*, Vol. 82, No. 4, pp. 1237–1255.
Kaldor, N. (1980). *The Role of Increasing Returns, Technical Progress and Cumulative Causation in the Theory of International Trade*, Paris, ISMEA.
Katz, N. L. and Shapiro, C. (1983). "Network Externalities, Competition and Compatibility", *Princeton University, Woodrow Wilson School, Discussion Paper No. 54*.
Kierzkowski, H. (Ed.) (1984). *Monopolistic Competition and International Trade*, Oxford, Oxford University Press.
Kornai, J. (1971). *Anti-Equilibrium*, Amsterdam, North-Holland.
Krugman, P. (1984). "Import Protection as Export Promotion: International Competition in the Presence of Oligopoly and Economies of Scale" in Kierzkowski (ed.), *op. cit.*
Levin, R., Klevarick, A. J., Nelson, R. and Winter, S. (1984). "Survey Research on R&D Appropriability and Technological Opportunity. Part I: Appropriability", Yale University, mimeo.
Luhman, N. (1975). *Macht*, Stuttgart, Ferdinand Euke Verlag.
Markusen, J. R. and Melvin, J. R. (1984). "The Gains-from-Trade Theorem with Increasing Returns to Scale" in Kierzkowski (ed.), *op. cit.*
Marris, R. and Mueller, D. C. (1980). "Corporation, Competition and the Invisible Hand", *Journal of Economic Literature*, Vol. 18, No. 1, pp. 32–63.
Metcalfe, J. S. (1985). "On Technological Competition", Manchester University, mimeo.
Metcalfe, J. S. and Soete, L. (1984). "Diffusion in Innovations and International Competitiveness" in Gibbons, Gummett and Udgaonkar (eds.), *op. cit.*
Mistral, J. (1982). "La Diffusion Inter-national Inégal de l'Accumulation et ses Crises" in Reiffers (ed.), *op. cit.*
Nelson, R. (1968). "A 'Diffusion' Model of International Productivity Differences in Manufacturing Industry", *American Economic Review*, Vol. 58, No. 5, pp. 1219–1248.
Nelson, R. (1981). "Assessing Private Enterprise", *Bell Journal of Economics*, Vol. 12, No. 1, pp. 93–111.
Nelson, R. (1982). "The Role of Knowledge in R&D Efficiency", *Quarterly Journal of Economics*, Vol. 97, No. 3, pp. 453–470.

Institutions and Markets in a Dynamic World   145

Nelson, R. (Ed.) (1982a). *The Government and Technical Progress*, New York, Pergamon Press.

Nelson R. (1984). *High Technology Policies: A Five Nations Comparison*, Washington, D.C., American Enterprise Institute.

Nelson, R. and Winter, S. (1977). "In Search of a Useful Theory of Innovation", *Research Policy*, Vol. 6, No. 1, pp. 36–76.

Nelson, R. and Winter, S. (1982). *An Evolutionary Theory of Economic Change*, Cambridge, Mass., The Belknap Press.

Noble, D. F. (1977). *America by Design*, Oxford, Oxford University Press.

Pasinetti, L. L. (1981). *Structural Change and Economic Growth*, Cambridge, Cambridge University Press.

Pavitt, K. (1984). "Sectoral Patterns of Technical Change: Towards a Taxonomy and a Theory", *Research Policy*, Vol. 13, No. 6, pp. 343–373.

Perez, C. (1983). "Structural Change and New Technologies", *Futures*, Vol. 15, No. 5, pp. 357–375.

Pizzorno, A. (1985). "Some Other Kinds of Otherness", Harvard University, Department of Sociology, mimeo.

Plott, C. R. (1982). "Industrial Organisation Theory and Experimental Economics", *Journal of Economic Literature*, Vol. 20, No. 4, pp. 1485–1527.

Polanyi, K. (1944). *The Great Transformation*, Boston, Ma., Beacon Press.

Polanyi, K. (1971). "Our Obsolete Market Mentality" in Dalton (ed.), *op. cit.*

Reiffers, J. L. (Ed.) (1982). *Économie et Finance Internationale*, Paris, Dunod.

Ricardo, D. (1951). *On the Principles of Political Economy and Taxation*, P. Sraffa (ed.), Cambridge, Cambridge University Press.

Rosenberg, N. (1976). *Perspectives in Technology*, Cambridge, Cambridge University Press.

Rosenberg, N. (1982). *Inside the Black Box*, Cambridge, Cambridge University Press.

Sah, R. K. and Stiglitz, J. E. (1985). "Human Fallibility and Economic Organisation", *American Economic Review*, Papers and Proceedings, Vol. 75, No. 2, pp. 292–297.

Salvati, M. (1985). "Diversita' e mutamento", *Economia Politica*, Vol. 2, No. 2, pp. 249–292.

Schelling, T. C. (1978). *Micromotives and Macrobehavior*, New York, Norton.

Scherer, F. M. (1980). *Industrial Market Structure and Economic Performance* (2nd Edition), Chicago, Rand McNally.

Scherer, F. M. (1982). "Inter-Industry Technology Flows in the U.S.", *Research Policy*, Vol. 11, No. 3, pp. 227–245.

Schumpeter, J. A. (1961). *The Theory of Economic Development*, Oxford, Oxford University Press.

Schumpeter, J. A. (1975). *Capitalism, Socialism, Democracy*, New York, Harper and Row.

Shonfield, A. (1965). *Modern Capitalism. The Changing Balance of Public and Private Power*, Oxford, Oxford University Press.

Silva, F. (1984). "Some Comparison in the Fields of Industrial Policy: Theory, the U.S., Italy", *Yale University, Institution for Social and Policy Studies, Working Paper No. 1016.*

Smith, A. (1976). *The Theory of Moral Sentiments*, Oxford, Oxford University Press.

Stiglitz, J. E. (1984). "Information and Economic Analysis: A Perspective", *Economic Journal, Conference Papers*, Vol. 95, pp. 21–41.

Teece, D. (1982). "Toward an Economic Theory of the Multiproduct Firms", *Journal of Economic Behavior and Organisation*, Vol. 3, No. 1, pp. 39–63.

Thirlwall, A. P. (1980). *Balance-of-Payment Theory and the United Kingdom Experience*, London, Macmillan.

de Tocqueville, A. (1969). *Democracy in America*, New York, Anchor Books.

Veblen, T. (1915). *Imperial Germany and the Industrial Revolution*, London, Macmillan.

Williamson, O. (1979). *Markets and Hierarchies*, New York, Free Press.

Williamson, O. (1981). "The Modern Corporation: Origin, Evolution, Attributes", *Journal of Economic Literature*, Vol. 19, No. 4, pp. 1537–1568.

Winter, S. (1982). "An Essay on the Theory of Production" in S. H. Hymans (ed.), *Economics and the World Around It*, Ann Arbor, Mich., University of Michigan Press.

Zysman, J. (1983). *Governments, Markets and Growth. Financial Systems and the Politics of Industrial Change*, Ithaca, N.Y., Cornell University Press.

[20]

Journal of Institutional and Theoretical Economics (JITE) 144 (1988), 635–657
Zeitschrift für die gesamte Staatswissenschaft

Economic Change and the Boundaries of the Firm

by

Richard N. Langlois *

Introduction

The study of economic change – including technological change – has long been a subject of fascination to economists. It is also a subject that has proven refractory to most attempts to capture it adequately. This essay is an attempt to walk a small piece of this difficult ground. Specifically, it aims to examine the problems that economic change poses for the explanation of the organization of firms. By this I mean the problem of explaining the boundaries of the firm – explaining the extent of internal organization or vertical integration.

What follows is an intellectual progress report rather than a polished theory. In an earlier foray into the field (LANGLOIS [1984]), I tried to sort out some of the methodological issues that would attend an explanation of vertical integration in a regime of rapid economic change. That paper was in part an attempt to locate the connections between a transaction-cost approach to the study of internal organization (WILLIAMSON [1985]) and an evolutionary or process discussion of economic change (NELSON and WINTER [1982]). I suggested then that any explanation of internal organization in a regime of rapid change ought to take into account two factors: disequilibrium and path-dependency. The present paper sets out to elaborate such an explanation, incorporating both my own more recent ideas on the subject and the relevant work of such writers as SILVER [1984] and TEECE [1984, 1986a, 1986b].

Economists confronting a phenomenon as complex as internal organization are faced with an inevitable tradeoff. On the one hand is the impulse to multiply variables and auxiliary conditions in order to capture a passable likeness of the world. On the other hand is the quite sensible desire to edit out such entities, even at the risk of leaving the best scenes on the cutting-room floor. The tendency in the management literature is generally to err in the former direction; this is what makes that literature so rich and, for economists, so

* The author would like to thank Bo Carlsson, Gunnar Eliasson, Ken-ichi Imai, Brian Loasby, Richard Nelson, Paul Robertson, and L. G. Thomas for helpful suggestions and discussions.

frustrating. Economic theories of vertical integration tend, by contrast, to the other extreme. They try to explain the phenomenon of vertical integration by at most one or two variables. This is why such theories are typically stark and, in the end, unsatisfying. In the spirit of the transaction-cost approach – and the "New Institutional Economics" more broadly – I will try to keep a middle ground in this essay. Much of the analysis will proceed by examining arguments carefully, and therefore by making distinctions. But I hope to keep these distinctions few enough that they might eventually serve as elements for a coherent dynamic theory of internal organization.

Theories of Vertical Integration

Economic theories of vertical integration fall into a number of distinct categories.[1]

One kind of theory involves what WILLIAMSON [1985, pp. 86–89] calls technological determinism: it is the production technology that alone (or primarily) shapes the organization of the productive unit. Such theories are unsatisfactory for a number of reasons, not the least of which is empirical. If the advent of centralized water and stream power gave us the factory system, why did not the advent of small electric motors destroy that system?[2] To put the matter more generally, we observe far more organizational integration than is explicable on grounds of technological indivisibilities alone.[3]

Another class of explanations are those of standard Marshallian price theory and the "structure-conduct-performance" paradigm, now somewhat quaint and old-fashioned, that grew out of it. For both descriptive and normative purposes, this approach swings on a single analytical hinge: the concept of "monopoly" or "market power", conceived of as arising naturally, but for reasons unexplained, within the competitive system. To appraise this class of theories properly would take us far afield. But it would not be unduly harsh to say that explanations of vertical integration from this direction have been singularly unilluminating when not downright wrong.[4]

---

[1] There have been a number of recent surveys of the theory of vertical integration. See especially BLAIR and KASERMAN [1983], CASSON [1984], and WILLIAMSON [1985].

[2] An example borrowed from LEIJONHUFVUD [1986], p. 205.

[3] This problem also limits the generality of the analysis of ALCHIAN and DEMSETZ [1972], which is an economic reincarnation of technological determinism. In this case internal organization results because of the monitoring costs that attend the common-pool problem in team production. But what makes team production necessary? The (given) production technology.

[4] This should not be entirely surprising, since Marshallian theory (or, more correctly, post-Pigovian theory) takes the equilibrium firm as a constituent given. It would be unfair to expect any theory to explain its own assumptions. (On the difference between the Marshallian and Pigovian versions of the firm, see MOSS [1984].)

Almost all modern economic theories of vertical integration are transaction-cost explanations.[5] We can imagine production as taking place in various stages. Considering production costs alone tells us nothing about whether each stage is likely to be a separate firm or whether some stages are likely to be jointly owned.[6] Indeed, if there were no costs but production costs, we would expect the least possible vertical integration: every stage would be its own firm, and each thus could take best advantage of the particular production economies open to it. Production would be fully decentralized, and all coordination would be a matter of price-mediated spot transaction. As COASE [1937, p. 390] pointed out, however, there is "a cost of using the price mechanism" in this way. There are other costs – transaction costs – in addition to production costs; and it is these transaction costs that determine the extent of internal organization. As WILLIAMSON [1985] would now articulate it, the level of vertical integration we observe in the economy largely reflects a minimun of the sum of production and transaction costs.[7]

But what are these transaction costs? And where do they come from? The problem is not that we have no answer to these questions; rather, it is that we have far too many. At some level, we could say that a transaction cost arises from any impediment to price-mediated spot exchange that makes internal organization a less-costly alternative; the transaction cost would thus equal the opportunity cost of market exchange. This is, of course, rather unhelpful. So economists have set about finding specific costs of market exchange. The resulting cornucopia includes asymmetric information (ARROW [1975]); techno-logical indivisibilities in team production (ALCHIAN and DEMSETZ [1972]); and differential risk perception (BLAIR and KASERMAN [1978]). Most of these explanations suffer from a lack of generality, and many from a failure to ask whether there might not exist contractual alternatives that cope with these problems quite as well as vertical integration.

The dominant – and perhaps most appealing – set of explanations today centers on the concept of asset specificity (KLEIN, CRAWFORD and ALCHIAN [1978]; WILLIAMSON [1985]). Efficient production frequently requires the use of specialized assets – unique machinery, for example – that have few alternative uses. The owners of such assets are vulnerable to the appropriation of their rents by their contractual partners. One alternative would be to use less-specialized equipment, but that frequently means a sacrifice of production efficiency. Another alternative is internal organization[8] – common ownership

---

[5] Such explanations are sometimes also called "market failure" explanations. This is Pigovian terminology, and it is arguably both prejudicial and misleading. On this see COASE [1960], DEMSETZ [1969] and DAHLMAN [1979].

[6] Or about any of the many other organizational alternatives.

[7] On the methodological implications of this assertion, see LANGLOIS [1984]. We will also return to the issue below. I should note that Williamson allows for the possibility of what he calls "mistaken" vertical integration.

[8] Yet another alternative might be a hostage. See WILLIAMSON [1985], chapters 7 and 8.

of both the specialized asset and the relevant surrounding stages of production. This eliminates the threat of expropriation and renders unproblematical the choice of the efficient specialized technology.

In Williamson's work, asset-specificity has become the centerpiece of the explanation of vertical integration. But it is not by any means the whole story. Most theories of internal organization, Williamson's included, are static theories in an important sense. They take the circumstances of production as given and investigate comparatively the properties of market-contract arrangements, internal organization, and sometimes other modes of organization. What happens, however, when the technologies of production – and perhaps other environmental factors – are changing rapidly? In Williamson's view, the approach from asset specificity alone may then be less persuasive. "The introduction of innovation," he writes, "plainly complicates the earlier-described assignment of transactions to markets or hierarchies based entirely on an examination of their asset specificity qualities. Indeed, the study of economic organization in a regime of rapid innovation poses much more difficult issues than those addressed here" (WILLIAMSON [1985], p. 143).

Innovation

We can begin to approach the problem by asking this question: is rapid economic change likely to make market contracting more costly or less costly relative to internal organization? Almost without exception, writers who have asked this question (in one form or another) have concluded that, in such circumstances, internal organization is clearly superior to arms-length contracting on transaction-cost grounds.

One way to think about this is in terms of the flexibility of internal organization in comparison with that of a decentralized system of market contracts.[9] The firm, it is often remarked, is a nexus of imperfectly specified contracts; this is in contrast with the more fully specified contracts of arms-length transaction. In the face of rapid change, imperfect specification allows some maneuvering room to adapt adroitly. To put it another way, the decentralization of markets makes it difficult to coordinate a complex reorientation of production in the face of change; a more-centralized arrangement, by contrast, might face lower costs of radical change, all else equal.

To be successful, an innovation must mesh with the complex system of production of which it is a part. Sometimes this is easy because the innovation fits neatly into the existing system. Sometimes, however, an innovation is sufficiently radical that its success requires significant changes elsewhere in the

---

[9] We might trace this observation back as far as KNIGHT [1971], p. 268.

system. The first kind of innovation is what TEECE [1984] calls an *autonomous* innovation; the second is a *systemic* innovation. The costs of coordinating a systemic innovation among many decentralized market participants is likely to be high – higher, at any rate, than the costs of coordinating the change within a single organization that owns most or all of the relevant stages (ADELMAN [1955]; SILVER [1984]; TEECE [1984]).

In a marvelous but neglected article, G. B. RICHARDSON [1972] articulated a number of ideas useful in developing this hypothesis. He begins by drawing on Edith PENROSE's [1959] notion of the *capabilities* of a firm. Production is not (as the production-function model would have it) a matter of combining resources according to explicit blueprints of some sort. Rather, production is a matter of human skill and experience. The organization puts its capabilities to use in the coordination of the various *activities* that go into producing goods and services. These activities correspond more or less to what I have called stages of production: research and development (R & D); the various stages of manufacturing; marketing; etc. The firm's boundaries will depend on its capabilities; it will undertake activities to which its capabilities are appropriate and leave other activities to the market. In general, the firm will undertake *similar activities*, activities that require similar capabilities.

The systemic character of production means that activities are related or, in Richardson's terms, *complementary* to one another. Complementary activities are those that must be coordinated in the process of production; in the context of systemic innovation, they would be those that must be adapted for the innovation to succeed. Clearly, not all complementary activities will be similar. Producing random-access memory chips is probably an activity similar to producing logic chips; but complementary activities like producing the capital equipment used in fabricating chips or the computers into which the chips are plugged are not particularly similar.[10]

Richardson's thesis is that when complementarity requires close coordination – he speaks of *closely complementary* activities – but the firm involved does not possess the necessary capabilities, the result may be an intermediate form of organization like licensing, joint venture, or equity investment. These intermediate modes allow some degree of coordination without incurring the high costs of complete vertical integration into activities for which the firm's capabilities are ill adapted.

More recently, TEECE [1982, 1986a, 1986b] has developed (apparently independently) a strikingly similar framework that extends these ideas in a number of ways. He too is influenced by Penrose and by the idea that a firm possesses capabilities – various skills and experience, some explicit, some

---

[10] For example, the optical stepper, a device used in the photolithography of semiconductors, is produced by firms with specialized capabilities (like GCA near Boston) or by firms specializing in similar – but non-complementary – activities (like camera-manufacturer Nikon).

tacit[11] and inexplicit. Rather than speaking of complementary activities, Teece talks of complementary *assets*. This formulation connects with the literature emphasizing asset specificity. It differs from Richardson in its focus on the asset rather than the activity, but these notions are surely related at some level.

TEECE [1986 b] distinguishes complementary assets according to whether they are *specialized* or *cospecialized*. A specialized asset is one whose relationship to the innovation is unilateral. For example, the value of an asset may depend on the success of a particular innovation – but the success of the innovation does not depend on the availability of the asset. Sometimes the reverse is true: the success of an innovation may depend on the availability of a particular asset – but the value of the asset does not depend much on the success of the innovation. When the dependence is mutual, however, the assets are cospecialized. To use Teece's example, the innovation of containerized cargo required the coordination of both containerized ships and specialized equipment in port. Both sets of assets had to be called into existence and were thinly supplied (at least at first).[12] Notice that the notion of cospecialization bears a striking resemblance to Richardson's idea of close complementarity.

The other factor Teece brings in is *appropriability*, the capacity of one party (in this case the innovator) to appropriate the rents or quasirents of the innovation. The innovator's ability to appropriate these rents will determine the extent of internal organization. And that ability will depend both on the degree of complementarity and on the "regime of appropriability," the ability – both practical and legal – to create and enforce property rights in the innovation (TEECE [1986 a], p. 188).

The innovator need not own all complementary assets in order to profit from his or her innovation; one need only take positions in those assets, long positions in assets likely to appreciate and short positions in assets likely to decline in value. But when the assets involved are cospecialized, the familiar problems of "holdup" and "opportunistic recontracting" are possible. This creates the usual motive for single ownership of all the relevant assets. The innovator may also have a motive to integrate into assets not cospecialized if imitators could otherwise quickly enter and bid away the quasirents of innovation. Where the knowledge involved is of a sort easily protected by patent (as in pharmaceutical),[13] licensing may obviate complete internal organization; but where this is not the case (as in most process technologies, such as semiconductor fabrication), internal organization may be the most effective way of protecting the quasirents.

---

[11] In the sense of POLANYI [1958].

[12] By contrast, the trucks needed to bring the containers inland from the port were specialized assets, since existing trailers could be easily modified to the task. The success of the innovation depended on the availability of trucks, but those assets were already in existence and thickly supplied.

[13] LEVIN *et al.* [1987].

Notice that much of the story here involves what we would ordinarily call "bottlenecks" in the innovation process. In Teece's story, bottlenecks cause transaction costs because they pose the threat of strategic expropriation of rents. "The owner of the bottleneck asset, realizing its strategic importance to the innovator, is in a position to threaten to withhold services, causing the price of its services to be raised" (TEECE [1986a], p. 188). What is interesting is that SILVER [1984] uses many of the same building blocks – especially the notion of bottlenecks – to create an explanation of vertical integration with a somewhat different slant.[14]

Citing SCHUMPETER [1934], Silver begins with the observation that innovation frequently involves the qualitatively new. The individual – the entrepreneur – who attempts to introduce the qualitatively new often meets with strong resistance. Such resistance may be cultural and psychological, as Schumpeter emphasized. But, more interestingly, it may also be informational. As we saw, the success of an innovation often requires the adaptation of complementary activities; if the innovation is indeed qualitatively new, many of the necessary activities will also be qualitatively new (and thus normally specialized to or cospecialized with the innovation). The problem for the innovator is to call forth these specialized activities. To do this through arms-length contracting, the innovator would have both to inform and to persuade those with the necessary capabilities. Since the innovator's vision is novel and idiosyncratic virtually by definition, this may not be an easy task. The innovator's potential contracting parties may have to invest in specialized assets, and it may take a high price to get them to bear the risk of an irreversible investment under such circumstances. This may make it less costly for the innovator to integrate into the cospecialized activities and to employ those parties with the relevant capabilities instead of contracting with them. Silver sees the benefits to this largely in informational terms: the innovator can communicate the procedures and routines the employee is to follow more easily than the detailed specifications of end-product a contractor would need. There is also a cost to such internal organization: the innovator will likely be integrating into areas to which his or her own capabilities are relatively less adapted, that is, into relatively dissimilar activities.

This story is clearly quite akin to that of Teece; but it is also different in a crucial way. Silver has picked up the Richardsonian thread more clearly. He emphasizes the costs of coordination in a regime of economic change, the costs of transmitting information that is novel and fundamentally qualitative in nature.[15] Asset specificity enters in a secondary way. But the threat to the

---

[14] The notion of bottlenecks as a motive for vertical integration was first suggested by ADELMAN [1955].

[15] This was also the theme of LANGLOIS [1984].

specialized assets arises not from the opportunism of fully convinced asset-holders; rather it arises from the uncertainty in the innovation process, as perceived by asset-holders who may not fully grok the innovator's vision. "In my scenario," says Silver,

"... the entrepreneur does not "do it himself" in order to keep the profitability of good X a secret (MAGEE [1981]). Just the opposite is the case! The innovator would prefer to concentrate his managerial resources narrowly on X. His problem is that he cannot, at reasonable cost, convey his implausible "secret" to those with the technical capabilities needed to produce the required operations at the lowest cost. Finding himself unable to secure the cooperation of the latter producers, the entrepreneur must direct his finite managerial resources into areas for which he does not have a comparative advantage. This in fact reduces the profitability of his innovation." (SILVER [1984], p. 17.)

In order to distinguish these two variants of the theory, I will call Teece's the *appropriability* version and Silver's the *entrepreneurial* version. In both cases, of course, the innovator is motivated to integrate by a desire to "appropriate" the rents of innovation. But in Teece's case, he or she does so in order to prevent others from grabbing the rents, whereas in Silver's case, he or she integrates in order to create rents that otherwise wouldn't exist (or wouldn't be as great).

I don't propose to choose between these variants. Instead, I intend to try to bring them together – to determine the circumstances under which each is applicable and to fit them both into a slightly roomier story. In order to do this, however, I'm afraid that some additional preliminaries are in order.

The Division of Labor

In one sense, of course, the dynamics of organization is a concern that goes back over 200 years in economics. One might even say that, in one form, it was the starting point for Adam Smith in the *Wealth of Nations*. Smith's theme was the division of labor. And his observation that the division of labor is limited by the extent of the market suggests a possible link between vertical integration and economic change in the form of market growth.

One economist who sees such a link is George Stigler. In a well-known 1951 article, he attempts to unpack the implications of Smith's observation by considering the various activities – he calls them "functions" – in terms of their individual (Marshallian) cost curves. Why do firms with increasing-returns technologies not grow indefinitely large? he asks. His answer is that the increasing-returns activities are held back by other activities within the firm that exhibit decreasing returns. As the market for the final product expands, however, it becomes profitable for the increasing-returns activities to spin off and exploit their economies of scale by aggregating the demands for their services across the industry.

Stigler draws from this analysis his much-discussed hypothesis about vertical integration.[16] Since a larger market means more of this "spinning off", he concludes, "Smith's theorem suggests that vertical disintegration is the typical development in growing industries, vertical integration in declining industries" (STIGLER [1951], p. 189). I will argue presently that this conclusion is unwarranted and, if taken narrowly, is probably exactly backwards. Before making that case, however, let me recast Stigler's analysis somewhat. Following LEIJONHUFVUD [1986], we can open up the black box of the Marshallian cost curve and look in a more Smithian fashion at the structure of production and the sources of economies of scale.

Consider first the paradigm of wholly undivided labor: crafts production. Here a single individual undertakes many of the relevant activities of production. Figure 1a shows this pictorially. Each of the artisans (*a* through *e*) performs sequentially all of the tasks (1 through 5). Consider now the reorganization of production in the manner of Smith's pin factory. In Figure 1b, each artisan now performs only one task: *a* performs only task 1, *b* performs only task 2, etc. This allows for specialization and comparative advantage, permitting production to partake of all the economies with which Smith was impressed: the increase in individual dexterity; the saving of time otherwise lost "sauntering" between tasks; and the concentration of attention, which would lead workers to perceive opportunities for mechanization and (autonomous) innovation.

There are several differences of note between crafts and factory production. In crafts production, each artisan requires relatively broad capabilities (in Penrose's sense). The artisan must be adequately skilled in all the tasks necessary to complete the product. This implies a certain degree of flexibility. Innovation of a stage-specific, efficiency-enhancing sort is, as Smith argued, less characteristic of crafts production. But innovation of a more systemic sort is likely: for the artisan, systemic innovation – innovation across the stages of production under his or her command – is in fact autonomous. This accounts for the distinctiveness of, and the lack of standardization in, a crafts product. It also suggests, once again, that an artisanal product is more protean, and that more-or-less radical product modification is cheap in this mode of production. Notice also that each artisan is the rival of all others, a factor that further encourages differentiated and nonstandard products.[17]

---

[16] Actually, he proposes *two* hypotheses in this article. The second – perhaps equally well-known – hypothesis is that taxes and other government-induced distortion of market prices accounts for much vertical integration.

[17] A complicating issue, of course, is the existence of cospecialized activities elsewhere in the system that militate in favor of standardization: the need for replacement parts, for example, or for irreversible human-capital investments by users. But this is getting ahead of the story.

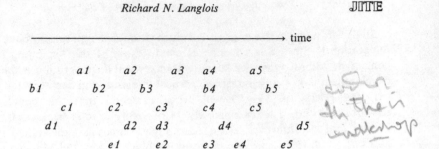

───────────────────────────────→ time

```
      a1        a2        a3    a4    a5
 b1        b2        b3        b4        b5
      c1     c2       c3       c4    c5
 d1             d2    d3       d4             d5
           e1        e2       e3    e4    e5
```

a. Crafts production.

```
a1   b2   c3   d4   e5
     a1   b2   c3   d4   e5
          a1   b2   c3   d4   e5
          etc. ...
```

b. Factory production.

```
a1   b2   c3        e5
               d4
f1   g2   h3        i5
```

c. Parallel-series scale economies.

Note: letters represent artisans, numbers represent tasks.
Source: LEIJONHUFVUD [1986].

Figure 1. The Vertical and Horizontal Divison of Labor.

In factory production, by contrast, the artisan's on-the-job capabilities are narrower in scope. This increases the efficiency of production, and even increases innovation – but innovation of a stage-specific, efficiency-enhancing sort. For the artisan in factory production, the opportunities for autonomous innovation are no longer more-or-less coextensive with those for systemic innovation. Increased production efficiency comes at the price of reduced flexibility, including product flexibility, implying standardization, interchangeable parts, etc. At the same time, however, the machinery used in production becomes more idiosyncratic and specialized (LEIJONHUFVUD [1986], p. 215). Notice also that the factory operatives are now *complementary* to one another rather than rivals.

This reorganization in the manner of the pinshop is what most people have in mind when they speak of the division of labor. But it is by no means the entire story. Factory production requires that the stages of production be closely coordinated in time. Since the various stages are unlikely to be uniformly efficient, however, some stages may be bottlenecks.[18] More interestingly, some stage may be anti-bottlenecks, that is, they may have excess capacity. Suppose one stage of production – stage 4, for example – is running at half capacity. If the firm were to double its sale of final product, it could run two assembly lines, both feeding into the same stage 4 (see Figure 1 c). The doubled output comes at the expense of less than twice the inputs. These economies of scale arise from organizational change not from technology, although mechanical innovation can renew the potential for generating economies by increasing the capacity of the stages.

Stage 4 in Figure 1 c can be "spun off" as in Stigler's story. Notice, however, that this spinning-off process is a manifestation of the division of labor quite different from what is implied in the pinshop reorganization. In Smith's terms, stage 4 has become a "peculiar trade" of its own. Leijonhufvud calls this spinning-off process the *horizontal* division of labor to distinguish it from the *vertical* division of labor implied in the pinshop reorganization. One important difference between the two is that the horizontal division of labor does not necessarily carry the implication of narrowed capabilities (or lowered human-capital requirements) on the part of workers; it may in fact mean an *increase* in human capital per worker (LEIJONHUFVUD [1986], p. 212). Eventually, of course, the "spun off" stage will itself subdivide labor in vertical fashion as the market for its (intermediate) product grows.

The important point to notice about the division of labor story so far – whether it is Smith's or Stigler's or Leijonhufvud's – is that it is incomplete in a crucial way. The division of labor is at base a matter of *production* costs alone. And, as we saw earlier, one cannot say much about the extent of internal organization without an overlying consideration of transaction costs. The horizontal division of labor can take place within a firm, as the assembly-line picture of Figure 1 c perhaps implies. Or it can take place through the creation of a legally separate entity, as when the anti-bottleneck stage becomes a firm of its own. Production efficiencies by themselves say nothing about the choice. This is precisely the difficulty with Stigler's analysis: he has made a case that there should be more (horizontal) division of labor when the market is growing (or, more correctly, when the extent of the market is large) and less division

---

[18] And, as ROSENBERG [1976, p. 125] has argued, such bottleneck stages are the most likely targets for innovation.

when the market is contracting (when the extent of the market is less). He assumes that this translates directly into statements about vertical integration; but without additional argument, it really does not.

Disequilibrium

We could, of course, simply overlay this analysis of the division of labor with a transaction-cost story based around asset specificity and appropriable rents. Both Leijonhufvud and Williamson do in fact tell the story this way. As we saw, the (vertical) division of labor leads to a reduction in the human-capital requirements (the crafts skills) of labor while at the same time increasing the idiosyncrasy and specificity of capital used in production. If each stage of production were owned separately – that is, if labor hired capital – the various capital owners could threaten, in the usual way, to withhold the services of their machines in order to appropriate more of the rents of production. This would lead to costly bargaining, disruptions of production, or the use of less efficient technology. If instead the owners of capital do not own specific machines but instead own shares in all the machines (*voilà* the capitalist firm), these problems disappear. The capitalists hire labor to run the machines; but, because labor has become "deskilled" (as the radicals put it),[19] the labor market is, in effect, contestable. There are still labor unions to contend with; but bargaining with a single agent is less costly than dealing with many individual threats.

This explanation has much to recommend it. In the large, it is probably right. But notice that it really has the most to say about the motives for integration that arise from the *vertical* division of labor. It says less about whether newly created "peculiar trades" will be carried out internally or by separate firms. Since the horizontal division of labor need not involve "deskilling," the labor input to the stage may be just as specialized as the capital component. It is thus ambiguous whether there are advantages to pooling the capital of this stage with the rest of the larger firm's capital.

Moreover, it is the thesis of this essay that rapid economic change may introduce other sources of transaction costs – costs that may dominate those from asset specificity of this kind. Consider Stigler's hypothesis once again: vertical disintegration should be characteristic of growing industries and vertical (re)integration characteristic of declining ones. Using the words "growing" and "declining" seems to imply an emphasis on rates of change. In fact, I would argue, Stigler means nothing of the sort. His analysis, like Smith's is about the *extent* of the market – not about the *rate of change* of the extent of the market. This difference is probably inessential for the analysis of the division of labor – of production costs – alone. But for the analysis of vertical integration, the difference may be a crucial one.

---

[19] MARGLIN [1974].

If we link together the ideas of growth and innovation as manifestations of economic change, then we can apply our earlier analysis in a straightforward way. Growth – or rapid growth, at any rate – must involve a large degree of systemic innovation. The costs of coordinating such innovation through arm's-length transaction suggest that vertical integration is in fact more typical of growing industries; and there does seem to be some empirical support for this possibility (JEWKES [1930]; ADELMAN [1955]; HARRIGAN [1985]).

We can also mount the complementary argument: where the market is not growing rapidly – where systemic innovation is not occurring on a significant scale – we should expect that the horizontal division of labor will take place through the formation of separate firms rather than internally. Internal organization also has its (transaction) costs.[20] These arise from the limits to the capabilities of managers and management structures. Now, one can enlist the division of labor in management as well as in production,[21] and thus try to limit these costs through decentralization; this is part of the logic behind the M-form structure (WILLIAMSON [1985], ch. 11). In the extreme, however, the least-costly structure of internal management is complete decentralization – vertical disintegration into the price system. If there is little economic change, and therefore no transaction costs to market organization, the only reason to bear the costs of internal organization would be whatever "static" sources of transaction costs happen to arise in the particular case. We would thus expect vertical integration to be lower when economic change is less, all else (including extent of the market) equal.

One implication of this hypothesis is that the evolution of industry structure in response to an increase in the extent of the market will depend crucially on the time pattern of growth.

If growth is gradual and innovation incremental, something like Stigler's story is probable. Firms will start off relatively integrated. They will slowly increase their division of labor as markets grow, spinning off (or calling forth) a web of specialist firms who will work on contract. As the industry declines and demand for final product diminishes, the division of labor will be forced to recede, and the firms will reintegrate. In this scenario, organization is driven by the division of labor, and production-cost considerations dominate transaction-cost considerations. What integration remains will be dictated by static transaction costs particular to the case.

If, by contrast, growth comes in spurts or is the result of radical innovation, the picture may be rather different. The times of rapid change are periods of "disequilibrium" (to use the word loosely) in which the transaction-cost disadvantages of markets outweigh the disabilities of internal management.

---

[20] Vertical integration can also increase production costs, of course, to the extent that an anti-bottleneck stage is not as fully utilized within the firm as it would be if "spun off" to aggregate demands across firms in the industry.

[21] An observation going back at least to BABBAGE [1835].

Holding the extent of the market constant, the disequilibrium industry is more integrated. As the industry matures, two potentially countervailing effects will come into play. First of all, the market will be increasing in size, which means that the division of labor will be increasing. At the same time, maturity means that the pace of change is slowing and that learning is taking place. What effects are stability and learning likely to have on the extent of internal organization?

As SILVER [1984, pp. 47–50] notes, the effects of stability and learning are somewhat ambiguous. On the one hand, learning will occur within the already-integrated firm: the cost of internal management decreases as managers develop their capabilities and as they institute managerial innovations of various kinds. On the other hand, learning will also take place within the economic system as a whole. In Silver's terms, the success of the integrated venture means that potential contractors no longer need be persuaded to invest in the necessary cospecialized assets. So the costs of market contract are also declining. On average, though, it seems likely that stability and learning will shift the balance in favor of disintegration. Silver's argument[22] is that learning may reduce or leave unchanged the level of vertical integration that minimizes the sum of production and transaction costs; but it would not *increase* the cost-minimizing level. Thus, on average, vertical integration should diminish with stability and learning (SILVER [1984], p. 48). Moreover, it is clear that in the limit – as the system of production becomes completely stable, with no change or qualitative uncertainty[23] to disturb it – most sources of transaction costs disappear, leaving market contracts, with their superior incentive attributes, clearly in the superior position (LANGLOIS [1984]). In this (admittedly unrealistic) world, even such sources of transaction costs as asset-specificity would disappear as contingent-claim markets develop and as behavioral norms appear within the contracting process to help mitigate opportunism.[24] Let us operate, then, on the assumption that stability and learning favor disintegration. Industry maturity – a stable or slowly growing phase of the life-cycle – would then mean decreased internal organization. Finally, a phase of decline would mean reintegration, both because the division of labor is receding and because the transaction costs of change are once again stirred up.

There may also be an intermediate case. In describing the rapid-change scenario, I relied implicitly on the entrepreneurial version of the theory rather than the appropriability version. The source of transaction costs in this story was the information costs of alerting contractors to, and persuading them of the

---

[22] Which he supports with a graphical analysis that I will not reproduce.

[23] As I argued in LANGLOIS [1984], it is qualitative – what I called "structural" – uncertainty that matters here. Uncertainty of a more routine sort, such as uncertainty about parameters like price or demand, poses no fundamental problems for market contracting. Indeed, HARRIGAN [1985] found empirically that uncertainty about price and demand actually *decreases* the observed level of vertical integration.

[24] On this latter possibility see, e.g., ULLMANN-MARGALIT [1978], SCHOTTER [1981] and AXELROD [1984].

benefits of, the qualitatively new. We could, however, also imagine an industry that is growing and innovating but in which the costs of alerting and persuading potential contracting partners is relatively low. In such an industry, the motives for integration may hinge to a far greater extent on questions of appropriability.

What kind of an industry might this be? One answer is that it may be an industry in which innovation is relatively less radical in some sense. The changes involved may be more or less systemic, but the economic system is not entirely unprepared for them. Indeed, potential contracting parties (and others) may have the capabilities, flexibility, and alertness not only to work with the innovating firm but actually to compete with it. In such an industry, a firm that has its hands into many of the relevant cospecialized activities may be in a better position to appropriate the rents of its innovation – and thus to prosper in the face of competition – than a firm less integrated.[25]

We are now in a position to articulate the refined version of the hypothesis more clearly. There are now two dimensions that matter: the extent of the market and the pace of change. Figure 2 illustrates this.

Extent of the Market

	small	large
slow change	Division of labor: low Internal organization: high Example: The highlands of Scotland, 1776.	Division of labor: high Internal organization: low Example: 19th-century gun manufacture.
rapid change	Division of labor: low Internal organization: high Example: Apple Computer, 1976	Division of labor: high Internal organization: high Example: "The Visible Hand." Japanese firms?

Figure 2. The Hypothesis Refined

In the upper-left-hand corner, we have little economic change and a market of small extent. This is the case of largely crafts production from which Smith began, a world exemplified for him by "so desert a country as the Highlands of Scotland," where "every farmer must be butcher, baker and brewer for his own family" (SMITH [1976], I.iii.2, p. 31).

In the upper-right-hand corner, we have relatively slow economic change but a larger market. Here the division of labor is extensive, and the horizontal

---

[25] There are, of course, methods of coordination intermediate between arm's-length contracting and complete vertical integration. For a particularly illuminating discussion in a relevant context, see IMAI and ITAMI [1984].

division of labor manifests itself as a network of independent contractors connected by market exchange. An example of this might be nineteenth-century firearms manufacture, which was characterized by "inside contracting" to specialized but independent artisans (ALLEN [1929], BUTTRICK [1952]); but there are other examples, dating back at least to the fourteenth-century arsenal of Venice (LANE [1973]).

In the lower-left-hand corner, we have rapid economic change and a small market. The extent of the market here will dominate, making extensive division of labor – and thus extensive contracting – unprofitable. Even in a high-tech world, the firm with a small market for its product is a crafts shop. An example would be any of the small, high-tech startups that have attracted so much attention in the last couple of decades.

Finally, in the lower-right-hand corner, we have rapid economic change and a relatively extensive market. Here we might expect to find the degree of vertical integration higher than in the upper-right-hand box. This may be for reasons emphasized by the entrepreneurial variant of the theory. Much of Alfred Chandler's discussion of the "Visible Hand," the evolution of large, vertically integrated firms in the nineteenth century, is probably consistent with this view (CHANDLER [1977]; and cf. SILVER [1984]). There may also be examples of integration under these conditions that stems from motives suggested by the appropriability variant. One interpretation would locate the success of Japanese microelectronics firms (compared with their American counterparts) in the greater ability to appropriate the benefits of innovation that their more-integrated structure confers upon them.

Path-Dependency

This elaboration of the theory of internal organization under conditions of economic change is clearly somewhat richer than hypotheses that do not distinguish between the effects of change and the effects of the extent of the market. Moreover, this elaboration begins to make room for both the entrepreneurial and the appropriability variants of the theory.

Unfortunately, the result so far is still rather unsatisfactory. Some further elaboration – and some cautions – are in order.

Throughout the essay so far I have operated on the methodological framework standard in transaction-cost analysis. I have assumed that an argument about which form of organization minimizes the sum of production and transaction costs is also immediately an argument about which form of organization we ought to observe under the conditions specified. In fact, of course, this assumption makes sense only with the collateral argument that something is enforcing cost-minimization on the system. To put it another way, we need to assume that some kind of "selection mechanism" is not only operating but operating tightly: organizations that do not minimize the sum of production and transaction costs are somehow more-or-less filtered out.

This is not a wholly unreasonable assumption. It is a fundamental insight of economics that a competitive system incorporates not only an invisible hand but also various kinds of invisible feet that go around prodding the ill-adapted. At the same time, of course, it *is* unreasonable to believe that such selection mechanisms always operate instantly and completely. To the extent that they do not, we may in fact observe to exist forms of organization that do not minimize cost.[26] We may also observe competing forms of organization to co-exist, either because selection pressures have not yet weeded out the inefficient or because the competing forms do not differ much in their survival value.

What this means is that, in a quite specific sense, history matters in the explanation of organizational form. The forms we observe today may be the result not (only) of conditions existing today but also of a constellation of past events. Indeed, if the alternative organizational forms are (or were) relatively similar in survival value, the explanation of the ones now in existence may come down in part to "historical accident", specific events that shunted history onto one track rather than another.[27]

The possibility of path-dependency has already thrown its shadows on our discussion. It appeared in the context of organizational learning. Suppose, I suggested, that rapid change motivates a high degree of internal organization (relative to what we would have expected with the same extent of the market under more tranquil conditions). How, I asked, will stability and learning affect the level of internal organization, all else equal? The tentative verdict was in favor of greater decentralization on balance. But notice that the question hinted at path-depency. If both the highly organized and the decentralized structure improve in efficiency with learning, and if the advantages of decentralization are modest (either inherently so or because of relaxed selection pressure), might not the degree of internal organization we observe (for a given

---

[26] The issues here are in fact more complicated even than this. For example, one has to be extremely careful about what one means by cost minimization in a dynamic context. As SCHUMPETER [1942, chapter 8] pointed out, a firm that appears to be inefficient from a static point of view (that is, from a point of view that excludes past and future) may actually be quite efficient from a dynamic point of view. For a more detailed discussion see LANGLOIS [1984, 1986a].

[27] This sort of path-dependency has always been a concern of economic historians. One of these is DAVID [1985, 1986], who has tried to find cases in which, when faced with a choice of competing technologies, history chose essentially by accident – and may not have chosen the more efficient alternative. In some ways, however, his examples are not perhaps as persuasive to theorists as the historian might like. His cases – the choice of the QWERTY layout for the typewriter keyboard or the choice of AC over DC power for electric generation – all hinge on network externalities of a sort that are the meat of neoclassical theory (KATZ and SHAPIRO [1985]). If path-dependency occurs only under such restricted circumstances, then the very peculiarity of QWERTY-like phenomena is actually testimony to the power of selection mechanisms to make history irrelevant. By contrast, the economics of organization may be a field in which path-dependency matters for more general reasons rather than because of theoretically tractable externalities of this sort.

extent of the market) depend crucially on past history? Consider two identical hypothetical industries. In one, change occurs slowly but steadily within a decentralized structure; in the other, market size and technological change come in periodic gulps. We observe the same extent of the market (and probably something like the same division of labor) in both. But the former may have a good deal less internal organization than the latter. And we would not be able to explain the difference without appeal to history.

What makes this all significant is that the possibility of alternative regimes of this sort may not always be so hypothetical. Consider the case of national or regional economies that develop (or enter into a particular technology or market) at different rates. Because of their different starting points, the various competing economies may ride quite different organizational tracks – yet may be equivalently efficient over some period of time. Indeed, the issue arises in a somewhat milder form within any given economy: for might not new entrants choose a different degree of organization from that found in incumbent production?

We can quickly give these abstract questions some life. For it is a central consideration in present-day discussions of international competitiveness that both Europe and Japan found themselves in a technological and institutional position quite different from that of the United States after World War II (ROSENBERG [1982], chapter 12). Devastated by the war, these economies were forced to rebuild both their technological and their organizational capabilities. They naturally looked to the United States for technology; but, both for internal historical reasons and probably for efficiency reasons as well, they often chose organizational structures quite different from those in the United States. In microelectronics, for example, the Japanese industry consists of ten or so large, vertically integrated systems firms, in contrast with a much more diverse and decentralized American industry that includes many small, unaffiliated "merchant" firms (LANGLOIS *et al.* [1988]). In other industries – like automobiles – the picture is more nearly reversed; though large, Japanese car companies are less vertically integrated than their American counterparts, a structure widely held to be one part of the Japanese success story (ALTSHULER et al. [1984], pp. 147–48).

A key issue in all this, it seems to me, is the relationship between technological capabilities and organizational form. One way to look at the issue is in terms of the proximity of an economy to the mythical "technological frontier." This may give us a way of analyzing more carefully the learning properties of relatively decentralized as against relatively integrated regimes. And this in turn may give us a clue to the dynamic properties of the various organizational paths that firms and economies may embark upon.

As NELSON and WINTER [1977] point out, the technological frontier is a place fraught with a quite dramatic and largely qualitative kind of uncertainty. No one knows which technological strategies will work or which working technologies will pay off; the tests are all ultimately empirical. If the frontier is advancing rapidly, it is a time of surprise and of rapid trial-and-error learning. And diversity – the trying out of many paths – is what keeps the frontier advancing. Under these circumstances, a decentralized structure may have advantages: there is likely to be some duplication of effort if many firms are working in isolation, but there is also likely to be a healthy pluralism of alternatives.[28]

Notice that we are now in the lower-left-hand box of Figure 2. The market is small, and the decentralized firms are all flexible craft shops able to modify the product quickly. As the market expands and the technical winners begin to emerge, the imperative to the subdivision of labor and associated process innovation will gain force. Whether this leads to much vertical integration will depend on the web of complementary activities already in place. For an economy alone at a frontier it created – like Britain in the nineteenth century or the United States after World War II – that web is likely to be woven relatively densely. This means that the entrepreneurial costs of introducing an innovation – even a more-or-less systemic one – are likely to be lower than in an economy not at the forefront.[29]

But it is important to keep in mind that it is often organizational innovation rather than technological innovation that drives economic change. And organizational innovation very often operates *behind* the technological frontier, seizing upon technological possibilities whose outlines are already fairly clear. Sometimes such innovation is revolutionary because it is entrepreneurial – it takes place in the absence of a well-developed network of complementary activities. But sometimes organizational innovation is revolutionary because it *supersedes* an existing – and perhaps passably efficient – web of activities. And sometimes an organizational innovation that owes its origins to the entrepreneurial motive can end up surviving because of its strategic or appropriability attributes.

Consider the case of Japanese microelectronics firms. Although Japan entered the semiconductor business quite early, its firms until recently operated behind the frontier of both product and process technology. They had no need for a structure well-adapted to advancing the frontier; they needed to get there in the first place. For this and other reasons, the Japanese industry developed within a relatively integrated stucture. Since their technology was imitative, system-wide trial-and-error learning was less important. And, since Japan did not possess the web of complementary activities that the United States did (and because Japanese government policy discouraged tapping directly into that web

---

[28] This also seems to have been Smith's view. See LANGLOIS [1986 b].

[29] I tend to think of this situation as akin to what Marshall had in mind when he advanced the idea of "external economies" as an explanation for why industries seem to exhibit decreasing costs even though individual firms ought eventually to encounter increasing costs. The existence of thick markets for complementary assets is a benefit external to the individual firm, though not, of course, to the economy as a whole.

through imports and foreign investment), each Japanese firm needed to generate a good many related activities internally. As the market for Japanese semiconductors grew (spurred by import restrictions and government procurement), the firms subdivided labor, mechanized, and mastered the "experience curve" internally. Japan is now up to the frontier – and ahead of most American firms except probably IBM – in process technology; there is no longer a lack of complementary activities in the Japanese system. But, not only does the integrated structure of the Japanese industry persists, it is displaying a survival value distressing to the American competition. The point, however, is that what called that integrated structure into existence is not what now gives it survival value.

A similar example might be Amercian competition with Britain in the nineteenth century. In small-arms manufacture, for instance, the "American system" of interchangeable parts came to surpass a British system relying more heavily on crafts production. This is normally discussed in terms of the technological innovation of interchangeability; but the real innovation was that Samuel Colt and others applied the techniques of factory production to a greather degree than did British firms. The reasons for this were likely consistent with the entrepreneurial variant: there were far fewer trained craftsmen in the United States. Contrary to popular perception (fostered by Colt) that factory production was cheaper than British crafts production, the reverse was probably true initially (CLARKE 1985). But factory production put the Americans in a position to learn process skills and mechanize more rapidly, so that American firms eventually surpassed the British. The same is probably true of the Japanese in microelectronics: starting from scratch with an integrated structure was originally much more costly than buying the intermediate products from the United States; but it put those firms on a trajectory that allowed them to learn and eventually master high-volume production more effectively. Once again, this is all consistent with Chandler's account of the "Visible Hand": what was important was organizational not technological innovation, and the advantage conferred by internal organization was the ability to learn and perfect mass-production – and to appropriate the rents of doing so.

None of this is to suggest that internal organization of the "Visible Hand" kind must always be superior to decentralized production. The case of the automobile industry seems to be a counterexample. When the visible hand of Henry Ford and others scrunched the young automobile industry together, it put that industry on a path of extensive vertical integration.[30] But here the Japanese success in manufacturing was apparently accomplished with less integration – more subcontracting – than had been prevalent in American

---

[30] For an analysis of vertical integration in the auto industry before 1940, see ROBERTSON and LANGLOIS [1988].

industry, and the American response seems to be involving an increase in subcontracting (ALTSHULER et al. [1984], p. 148). This should not be surprising.

The manufacture of automobiles is a business in which the basic parameters of product and process are much better known – are changing far less rapidly – than in microelectronics. The costs of market coordination are thus much lower, and the benefits of vertical integration correspondingly less in relation to its costs.

Summary

This paper attempts to synthesize and extend the theory of vertical integration in a regime of rapid economic change. In particular, the paper develops a tentative theory in which the degree of vertical integration in an industry depends on such factors as the extent of the market; the rate of change of the extent of the market; the level of Marshallian "external economies"; and past history. Asset specificity – the variable stressed in the most influential of modern transaction-cost theories – appears as only one strand in a larger tapestry.

Zusammenfassung
Ökonomischer Wandel und die Grenzen der Unternehmung

In diesem Artikel wird versucht, die Theorie der vertikalen Integration innerhalb eines Regimes schnellen ökonomischen Wandels zusammenzufügen und zu analysieren. Insbesondere wird versucht, eine vorläufige Theorie zu entwickeln, in der das Ausmaß der vertikalen Integration in einer Industrie von Faktoren abhängt wie: Größe des Marktes, Änderungsrate der Größe dieses Marktes, Niveau der externen Effekte im Sinne von Marshall, vorausgegangene Entwicklung. „Asset specificity" – die Größe, die in den einflußreichsten modernen Transaktionskostentheorien im Vordergrund steht – erscheint nur als ein Strang in einem größeren Gebilde.

References

ADELMAN, M. [1955], "Concept and Statistical Measurement of Vertical Integration", pp. 281–330, in: *Business Concentration and Price Policy*, Report of a National Bureau of Economic Research Conference, Princeton.

ALCHIAN, A. A. and DEMSETZ, H. [1972], "Production, Information Costs, and Economic Organization", *American Economic Review*, 62, 777–795.

ALLEN, G. C. [1929], *The Industrial Development of Birmingham and the Black Country, 1860–1927*, London.

ALTSHULER, A., ANDERSON, M., JONES, D., ROOS, D., and WOMACK, J. [1984], *The Future of the Automobile: The Report of MIT's International Automobile Program*, Cambridge.

ARROW, K. J. [1975], "Vertical Integration and Communication", *Bell Journal of Economics*, 6, 173–183.

AXELROD, R. [1984], *The Evolution of Cooperation*, New York.

BABBAGE, C. [1835], *On the Economy of Machinery and Manufactures*, London.

BLAIR, R. D. and KASERMAN, D. L. [1978], "Uncertainty and the Incentive for Vertical Integration", *Southern Economic Journal*, 45, 266–272.

—— [1983], *Law and Economics of Vertical Integration and Control*, New York.

BUTTRICK, J. [1952], "The Inside Contract System", *Journal of Economic History*, 12, 205–221.

CASSON, M. [1984], "The Theory of Vertical Integration: A Survey and Synthesis", *Journal of Economic Studies*, 11, 3–43.

CHANDLER, A. D. [1977], *The Visible Hand: The Managerial Revolution in American Business*, Cambridge.

CLARKE, B. N. [1985], *Early American Technology: A Reexamination of Some Aspects of Connecticut's Industrial Development*, Unpublished M. A. thesis, University of Connecticut.

COASE, R. H. [1937], "The Nature of the Firm", *Economica (N. S.)*, 4, 386–405.

—— [1960], "The Problem of Social Cost", *Journal of Law and Economics*, 3, 1–44.

DAHLMAN, C. [1979], "The Problem of Externality", *Journal of Law and Economics*, 22, 141–162.

DAVID, P. [1985], "Clio and the Economics of QWERTY", *American Economic Review*, 75, 332–337.

—— [1986], *Technological System Rivalries: Lessons from History*, Paper presented at the Economic History Association annual meeting, September, Hartford, Connecticut.

DEMSETZ, H. [1969], "Information and Efficiency: Another Viewpoint", *Journal of Law and Economics*, 12, 1–22.

HARRIGAN, K. R. [1985], "Vertical Integration and Corporate Strategy", *Academy of Management Journal*, 28, 397–425.

IMAI, K. and ITAMI, H. [1984], "Interpenetration of Organization and Market: Japan's Firm and Market in Comparison with the U. S." *International Journal of Industrial Organization*, 2, 285–310.

JEWKES, J. [1930], "Factors in Industrial Integration", *Quarterly Journal of Economics*, 44, 621–638.

KATZ, M. L., and SHAPIRO, C. [1985], "Network Externalities, Competition, and Compatibility", *American Economic Review*, 75, 424–440.

KLEIN, B., CRAWFORD, R. G., and ALCHIAN, A. A. [1978], "Vertical Integration, Appropriable Rents, and the Competitive Contracting Process", *Journal of Law and Economics*, 21, 297–326.

KNIGHT, F. [1971], *Risk, Uncertainty, and Profit*, Chicago.

LANE, F. C. [1973], *Venice, A Maritime Republic*, Baltimore.

LANGLOIS, R. N. [1984], "Internal Organization in a Dynamic Context: Some Theoretical Considerations", pp. 23–49, in: M. Jussawalla and H. Ebenfield (eds.), *Communication and Information Economics: New Perspectives*, Amsterdam.

—— [1986a], "Rationality, Institutions, and Explanation", pp. 225–255, in: R. N. Langlois (ed.), *Economics as a Process: Essays in the New Institutional Economics*, New York.

—— [1986b], *Science, Technology, and Public Policy: Lessons from the Classicals*, Paper presented at the American Economic Association annual meeting, December 28, 1986, New Orleans.

—— PUGEL, T. A., HAKLISCH, C. S., NELSON R. R., and EGELHOFF, W. G. [1988], *Microelectronics: An Industry in Transition*, London.

LEIJONHUFVUD, A. [1986], "Capitalism and the Factory System", pp. 203–223, in: R. N. Langlois (ed.), *Economics as a Process: Essays in the New Institutional Economics*, New York.

LEVIN, R. C., KLEVORICK, A., NELSON, R. R., and WINTER, S. G. [1987], "Appropriating the Returns from Industrial R & D", *Brookings Papers on Economic Activity*, 3.

MAGEE, S. P. [1981], "The Appropriability Theory of the Multinational Corporation", *Annals of the American Academy of Political and Social Science*, 458, 123–135.

MARGLIN, S. A. [1974], "What Do Bosses Do? The Origin and Function Hierarchy in Capitalist Production", *Review of Radical Political Economics*, 6, 60–112.

MOSS, S. [1984], "The History of the Theory of the Firm from Marshall to Robinson and Chamberlin: the Source of Positivism in Economics", *Economica*, 51, 307–318.

NELSON, R. R. and WINTER, S. G. [1977], "In Search of Useful Theory of Innovation", *Research Policy*, 5, 36–76.

— — [1982], *An Evolutionary Theory of Economic Change*, Cambridge.

PENROSE, E. [1959], *The Theory of the Growth of the Firm*, Oxford.

POLANYI, M. [1958], *Personal Knowledge*, Chicago.

RICHARDSON, G. B. [1972], "The Organisation of Industry", *Economic Journal*, 82, 883–896.

ROBERTSON, P. L. and LANGLOIS, R. N. [1988], *Innovation and Vertical Integration in the American Automobile Industry, 1900–1940*, paper presented at the Economic History Association annual meeting, September 24, Detroit.

ROSENBERG, N. [1976], *Perspectives on Technology*, New York.

— — [1982], *Inside the Black Box: Technology and Economics*, New York.

SCHOTTER, A. [1981], *The Economic Theory of Social Institutions*, New York.

SCHUMPETER, J. A. [1934], *The Theory of Economic Development*, Cambridge.

— — [1942], *Capitalism, Socialism, and Democracy*, New York.

SILVER, M. [1984], *Enterprise and the Scope of the Firm*, London.

SMITH, A. [1976], *An Inquiry into the Nature and Causes of the Wealth of Nations*, Glasgow Edition. Oxford.

STIGLER, G. J. [1951], "The Division of Labor is Limited by the Extent of the Market", *Journal of Political Economy*, 59, 185–193.

TEECE, D. J. [1982], "Towards an Economic Theory of the Multiproduct Firm", *Journal of Economic Behavior and Organization*, 3, 39–63.

— — [1984], "Economic Analysis and Strategic Management", *California Management Review*, 26, 87–110.

— — [1986a], "Firm Boundaries, Technological Innovation, and Strategic Management", pp. 187–199, in: L. G. Thomas (ed.), *The Economics of Strategic Planning*, Lexington, Mass.

— — [1986b], "Profiting from Technological Innovation: Implications for Integration, Collaboration, Licensing, and Public Policy", *Research Policy*, 15, 285–305.

ULLMANN-MARGALIT, E. [1978], *The Emergence of Norms*, New York.

WILLIAMSON, O. E. [1985], *The Economic Institutions of Capitalism*, New York.

Richard N. Langlois
Associate Professor
Department of Economics
The University of Connecticut
U 63 Storrs, CT 06268
U. S. A.

Cambridge Journal of Economics 1991, 15, 315–342

Property rights, asset specificity, and the division of labour under alternative capitalist relations

Ugo Pagano*

Introduction

The relationship between property rights and the organisation of work has been one of the fundamental issues examined in the 'new institutional' literature[1] and that on the 'labour process'.[2] The variety and the complexity of the contributions present in both streams of the literature makes any definition of the general characteristics which may distinguish one set of writers from the other difficult and imprecise. Nevertheless, in my opinion, it can be said that one important difference lies in an evaluation of the relative importance of the causal relationships existing between property rights and the organisation of work. The new institutional literature has emphasised one direction of causality, that running from the needs of an efficient organisation of work to the formation of an adequate structure of property rights and of governance. By contrast, the labour process literature has emphasised the opposite direction of causality, pointing out how the property rights and the other institutions which define an economic system shape the organisation of work and the technology of that system.

Consider the following question: does the often very detailed and hierarchical division of labour, which characterises many firms under capitalism, exist because of transaction costs and technological efficiency or because of capitalism?

The new institutional literature has provided arguments supporting the first possibility. Here, capitalist property rights and the hierarchical division of labour are considered as an endogeneous outcome of the necessities of transaction and technological efficiency. By

Manuscript received 11 September 1989; final version received 21 August 1990.

*University of Siena. This paper is a substantially revised and enlarged version of Pagano (1988) which was presented at the Workshop on Economics and Institutions of the International School of Economic Research held at the Certosa di Pontignano (University of Siena) in July 1988. I wish to thank the other participants to the Workshop for their comments and, in particular, Sam Bowles, Robert Clower, Marcello De Cecco, Axel Leijonhufvud, Edmund Phelps, Robert Rowthorn and Herbert Simon. I have also received additional useful comments from Partha Dasgupta, Ernst Fehr, G. C. Harcourt, Geoffrey M. Hodgson, R. Ramana, Frank Wilkinson and two anonymous referees of this *Journal*. The responsibility for any mistake is mine alone.

[1] The most complete exposition of the new institutional literature is Williamson (1985). Useful guides are Putterman (1986), which also includes some contributions from the labour process literature, and Langlois (1986). The new institutional literature is usually defined to include what are sometimes called 'transaction costs' and 'property rights' literature. Important contributions are Coase (1952), Demsetz (1967), Alchian and Demsetz (1972), Posner (1973), North and Thomas (1973), North (1981) and Alchian (1987).

[2] The recent labour process literature stems from Marx's analysis of the factory system and starts with Braverman (1974) and Marglin (1974). It includes Edwards (1979), Littler (1982), Wood (1982), and Bowles and Gintis (1983, 1986). Useful introductions to this stream in the literature are Thompson (1983) and the first two chapters of Sawyer (1989). Pagano (1991B) provides a short evaluation of Braverman's contribution.

316   U. Pagano

contrast, the labour process literature has given reasons and considered numerous historical cases providing evidence for the second possibility: that exogenously given (capitalist) property rights dictate a technology and a division of labour which has very little to do with the dictates of efficiency.

The main object of this paper is to deal with this particular instance of the relationship among property rights, division of labour and technology. An attempt will also be made to make more general observations about the relationship itself and it may be useful to emphasise immediately that the two different approaches outlined above arise in many other instances and cut across the traditional divisions between Marxian and neoclassical economics.[1]

The first section of this paper examines the principles of the division of labour which should be applied to obtain an optimum organisation of work. These are Gioia–Babbage, the Smithian, and the Workers Preferences principles. Here it is shown that the Babbage principle provides a powerful explanation for the existence of hierarchies and a strong argument for their relative efficiency. By contrast, the Smithian and the Workers Preferences principles imply that less hierarchical and possibly more democratic forms of organisation could be advantageous. However, an 'optimal' division of labour would require that the effects of all the principles considered should be taken into account.

The second section examines the effects of exogenously given capitalist property rights on the division of labour. This examination is close to the spirit of the labour process literature. It tries to show how capitalist property rights have an important part in explaining the nature of the division of labour of the firm under capitalism and its possible departure from the optimal division of labour examined in the first section. However, the analysis utilises one concept developed in the new institutional literature: the concept of asset-specificity or of assets which can be deployed in other organisations only at substantial costs. The concept of asset-specificity plays an important role in the claim that the organisation of work may be inefficient under capitalism because of an underapplication of the Smithian and Workers' Preferences principles and of an overapplication of the Babbage principle. Another inefficiency of 'classical' capitalism is shown to lie in the existence under that system of the Ure–Marx effect—that is, the tendency to invest more in physical than in human capital and a bias to choose machines requiring little firm-specific human skill for their operation.

We consider in the third section a 'new institutional' argument: that inefficiencies such as those examined in the second section would endogenously generate new property rights and/or governance structures which would tend to eliminate these inefficiencies. This argument is criticised by showing that, in spite of their inefficiencies, the property rights of 'classical' capitalism can be self-sustaining. Factors contributing to the institutional stability and those contributing to the institutional instability of 'classical capitalism' are also examined in this section.

[1] Indeed, neoclassical economics has usually assumed exogenously given property rights. On the other hand the recent work by Coase, Alchian and Demsetz (see, p. 315, n. 1) has attempted to use the powerful neoclassical theory of externalities to study the implications of technological changes for property rights. This approach, enriched by some elements of the Marxian tradition, has been developed and used by North (1981) to provide a framework for the interpretation of history. The co-existence (and the conflict) of these two approaches within the Marxian tradition is striking. Marx himself provides (but does not integrate) the outlines of both theories. On one hand, the development of technology is seen as the ultimate cause for the change of property relations. On the other hand, property relations (influenced, in turn, by class struggle) influence the development of technology. To my knowledge, the best case for the first theory is provided by Cohen (1978), whereas the best illustration for the second theory can be found in Brenner (1986) and his contributions in Aston and Philpin (1988). Roemer (1988, ch. 8) provides a useful introductory survey.

Finally, in the last section we consider two alternative forms of capitalist property rights which may offer some solution to the problems which are solved so unsatisfactorily under 'classical capitalism'. Comparing them with 'classical capitalism' allows a better evaluation of the factors determining the institutional stability of these systems. In particular, one finding of this analysis is that the market itself, far from being a neutral environment where efficient institutions necessarily evolve, is an institution the survival and stability of which is itself dependent on the existence of the institutions which it is supposed to select.

1. The principles of the 'optimal' division of labour

The existence of hierarchical firms characterised by an authoritarian organisation of work and a detailed division of labour can be explained by the following principle formulated by Charles Babbage in 1832:[1]

> That the master manufacturer, by dividing the work to be executed into different processes, each requiring different degrees of skills or force, can purchase exactly that precise quantity of both which is necessary for each process; whereas, if the whole work were executed by one workman, that person must possess sufficient skill to perform the most difficult, and sufficient strength to execute the most laborious, of the operations in which that art is divided (Babbage, 1832, pp. 137–138).

After discovering this principle independently, Babbage generously acknowledged that he had been anticipated by Melchiorre Gioia (1815). However, there is a difference between the two formulations: whereas Babbage refers to the advantages of the division of labour for a cost-minimising 'master manufacturer', Gioia considers the same advantages for a rational society taken as a whole. Indeed one could speak of a joint Gioia–Babbage principle which illustrates the very same advantages of the division of labour occurring for society and for a cost-minimising employer: thus, following his own self interest, the latter happens to do what is in the interest of the former. In both cases these advantages are due to the principles of comparative advantage and of the minimisation of learning time.

The division of labour entails the exploitation of the principle of comparative advantage because it allows each individual to perform only that activity in which s/he is comparatively more gifted. More important, the division of labour also implies a dramatic saving of training time. If each worker is performing all the tasks necessary for a certain productive process, it also becomes necessary for each worker to learn all these tasks. By contrast, if a very detailed division of labour happens to be introduced, and each worker is assigned only one task, then s/he obviously has to learn that task only. In other words, the Babbage principle indicates that a very detailed division of labour minimises training time; productivity is increased by the simple fact that, since less time is required for learning, more time is spent on producing useful goods. Productivity can be increased up to the point where all jobs imply performing only one task, require the minimum amount of learning and entail the full exploitation of the principle of comparative advantage (see point (i) of the Appendix).

The Gioia–Babbage principle therefore indicates the efficiency of a fairly rigid hierarchy. It suggests that only a few people should be assigned to the more skilled jobs and the other workers to the less skilled, or completely unskilled jobs.

[1] The Babbage principle was extensively used by Marx (1967, vol. 1) and has had a central role in Braverman's (1974) analysis of labour process. Leijonhufvud (1986) also contains a clear exposition of what is described in the present paper as the Gioia–Babbage principle which Leijonhufvud calls (in my opinion, misleadingly) the 'efficient, Smithian technology' (p. 221).

318   U. Pagano

It also suggests that the planning, co-ordination, monitoring and, in general, the management tasks should be separated from the other activities. The separation of the management of tasks from their execution would allow a remarkable saving of training time. Only a few people would then have to learn these management activities, and the large majority of people simply learn how to execute what they are being told to do.

Braverman (1974) pointed out how the three main principles of Taylor's 'scientific management' implied respectively the dissociation of the labour process from the skills of the workers, the separation of conception from execution, and the use of management's knowledge of the productive process to plan and control each step of the productive process. In this respect 'Taylorism' can be considered as a detailed set of corollaries of the Gioia–Babbage principle.

In other words, the Gioia–Babbage principle gives powerful reasons for the relative efficiency of an authoritarian and detailed division of labour. It offers a normative justification for the hierarchical structure of the firm: hierarchies increase productivity, and therefore human welfare, because they save on the learning necessary to acquire new skills and use given skills more efficiently because of the principle of comparative advantage. In the opinion of the present writer the recently popular question—why do firms' hierarchies exist?—has already found in the Gioia–Babbage principle one of its most convincing answers.[1] Entrepeneurs had an incentive to organise hierarchical firms characterised by a very detailed division of labour because it minimised their costs. And this also happened to maximise the welfare of society.

I wish now to consider an alternative mechanism by which the division of labour can influence productivity and welfare. This mechanism was spelt out by Adam Smith and happens to be so well known that it may seem inappropriate to spend time on it. Nevertheless, I feel that this is necessary because it is often confused with the Gioia–Babbage principle, whereas there is a substantial difference between the two.

The first difference between the Smithian and the Gioia–Babbage principles is that Smith considers the difference in skills more a consequence than a cause of the division of labour. From the Smithian point of view there is little comparative advantage to be exploited before the introduction of the division of labour. The differences in skills arise as a consequence of the introduction of the division of labour.

---

[1] The literature inspired by Coase's (1952) famous article on the nature of the firm explains its existence by referring to the market transaction costs that would otherwise arise if the firm did not exist. The Gioia–Babbage principle seems to imply that firms might well exist even if market transaction costs were equal to zero. For, even in this case, somebody managing other people, who execute his commands, can be cheaper than each person managing himself and executing the commands conceived by himself. In other words, the Gioia–Babbage principle seems to imply that specialisation in command giving and taking is advantageous independently of any positive market transaction costs argument. This would seem to support Demsetz's (1988) idea that increasing returns to management are a sufficient explanation for the existence of firms and they can also arise in an ideal situation of zero market transaction costs. However, a possible objection to this argument is that, in a world of zero transaction costs, commands could themselves be traded and managers could even be hired by workers as consultants. Still, in order for the workers to buy commands, they should engage in some form of costly evaluation of the commands themselves which would violate the Gioia–Babbage principle. If the resources expended in the evaluation of commands are defined as market transaction costs, then it can still be maintained that firms exist because of market transaction costs. A discussion of the ambiguities contained in the definition of market transaction costs can be found in Dow (1987) and ch. 9 of Hodgson (1988).

A limit to the traditional transaction costs explanation of the existence of the firm is that it has concentrated its attention on the information and enforcement costs which can be observed in a situation of market equilibrium. Pagano (1991A) tries to show that 'disequilibrium transaction costs' are very important in explaining the relative advantages and the existence of firms.

The second and more important difference can only be understood after re-examining the famous Smithian principles of the division of labour. According to Smith, improved dexterity, saving of time otherwise spent on changing occupation, and the invention of machines by workmen are the main reasons why the division of labour improves productivity and welfare. These principles can be summarised by stating that each worker, by specialising in particular activities, acquires better job-specific skills than would be the case if s/he were performing a more numerous set of tasks. The more a worker performs a particular activity the more he learns that activity and therefore his productivity also increases. The division of labour increases productivity because it aids a process of learning-by-doing.

We can now try to compare the Smithian and the Gioia–Babbage principles.

Smith emphasises the advantages of the division of labour due to a greater acquisition of new skills, whereas Gioia and Babbage concentrate on its advantages due to an optimal utilisation of given skills. Babbage and Gioia say that the division of labour increases productivity because it minimises the amount of learning which is required for doing. Smith says that the division of labour increases productivity because it maximises the amount of learning acquired by doing. Or, to put it in another way, for Babbage and Gioia the learning necessary for the doing is minimised whereas for Smith the learning due to the doing is maximised.

The distribution, over time, of the benefits of the Gioia–Babbage and Smith principles is different. The first occur immediately, by reducing the training time spent on the workers. The second take more time. They occur after the workers have acquired additional skills as a result of the learning-by-doing process.

We cannot rule out a priori the fact that the same particular division of labour may optimise the use of both principles. Or that the division of labour which minimises the learning required before doing, also happens to be the one which maximises learning by doing. But there are good reasons to believe that this is not the case and that the overall optimisation problem of productivity over time often involves some compromise between the degrees of specialisation suggested by the Gioia–Babbage and the Smithian principles.

Indeed, there are good reasons to believe that the Smithian principles involve a less detailed division of labour than that which the Gioia–Babbage principle does. A very detailed division of labour may minimise the learning required for doing certain activities, but it may also inhibit the future advantages to be gained from the learning-by-doing process. In this case, enlarging the job may be a way of exploiting the Smithian advantages. This may be convenient even if there is some loss of the Gioia–Babbage benefits. Enlarging a job, which is specialised on the basis of the Gioia–Babbage principle, may imply that the worker can acquire a greater understanding of how some tasks are linked together and, therefore, can learn by doing to reorganise these tasks more efficiently (see point (ii) of the Appendix). This enlargement of the job may require much more preliminary knowledge of the productive process than that which is implied in the Gioia–Babbage principle. Still, the Smithian dynamic benefits of having a less detailed division of labour can be greater than the additional training costs.

Moreover, the Smithian principles do not seem to imply that a rigid separation of planning and co-ordination from execution activities is necessarily beneficial. Executing a job without understanding the reasons and the purposes for which it is performed is likely to be more an obstacle than an advantage for the learning-by-doing process.

320   **U. Pagano**

To conclude, choosing a very detailed division of labour on the lines of Gioia and Babbage may imply foregoing some of the future learning-by-doing advantages for the immediate minimum learning benefits.

The Smith and Gioia–Babbage principles suggest two ways by which the division of labour can increase human welfare. In both cases, the intermediate step is given by the effects of the division of labour on (the present or future) productivity of work. But the division of labour and, in general, the organisation of work also directly influences human welfare. Workers are usually not indifferent to the different types of job which they perform nor to the type of organisation for which they work. This simple fact is obviously very important. However, it has been usually ignored by orthodox economists, who have assumed that the only arguments of the utility functions are consumption goods and leisure and that work affects utility only indirectly either because of the products of work or as forgone leisure.[1] When the preferences of the workers for their own work are taken into account, increases in the productivity of work do not necessarily imply higher welfare. The increase in welfare obtained by increases in the productivity of work may be offset by the decrease in welfare due to an increase in the disutility of work. Narrow jobs, organised on the basis of the Gioia–Babbage principles, may well imply an increase of the disutility of work greater than the increase of utility due to the increase of the product of work obtained by an application of these principles (Pagano, 1985).

Two consequences of taking workers' preferences into account (or the Workers' Preferences principle) are important here. First, the workers may rather enjoy the process of learning by doing and the necessary preliminary learning, so that the Workers' Preferences principle may imply that the division of labour should be less detailed than even a joint application of the Gioia–Babbage and Smithian principles suggests. Second, the workers may prefer a greater variety of activities and participation in management decisions than is implied by these principles (see point (iii) of the Appendix). These consequences of the workers' preferences may hold even when they come together with a lower productivity and a lower level of consumption.

In general, an optimal division of labour should take into account the effects of the Gioia–Babbage principles on present productivity and of the Smithian principles on future productivity as well as the effects that the division of labour has on the disutility of work because of the Workers' Preferences principle. Giving different weights to these principles implies a different division of labour and organisation of work. A greater weight given to the Gioia–Babbage principle implies a more authoritarian and detailed division of labour and the existence of rigid hierarchies. By contrast, a greater weight given to the Smithian and Workers' Preferences principles implies a less detailed division of labour and less hierarchical and more democratic organisation of work (see point (iv) of the Appendix). The purpose of the next section is to examine the influence of property rights, defining a 'classical' capitalist system, on the weight given to the application of each one of these principles.

2. Asset specificity and 'classical' capitalism

A claim advanced in some of the works of the labour process literature is that capitalism has degraded and deskilled work, introducing an undesirable division of labour. In

---

[1] There are, however, remarkable exceptions in the history of the classical and neoclassical schools. Marx had an original position on this point because he believed that workers' preferences were important for the construction of future society but irrelevant for understanding the economic institutions of capitalism. On this see Pagano (1985).

particular, in his book *Labour and Monopoly Capital* (1974), Braverman argued that there is empirical evidence to support this claim. The extent and the validity of the de-skilling tendency has, however, been questioned by other contributors to this stream of the literature.[1]

The purpose of the present paper is not to deal with whether or not there is empirical evidence to support this thesis. Instead I will try to advance a different view point: one can give a definition of the property rights defining 'classical capitalism' which, in my opinion captures rather well some aspects of the capitalist societies of the past and also, perhaps, some characteristics of some contemporary capitalist societies. Then, it is possible to show that this particular set of property rights defining 'classical capitalism' is likely to bring about institutions characterised by some of the features described by Braverman, in particular, firms characterised by an undesirably hierarchical and detailed division of labour. This division of labour cannot be justified by technological or transaction efficiency alone but must be seen through the constraints posed by the property rights system of a 'classical' capitalist society.

In order to maintain that the property rights system of 'classical' capitalism produces an undesirably hierarchical and detailed division of labour, I will try to show that this system brings about an overapplication of the Gioia–Babbage principle and an underapplication of the Smithian and Workers' Preferences principle (see point (iv) of the Appendix). This claim is not meant to imply that the Smithian and Workers' Preferences principles do not have any role under capitalism, but rather to point out that they have less influence than they would if the system were not constrained by capitalist property rights.

The property rights of 'classical' capitalism are here simply defined by the fact that, under this system, all the agents own their labour power and it is possible for some agents to hire and fire the labour power of other agents. On the one hand, this differentiates capitalism from slavery or a feudal system, where agents are allowed to have all or some property rights on the labour power of other individuals. On the other hand, the possibility of hiring and firing labour power differentiates capitalism from systems where people can only work for a organisation if they are given some property rights in the organisation itself. In fact, the typical capitalist firm is characterised by the fact that the firm does not have any property rights over the worker and the worker, in turn does not have any property rights in the firm and/or his/her job.

I will now use one of the fundamental concepts developed by the new institutional literature: the concept of asset-specificity, or the concept of assets specific to certain organisations or firms, which cannot be redeployed somewhere else without substantial losses. In situations characterised by uncertainty, bounded rationality and goal incongruence or opportunism,[2] market relations cannot cope with asset-specificity. For, in

---

[1] In particular, Edwards (1979) has observed that skilling and de-skilling occur simultaneously for different groups of workers, so that the overall tendency is not clear. This point emerges also from the contributions contained in Wood (1982). For an introduction to the debates concerning Braverman's de-skilling thesis see Thompson (1983), Sawyer (1989) and Pagano (1991A).

[2] Some of these concepts have a particular meaning in new institutional economics and, in particular, in the often 'book-specific' terminology used by Williamson (1985). Bounded rationality is mainly related by Williamson to the human incapacity of dealing with the future by writing complete contingent contracts and is not grounded in the more fundamental concept of limited computational capacity considered by Herbert Simon. On this point see Hodgson (1989). The fundamental meaning of opportunism in Williamson is the tendency of the agents to interpret and exploit necessarily incomplete market contracts to their own advantage. A discussion of the role of opportunism in transaction cost economics is contained in Hodgson (1988) and Langlois (1984).

322   U. Pagano

cases of unforeseen events, not well specified in market contracts because of bounded rationality, each agent cannot defend him/herself against the opportunism of other agents by changing trading partner at a low cost. This implies that transactions to be supported by asset-specific investment may not take place in the absence of a governance structure or of a redefinition of property rights. Instead, there will be a tendency to use transactions which do not involve any asset-specificity and are supported by general purpose assets. In other words the asset-specificity problem arises because, under existing property rights, some transactions generate externalities which make it difficult or impossible to carry out the transactions themselves. This is because they involve the development of assets over which property rights are ill-defined.[1]

It is easy to see that the application of the Gioia–Babbage principle does not involve the creation but rather the elimination of elements of asset-specificity. Consider, for example, that some of the learning which is necessary for production is likely to be specific to a particular organisation and, therefore, involves investment in human capital specific to that organisation. Now, the application of the Gioia–Babbage principle, which implies the minimisation of all the learning necessary for the doing, also involves the minimisation of this organisational-specific learning. In other words, the very detailed and hierarchical division of labour implied by the Gioia–Babbage principle is usually the means by which the asset-specificity problem can be suppressed.

Let us now consider the effects on the creation of asset specificity of the Smithian principles which, as already pointed out, rely on the maximisation of learning-by-doing. First, some of the additional preliminary learning which may be required for enjoying their advantages may happen to be firm-specific. Second, a great deal of the learning acquired by doing is also likely to be specific to the organisation itself and not redeployable in other firms. Thus, contrary to the Gioia–Babbage principle, the Smithian principle involve the creation of assets which are specific to the particular organisation where they happen to be applied.

Finally, let us consider the Workers' Preferences principle. Insofar as the workers would prefer a division of labour where they enjoy the process of learning-by-doing, this may simply accentuate the problem posed by the application of Smithian principles. This is because learning-by-doing which is partially firm-specific will have to be more than that which is implied by the Smithian principles. Moreover, insofar as workers wish to acquire knowledge and to participate in the organisation's decisions, this involves an additional investment which is also clearly firm-specific. Finally, taking account of workers' preferences involves changes in the work environment, which may imply expenditure on certain durable assets. These durable assets may have a strong element of firm-specificity. They may turn out to be valuable for the workers employed during the current period but prove less valuable for the workers joining the firm in the future. In other words, they may not be redeployable for other workers at low cost.

Indeed, the Workers' Preferences principle may also find little application under capitalism. The workers may have very little incentive to make their working environment more pleasurable. This is because they know that the effort spent on, or the income forgone in, improving the organisational environment may be lost if they happen to be

---

[1] The concept of asset-specificity is usually used in the new institutional literature to show how its existence involves the endogenous development of new forms of organisations and property rights. Here property rights are exogenously given and the focus of the analysis is on the implications of asset-specificity on the forms of organisation suggested by the principles of the division of labour considered in the previous section.

fired. The employers also may be little inclined to spend on assets which may be expropriated if the workers leave the firm and which cannot be easily redeployable to new workers.

Thus, the application of the Smithian and the Workers' Preferences principles involves the creation of substantial elements of asset-specificity, while the application of the Gioia–Babbage principle eliminates asset-specificity. For this reason it can be argued that the Gioia–Babbage principle is 'overapplied' and the Smithian and Workers' Preferences principles are 'underapplied' under 'classical' capitalism.[1]

For instance, consider what happens to the human firm-specific capital in a system where firms can fire workers and workers, in turn, can quit the firm, that is to say, a system in which firms do not own the workers and workers do not own the firms. On the one hand, workers do not have well-defined property rights in their human capital, because they can easily be relieved of these assets by being fired. On the other hand, the owners of the firm also do not have well-defined property rights in the human capital of the workers, because the workers can just leave the firm.

Consider also the physical capital, which is complementary to this firm-specific human capital and workers' preferences. It is again not easily redeployable with other workers and the workers are also not easily redeployable with other machines. Both lose part of their value if they happen to be separated from each other This also happens to be true for the part of physical capital which is invested to satisfy specific workers' preferences.

Hence property rights are not well-specified and a strong externality exists.

The same problem does not arise in the case of firm-specific physical capital which, however, is not specific to workers' preferences or skills.

Unlike human capital, machines can be owned rather than being hired by the firm. By contrast, owning rather than hiring labour is incompatible with capitalist property rights, for it would imply a reintroduction of slavery.[2] This fundamental difference between human and non-human capital has two important consequences for the technology and organisation of work which is likely to be chosen under a system of classical capitalism.

---

[1] The exact meaning of 'overapplied' and 'underapplied' is clarified in the Appendix where we define the social welfare function which should be optimised in order to achieve maximum total utility. Of course, it is rather unsatisfactory to compare social systems with the 'Nirvana' solutions maximising the social welfare function. A proper criticism of a given system of property rights must be based on its comparison with alternative property rights systems which are likely to offer some solutions to its failures. This comparison is carried out in Section 4 of this paper.

[2] Indeed one might think that an introduction of slavery or feudalism might, paradoxically, solve some of the externality problems which have been examined. For, under these systems property rights seem to be well-defined because the master or the lord can enjoy all the fruits of the investment made in the human capital of the workers without fearing that the workers may quit. But the problem is that even under slavery the property rights that one individual can have over another individual are somewhat limited. Thus it is rather difficult to make slaves work hard and exploit their human capital if they do not have any incentive to do so. Feiner (1986) and Genovese (1969) illustrate how this was the cause of the low productivity of the slave mode of production. On the other hand, there is some evidence that the masters did invest in the human capital of their slaves. This may be somewhat overstated in Fogel and Engerman (1976) but it is not completely denied in the critical reviews contained in David *et al.* (1976). The antiliteracy laws, existing in the majority of the American Southern states under slavery and their violation by single slave owners (Genovese, 1975, pp. 561–565) seem to imply that there was a contradiction between the general interest of the slave owners in keeping the slaves illiterate (to prevent the possibility of their reading abolitionist publications and organising mass revolts) and the individual interest of single slave owners in having some educated slaves (a 'private' interest which was not dangerous to follow as long as the other slave owners did not do the same).

First, under 'classical capitalism' there is a tendency to invest more in machines than in workers.[1] This is due to the fact that the asset specificity investment problem can be rather easily overcome for machines but not for workers. The user of firm-specific capital can buy the machines from their producer. This guarantees both the user and the producer against the expropriation hazards which would arise if the user were renting the organisation-specific machines from the producer. In the latter case, neither the user nor the producer could change its partner at low cost and machines would be undersupplied because of the fear of post-contractual opportunistic behaviour. This post-contractual opportunistic behaviour is remarkably limited if the user of firm-specific machines buys the machines rather than renting them from the producer and takes all the benefits and the risks which are due to their firm-specificity. Under capitalism this solution is, obviously, impossible in the case of human capital.

Second, under classical capitalism, there is a tendency to invest in a particular type of machine. In particular, there is a tendency to choose machines which are complementary to non-firm-specific human capital.

These two consequences of the different status of human and non-human capital may be called 'the Ure–Marx effect' because both authors observed how the development of capitalism was based more on investment in machine skills than in human skills and, in particular, on machine skills 'independent' of human skills.[2]

An important corollary of the fact that machines can be bought rather than rented from their owner is that, unlike labour, they can also be easily commonly owned.

Indeed, the joint stock company is a fairly common type of capitalist organisation where machines are commonly owned and the capitalists own shares instead of machines. This has important consequences, because it implies that asset-specificity problems among machines can be overcome much more easily than asset-specificity problems among workers, and among workers and machines. In the joint stock company each share holder can withdraw shares but cannot expropriate or be expropriated by the withdrawal of asset-specific machines. Thus, investment in mutually specific machines is not inhibited by the fear of expropriation problems.[3]

The same solution is not easily available for the firm-specific investment relations existing among workers and among workers and machines. This difference between relations among machines, on the one hand, and relations among workers and machines and among workers themselves, on the other hand, reinforces the 'Ure–Marx effect'. It contrasts sharply the almost unlimited potential of investment in machines, existing under 'classical' capitalism, with the very limited potential for investment in people offered by this system of property rights.

---

[1] More precisely, the ratio of the capital-to-worker investment tends to be inefficiently high under 'classical capitalism' with respect to alternative modes of production, such as the models of 'company workers' capitalism' and 'unionised capitalism' examined in Section 4. There, we will show that in these systems the property rights problems of 'classical capitalism' can find some solution.

[2] Referring to the learning-by-doing advantages of the division of labour exposed by Adam Smith, Ure (1835) claims that 'what was in Dr. Smith's time a topic of useful illustration, cannot now be used without the risk of misleading the public's mind as to the right principle of the manufacturing industry' (p. 19). 'On the contrary, whenever a process requires particular dexterity and steadiness of hand it is withdrawn as soon as possible from the "cunning" workman who is prone to many kinds of irregularities, and it is placed in charge of a particular mechanism, so self-regulating that a child could supervise it' (p. 19). Marx (1967) based his analysis of the capitalist factory on Ure (and Babbage) and observed that the capitalist mode of production implied some form of skilling of machines and de-skilling of the workers.

[3] This point is nicely put forward in Leijonhufvud (1986) where he also considers a possible solution of the Dahlman paradox: that the industrial revolution implied the simultaneous institution of private property of land (enclosures) and common property of capital (joint-stock company).

In conclusion, 'classical capitalism' is characterised by an unsatisfactory definition of property rights.[1]

A first consequence of this is the 'Ure–Marx effect'; that is, a greater incentive to invest in machines rather than in workers and, in particular, in machines involving the complementary use of little human capital.

A second, related consequence is that Gioia and Babbage rather than Smith are likely to be the source of inspiration for the organisation of work under capitalism—this implying a too hierarchical and detailed division of labour within the firm.

Finally, the Workers' Preferences principle may also find little application under capitalism.

Hierarchical firms, characterised by an inefficient quantity and quality of machines, a detailed and authoritarian organisation of work and an unpleasant working environment, may well be generated by the property rights of 'classical capitalism'.

3. Self-sustaining and inefficient property rights

In the Introduction I considered the following question: is the often very detailed and hierarchical division of labour which characterises many firms under capitalism the result of transaction costs and technological efficiency or the result of capitalism?

The overapplication of the Gioia–Babbage principle, and the Ure–Marx effect considered in the preceding section, give some support to the second possibility—a possibility which is often advanced in the labour process literature.

Still, a powerful objection, inspired by the new institutional economics, needs to be considered. Capitalism forbids the owners of firms to own the workers, but does not forbid the workers to own firms, or to develop alternative contractual relationships by which, for example, the workers 'own' their jobs. So, if the effects of the typical property rights arrangements are so unpleasant why do we not see the development of organisations and firms based on a different set of property rights? Or, in other words, why do rational agents not evolve a system of property rights and a governance system which adapts itself to the dictates of technological and transaction cost efficiency?

Posing these questions challenges what has been the underlying assumption of the preceding section: that property rights are exogenously given and determine the technological and transaction structure of the economy. Indeed, it inverts the direction of causality and makes the 'needs' of an efficient technological and transaction structure dictate the property rights system of the economy.[2]

---

[1] This statement, as well as the following ones of this section, will become clearer in Section 4 where 'classical capitalism' is compared to alternative models of capitalism which are characterised by a more satisfactory definition of property rights. In fact, it is only by comparative analysis that the shortcomings of a particular system can be more precisely evaluated.

[2] This approach is taken by the property rights literature. See Demsetz (1967) where he claims that: 'property rights develop to internalize externalities when the gains of internationalization become larger than the cost of internalization. Increased internalization, in the main, results from changes in economic values, changes which stem from the development of new technology and the opening of new markets, changes to which old property rights are poorly attuned' (p. 350). This approach shares some aspects of Marx' theory of history, brilliantly examined and defended by Cohen (1978). In the Marxian theory, changes in property rights stem from their inability to cope efficiently with a certain level of productive forces. The level of the productive forces expresses how much labour needs to be spent to make specified products if the productive forces are to be used in their optimal combination. It is, therefore, defined by the technology and the potential uses of resources which are available at a certain moment of time. Relations of production or property rights can 'fetter' productive forces. Or, in other words, they inhibit their development and their optimal use. Also here, when this 'fettering' takes place, there is a tendency to displace the old system of property rights. According to Brenner, an alternative and more convincing theory of history can also be found in Marx (see p. 316, n. 1).

326   U. Pagano

Consider the following theory of the property structure of the firm put forward by Professor Alchian (1987). In order to simplify the analysis, Alchian assumes that there are owners of just firm-specific resources and owners of just 'general' resources. Then, he writes:

A firm, then, is a group of firm-specific and some general inputs bound by constraining contracts, producing a non-decomposable-end product value. As a result, the activities and operation of the firm will be most intensively controlled and monitored by the firm-specific input owners who gain or lose the most from the success or failure of the 'firm'. In fact, they are typically considered the 'owners' or 'employers' or 'bosses' of the firm, though in reality the firm is a cooperating collection of resources owned by different people.[1]

This argument takes as given which assets are general and which assets are firm-specific. Given the general thrust of the argument (which is intended to show that the resulting configuration of property rights is efficient) we must assume that technological efficiency is given and determines the general or the firm-specific nature of the assets. Given this efficient configuration of the assets, it can be reasonably argued that rational agents will achieve an efficient set of property rights which minimise transaction costs. The owners of the firm-specific assets will be the ones which will be willing to pay the most for the ownership of the firm and, in particular, for the right to hire and fire the other members, whereas the owners of general assets will value these property rights much less because they can leave the firm at low cost in the case of substantial disagreement with the other partners. In this approach, capital hires and fires labour, or owns the firm only when capital is firm-specific and labour is the general input of production. When the opposite is true the theory predicts that labour will hire capital.

Under the market system the factor which needs to safeguard its firm-specific investment will acquire the property of the firm. This factor is also likely to be that which is willing to spend the greatest effort on its efficient management because it cannot exist from the firm at low cost.[2] Thus, the efficient property rights structure of the firm is endogenously generated by the market system. Co-operatives and capitalist forms of organisation will prevail because of their relative efficiency. Property rights arrangements which are not efficient are institutionally unstable in a market economy.

This endogenous generation of efficient organisational structures is extended in the new institutional literature to cover more complex cases where both machines and labour are firm-specific. Governance systems, exchange of hostages, formations of unions and the modern corporation are all institutions through which the agents can efficiently protect asset specific investments against the expropriation hazards due to the opportunism of other agents in unforeseen circumstances.[3]

---

[1] See Alchian (1984, 1987) where he also maintains that 'industrial democracy arrangements are rare, because the owners of more general resources have less interest in the firm than those of specific resources' (p. 1032).

[2] In other words, these agents become the owners of the firm because they need a 'voice' since asset-specificity prevents them from exercising the 'exit' option to safeguard their interests. On 'voice' and 'exit' see Hirshman (1970).

[3] The most complete exposition of the results obtained by following this approach is Williamson (1985). An important limit to the new institutional economics is pointed out by Nutzinger (1982). He argues that the transaction costs which characterise each institutional arrangement are not independent of the co-existing institutions. Thus, it is only by making a strong *ceteris paribus* assumption that we can compare the relative efficiency of alternative institutions. 'From this follows: Whenever the property right economists claim to have provided a generalisation of the standard model of production and exchange, then this claim, strictly speaking, has to be confined to models of partial equilibrium in the tradition of Marshall, and cannot be easily extended to general equilibrium situations in the sense of Walras' (p. 181).

The aim of rational human agents to achieve technological and transaction cost efficiency is important for understanding the evolution of property rights. Still, the argument is incomplete because property rights do also have an important role in shaping the technological and transaction structure of the economy. In a world where transaction costs are not zero, property rights cannot be easily transferred to the agents who can use more efficiently the resources over which they are defined; nor can property rights be easily redefined according to the dictates of efficiency. Instead of being simply shaped by efficiency, the actual distribution of property rights is also likely to constrain efficiency and limit the choices which are feasible for individuals by influencing the set of possible techniques and transactions. And, once these choices are implemented, even in an ideal world of zero transaction costs, a new set of property rights (different from the rights which were efficient before the implementation of these choices) becomes efficient.

Consider again Professor Alchian's statement. As we saw in the preceding section, the general and firm-specific characteristics of the inputs depend on the property rights existing at a certain moment of time. Thus, if it is true that technology influences property rights, the opposite also is true: property rights influence technology. This implies that we have to face very complicated cumulative processes where property rights influence themselves via technology and technology influences itself via property rights.

In this context, simple efficiency stories may well lose their meaning. Each outcome is likely to be path dependent and inefficient interactions between property rights and technology are likely to characterise the history of economic systems.[1]

Suppose that the property rights of 'classical' capitalism happen to be the dominant form of property rights and that the inefficiencies considered in the preceding section can be overcome by the development of new organisations characterised by different property rights. Suppose, in particular, that workers' co-operatives, or other organisations where the workers have some property rights in their jobs, could overcome the asset-specificity problem by making the workers own their firm-specific human capital. Then, we can easily see how the need and the success of these organisations may require an alternative technology which, in turn, requires that the property rights defining these organisations already exist—an impossibility which may imply the institutional stability of inefficient organisations.

Recall that the existence of firms characterised by the property rights of 'classical' capitalism gives rise to an organisation of production where asset-specific investment is mainly concentrated in physical capital and comparatively little asset-specific investment is made in human capital. Consider also that some learning-by-doing is acquired by managers and specialists in the use of this set of techniques. This has three consequences. In the first place, the need to redefine property rights in such a way as to solve the human capital specificity problem is overshadowed by the fact that little human asset-specificity is generated by the technology used by the system.[2] In other words, the property rights problem may not be visible to the agents because the asset over which the problem would arise is not generated under the property rights of 'classical'

---

[1] A formalisation of the concept of self-sustaining 'property rights equilibria' and an examination of their properties of 'institutional stability', are considered in Pagano (1991C).

[2] For note 2, see next page.

328   U. Pagano

capitalism. Secondly, even if the agents realise that an alternative arrangement of property rights which favours human asset specificity may yield higher benefits, redefining or transferring property rights is costly and requires time. As a consequence, for some time, investment continues to be concentrated on capital rather than labour. Thirdly, after a period of time in which these property rights constrained techniques have been used, the learning generated by their application may make them more efficient than the techniques unconstrained by inefficient property rights. Or, in other words, the other techniques, unconstrained by an inferior property rights system, would have been more efficient if they could have been used and enjoyed a process of learning by doing. But, given that this has not happened, they are now less efficient given the current state of technological knowledge.

Thus, the existence of classical capitalist property rights generates technological conditions which make capital the asset characterised by a higher degree of asset-specificity relative to labour. This, following Alchian, implies that capital should hire labour and that, in fact, the property rights of classical capitalism will be regenerated by the agents of a market economy. This regeneration of capitalist property rights occurs even if we have assumed that co-operatives, or organisations characterised by some form of job ownership, are more efficient because they allow investment in firm-specific human capital. In order to generate the new superior property rights which we have assumed to be provided by co-operatives, these organisations should already exist. This vicious circle, which may prevent the formation of co-operatives, is due to the fact that only when human asset specificity already exists does this form of property rights become clearly convenient. But this investment in human-specific capital requires that co-operatives have had the time to generate the technology consistent with their property rights.

Thus, the system of property rights which characterises 'classical' capitalism can be self-sustaining even when it is less efficient than alternative property rights systems which do not discourage investment in firm-specific human capital.

It is worth observing that under 'classical' capitalism the existence of a competitive labour market is not inconsistent with the existence of rigid hierarchies based on an overapplication of the Gioia–Babbage principle. By contrast, the existence of rigid hierarchies, where the workers at the bottom of the hierarchy are simply told to execute simple movements, creates the conditions for a flexible labour market for these workers. It minimises the firm-specific human capital which is lost when they change organisations and, therefore, implies low market transaction costs. Indeed, it can be said that a flexible competitive labour market is made possible by the existence of rigid hierarchies which offer little learning-by-doing, no promotion possibilities and little realisation of the

---

[2] In a world of perfect knowledge and zero transaction costs this would not happen. The problem would not be 'overshadowed' by the fact that the asset to be generated under the new system of property rights does not yet exist. The agents would know the value of these future assets (or the value of the externality). Moreover, in that world the identity of the owners would not matter for an efficient internalisation of the externality. On this point see Demsetz (1988B, ch. 2). However, in a world of imperfect knowledge and positive transaction costs it seems relevant to distinguish between existing and future assets over which property rights are ill-defined. The traditional examples of the property rights literature concern existing assets, such as air spaces and television channels, which were previously commonly owned and over which property rights were defined after the increase in the value of these assets. Here, the asset, its value and the competing property claims are clearly visible and an effort to redefine the property rights over the existing assets is likely to arise. By contrast the value of an asset which does not yet exist is likely to be relatively invisible to the agents and competing property claims on a non-existing asset are less likely to arise. As a consequence, the effort to redefine property rights is less likely to occur.

workers' preferences for more interesting jobs and a better working environment. A competitive market for labour power, together with rigid hierarchies, exists here because of the failure of the property rights of classical capitalism to internalise the externality posed by workers' firm-specific assets and it is far from being associated with any Pareto optimality property.

In spite of this failure, the property rights of classical capitalism may exhibit some 'institutional stability'. This is because they may help to generate not only a technology but also a set of values which may make these property rights self-sustaining.

Indeed, under classical capitalism, another vicious circle may arise between values and property rights which prevents their change. Again, the need and the success of organisations where the workers have at least some property rights in their jobs may require a new set of values which in turn, partially, depends on the fact that these organisations already exist. The case of 'positive' and 'negative' freedom values illustrates this possibility and also some other relevant points.

Traditional liberal values put a lot of stress on negative freedom or 'freedom from' instead of on positive freedom or 'freedom to'. I feel that both concepts of freedom are appealing and I find it somewhat discouraging to believe that there may be a trade-off between the two. Still, I am afraid that this problem exists. Negative freedom implies that we can easily break the constraints of pre-existing relations and move to relations which we prefer. Positive freedom implies the ability to do things within a certain set of relations and includes the possibility of investing in these relations without fearing the fact that they are going to be broken. The advantage of negative freedom is that we are not stuck in undesirable relations because we can always break them. Clearly, positive freedom is based on the opposite characteristics: it involves the ability to make specific investments in relations. But these specific investments in relations make their break-up very costly. In other words, positive and negative freedoms put severe limitations on each other.

Consider a set of traditional capitalist firms all using a technology characterised by a very pronounced application of the Gioia–Babbage principle. Consider also the position of the worker in that system. The workers enjoy a lot of negative freedom and very little positive freedom. In that system relations can be easily broken because no asset-specific investment is made by the worker in the organisation nor by the organisation in the worker. Changing organisations is cheap, but a necessary companion of market mobility is a hierarchical and detailed division of labour which gives very limited possibilities for the worker to enjoy positive freedom.

Consider now a system of firms where different property rights have produced an organisation of work based on the learning-by-doing and Workers' Preference principles. Here, the worker enjoys a lot of positive freedom but his/her negative freedom is somewhat limited. This new set of property rights and the consequent alternative organisation of work imply that s/he has invested a lot in firm-specific assets which make it very costly for her/him and the organisation if s/he happens to move to another organisation.

Developing a strong taste for positive freedom, such that one is ready to give up some negative freedom, is partially dependent on the existence of organisations where positive freedom can show its advantages. Still, the very existence and success of these organisations, as well as the need for them, is conditional upon the existence of people who have already developed a taste for positive freedom and a sense of commitment to the organisation even when this limits their negative freedom. New organisations, based on an alternative structure of property rights, may require new values and the new values may require that such organisations already exist.[1] A vicious circle between values and property rights similar to that existing between technology and property rights may prevent the formation of these organisations.[2]

Thus, the property rights of classical capitalism favour technology and values that may make them self-sustaining. Other factors contribute to their institutional stability.

The system can cope rather well with technological innovations insofar as they imply that the workers should be assigned to different tasks. Neither the workers nor the employers have invested substantially in either job-specific or firm-specific skills which become redundant as a consequence of the innovation. Thus, the resistance to technological change is likely to be low.

Moreover, monitoring jobs with little task and skill content is relatively cheap and simple. And, insofar as there is a relative abundance of unskilled labour and workers are not unionised, their bargaining power is low because they can be replaced cheaply by other workers. Indeed, any change in the property rights system which encourages workers' investment is going to alter these conditions and increase the bargaining power of the workers. The same change is going to have both efficiency and distributional consequences and may be opposed by the employers for these latter reasons.

At the same time, many factors can threaten the institutional stability of the property rights of classical capitalism. Technological innovations may render particularly inefficient a system of property rights biased against firm-specific investment in human capital and make relatively visible the human capital externality which the property rights of classical capitalism are not able to internalise. The workers may increasingly dislike the values which sustain the property relations of that system. For instance, they may feel the relative emptiness of the concept of negative freedom which underlies the legitimacy of the system. The sense of non-belonging to the organisation may make monitoring very expensive. Unions may be formed and, even simply for distributional purposes, may gain some forms of property rights for their members in the jobs which they perform and the organisations where they work. Finally, competitors who have succeeded in the internalisation of the human capital externality and moved to a superior system of property rights may threaten to drive the firms of 'classical' capitalism out of the market.

4. Institutional (in)stability of alternative capitalist relations

A better assessment of the institutional stability of 'classical capitalism' involves an evaluation of the comparative institutional stability of the alternative forms of property rights which may offer a partial solution to the inefficiencies due to its inability to favour firm-specific investment. Two alternative arrangements of property rights can offer and sometimes have offered a solution to the typical property rights problem of 'classical capitalism'.

Under the first arrangement, which can be called 'company workers' capitalism', the workers of a particular firm acquire some property rights in that firm. The owners of the physical capital of the firm lose the right of firing workers at their discretion and the workers acquire some form of job ownership in that particular firm. An internal labour

[1] In other words, the development of a compatible ideology is of fundamental importance for the success of a certain set of property rights. This point is correctly emphasised by North (1981).
[2] Another vicious self-sustaining circle between capitalist property rights, values and technology is illustrated by Marx (1967) in his illustration of commodity fetishism. I have examined this vicious circle in ch. 3 of Pagano (1985). Other similar interesting vicious circles are considered in Putterman (1982).

market, or some bureaucratic rules, characterise the allocation of jobs to the workers after they have joined the firm: the understanding is that the insiders have a right to a job, even if not a right to a particular job in the firm, and they have priority over outsiders when some 'better' jobs, compatible with the skills they have acquired, are available in the firm. Under 'company workers capitalism' rigid hierarchies have become flexible bureaucracies: some workers can climb the ladder and seniority is rewarded. Under 'company workers capitalism' investing in firm-specific skills is not subject to expropriation hazards and it is remunerated within the firm. Under this new arrangement of property rights the externality typical of 'classical capitalism' is internalised in each particular firm.

The second arrangement may be called horizontally 'unionised capitalism' in that all workers involved in a particular occupation, or their union, acquire some property rights in a particular job performed in many different firms. In particular, they acquire the right of determining, together with the association of the employers, job specification and on-the-job training and they use this property right to make each firm develop human skills which can be transferred to other firms without substantial losses. Thus, the employers of each firm lose the property right of determining job specification and on-the-job training—a right that they keep under 'company workers' capitalism'. On the other hand, under this arrangement each firm keeps the right of firing workers—a right which is lost or seriously limited under 'company workers' capitalism. And this last right can be kept without diminishing the workers' incentive to invest in the skills required by the organisation. For, under this system of property rights, jobs have been standardised and any learning acquired in one firm can be used in another firm. Even if the workers change firm fairly often, they can climb the ladder of an occupational career. Their level of ability is certified by some authority outside the firm. This authority also ensures that the training and the jobs in each organisation are not firm-specific and can be used in other organisations.[1]

Either 'company workers' capitalism' or 'unionised capitalism' represent property rights arrangements which allow for a certain internalisation of the externality typical of 'classical capitalism'[2]—an externality which we have seen to imply that the property rights concerning firm-specific human assets and assets complementary to them are ill-defined. In the case of 'company workers' capitalism, the externality is internalised by giving the workers of each firm some property rights in that firm. In the case of 'unionised'

---

[1] However, only some forms of firm-specificity can be eliminated by this institutional arrangement. Still, it is important to emphasise that firm-specificity can often be due to the absence of standardisation. Consider the following example. Two firms are characterised by identical productive processes. In particular, in both firms four tasks (a, b, c, d) are performed. However, in the first firm there are two jobs respectively defined by tasks (a, b) and tasks (c, d). In the second firm there also two jobs but they are respectively defined by tasks (a, d) and tasks (b, c). Given this definition of the jobs in the two firms, jobs are firm-specific in spite of the fact that the tasks performed at the two firms are identical. In this important class of cases standardisation can eliminate firm-specificity. Observe that, in absence of the co-ordination and the monitoring provided by the property rights of 'unionised capitalism, the (over)application of the Gioia–Babbage system, typical of 'classical capitalism' can standardise jobs but only at the lowest level. In this case the jobs in both firms will be identically defined by (a), (b), (c) and (d).

[2] In some ways the distinction outlined here between the workers of 'unionised capitalism' and 'company workers capitalism' resembles the distinction between the members of the scientific and technological community considered by Dasgupta and David (1988). Indeed, like the scientist, the 'unionised worker' acquires rights which are not specific to a particular firm and which are commensurate to his/her level of ability which is evaluated by the other members of the community of people employed in the same occupation. By contrast, the 'company worker', similarly to the technologist, acquires rights which are specific to a particular firm and are commensurate to his/her level of ability which is evaluated by the other members of the firm.

332   U. Pagano

capitalism the externality is eliminated by making 'general purpose' some previously firm-specific assets which become occupation-specific assets owned by a union—an institutional solution which allows the formation of a market for the previous externality. In this respect, both systems are potentially Pareto-superior alternatives to 'classical capitalism'. In both systems we should expect that the overapplication of the Gioia–Babbage principle and the underapplication of the Smithian and Workers' Preference principles are somewhat contained, and that the impact of the Ure–Marx effect is less pronounced than under 'classical capitalism'. Still, we have to consider the conditions of institutional stability of these alternative property relations.

In some ways, as with 'classical capitalism', each one of these systems can develop a technology and a set of values which makes each one of this set of property rights self-sustaining.

Consider 'company workers' capitalism'. Under this system of property rights, the workers have an incentive to invest in firm-specific assets. The resulting technology implies that the workers, owning firm-specific resources, will greatly value the property rights that they have in the firm. Moreover, under this property rights system, the workers, perceiving that their advancement is linked to success of the firm, are likely to develop a system of values that implies a certain loyalty to the organisation. In turn, this sustains the property rights system which requires that the workers have that sense of loyalty and are not going to 'misuse' their rights against the general interests of the organisation.

Examine now the case of 'unionised capitalism'. Under this system of property rights the workers have an interest in investing in occupational specific assets. The latter are valuable only insofar as each firm does not change job specification and training—a condition that is satisfied insofar as the union, together with the association of employers, is able to enforce the property rights that it has in each firm. Again the property rights system is technologically self-sustaining. The resulting technology implies that workers have invested in occupational-specific assets and have a vested interest in supporting the union which defends their property rights in those assets. Furthermore, the interaction between values and property rights follows a similar pattern. Under that system of property rights, the workers realise the benefits of the union supporting those property rights and develop a sense of loyalty to the union—such a sense of loyalty making the union able to sustain and enforce these property rights.

Moreover, as with the case of 'classical capitalism', the technology and the values of 'company workers' capitalism' and 'unionised capitalism' may enjoy learning-by-doing which further contributes to the institutional stability of the corresponding property rights after they have prevailed for a sufficiently long time. Thus path dependence, in the form of lock-in effects, characterise each one of the three property rights systems which we have examined.

In other respects, 'company workers' capitalism' and 'unionised capitalism' differ as to the factors which contribute to their institutional stability or instability.

'Company workers capitalism' is characterised by firms' internal flexibility but by external labour market inflexibility. Within certain limits the firm has the possibility of redefining jobs within the organisation and reallocating and retraining its workers. This contributes to its institutional stability by permitting adaptation to changes in demand and technological innovation. On the other hand, the firm cannot rely on an external occupational market to adapt to these changes. Trained workers for standardised jobs are not there and, in any case, insiders cannot be substituted for by outsiders without upsetting the property rights which lie at the institutional foundation of 'company workers capitalism'.

This inflexibility contributes to the institutional instability of 'company workers capitalism' in the face of changes in demand and technological innovation. For, when adaptation fails the workers realise that the property rights, acquired in firm-specific assets, lose their value. They may react by reducing firm-specific investment and feel less loyalty for the organisation—a reaction which creates a inhospitable environment for the property rights of 'company workers' capitalism'. This may degenerate into an institutional crisis in the firm founded on that system of rights. Each group of workers may be tempted to use their firm-specific assets to bargain for an increased share of the firm's falling joint surplus and to resist changes in job specifications. In trying to do so they may discover the advantages of union action involving the participation of workers external to the firm. Unions may enforce standardised jobs and impose a uniform remuneration for all the workers doing the same job. In this case the system collapses into 'unionised' capitalism. Or, they may simply support the struggle of workers defending their firm-specific investment and help by arbitrating, together with employers associations, in disputes arising in specific firms.[1] On the other hand, the latter may be tempted by the 'classical' capitalism model which diminishes the bargaining power of the workers by eliminating their firm-specific assets. And this solution may be tempting not only when the firm cannot cope with a difficult external environment but also, simply, each time a group of workers uses their firm-specific assets to 'blackmail' the other members of the organisation.

The situation of horizontally 'unionised capitalism' lies at the opposite pole. Under this system the firm can rely on external labour market flexibility but not on the kind of internal flexibility which we have seen to characterise the firm defined by the property rights of 'company workers' capitalism'. Under 'unionised capitalism' the firm can react to demand and technological shocks which involve changes in the composition of its work force by hiring and firing workers. In this way it can have a greater number of workers doing some standardised jobs and a lower number of workers performing some other standardised jobs. Thus, under 'unionised capitalism' the firm enjoys the advantages of market flexibility for skilled labour. Contrary to the traditional view, which sees the unions only as an impediment to market flexibility and as source of monopolistic power, the union here is a precondition for having a market for skilled labour requiring substantial on-the-job training. Without a union determining, in collaboration with the employers' association, the standardised nature of jobs and training, occupational markets for skilled labour collapse. A tendency to develop the property relations of either 'company workers' or 'classical capitalism' would replace occupational markets for skilled labour either with internal markets for firm-specific labour or with unskilled labour markets or with some combination of both.

---

[1] A valuable example of the importance of the role of unions under 'company workers capitalism' is suggested by Wilkinson (1977) and Elbaum and Wilkinson (1979) in their account of industrial relations in the British steel industry. 'With the development of promotion by seniority, the institutionalised horizontal division created by skilled unionism was replaced by institutionalised vertical divisions between plants.' Still, the union had an important role in settling disputes and ensuring peaceful agreements at industry level. Moreover, 'the trade union card gave the worker the right to a place in the promotion line and hence the right to a series of jobs which made up the promotion line. Skills, or job opportunities were transferable neither to other industries, nor within the iron and steel industry, and therefore the iron and steel process workers had the status of unskilled worker outside the plant in which they were employed' (Wilkinson, 1977, p. 129). According to Elbaum and Wilkinson (1979) this arrangement explains the successful resistance of British steel workers to Taylorism which differentiated the British and the American steel industries.

334   U. Pagano

Indeed, a great source of institutional instability for 'unionised capitalism' lies in the fact that under this arrangement each firm may have an incentive to free ride on job training and specification. Under this arrangement each firm may gain by providing cheaper training which is only firm-specific and having jobs which satisfy better the specific needs of that firm; for each firm it pays to deviate from the agreed standardised training and job specification, provided that other firms do not do the same. If many firms free ride, then the public good, the occupational market that they jointly 'own' with the union, is destroyed and each firm as well as each worker is worse off. Thus a public good problem is the source of institutional instability of the only true market solution for skills acquired in the organisation.[1] It well illustrates how the market, far from being an exogenously given environment within which institutions evolve (possibly efficiently), is itself an institution supported and sustained by other institutions. If the union and the employers' associations fail to enforce their property rights in each firm,[2] then the occupational markets for skills are replaced by other market institutions supported by other institutions steming from alternative systems of property rights: namely, markets for unskilled labour (supported by the rigid hierarchies of 'classical capitalism') and internal labour markets (which is a disputable alternative name for the flexible bureaucracies of 'company workers capitalism').

Still, the public good problem examined above is not the only source of institutional instability for 'unionised capitalism'.

Technological and product innovation often put under stress the division of labour which has been agreed between unions and employers associations. Standardised jobs and training need to be continuously redefined and, together with them, the property rights of each single union. This redefinition is not easy because the interests of different employers and unions are likely to be different. If a compromise is not achieved, the system is likely to move towards some mixture of the other two forms of capitalism examined above—a result which is very likely when the unions themselves cannot agree on the property rights to be attributed to each single union.

Another source of institutional instability is the monopoly power which each union can exercise in each firm using the occupational-specific assets owned by the members of the union. Each union can exploit the fact that its members own assets which are indispensable for the production process in many firms and bargain for higher wages, which squeeze the remuneration of the other owners of both specific and general resources employed in the firm. In particular, since the human capital owner by each union is only valuable if

---

[1] Ryan (1984) observes that 'there is usually the possibility of specialising trainees for particular job tasks in order to make them relatively productive at an early stage of their training—at the expense, of course, of their training. Cheap trainee labour presents an incentive to do just that; the control of management over production methods provides it with the opportunity to do so (p. 199). He points out how, with the impossibility of writing and enforcing complete employment contracts, 'the superior alternative is to remove the incentive to management to engage in the intensive use of trainee labour by limiting the trainee differential in pay). In his very stimulating book, *The End of Economic Man*, Marsden (1986) examines the role of the union in limiting the tendency to free ride of each employer and creating the very conditions for the existence of occupational markets.

[2] However, cooperation can evolve in more informal ways when the different units can easily monitor each other and they are likely to interact very often in the future creating the conditions for a repeated game of the sort considered by Axelrod (1984). These conditions seem likely to arise in the case of the 'Marshallian industrial districts' considered in Brusco (1982), Sabel (1982), Piore and Sabel (1984) and Becattini (1987). Moreover, as is pointed out in this very interesting literature, the sense of trust and of belonging to a community can be an even more important factor for the development of skills, which may be specific to the industrial district but general within it. Informal exchanges of ideas and trust may favour the informal development of common standards. Specific working experiences may be more easily generalised in the 'atmosphere' of the industrial district.

used together with the human capital owned by the other unions, each union may try to hold up its resources and squeeze the rewards obtained by the members of the other unions. Moreover, each union may restrict entry either by limiting (by some form of legal power) the number of the trainees who undergo organisational apprenticeship or by increasing the wage to be paid to them while training.[1] Again, a move to the property rights of 'classical' or 'company workers' capitalism may be the organisational answer favoured by the owners of the other assets cooperating in the firm.[2]

Thus, technological change and unions' monopoly power, together with the public good problem examined above, pose a constant threat to the institutional stability of 'unionised capitalism'. Still, a movement towards 'company workers' and/or 'classical capitalism' is not the necessary result of an institutional crisis of 'unionised capitalism'. Indeed, a centralisation of the unions may be an alternative institutional solution to the problems of 'unionised capitalism' as well as to the problems of 'company workers capitalism'. This arrangement, which is often referred to in the literature as 'solidaristic corporatism',[3] is a system where centralised bargaining takes place between two central organisations: the association of employers and the association of unions. 'Solidaristic corporatism' can be defined as a system of property rights where each worker has a right to a job of quality close to the social norm but not to a job in a particular firm or occupation. 'Solidaristic corporatism' is difficult to create and to sustain. Even if the other workers keep acting in accordance with the general interest, for each group of workers it pays to pursue their particular interest. The solution of this problem requires that the unions, representing the interests of the workers engaged in particular firms or occupations, give up some of their rights to a single centralised union.

Indeed, under 'centrally unionised' capitalism the workers do something similar to what is accomplished by the owners of physical capital when they give up the property of single machines and become shareholders: workers give up property rights in single specific jobs and become owners of a right to a job of quality close to the social norm. In this way, as for the case of shareholders, they can diversify risk and eliminate some expropriation problems. However, the analogy is far from being complete. By its very nature, work cannot be similarly standardised and separated from the individuals performing it. Thus not only the institution of this arrangement but also its institutional stability is much more problematic. A continuous tension between particular and general interest is bound to exist and may eventually bring about the collapse of 'solidaristic corporatism' either into 'unionised' capitalism or 'company workers' capitalism or, even, into 'classical capitalism'. This collapse may, also, be favoured by employers if the unions use their centralised power to obtain conditions particularly unfavourable for the employers.

[1] For an alternative but not incompatible reason pushing up the wage of the trainees, see p. 334, no. 1.

[2] The choice of one of these systems is therefore due to the social history of a particular industry and country rather than determined by technology. An empirical study supporting this thesis is offered by Maurice, Sellier and Silvestre (1984). In Pagano (1991C) I try to argue that the different self-sustaining 'property rights equilibria' which characterise the three major industrialised countries are due the strong shocks which these countries experienced after the end of the Second World War.

[3] Rowthorn (1988) defines solidaristic corporatism as a variant of capitalism where there is centralised bargaining between strongly organised workers' and employers' organisations and where 'the centralized trade union movement, and its associated political party (or parties), pursue the egalitarian objective of full employment. By full employment is meant not just a job of any kind at any price, but a satisfying job with a wage close to the average. Thus the objective is to equalise in so far as possible employment opportunities for all the workers'. The following analysis of 'solidaristic corporatism' owes a great deal to Rowthorn (1988) as well as to discussions with the author.

336   U. Pagano

Still, the system has several advantages which may contribute to its institutional stability.

Under this system the workers, taken as whole, have greater bargaining power than under a system of decentralised unions. The possibility that one group of workers expropriates the employers and the other workers of their specific investment is greatly decreased under 'solidaristic corporatism'.The centralised union may realise that this behaviour damages not only the owners of physical capital but also the other workers whose interest the union is supposed to defend. Thus, if there are reasons for which employers may fear centralised bargaining, there are also reasons for which employers as well as workers may prefer this system.[1]

Under 'solidaristic corporatism' each particular worker can invest in assets specific to certain occupation and/or firms and, at the same time, insure her/himself against circumstances such as technological and demand structure changes which may decrease the value of those assets. In these cases the worker has a right to be subsidised and/or retrained. This insurance may create 'moral hazard' problems. For, each worker, being aware of the fact that her/his occupation-specific assets are insured if they become useless for society, may lose the incentive to look for occupations which are in short supply. Still, the problem can be solved by some degree of central allocation of work, carried out by the single centralised union; the worker who has redundant skills is subsidised only if he agrees to be retrained for some socially useful occupation.

Standardised jobs and the corresponding occupational markets as well as firms' internal markets can be redefined without substantial resistance when this is required by technological innovations. The workers are insured against losses of occupational-specific and/or firm-specific assets. Thus, the system can enjoy the benefits of a frequent and flexible redefinition of occupational and 'internal' markets which makes them consistent with the needs of technological change. Moreover, under 'solidaristic corporatism' there is no occupational or company union which may limit entry to new trainees and exercise monopoly power. By contrast, the single centralised union can ensure a right to a job of approximately average quality for all its members by creating conditions where no skill is comparatively oversupplied or undersupplied. A limitation of entry to particular firms and/or occupations and an exercise of monopoly power would be inconsistent with these conditions. It would give an unfair advantage to some workers and damage other workers, contradicting the right to a job of average quality which is the institutional basis of 'solidaristic corporatism'.

Finally, as to the particular problems of occupational markets, centralised unions have a better chance of overcoming the typical public good problem of 'unionised capitalism': that each employer has an incentive to deviate from the standardised training and job definition. On the one hand, enforcement is easier when a deviant employer is controlled and, eventually, punished by a union representing all the workers. On the other hand, the incentive to deviate is weaker if the unions are ready to adjust job definition, without major internal contrasts, when circumstances change. Thus, occupational markets for skilled labour are conditional on the existence of a union which, together with the association of the employers, establishes and enforces uniform standards in job training and definition. Or, in the terminology of the present paper, they are dependent on the existence of the property rights of horizontally 'unionised capitalism'. But an approximation to flexible

---

[1] Calmfors and Driffill (1988) point out how the centralisation of bargaining involves an internalisation of the negative externality, induced by an increase of the wage of a group of workers, on inflation and unemployment. A similar point is argued in Freeman (1988).

markets, relatively free from the expropriation hazards of monopoly power and characterised by flexible job definitions, requires a centralisation of the unions. Or, in the
terminology of the present paper, it requires the property rights defined by 'solidaristic
corporatism'. It is ironic that the only fairly close approximation to the competitive
markets ideal of general equilibrium analysis can only, perhaps, be achieved by a system of
property rights which requires the most centralized organizations.

Conclusions

In the Introduction to this paper, we considered the following question: is the often very
detailed division of labour and hierarchical division of labour which characterise many
firms under capitalism the result of transaction costs or of capitalism?

The preceding sections suggest that this question itself need to be questioned. One
should ask: 'which type of capitalism is the question referring to?'

Indeed, in this paper, after considering the principles which define an optimal division
of labour, three types of capitalism, characterised by different sets of property rights,
have been defined and an attempt has been made to show that the answer changes according to the type of capitalism we are referring to. Whereas 'classical capitalism' implies
an excessively detailed and hierarchical division of labour, 'company workers' and
horizontally 'unionised' capitalism offer some remedies for this situation.

Do these remedies necessarily come about? Do efficient property rights arise
spontaneously? Do efficient institutions necessarily evolve in a market environment?

A positive answer to this question characterises a great deal of the new institutional
economics. The conclusions of this paper do not share this positive answer and are in this
respect closer to the spirit of the 'labour process literature'. Each one of these forms of
capitalist property rights has been shown to be to a certain extent self-sustaining and each
one of them has its own factors of institutional (in)stability. Thus, it seems that there is no
well founded argument that justifies the necessary emergence of efficient property rights.

In particular, the argument that, in a market environment efficient institutions based on
efficient property rights tend to emerge, has also been criticised by pointing out that the
market itself, far from being the 'neutral' environment where efficient institutions are
selected, is also itself an institution, the survival and the existence of which depends on
these institutions.

The possibly competitive and flexible but also suboptimal markets for unskilled labour
of 'classical capitalism' must live in symbiotic complementarity with the rigid hierarchies
which also stem from this system of property rights. The internal markets or the flexible
bureaucracies of 'company workers capitalism' mean a substantial limitation of what is
commonly meant by a market economy which becomes supported or substituted for by a
cobweb of bureaucratic rules specifying the property rights of the workers in their
companies. Finally, the markets for skilled labour of 'unionised capitalism' must see the
foundations of their life in the existence of unions and employers associations.[1]

---

[1] Observe that some sort of completely self-regulating labour market is only consistent with 'classical
capitalism' and only for those workers who are outside its rigid hierarchies. Thus, a completely self-regulating
labour market is likely to be a very unsatisfactory institution where workers do not acquire skills, attachment
to trades and/or firms and do not experience any form of positive freedom and work satisfaction. Polanyi
(1944) pointed out the devastating consequences of the institution of a completely self-regulating labour
market. He argued that other institutions, which integrated or replaced the market institution with alternative
regulation systems, had to be developed. Otherwise, society itself would have not survived the consequences
of self-regulating markets. A modern presentation of Polanyi's ideas is offered by Stanfield (1986). The
possibility that some of Polanyi's propositions can be re-considered by using the tools of new institutional
economics is advanced by North (1977).

338   U. Pagano

I hope that it is not overambitious to conclude by indicating briefly one way in which the content of this paper may relate to the current issues concerning the transformations occurring in contemporary advanced capitalist economies and the economic policies intended to favour their development.

There is widespread consensus on four facts. The first is that we are living in a period of fast structural change characterised by the application of new technologies and by different demand patterns. The second is that both new goods and new technologies require more human knowledge-intensive production processes. The third is that the need for a better quality of working life is becoming more powerful as people already own a fair amount of consumption goods. The fourth is that only countries developing the appropriate institutions will be able to succeed in meeting this challenge.

A popular interpretation of these statements has been that more labour market flexibility is required.[1] There is some obvious truth in this statement insofar as in a changing word people need to do different things. But the statement has also acquired a different meaning: that all the rights of the workers, either at company level or at occupational level, are simply an impediment to market flexibility: property rights in particular firms or occupations, industrial democracy or union activity prevent the efficient working of the market system. The institution, able to cope with the new problems, is the market system and the other institutions, which it is able to select efficiently when the collective action of organised groups of workers do not impose inefficient institutions.

Of course, collective action can often bring about inefficient institutions which may be an obstacle to the required changes. But limiting job property rights does not necessarily imply that the market selects the appropriate institutions. It may rather mean that by selecting this new set of property rights we are selecting a certain type of market: that for relatively unskilled labour, which is typical of 'classical capitalism'. And, if the change was intended to be towards the generation of more on-the-job learning and a better quality of working life, we are certainly choosing the wrong set of property rights *and* the wrong markets. A positive change in this direction can only be obtained by accepting the importance for productivity and welfare of the workers' rights in their jobs and being aware of the new problems which these imply. It cannot be obtained by destroying them in name of market flexibility.[2]

Bibliography

Alchian, A. 1984. Specificity, specialization and coalitions, *Journal of Institutional and Theoretical Economics*, vol. 40, March

Alchian, A. 1987. Property rights, in Eatwell, J., Millgate, M. and Newman, P. (eds.), *The New Palgrave*, London, Macmillan

Alchian, A. and Demsetz, H. 1972. The property rights paradigm, *Journal of Economic History*, vol. 33, March

Aoki, M. 1984. *The Co-operative Game Theory of the Firm*, Oxford, Clarendon Press

Aston, T. H. and Philpin, C. H. E. (eds.) 1985. *The Brenner Debate. Agrarian Class Structure and Economic Development in Pre-Industrial Europe*, Cambridge, CUP

[1] 'Flexibility' is a very ambiguous word which has a surprising number of different meanings. This is pointed out in ch. 10 of Boyer (1988), ch. 12 of Morroni (1990) and Vercelli (1988).
[2] While this paper was being refereed and revised, an even more important economic policy issue has become the introduction of markets and of a new set of property rights in Eastern European economies—a transition which is popularly described as the introduction of 'capitalism' in these economies. An implication of this paper is that in theory as well as in reality 'capitalism' is far from being an unambiguous word. I believe it would be a great tragedy if the type of capitalism, that is introduced turns out to be some sort of 'classical capitalism'.

Axelrod, R. 1984. *The Evolution of Cooperation*, New York, Basic Books

Babbage, C. 1832. *On the Economics of Machines and Manufactures*, London, Charles Knight

Becattini, G. (ed.) 1987. *Mercato e forze locali: il distretto industriale*, Bologna, Il Mulino

Bowles, S. 1985. The production process in a competitive economy: Walrasian, neo-Hobbesian, and Marxian models, *The American Economic Review*, vol. 75, May, reprinted in Putterman (1986)

Bowles, S. and Gintis, H. 1983. The power of capitalism: on the inadequacy of the conception of the capitalistic firm as private, *Philosophical Forun*, vol. 14

Bowles, S. and Gintis, H. 1986. *Democracy and Capitalism*, New York, Basic Books

Boyer, R. (ed.) 1988. *The Search for Labour Market Flexibility: the European Economies in Transition*, Oxford, Clarendon Press

Braverman, H. 1974. *Labour and Monopoly Capital*, New York, Monthly Review Press.

Brenner, R. 1986. The social basis of economic development, in Roemer (1986)

Brusco, S. 1982. The Emilian model: productive decentralisation and social integration, *Cambridge Journal of Economics*, vol. 6, no. 2

Calmfors, L. and Driffill, J. 1988. Centralization of wage bargaining, *Economic Policy*, April

Coase, R. H. 1952. The nature of the firm, *Economica* (1937), reprinted in Stigler, G. H. and Boulding, K. E. (eds.), *Readings in Price Theory*, Homewood, Richard D. Irwin

Cohen, G. A. 1978. *Karl Marx's Theory of History: a Defence*, Oxford, Oxford University Press

Dasgupta, P. and David, P. 1988. 'Priority, Secrecy, Patents and the Socio-Economics of Science and Technology', Center for Economic Policy Research, Stanford University, Publication No. 127

David, P. A., Gutman, H. G., Sutch, R., Temin, P. and Wright, G. 1976. *Reckoning with Slavery*, Oxford, Oxford University Press

Demsetz, H. 1967. Toward a theory of property rights, *American Economic Review. Papers and Proceedings*, no. 2

Demsetz, H. 1988A. The theory of the firm revisited, *Journal of Law, Economics and Organization*, vol. 4, no. 1, reprinted in Demsetz (1988B)

Demsetz, H. 1988. *Ownership Control and the Firm. The Organization of Economic Activity*, Oxford, Basil Blackwell

Dow, G. K. 1987. The function of authority in transaction cost economics, *Journal of Economic Behaviour and Organization*, no. 8

Edwards, R. 1979. *Contested Terrain*, New York, Basic Books

Elbaum, B. and Wilkinson, F. 1979. Industrial relations and uneven development: a comparative study of the American and the British steel industries, *Cambridge Journal of Economics*, vol. 3, no. 3

Feiner, S. F. 1986. Property relations and class relations in Genovese and the modes of production controversy, *Cambridge Journal of Economics*, vol. 10, no. 1

Fogel, R. W. and Engeman, S. L. 1976. *Time on the Cross. The Economics of American Negro Slavery*, London, Wildwood House

Freeman, R. 1988. Labour markets, *Economic Policy*, April

Genovese, E. 1969. *The Political Economy of Slavery: Studies in the Economy and the Society of the Slave South*, New York, Vintage Books

Genovese, E. 1975. *Roll, Jordan, Roll. The World the Slaves Made*, London, Andre Deutsch

Gioia, M. 1815. *Nuovo Prospetto delle Scienze Economiche*, vol. 1, Lugano, Presso Guis.

Hirshman, A. D. 1970. *Exit, Voice and Loyalty*, Cambridge, Mass., Harvard University Press.

Hodgson, G. M. 1988. *Economics and Institutions*, Oxford, Polity Press

Hodgson, G. M. 1989. Institutional economic theory. The old versus the new, *Review of Political Economy*, vol. 1, no. 3

Langlois, R. N. 1984. Internal organization in a dynamic context: some theoretical considerations, in Jussawalla, M. and Ebenfield, H. (eds.), *Communication and Information Economics: New Perspectives*, Amsterdam, North Holland

Langlois, R. N. 1986. *Economics as a Process, Essays in the New Institutional Economics*, Cambridge, CUP

Leijonhufvud, A. 1986. Capitalism and the factory system, in Langlois (1986)

Littler, C. R. 1982. *The Development of the Labour Process in Capitalist Societies*, London, Heineman

Marglin, S. 1974. What do bosses do?, *Review of Radical Political Economy*, vol. 6

Marsden, D. 1986. *The End of Economic Man*, Brighton, Wheatsheaf

340   U. Pagano

Marx, K. 1967. *Capital*, New York, International Publishers

Maurice, M., Sellier, F. and Silvestre, J. 1984. The search for a societal effect in the production of company hierarchy: a comparison of France and Germany, in Osterman (1984)

Morroni, M. 1990. 'Production Process and Technical Change', *Quaderni del Dipartimento di Scienze Economiche. Istituto Universitario di Bergamo*, Bergamo

North, D. C. 1977. Markets and other allocation systems in history: the challenges of Karl Polany, *Journal of European Economic History*, vol. 6

North, D. C. 1981. *Structure and Change in History*, New York, Norton

North, D. C. and Thomas, R. P. 1973. *The Rise of the Western World*, Boston, Harvard University Press

Nutzinger, H. G. 1982. The economics of property rights—a new paradigm in social science? in Stegmuller, W., Balzer, W. and Spohm, W. (eds.), *Philosophy of Economics*, Berlin, Springer-Verlag

Osterman, P. 1984. *Internal Labour Markets*, Cambridge, Mass., The MIT Press

Pagano, U. 1985. *Work and Welfare in Economic Theory*, Oxford, Basil Blackwell

Pagano, U. 1988. 'Asset Specificity and the Labour Process Literature'. Lecture Notes for the I.S.E.R. workshop on Economic and Institutions, University of Siena-C. N. R., Siena

Pagano, U. 1991A. Authority, coordination and disequilibrium: an explanation of the co-existence of markets and firms, *Structural Change and Economic Dynamics*, forthcoming

Pagano, U. 1991B. Braverman, in Arestis, P. and Sawyer, M. C. *Biographical Dictionary of Dissenting Economists*, Cheltenham, Edward Elgar

Pagano, U. 1991C. Property Rights Equilibria and Institutional Stability, *Economic Notes*, no. 2

Piore, M. and Sabel, C. 1984. *The Second Industrial Divide*, New York, Basic Books

Polanyi, K. 1944. *The Great Transformation*, New York, Rinehart

Posner, R. 1973. *Economic Analysis of Law*, Boston, Little, Brown

Putterman, L. 1982. Some behavioural perspectives on the dominance of hierarchical over democratic forms of enterprise, *Journal of Economic Behaviour and Organization*, vol. 3

Putterman, L. 1986. *The Economic Nature of the Firm. A Reader*, Cambridge, CUP

Roemer, J. 1986. *Analytical Marxism*, Cambridge University Press

Roemer, J. 1988. *Free to Lose. An Introduction to Marxist Economic Philosophy*, London, Radius

Rowthorn, R. 1988. Solidaristic corporatism and labor process performance, in *Economics and Institutions*. Proceedings of the International School of Economic Research, Siena

Ryan, P. 1984. Job training, employment practices, and the large enterprise: the case of costly transferable skills, in Osterman (1984)

Sabel, C. 1982. *Work and Politics. The Division of Labour in Industry*, Cambridge, CUP

Sawyer, M. C. 1989 *The Challenge of Radical Political Economy*, London, Harvester Wheatsheaf

Smith, A. 1976. *An Inquiry into the Nature and Causes of the Wealth of Nations*, edited by E. Cannan, University of Chicago Press, Chicago

Stanfield, R. 1986. *The Economic Thought of Karl Polany*, London, Macmillan

Thompson, P. 1983. *The Nature of Work. An Introduction to Debates on the Labour Process*, London, Macmillan

Ure, A. 1935. *The Philosophy of Manufactures*, Charles Knight, London

Vercelli, A. 1988. 'Technological Flexibility, Financial Fragility and Recent Revival of Schumpeterian Entreprenurship', Reserches Economique du Louvain, Louvain

Wilkinson, F. 1977. Collective bargaining in the steel industry in the 1920s, in Briggs, A. and Saville, J. (ed.), *Essays in Labour History 1918–1939*, London, Croom Helm

Williamson, O. E. 1985. *The Economic Institutions of Capitalism*, New York, The Free Press

Wood, S. 1982. *The Degradation of Work: Skill De-skilling and the Labour Process*, London, Hutchison

Appendix

(i) Denote by $T = 1 \ldots t \ldots m$ the tasks to be performed to produce a product Y and by n the number of workers employed in the production process. Call $t_1, t_2 \ldots t_n$ the number of tasks performed respectively by workers $1, 2 \ldots n$.

Then $\mathcal{J} = (t_1 + t_2 + \ldots + t_n)/n$ denotes the average number of tasks per worker or the average task content of a worker's job. Define L as the learning per worker necessary to start the production process and assume that it is a continuous function differentiable in $\mathcal{J}^*$

$$L = L(\mathcal{J}) \quad \text{and} \quad L'(\mathcal{J}) \geq 0 \tag{1}$$

(1) says that learning per worker increases with the number of tasks per worker.

Denote by h the total production time spent by an (average) worker, then

$$h - L(\mathcal{J}) \tag{2}$$

expresses the average direct production time (net of training time) performed by a worker.

Call productivity or product per worker by $y = Y/n$. The Gioia–Babbage principle assumes that productivity is a function:

$$y = y[(\mathcal{J}), L(\mathcal{J}), h - L(\mathcal{J})] \tag{4}$$

We will now try to understand the reasons for which, according to Gioia and Babbage, y is a decreasing function of $\mathcal{J}$ for $\mathcal{J}$ greater than 1 and, therefore, it is maximised when $\mathcal{J}$ is equal to 1, or when the task content of each job is at a minimum. This can be done by showing that y is a decreasing (in one case constant) function of each one of the three arguments considered in (4).

An increase in $\mathcal{J}$ decreases y because a lower number of tasks per worker entails a greater exploitation of the principle of comparative advantage. Beside being directly a decreasing function of $\mathcal{J}$, y is also indirectly affected by $\mathcal{J}$ because an increase in $\mathcal{J}$ requires an increase in learning time. The increase in learning does not directly increase productivity. If the worker learns and performs more than one task, we could always obtain the same productivity by having each worker learning and performing only one task. Thus, productivity is a constant direct function of $L(\mathcal{J})$. On the other hand, this increase in learning time, due to an increase in $\mathcal{J}$, decreases productivity indirectly because it reduces $h - L(\mathcal{J})$ or the production time net of learning time. Thus, y is a decreasing function of $h - L(\mathcal{J})$.

Therefore the maximisation of y is achieved for $\mathcal{J} = 1$. This maximisation may be constrained by the fact that the scale of production does not allow the employment of such a number of workers that one worker performs one task only. In this respect the Gioia–Babbage benefits of the division of labour are limited by the extension of the market and imply increasing returns to scale until the quantity produced is such that each worker performs only one task.

(ii) Denote by L_f the future learning by doing per worker and by y_f the future productivity of labour. The Smithian principle implies that future productivity is a function of future learning due to the present division of labour or:

$$y_f = y_f[L_f(\mathcal{J})] \tag{5}$$

On the one hand, maximising productivity by maximising learning-by-doing involves the task content of jobs not being too large, otherwise we do not acquire sufficiently 'deep' knowledge to improve our activities. On the other hand, it requires that the task content of jobs should not be too narrow, otherwise we do not acquire a sufficiently 'wide' knowledge to enable us to improve them. Thus, (5) can be represented as strictly concave function in $\mathcal{J}$ having a maximum $\mathcal{J}^*$ for $\mathcal{J} > 1$. Also, in this case the scale of production may not be sufficiently large to allow a sufficiently small number of tasks per workers compatible with the unconstrained maximisation of (5). This was a major theme in Smithian economics, embodied in the famous statement that the division of labour is limited by the extent of the market. Denote by $\tilde{\mathcal{J}}$ the minimum number of tasks per worker which is possible for a certain extent of the market. The implications of the Gioia–Babbage and the Smithian principles coincide for: $\tilde{\mathcal{J}} > \mathcal{J}^*$. But they diverge for: $\tilde{\mathcal{J}} < \mathcal{J}^*$. In the first case, both principles imply that productivity can be maximised by jobs having the minimum average task content compatible with the extension of the market. In the second case, the Gioia–Babbage principle yields the same conclusion whereas the Smithian principle implies that productivity can be increased by increasing the average task content of a worker's job above the minimum value compatible with the extension of the market.

(iii) The Workers' Preferences principle implies that the task content of jobs, $\mathcal{J}$, the preliminary learning, L, and the future learning acquired by doing influence the job satisfaction per worker function:

342   U. Pagano

$$s = s[\mathcal{J}, L(\mathcal{J}), L_f(\mathcal{J})] \tag{6}$$

Assume that workers dislike too low a task content of jobs and the too limited amount of preliminary and future learning associated with it. Then a maximum of (6) is likely to occur for $\mathcal{J} > 1$.

(iv) An optimal division of labour or an optimal task content of jobs requires the maximisation of the benefits due to present and future productivity and to job satisfaction; that is the maximisation of the weighted sum of y, y_f and s. Or, it requires the maximization of a function W such that:

$$W = ay[(\mathcal{J}), L(\mathcal{J}), h - L(\mathcal{J})] + by_f[L_f(\mathcal{J}) + cs[\mathcal{J}, L(\mathcal{J}), L_f(\mathcal{J})]$$

where a, b and c are the optimal social weights given respectively to present productivity, future productivity and job satisfaction.

The weights a, b and c are also the weights given respectively to the Gioia·Babbage principle, the Smithian principle and the Workers' Preferences principle (see (4), (5) and (6)). Thus, an optimal division of labour requires the joint application of all these three principles. The greater the weight of a relatively to b and c, the smaller are the values of $\mathcal{J}$, L and L_f which maximise W. If b and c are equal to zero and a is equal to 1, then the maximisation of W implies $\mathcal{J}$ equal to 1 and the minimisation of learning associated with the application of the Gioia–Babbage principle. Any departure of a, b and c from the optimal social weights is referred to in the text as an underapplication or an overapplication of one of these three principles.

[22]

Structural Change and Economic Dynamics, vol. 3, no. 1, 1992

AUTHORITY, CO-ORDINATION AND DISEQUILIBRIUM: AN EXPLANATION OF THE CO-EXISTENCE OF MARKETS AND FIRMS

UGO PAGANO[1]

The explanation of the causes for the existence of the firm relies on market transaction costs, such as monitoring and enforcement costs, which can be observed in an equilibrium situation. The purpose of this paper is to show that 'disequilibrium transaction costs' can be even more important than 'equilibrium transaction costs' in explaining the nature of the firm, and the co-existence of markets and firms. Managers are not only dealing with organizational issues; they also try to balance supply and demand. In order to explain the co-existence of markets and firms, their success must be compared with the performance of the market.

1. INTRODUCTION

Questions like 'why do firms exist?', 'why do markets exist?', and 'why is firm-organization more extended in some sectors than in others?' have recently attracted the interest of economists. The starting point for recent literature has been the seminal article by Coase (1952). Coase observed that if markets provided a cost-free way of organizing economic activity, then the existence of firms could not be justified. He suggested that a comparative analysis between firms and markets is necessary in order to understand the existence and the properties of these organizations. Coase concentrated his attention on the costs of finding the relevant prices and the costs of writing and enforcing market contracts. These costs share an important property: they can be observed in a situation of market equilibrium.

Coase's line of inquiry has been influential. Explanations for the existence of firms based on 'the equilibrium costs' of the market economy, have also characterized subsequent explanations for the existence of firms advanced in the 'New Institutional Literature': the cost of specifying from the outset all the actions which should be performed in each particular state of the world (Simon, 1957), the monitoring costs in team production (Alchian and Demsetz, 1972) and, more generally, the agency costs in situations of asymmetric information (Jensen

[1] I would like to thank Fabio Petri, Bob Rowthorn and R. Ramana for useful discussions. Particular thanks go to Frank Hahn and Alessandro Vercelli for their useful comments to a preceding version of this paper (Pagano, 1989). Finally, three anonymous referees gave me valuable suggestions for which I am very grateful. The usual caveats apply.

and Meckling, 1976). The costs incurred in compensating an agent who invests in specific resources in a world characterized by uncertainty and opportunism (Williamson, 1985) are all costs which do not disappear in a market equilibrium and can be conveniently studied in an equilibrium framework.

In my opinion, a limit of the 'New Institutional Literature', stemming from Coase's article, is that the transaction costs existing in a market equilibrium provide only a partial explanation for the existence of the firm.[2] This explanation puts an exaggerated emphasis on the comparative advantages of the 'policing' activity of firms' managers in situations where market contracts would be very costly to write and enforce. Indeed, if we start from a market equilibrium, the 'simplification' of market contracts and their enforcement is all that is left to explain the existence of firms. The main issue is whether 'the authority of competition', existing on the market, can do better than the 'authority of command' existing within the firm.[3]

The situation changes if we take as our starting point not 'market equilibrium transaction costs' but 'market disequilibrium transaction costs'. In this case, the existence of firms can be explained with reference not only to their 'policing' advantages but also to their co-ordination advantages with respect to the markets.[4]

The introduction of disequilibrium introduces a new dimension in the comparison between firms and markets. The main issue becomes the way in which disequilibrium is to be eliminated and, specifically, whether there is an attempt to eliminate disequilibrium before or after the implementation of economic decisions. Following the Marxian terminology, I will denote the first case by 'ex-ante

[2] Williamson himself has maintained that a limitation of the New Institutional Literature is that 'possible disequilibrium features are ignored' (Williamson, 1985, p. 272). Other aspects of this literature are considered in Pagano (1991a, b), where its results are compared to and integrated with those of the Radical and/or Labour Process Literature.

[3] The terms 'authority of competition' and 'authority of command' are used by Marx (1967). In the New Institutional Literature the term 'authority of command' and 'authority of competition' are respectively replaced by the terms 'authority relation' and 'competition' or 'market discipline'. Coase (1952) and Simon (1957) consider the authority relation as the fundamental characteristic of the firm. This view is shared by Williamson (1985), who also considers the concept of governance which emphasizes the importance of complex forms of shared authority. By contrast, in their famous monitoring explanation of the firm, Alchian and Demsetz (1972) rejected the 'authority relation' as a fundamental characteristic of the employment relationship. They argued that, since monitoring is voluntarily accepted by the workers, it does not involve any form of authority. They seem to believe that authority is such only when it is involuntarily accepted. In my opinion they are wrong. As other authors show, authority can be voluntarily accepted. Indeed, Hobbes' (1968) theory of the State is founded on the *voluntary* acceptance of the *absolute* authority of the King and the solution of many problems of *collective action* (Olson, 1965, 1982) involves that some form of authority is (*often voluntarily*) accepted.

[4] Of course, the opposite argument is also possible. The existence of markets could be explained by their relative efficiency with respect to firms when the latter do not have simply to enforce decisions but also to co-ordinate them. We could either start from an economy completely organized by markets and 'discover' the reasons for the existence of firms or start with a 'single firm economy' and 'discover' the reasons for the existence of markets. The issue of state intervention (in what many economists call 'market economies' but are in fact 'mixed markets–firms economies') is strictly related to this analysis. For instance, the arguments in favour of 'complete state intervention' can be similar to those supporting a 'single firm economy' (which is equivalent to a 'centrally planned economy').

co-ordination' and the second case by 'ex-post co-ordination'. Ex-ante co-ordination and ex-post co-ordination together with authority of command and competition give rise to four possible combinations. This provides the structure of the table of organizations that I am introducing in this paper and that will be used to re-examine the issues of the existence of firms and of their relative efficiency.

I will identify Marx, Hayek, Lange and the Rational Expectations theorists as the advocates of each one of the four possible combinations of forms of authority and co-ordination embodied in our table of organizations.

Using these economists as the authors of an entry in our table has left me feeling somewhat uncomfortable. Certainly, limiting them to a box in a table insults the complexity of their contributions. Still, I found no better way of expressing these different organizational possibilities than using a stylized exposition of their contributions and of their 'revealed preferences' for a particular solution.

I will try to show that no single organizational solution advocated by these economists is likely to be optimal for the economy taken as a whole. Each solution has its own disequilibrium costs and has some relative advantages. These relative advantages are likely to imply that each solution is appropriate for different situations and for different decisions. There are some good 'a-priori' reasons to believe that these solutions may have to co-exist in real-life economies in spite of the possible reciprocal distaste of their advocates. In other words, I will conclude by trying to show that, when these authors are 'forced to co-exist' in a single analytical framework (as their organizational solutions are 'forced to co-exist' in real-life economies), they can jointly offer an explanation of the limits of market and non-market organization which integrates and improves on the explanations given by New Institutional Economics.

2. MARX'S DYNAMIC 'COASIANISM' AND THE 'FATAL ATTRACTION' OF A SINGLE-FIRM PLANNED ECONOMY

Marx (1967, in particular pp. 354–359) proposes two pairs of categories which can help us to answer the question 'why do firms exist?' (Coase's famous question). The first pair is used to distinguish between different sequences of co-ordination and implementation of economic decisions while the second is used to distinguish between different forms of authority.

The sequence between co-ordination and implementation of decisions is distinguished in 'ex-ante' and 'ex-post' co-ordination. A set of desired actions is said to be co-ordinated 'ex-ante' if they are implemented only after the agents try to make them mutually consistent. In other words, in the case of 'ex-ante' co-ordination, co-ordination precedes implementation. 'Ex-post' co-ordination defines an opposite system. In this case the implementation of desired actions is carried out without any 'ex-ante' co-ordination. If the desired actions are mutually inconsistent, then some of them cannot be implemented and actual actions will differ from desired actions. The system is, however, characterized by 'ex-post' co-ordination only if it satisfies the additional condition that it tends to

56   UGO PAGANO

react to mutual inconsistencies by generating a new set of desired actions such that at least some of these inconsistencies are eliminated.

The second distinction used by Marx is that between the authority of command and the authority of competition. The authority of command is based on a direct sanction that the command giver can apply on the command taker if the latter does not implement the orders of the former. The authority of competition is based on different principles. It relies on the fact that an agent can punish a trading partner by breaking their trading relationship and moving into a new one. Unlike the authority of command, the authority of competition does not involve any direct power relation; it involves simply the fact that each one of these two agents can establish a relation with other agents if he thinks that this could be more advantageous to himself.

Marx uses these categories to define and distinguish between firm-type and market-type co-ordination. Firm-type organization is defined by two fundamental ingredients: ex-ante co-ordination and the authority of command. By contrast, ex-post co-ordination and the authority of competition define market-type organization.

Within a firm, a central agent (the management) works out a production plan before production takes place. The purpose of the plan is to co-ordinate *ex ante* the production activities to be implemented. The central agent also has the authority to give some commands and can apply some sanctions against the individuals who do not carry out this plan.

In a market economy there is no central agent who tries to work out a production plan co-ordinating 'ex-ante' production activities. In contrast, the market economy is characterized by 'ex-post' co-ordination: there is a tendency in the market system to correct the mistakes implemented by the agents in the previous period by generating a new set of desired actions such that some inconsistencies are eliminated. Because of the lack of 'ex-ante' co-ordination, it is possible that in a market economy the individuals produce commodities that turn out to be in excess supply. In this case the actions which the agents desired to perform (i.e. to produce a commodity which could be sold at least at the cost of production) cannot be implemented. However, as a result of this failure, the agents will try to reduce the production of an unprofitable, oversupplied commodity and try to move on to the production of a profitable, undersupplied commodity. In this way each agent contributes to a movement towards equilibrium or, in other words, towards a situation where the actions desired by the agents are mutually consistent. Therefore, even if the market has no 'ex-ante' system to ensure the consistency of economic decisions, it has, according to Marx, an 'ex-post' co-ordination mechanism which tends to eliminate inconsistencies.[5]

Moreover, even if no central agent can give orders to the other agents, the market is characterized by a mechanism which has a function similar to the

[5] The 'ex-post' elimination of inconsistencies can generate new inconsistencies. The market can therefore be in a permanent situation of disequilibrium. For this reason, Marx observes that, in a market economy, the 'constant tendency to equilibrium of the various spheres of production is exercised only in the shape of a reaction against the constant upsetting of this equilibrium' (p. 356).

authority of command. Suppose that a worker is taking more time than the other workers to produce a unit of output. If the worker is the employee of a firm, the employer can apply some sanctions against him, such as lowering his pay, or even firing him. But suppose that the worker is an independent producer who sells his products on a competitive market. The authority of competition now has an effect similar to the authority of command existing in a firm. The producer will have to sell his product at the same lower price at which his more efficient competitors sell it. His per hour pay will be lower than that of his competitors; sometimes, it can be so much lower as to push him out of business. Thus, market-type and firm-type discipline can have similar effects.

These results are collated in Table 1, where markets and firms are defined as combinations of alternative forms of authority and co-ordination. We put the name of Marx in brackets to indicate that, according to Marx, firm-type organization (or planning) is the best economic system and we will follow the same convention for the optimality claims advanced by the other authors.

 The Marxian approach starts by considering a single-firm economy and a complete market economy. These two ideal types are used as analytical tools to define other organizations. In particular, capitalism is defined as an economy where both firm-type and market-type organizations co-exist. According to Marx, the employment contract defines the boundaries between these two organizations.[6] Before the signature of the employment contract the employer and the employee are two agents of the market economy; after that, the market is replaced by the firm—the organization within which the employer allocates and uses the labour power he has bought on the market.

Marx believed that firm-type co-ordination was more efficient than market-type

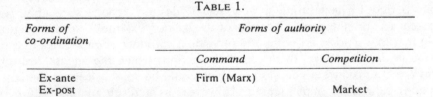

TABLE 1.

Forms of co-ordination	Forms of authority	
	Command	Competition
Ex-ante	Firm (Marx)	
Ex-post		Market

 [6] In the Marxian theory, the employment contract is defined as a peculiar market transaction by which labour power is exchanged for a wage. Labour power, or capacity for labour, is defined by Marx as the 'aggregate of those mental and physical capabilities existing in a human being which he exercises whenever he produces a use value of any description' (Marx, 1967, Vol. 1, p. 167). Labour power (or capacity for labour) is exchanged on the market and its allocation among firms is co-ordinated by the market mechanism. By contrast, labour itself (or the use of labour power) is co-ordinated by the employer who, after the signature of the employment contract, acquires the right to the capacity for labour of the employee for a certain length of time. According to Marx, under capitalism the use of labour power (labour itself) is not the object of a market transaction. The organization by which the allocation of labour is carried out is the firm and not the market. In other words, the employment contract defines the 'boundary' between the two organizations—the market and the firm—which, according to Marx, co-exist under capitalism. A detailed assessment of the comparative analysis of firms and markets carried out by Marx can be found in Chapter 3 of Pagano (1985). In this chapter the relationship between this analysis and the Marxian alternatives to capitalism is also considered.

58 UGO PAGANO

co-ordination in the management of a modern industrial society. According to Marx, modern technology implies a strong interdependency of irreversible investment decisions. In this situation, the ex-post co-ordination system, which characterizes ex-post market co-ordination, can correct mistaken economic decisions only by a terrible waste of real resources. The tendency to eliminate inconsistencies arises too late, only after major irreversible investment decisions have been implemented. In contrast, the ex-ante co-ordination which charac-terizes firm-type organization allows the elimination of these inconsistencies before their implementation.[7] He interpreted the growth of big industrial conglomerates under capitalism as evident proof of this greater efficiency of firm-type co-ordination. However, in his view, this clear tendency to replace the market by the firm was still too slow and too weak under Capitalism. Under the capitalist system the existence of many private producers implied that their numerous independent decisions had to be mediated by the market. Only under Socialism, after the abolition of private ownership of the means of production, could the economy be managed as one single big firm.

3. GENERAL EQUILIBRIUM INSTITUTIONAL CONFUSIONS

The Walrasian description of the working of a market economy uses the device of a ticket economy. It is assumed that an auctioneer announces a set of prices and asks the agents of the economy to write down on a ticket the quantities of the commodities which they desire to sell, buy and produce at those prices. The auctioneer collects these tickets and, for each commodity, calculates whether there is an excess demand or excess supply at the prices he has declared. The auctioneer then announces a new price vector such that all the prices of the oversupplied commodities are decreased and all the prices of the undersupplied commodities are increased. Given some special assumptions, such as gross substitutability, an equilibrium price vector can be obtained by repeating this procedure several times.[8]

How should we classify the Walrasian mechanism within the Marxian table of organizations considered in the preceding section?

It can be argued that, in spite of the fact that the Walrasian mechanism was intended to approximate to the working of a market economy, it should be included in the north-west corner which, according to Marx, describes planning

[7] There is no doubt that, after more than a hundred years, the Marxian answer appears fairly weak and extreme. In our time few economists would exaggerate the advantages of a centrally planned single firm economy as Marx did. But, in spite of the weakness of his answers, Marx' way of setting out these questions still has some methodological lessons to teach us. Of course, this claim can only be substantiated by comparing the Marxian theory with the ones accepted in our time by the majority of the profession. This is what we are going to do in the following sections.

[8] Walras was aware of the institutional differences between his 'ticket economy' and a market economy. But his main aim was to construct a model of an ideal economy where social justice and maximization of 'material welfare' were mutually consistent. He was aware that this goal could be realized by the 'ticket economy' and not by the market economy. On the other hand, he believed that the market economy could be reformed on the lines implied by his ticket economy. On this point see Pagano (1985, Chapter 6).

AUTHORITY, CO-ORDINATION AND DISEQUILIBRIUM   59

and/or firm-type co-ordination. This conclusion can be justified by observing that
the Walrasian ticket economy is characterized by ex-ante co-ordination and some
authority of command. Ex-ante co-ordination characterizes the ticket economy
because the decisions are first co-ordinated by an exchange of tickets and prices
between auctioneer and economic agents and, only after that, are they implemented. Before the achievement of the equilibrium (i.e. before the co-ordination
of the actions desired by the individuals) no production or trade decisions are
implemented. Moreover, it may be argued that some authority of command exists
in the ticket economy. A central agent (the auctioneer?) must have the authority
to make the agents write their 'true' production and trading intentions on the
tickets. The central agent must also have the authority to prevent the other agents
from implementing their decisions before the achievement of the equilibrium and
the power to enforce their decisions at equilibrium prices.

The 'auctioneer parable' can give us a misleading representation of the market
economy. An idealized form of planning (more precisely, decentralized planning)
is used as a model of a market economy. Characteristics of firm-type organization, such as ex-ante co-ordination and the existence of a central agent, are
employed to represent the working of the market mechanism. Furthermore, the
optimality properties of the model are used to ensure that the 'hidden hand' of
competition does not require the help of the 'visible hands' of planners and
managers to allocate economic resources efficiently.[9] In fact, once the optimality
of the market mechanism is shown by approximating its mechanism to that which
is only possible in an idealized single-firm economy, a paradoxical question arises:
'why do firms exist?'. If markets can optimally organize economic activity without
cost, the existence of firms is left unexplained.

The answer to this question has been the starting point of the New Institutional
Literature. But an interesting and different answer is already contained within the
Marxian framework. Firms exist because ex-ante co-ordination and authority of
command have some relative advantages over ex-post co-ordination and the
authority of competition. From the Marxian point of view the optimality results

---

[9] In other words, what is simply an 'auctioneer equilibrium' is called a 'competitive equilibrium'.
Two good reasons run against this interpretation. Firstly, when production and exchange are allowed
in disequilibrium, the endowments of the agents change. Whereas the 'auctioneer equilibrium' can be
defined on the basis of the initial endowments, a 'competitive equilibrium' must be defined on the
basis of endowments which are also the result of the adjustment process. Secondly, the agents of the
auctioneer economy (except the auctioneer himself) can be defined as price takers (because prices are
changed by the auctioneer) whereas the agents of a market economy must set prices. In disequilibrium
situations, because of the possible existence of unsatisfied buyers, the agents will not face perfectly
elastic demand curves. This circumstance is inconsistent with the concept of perfect competition,
which requires the agents to be price takers and/or to face perfectly elastic demand curves. However,
the terminology is confusing because the definition of perfect competition itself is consistent with the
characteristics of an auctioneer economy but contrasts with the institutional characteristics of market
competition and with a reasonable concept of competitive equilibrium, where the fact that the agents
set prices should be taken into account. We may conclude with Frank Hahn (1987, p. 137): '... the
behaviour postulated for the auctioneer will implicitly define what we are to mean by equilibrium: that
state of affairs when the rules tell the auctioneer to leave prices where they are. But the auctioneer's
pricing rules are not derived from consideration of the rational actions of agents on which the theory
is supposed to rest. Thus the equilibrium notion becomes arbitrary and unfounded.'

of the Walrasian model can only reinforce this conclusion. The optimality properties of the Walrasian model could be used to support the Marxian claim that planning or firm-type organization is superior to market-type organization. This follows from the fact that, unlike market organizations, planning and the auctioneer economy share common institutional characteristics—namely ex-ante co-ordination and the existence of a central agent.[10]

The institutional similarity between planning and the auctioneer is therefore suggestive and, in some respects, more appropriate than that between the auctioneer and the market. But it can be equally misleading. Although planning and the auctioneer economy are both characterized by ex-ante co-ordination and the existence of a central agent, they are substantially different. For instance, in the auctioneer economy, the central agent (the auctioneer himself) is implicitly assumed to work for nothing and does not consume real resources. In contrast, under 'feasible' planning, the central agent (the planning office) does not work for nothing: bureaucrats and planners do consume real resources which could be used in the production of useful goods. Moreover, the managers of the auctioneer economy maximize profits. There is no reason to believe that the bureaucrats of a planned economy would do the same only because the central planners instruct them to do so.

4. NOBODY CAN BE A RATIONAL 'PLANNER': THE AUSTRIAN DEFENCE OF THE MARKET INSTITUTION

The costs of economic planning were discussed in the famous controversy about the economics of socialism initiated by the Austrian economist von Mises (1920). Von Mises questioned, in this context, the economic rationality of central planning. In his opinion, rational economic decisions are only possible if the costs of the resources or their estimated values for some alternative uses are known to the agents. The market makes these values known. Agents, planning to employ the resources in alternative ways, compete by offering prices related to their estimate of the value of the resource for these alternatives. Therefore, the market prices provide each agent with information about the cost of the resource or information about its estimated value for the alternative uses planned by rival agents. Without this rivalry among alternative plans, which is only possible under market competition, price would not be attached to the costs of resources, and taking rational decisions would be impossible.

As Hayek (1935) clarified by developing von Mises' argument, under a system of collective property, a central agent decides how the resources of the whole

---

[10] Indeed, Walrasian models of the ticket economy, where the auctioneer has been substituted for a planning office, have been explicitly used as planning models. The co-ordination advantages of this procedure have also been compared with those of other planning procedures. Alternative planning procedures can improve on the properties of the auctioneer–planner model. For instance, this can be done either by letting the planner have some 'cumulative memory' of the preceding steps of the procedure (Malinvaud) or by 'inverting' the information flows between the planning office and the agents (Kornai and Liptak). For a presentation of these viewpoints and a general survey of this literature see Heal (1973).

society should be used. But the knowledge concerning the expected net benefits of each of these uses is dispersed among the agents who know their production and consumption opportunities. In the absence of a market economy, the agents cannot communicate the opportunities which they perceive to the other agents because the competitive bidding for economic goods cannot take place. Under central planning the knowledge of the agents is, therefore, locked in their minds. The central planning office, being unaware of the opportunities available to the agents of the economy, cannot take rational decisions. Society is not able to make an efficient use of the knowledge acquired by its members.

In spite of their different conclusions, Marx, Hayek and von Mises have some points in common which differentiate them from the Walrasian approach. In both approaches the market is analyzed as an institution where individuals, having ex-ante un-coordinated plans, compete with each other to utilize resources in employments where they expect the greatest benefit. Both Marx and the Austrians consider the market as a system characterized by a permanent disequilibrium[11] and share the idea that in a market economy there is no necessary ex-ante compatibility among the competing plans of the agents but simply a tendency to eliminate some inconsistencies ex-post. According to both approaches, it does not make sense to evaluate the advantages and disadvantages of a market economy in an ideal situation of equilibrium where, under certain conditions, it could be characterized by Pareto optimality. The Marxian and the Austrian schools maintain that the institutional characteristics of each system have to be described and evaluated by examining their systems of coordination and implementation of economic decisions. Obviously, this cannot be done in an equilibrium situation where decisions have already been co-ordinated by some mythical figure (the auctioneer) and contracts have the property of being self-enforcing (so that no authority is necessary for their implementation).

Although Marx and the Austrians employ many of the same criteria in the comparison of alternative economic institutions they arrive at opposite assessments of the relative merits of the market and central planning. According to Marx, the waste of real resources, due to the inconsistencies arising in the course of the ex-post adjustment process of the market economy, justifies the replacement of the inefficient market economy by central planning. In contrast, according to Hayek and von Mises, the costs, or even the impossibility, of constructing a plan ex-ante for the whole economy are such that the only rational solution is to break the central plan into many independent sub-plans co-ordinated by the market. According to the Austrians, the market is not 'optimal' and does not eliminate all inconsistencies ex-ante. But it is the only system by which economic activity can be organized when one considers that all the relevant information only exists dispersed in the minds of the individuals. Or, to put it another way, according to

[11] The similarities between the Austrian and Marxian approaches and their difference with the General Equilibrium school are nicely illustrated by Lavoie (1985) who also clarifies how Lange and Lerner failed to give an adequate answer to von Mises. Hayek (1949) criticizes the equilibrium approach of mainstream economics.

62 UGO PAGANO

the Austrians the market is optimal in the 'strong' sense that it is the only feasible organization by which dispersed knowledge can be transmitted.

5. FALSE EQUIVALENCE RESULTS FOR AN ADDITIONAL OPTIMALITY CLAIM

The discussion of the relative 'disequilibrium' merits of firm-type and market-type organization had promising foundations in the opposite arguments and conclusions of Marx and the Austrian economists. Unfortunately, the development of the discussion was somewhat blocked by Oskar Lange's famous work[12] on the economic theory of socialism. Lange appeared to prove a substantial equivalence of markets and the planning activity which could be carried out in a single-firm socialist society. This is an unfortunate consequence of Lange's contribution. His 'equivalence' result neglects fundamental institutional differences which underlie the dynamics of firm-type organization (or planning) and market organization. I will suggest that Lange's model does not show any equivalence between the organizational solutions considered in the preceding sections and is not equivalent to any of them.

Lange's famous answers to the objections of von Mises and Hayek against planned systems were based on the general equilibrium theory of Walras. Lange interprets the Walrasian disequilibrium adjustment as a real market process where prices move according to the actual imbalances between demand and supply which occur in a competitive economy.[13] He re-exposes the process by which the equilibrium is achieved in the Walrasian system without mentioning the role of the auctioneer in both co-ordinating decisions before their implementation and setting prices. Lange does not seem to be aware of the importance these assumptions have in showing the convergence of a market economy to an equilibrium position. He stresses the 'parametric function of prices' (Lange 1936a, p. 26) without realizing that, in the Walrasian system, prices can be regarded as parameters and the individuals can be regarded as price takers only because the auctioneer performs the task of setting prices.[10] More important, he does not perceive that von Mises' and Hayek's arguments on the informational function of prices can only be understood by considering the agents as price setters who compete for resources offering prices related to their expected benefits. According to the Austrians, under a market economy the freedom of price-setting according to the subjectively perceived opportunities enables each individual to gain immediate information about the opportunities perceived by the other individuals. Thus, Lange misses the 'Austrian' point. He does not really understand the 'Austrian' argument about the informational role of prices when he emphasizes that the *parametric function* of prices is the essence of competition.

[12] Lange (1936a, b); see also Lerner (1936). Lange was not the first to contribute to the economic theory of Socialism by a re-interpretation of the general equilibrium theory. The most complete statement of this view was advanced by Barone (1908).

[13] Indeed, the only difference which Lange considers between the Walrasian model and the real market economy is that, whereas in the former case we 'start with a set of prices given at random' (Lange 1937, p. 26), in the latter 'it is the *historically* given prices which serve as a basis for the process of successive trials'.

At the same time, Lange does not realize that the equilibrium is eventually reached in the Walrasian economy only because the auctioneer ensures that decisions are implemented when the opportunities perceived by the agents are mutually consistent. In this way, Lange also misses the 'Marxian' point about the existence of permanent disequilibrium and waste of resources in a market economy.

The main difference between Walras and Lange's interpretation of Walras is that the former refers to an idealized 'ex-ante' co-ordination system where adjustments occur on paper, whereas the latter attributes the properties of this idealized system to real markets reacting 'ex-post' to real imbalances between demand and supply. This must be kept in mind when one considers Lange's own model of planning because this is intended to show that planning can replicate (his model of) the market system. In fact, as in Lange's model of socialism, the planning office adjusts 'ex-post' real imbalances between demand and supply by increasing (decreasing) prices when there is excess demand (supply) and the agents take these prices as parameters. Under planning, 'the parametric function of prices must be imposed on them by the Central Planning Board as an accounting rule' (Lange, 1936a, p. 30). Moreover, the prices fixed by the Central Planning Board have the same function as market prices. 'Any price different from the equilibrium price would show at the end of the accounting period a surplus or a shortage of the commodity in question' (Lange, 1935a, p. 31). 'Thus the accounting prices in a socialist economy can be determined by the same process of trial and error by which prices on a competitive market are determined' (Lange, 1936a, p. 33). This procedure could work '*much* better in a socialist economy than it does in a competitive market. For the Central Planning Board has a much wider knowledge of what is going on in the whole economic system than any private entrepreneur can ever have; and, consequently, may be able to reach the right equilibrium prices by a much shorter series of successive trials than a competitive market' (Lange, 1936a, p. 34).

There is a substantial difference between the Walrasian auctioneer and Lange's planning office. In Lange's model, the central planning office works by correcting 'ex-post' the imbalances which arise in the real economy; it increases (decreases) the price of goods whenever there is excess demand (supply) in the economic system. In contrast, in Walras' model the auctioneer works by correcting ex-ante the imbalances which arise in the ticket economy where production and exchange decisions are written simply on paper and are not implemented until all the imbalances have been eliminated. It follows that, if we accept the institutional definitions given by Marx, the Walrasian auctioneer, who was intended to be an approximate description of the working of a market economy, is much more a 'true planner' than Lange's planning office. Unlike the auctioneer, who co-ordinates decisions ex-ante, Lange's planning office shares the characteristic of ex-post co-ordination with the market economy.

Lange's model was intended to prove a substantial equivalence between the planning and the market systems. But it is very different from both systems (if we accept Marx's and Hayek's definition of these systems). If we refer to Table 1,

64 UGO PAGANO

Lange's model fits in the south-west corner, which describes ex-post co-ordination through command—a box which is not occupied by either the planning or the market institutions (when these institutions are defined according to the common Marx–Hayek terminology). On the one hand, unlike the case of 'Marxian' planning or firm-type co-ordination, Lange's model contemplates only the possibility of ex-post intervention of the central authority who corrects imbalances which arise in the real economy by changing accounting prices. On the other hand, unlike the case of Hayek's and Marx's market economy, in Lange's model a central authority exists and commands the firms' managers, instructing them to take prices as parameters and to maximize profits.

Thus, the equivalent claims advanced by Lange are based on a re-definition of market and planning which in turn is based on a (mis)reading of Walras. In his view the two systems can achieve almost equivalent results only because they are both interpreted as a (modified) Walrasian auctioneer economy. Instead of proving a substantial equivalence between the two systems contrasted by the Austrians and Marx, Lange proposes a model which is different from both.

It could be argued that his model represents a successful compromise between markets and central planning. His model of 'market socialism' could handle some Marxian objection to markets in that the planning office could, according to Lange, react more quickly to disequilibrium than markets and change (accounting) prices with greater speed. Moreover, his model of 'market socialism' could answer some Austrian objections to planning in that the planning office only needs to know aggregate excess demand and supply in order to set 'rational' prices.

However, it can also be argued that Lange's solution has the worst characteristics of both markets and planning, and leaves both the Marxian and Austrian arguments without a satisfactory answer. On the one hand, from the Marxian standpoint, Lange's planning does not have the main advantages of firm-type organization (i.e. ex-ante co-ordination).[14] On the other hand, from the Austrian stand-point, Lange's accounting prices cannot perform the role of efficient transmitters of the information dispersed among the agents. In Lange's model, the agents are not free to set prices according to the subjective opportunities which they perceive. Thus, even if the socialist managers have the same incentives as private entrepreneurs, they are unable to transmit information immediately about the positive opportunities perceived by them, because they cannot increase the prices of the resources employed in the exploitation of these opportunities. They can only increase the demand for these resources at the price given by the planning office. Their additional demand implies that all the users of that resource (including themselves) will be 'rationed' until the planning office adjusts prices. The agents perceiving the new positive opportunities cannot immediately acquire amounts of resources greater than their competitors by offering a higher price. Thus, resources are not immediately moved to a use where they have a higher value and the other competing agents are not

---

[14] This 'Marxist' criticism was expressed by Maurice Dobb (1933) and (1935).

AUTHORITY, CO-ORDINATION AND DISEQUILIBRIUM   65

immediately aware of the increased opportunity cost of the resource which they employ.

Lange believed that he had found the optimal synthesis between market and planning. It is an open question, which goes beyond the scope of this paper, whether his model combines the advantages or the disadvantages of both systems. It is certainly different from both of them for reasons more substantial than those advanced by Lange. For this reason, his optimality claim has to be added to that of Marx and the Austrians as a claim advanced for a different model. We will see that a similar argument can be developed for the Rational Expectations school, which we are going to examine in the following section.

6. COMPETITION MAKES EVERYBODY A RATIONAL PLANNER: INTUITIONS AND PARADOXES OF THE RATIONAL EXPECTATIONS SCHOOL

In both the Marxian and the Austrian models the market economy is characterized by ex-post co-ordination and the absence of a central authority. No central agent ensures that decisions are taken only on the basis of equilibrium prices. The agents decide on the basis of current prices. They do not try to guess whether the current prices are (dis)equilibrium prices and whether they are likely to stay unchanged in the future. If production takes time, current prices may provide misleading information for making economic decisions. Suppose that disequilibrium prices prevail on the market. Cobweb theories have shown how the agents could keep on making wrong decisions *ad infinitum* if they base their decisions on current prices. If all the agents make their production decision on the basis of a high (low) price due to an undersupplied (oversupplied) market, the opposite situation will prevail in the following period.[15]

What is possible for one small agent—selling a different quantity at the current price—is not possible for all of them. Each agent ignores the effects of the reactions of all the other agents to the same current price and contributes to the endless repetition of the same mistake. In the case of cobweb theories, the market provides an ex-post co-ordination in the sense that an inconsistency of the previous period (excess demand) is eliminated. But this ex-post co-ordination mechanism is here particularly weak in that inconsistencies may be eliminated only at the cost of recreating new inconsistencies at the opposite extreme (excess supply).

Within the framework of the theories we have so far considered, the elimination of this unsatisfactory succession of mistakes at the opposite extreme

---

[15] From a formal point of view these oscillations will exist under the usual assumptions that the demand curve has a negative slope and the supply curve has a positive slope. These oscillations will be explosive, of constant amplitude or damped if the supply curve has a slope greater than, equal to or smaller than the absolute value of the slope of demand. The standard cobweb model implicitly assumes that the agents have static expectations in that the agents expect the future price to be equal to the current price. The paradoxical consequences of the cobweb model, which appeared particularly unrealistic for the case of explosive oscillations, stimulated the formulation of adaptive expectations by Nerlove (1958). Adaptive expectations were criticized by Muth (1961) on the grounds that they were rational only under special conditions.

66 UGO PAGANO

would seem to require some form of central intervention whereby the agents could internalize ex-ante the consequences of their decisions. A move away from the market mechanism in the direction of central planning would seem to be necessary for the ex-ante elimination of these recurrent mistakes.

Muth (1961) offered an alternative view of the market mechanism. He argued that the agents of a market economy were able, on average, to avoid these systematic mistakes by making an optimal use of the available information which would have been processed by employing the relevant economic theory. The expectations of the agents were not naively and mechanically based directly or indirectly on current prices. They were formed, on average, on the basis of the same relevant theory which was used by the economist to model the economy. This hypothesis of the formation of expectations—appropriately called 'rational expectations hypothesis'—was, according to Muth, supported by the principle of competition itself. 'If the predictions of the theory were substantially better than the expectations of the firms, then there would be opportunities for the 'insider' to profit from the knowledge by inventory speculation, if possible, by operating a firm or by selling a price forecasting service to the firms' (Muth, 1961, p. 318). Or, in other words, '. . . if expectations were not moderately rational there would be opportunities for economists to make profits . . .' (Muth, 1961, p. 330).

What is claimed here is that the systematic mistakes, like those predicted by cobweb theories, will not take place because the agents will predict the equilibrium prices, which allow the compatibility of their decisions as if they knew the theory and the information utilized by the economist. Or, to put it a different way, the agents of a market economy will not make systematic mistakes because, like economic theorists, they learn from past experiences and eliminate this type of mistake from future expectation formation. The type of expectation mistakes which they make are necessarily random and are uncorrelated with the information which was available when they formed their expectations.

According to the Rational Expectations Theorists, not only are ex-ante co-ordination and the authority of competition compatible but the former necessarily implies the latter because the authority of competition implies that all the opportunities for profits, including those arising from the use of processing information, are exploited. Thus, the agents will hold rational expectations about future prices which make their decisions ex-ante compatible.

The rational expectations theory completes our table of organizations by occupying the north-east corner of the table which joins together the authority of competition with ex-ante co-ordination. Like the other theories, the rational expectations model has tried to describe an optimal world. But, like the other theories, it fails to take into account the organizational assumptions and costs which are required for achieving this type of configuration of the economy.

If we assume that the agents have all the necessary information on the economy and can use that information efficiently to compute the equilibrium solution, we are making assumptions much stronger and unrealistic than those Hayek believed to be necessary for the feasibility of the central planning solution. In the case of central planning we are assuming that only one agent (the planning office) collects and processes this information. Here, we are assuming that all the agents achieve this result which, according to Hayek, is impossible for one complex organization. In the rational expectations case, the collection and the processing of information is much more costly than under central planning. Moreover, in the rational expectations case, each individual must be sure that all the other individuals are performing the same collection and the same processing of information as he is. Each individual must also know that this is done by all the other individuals on the basis of the same 'true' model and without making mistakes. If a relevant number of individuals use a different model of the economy, or fail to collect and process relevant information, or simply make mistakes, then the other individuals' efforts of predicting the 'correct' equilibrium outcome is useless. The outcome will be influenced by the actions that a number of individuals make on the basis of a wrong assumption. It can be observed that this problem does not arise for a central planner if he can be sure that the individuals will abide by his plan. Or in other words, unlike the agents of a market economy, the central planner does not have to pay attention to the actions that other agents would make on the basis of their own expectations.

Indeed, for several reasons, it would be extremely misleading to say that the rational expectations model has shown that the market can attain the same ex-ante co-ordination achieved by some idealized form of central planning, and that the authority of competition succeeds where the authority of command would fail.

In the first place, the possibility that different agents may choose on the basis of different models is simply ruled out by using the strange argument that 'expectations, since they are informed predictions of future events, are essentially the same as the prediction of the relevant economic theory' (Muth, 1961, p. 316). Thus, the co-existence of different agents with competing economic theories is ignored and each economist having a different economic theory can comfortably assume that each modelled agent shares the same theory as the author of the model. As Frydman and Phelps (1983, p. 27) have observed 'the rational expectations program of policy analysis logically requires the authority of a single model'. Thus it is appropriate to say that rational expectations replace the authority of command with the authority of a single model or theory imposed on the agents.[16]

Secondly, even if one accepts that the different agents act under the authority of a single theory and share the same model of the economy, rational expectations theorists are far from showing that a competitive economy can achieve ex-ante co-ordination. Even if people share the same theory, they are going to have heterogeneous information because of the dispersion of knowledge existing in society. Heterogeneous information implies that the information

---

[16] Assuming that the authority of a single theory may ever be accepted is not only highly unrealistic, it also contrasts with the moral beliefs which are at the foundation of liberal democracies. These moral beliefs claim that accepting and promoting competing theories saves us from serious mistakes. In contrast, in the rational expectations world, the authority of a single theory is a necessary condition for avoiding mistakes.

68 UGO PAGANO

available to each individual is not sufficient to forecast the expectations of other people. This is true even if each individual not only shares the same theory but also knows that all individuals know that he knows that they know that he knows (and so on) that each individual shares the same theory by which he processes information and forms his expectations.[17] Even in this case, each individual has to form expectations of other people's expectations, which he cannot assume to be the same because they are conceived on the basis of different pieces of information. Expectations of expectations, or expectations of a higher order, will introduce a situation of behavioural uncertainty.

In other words, in a situation of heterogeneous information the agents will be in the situation described by Keynes in his 'beauty contest' example, where the issue is to guess not which face is more beautiful but which is, according to the majority of people, more beautiful (Keynes, 1937, p. 156). Each agent attempting to guess average expectations tries to formulate his expectations of the expectations of the other agents, the expectations of the other agents of his expectations, his expectations of the expectations of the other agents of his expectations, and so on. The result is an infinite regress where average expectations are unlikely to be determined by any one of the agents. In this situation it is difficult to believe that the agents have any rational basis on which to form their expectations.

The fact that heterogeneous information generates a 'beauty contest' type of uncertainty has been shown in the context of the 'market island paradigm'[18] and in the case of the cobweb model.[19] In the former case, each agent knows the

---

[17] Phelps (1983) considers the case in which all the individuals share the same theory but each individual does not know that the other individuals share this theory and is uncertain about their expectations. Then convergence to the rational expectations equilibrium is highly problematic even if each individual processes homogeneous information by means of the same theory. The infinite regress problem of expectations of expectations also arises in this case.

[18] The 'market island paradigm' was originally formulated by Phelps (1970) and has been extensively used by Lucas (1972, 1973, 1975). Frydman (1983) has shown that the informational assumptions of the model are not consistent with the rational expectations assumption. In order to form rational expectations, the agents should know not only the supply parameters of their own market island, but also the supply parameters of the agents living in other market islands. This assumption is not only inconsistent with the 'market island paradigm' adopted by Lucas himself, but also with the assumption of the decentralization of information in market economies. Indeed, from the latter point of view, the market island paradigm itself is too demanding because it implies that the agents know the supply parameters of the agents operating in their 'market island'. From this point of view, the cobweb framework is more appropriate than the 'market island paradigm'. It shows that agents can have heterogeneous information even if they operate on the same 'market island' but face different supply shocks.

[19] A complete analysis of this problem in the cobweb framework is provided in Chapter 4 of Pesaran (1987). Pesaran shows how the infinite regress problem of expectations of expectations, due to the behavioural uncertainty arising in beauty contest situations, does not admit any plausible solution in cases of real heterogeneous information. In particular, the formation of rational expectations is not possible when each firm knows only its own supply shocks which are serially correlated and when each different firm knows only its own adjustment costs. To assume otherwise would contrast with any assumption of the decentralization of information in competitive markets. Pesaran convincingly argues that the assumption of identical firms processing homogeneous information is hidden under the analytical framework of a single representative firm used by the rational expectations school (see, for example, Sargent, 1978). Observe that Pesaran is (at least implicitly) assuming that heterogeneous information causes problems only in inter-firm co-ordination and not in intra-firm co-ordination. This point will be examined in the concluding section.

current prices in its own market but has no information on current average prices, whereas in the latter, each firm knows its own supply shocks but has no information about other firms' supply shocks. Both results introduce serious doubts about the possibility that competition can generate any form of successful ex-ante co-ordination independently of norms, customs and rules internalized by the agents. Indeed, the latter could be the decentralized institutions which may stabilize real-life markets and promote some form of ex-ante co-ordination. However, an examination of this point is beyond the scope of this paper. Here, it is sufficient to observe that the market cannot be described as an idealized case of central planning when a central planner imposes the authority of a single model and of a single set of information to be processed by the model. In a market economy no such authority exists and the agents are likely to process heterogeneous information by means of different models.[20]

Finally, even if we assume that all agents use the same model to process the same homogeneous information, and also assume that everyone knows that everyone knows that everyone knows etc. that this is the case, we are still very far from the possibility that the market can achieve ex-ante co-ordination. If we say that rational expectations are possible because in an ideal situation of rational expectations equilibrium people can estimate the parameters of the model, then we are simply assuming what has to be shown. This is because the economy can be in a rational expectations equilibrium only when all the agents have rational expectations or they have already learnt the equilibrium relations of the economy.[21] Then, in order for the rational expectations solutions to be calculated, each agent should solve the same information and calculation problem that, according to Hayek, was impossible to solve for a single central agent. Even if all the agents accept the authority of a single model to process homogeneous information, and even if this is common knowledge, it is very difficult to believe that each agent could ever achieve this result. The issue is therefore how, starting from a disequilibrium situation, they can learn and converge to a rational expectations equilibrium without having to calculate this equilibrium solution. Typically, learning involves the following problem: while learning, the agents' actions will be influenced by their learning mistakes, but these learning mistakes change the economy about which they are trying to learn. In other words, the learning process is characterized by a feedback of learning on outcomes. Therefore disequilibrium learning mistakes may well inhibit the possibility of

[20] This is not necessarily a relative disadvantage of a market economy. Indeed, it may be its virtue. But this is far from being captured by the rational expectations model.

[21] In order to give operational meaning to the rational expectations hypothesis Lucas (1975) restricted his analysis 'to the situation in which the relevant distributions have settled to stationary values' (p. 1121). Frydman (1983) observes that this solution involves a vicious circle. The major problem with this justification of the rational expectations hypothesis is that the relevant distributions can be at their 'stationary values' if and only if every agent 'knows' the parameters of these stationary distributions. Stated differently, the markets are in the rational expectations equilibrium if, and only if, every agent forms its expectations according to the rational expectations equilibrium forecast function. Thus, the assumption that relevant distributions have settled down to stationary values cannot be used to give 'operational meaning' to the assumption that the agents 'know' the parameters of those distributions (pp. 110–111).

70 UGO PAGANO

reaching a stationary state where the expectations of the individuals coincide with the actual outcomes of the economy. Learning implies that the economy cannot be in a stationary state even if it is assumed to be so in all other respects.

Two approaches have been taken into account in dealing with this problem: one is defined as 'rational learning' and the other is defined as 'boundedly rational learning'. Under 'rational learning' the individuals are assumed, except for a limited number of parameters, to know the true equilibrium relations of the economy in their structural form (and that everyone knows that they know that he knows etc.). 'Rational learning' involves various iterations due to the feedback of the disequilibrium estimation mistakes on the outcomes of the economy. In general 'rational learning' can be shown to converge to an equilibrium, but not necessarily to the rational expectations equilibrium, because the disequilibrium learning mistakes change the final equilibrium outcome.[22] 'Rational learning' does not solve the learning problem because the agents are assumed to know, except for some subjective uncertainty for a limited number of parameters, the structural form of the equilibrium relations of the economy from the outset. Thus 'rational learning' departs very little from the assumption that the agents know the rational equilibrium relations. The fact that this assumption is incredibly demanding on the abilities of the individuals underlies the attempt made in the 'boundedly rational learning' models. At first sight the 'boundedly rational learning' models[23] have some attractive features. The individual needs to know and stick to a relatively simple learning rule. This requires the knowledge of the reduced form equations of the true model (apart from the values of a limited number of parameters) but it does not require the knowledge of the model. In spite of the usual feedback from learning to the outcomes, convergence to a rational expectations equilibrium (or at least to an equilibrium) can be shown to occur under these circumstances which seem to be considerably less demanding on rationality. But the attractiveness of 'boundedly rational learning' is largely deceptive. Indeed, the simplification of the learning process is only achieved by increasing the complexity of what is implicitly or explicitly done before the learning process starts. This is because convergence requires that the agents choose *ex ante* a good learning rule and accept its authority during the learning process. In turn the choice of a good learning rule can only be made by knowing the 'rational expectations equilibrium'.[24]

When we add that in all the learning models the acquisition of information is

---

[22] This general result of 'rational learning' comes from M. M. Bray and D. M. Kreps (unpublished data).

[23] As an example of this class of models see Bray (1983). Some limitations of the model are considered by Bray herself and by Roy Radner in his comment of Bray's paper. A full list of references is provided in Chapter 3 of Pesaran (1987).

[24] As Pesaran (1987) observes, '. . . all the authors who have studied the problems of convergence in boundedly rational learning models have assumed that the agents' choice of the learning rule is based on some common a priori knowledge of REE'.

assumed not to be costly,[25] and that continuous market clearing is assumed to hold during the learning process (this seems to require a Lange-type planner/auctioneer acting *ex post* with infinite speed), then it is difficult to avoid the conclusion that the rational expectations literature has dramatically failed to show that the authority of competition can achieve ex-ante co-ordination. One cannot avoid the feeling that a lot of unnecessary confusion is generated when a fair number of economists are persuaded by the claim that rational expectations are a simple extension of utility maximization[26] to expectations formation, or that consistency requires the modelled agents to have the true expectations generated by the model.

Still, this literature has made some useful contributions. The fact that the agents of a market economy take into account more information than current prices and may make an (only sometimes successful) attempt to forecast future prices and to achieve ex-ante co-ordination is a reasonable assumption. Moreover, the fact that some systematic mistakes can sometimes be eliminated also makes sense if one admits the existence of the disequilibrium and information costs involved in the elimination of these mistakes. Finally, the 'negative results' obtained by the literature stimulated by the defence or the criticism of the rational expectations hypothesis have clarified, together with the limits to rational expectations, the limits of the market system itself.

Indeed, the rational expectations hypothesis has stimulated the exploration of the only combination which has not yet been fully considered in the history of economic analysis: that between ex-ante co-ordination and the authority of competition. Like Marx, Lange and Hayek, the Rational Expectations theorists have not resisted the claim that their combination was the optimal one. The fact that their claim was even harder to justify can be considered a merit or a liability. It has certainly the very limited merit of completing our table of organizations (Table 2), which now shows an optimality claim for all the possible combinations of authority and co-ordination.

---

[25] If information is costly, then the agents will collect additional information only when its expected marginal benefit of search outweighs its marginal cost. But the expected marginal benefit will depend on their a priori beliefs, which can be wrong because there is no way one can be certain about the value of additional information before one has collected it (Stigler, 1961). Thus the individuals can be trapped in wrong beliefs which are not changed because the collection of information, which would show them to be wrong, is (wrongly) assumed to be costly. Thus, there is no successful reformulation of the rational expectations hypothesis which deals satisfactorily with the problems stemming from costly information. Nor is it possible to appeal to any equilibrium solution of the problem because if a competitive equilibrium is defined as a situation where all the arbitrage profits are eliminated, then in equilibrium there are no returns for those who eliminate systematic mistakes. 'Hence the assumptions that all markets, including that for information, are always in equilibrium and always perfectly arbitraged are inconsistent when arbitrage is costly' (Grossman and Stiglitz, 1980, p. 393). In fact, equilibrium analysis, far from solving the problem, simply shows one of the 'paradoxes of the pure equilibrium method' (Vercelli, 1989, pp. 26–29). Some 'equilibrium degree of disequilibrium' (Grossman and Stiglitz, 1980, p. 393) can be used to solve the existence problem, but not to show that competition eliminates all systematic mistakes.

[26] For instance, Kantor (1979, p. 1429) maintained that the rational expectations hypothesis was an extension of 'the maximization assumption to the use of information'.

72   UGO PAGANO

TABLE 2.

Forms of co-ordination	Forms of authority	
	Command	Competition
Ex-ante	(A) firm planning (Marx)	(B) markets (Rational Expectations)
Ex-post	(C) planning (Lange)	(D) markets (Hayek)

7. COMPARING 'PERFECT' MODELS: THE SUPERIOR 'IMPURITY' OF REALITY

We will now try to summarize the comparative analysis which, in spite of their optimality claims, emerges from the examination of the authors considered above. This will be done by comparing each one of the four entries[27] of Table 2 with all the others.

(A–D) Markets have relatively lower co-ordination costs because decisions are taken on the basis of cheap current price information, whereas firms have higher co-ordination costs because decisions are taken on the basis of relatively costly planning decisions. On the other hand, the planning taking place inside firms may save the resources which would be wasted by the inconsistencies arising in the framework of the ex-post adjustment existing in a market economy where the agents base their decisions on current prices.

(A–B) The disequilibrium cost of a market economy becomes lower if we assume that, under competitive pressure, the agents will try to forecast future prices and eliminate some inconsistencies. In this respect, the gap between the waste of real resources due to disequilibrium between market-type and firm-type organization can be reduced. However, it cannot be completely eliminated because the organizational requirements which are necessary for a market economy to eliminate this waste are too costly (they require multiplication of a single model or of a single learning rule by different agents and homogeneous information). On the other hand, a partial elimination of inconsistencies may be achieved. Insofar as this partial elimination of inconsistencies is less costly in the market than in the firm, this saving of organizational costs may be greater than the benefit of the more complete elimination of inconsistencies achieved within the firm.

[27] Indeed, other entries could also be considered as intermediate cases among the 'pure' cases examined in Table 2. For instance, 'indicative planning' can be described as an intermediate case between (A) and (B) where a central agent provides forecasts which are used by the agents to form their expectations about future trends in the economy. Information costs may be decreased if the state centralizes this function. Behavioural uncertainty can be reduced if the state can build a reputation for being reliable. 'Keynesian demand management' can be regarded as an intermediate entry between (C) and (D) where the agents act on the basis of current prices and the state steps in to correct the inconsistencies which arise at aggregate level. The concentration of the state on the intervention at aggregate level could be defended on two grounds: first, it is less costly to intervene on aggregate levels because it requires less information; and second, aggregate inconsistencies are more costly for the economy than simple mismatching of demand and supply in particular sectors. In this paper I only consider 'pure cases' because they are simpler and more important for understanding the disequilibrium reasons for the existence of firms.

AUTHORITY, CO-ORDINATION AND DISEQUILIBRIUM   73

(A–C) The organizational costs of planning may be decreased if management simply intervenes *ex post* to eliminate inconsistencies. Indeed, this is close to the idea of 'managing by exception', which is applied in actual firm management when the hierarchically superior managers intervene only when inconsistencies arise (Radner, 1989, p. 15). Again, the organizational costs to be sustained to eliminate inconsistencies should be compared with the benefits of this improved consistency. This way of reasoning can be illustrated by observing that a central agent acting like a Walrasian auctioneer will be able, by the exchange of tickets occurring in that economy, to eliminate inconsistencies after a certain number of iterations. These iterations are costly and the cost can be reduced by a central agent who, acting *à la* Lange, observes the real economy and changes prices when imbalances occur. But this decrease in planning costs is only achieved by increasing the cost of the waste of real resources because inconsistencies are not anticipated but only corrected *ex post* after some time.

(B–D) It is questionable whether 'Rational Expectations markets' ('weakly' defined as markets where the agents try to achieve some ex-ante co-ordination by trying to forecast future equilibrium prices on the basis of available information) are more efficient than markets *à la* Hayek, where the agents take their decisions on the basis of current prices. It is doubtful whether 'Rational Expectations markets' can reduce co-ordination failure. Moreover, when they succeed, the benefits of decreasing co-ordination failure should be compared to the greater computational and information costs which Rational Expectation markets imply in comparison with the markets *à la* Hayek. It seems reasonable to assume that the agents of a market economy take many decisions on the basis of current prices and make an effort to predict future prices only for 'major decisions'. Only in the case of major decisions may the cost of forecasting activity be compensated by the saving of real resources otherwise wasted because of co-ordination failure. In other words, the pressure, or the authority of competition, can have different effects on expectation formation in the two cases. In the case of 'major decisions', where mistaken forecasts of future equilibrium prices imply considerable losses, competitive pressure is likely to make the agents spend time and resources trying to form 'rational', or, rather, more 'reasonable' expectations. In contrast, in the case of 'minor decisions', where mistaken future equilibrium prices do not imply great co-ordination losses, competitive pressure is likely to make the agents save time and effort by taking their decisions on the basis of current prices. In other words, B and D, or Hayek's and the Rational Expectations theories taken in their 'weak' versions, are not necessarily two incompatible and competing models of the nature of competition. In contrast, they can be interpreted as two alternative real forms of co-ordination which the 'authority of competition' may imply for different decisions.

(C–D) A central authority may sometimes be faster than the market in correcting inconsistencies *ex post*. When and if this arises, real resources may be saved by centralizing decisions within a firm. This saving of real resources should be compared with a possible increase of organizational costs.

(B–C) A similar case can be made even when the agents of a market economy

74 UGO PAGANO

try to eliminate inconsistencies *ex ante*. They may be unable to eliminate all inconsistencies or able to eliminate them only at considerable costs. Then it is possible that the commands of a central authority do better than competition, even if the central authority tries to eliminate inconsistencies only ex-post. If the ex-post intervention of the central authority is sufficiently fast, the costs of co-ordination failure may be lower than those existing in 'Rational Expectations markets'. Moreover, the organizational costs of central ex-post co-ordination may be lower than the costs to be sustained when many agents attempt to achieve ex-ante co-ordination by trying to form 'rational expectations' about future equilibrium prices.

In general, different systems are likely to have different organizational costs and different results in the elimination of inconsistent decisions. For instance, one may argue that moving from ex-ante to ex-post co-ordination, and from the authority of command to the authority of competition, organizational costs decrease but the costs due to the inconsistencies of the decisions increase.[28] In this sense no organizational form is optimal. In contrast, there is a trade-off between organizational costs which have to be organized. For each particular set of actions the inconsistencies which would arise in the absence of a particular organization should be compared with its organizational costs. Given the variety of actions that we have in reality, it is reasonable to expect that a plurality of organizational solutions exist, and this is in fact the case: different forms and sizes of firms and markets do characterize different sectors of real life economies. This does not mean that what we have in reality is optimal or efficient, but simply that the 'impurity' of reality is much more 'reasonable' than any 'pure' application of the four solutions contained in our table of organizations.[29]

8. CONCLUSION: WHY DO FIRMS EXIST? A DISEQUILIBRIUM ANSWER

Questions like: 'why do firms exist?', 'why do markets exist?' and 'why is firm-organization more extended in some sectors than in others?' find some answers when we observe the disequilibrium[30] costs of each institution. These answers should be considered to be complementary to the answers given by the New

[28] However this summary statement should be taken with some caution. An excessive reliance on ex-ante co-ordination and authority of command (as well as an excessive reliance on ex-post co-ordination and authority of competition) can increase both the costs of inconsistencies and organizational costs.

[29] The importance of the 'impurity principle' is forcefully underlined in Chapter 7 of Hodgson (1988).

[30] As Vercelli (1989) points out, many economists consider disequilibrium analysis to be irrelevant. He analyses the disappointing consequences that this approach has for macroeconomic analysis, and provides a full criticism of this methodology. I wish to stress that, quite unfortunately, the same criticism applies to New Institutional Economics, which has often taken the Arrow–Debreu equilibrium model with incomplete contracts as its implicit foundation. This paper confirms the point that 'it should never be forgotten, however, that the equilibrium configuration is much poorer in information than the "dynamic" representation. Any conclusion drawn from the subset of information which characterizes the equilibrium configuration may be gravely misleading if the real system is not guaranteed to be and remain in equilibrium' (Vercelli, 1989, p. 21). It can be added that, even if and when the dynamic analysis cannot achieve the same deterministic precision of equilibrium analysis, it is better to be roughly right than precisely wrong.

Institutional approach by introducing more realistic features in the equilibrium situation of an economy. It can be argued that the New Institutional Literature has concentrated its attention only on one of the two distinctions considered in our table of organization (i.e. that between authority of competition and authority of command), and has ignored the other (i.e. that between ex-ante and ex-post co-ordination). This is due to its 'equilibrium approach'. In equilibrium, the ex-ante versus ex-post co-ordination issue does not arise because it is implicit in the notion of equilibrium that some co-ordination of decisions has already been achieved. In equilibrium it is only possible to study the institutions by which equilibrium (incomplete) contracts can be best implemented, and to compare the relative efficiency of the authority of command competition, but it is impossible to compare the relative efficiency of alternative co-ordination systems.

In contrast, an important reason for the existence of management and an important aspect of the work of managers is to try to balance supply and demand within the firm in a way different from, and often superior to, the market when the latter is considered in a disequilibrium situation. When this superiority emerges (and I have tried to show that this is not necessarily the case), this may be due to the various means which are available to the firm in dealing with disequilibrium, which either are not available or are available at greater costs to the market: namely within a firm, its members (i) can act under the authority of a single plan derived from a single model; (ii) can learn how to formulate the plan according to consistent learning rules, the authority of which is accepted by the members of the firm; (iii) can save the costs which they would incur if each member of the firm had to formulate their own complete plan on the basis of their own model; (iv) can avoid costly inconsistencies by co-ordinating *ex ante* the actions before they are implemented; and (v) can eliminate unforeseen ex-post inconsistencies in the plan by constantly monitoring the emergence of ex-post imbalances. Or, in other words, firm-type co-ordination can within certain limits: reduce behavioural uncertainty (i and ii), decrease computation and information costs (iii) and save on mismatching between demand and supply (iv and v).

It is a worrying thought, given the enormous size of many firms, that the cause of their success is that the people working within them leave outside the firms that plurality of theories, models, plans and ideas which it is possible to implement in the context of a market economy, and accept the authority of some people formulating a plan on the basis of a single model. But if, within the firm, some form of authority of command can do better than the authority of competition, the organizational answer to these worries cannot be competition itself. It must, instead, be found in some form of internal decentralization of decisions and of democratic control of that authority. A solution to this problem is not easy but an effort in this direction may be highly rewarding.

REFERENCES

ALCHIAN, A. (1984). 'Specificity, Specialization and Coalitions', *Journal of Institutional and Theoretical Economics*, **40**, 34–9.

76 UGO PAGANO

ALCHIAN, A. (1987). 'Property Rights', in Eatwell, J., Milgate, M. and Newman, P. (eds), *The New Palgrave*, 1031–4. Macmillan, London.

ALCHIAN, A. and DEMSETZ, H. (1972). 'Production, Information Costs and Economic Organization', *American Economic Review*, **62**, 777–795.

ARROW, K. J. and HAHN, F. H. (1971). *General Competitive Analysis*, Oliver & Boyd, Edinburgh.

BARONE, E. (1908). 'The Ministry of Production in the Collectivistic State', in A. Nove and D. M. Nuti (eds), *Socialist Economics*, Penguin, Harmondsworth.

BRAY, M. M. (1983). 'Convergence to Rational Expectations Equilibrium', in R. Frydman and E. S. Phelps (eds), *Individual Forecasting and Aggregate Outcomes. Rational Expectations Examined*. Cambridge University Press, Cambridge.

COASE, R. H. (1952). 'The Nature of the Firm'. *Economica*, (1937), **4**, 386–405; reprinted in G. H. Stigler and K. E. Boulding (eds), *Readings in Price Theory*. Richard D. Irwin, Homewood.

DOBB, M. H. (1933). 'Economic Theory and the Problem of a Socialist Economy', *Economic Journal*, **19**, 589–98.

DOBB, M. H. (1935). 'Economic Theory and a Socialist Economy: a Reply', *Review of Economic Studies*, **3**, 144–51.

FRYDMAN, R. (1983). 'Individual Rationality, Decentralization and the Rational Expectations Hypothesis', in R. Frydman and E. S. Phelps, (eds) *Individual Forecasting and Aggregate Outcomes. Rational Expectations Examined*, Cambridge University Press, Cambridge.

FRYDMAN, R. and PHELPS, E. S., (eds) (1983). *Individual Forecasting and Aggregate Outcomes. Rational Expectations Examined*, Cambridge University Press, Cambridge.

GROSSMAN, S. and STIGLITZ, J. E. (1980). 'On the impossibility of informationally efficient markets', *American Economic Review*, **70**, 393–408.

HAHN, F. H. (1987). 'Auctioneer', in Eatwell J., Milgate, M. and Newman, P. (eds), *The New Palgrave*. Macmillan, London.

HAYEK, F. A. (1935). *Collectivist Economic Planning*. Routledge, London.

HAYEK, F. A. (1949). *Individualism and Economic Order*. Routledge, London.

HEAL, G. M. (1973). *The Theory of Economic Planning*. North Holland, Amsterdam.

HOBBES, T. (1968). *Leviathan*. Penguin, Harmondsworth.

HODGSON, G. M. (1988). *Economics and Institutions*. Polity Press, Cambridge.

JENSEN, M. and MECKLING, W. (1976). 'The Theory of the Firm: Managerial Behaviour, Agency Costs and Capital Structure', *Journal of Financial Economics*, **3**, 305–60.

KANTOR, B. (1979). 'Rational Expectations and Economic Thought', *Journal of Economic Literature*, 1422–41.

KEYNES, J. M. (1937). *The General Theory of Employment, Interest and Money*. Macmillan, London.

LANGE, O. (1936a). 'On the Economic Theory of Socialism: Part I.' *Review of Economic Studies*, **4**, 53–71; reprinted in M. J. Farrel, (1973). *Readings in Welfare Economics*. Macmillan, London.

LANGE, O. (1936b). 'Mr Lerner's "Note on socialist economics," *Review of Economic Studies*, **4**, 143–4; reprinted in M. J. Farrel, (1973). *Readings in Welfare Economics*. Macmillan, London.

LANGE, O. (1937). 'On the Economic Theory of Socialism: Part II', *Review of Economic Studies*, **4**, 123–42; reprinted in M. J. Farrel (1973). *Readings in Welfare Economics*. Macmillan, London, UK.

LANGLOIS, R. N. (1986). *Economics as a Process, Essays in the New Institutional Economics*. Cambridge University Press, Cambridge.

LAVOIE, D. (1985). *Rivalry and Central Planning*. Cambridge University Press, Cambridge.

LERNER, A. P. (1936). 'A Note on Socialist Economics', *Review of Economic Studies*, **4**, 72–6; reprinted in M. J. Farrel (1973). *Readings in Welfare Economics*. Macmillan, London.

LUCAS, R. E. (1972). 'Expectations and the Neutrality of Money', *Journal of Economic Theory*, **4**, 103–24.

LUCAS, R. E. (1973). 'Some International Evidence on Output–Inflation Trade-offs', *American Economic Review*, **63**, 326–44.

LUCAS, R. E. (1975). 'An Equilibrium Model of the Business Cycle', *Journal of Political Economy*, **83**, 1113–44.

MARX, K. (1967). *Capital*. New York International Publishers, New York.

MUTH, J. F. (1961). 'Rational Expectations and the Theory of Price Movements', *Econometrica*, **29**, 315–35.

NERLOVE, M. (1958). 'Adaptive Expectations and Cobweb Phenomena', *Quarterly Journal of Economics*, **72**, 227–40.

OLSON, M. L. (1965). *The Logic of Collective Action*. Harvard University Press, Cambridge, MA.

OLSON, M. L. (1982). *The Rise and Fall of Nations*. Yale University Press, New Haven, CT.

PAGANO, U. (1985). *Work and Welfare in Economic Theory*. Basil Blackwell, Oxford.

PAGANO, U. (1989). 'Firms, Co-ordination and Disequilibrium', *Quaderni del Dipartimento di Economia Politica*, **93**, Siena.

PAGANO, U. (1991a). 'Property Rights, Asset Specificity and the Division of Labour under Alternative Capitalist Relations', *Cambridge Journal of Economics*, **15**, 315–42.

PAGANO, U. (1991b). 'Property Rights Equilibria and Institutional Stability', *Economic Notes*, **20**, 189–228.

PESARAN, H. M. (1987). *The Limits to Rational Expectations*. Basil Blackwell, Oxford.

PHELPS, E. S. (1970). 'Introduction: the New Microeconomics in Employment and Inflation Theory', in E. S. Phelps *et al.* (eds), *Microeconomic Foundations of Employment and Inflation Theory*. Macmillan, London.

PHELPS, E. S. (1983). 'The Trouble with "Rational Expectations" and the Problem of Inflation Stabilization', in R. Frydman and E. S. Phelps (eds), *Individual Forecasting and Aggregate Outcomes. Rational Expectations Examined*, Cambridge University Press, Cambridge, UK.

PUTTERMAN, L. (1986). *The Economic Nature of the Firm. A Reader*. Cambridge University Press, Cambridge.

RADNER, R. (1989). Hierarchy: The Economics of Managing, Marshall Lecture, Cambridge.

SARGENT, T. J. (1978). Estimation of dynamic labour demand schedules under rational expectations, *Journal of Political Economy*, **86**, 1009–1044.

SIMON, H. A. (1957). *Models of Man*. New York, John Wiley.

STIGLER, G. J. (1961). 'The Economics of Information', *Journal of Political Economy*, **69**, 213–25.

VERCELLI, A. (1989). *Keynes after Lucas*. Mimeo, Siena.

VON MISES, L. (1920). 'Economic Calculation in the Socialist Commonwealth', in A. Nove and D. M. Nuti (eds), *Socialist Economics*. Penguin, Harmondsworth.

WILLIAMSON, O. E. (1985). *The Economic Institutions of Capitalism*. The Free Press, New York.

Part VI
Institutional Change and Economic Growth

[23]

Jel *JOURNAL OF ECONOMIC ISSUES*
Vol. XVI   No. 3   September 1982

The Evolution of the Veblenian Dichotomy: Veblen, Hamilton, Ayres, and Foster

William T. Waller, Jr.

This article will reexamine the concept of "institution" and discuss its relationship to the concept of technology, in pursuit of a unified reevaluation and refinement of the Veblenian dichotomy. The article will first examine the historical development of the dichotomy by economists in the Veblen-Ayres tradition. Second, it will discuss refining the concept of institution's role in the evolution of the meaning of technology within the dichotomy, and some implications will be drawn.

The Veblenian dichotomy is the central analytical tool of institutional economists in the Veblen-Ayres tradition. In his work, Thorstein Veblen expressed the dichotomy in many particular forms.[1] The particular form of interest here, one of the most general, has thus come to be the representative expression: the distinction between what Veblen called "institutions" and "technology."[2]

The concept of technology has been a recent center of controversy among institutional economists.[3] Institutionalists are refining the meaning of "technology," as well as reexamining its usefulness as a tool of analysis. The particulars of this debate will be discussed later. The fact that the debate is taking place may be more important than the issues involved, for the reason that the institutionalists' concept of a technological process is an abstraction, a working hypothesis about human behavior. All hypotheses, and all elements of scientific knowledge for that matter, are tentative. The institutionalists' concept of the technological process includes testing hy-

The author is Assistant Professor of Economics, Hobart and William Smith Colleges, Geneva, New York.

potheses to see if they have "linkages" with the rest of the hypotheses judged by the community of scholars to be warranted knowledge. Or, more simply, each hypothesis is compared and evaluated as to its consistency with those hypotheses currently judged to be most correct. Since this warranted knowledge is itself only tentative, the process of reevaluating hypotheses must be constant and ongoing.[4] The very meaning of the technological process calls for its own reevaluation.

The reevaluation of hypotheses of human behavior, for example, is one of the main differences between the institutionalists and their orthodox counterparts. The institutionalists view human behavior as a process of cumulative adaption to changing circumstances within the cultural context in which the behavior takes place. This view is acknowledged to be tentative and subject to change in the light of evidence to the contrary. Unlike the institutionalists, the orthodox economists make an a priori assumption about the nature of human behavior, and do not subject it to any testing process. This assumption can be seen in the following statement from a widely used contemporary, intermediate micro-theory text:

> The postulate of rationality is the customary point of departure in the theory of the consumer's behavior. The consumer is assumed to choose among the alternatives available to him in such a manner that the satisfaction derived from consuming commodities (in the broadest sense) is as large as possible. This implies that he is aware of the alternatives facing him and is capable of evaluating them. All information pertaining to the satisfaction that the consumer derives form various quantities of commodities is contained in his *utility functon*.[5]

It seems clear that in order to continue developing a scientific paradigm, the institutional economists must use their analytical tools to evaluate their own concepts, as well as the usefulness of the conceptual constructs of their orthodox counterparts. The debate referred to above seems to indicate that this is in fact an ongoing reexamination of the concept of the technological process. Notably absent is a similar reevaluation of Veblen's concept of "institutions" or "institutional behavior." Reevaluation of technology without a similar reevaluation of the concept of institutions must be looked upon as truncated analysis. Veblen was analyzing behavior as being made up of technological aspects in association with institutional aspects in a social context. This implies that the concept of "technology" only has meaning when used in conjunction with the concept of "institution." To reevaluate one without reevaluating the other may lead to a distorted view of the institutionalists' contribution.

In an effort to rectify what I see as a serious omission from the debate, this article will reexamine the concept of "institution" and its relationship to the outcomes of the current discussion of technology, in the hope that this will lead to a clarification and refinement of the dichotomy.

Early Development

We begin with an examination of the evolutionary development of the concept of "institution." The logical place to start is with Veblen.

Veblen

Veblen extended and elaborated his definition of "institution" throughout his work. In an early work he spoke of institutions as aggregates of spiritual attitudes:

> The institutions are, in substance, prevalent habits of thought with respect to particular relations and particular functions of the individual and of the community; and the scheme of life, which is made up of the aggregate of institutions in force at a given time or at a given point in the development of any society, may, on the psychological side, be broadly characterized as a prevalent spiritual attitude or a prevalent theory of life.[6]

He extended that definition in another article: "As a matter of course, men order their lives by these principles and, practically, entertain no question of their stability and finality. That is what is meant by calling them institutions; they are settled habits of thought common to the generality of men."[7] In one of his last works he defined an institution as "of the nature of a usage which has become axiomatic and indispensable by habituation and general acceptance."[8] Veblen used many variations of the dichotomy, each tailored to the particular aspect of society he was analyzing.[9] But his concept of "institution" remains substantially intact and consistent throughout his analysis.

An important aspect of this definition is that by "institution" Veblen is referring to behavior patterns or functions that exhibit the characteristics he attributes to them in his definitions. These institutional behavior patterns take place in a structural context. While the behavior patterns and structural context are two aspects of the same phenomena, it seems clear that Veblen was interested primarily in analyzing the behavior patterns.

Other authors have referred to these behavior patterns as "function," and to the structural context as "structure." It must be kept in mind that this distinction between "structure" and "function" is an analytical one. Although behavior patterns have been described as resulting from "con-

scious, deliberate choice making on the part of people holding and using power to establish structure," through repetition the "institutions" become habitual.[10] The original conscious decision-making processes which
brought them into being are forgotten, and the "institutions" appear and
are thought to be "natural" and "eternal."[11]

The sense in which these behavior patterns are habitual is that they are
used but not questioned. Their authenticity or appropriateness to the circumstance in which they are employed is generally explained by recourse
to common sense or tradition. The appeal to tradition for verification is
tantamount to religious justification of questioned beliefs or behaviors.[12]

A second important aspect of Veblen's concept of "institution" is that
institutions are a non-dynamic factor in cultural development:

> It is to be noted then, although it may be a tedious truism, that the institu-
> tions of to-day—the present accepted scheme of life—do not entirely fit
> the situation of to-day. At the same time, men's present habits of thought
> tend to persist indefinitely, except as circumstances enforce a change.
> These institutions which have so been handed down, these habits of
> thought, points of view, mental attitudes and aptitudes, or what not, are
> therefore themselves a conservative factor. This is the factor of social in-
> ertia, conservatism.[13]

That Veblen's concept of "institutions" is part of an analysis of behavior
on the cultural level is evident:

> To any modern scientist interested in economic phenomena, the chain of
> cause and effect in which any given phase of human culture is involved,
> as well as the cumulative changes wrought in the fabric of human conduct
> itself by the habitual activity of mankind, are matters of more engrossing
> and more abiding interest than the method of inference by which an indi-
> vidual is presumed invariably to balance pleasure and pain under given
> conditions that are presumed to be normal and invariable.[14]

Hamilton

The next major development in the evolution of the "institution" concept occurred in the 1930s and 40s, in the work of R. A. Dixon and Walton Hamilton.[15] The analysis will center on Hamilton for two reasons.
First, he is generally credited with naming Institutional Economics, and
second, he made an explicit, in-depth attempt to define "institution."[16]
This attempt at definition was probably a result of the danger Hamilton
recognized in naming a branch of economics with a term that had a mean-

ing and usage in the vernacular that did not correspond to the specific meaning that these particular economists attributed to it.[17]

Hamilton's concept of an institution is very complex. To see the concept in a processual context, we will begin by comparing Hamilton's definition with Veblen's. We can then see how Hamilton expanded Veblen's view of "institution."

It can easily be seen that Hamilton includes in his definition those patterns of behavior that Veblen identified as "institutions." Both Veblen and Hamilton agree that institutions are cultural constructs; according to Hamilton, "our culture is a synthesis—or at least an aggregation—of institutions . . . . The function of each is to set a pattern of behavior and to fix a zone of tolerance for an activity or complement of activities."[18] Both point out the role of habit and custom in institutions. Hamilton believed that the concept of institution "connotes a way of thought or action of some prevalence or permanence, which is embedded in the habits of a group or the customs of a people."[19] They also agree that compliance with the requirements of the institution is usually unquestioned, that "as long as it remains vital, men accommodate their actions to its detailed arrangements with little bother about its inherent nature or cosmic purpose."[20]

A vital institution is a behavior pattern that is organizing activities still of technological importance to the community. An institution that interfered with technologically essential activities would in fact eventually be questioned. This reflects Hamilton's notion of evolving institutions, which is dealt with in the next section. Even while acknowledging this diference Hamilton clearly recognized the aspect of culture Veblen called institutions.

There are also, however, two crucial differences in the usage of the term "institution" by Veblen and Hamilton. The first concerns the role of institutions in cultural change. As stated earlier, Veblen saw institutions as a non-dynamic factor in cultural development. More specifically, changing technological circumstances force institutions to change; institutions do not generate changes within a culture. Instead the source of the cultural change is outside the institution and "enforces" a change in the institutional patterns.[21] Hamilton does not specifically disagree with this description of institutional change.[22] In fact, his statement that "as an institution develops within a culture it responds to changes in prevailing sense and reason" shows an undeniable similarity to Veblen's thinking.[23]

But while Hamilton does state that institutions change in response to changes in outside circumstances, he also allows for the possibility that change in the institution is a cause of change in the outside circumstances:

"In this continuous process of the adaption of usage and arrangement to intellectual environment an active role is assumed by that body of ideas taken for granted which is called common sense. Because it determines the climate of opinion within which all others must live it is the dominant institution in society."[24] Hamilton also saw an institution as "a folkway, always new yet ever old, *directive* and responsive, *a spur to* and a check upon *change*, a creature of means and a master of ends."[25] This concept of an institution as "a spur to change" seems fundamentally different from Veblen's concept of institutions as a drag on cultural change.

This is consistent with the second crucial difference between Hamilton's and Veblen's definition of an institution, illustrated by Hamilton's statement: "Moreover the way of knowledge is itself an institution."[26] Veblen, however, would place "the way of knowledge" in the realm of that behavior he describes as "technology." Veblen's theory treats technological behavior as the dynamic element of cultural change. Hamilton's definition is much broader than Veblen's since he includes both Veblen's "institutional" behavior and "technological" behavior in his definition of "institution." Since he includes Veblen's "technology" in his definition of "institution," it follows that he would see institutions as a dynamic force in cultural change. But Veblen is analyzing the institutional *and* technological aspects of cultural behavior, while Hamilton includes both aspects in his definition of institutions, so it is clear that their concepts of institution are fundamentally different. What makes this important is that both definitions are in the literature of institutional economics and both definitions affected later scholars. While the similarities are often noted or assumed, the differences between the usages are not.[27]

Ayres

Historically and analytically the next major development of the concept of "institution" was to come in the work of C. E. Ayres. Ayres's concept clearly represents an extension of Veblen's.[28] Ayres is in agreement with Veblen in that he emphasizes the analysis of "institutional" behavior patterns rather than of social structures. While "institutions" are both functional and structural, Veblen and Ayres emphasize the functional rather than structural aspects. For Ayres, "the term 'institution' is not a structural category. That is, it does not refer merely to the division of the total substance of society into its constituent parts. It is, rather, a functional category. As such it has reference to a certain type of social organization, or certain aspect of social behavior, which is qualitatively different from another aspect."[29] Ayres also takes the Veblenian view of the role of institutions in social change: "By virtue of its peculiar character, the institutional function is essentially static. In the process of social change, institutional function plays a negative part. It resists change."[30]

Like Veblen, Ayres is trying to separate out and analyze a particular aspect of culture that is non-dynamic and habit-oriented. Ayres also recognizes the danger of using the word "institution" to denote this aspect of culture.[31] He points out that "no word is more frequently or more vaguely used in contemporary social science than 'institution,' "[32] and that "it is not necessary to be an accomplished scholar to realize that we use this term very loosely in common speech."[33]

To rectify the confusion over the term "institution," Ayres suggests a look back to Veblen. He does this by using the term "ceremonial function" to describe that aspect of culture that he and Veblen are trying to separate out, previously denoted by the term "institution."[34] A great many institutionalists in the Veblenian tradition followed suit and the Veblenian dichotomy became the ceremonial-technological distinction.

This substitution of "ceremonial function" for "institution" had two major effects. It eliminated the vagueness associated with the term "institution," because "ceremonial" does not have such common usage or a different vernacular meaning.[35] It also eliminated confusing associations with Walton Hamilton's wider conception of "institutions," also in use at this time.

Ayres also made a major contribution by way of making more explicit some aspects of the ceremonial function. He notes that "one peculiar feature which 'typical' institutions all seem to exhibit is that of determination of authorities. . . . [I]nstitutional authority is authority, defined and supported and limited by custom."[36] This authority organizes society into a hierarchical structure of privilege and subservience. The hierarchical structure persists because of habit and a ceremonial verification system: "Mores are always accompanied by legends; and these legends, of which every community has so rich a stock, invariably point to a moral. The mores are the morals to which the legends point; and the legends do not merely tell a story. The story which they tell is invariably a mythical explanation of the legendary reasons for the mores."[37]

These mythical explanations are believed as an act of faith and are beyond question, since they occurred in the ancient past, and were unique events. Ayres spent a large portion of his prolific career expanding the ceremonial-technological distinction.[38] Further examination of this distinction is unfortunately outside the scope of this article.

Foster

The next important contribution grows out of the work of a student of C. E. Ayres, J. Fagg Foster. Foster is associated with the so-called "oral tradition" in institutional economics. Since Foster has published very little, we must look at definitions of "institution" attributed to him by his students.

In his recent book *The Discretionary Economy*, Marc Tool attributes the following definition to Foster: "The term institution means any prescribed or proscribed pattern of correlated behavior or attitude widely agreed upon among a group of persons organized to carry on some particular purpose."[39] Another student of Foster's, Paul D. Bush, defines institution in a recent paper as "a set of socially prescribed patterns of correlated behavior."[40] A third student of Foster's, Louis Junker, in an unpublished manuscript quoted Foster defining institution as "prescribed patterns of correlated human behavior with (a) instrumental aspects and (b) ceremonial aspects."[41]

This definition by Foster is, or at least allows, a more expansive view of institutions, permitting the definition in some ways to recover some of the flavor of the usage we have associated with Walton Hamilton. This expansion of the definition was mentioned by Junker in an earlier work:

> Clarification of this issue must be ascribed to Professor J. Fagg Foster of the University of Denver, who has broken down institutional structures into their instrumental aspects (after John Dewey) and their ceremonial aspects. This broadens Veblen's viewpoint considerably because he did not *concentrate* on this point but seemed to be always contrasting obstructionary institutions against dynamic technology only. Thus Foster is making amends to Veblen's analysis by accounting for social behavior patterns that are in rapport with modern technology, and thus are efficient organizational structures. Veblen merely hints around the issue at times. . . .[42]

Foster's ceremonial-instrumental dichotomy is such a significant refinement of the institution-technology dichotomy that it can be considered qualitatively different. This "new" version of the Veblenian dichotomy eliminated problems that arose consistently in the use of the institution-technology dichotomy. It also allows for the application of the dichotomy to new areas of inquiry about social behavior, as well as allowing us to be more precise about our reevaluation of past analysis. For example, it totally eliminates the structure-function problem. If someone uses "institution" in the structural sense, the ceremonial functions of this particular institutional structure can still be analyzed without the semantic difficulty encountered previously.

The new version also eliminates a similar difficulty on the "technology" side of the dichotomy. Technological behavior has been described by one prominent institutionalist as "organized intelligence in action."[43] This process is considerably more than simply tools and tool skills, but institutionalists have at times allowed themselves to slip back and forth from the "organized-intelligence" definition to the "technology-as-tools" definition. By substituting "instrumental behavior" for "technology," this slipperiness can be avoided.

Possibly the most significant aspect of Foster's refinement is that he isolated that aspect of culture that Veblen wished to analyze and called it ceremonial behavior, in addition to isolating those behaviors that oppose ceremonial behavior and calling them instrumental behavior. This allowed the dichotomy to be used as a tool of analysis not only to evaluate human behavior and identify its instrumental and ceremonial qualities, but also to evaluate their earlier version of the dichotomy itself.

*Earlier and More Recent Developments
and Their Associations with the
"Technology Controversy"*

In reviewing the recent controversy over technology mentioned earlier, we find it to be only an example of a problem that has pervaded the writing of economists in the Veblen-Ayres tradition for several years. The articles cited concern a disagreement over the meaning of "appropriate technology," but in fact the disagreement among the authors is on a much more fundamental level. By this I mean that they are not arguing over the "appropriateness" of technology, rather their disagreement stems from a dual meaning of "technology."

On one side of the disagreement is the concept of "technology" as it appears in the "old" dichotomy. There the technological process is the source of dynamic progressive change in a culture. It is that behavior which promotes the continuity of the life process. Unfortunately "appropriate" technology advocates are not using the word "technology" in this way. They are using "technology" to mean "tools," and their use.[44]

Inevitably in the analysis of this issue by institutional economists there is confusion over which definition of technology the authors intended to use. For example, one author writes: "Institutionalism views technology as the dynamic force for economic change."[45] In this case he appears to mean technological behavior. But in the same paragraph he also writes: "But from an institutionalist or evolutionary economics perspective, merely removing traditional elites from power does not automatically liberate technology."[46]

If the author means technology as used in the "old" dichotomy, this statement is contradictory. Behavior which by definition is liberating does not need to be liberated. If the author means technology as tools, the statement makes perfect sense. This is not intended as a criticism of the above-cited author; in fact all of the institutionalists involved in this controversy have the same difficulty. It is the term that causes the confusion. This confusion over usage of the term "technology" in some cases leaves the impression that the author would uncritically applaud any application of a tool or gadget as part of the technological process, irrespective of its impact on the life process. In fact the "old" version of the dichotomy particularly lends itself to this sort of confusion.

Those on the other side of this controversy are responding to this impression. They in fact are using the "new" dichotomy. They say that any application of tools can be evaluated; its adequacy for solving a problem can be adjudged from its consequences. And tool application as human behavior can be evaluated for its instrumental *and* ceremonial aspects. The confusion over the meaning of technology is avoided by those using the "new" dichotomy, since in their analysis the word never need be used.

Neither side disagrees with the other on the definition of the technological process. But instead the disagreement is one over the use of the "old" dichotomy as opposed to the "new" dichotomy. If it were simply a matter of semantics this controversy would be an example of pedantry of the worst sort. But in examining another issue of current interest among institutional economists, that of "ceremonial encapsulation," we can see it is a substantive disagreement.

Bush and Junker, both students of Foster, have been simultaneously developing the notion of ceremonial encapsulation of technology using the "new" dichotomy.[47] Junker describes this phenomena:

Spurious 'technological' developments, on the other hand, are those which are encapsulated by a ceremonial power system whose main concern is to control the use, direction, and consequences of that development while simultaneously serving as the institutional vehicle for defining the limits and boundaries upon that technology through special domination efforts of the legal system, the property system, and the information system. These limits and boundaries are generally set to best serve the institutions seeking such control. . . . This is the way the ruling and dominant institutions of society maintain and try to extend their hegemony over the lives of people.[48]

Junker goes on to point out that this is not consistent with promoting the continuity of the life process but instead "it serves to shackle mankind."[49] Bush's development of this concept is essentially the same, while using slightly different terminology.

It is significant that the concept of ceremonial encapsulation of technology is being developed by institutionalists using the "new" dichotomy. Using the "old" dichotomy the concept of "ceremonial" technology has no meaning. Using the "new" dichotomy it can be analyzed in the manner of Junker and Bush. This illustrates the fact that the "new" dichotomy leads to innovative social analysis in areas previously neglected, though not ignored, by institutionalists.

Inherent difficulties in the "old" dichotomy resulted in (1) a lack of emphasis on analysis of the type being done by Bush and Junker, and (2) the "appropriate technology" debate. These difficulties are a result of the dual usage of the concepts of "institution" and "technology" in the "old" dichotomy. This is not a matter simply of correcting the dual usage problem; more careful usage of these terms might clear up some of the confusion, but it would not eliminate another substantive problem also related to the "old" dichotomy and particularly apparent in the concept of "technology."[50]

The meaning of "technology" in the vernacular is associated with implements and their application. The institutionalists' conception of the "scientific-technological process" is larger and more encompassing. Even if institutionalists focus on the correct version for their analysis, the term "technology" has a tendency to shift the focus of the analysis to techniques.

One problem resulting from this is difficulty in correctly identifying the problem or in asking the correct question. The scientific-technological process is a problem-solving process. If we focus on tools, scientific apparatus, and techniques, as we are apt to do in our complex society, we sometimes define the problems in terms of the techniques we use to solve them. An example of this in economics is when economists discuss at great length in the literature the use of sophisticated mathematical techniques to solve problems of choice involving risk by maximizing expected utility, while ignoring the issue of the meaningfulness of the concept of maximizing expected utility. We have concentrated on the use of a sophisticated tool while ignoring whether the application we have chosen is appropriate.

This emphasis on technique is like two individuals arguing over whether an ocean liner or a rowboat is more appropriate for crossing a lake, without ever considering walking around it. They have missed the point that the real question is how to get from one point to the other; emphasizing the techniques leads to misidentifying the question. Since we evaluate solutions to problems on the basis of all their consequences, we cannot properly evaluate all the consequences without examining all the alternatives.

A similar misidentification of the correct question can be found on the "institution" side of the "old" dichotomy. This occurs when "institution" in the structural sense is confused with institutional behavior. For example, if we identify the nuclear family or the Catholic Church as institutions, we have a tendency to overlook the fact that these structures are made up of technological (instrumental) behaviors as well as institutional (ceremonial) behaviors.

The dual usage problem may also lead to evaluating behaviors out of context. The best solution to a problem cannot be found if the social milieu in which the problem occurs is not considered completely. This is not a relativist position; the social milieu does not determine the correct or better solution to a problem. But all the consequences of proposed solutions cannot be evaluated without considering the environment in which this proposed action is to take place. This has not been a significant problem among institutionalists; in fact their explicit consideration of the social milieu is one of the main things that differentiates them from their orthodox counterparts. But the "new" dichotomy, particularly through the concept of ceremonial encapsulation, makes this difference more pronounced and more explicit.

Implications

These problems, present in the old dichotomy *to whatever degree,* have achieved a crucial level of importance in recent years. The institutional economist in the Veblen-Ayres tradition evaluates actions on the basis of all the effects of that action on the continuity of the life process. This evaluation process obviously requires the best information possible about potential consequences. That methodology which best makes us aware and anticipates consequences has always been the most desirable. We have recently been reminded that it is crucial.

The revelation in the last few years of the extent of the consequences of dumping toxic waste into the environment in general, and our water supply in particular, has served to remind us of the importance of unanticipated or ignored consequences. It has also served to illustrate the even greater importance of anticipating these consequences, because some have the quality of being irreversible. The irreversibility of some consequences is not new, but the scale of these consequences is unprecedented. Their destructive capacity has expanded to encompass the entire planet. In recent years alone we have seen the examples of potential nuclear destruction, destruction of the environment through pollutants in general, the possible destruction of the ozone layer, and the reduction in the size of the gene pool of crucial agricultural plants. The list could, of course, go on. We discovered these consequences and the process of solving these problems is underway.

Discovering these consequences was crucial to the continuity of the life process. The improvement and refinement of our analytical tools to better anticipate consequences of this type, and to discover ways of solving problems resulting from our actions, is the most important task before the human race.[51]

The current discussion among institutionalists on the methodological questions characterized in this paper as a conflict between the "old" and "new" dichotomy is in fact an attempt to refine their tools of analysis. The purpose of this paper has been to reemphasize that the dichotomy is an evolving tool of analysis and that it is necessary to frame current controversies among institutionalists in terms of the meaning of the evolving dichotomy for future analysis. If what I have described as the "new" dichotomy is a superior tool of analysis, it should be used. This can only be determined if the controversy over the meaning of the dichotomy is addressed as a crucial methodological question, rather than on an issue-by-issue basis.

Notes

1. For a rather extensive listing see Marc R. Tool, "Philosophy of Neo-Institutionalism: Veblen, Dewey, and Ayres" (Ph.D. diss., University of Colorado, 1954).
2. The generality of this particular formulation is attested to by the fact that later institutionalists have seen fit to spend a great deal of time defining these particular terms, rather than other formulations, when writing economics texts. See, for example, C. E. Ayres, *The Industrial Economy* (Cambridge, Mass.: Riverside Press, 1952), p. 42; W. Nelson Peach, *Principles of Economics* (Homewood, Illinois: Richard D. Irwin, 1960), p. 10; Marc R. Tool, *The Discretionary Economy* (Santa Monica: Goodyear, 1979), p. 73.
3. For a representative sample of this discussion see the exchange between Hayden and DeGregori in *Journal of Economic Issues* 14 (1980).
4. This discussion is drawn from Jacob Bronowski's discussion of genuine knowledge in his book *The Origins of Knowledge and Imagination* (New Haven: Yale University Press, 1978).
5. J. Henderson and R. Quandt, *Micro Economic Theory: A Mathematical Approach* (New York: McGraw-Hill, 1971), p. 6 (emphasis in original).
6. Thorstein Veblen, *The Theory of the Leisure Class* (New York: Modern Library, 1934), p. 190.
7. Thorstein Veblen, *The Place of Science in Modern Civilization and Other Essays* (New York: Viking Press, 1919), p. 239.

770   William T. Waller, Jr.

8. Thorstein Veblen, *Absentee Ownership and Business Enterprise in Recent Times* (Boston: Beacon Press, 1967), p. 101.
9. Tool, *Philosophy of Neo-Institutionalism.*
10. Tool, *The Discretionary Economy*, p. 75.
11. This discussion is drawn from Marc Tool's *The Discretionary Economy*, pp. 73–78. What we are concerned with in this context is Veblen's interest in the habitual nature of behavior patterns. I find Tool's discussion to be consistent with Veblen's views, but it should be recognized that Tool's analysis expands and extends Veblen's analysis significantly.
12. An excellent analysis of the religious character of explanations based on "tradition" is provided in Lord Raglan's *The Hero: A Study in Tradition, Myth, and Drama* (New York: Vintage Books, 1956), particularly Part 1.
13. Veblen, *The Leisure Class*, p. 191.
14. Veblen, *The Place of Science*, p. 191.
15. Russell A. Dixon, *Economic Institutions and Cultural Change* (New York and London: McGraw-Hill, 1941), pp. 3–30; Walton Hamilton, "Institutions," *Encyclopedia of the Social Sciences* (New York: MacMillan Co., 1932), vol. 7, pp. 84–89.
16. Walton Hamilton, "The Institutional Approach to Economic Theory," *American Economic Review* 9 (1919); Hamilton, "Institutions."
17. Hamilton, "The Institutional Approach."
18. Hamilton, "Institutions," p. 84.
19. Ibid.
20. Ibid., p. 87.
21. Veblen, *The Leisure Class*, pp. 190–98.
22. In fact R. A. Dixon, in his *Economic Institutions and Cultural Change*, uses Hamilton's definition of institutions, but quotes Veblen (see footnote 21) on institutional change, and sees the two as completely compatible.
23. Hamilton, "Institutions," p. 85.
24. Ibid.
25. Ibid., p. 89 (emphasis added).
26. Ibid., p. 88.
27. See, for example, John R. Commons, *The Economics of Collective Action* (New York: MacMillan Co., 1950), p. 21; Peach, *Principles of Economics*, p. 76, for definitions that incorporate both Veblen's and Hamilton's usage; also Dixon, *Economic Institutions*, chap. 1. The differences in the definitions are noted in D. Hamilton, *Evolutionary Economics* (Albuquerque: University of New Mexico Press, 1974), pp. 76–9.
28. C. E. Ayres, *Science: The False Messiah and Holier Than Thou* (Clifton, N.J.: Augustus M. Kelley, 1973). See particularly the introduction, "Prolegomenon to Institutionalism."
29. C. E. Ayres, *The Industrial Economy* (Cambridge, Mass.: Houghton Mifflin; The Riverside Press, 1952), pp. 42–3.
30. Ibid., p. 49.
31. This is characteristic of Ayres's early work. A shift has been noted by some writers. See Marc Tool, "A Social Value Theory in Neo-institutional Economics," *Journal of Economic Issues* 11 (1977): 823. See particularly footnote 75 on p. 845. This shift is to a view similar to J. Fagg Foster's. I would like to acknowledge my debt to one of the referees for pointing this out in a review of an earlier draft.

32. C. E. Ayres, *The Theory of Economic Progress* (Kalamazoo, Mich.: New Issues Press, Western Michigan University, 1978), p. 178.

33. Ayres, *The Industrial Economy*, p. 42.

34. The innovation by Ayres was not in the use of the term "ceremonial." Veblen used this term in *Imperial Germany and the Industrial Revolution* (New York: Viking Press, 1939). The innovative aspect is his consistent use of "ceremonial" in place of "institution" in the Veblenian dichotomy.

35. This type of problem was not completely eliminated, but appears to be reduced. See Ayres, *The Theory of Economic Progress*, p. 156.

36. Ayres, *The Industrial Economy*, p. 43.

37. "Mores" is William Grahm Summers's term; Ayres sees it as similar, but not identical, to "institution." See also Ayres, *The Industrial Economy*, p. 44.

38. For an excellent discussion of C. E. Ayres's contribution see Louis Junker, *The Social and Economic Thought of Clarence Edwin Ayres* (Ann Arbor: University Microfilms, 1962).

39. Tool, *The Discretionary Economy*, p. 74.

40. Paul D. Bush, "The Ceremonial Incapsulation of Capital Formation in the American Economy" (Paper read before the Economics section at the Annual Meeting of the Western Social Sciences Association, Lake Tahoe, Nevada, 27 April 1979), p. 2.

41. Louis J. Junker, "Institutionalism and the Criteria of Development," mimeographed (Kalamazoo: Western Michigan University, approximately 1969), p. 10.

42. Junker, *Social and Economic Thought of Ayres*, p. 46.

43. This definition of technology is from the lectures of Professor David Hamilton of the University of New Mexico.

44. See for example E. F. Shumacher's *Small is Beautiful: Economics as if People Mattered* (New York: Harper and Row, 1973).

45. T. DeGregori, "Technology and Economic Dependency: An Institutional Assessment," *Journal of Economic Issues* 12 (1978): 472.

46. Ibid.

47. Bush, "Ceremonial Encapsulation," p. 6; Louis J. Junker, "Markings on the Nature, Scope, and Radical Implications of the Ceremonial-Instrumental Dichotomy in Institutional Analysis" (Paper read before the Economics section at the Annual Meeting of the Western Social Sciences Association, 24 April 1980).

48. Ibid., pp. 3–4.

49. Ibid., p. 4. I would contend that what I have called the "new" dichotomy is in fact the "radical" implications of the dichotomy to which Junker's paper refers.

50. It is interesting to note that Ayres thought the dual-usage problem significant enough to address it in his Addendum to *The Theory of Economic Progress*, and indicates that resolution of this problem would be a major benefit.

51. Anne Mayhew provides an excellent analysis of these types of problems and their implications on the Ayresian view of technology in her article "Ayresian Technology, Technological Reasoning, and Doomsday," *Journal of Economic Issues* 15 (1981): 513–20.

[24]

Jei *JOURNAL OF ECONOMIC ISSUES*
Vol. XXI   No. 3   September 1987

The Theory of Institutional Change

Paul D. Bush

If institutional economics is truly an "evolutionary" economics, it is because it has the capacity to explain the phenomenon of institutional change and because it incorporates the principles of that explanation in both theoretical and applied inquiry. While it cannot be argued that all that has been labeled "institutional" economics in the past rests either explicitly or implicitly on a coherent theory of institutional change, contemporary institutionalists generally agree that such a theory is, and must be, the diagnostic characteristic of the institutionalist perspective.

The purpose of this article is to set forth a systematic statement of the institutionalist theory of institutional change. The theory presented is a synthetic statement of what the author understands to be (at its present state of development) the theory of institutional change that informs all analytically grounded contributions to the institutionalist literature. The classical foundations of the theory were laid by Thorstein B. Veblen, John R. Commons, John Dewey, and Clarence E. Ayres. Contemporary refinements of the theory are to be found in the works of J. Fagg Foster, William Dugger, David Hamilton, F. Gregory Hayden, Louis Junker, Philip Klein, Anne Mayhew, Walter C. Neale, Baldwin Ranson, Marc Tool, and others who have offered explicit dem-

The author wishes to thank William M. Dugger for his thoughtful comments on the initial design of this article, James A. Swaney for his careful review and critique of earlier works upon which this article draws heavily, and Marc R. Tool for his patience and encouragement in seeing this project through to the end. They are, of course, absolved of any blame for the deficiencies that careful readers will undoubtedly discover.

onstrations of the theory of institutional change in their theoretical and applied investigations. The theory, like the phenomenon it purports to explain, has undergone evolutionary change. As the intellectual pace in institutional economics has quickened in recent years, contributions to the theory of institutional change have likewise appeared at an increased rate. The following presentation attempts to capture not only those classical principles set forth by Veblen at the turn of the century, but also the most recent contributions that have extended the theory and pointed it in new directions.

The article is organized into six major sections. The first section presents a discussion of the institutional structure and the concept of "behavioral patterns." The second section is devoted to an explication of the "institutional" dichotomy, which is a fundamental tenet of most contemporary institutionalist analyses. The third section examines the concept of the "technological dynamic," which institutionalists believe identifies the basic evolutionary force in social change. The fourth section describes the manner in which "institutional space" is partitioned by the knowledge fund and the value structure of the institution. The fifth section develops the concept of "ceremonial encapsulation" and explains both "progressive" and "regressive" institutional change. The article concludes with some observations on the discretionary character of social evolution.

The Institutional Structure of Society

The theory of institutional change must begin with a theoretical formulation of the institutional structure. This section and the next are devoted to that formulation. The primary focus in both will be the significance of the value system of the society in determining the character of the institutional structure.

Definition of the Term "Institution"

"Society" may be thought of as a set of institutional systems. An "institutional system," in turn, may be thought of as a set of institutions. And an "institution" may be defined as *a set of socially prescribed patterns of correlated behavior*. In each of the above sentences, the term "set" refers to functionally interrelated elements.

Social Prescriptions

When employing this definition of an institution, institutionalists lay stress on the term "socially prescribed." While it is entirely possible for human behavior to exhibit random characteristics, institutionalists argue that all behavior within a community is ultimately subject to social prescriptions or proscriptions. This is especially true of all problem-solving (purposive) behavior. The community at large has a stake in the manner in which its tools and intelligence are brought to bear on its life processes. Those patterns of behavior perceived to be vital to the survival of the community are the most carefully prescribed and carry the heaviest sanctions.

It is a well-established point in the fields of sociology and child psychology that social conditioning begins prior to an infant's capacity to walk or talk.[1] Throughout one's life, the process of habit formation is the mechanism by which socially prescribed behavior is internalized. While some habits may be learned only through conscious effort, most habit formation is probably unconscious. Such unconscious habituation gives rise to the impression that certain patterns of behavior are "natural" and not amenable to discretionary change. The fruitless "nature" versus "nurture" debate is grounded in the misapprehension of unconscious habituation. Institutionalists hold the view that all socially relevant behavior is learned and is, for the most part, habitual.[2] While unconscious habituation may account for most observed behavior, particularly "traditional" behavior, this fact must not be allowed to obscure the discretionary nature of the social prescriptions that are thereby internalized. Socially prescribed behavior arises from social choices, and the critical history of any culture is the story of how these choices evolved in the life experience of the community. As will be argued at length below, institutional change is discretionary precisely because all social prescriptions are the outcomes of conscious choices made at some point in the life history of the culture.[3]

Behavioral Patterns

The term "patterns of correlated behavior" embodies two important concepts: (1) the notion that behavior within an institution is not random but purposeful and correlated; and (2) the notion that "values" function as the "correlators" of behavior within and among patterns of behavior. The term "behavioral pattern" (singular) may be thought of as two behaviors (or activities) correlated by a value. This conception of a "behavioral pattern" clearly indicates the social significance of "values." Values function as the standards of judgment by which behavior is correlated. Values not only correlate behavior within the behavioral pattern, they also correlate behavioral patterns with one another. The interconnection among behavioral patterns may be envisioned as the correlation of one behavior of one behavioral pattern by a given value with the behavior from another behavioral pattern. In essence, the interconnection among behavioral patterns is accomplished by a behavioral pattern.

In order to clarify these relationships, it may be helpful to symbolize a behavioral pattern as follows: B^1 V^1 B^2, where "B^1" is one behavior or activity, "B^2" is another behavior or activity, and "V^1" is the value that correlates B^1 with B^2. A second behavioral pattern might be identified as follows: B^3 V^3 B^4. The correlation of the first behavioral pattern with the second is accomplished through the use of an additional value, V^2, such that B^2 is correlated with B^3 through V^2, which produces a third behavioral pattern: B^2 V^2 B^3. Thus "behavioral patterns" (plural) are correlated by values, and the correlation of behavioral patterns entails a behavioral pattern. It is, then, the value system of the institution that provides the functional interrelationship of all patterns of behavior within the institution.[4] These comments on the nature of the correlation of behavior within and among behavioral patterns requires a further statement about the focus of the social prescriptions that give shape and form to the institutional structure. Clearly, what is prescribed are the values that will be employed as correlators of behavior. In other words, a given pair of behaviors or activities can be found in a number of different social contexts, but their relationship to one another will change depending on the value system under which they are correlated. This will be discussed at length below. Thus the diagnostic characteristic of an institution is the value structure that correlates the behavior within it. It follows from this that institutional change must entail a change in the value structure of the institution. This matter will also be explored at length later. But another concept fundamental to institutional analysis must be discussed first. It is the notion of the ceremonial-instrumental dichotomy.

The Ceremonial-Instrumental Dichotomy

Given the central importance of values to the structure of institutions, inquiry into the nature of institutions and the processes of institutional change is inherently normative. All inquiry involves interpretation, and interpretation requires judgment.[5] When the subject matter under investigation is the value system of society, interpretations and their attendant judgments must be made about the value system. The methodology of institutional economics faces this intellectual responsibility squarely by incorporating a philosophy of value that permits a straight-forward analysis of the value system. In contrast, all schools of mainstream economics attempt to evade this intellectual responsibility by purporting to adhere to the value-knowledge dualism in their methodologies. This positivist tenet is the foundation for claims of "objectivity" in mainstream economics. In the long history of the institutionalist critique of mainstream economics (from Veblen to Tool), this *wertfrei* methodology has been shown to be not only sterile, but counterproductive: normative considerations are not eschewed, they are merely suppressed, thereby obfuscating the true import of the inquiry; and the notion of "objectivity" is held hostage to the positivist dualism. As a consequence of these methodological strictures, mainstream economists have evaded the study of institutional structure (let alone institutional *change)* by relying on "methodological individualism."[6] The philosophical foundations of the institutionalist approach to the study of the value system of society is grounded in the classical works of Veblen and Dewey. Their works were synthesized and refined by Clarence E. Ayres. Ayres's student, J. Fagg Foster, and his student, Marc R. Tool, have brought "social value theory" to its present state of development. It is this particular line of institutionalist thought that informs the treatment of values in this essay.[7]

Ceremonial Values

The institutional structure of any society incorporates two systems of value: the ceremonial and the instrumental, each of which has its own logic and method of validation. While these two value systems are inherently incompatible, they are intertwined within the institutional structure through a complex set of relationships.

Ceremonial values correlate behavior within the institution by providing the standards of judgment for invidious distinctions, which prescribe status, differential privileges, and master-servant relationships, and warrant the exercise of power by one social class over another. The logic of the ceremonial value system, as Veblen put it, is one of "sufficient reason." Validation of ceremonial values is found in appeals to tradition and in the formulation of suitable myths (ideologies) that mystify the origin and legitimacy of their existence. Ceremonial values are by their very nature beyond inquiry in the sense that they may not be subjected to critical scrutiny. They may be rationalized through plausible argument, but they are never subjected to any sort of test of refutability. They are accepted on authority and regarded as absolute. Presumably, they emanate from human nature and, therefore, are not subject to human discretion. Patterns of behavior in which behaviors are correlated by ceremonial values are referred to here as "ceremonially warranted" patterns of behavior. The operative criterion by which such patterns of behavior are judged within the community is that of "ceremonial adequacy."

Instrumental Values

Instrumental values correlate behavior by providing the standards of judgment by which tools and skills are employed in the application of evidentially warranted knowledge to the problem-solving processes of the community. Using Veblen's language once again, the logic of the instrumental value system is that of "efficient cause." Instrumental values are validated in the continuity of the problem-solving processes. Patterns of behavior correlated by instrumental values are referred to as "instrumentally warranted" patterns of behavior. The criterion by which the community judges instrumentally warranted patterns of behavior is that of "instrumental efficiency."

Instrumental values are not, however, fixed or immutable. The problem-solving processes of the community, being dependent on the processes of inquiry and technological change, are inherently dynamic, requiring changes in habits of thought and behavior. As new patterns of behavior are required to accommodate the absorption and diffusion of new technology, instrumentally warranted patterns of behavior must change accordingly; and this requires changes in the instrumental values that correlate such behavior. H.H. Liebhafsky has referred to this capacity for change in the instrumental value system as "self-correcting value judgments."[8] A specific standard of judgment is warranted only as long as it provides for instrumental efficiency in maintaining the causal continuity of the problem-solving process. When such a standard loses its capacity to do so, it is replaced by a more appropriate standard. The process is "self-correcting" by virtue of the fact that the processes of inquiry upon which the problem-solving processes depend involve a conscious awareness of the method by which behavior is correlated. The causal continuity of the problem-solving process is, in principle, open to the surveillance of the community. When a sensed awareness of a disrapport between current institutional practices and instrumental efficiency arises within the community, the community has the capacity to opt for the discretionary change of those patterns of behavior that are no longer appropriate to the problem-solving processes.

The "Dialectical" Nature of Behavior

Whereas the value system of an institution is dichotomous, behavior is "dialectical" in the sense that Nicholas Georgescu-Roegen has used the term; that is to say, behavior may possess either ceremonial or instrumental characteristics, or possess *both* ceremonial and instrumental characteristics.[9] This fact adds considerable complexity to the forms that behavior patterns may take. As will be shown below, a ceremonially warranted pattern of behavior may incorporate instrumental behavior, and an instrumentally warranted pattern of behavior may incorporate behavior that has ceremonial characteristics.

A few examples may help to clarify the notion of the dialectical nature of behavior. Some examples of purely ceremonial behavior (B_c) would include: discrimination on the basis of race, color or creed; "wrapping oneself in the flag"; making a sacrificial offering; using deceit or coercion in manipulating the behavior of others; and kow-towing to those in authority. Some examples of purely instrumental behavior (B_i) would include: sawing a board; practicing the clarinet; painting a picture; dialing a telephone; programming a computer; using persuasion to obtain the cooperation of others; solving a mathematical problem; and taking medicine under a doctor's prescription. Three examples of behavior that possess both ceremonial and instrumental characteristics (B_{ci}) are: taking a bath; giving an order; and standing behind a lectern. Let us turn briefly to an explanation as to why each of the behaviors in this last set are dialectical.

The example of "taking a bath" is borrowed from Clarence Ayres's discussion of the "cult of the tub."[10] Noting Veblen's comments on the "ceremonial cleanliness" of the upper classes, Ayres discusses the ceremonial implications of the cult of the tub; but he also points out that whatever may be the ceremonial significance of cleanliness, regular bathing is instrumental to both personal and public hygiene. Similarly, the act of "giving an order" may at once announce one's status as well as perform the instrumental function of supervising the work of others. Most of us can tell the difference between the situation in which the boss issues orders just to remind everyone that he/she is in charge and the situation in which the boss issues orders that are instrumental to the supervision of an employee's work. Lastly, "standing behind a lectern" in a classroom clearly establishes the ceremonial status of the professor; but it is also an instrumentally efficient position from which to deliver a lecture.[11]

Whether a dialectical behavior will carry primarily ceremonial or instrumental significance in a given instance depends on the social context in which it occurs. Under the theory presented here, that social context is defined by the behavioral pattern in which the behavior is correlated with other behavior in the institutional arrangement. And that correlation is uniquely the function of the value that defines the behavioral pattern. If the value that correlates behavior is ceremonial, the dialectical behavior will take on ceremonial significance: thus, "taking a bath" performs the ceremonial function of displaying status; "giving an order" is intended to let everyone know who the boss is; and "standing behind a lectern" establishes the superior status of the professor over his/her students. If, on the other hand, the value is instrumental, the dialectical behavior takes on instrumental significance: bathing is understood to be necessary to maintenance of both personal and public health; orders are understood to be necessary to the instrumentally warranted process of supervision; and the physical location assumed by the professor is understood to be a function of his/her need to communicate effectively.

Types of Behavioral Patterns

The principle that the mode of valuation (that is, ceremonial or instrumental) will determine the ceremonial or instrumental significance of dialectical behavior is closely related to another important principle governing the formation of behavioral patterns in general. It was stated earlier that ceremonially warranted patterns of behavior can contain instrumental behavior and that instrumentally warranted patterns of behavior can contain behavior that has ceremonial characteristics. These possibilities emerge because there are a number of ways in which values and behaviors of a ceremonial or instrumental type can be combined. It has been demonstrated elsewhere that the number of possible combinations is finite.[12] Using the symbols introduced above, the possible types of behavioral patterns may be enumerated as follows:

Ceremonially Warranted Patterns	Instrumentally Warranted Patterns
(C-1) $B_c \ V_c \ B_c$	(I-1) $B_i \ V_i \ B_i$
(C-2) $B_c \ V_c \ B_i$	(I-2) $B_i \ V_i \ B_{ci}$
(C-3) $B_c \ V_c \ B_{ci}$	(I-3) $B_{ci} \ V_i \ B_{ci}$
(C-4) $B_{ci} \ V_c \ B_i$	
(C-5) $B_{ci} \ V_c \ B_{ci}$	

Several important observations may be made by reference this tabeau of behavioral patterns.

First, it should be noted that there are five possible types of ceremonially warranted behavioral patterns as compared with only three types of instrumentally warranted behavioral patterns. This reflects the fundamental differences in the two modes of valuation. The instrumental mode of valuing requires an open-ended process of inquiry capable of evaluating the consequences of the application of any particular standard of judgment in the correlation of behavior. The logic of instrumental valuation is, therefore, embedded in the causal continuity of the problem-solving process. This delimits the types of behavior to which instrumental values are relevant as correlators. The logic of instrumental valuation is relevant only to behavior that is somehow involved in the tool-skill nexus of the technological continuum. This is symbolized in the above tableau by the appearance of the $"i"$ subscript in all behaviors shown in each of the three cases of instrumentally warranted behavioral patterns. Note the complete exclusion of any behavior exhibiting *only* a $"c"$ subscript. In other words, instrumental valuation cannot rationalize purely ceremonial behavior. The values that correlate behavior in the pursuit of the arts and sciences cannot validly be made to justify such things as the imposition of invidious distinctions on the social structure of the community, the use of dishonesty and deceit in human affairs, or the denial of access to knowledge vital to the problem-solving processes of the community by vested interests.

In contrast, the ceremonial mode of valuation does not entail such limitations. As shown in the tableau, combinations of all three types of behavior can be correlated through ceremonial values. This is made possible by the very nature of the logic of ceremonial valuation. Resting as it does on the notion of "sufficient reason," the logic of ceremonial valuation may be used to rationalize any combination of behaviors. All that is required is a plausible argument to validate any particular correlation of behavior. The boundaries of the logic are as limitless as the human imagination. A particular pattern of behavior may be required "because the memory of man does not run to the contrary," or because "it is the will of God," or because "blacks are inherently inferior to whites," or because "it is consistent with the requirements of national security."

There should be no difficulty in seeing that purely ceremonial behaviors will be correlated by a ceremonial value. But what can be said about those patterns of behavior in which a ceremonial value correlates a ceremonial and an instrumental behavior? Such cases arise in C-2 and C-4 in the tableau. (Note that they do not arise in C-3 or C-5 where the ceremonial value gives ceremonial significance to the behaviors designated "B_{ci}.") In these instances, instrumental behavior is "encapsulated" within a ceremonially warranted behavioral pattern, thereby incorporating instrumental behavior in a ceremonially prescribed outcome.

Bronsilaw Malinowski provided a detailed description of such behavioral patterns in his account of the canoe-building practices of the Trobriand islanders.[13] According to Malinowski, two kinds of behavior are clearly involved in the canoe-building activities of the Trobrianders; one is ceremonial, the other instrumental. "The building of the sea-going canoe," he says, "is inextricably bound up with [the rituals of the Kula magic]. . . . the technicalities of construction are interrupted and punctuated by magical rites."[14] For example, before the tree from which the canoe will be carved can be felled, the magician must make an offering to the woodsprite that presumably inhabits the tree and utter an incantation designed to persuade the woodsprite to leave the tree. It is only after this ritual has been performed that the canoe builder can proceed to chop down the tree.

The Trobrianders are aware of the differences in the behavior of the magician and the craftsman. They apply instrumental criteria to the evaluation of the technical competence of the craftsman and the results of his efforts. It is clear that they understand that the rituals performed by the magician, however mystically potent they are presumed to be, "will not make up for bad workmanship." Nevertheless, the Trobrianders would never consider building a canoe except under the guidance of the Kula magic, for they believe that "a canoe built without magic would be unseaworthy."[15] It is the logic of magic and ritual, not the logic of the tool-skill nexus of canoe-building technology, that determines the correlation of the magician's behavior with that of the craftsman in the above example. In this instance, ceremonial considerations are dominant, and a ceremonially warranted standard of judgment correlates the behaviors of the magician and the craftsman. The instrumental behavior of the craftsman is "encapsulated" within a ceremonially warranted pattern of behavior. It should be obvious that there could be no instrumental warrant for this pattern of behavior because the technology of canoe-building is a causal continuum confined to the realm of evidentially demonstrable consequences within which the ritualistic behavior of the magician has no meaning.

The Concept of Ceremonial Dominance

The fact that an instrumental behavior can be encapsulated within a ceremonially warranted pattern of behavior leads to a broader set of considerations. In the case of the Trobrianders, Malinowski argues that magic is not merely an extraneous function "having nothing to do with the real work or its organisation." The presumed mystical powers of the magician give him the invidious status of a "natural leader whose command is obeyed, who can fix dates, apportion work, and keep the worker up to the mark."[16] In the language of present analysis, Malinowski is saying that the entire range of the division of labor in the canoe-building process is dominated by ceremonial considerations.[17] For the Trobrianders, the division of labor inherent in the technology of canoe-building is not a sufficient basis for the correlation of behavior. Something more is required to integrate the particular activities of canoe-building with other aspects of the culture; it is the function of magic to meet this requirement. Consequently, the instrumental warrant for the correlation of behavior inherent in the technology of canoe-building is dominated by a "higher order" of warrantability as the division of labor in this critical enterprise is required to meet the standard of "ceremonial adequacy."

This is the phenomenon of ceremonial dominance, and it is by no means confined to the Trobriand society. Institutional economists believe that it is a characteristic of all cultures. In modern, industrial societies, ceremonial dominance is rationalized not through magic but through ideologies. The magician's incantations are replaced by the harangues of the ideologue. Mystical potency is no longer perceived as the ability to drive out the demons of the lagoon; it is now perceived as the capacity to mobilize the *Herrenvolk,* or to awaken entrepreneurial spirit from its slumbers, or to inspire greater productive efforts by the new socialist man. All ideologies possess ritualistic language that serves to block inquiry and to mystify the warrant for socially prescribed patterns of behavior. Thus the *"untermensch"* may be sent to the gas chambers, "property rights" may be viewed as superior to "human rights," and "counterrevolutionaries" may be sent to the gulags.[18]

Clarence E. Ayres argued that ceremonially warranted patterns of behavior stifle progress precisely because they are "past-binding" and inhibit technological innovation.[19] He noted, however, that ceremonial practices are believed by members of the culture to be the source of instrumental efficiency; thus the Trobrianders believed that a canoe, no matter how well built, would not be sea-worthy unless the prescribed magic rituals were performed. This confusion abounds, Ayres said, because "'ceremonial adequacy' is an imitation of technological efficiency. The tribal medicine man purports to be altering the course of events in imitation of the tool activities by which technicians really do alter the course of events."[20] As indicated above, it is the encapsulation of instrumental behavior within a ceremonially warranted behavioral pattern that gives plausibility to this imitation of instrumental efficiency by ceremonial adequacy.

Ayres argued that the degree to which the ceremonial practices of the community inhibit technological innovation will vary from culture to culture and from one historical epoch to another. The fact that technological innovations appear to occur with greater frequency in one culture as compared to another is in part because of the relative degree of "permissiveness" in the ceremonial practices of the two cultures.[21] For example, the ceremonial practices of feudalism were less permissive of technological innovation than the ceremonial practices of the system of mercantile capitalism that emerged from the "cracks and crevices" of feudalism. The permissiveness of the ceremonial practices of a culture is a function of ceremonial dominance as defined above. In the analysis that follows, the phrase "index of ceremonial dominance" will be used to indicate the degree of permissiveness within the institutional structure. The two concepts are inversely related; thus a high index of ceremonial dominance would indicate that the institution has a very low degree of permissiveness with respect to technological innovation.[22]

The Dynamic Character of Technological Innovation

The foregoing analysis of ceremonial dominance required the premature introduction of the concept of technological innovation. Since this concept is fundamental to the institutionalist theory of institutional change, it requires careful consideration, and it is to that task the discussion now turns.

The Meaning of "Technology"

The term "technology" has been defined in various ways by institutionalists. While there is a continuity of meaning to the various definitions, the term continues to produce confusion and often heated dispute.[23] Part of the problem arises from the failure of institutionalists always to distinguish clearly technology as a process from the tools or machinery that embody technology. Sloppy conceptualization along these lines was encouraged by Veblen's (almost) invariant coupling of the words "machine" and "technology." Despite the fact that he habitually used the term "machine technology," it is clear that he never intended the term to be confined to "machines" as such. Accordingly, when speaking of the relationship of technological change to economic development, he says,

> the changes that take place in the mechanical contrivances are an expression of changes in the human factor. Change in the material facts breed further change only through the human factor. It is in the human material that the continuity of development is to be looked for; and it is here, therefore, that the motor forces of the process of economic development must be studied if they are to be studied in action at all.[24]

Technology for Veblen was a process that arose out of the human proclivity for workmanship and the exercise of intellectual curiosity. It was embodied in the tool-skill nexus of problem-solving activities. The essence of technological change, therefore, was the change in "prevalent habits of thought" associated with a given state of the arts and sciences. Veblen saw technological change as a process of "cumulative causation." The problem-solving processes of the community generate innovations in the ways of "bringing material things to account," thereby changing the industrial environment in which the community works; and this changed environment produces further changes in prevalent habits of thought about how to conduct the community's affairs.

Clarence Ayres endeavored to explicate the broad implications of Veblen's notion of machine technology. Comparing Veblen's analysis with John Dewey's philosophy, Ayres argued that Veblen's conception of the technological process was the logical equivalent of Dewey's notion of "instrumentalism."[25] According to Ayres, Dewey faced the problem of formulating a concept that would "identify the intellectual procedures of science with the use of instruments and at the same time . . . identify the instruments of scientists with the tools which are in still wider use by artisans and craftsmen."[26] This is precisely what Veblen had accomplished in his overall treatment of the interplay of science and technology in his description of the manner in which the evolution of the scientific point of view had transformed society.[27] In Ayres's view, the confluence of the ideas of Veblen and Dewey require us to think of "technology" in the broadest possible terms. "So defined, technology includes mathematical journals and symphonic scores no less than skyscrapers and assembly lines, since all these are equally the product of human hands as well as human brains."[28]

This broadening of the conception of technology to incorporate the full sweep of the arts and sciences, does not render the notion vacuous; on the contrary, it enhances its theoretical precision. As Anne Mayhew has argued so convincingly, Ayres's integration of Veblen and Dewey brings us to the recognition that the essence of the technological process is "instrumental valuing."[29] The instrumental mode of valuation is the thread of continuity running through all of the arts and sciences which permits "the evaluation of the consequences of any particular use of a tool."[30] With reference to the foregoing discussion of the ceremonial mode of valuation, it is useful to note that Mayhew cites H.H. Liebhafsky's telling observation that ceremonialism inhibits progress precisely because it "inhibits . . . the free inquiry necessary for instrumental valuing."[31]

Thus "technology" is broadly conceived in the institutionalist literature. This is consistent with the "holistic" nature of the institutionalist methodology, which facilitates an understanding of the workings of the economic system as a cultural process.[32] From this perspective, the fund of knowledge available to the community for problem-solving purposes is composed of the instrumentally warranted knowledge generated across the full range of the arts and sciences. "Technological innovation," therefore, can originate in any field of inquiry or creative endeavor. This broadened view of technology also encompasses the notion that the knowledge fund is expanded through the efforts of the entire community, not just some academic or scientific elite. The proclivities for workmanship and intellectual curiosity, the well-springs of the pursuit of instrumentally warranted knowledge, are the common heritage of all members of the community. Incremental contributions to the knowledge fund occur on a daily basis through the efforts of individuals found in all walks of life and at all levels of the socioeconomic structure of the community. This idea was captured brilliantly in a statement that Solomon Fabricant made before the Joint Economic Committee of the U.S. Congress in 1978.

> In short, the high productivity of the American economy is the end result of a great many different activities involving decisions by millions of scientists, engineers, and technicians in laboratories and industry; educators in schools, universities, and training centers; managers and owners of production facilities; workers and their families and unions; and government officials. Increase of this country's output per hour over the long run is the result of the energy, ingenuity, and skill with which all of us, individually and as a Nation, manage our resources of production.[33]

The institutionalist view that "capital" can only be meaningfully identified as the "immaterial capital" of the knowledge and skills possessed by the community at large is founded on the kind of evidence to which Fabricant alludes in this statement.[34]

The Technological Dynamic

The technological process is inherently dynamic. Technological innovation creates new possibilities for inquiry and problem-solving. Whether it takes the form of ideas embodied in a new mathematical equation, a new physical implement, or a new technique for organizing problem-solving activity, technological innovation involves a change in behavior, and changes in behavior create new problems for the community in the correlation of behavior. This is the process that Veblen called "cumulative causation." He captures the essence of the process in the following passage:

> All economic change is a change in the economic community—a change in the community's methods of turning material things to account. The change is always in the last resort a change in habits of thought. This is true even of changes in the mechanical processes of industry. A given contrivance for affecting certain material ends becomes a circumstance which effects the further growth of habits of thought—habitual modes of procedure—and so becomes a point of departure for further development of the methods of compassing the ends sought and for further variation of ends that are sought to be compassed.[35]

The observation that the solution of one problem creates a whole host of new problems, trite though it may be, is nevertheless, pertinent. The expansion of the community's fund of knowledge is not only instrumental to the solution of problems, it is the means by which new problems are identified.

It would appear that anthropological research and studies of the history of technology support the proposition that technological innovation is developmental in the sense of being cumulative, combinatorial and accelerating in character. As a cumulative process, it exhibits a one-way time vector; the expansion of the knowledge fund through technological innovation is an irreversible process through time. This is true because the emergence of new technologies involves the combination of previously existing technologies. The time rate of technological innovation appears to approximate an exponential function, exhibiting a very flat curve through history until the last three centuries. William F. Ogburn, among others, attributed the exponential expansion of the community's knowledge fund to the cumulative nature of its growth. As Ogburn puts it: "The fact that material culture is accumulative, that is, new inventions are not lost but added to the existing stock, and the fact (if it be a fact) that the larger the stock the greater the number of new inventions, suggests at first glance the compound interest law."[36] Marc R. Tool uses a graphical presentation of this proposition in his book *The Discretionary Economy* to illustrate the "exponential growth in the knowledge of continuum."[37] These, then, are the major premises upon which the institutionalist hypothesis of the technological dynamic is based.

Clarence Ayres laid particular emphasis on the combinatorial aspect of technological innovation. The thrust of his argument is contained in the following passage:

> knowledge and skills accumulate. They do so . . . because knowledge and skills are objectified in tools and symbols. . . .
> The importance of such objectification of this whole aspect of culture is not merely that of accumulation. Rather accumulation is only the minor premise to innovation. The major premise is the combining of previously exisiting "culture traits" to form new ones.[38]

Ayres's emphasis on the idea that technological innovation is a combinatorial process bears a striking resemblance to Nicholas Georgescu-Roegen's conception of evolution as "the emergence of novelty by combination."[39] In both formulations, the evolutionary process is couched in terms of a "developmental continuity" that rises out of a combination of previously existing traits. Unlike the evolutionary processes of the biological and physical realms, the emergence of novelty by combination in human culture results from the choices made in the problem-solving processes. In other words, the rate and direction of social evolution is subject to the discretionary control of mankind. Using terminology established earlier in this discussion regarding patterns of behavior, technological innovation involves changes in instrumentally warranted patterns of behavior. Such changes are made possible by the mode of instrumental valuation, which permits changes in the standards of judgment by which behavior is correlated. J. Fagg Foster used the term "developmental continuity" to identify both the meaning of evolution and the method by which it was accomplished, that is, instrumental valuing.[40] Thus it can be seen that the institutionalist hypothesis regarding the technological dynamic is conceptually linked to the instrumental theory of value.

The Interface of the Knowledge Fund and the Institutional Structure

At any given point in time, the institutional structure of society incorporates a given fund of knowledge that is distributed between ceremonial and instrumental patterns of behavior. Knowledge is either "encapsulated" within ceremonial patterns or "embodied" within instrumental patterns of behavior. This distinction in language is required to indicate that the index of ceremonial dominance determines the permissable use of existing knowledge in the community's problem-solving processes. The knowledge fund is translated into problem-solving activities through instrumentally warranted patterns of behavior. But because of the phenomenon of ceremonial dominance, only that part of the knowledge fund that can be reconciled with the existing value structure of the community would be sanctioned for problem-solving purposes. In other words, the instrumental behavior that is permitted within the community is required to meet the standard of ceremonial adequacy. Thus knowledge that cannot be reconciled with the need to justify existing patterns of status, power, and other forms of invidious distinctions would not be intentionally sanctioned.

While ceremonial dominance determines the ceremonial feasibility of the range of permissable behavior, it is the knowledge fund that determines the instrumental feasibility of problem-solving activities. When these two standards of feasibility are taken into account, the interface of the fund of knowledge with the institutional structure defines an "institutional space" that may be partitioned into four sectors delineating the ceremonial and instrumental feasibility of behavioral patterns.[41] These four sectors are presented schematically in Figure 1 and can be identified as follows:

Sector I.   In which the behavioral patterns are both ceremonially and instrumentally feasible.

Sector II. In which behavioral patterns are instrumentally feasible but ceremonially nonfeasible.

Sector III. In which the behavioral patterns are ceremonially feasible but instrumentally nonfeasible.

Sector IV. In which behavioral patterns are both ceremonially and instrumentally nonfeasible.

Each of these sectors will be discussed in turn.

Sector IV can be immediately disregarded since it is an empty set. Behavioral patterns in this sector, even if they could be imagined, are both ceremonially and instrumentally nonfeasible; they would not fall within either the myth structure or the technology of the community. Sector I, on the other hand, is that sector in which the actual institutional structure exists. The patterns of behavior in this sector are tech-

1092   Paul D. Bush

	INSTRUMENTALLY FEASIBLE	INSTRUMENTALLY NONFEASIBLE
CEREMONIALLY FEASIBLE	SECTOR I (Sector of Ceremonial Encapsulation)	SECTOR III (Sector of Lysenko Effects)
CEREMONIALLY NONFEASIBLE	SECTOR II (Sector of Lost Instrumental Efficiency)	SECTOR IV (Empty Set)

Figure 1. *The Partitioning of Institutional Space by the Interface of the Knowledge Fund and the Value Structure of the Institution.*

nologically feasible, and they meet the standard of ceremonial adequacy. Sector II defines, for a given state of the knowledge fund, the technological possibilities of the community that are denied to it by the existing level of ceremonial dominance. As will be shown below, it is into this sector that the community would move if "progressive" institutional changes reduced the degree of ceremonial dominance. Sector III may at first blush appear to be socially irrelevant, but as the subsequent discussion will show, it has always been a factor in human history, particularly in the history of the twentieth century. Sector III contains behavioral patterns that involve an extension of the myth structure that not even the ceremonial encapsulation of instrumental behavior can sustain without a loss of instrumental efficiency to the community at large. Such extensions of the myth structure will be referred to later as "Lysenko effects." It is into this sector that the community would move if "regressive" institutional change increased the degree of ceremonial dominance.

The Process of Institutional Change

This discussion has now reached the stage where the process of institutional change can be brought under direct inspection. Both the "regressive" and "progressive" forms of institutional change will be delineated. Fundamental to a discussion of either is the concept of "ceremonial encapsulation." In the case of "regressive" institutional change, a particular type of ceremonial encapsulation, the "Lysenko" type, will be shown to be the cause of what might be called the *absolute* "triumph of imbecile institutions over life and culture."[42]

Ceremonial Encapsulation

In the foregoing discussion of the technological dynamic, it was argued that the dynamic force for change in the institutional structure is the growth of the community's fund of knowledge. The phenomenon of ceremonial dominance, however, poses an obstacle to the absorption and diffusion of the new knowledge in the form of technological innovation. Consequently, a new discovery in the arts or sciences will be incorporated into behavioral patterns only to the extent that the community believes that the previously existing degree of ceremonial dominance can be maintained. Technological innovations will be permitted only if it is anticipated that they will not disrupt the existing value structure of the community. This will involve changes in behavioral patterns, but any increase of instrumentally warranted behavioral patterns will be offset by concomitant increases in ceremonially warranted patterns of behavior. The new ceremonially warranted patterns are required to "encapsulate" the increase in instrumentally warranted behavioral patterns. It is through this process that the community seeks to attain a *status quo ante* with respect to its value structure. Hence, ceremonial encapsulation, to the extent that it is successful, denies to the community those technological innovations that the existing knowledge fund is capable of generating, thereby depriving the community of higher levels of instrumental efficiency in the problem-solving processes.[43]

Two important qualifications must be introduced to the discussion at this point. First, it should be noted that the theoretical formulation of "ceremonial encapsulation" does not require the assumption that the community is omniscient in its effort to "encapsulate" new knowledge. There may be considerable slippage in the process, and technological innovations inconsistent with the existing value structure may indeed be adopted without a full comprehension of the consequences of doing so. To the extent that such innovations "slip through" the ceremonial net, so to speak, some amount of "progressive" institutional change (as defined below) will take place.[44] Second, it must be noted that both anthropological and contemporary studies indicate that all societies attempt to maximize the efficiency with which they employ their existing (ceremonially encapsulated) technology. Whatever the community's taboos may be that bound use of knowledge, the knowledge that is deemed ceremonially adequate is used to the fullest. If one must grow rice with little more than one's bare hands, it would be wise to study the rice-growing methods of the Vietnamese peasant. And if one must navigate among the South Pacific archipelagos in an outrigger canoe, it would be desirable to do so in one built by the Trobrianders. Veblen's "instinct of workmanship" appears to manifest itself even under the most trying ceremonial circumstances.

It is the attempt to preserve the existing value structure in the face of technological innovation that gives the ceremonial practices of the community what Ayres called their "past-binding" character.[45] This notion is similar to Ogburn's concept of "cultural lag," which he formulated to explain the lag in the correlation of adjustments between two interrelated aspects of culture.[46] The concept of ceremonial encapsulation offers a precise explanation of the cultural lag involved in the institutional response to technological innovation. It focuses on the fact that although "past-binding," the ceremonial practices of the community are "permissive" in the sense that some aspects of the expanding knowledge fund will be absorbed into the behavioral patterns of the community. As indicated above, this involves the effort to preserve the existing value structure. Thus it is the value structure that correlates behavior within the institution that "lags." Even though there is some technological innovation, as long as the value structure remains unchanged, it cannot be said that an "institutional change" has taken place. Under the logic set forth in the present analysis, an "institutional change" does not take place unless there is a change in the index of ceremonial dominance; which is to say, an institutional change occurs only when there is a change in the value structure of the institution.

There are three identifiable types of ceremonial encapsulation of the knowledge fund.[47] For purposes of identification, the three types of ceremonial encapsulation will be called: (1) the "past-binding" type, (2) the "future-binding" type, and (3) the "Lysenko" type.

The "past-binding" type. The first type of ceremonial encapsulation for which the term "cultural lag" is most appropriate involves the "past-binding" resistance of the traditions of the community to the absorption and diffusion of technological innovations. The community responds to unanticipated advances in the arts and sciences (either indigenous or borrowed from other cultures) by attempting to minimize the impact of the technological innovation on existing habits of thought and behavior. Since technological innovation requires changes in instrumentally warranted patterns of behavior, it carries with it a threat to the stability of the ceremonially warranted patterns of behavior that traditionally encapsulate the knowledge fund that is the common heritage of the community. In the face of this threat, conscious efforts are made to shore up the existing value structure by an elaboration of ceremonial practices designed to minimize the innovation's dislocation of the status quo. Veblen described this type of ceremonial encapsulation as follows: "The innovation finds its way into the system of use and wont at the cost of some derangement to the system, provokes new usages, conventions, beliefs, and principles of conduct, in part directed

advisedly to its utilisation or to the mitigation of its immediate consequences, or to the diversion of its usufruct to the benefit of given individuals or classes."[48] While this type of ceremonial encapsulation is
most easily identified in traditional, preindustrial cultures, which exhibit very slow time rates of technological diffusion, the cultural lags it
produces are also quite evident in modern society. For example, Ogburn argued that the historical delay in the development of workmen's
compensation laws, coming almost a century after the onset of the industrial revolution, constituted a major cultural lag.[49] But perhaps the
most widely recognized evidence of this type of ceremonial encapsulation in the standard economics literature is to be found in those studies
that report the frustration of the best-laid plans for economic development in less developed economies.

The "future-binding" type. The second type of ceremonial encapsulation involves the active development of technological innovations for
the purpose of strengthening and extending the control of vested interests over the life of the community. In this case, the introduction of
technological innovations into the life processes of the community is
carefully coordinated with the formulation of an appropriate mythol-
ogy and related ceremonial practices that rationalize and enforce the
legitimacy of the control over the technology by the vested interests
that have captured it. The strategy is to promote, capture, and control
all those technological innovations that can reasonably be anticipated
to have a bearing on the ceremonially warranted exercise of power by
the vested interests over the life processes of the community. To the
extent that vested interests can maintain control over the process of
technological innovation, they effectively control the future of the community, hence the term "future-binding."

It is this second type of ceremonial encapsulation that has been the
main preoccupation of institutional economists from Veblen to the present. Veblen formulated the problem in terms of his distinction between "pecuniary" and "industrial" employments, in which the
ceremonially warranted pecuniary employments were dominant over
the instrumentally warranted industrial employments.[50]

Contemporary institutionalists have identified this type of ceremonial encapsulation in several recent works. F. Gregory Hayden has
offered extensive evidence of the capacity of giant enterprises in the
chemical, farm machinery, and agribusiness industries to encapsulate
science and technology for the purpose of increasing their own power
and profits at the expense of instrumental efficiency in maintaining a
healthy food chain, the conservation of viable agricultural acreage, and
the preservation of vital social and ecological systems.[51] The late Louis

J. Junker analyzed the ceremonial encapsulation of knowledge pertaining to diet and health by what he called the "American food power system." While many of the conclusions he drew in this study are highly controversial, he offered compelling evidence that those industries involved in the production, distribution, and sale of commodities and services relating to nutrition and health have the power to prevent the community from utilizing the complete fund of knowledge available for the proper maintenance of health and dietary practices. In the concluding paragraphs of his study, Junker summarizes the social significance of this "future-binding" type of ceremonial encapsulation as follows:

> As a general theoretical principle, the ceremonial-instrumental dichotomy posits the existence of a gap between the growing knowledge fund (and the value structure it entails) and the vested interests of the existing power system that governs and exploits its use. All the forces that encapsulate and control knowledge for the benefit of limited vested interests create master-servant relationships between themselves and the community at large, and this produces organized waste. Genuine knowledge sets the outer limits of human potential. But ceremonial forces encapsulate genuine knowledge, and thus the human potential, by confining the use of knowledge within the framework of the core values of the established power structure. This encapsulation reduces the community's flexibility and adaptivity to the potentialities of the new knowledge. In the case of the food power system, the encapsulation can lead quite literally to death.[52]

The Hayden and Junker studies, while focusing on specific industrial clusters, lay bare the underlying process of ceremonial encapsulation that is endemic to the economy as a whole. Other institutionalists have produced works that reveal the specific means by which the process contaminates the entire society.

William M. Dugger's study of "corporate hegemony" analyzes the social mechanisms by which this type of ceremonial encapsulation is transmitted throughout the community.[53] It is Dugger's contention that the corporation has become the dominant institution in American society and that this dominance is manifest in its hegemonic influence over all other institutions of the society. This hegemony is maintained, he says, "not through a conspiracy, but through four social mechanisms": subordination, contamination, emulation, and mystification. He identifies each as follows: "Subordination ties all institutions together so that noncorporate institutions are used as means to corporate ends. Contamination puts corporate role motives into noncorporate roles. Emulation allows corporate leaders to gain acceptance, even respect, in non-corporate leadership roles. And mystification covers the corporate hegemony with a protective (magic) cloak."[54] It is through these mechanisms, Dugger argues, that the corporate interests are able to control the availability and use of knowledge throughout the society. One of the most significant features of his analysis is his treatment of the ceremonial encapsulation of institutions of higher learning by corporate interests.[55] He shows how the university's instrumentally warranted social goals to pursue unfettered inquiry and to expand the intellectual horizons of its students have been subordinated to the ceremonially warranted corporate goals of industry-specific research and the vocationalization of the curriculum. Beginning with Veblen's *The Higher Learning in America,* institutionalists have stressed the critical importance of the educational system (most particularly, the system of higher education) to the development of society's capacity to adapt to growth in the knowledge fund.[56] Dugger's analysis reveals how this critical educational mission has been ceremonially encapsulated to the detriment of the community.

John Munkirs has also produced a powerful analysis of the American economy that comes to rest, in part, on his identification of the ceremonial encapsulation of technology by what he calls the system of centralized private sector planning (CPSP), which is dominated by giant financial and industrial corporations. One of his main contentions is that the reality of centralized private sector planning is only dimly perceived by policy makers and the public at large because their view of the real world is obscured by the mythical *Weltanshauung* of capitalist ideology. In the language of the present analysis, this ceremonially warranted perception of reality has impaired our society's capacity to develop instrumentally warranted social policies. Munkirs sums up the matter in the following passage:

> Unfortunately, in America, the real choices that our technological knowledge make possible (choices between different production and distribution systems, for example, centralized versus decentralized) have been circumscribed by, or encapsulated within, our capitalistic ideology and, in particular, by the values of self-interest, profit seeking, and laissez-faire. In brief, the particular type of centralized planning that exists in America today is due neither to technological determinism nor to conspiratorial machinations. Rather, CPSP is a direct result of combining the values of self-interest, profit seeking, and laissez-faire with certain technological possibilities.[57]

Munkirs's detailed analysis of the structure and functioning of the centralized private sector planning system provides dramatic evidence of the existence of "future-binding" ceremonial encapsulation throughout the entire economy of the United States.

While space does not permit an extended discussion of the subject, it must be noted that a driving force for "future-binding" ceremonial encapsulation in the twentieth century has been the military-industrial complexes of the nations of the world. Veblen set forth the first systematic analysis of the military-industrial complex in 1917. He demonstrated how the ceremonial preoccupation with nationalism, patriotism, and the pecuniary employments encapsulate technology and the industrial employments at the expense of life and culture.[58] Fortified by appropriately formulated myths (for instance, "the balance of powers," "mutually assured destruction," "strategic defense initiative"), the military-industrial complex has virtually unlimited capacity to produce, capture, and control modern technology. The degree of ceremonial dominance enjoyed by the military-industrial complex in the United States is indicated by the fact that most Americans take it for granted that not only national security but economic stability is dependent on a "strong national defense."

The "Lysenko" type. In the "past-binding" and "future-binding" types of ceremonial encapsulation, genuine knowledge is encapsulated by the ceremonial beliefs and practices of the community. In the "Lysenko" type of ceremonial encapsulation, on the other hand, the community attempts to achieve instrumentally nonfeasible outcomes through ceremonially warranted behavioral patterns. This is the extreme case of ceremonial practices imitating instrumental efficiency. Under the concept of institutional space set forth earlier, such an effort pushes the community into Sector III, which entails ceremonially feasible, but instrumentally nonfeasible patterns of behavior. Spurious "knowledge" is substituted for genuine knowledge, and ceremonially warranted patterns of behavior *displace* instrumentally warranted patterns of behavior in critical areas of the community's problem-solving processes.

This type of ceremonial encapsulation is called the "Lysenko" type, after Trofim D. Lysenko, whose name has become synonymous with the corruption and manipulation of science for ideological purposes. Lysenko was the Russian "agrobiologist" who argued that genetic change could be induced through the environmental conditioning of biological organisms. Although his theories were diametrically opposed to the evidentially warranted hypotheses developed over the previous century in the field of genetics, they were embraced by Stalin as the only biological theories consistent with Marxist-Stalinist ideology. Ly-

The Theory of Institutional Change   1099

senko's theories became the official dogma in agronomy and the supporting biological sciences. The application of Lysenko's theories to the growing of field crops produced disastrous results; nevertheless, Lysenkoism dominated Soviet science for thirty years. But perhaps the most devastating effect Lysenkoism had on the reduction of instrumental efficiency in the Soviet Union was not its impact on the practice of agriculture, but its impact on the practice of science.[59]

History offers numerous examples of the "Lysenko" type of ceremonial encapsulation, but space limitations permit only a brief mention of two cases (one historical, and the other potential) that have emerged in the twentieth century. The most notorious historical case is, of course, the Nazi theory of Ayrian racial supremacy. The Nazis did not invent anti-Semitism and racism; these virulent forms of invidious discrimination were the cultural heritage of Europe. The Nazi innovation was to formulate a theory that would provide a cloak of "scientific" legitimacy for the racial laws adopted in the Third Reich. The new, spurious "science" displaced genuine science, thereby providing the intellectual foundation for the monstrous crimes against humanity that followed. Turning to the potential case, while it is perhaps not the same threat to civilization that the Nazi racial theories were, the so-called science of "creationism" is, nevertheless, a contemporary example of a "Lysenko" type of ceremonial encapsulation going somewhere to happen. Creationists, encouraged by the moral support of President Reagan, are engaged in a nationwide campaign to place "creationism on a par with classical evolution in public school instruction."[60] Aside from the damage this would cause to the teaching of science, one can only speculate on the broader social ramifications of a successful creationist campaign to substitute religious dogma for the processes of inquiry.

The Definition of Institutional Change

Institutional change takes the form of a change in the value structure of the institution. A change in the value structure may be measured theoretically by a change in the institution's index of ceremonial dominance. The index of ceremonial dominance reflects the dominance of ceremonially warranted values over instrumentally warranted values in the correlation of behavior in the behavioral patterns of the institution. An increase in the index of ceremonial dominance entails the displacement of instrumentally warranted values by ceremonially warranted values in the correlation of behavior. An increase in the index of ceremonial dominance signifies a "regressive" institutional change. A decrease in the index of ceremonial dominance entails the displacement of ceremonially warranted values by instrumentally warranted values in the correlation of behavior. A decrease in the index of ceremonial dominance signifies a "progressive" institutional change. As already indicated in the foregoing discussion of "past-binding" and "future-binding" ceremonial encapsulation, the index of ceremonial dominance may remain unchanged if ceremonially warranted patterns of behavior increase at a rate sufficient to encapsulate increases in instrumentally warranted patterns of behavior brought about by changes in the community's fund of knowledge. In such cases, there is no institutional change.

"Regressive" Institutional Change

The "Lysenko" type of ceremonial encapsulation (called a "Lysenko effect") generates "regressive" institutional change by causing the *displacement* of instrumentally warranted patterns of behavior by ceremonially warranted patterns of behavior, thereby raising the index of ceremonial dominance in the community. This is a quite different outcome from the institutional adjustments associated with either "past-binding" or "future-binding" ceremonial encapsulation. In those cases, the index of ceremonial dominance remains unchanged, and there is a *net increase* in the instrumental efficiency of the community, meager though it may be. In the case of a "Lysenko effect," there is a *net loss* of instrumental efficiency because there is no way to maintain legitimate scientific or technological practices in those parts of the community affected directly or indirectly by the intrusion of the spurious "science." The Russian agronomists and biologists who opposed Lysenkoism were expelled from the academies or worse. Agricultural practices were modified to meet the Lysenkoist criteria, and agricultural productivity declined. A similar fate befell the German scientists, intellectuals, and ordinary citizens who disputed Nazi dogma. Their options were: (1) remain on the faculties, join the party, and teach the despised doctrines; (2) speak out against these intellectual outrages and risk death or the concentration camps; or (3) emigrate. The loss of instrumental efficiency to the community was measured ultimately by the Holocaust and the death and destruction of World War II.

While one can be sanguine that "regressive" institutional changes are ultimately reversible, since the demonstrable adverse consequences of spurious "knowledge" cannot be long endured in the life processes of the community without a sensed awareness that something is amiss,

Veblen admonished us to remember that "history records more frequent and more spectacular instances of the triumph of imbecile institutions over life and culture than of peoples who have by force of
instinctive insight saved themselves alive out of a desperately precarious institutional situation."[61] Lysenkoism lasted for thirty years in
Russia; and while the Third Reich lasted for only twelve, the cost of
reversing the "regressive" institutional changes it spawned were ultimately borne by the entire world.

Progressive Institutional Change

"Progressive" institutional change occurs when, *for a given fund of
knowledge,* ceremonial patterns of behavior are displaced by instrumental patterns of behavior.[62] This entails an increased reliance on instrumental values in the correlation of behavior within the community,
thereby lowering the index of ceremonial dominance. The displacement of ceremonial patterns by instrumental patterns of behavior
moves the institution into Sector II, which was defined by the interface
of the knowledge fund and the original index of ceremonial dominance.
Sector II, it will be recalled, isolates that institutional space in which
behavioral patterns are instrumentally feasible but ceremonially nonfeasible. In other words, this sector contains those behavioral patterns
that the knowledge fund makes possible but which cannot be undertaken because of ceremonial restraints on behavior. "Progressive" institutional change involves technological innovations that break down
those ceremonial barriers.

To reiterate, innovations in the arts and sciences bring about growth
in the fund of knowledge, but the new knowledge is incorporated into
the problem-solving processes only to the extent that it is possible for
the community to maintain the previously existing level of ceremonial
dominance. With the exception of the "Lysenko" type, the process of
ceremonial encapsulation involves some technological innovation.
This *is the first phase of institutional adjustment.* Even though the new
instrumental patterns of behavior generated through the technological
innovation are ceremonially encapsulated, they *are* integrated into the
experience of the community. The new standards of instrumental valuing they bring to the problem-solving processes have demonstrable
consequences that become known to the community. As the community becomes habituated to employing these new standards of judgment in the correlation of behavior, the learning process reveals new
opportunities for their application elsewhere in the problem-solving

processes. The diffusion of the new instrumental values throughout the community erodes the ideological foundations of those ceremonial practices that are dominant in the affected areas of activity. Eventually, instrumental standards of judgment displace ceremonial standards of judgment in the correlation of behavior in a range of problem-solving activities not contemplated in the original technological innovation. *"Progressive" institutional change is,* then *the second phase of the institutional adjustment* brought about by innovations in the arts and sciences.

Veblen's conception of "cumulative causation" explains the dynamics of the process that produces "progressive" institutional change. Technological innovation changes the objective circumstances of the community; the new set of circumstances alters habits of thought and behavior; these new habits of thought and behavior are projected into other areas of the community's experience, giving rise to further innovations in the arts and sciences, which, in turn, produce new technological innovations in the community's efforts "to turn material things to account."[63] Veblen believed that the change in the material circumstances of the culture brought about through the introduction of machine technology during the Industrial Revolution conditioned working people to think in terms of cause and effect. "The machine," he said, "throws out anthropomorphic habits of thought."[64] This affects not only the ability of working people to become consciously aware of the manner in which their behavior is correlated in the workplace, but also their ability to think in causal terms about broader social relationships that affect the life processes of the community. Machine technology creates the material circumstances that are inhospitable to those habits of thought that rationalize ceremonial patterns of behavior. "Its scheme of knowledge and of inference is based on the laws of material causation, not those of immemorial custom, authenticity, or authoritative enactment."[65] Thus the working people in an industrial society are less likely to submit to the kind of master-servant relationship that existed under feudalism. The industrial system gives rise to an "animus of insubordination" and the individual's status shifts from "subject" to "citizen."[66]

A critical factor in bringing about "progressive" institutional change is a sensed awareness within the community that there is a need to modify habitual patterns of thought and behavior in order to achieve a higher level of instrumental efficiency in the problem-solving processes. Veblen saw this sensed awareness arising out of the change in the material circumstances of the community brought about by the introduction of machine technology. Other factors affecting the material circumstances of the community can also bring about such a sensed awareness. Clarence Ayres stressed the importance of the "frontier experience" in breaking down the allegiance to traditional patterns of behavior.[67] Environmental catastrophes that disrupt the physical habitat of the community can also have a profound effect on the community's willingness to consider alternative patterns of behavior as a simple matter of survival. Finally, contact with other cultures through war or trade can induce a sensed awareness of new possibilities for social adaptation.[68]

One additional brief comment must be made on a subject that should be given detailed attention, and that is the dynamic interrelationship between "progressive" institutional change and growth in the knowledge fund. It is clear that there is a feed-back relationship between "progressive" institutional change and further growth in the knowledge fund. As the theory has been formulated so far, it is the change in the fund of knowledge, generated by the community-wide problem-solving processes (incorporating both formal and informal processes of inquiry), that provokes institutional adjustment. As the second phase of institutional adjustment ("progressive" institutional change) lowers the index of ceremonial dominance in the community, it becomes easier to absorb and diffuse technological innovations; *but it is also this process that accelerates the growth of knowledge.* As Milton Lower puts it, "knowledge increases in the degree that it is used."[69] The higher rates of technological innovation made possible by a lower index of ceremonial dominance provide the social environment conducive to the processes of inquiry throughout the culture. Thus, the growth of knowledge is both the cause and consequence of "progressive" institutional change. The dynamic relationship between the growth in knowledge and "progressive" institutional change is presented schematically in Figure 2.

The Limits to "Progressive" Institutional Change

There is, of course, nothing inevitable about "progressive" institutional change. Veblen expressed his generally pessimistic view about it when he warned of the "triumph of imbecile institutions over life and culture." The historical reality of "regressive" institutional change has already been acknowledged. Given the present state of the theory presented here and the level of empirical work associated with it, predictions regarding either the time rate or the direction of institutional

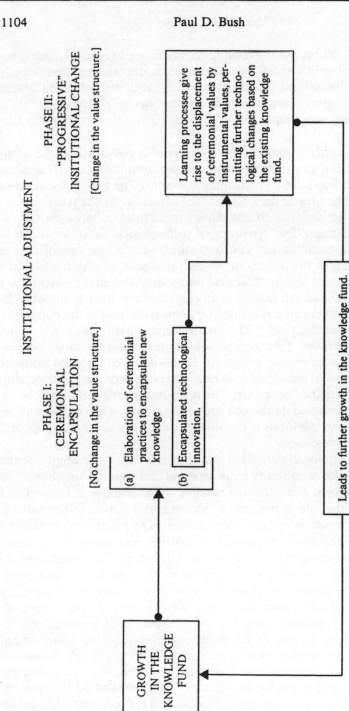

Figure 2. *The Dynamics of the Relationship between Growth in the Knowledge Fund and the "Progressive" Institutional Change.*

INSTITUTIONAL ADJUSTMENT

PHASE II:
"PROGRESSIVE"
INSTITUTIONAL CHANGE

[Change in the value structure.]

Learning processes give rise to the displacement of ceremonial values by instrumental values, permitting further technological changes based on the existing knowledge fund.

PHASE I:
CEREMONIAL
ENCAPSULATION

[No change in the value structure.]

(a) Elaboration of ceremonial practices to encapsulate new knowledge

(b) Encapsulated technological innovation.

Leads to further growth in the knowledge fund.

GROWTH IN THE KNOWLEDGE FUND

The Economics of Institutions

change on anything but the most narrowly defined range of cultural activity is probably impossible. Nevertheless, the theory does specify qualitative limitations on the generation and rate of institutional change. They are: (1) the availability of knowledge; (2) the capacity for understanding and adaptation; and (3) the principle of minimum dislocation.[70]

The availability of knowledge. The breadth and depth of the accumulated fund of knowledge available to the community clearly sets the limits to the feasibility of institutional change. The greater the fund of knowledge, the greater the potential for institutional change. Scientifically primitive societies do not exhibit rapid rates of "progressive" institutional change. The dynamics of technological innovation are at work in these communities as in any other, but the time rate of change is constrained by the paucity of the technological base from which the innovations must spring. "Cultural borrowing" can make a significant difference to the rate of change in any society since the transfer of technology from other cultures creates a quantum increase in the borrowing culture's knowledge fund.[71] The institutional consequences of this fact have been the focus of the institutionalist literature on economic development.[72] Development programs involving technological transfer from advanced to less-developed economies, in order to be successful, must anticipate the "progressive" institutional changes that will be required to accommodate the new technology; otherwise ceremonial encapsulation will significantly diminish the culture's ability to adopt and diffuse the technology.[73]

The capacity for understanding and adaptation. The ability of the members of the community to understand and adapt to the changes in habits of thought and behavior entailed by technological innovations affects the time rate of both the adoption and diffusion of the innovations. There must be some social mechanism to facilitate the changing of habits of thought if "progressive" institutional change is to occur. Veblen's analysis of the impact of the "discipline of the machine" on the institutional structure was premised on the fact that a broad cross-section of the population came into contact with machine technology on a daily basis. The workplace served as a "school of hard knocks" so to speak. Contemporary institutional economists lay greater stress on the educational system of the culture as the most important social mechanism performing this function. But, as the earlier discussion of Dugger's theory of corporate hegemony revealed, it is clear that the educational system can be so organized as to inhibit rather than enhance "progressive" institutional change. If it is organized along invidious lines that reflect the existing occupational structure, it will simply reinforce the status quo and contribute to increasingly sophisticated strategies for the ceremonial encapsulation of the knowledge fund. If it is to contribute to the community's capacity for understanding of and adaptation to advances in the knowledge fund, the educational system must be organized for that purpose. Baldwin Ranson states the matter plainly.

> Educational planners can promote economic progress by providing everyone with the skills necessary to master the best technology. That planning objective is not dictated by any occupational structure, but rather by the nature of technological progress: the more the community knows, the more it can learn. Transmitting the ability to adapt to evolving technological opportunities will maximize economic progress as well as educational excellence, not as measured by competitive superiority of one group over another, but by the growing potential for economic and social wellbeing of the entire community.[74]

In sum, the time rate of "progressive" institutional change is bounded by the community's capacity to learn the adaptive skills necessary to absorb technological innovation.

The principle of minimal dislocation. The principle of minimal dislocation is critical to an understanding of both the direction and rate of "progressive" institutional change.[75] The principle states that while technological change always involves dislocation in the institutional structure, the interdependence of the institutional structure is such that "progressive" institutional change is possible only if it involves a minimal dislocation of the behavioral patterns of the community. Technological innovation in the context of "progressive" institutional change always involves the displacement of ceremonial patterns of behavior, and it may also involve the displacement of outmoded technology. Such dislocation of the institutional structure is inherent in the process. But those patterns of behavior that are displaced by the technological innovation are interlinked with other patterns of behavior (both ceremonial and instrumental) throughout the institutional structure of the society. As the earlier analysis of behavioral patterns indicated, the variety of forms that behavioral patterns can take introduce considerable complexity into the institutional structure. Ceremonially warranted patterns of behavior may contain instrumental behavior as well as ceremonial behavior.[76] Thus care must be taken not to displace ceremonial practices that encapsulate instrumental activities vital to the problem-solving processes of the community.

To illustrate the argument, recall the case of canoe-building in the

Trobriand culture. The division of labor within the culture as a whole that regulated not only the tasks of the craftsmen in building the canoe but also the correlation of canoe-building with other activities of the culture was ceremonially encapsulated by a system of magic and ritual. A "progressive" institutional change that would free the division of labor in canoe-building from magic and ritual, but would not somehow provide for the reintegration of canoe-building with other activities of the community still under the rule of magic and ritual, would entail a maximum dislocation of the institutional structure. The attempt to introduce an instrumentally warranted division of labor in one part of the culture would disrupt the instrumentally vital (but ceremonially encapsulated) division of labor on a culture-wide basis. It is highly unlikely that any community (scientifically primitive or advanced) would knowingly undertake institutional changes that entail a maximal dislocation of the institutional structure, but this does not preclude the possibility that errors in judgment or lack of knowledge could lead to maximal dislocation. Thus the principle of minimal dislocation provides insight into the problems that must be addressed in any form of social or economic planning.[77]

The Discretionary Character of Institutional Change

Marc Tool describes "progressive" institutional change as change that "provides for the continuity of human life and the noninvidious recreation of community through the instrumental use of knowledge."[78] This language is descriptively accurate of the process in which ceremonially warranted patterns of behavior are displaced by instrumentally warranted patterns of behavior under conditions of minimal dislocation. It is the institutionalist view that this is *in fact* what happens when the community alters its behavior to accommodate the use of existing knowledge. But it is also clear that Tool's language states a social value principle that is applicable to the formulation of social policy. It provides a criterion for selecting among alternative institutional arrangements when the purpose is to achieve genuine progress in the community's problem-solving processes. Thus the theory of institutional change presented here achieves a dual purpose: it provides an explanation of the process of institutional change while at the same time it reveals the social value criterion most appropriate to the planning of the process.

It would not be historically accurate to suggest that all institutional changes result from the conscious formulation of social policy, and it has not been the author's intention to make such an argument. What has been argued is that the evolution of a culture results from the choices made to adopt or not to adopt the technological innovations. The intentional choice to improve the instrumental efficiency of the community through the adoption of a technological innovation does not necessarily involve the intention to throw over some aspect of the ceremonial practices of the culture. The displacement of ceremonially warranted patterns of behavior by instrumentally warranted patterns of behavior is a consequence of the extension of instrumental valuing in the correlation of behavior. The "progressive" institutional changes that have brought modern cultures to their present stage of development may have appeared to have been quite unremarkable at the time of their occurrence. This is most likely to be true of the process of technological diffusion wherein the adaptation to new technology requires incremental adjustments in the habits of thought and behavior over a broad cross-section of the community. Nevertheless, no matter how subtle the process, it involves the making of choices, and these choices define the evolutionary continuum of the culture.

A conscious awareness of the nature of the choices made in the process of social evolution is a precondition to the planning of that process. By revealing the nature of these choices, the institutionalist theory of institutional change demonstrates that social evolution is subject to the discretionary control of mankind. It is this realization that informs the institutionalist approach to public policy formation. In the institutionalist view, social problems arise when the institutional structure is unable to accommodate the noninvidious application of instrumentally warranted knowledge to the support of the life processes of the community. The solutions to social problems take the form of "progressive" institutional changes that will alter those ceremonially warranted patterns of behavior that thwart the extension of instrumental valuing in the problem-solving processes.

Tool argues that the social value principle that emerges in this theory of institutional change has the greatest potential for successful application within a democracy polity.[79] Those habits of thought that make instrumental valuing possible are most likely to be nurtured in a system of democratic self-governance.[80] He cites three reasons for this affinity: (1) because democracy "encourages the development of distinctively human potentialities for creative and reflective use of the mind"; (2) because it "engenders an experimental approach to social change"; and (3) because "self-rule generates consequences that must be endured, a democratic public becomes increasingly self-conscious about the character of the value theory it employs."[81] As Ayres put it, "The essence of democracy is not the fact of majority rule, but rather the process by which majorities are formed."[82] For the institutionalist, the process by which majorities of a democracy are formed is identical with the process of inquiry upon which instrumental valuing depends. Thus, democracy is the political process most likely to nurture the conscious exercise of human discretion over the evolution of the society.

Notes

1. One of the earliest classics in the field is Charles H. Cooley's *Human Nature and the Social Order* (New York: Schocken Books, 1964 [1902]).
2. For an authoritative statement of the institutionalist position on the "nature versus nurture" debate, see William M. Dugger, "Sociobiology: A Critical Introduction to E. O. Wilson's Evolutionary Paradigm," *Social Science Quarterly* 62 (June 1981): 221–33.
3. This theme is developed most fully by Marc R. Tool in *The Discretionary Economy: A Normative Theory of Political Economy* (Santa Monica: Goodyear Publishing Co., 1979).
4. The notation used here for behavioral patterns was first developed by the author in "An Exploration of the Structural Characteristics of a Veblen-Ayres-Foster Defined Institutional Domain," *Journal of Economic Issues* 17 (March 1983): 35–66.
5. See John Dewey, *Reconstruction of Philosophy,* enlarged edition (Boston: Beacon Press, 1948 [1920]): and John Dewey, *Theory of Valuation* (Chicago: University of Chicago Press, 1939). See also, Jacob Bronowski, *Science and Human Values,* revised edition (New York: Harper & Row, 1965).
6. These matters have been discussed at greater length by the author in "The Normative Implications of Institutional Analysis," *Economic Forum* 12 (Winter, 1981–82): 9–29.
7. Space constraints do not permit a detailed review of this literature in this essay. For a systematic treatment of the institutionalist approach to value theory see Steven Hickerson's "Instrumental Valuation: The Normative Compass of Institutional Economics" in this volume.
8. H. H. Liebhafsky, *The Nature of Price Theory,* revised edition (Homewood: Dorsey Press, 1968), p. 523.
9. Nicholas Georgescu-Roegen, *The Entropy Law and the Economic Process* (Cambridge: Harvard University Press, 1971), p. 14.
10. Clarence E. Ayres, *Toward a Reasonable Society* (Austin: University of Texas Press, 1971), p. 241.
11. It is interesting to note that Veblen treated "conspicuous consumption" as dialectical behavior. Accordingly, he says, "an article may be useful and wasteful both, and its utility to the consumer may be made up of use and

waste in the most varying proportions. . . . It would be hazardous to assert that a useful purpose is ever absent from the utility of any article or of any service, however obviously its prime purpose and chief element is conspicuous waste." Thorstein Veblen, *The Theory of the Leisure Class* (New York: Augustus M. Kelley, 1975 [1899]), pp. 100–101.

12. See Bush, "An Exploration of the Structural Characteristics," pp. 39–42.
13. Bronislaw Malinowski, *Argonauts of the Western Pacific* (New York: E.P. Dutton, 1950 [1922]). See especially Chap. 5, "The Ceremonial Building of a Waga."
14. Ibid., p. 124.
15. Ibid., p. 115.
16. Ibid., p. 116.
17. This discussion of Malinowski's commentary should not be misinterpreted. It is not at all clear that Malinowski would have agreed with the treatment of his observations set forth here. See Clarence E. Ayres's remarks on Malinowski's analysis of the function of magic in the Trobriand culture in Ayres, *Toward a Reasonable Society*, p. 133.
18. Marc R. Tool provides an extensive analysis of the ceremonial functions of ideology in *The Discretionary Economy;* see especially: pp. 26–34, and pp. 275–78.
19. Clarence E. Ayres, *The Theory of Economic Progress* (Chapel Hill: University of North Carolina Press, 1944), pp. 177–202.
20. Ayres, *Toward a Reasonable Society*, p. 31.
21. Ayres, *The Theory of Economic Progress*, pp. 177–78.
22. A rigorous formulation of the index of ceremonial dominance appears in Bush, "An Exploration of the Structural Characteristics," pp. 48–51.
23. For example, see the exchange of notes between F. Gregory Hayden and Thomas R. DeGregori in the *Journal of Economic Issues* 14 (March 1980): 221–25. See also Warren Samuels, "Technology *vis-a-vis* Institutions in the *JEI*: A Suggested Interpretation," *Journal of Economic Issues* 11 (December 1977): 867–95; and David Hamilton, "Technology and Institutions are Neither," *Journal of Economic Issues* 20 (June 1986): 525–32.
24. Thorstein Veblen, "Why is Economics Not an Evolutionary Science," *The Place of Science in Modern Civilisation* (New York: The Viking Press, 1942 [1919]), p. 71–72.
25. Ayres, *Toward a Reasonable Society*, p. 277.
26. Ibid.
27. See Thorstein Veblen, "The Evolution of the Scientific Point of View," *The Place of Science in Modern Civilisation* (New York: Viking Press, 1942 [1919]), pp. 32–55.
28. Ayres, *Toward a Reasonable Society*, p. 278.
29. Anne Mayhew, "Ayresian Technology, Technological Reasoning, and Doomsday," *Journal of Economic Issues* 15 (June 1981), pp. 513–20.
30. Ibid.
31. Ibid., p. 514. The Liebhafsky observation was contained in a letter he had written to Warren Samuels and which Samuels quoted in his article, "Technology vis-a-vis Institutions." The Liebhafsky quotation appears on p. 887 of the Samuels article.
32. The term "holism" was first used in reference to institutional economics

by Allan G. Gruchy in *Modern Economic Thought: The American Contri-bution* (New York: Prentice-Hall, 1947). An excellent discussion of "holis-tic" methodology in institutional economics is to be found in Yngve Ramstad, "A Pragmatist's Quest for Holistic Knowledge: The Scientific Methodology of John R. Commons," *Journal of Economic Issues* 20 (De-cember 1986): 1067–1105. In a passing remark, Ramstad indicates that the kind of approach the present author took in "An Exploration of the Struc-tural Characteristics," (and, by extension, in this article) is incompatible with the "holistic" methodology. The author disagrees with Ramstad on this point, but this is not the place to argue the issue.

33. U.S. Congress, Joint Economic Committee, *Special Study on Economic Change*, Hearings, 95th Congress, 2d Session, June 8, 9, 13 and 14, 1978, (Washington: U.S. Government Printing Office), p. 517.

34. For some representative samples of the institutionalist view of the concept of capital, see: Thorstein Veblen, "On the Nature of Capital" in *The Place of Science in Modern Civilisation* (New York: Viking Press, 1942 [1919]), pp. 324–86; Louis J. Junker, "Capital Accumulation, Saving-Centered Theory, and Economic Development," *Journal of Economic Issues* 1 (June 1967): 25–43; Baldwin Ranson, "The Unrecognized Revolution in the The-ory of Capital Formation," *Journal of Economic Issues* 17 (December 1983): 901–13; and William Dugger, "Capital Accumulation and Techno-logical Progress," *Journal of Economic Issues* 18 (September 1984): 799–823.

35. Thorstein Veblen, "Why is Economics Not an Evolutionary Science?", in *The Place of Science in Modern Civilisation*, p. 75. See also W. F. Ogburn, *On Culture and Social Change* (Chicago: University of Chicago Press, 1964), p. 25; and Louis J. Junker, "Capital Accumulation, Savings-Centered Theory and Economic Development," p. 33. In footnote 33, on page 33, Junker provides a useful list of references on the notion of the exponential increase in the knowledge fund.

36. William F. Ogburn, *Social Change* (New York: The Viking Press, 1950 [1922]), pp. 103–42. See also, Thomas R. DeGregori, *A Theory of Technol-ogy* (Ames: The Iowa State University Press, 1985), p. 36.

37. Tool, *The Discretionary Economy*, p. 39. A smooth, continuous exponen-tial function, such as that used in Tool's illustration, is an oversimplification, as he would readily admit. Most institutionalists would agree that in real time there can be discontinuities and "quantum leaps" in the rate of growth that require the qualification that the function is only a rough approximation of an exponential curve. This qualification does not, however, reach to the notion of "developmental continuity" discussed in the following paragraphs.

38. Ayres, *Toward a Reasonable Society*, pp. 112–13. Ogburn also stressed the combinatorial aspect of the growth of technology and cultural traits; see Ogburn, *On Cultural and Social Change*, pp. 25–26.

39. Nicholas Georgescu-Roegen, *The Entropy Law and the Economic Process* (Cambridge: Harvard University Press, 1971), p. 13.

40. This attribution of the use of the term "developmental continuity" to Fos-ter is based on the author's recollection of Foster's lectures at the Univer-sity of Denver. The recollection is corroborated by Baldwin Ranson's

1112   Paul D. Bush

reference to Foster's use of the term in his review of Marc Tool's *The Discretionary Economy,* which appeared in the *Journal of Economic Issues* 14 (September 1980), p. 764. Another student of Foster's, the late Louis J. Junker, commented extensively on the principle of continuity in his article entitled "Instrumentalism, the Principle of Continuity and the Life Process," *American Journal of Economics and Sociology* 40 (October 1981): 381–400.

41. This discussion of the partitioning of "institutional space" is based on a mathematical modelling of these relationships developed by the author in "A Veblen-Ayres Model of Institutional Change: A Provisional Formulation," a paper presented at the Annual Meetings of the Western Economic Association, Anaheim, California, 21 June 1977.

42. The language, "the triumph of imbecile institutions over life and culture" is, of course, Veblen's ringing phrase. See Thorstein Veblen, *The Instinct of Workmanship* (New York: Augustus M. Kelley, 1964 [1914]), p. 25.

43. The term "ceremonial encapsulation" has only recently been introduced into the institutionalist literature. The author and the late Louis J. Junker, unbeknown to one another, began using the term almost simultaneously in their teaching and writing. The author's first effort to define the term rigorously appeared in "A Veblen-Ayres Model of Institutional Change: A Provisional Formulation." The author presented an application of its use in "The Ceremonial Encapsulation of Capital Formulation in the American Economy," a paper presented to the Western Social Science Association, Lake Tahoe, Nevada, 27 April 1979, and extended the rigorous treatment of the concept in "An Exploration of the Structural Characteristics," pp. 35–66. For Louis J. Junker's theoretical formulation of the concept, see: "The Ceremonial-Instrumental Dichotomy in Institutional Analysis: The Nature, Scope, and Radical Implications of the Conflicting Systems," *American Journal of Economics and Sociology* 41 (April, 1982): 141–50; and "The Conflict Between the Scientific-Technological Process and Malignant Ceremonialism," *American Journal of Economics and Sociology* 42 (July, 1983): 341–52. The dates of these articles do not accurately reflect the time frame in which Junker began using the term since both were published several years after the papers on which they are based were presented to various professional societies. Junker's most detailed application of the concept of ceremonial encapsulation to a specific problem area is to be found in his "Nutrition and Economy: Some Observations on Diet and Disease in the American Food Power System," *Review of Institutional Thought* 2 (December 1982): 27–58. The author has commented on the origin of the concept and Louis Junker's pioneering application of it in an article entitled "On the Concept of Ceremonial Encapsulation," *Review of Institutional Thought* 3 (December 1986): forthcoming. Whether the term "ceremonial encapsulation" is merely a new way of referring to well-established concepts in the institutionalist literature or, for better or worse, an extension of institutionalist analysis into new intellectual territory is a matter that must yet be settled. For two important contributions to the deliberations on this point, see William T. Waller, Jr., "The Evolution of the Veblenian Dichotomy: Veblen, Hamilton, Ayres, and Foster," *Journal of Economic Issues* 16 (September 1982): 757–71; and Hans E. Jensen's article on the "Theory of Human Nature" in this volume, pp. 1039–73.

44. A special case of this kind of "slippage" is discussed as the "add on" process in Bush, "An Exploration of the Structural Characteristics," pp. 59–61.
45. Ayres, *Toward a Reasonable Society,* pp. 30, 137, and 233.
46. See Ogburn, *On Cultural and Social Change,* pp. 200–213. The similarities between the works of Veblen and Ogburn have been widely noted, and the notion of the cultural lag is often attributed to Veblen. He did not, of course, use the term. Ogburn denied that his formulation of the concept was influenced by Veblen. There are some fundamental differences between the Veblen-Ayres approach and Ogburn's. Whereas Veblen and Ayres postulate technological innovation as the dynamic factor generating the cultural changes to which there is a lagged cultural response, Ogburn argued that changes in those aspects of culture identified by Veblen and Ayres as "ceremonial" could be the dynamic cause of a lagged cultural response. Nevertheless, Ogburn's comments on this point do not appear to offer a serious challenge to the arguments made by Veblen and Ayres. Virtually all of Ogburn's own studies treat technology as the "independent variable"; and in those instances where he would appear to make ceremonial practices the independent variable, a case can be made that he failed to probe far enough along the chain of causal events to discover the technological innovation that produced the change in the ceremonial practices. As will be demonstrated in the following paragraphs, "regressive" institutional changes prompted by purely ceremonial considerations force the community into Sector III, and this results in a loss of instrumental efficiency. This line of analysis directly contradicts Ogburn's speculations. See William F. Ogburn, *On Culture and Social Change: Selected Papers,* ed. Otis D. Duncan (Chicago: The University of Chicago Press, 1964), p. 87.
47. This discussion of the three types of ceremonial encapsulation is based on the author's presidential address to the Association for Institutional Thought entitled "On the Concept of Ceremonial Encapsulation" (Albuquerque, New Mexico, 29 April 1983), a revised version of which appears in *The Review of Institutional Thought* 3 (December 1986): forthcoming.
48. Thorstein Veblen, *Imperial Germany and the Industrial Revolution* (New York: Augustus M. Kelley, 1964 [1915]), p. 25.
49. Ogburn, *Social Change,* pp. 213–36.
50. Veblen developed this theme originally in "Industrial and Pecuniary Employments," *Publications of the American Economic Association* 2 (1901): 190–235, reprinted in *The Place of Science in Modern Civilisation,* pp. 279–323; and expanded upon it later in *The Theory of Business Enterprise* (Clifton, N.J.: Augustus M. Kelley, 1975 [1904]).
51. F. Gregory Hayden, "A Geobased National Agricultural Policy for Rural Community Enhancement, Environmental Vitality, and Income Stabilization," *Journal of Economic Issues* 18 (March 1984): 181–221.
52. Junker, "Nutrition and Economy," p. 50.
53. It should be noted that while Dugger does not employ the term "ceremonial encapsulation" in his discussion of corporate hegemony, there can be no question that the term applies to his analysis. See William M. Dugger, *An Alternative to Economic Retrenchment,* (New York: Petrocelli Books, Inc., 1984). This point is clearly established by William T. Waller, Jr. in "Ceremonial Encapsulation and Corporate Cultural Hegemony," *Journal of Economic Issues* 21 (March 1987): 321–28.

1114   Paul D. Bush

54. Dugger, *An Alternative to Economic Retrenchment*, p. 57.
55. Ibid., pp. 135–42.
56. Thorstein Veblen, *The Higher Learning in America: A Memorandum on the Conduct of Universities by Business Men* (New York: Augustus M. Kelley, 1965 [1918]). This book is often dismissed by serious scholars and university administrators alike as Veblen's angry "letter to the editor" about those who made his life so miserable in academia. Yet the book is a systematic piece of institutional analysis and may be more relevant to institutions of higher learning today than when Veblen wrote it. For an excellent institutionalist commentary on the role of education in progressive institutional change, see Baldwin Ranson, "Planning Education for Economic Progress: Distinguishing Occupational Demand from Technological Possibilities," *Journal of Economic Issues* 20 (December 1986): 1053–65.
57. John R. Munkirs, *The Transformation of American Capitalism* (Armonk, N.Y.: M.E. Sharpe, 1985), p. 179.
58. Thorstein Veblen, *The Nature of the Peace and the Terms of Its Perpetuation* (New York: Augustus M. Kelley, 1964 [1917]).
59. For an authoritative account of Lysenkoism, see David Joravsky, *The Lysenko Affair* (Cambridge: Harvard University Press, 1970).
60. *Los Angeles Times*, 21 October 1980, Part I, p. 3.
61. Veblen, *The Instinct of Workmanship*, p. 25.
62. As Ayres put it: "the progressive advance of technology means a similarly cumulative diminution of the extent and importance in the affairs of the community of superstition and ceremonial investiture." *The Theory of Economic Progress*, p. 245; see also page 201 where he refers to the process as the "displacement of ceremonial by technological functions." Ayres did not specify the requirement of a given fund of knowledge. This is an analytical refinement that has been developed by the author. Putting the matter of "progressive" institutional change in the context of problem solving, Marc Tool states that "The resolution of a problem consists of the reduction or removal of ceremonial behavior and attitudes and the creation or extension of instrumental behavior and attitudes." See Tool, "A Social Value Theory in Neoinstitutional Economics," *Journal of Economic Issues* 11 (December 1977): 823–46 at p. 837; this essay is reprinted in Tool, *Essay in Social Value Theory: A Neoinstitutionalist Contribution* (Armonk, N.Y.: M.E. Sharpe, 1986), pp. 33–44; the quotation appears on page 47.
63. Veblen discusses the process of "cumulative causation" throughout his works, but perhaps the most pertinent of his remarks on the subject for present purposes is to be found in *The Place of Science in Modern Civilisation*, pages 74–75.
64. Veblen, *The Theory of Business Enterprise*, p. 310.
65. Ibid., p. 311.
66. Veblen, *Imperial Germany and the Industrial Revolution*, p. 100. The question as to whether Veblen, in giving this account of institutional change, failed to distinguish adequately between what has been called "functional" rationality and "substantial" rationality has been given careful consideration by Rick Tilman in his masterful study of C. Wright Mills. See Rick Tilman, *C. Wright Mills: A Native Radical and His American Intellectual Roots* (University Park: Pennsylvania State University Press, 1984), pp. 97–98.

67. Ayres, *The Theory of Economic Progress*, pp. 137 ff.
68. In one of his most remarkable essays, Veblen described in some detail the mental processes involved in achieving the "sensed awareness" discussed here. In "The Intellectual Pre-eminence of Jews in Modern Europe," Veblen argues that the cultural alienation of the European Jew gave rise to a "skeptical animus" among Jewish intellectuals that emancipated them from the ceremonial practices of both the Christian culture and their own traditional heritage. Being thus released from the "dead hand of conventional finality," they were free to explore truly innovative approaches in all of the arts and sciences. The intellectual transformation of the European Jew was, for Veblen, a metaphor for the emergence of the scientific habit of thought. See "The Intellectual Pre-eminence of Jews in Modern Europe," in *Essays in Our Changing Order*, ed. Leon Ardzrooni (New York: Augustus M. Kelley, 1964 [1934]), pp. 219–31. The essay originally appeared in *The Political Science Quarterly* 34 (March 1919): 33–42.
69. Milton D. Lower, "The Industrial Economy and International Price Shocks," *Journal of Economic Issues* 20 (June 1986): 297–312, at p. 311.
70. These three limiting conditions of "progressive" institutional change were discussed by Marc Tool in *The Discretionary Economy*, pp. 172–76. They were originally formulated by J. Fagg Foster and presented in his lectures at the University of Denver in the late 1940s and early 1950s. A severely truncated version of his treatment of them appears in Foster, "Syllabus for Problems of Modern Society: The Theory of Institutional Adjustment," *Journal of Economic Issues* 15 (December 1981): 929–35.
71. "Cultural borrowing" is the term Veblen used to identify this phenomenon in *Imperial Germany;* see especially pp. 19–43.
72. See, for example, Louis J. Junker, "Capital Accumulation, Savings-Centered Theory, and Economic Development," pp. 25–43; and Philip A. Klein, "An Institutionalist View of Development Economics," *Journal of Economic Issues* 11 (December 1977): 785–807.
73. While David Seckler may not regard himself as an institutionalist, he has provided solid evidence of the correctness of the institutional position on this point in his article entitled "Institutionalism and Agricultural Development in India," *Journal of Economic Issues* 20 (December 1986): 1011–1027.
74. Baldwin Ranson, "Planning Education for Economic Progress," p. 1063.
75. While there can be no question that J. Fagg Foster formulated this principle, it is clear that Clarence Ayres had an intuitive grasp of it, as indicated by the following statement: "It is also true that the sudden nullification of the ceremonial system of any community would produce a grievous state of disorganization." See Ayres, *Toward a Reasonable Society*, p. 138.
76. To reiterate the point by way of an additional example, it should be recalled that Veblen found a "non-invidious residue" even in the ceremonial labyrinth of organized religion. He commented favorably on the instrumentally warranted" sense of communion with the environment, or with the generic life process—as well as the impulse of charity or of sociability," which he found to be encapsulated in religious life. See Veblen, *The Theory of the Leisure Class*, p. 334.
77. A matter of some importance in any discussion of "minimal dislocation" is the environmental impact of the technological innovations contemplated in "progressive" institutional change. The principle of minimal dis-

1116   Paul D. Bush

location requires that any technology be compatible with the sustainability
of the evolution of the ecosystem. This is a point that may not have been
given sufficient attention by institutionalists in the past. Space limitations
preclude any discussion of this vital issue. A most valuable discussion of
this matter is to be found in James A. Swaney, "A Coevolutionary Model
of Structural Change," *Journal of Economic Issues* 20 (June 1986):
393–400. The author's only quibble with this article has to do with Swaney's misapplication of the terms "ceremonial" and "instrumental" in his
discussion of ecosystem feedbacks.
78. Tool, *The Discretionary Economy*, p. 293.
79. Tool, *The Discretionary Economy;* see, in particular, pp. 199–213, and pp.
315–36. See also his essay entitled "The Neoinstitutionalist Perspective in
Political Economy," in Tool, *Essays in Social Value Theory*, pp. 3–30.
80. This theme runs throughout the institutionalist literature. It reflects the
heavy influence of John Dewey's philosophy on American Institutionalism. Clarence Ayres viewed democracy as the system of governance most
compatible with the emergence of the scientific point of view. See Ayres,
Toward a Reasonable Society, pp. 281–94. The thesis was advanced most
persuasively by the mathematician and philosopher Jacob Bronowski in
his elegant little book *Science and Human Values*. While Bronowski was
not an institutionalist, his philosophical writings have been most enthusi-
astically embraced by them.
81. Tool, *Essays in Social Value Theory*, pp. 25–26.
82. Ayres, *Toward a Reasonable Society*, p. 283.

[25]

Journal of Institutional and Theoretical Economics (JITE) 145 (1989), 67–84
Zeitschrift für die gesamte Staatswissenschaft

Institutional Persistence and Change:
The Question of Efficiency

by

BRIAN R. BINGER and ELIZABETH HOFFMAN*

1. Introduction

A great deal of recent research in economic history has focused on understanding the origins of institutions. (See, for example, ANDERSON and HILL [1975]; CHEUNG [1968]; COHEN and WEITZMAN [1975]; DAHLMAN [1980]; FENOALTEA [1975a, b, 1976, 1977, 1987]; GRANTHAM [1980]; HIGGS [1973, 1974]; HOFFMANN [1975]; LIBECAP [1978a, b]; McCLOSKEY [1972, 1975a, b, 1976]; NORTH and THOMAS [1973]; REID [1973, 1975, 1976]; UMBECK [1977a, b, 1981a, b]). In many cases the intent of the research has been to identify ways in which a particular institution "solved" some particular social or economic problem faced by a group of people. Moreover, the point is often made that whatever emerges as an abiding institution *must* be efficient in light of the constraints facing the society. Otherwise it would not persist.

While this approach has led researchers to carefully study the economic rationale behind such diverse institutions as the open field system (DAHLMAN [1980]; HOFFMANN [1975]; McCLOSKEY [1972, 1975a, b, 1976]; NORTH and THOMAS [1973]; FENOALTEA [1975a, b, 1976, 1977, 1987]), mineral rights in the American West (LIBECAP [1978a, b]; UMBECK [1977a, b, 1981a, b]), and share-cropping in the post-bellum American South (HIGGS [1973, 1974]; REID [1973, 1975, 1976]), it tends to ignore the very real possibility that an equilibrium outcome of a repeated coordination game is not necessarily efficient. Thus, while an institution may provide obvious benefits, it is not necessarily more efficient than alternative institutions just because it persists.

To illustrate this point, we argue that an institution is analogous to a public good. A well-functioning institution reduces transaction costs and facilitates cooperation, allowing individuals to benefit from social and economic exchange. Seen in that light, any well-functioning institution provides some benefits to some individuals. But, recognizing that benefits are provided is not the same as saying that the institution is efficient, even if we use a second-best

* The authors wish to thank the participants at the conference on New Institutional Approaches to Economic History for their helpful comments. NSF grant # SES–8608206.

notion of efficiency. Theoretical and experimental evidence suggest quite strongly that the voluntary provision of a public good is generally positive, but suboptimal. To the extent that an institution can be viewed as the equilibrium of a process of voluntary exchange involving positive externalities, the benefits provided cannot be presumed to exhaust the gains from exchange.

In this paper we use theoretical and experimental results from research in game theory, the voluntary provision of public goods, and public choice to try to understand the limits of what historians can say about institutional origins and institutional change. Institutions may arise as inefficient equilibria of repeated coordination games and persist because, though all would benefit from a change in joint strategies, no one individual can benefit from a unilateral change.

2. Institutions and Public Goods

The simple definition of a public good is a good which is consumed jointly by several individuals. However, the concept of a public good can also be applied to a wide variety of joint decisions. For example, if a group of homeowners is being polluted by a factory, any reduction in pollution is a public good. Similarly, if a group of firms can establish an effective cartel, their reduction in output, which has the effect of raising prices and profits, is also a public good to them. In fact, we can view the outcome of any beneficial collective action as a public good. (See BINGER and HOFFMAN [1988, chapter 21], for further exposition on this point.)

Economic and social institutions establish legal or normative guidelines for the conduct of human interaction. If they function relatively well they provide positive externalities (public goods) by reducing the transaction costs of production and exchange. Taking the most extreme example, if there were no accepted rules of interpersonal communication, we would have to come to agreement on a new set of rules every time we encountered a new individual. These rules would have to govern such diverse behavior as how we greet the person, how we stand when we talk, and what kind of economic exchange is legitimate. If more than two individuals wished to communicate with one another, all would have to agree on the rules. Needless to say, the transaction costs of human interaction would be very high in such a world.

Modern banking institutions provide a more concrete example. Before the development of banking institutions, most exchange took place through face-to-face barter or the exchange of coins. With the growth of overseas trade in the Middle Ages it became necessary to exchange payment over long distances. Banking houses became the middlemen who brokered such long-distance transactions, thereby reducing transaction costs. Today, our complicated economic system could not function without banks to bring together borrowers and lenders and spread risk. If every time someone who needed funds had to search for someone willing to lend exactly that amount at an agreeable interest rate, the transaction costs would quickly swamp the expected returns on a wide variety of potential projects. Society benefits from a much higher per capita income when more goods are produced at lower cost.

Just as we can view institutions as providing positive externalities (public goods), we can view more or less efficient institutions as being more or less effective at exhausting the public gains from exchange. Returning to the banking example for illustration, we could think of starting from an initial position of one-to-one barter and no banks at all. If we introduce only local banks we gain by bringing local borrowers and lenders together, but if we then introduce interstate and international banking we can spread risks much more efficiently. In some cases alternative institutions exist simultaneously; in other cases institutions evolve over time. In both cases we can gain understanding of the possible efficiency of such institutions by studying theoretical and experimental evidence on the allocation of public goods.

3. An Introduction to the Theory of Repeated Games

The theory of repeated games can be used as a powerful tool for arguing that persistent institutions are efficient. Although in the development of institutions there are likely to be many players and many possible institutional outcomes, it is instructive to begin by asking what strategies would be chosen by players in a two-person, infinitely-repeated prisoner's dilemma game (AUMANN [1978]; MOULIN [1982]; KURZ [1985]; AXELROD [1984]). To answer this question, we analyze the infinitely many future plays as one *supergame* and look at the sequence of moves each player will make contingent on what the other player does. We know that it is a dominant strategy to cheat in a one-shot prisoner's dilemma game. However, that strategy is not the only equilibrium of an infinitely repeated supergame.

Suppose, for example, that one player adopts the following long-term strategy: cooperate with the other player as long as that other player continues to cooperate; but, if the other player ever cheats once, then cheat for the rest of time. The best the other player can do against such a strategy is to adopt exactly the same strategy. As long as both players cooperate they get the efficient outcome, but if one cheats they get the inefficient outcome for the rest of time. Such strategies are referred to as *punishment strategies* in the repeated game literature. (See AUMANN [1978] and MOULIN [1982] for a formal proof that punishment strategies yield cooperation as a Nash equilibrium of the supergame.) In an infinitely repeated game the benefits from cheating once can never outweigh the loss of benefits from the efficient outcome for the rest of time. Thus, it is a weak Nash equilibrium for players in the infinitely repeated supergame to always cooperate.

The 2 × 2 prisoner's dilemma game is the most famous example of such games. However, the prisoner's dilemma is a generic concept which can be applied to understanding strategies and equilibria in the general class of games in which all benefit from cooperation but each player has a dominant strategy to defect. For example, consider the follwoing continuous n-person dilemma game. Each player is endowed with units of a private good (dollars) which he or she can donate to a common pool. For every dollar contributed, a center adds $ .50 and then divides the total equally among the participants. If the game is to be played only once it is a dominant strategy for each participant to contribute $ 0 to the common pool. This corresponds to the cheat-cheat equilibrium of the 2 × 2 prisoner's dilemma game. If the game is to be played an infinite number of times, however, any contribution from $ 0 to 100 % of the private endowments can be sustained as an equilibrium of the supergame. If each person contributes 100 % of his or her endowment, joint profits are maximized. However, any other jointly enforced set of contributions can also be sustained as an "inefficient" equilibrium.

While punishment strategies are effective, they are quite draconian: each player threatens to punish for the rest of time if any other player defects. It turns out, however, that many equilibria (both efficient and inefficient) can also be sustained with far less draconian strategies. (See, for example, AXELROD [1984]; GREEN and PORTER [1983]; KREPS, MILGROM, ROBERTS, and WILSON [1982]; KREPS and SPENCE [1985]; RADNER, MYERSON, and MASKIN [1986]; SAMUELSON [1987]).

The idea that cooperation can be the Nash equilibrium of a prisoner's dilemma supergame raises the possibility that humans can develop efficient institutions that persist as long as certain underlying parameters do not change very much. Yet, it is also the case that the cooperative equilibrium is only one of many possible Nash equilibria of an infinitely-repeated supergame. For example, the single-play prisoner's dilemma outcome is also a Nash equilibrium of the infinitely-repeated supergame. If one player cheats, the best the other player can do is cheat also.

If the game is to be played only a finite number of times, the cooperative outcome "unravels" from the last play backward. To analyze the equilibrium of a finitely-repeated game, we use a dynamic programming approach: start at the last play and analyze the optimal strategy at each play backwards from the end of the game. On the last play there are no future plays in which to be punished, consequently, it is a dominant strategy to cheat. Thus, everyone knows everyone will cheat on the last play. But, if everyone is going to cheat on the last play, it is a dominant strategy to cheat on the next-to-last play, since there are no future profits to protect. Similarly, it is a dominant strategy to cheat on the play before that, and so on all the way back to the first play. By backward induction, therefore, we conclude that on any play all future plays will involve cheating by one's opponent. Thus, it is a dominant strategy to always cheat.

What does this brief introduction to the theory of repeated games suggest about the efficiency of institutions? First, it raises the possibility that efficient institutions might develop as the outcome of a continuous n-person repeated prisoner's dilemma game. However, it also should caution us that institutions need not be efficient to persist. In both finitely-repeated and infinitely-repeated games inefficient supergame equilibria do exist. Moreover, in games with many possible strategies there are likely to be many possible inefficient equilibria, some of which are more or less efficient than others. Thus, just because we observe that an institution endures and seems to "do better" than some other institutions does not mean that it is necessarily efficient. Arguments to the effect that individuals will exhaust any gains from exchange and that institutions must be efficient do not apply when there are externalities and public goods.

A generally recognized example of a long-run inefficient equilibrium of a continuous n-person prisoner's dilemma is the organization of ocean fishing. Despite a long history and recognition that competitive fishing is severely depleting fishing stocks, fishermen have not developed institutions for defining and enforcing property rights in fish which have yet to be caught. Consequently, all continue to play a cheat-cheat strategy which involves each fisherman trying to catch as many fish as possible. In this case the competitive market institution which endures provides minimal (sometimes negative) profits to fishermen. An institution which defined and enforced property rights and restricted the catch would provide considerable benefits to both fishermen and future consumers of fish.

4. Experimental Evidence on the Voluntary Provision of Public Goods

If repeated games can have either efficient or inefficient equilibria, under what circumstances are we likely to observe one or the other kind of equilibrium developing? Such information would help us to judge the likelihood that a particular historical institution is efficient. Recent experimental literature on the voluntary provision of public goods provides the beginning of an answer to that question.

Most of the recent experimental work on the voluntary provision of public goods stems from a series of experiments by MARWELL and AMES [1979, 1980], which involved a game very similar to the n-person dilemma game described above. In those experiments, they gave subjects tokens which could be redeemed for cash in two different markets: a private goods market and a public goods market. In the private goods market there was a constant rate of exchange; but, in the public goods market the rate of exchange depended on how many other participants contributed. Moreover, it was efficient for all paritci-pants to exchange 100% of their tokens for the public good, where efficiency was measured as the percentage of the total possible profits actually earned by the participants. In the experiment the private good was labeled individual exchange and the public good was labeled group exchange.

MARWELL and AMES' [1979, 1980] results were somewhat mixed. Very few subjects contributed nothing to the group exchange; yet, very few subjects contributed 100% to the group exchange. Most contributed some tokens to each, leading to a positive, but still inefficient, level of provision of the public good.

This evidence provides some support for an argument that public goods will be provided in positive, but suboptimal amounts, even when it is a dominant strategy to provide zero units of a public good. However, their experiment did not allow for repeated plays of the game. Each subject made one contribution, was paid, and the experiment ended. To understand how institutions work, we need to understand more about repeated voluntary provision of public goods. ISAAC, WALKER, and THOMAS [1984] replicated the MARWELL and AMES [1979, 1980] experiments, with the added feature that they allowed subjects to revise their contributions in an iterative process and they told subjects the total number of tokens contributed each period. They also changed the payoff structure so that each subject had a dominant individual strategy to exchange 100% of his or her tokens for the private good. They found that the first period there were substantial, but suboptimal, contributions. This was the same result as MARWELL and AMES' [1979, 1980]. But, once those who had contributed a large number of tokens saw how few were contributed by others, they revised their contributions downward. Within a few iterations contributions to the group exchange had fallen practically to zero.

In a series of extensions of these initial experiments, ISAAC and WALKER [1987] tried various changes in their experimental design in an attempt to induce cooperation. They found that two treatment variables had a significant effect on the level of contributions to the group exchange. First, if subjects could discuss strategies before each iteration, efficiency was nearly 100%. This suggests that institutions in which people who stand to gain from cooperation communicate regularly are more likely to be efficient than those without such communication. Second, they found that if the individual returns from group exchange were raised, so that individuals had more of a "stake" in the group exchange, the level of provision rose. Thus, the experimental evidence suggests that when individuals gain more individually from the provision of a public good they are more likely to provide it in positive amounts. This suggests that institutions which provide relatively high individual benefits are likely to be more efficient than those which do not.

5. Efficiency and Equilibrium of Social Decision Processes

The above discussions of repeated games and the voluntary provision of public goods assume that all members of a society benefit from the public goods aspect of a particular institution. In reality, however, most social and economic institutions provide benefits to some members of society and impose costs on others. In such a situation, society is constantly reevaluating, in some way or another, the institutions under which it operates.

How it reevaluates depends upon the decision making institutions themselves. But, what is universal about social decision processes is that they cannot be counted on to generate efficient, consistent social decisions. (For an introduction to the public choice literature, see RIKER [1982] and MUELLER [1979]).

This point is illustrated with reference to ARROW's [1963] famous voting paradox. Suppose there are three possible alternative institutional arrangements being considered (x, y, and z) and three factions in society (A, B, and C). We might represent the preference orderings of the three factions over the three alternatives in the following form:

	Factions		
	A	B	C
	x	y	z
Preferences	y	z	x
	z	x	y

While this society might use any decision process to determine which alternative to adopt, we use the example of a set agenda for consideration, simple majority rule, and *Roberts's Rules of Order*. In this framework, the three alternatives might be labeled 1) an original motion on the floor, 2) an amended motion and 3) the status quo. First the original motion is compared to the amended motion. Then the majority rule winner (original motion or amended motion) is compared to the status quo.

If the agenda is to first compare x to y and the winner to z, the social outcome will be z, since A and C prefer x to y and then B and C prefer z to x. However, if the agenda is to first compare x to z and the winner to y, the outcome will be y: B and C prefer z to x and A and B prefer y to z. Finally, if the agenda is to first compare y to z and the winner to x the outcome will be x: A and B prefer y to z and A and C prefer x to y. Thus, the agenda determines the outcome: any of the three alternatives can be chosen by a suitable agenda. In fact, such a decision process always favors the status quo. The last outcome considered plays the role of the status quo under *Robert's Rules of Order* and wins in every agenda outlined above (see RIKER [1982] for further elaboration on this point).

In such a situation there is no "solution" to the public decision making process. Any outcome can be chosen by a suitable agenda. Moreover, since most agendas consider the status quo last in comparison to other proposals, institutions can persist for long periods of time, even when a majority of the members of society would prefer some other alternative.

While not all societies will make decisions using Robert's Rules of Order, the problem outlined above applies to all decision processes when faced with the above set of preferences. There is a cycle to the voting process and those in power can remain in power for long periods of time if they have control over the decision making agenda. If they do not have such control there can be frequent changes in policy, with each new policy being opposed by a majority of the population.

This example may seem extreme; we may argue that there is much more similarity in preferences in the average society we might study in history. However, as ARROW [1963] has shown, with just a few alternatives to consider and a few diverse factions in society, the probability of observing such a cycle in voting goes to 1 very fast as the number of participants and alternatives increases. Moreover, even in situations where there appears to be one alternative which is preferred to all others by majority rule, a different voting process can often lead to a different outcome. Thus, it is a fundamental problem in public decision making. In fact, ARROW [1963] showed that the only public decision process which can be counted on to give transitive outcomes is a dictatorship in which the dictator imposes his or her preferences on society.

Certain voting institutions mitigate the potentially chaotic effects of the voting cycle to a greater or lesser degree. For example, if all choices can be reduced to binary choices (x against only y), then the faction which loses does not see that some other alternative (like z) might be preferred. The U. S. two-party primary system does exactly that. By the time of a general election, it is generally the case that the electorate has only two viable choices left. However, all that is needed to upset such an apparently stable outcome is for some members of the opposition to find an issue which splits the winning party. If they are successful, the opposition will win the next time around and the party just ousted from power can try the same ploy itself. In such a situation, each election appears decisive, but power cycles from one group to the next.

This lack of consistency has profound implications for public decision making. For example, control of the agenda is a powerful tool for getting one's own preferred alternative enacted (PLOTT and LEVINE [1978]). Similarly, different voting rules yield different outcomes with the same set of underlying preferences. This leads to manipulation of the outcomes by misrepresenting preferences, proposing new voting procedures, or changing the agenda.

What all this adds up to is the potential for public decisions to be highly unstable and certainly not defensible as welfare improving. What does get enacted depends on the voting rule used and how the agenda was written, not on what is "best" for society, even if a "best" alternative could be identified. Moreover, when a group that has been out of power regains control of the agenda, public policy can shift dramatically with no change in the underlying preferences. Even when policy appears to be stable, there may be more preferred alternatives which are not being given a chance on the social agenda.

In the next section we apply the theoretical and experimental results summarized above to a review of the literature on the origins, persistence, and decline of one economic and social institution: the open field system.

6. The Open Field System

The open field system as an agricultural institution developed and spread through much of England and continental Europe during the eighth through the thirteenth centuries. While there was much variation in the organization and administration of the open fields and large areas of Europe never adopted an open field system, we might characterize an open field village as follows. Radiating from the village were long, narrow strips of arable land, with each family's strips intermingled throughout the arable land. This is usually referred to as scattering the strips throughout the open fields. The arable land with its scattered strips was then divided into two or three large groups of strips and decisions about planting and harvesting were made in common (as discussed below).

In a three-course rotation system, for example, all the land in one group of strips would be sown with a winter grain (such as winter wheat), all the land in the second group of strips would be sown with a spring grain (such as oats or barley), and all the land in the third group would lie fallow. In addition, the community's herd of beasts of burden would typically be allowed to graze on the fallow. This provided the animals with grass and served to manure the field. To keep the animals from trampling the planted fields, communities either erected temporary fencing or employed children to tend the animals.

We do not know how all open field villages made their planting and rotation decisions, but surviving evidence from medieval England suggests that decisions were made by a form of weighted majority rule: those who owned or leased more land had a proportionately larger say in the decision making process. Thus, it seems as though the open field system persisted largely because a majority of the more powerful peasants in each village continued to support it.

There are a number of explanations for the origin and persistence of the open field system and the scattering of strips. However, each is predicated on an assumption that the open field system provided an efficient solution to a problem in the allocation of public goods. For example, consider DAHLMAN'S [1980] thesis. He argues that there are substantial scale economies in the grazing of cattle when there is little fodder available for supplemental feeding. Cattle tend to stay together in herds and to quickly destroy the grass in any one spot if they cannot wander over a large area. Thus, it is better for an entire community with a limited amount of grazing land to graze its cattle in one herd over the grazing land and the stubble after the crops have been harvested. However, it is still in the individual interest of larger landowners to fence their land and graze their own cattle separately, since cattle grazing in large herds belonging to several people are more susceptible to disease, neglect, and theft. Dahlman argues that medieval open field farmers developed the institution of scattering the strips of farmers around the open fields in order to make it virtually impossible for any one individual to break the agreement to graze all cattle in common.

McCloskey [1975, 1976] and Fenoaltea [1975a, b, 1976, 1977, 1987] do not agree with Dahlman's explanation, but they do agree that the institutions of open field farming and scattering of strips developed as efficient solutions to specific kinds of problems in the medieval economy. In fact, in a recent working paper, Fenoaltea [1987] reiterates his position that such a persistent institution must have been efficient simply because it constituted a long-run equilibrium.

McCloskey argues that scattering was a form of crop insurance in a world in which insurance markets were virtually nonexistent. Fenoaltea argues that scattering developed because there were scale economies associated with having an entire village plant and harvest the same crops at the same time; yet, each family wanted to tend its own fields to avoid the principal-agent problem associated with having others tend one's fields. Both McCloskey and Fenoaltea then go on to argue that if it is efficient to scatter strips it is also efficient to have open fields, since it would be very costly to fence off each separately owned strip. In discussing the demise of the open field system in the 17th and 18th centuries, McCloskey [1972, 1975b] argues that the spread of market agriculture provided English farmers with much less costly insurance and Dahlman [1980] argues that the development of fodder crops as part of the rotation system virtually eliminated the scale economies from mass grazing.

Hoffmann [1975] develops yet another argument which depends on population growth as the explanatory variable. He presents evidence that before the development of the open field system European peasants neither scattered their strips nor made common decisions regarding planting, harvesting, and rotation systems. Each peasant made his own decisions regarding the cultivation of his own land, which was generally in a single parcel. Moreover, there was no need to graze cattle on the stubble, since there was plenty of "waste" for pasture. However, with rapid population growth, this system was threatened. First, inheritance by several sons, each of whom would want some of the best land, tended to fragment land into scattered parcels. Second, population growth forced communities to expand arable production until the pasture was insufficient to maintain the herds. The solution was convertible arable and pasture. Whichever piece of arable land was lying fallow became temporary pasture.

This system quickly developed severe externalities in a world of scattered strips and individual decision making. Cattle grazing on the fallow stubble would have to be tethered and moved from place to place to maintain the grass and spread the manure naturally. But, without fences, there is a powerful individual incentive to tether one's cattle very loosely and allow them to wander into the neighbor's corn. It is the classic farmer-rancher problem first identified by Coase [1960].

Hoffmann [1975] then identified two possible institutions to solve this externality problem. On the one hand, peasants could have redistributed land to maintain consolidated plots and required each family to fence its own cattle when grazing in the fallow. On the other hand, they could have joined together to coordinate planting, fallowing, and grazing on the already scatterd strips. We know that over much of Europe the latter institution developed.

Hoffmann argues that joint decision making and continued scattering was adopted because the peasants saw it as the best way of maintaining a minimal level of subsistence for all members of a society which was not oriented towards the market. An individualistic agricultural organization might have produced more total output, but it would have tended to produce large inequalities among peasants. Some would have starved, while others would have generally had excess grain in storage. A communal system ensured a more equitable distribution of what was produced. It was a form of communal insurance.

With the spread of market agriculture in the 17th and 18th centuries, HOFF-MANN [1975] argues that an increasing number of peasants saw the benefits of consolidation and individual decision making. In particular, peasants who could produce more could now sell their surpluses instead of simply storing them. Consolidation and individual decision making were seen by many as the only institution which would allow them to adopt new technology and increase yields.

While as historians we may find one of these explanations more convincing than the others, what is important for our purposes here is that each author is assuming the existence and possibility of an efficient cooperative solution. However, just because an institution appears, *ex post*, to solve some prisoner's dilemma problem, does not mean that other, more efficient, institutions existed but were not realized.

The experimental and theoretical discussions point up the problems associated with historical explanations of the origins of institutions which view those institutions as solutions to a prisoner's dilemma problem. We can never know whether an institution represents a "solution" or simply an inefficient equilibrium. Adam Smith's invisible hand may work in competitive markets for private goods. But, it cannot be presumed to work in the allocation of public goods and externalities. Moreover, since many inefficient equilibria of such a repeated game exist, it is very risky to develop a predictive theory of the origin of social institutions from *ex post* theorizing, based on historical evidence. We may develop potentially *testable hypotheses* from reviewing such evidence, but in the absence of adequate data they remain no more compelling than any other hypotheses. In particular, such hypotheses cannot then be used to *explain* similar phenomena observed elsewhere.

One recent branch of economics has tried to do just that by introducing the concept of transaction costs (WILLIAMSON [1979]). Extending the Coase theorem (COASE [1960]), which predicts that agents who can do harm to one another will bargain until the gains from trade are exhausted if property rights are clearly defined, the transaction cost literature redefines the concept of efficiency in terms of second best. A second best optimum gives the highest joint profits, given transaction costs. These transaction costs can include bargaining costs, information costs, and principal-agent problems.

While this approach has enriched our understanding of how efficient it is realistically possible for institutions to become, there is a serious problem of circularity when such reasoning is applied to analyses of the origins of institutions in history. Since historical agents did not keep records of relevant transaction costs, we can only infer them. But, when we do so, we miss the fact that our models are not fully specified. It is very tempting to analyze an institution that appears somewhat inefficient from today's standpoint, but which goes part way in solving some obvious prisoner's dilemma problem and conclude that transaction costs prevented the society from achieving the fully efficient solution. However, once we recognize that we can fail to reach full efficiency either because of transaction costs or because the society has become stuck in an inefficient equilibrium, it is clear that we do not have enough information to judge the first- or second-best efficiency of any particular historical institution.

To illustrate this point, we consider the persistence and final demise of the open field system discussed above. Observing the medieval agricultural economy from today's perspective, no one would disagree that society gets more agricultural output and farmers get higher incomes and are less susceptible to crop failures if grain crops are grown in rotation with fodder crops and farm animals are given supplemental feed. Moreover, the technology of growing fodder crops was not discovered *de novo* in the 17th century. Pliny's writings on agricultural technology mentions the growing of fodder crops in rotation, the medieval rotation system included oats, and there is evidence that nitrogen-fixing crops were grown on some manors in the Netherlands (SLICHER van BATH [1963]) and England (CAMPBELL [1983, 1988]) in the 13th century. If the open field system was an efficient institution, given the constraints prevailing at the time, why did this new, superior technology, which would ultimately make the open field system unnecessary, not diffuse until the 17th to the 19th centuries? Simply changing rotation systems was possible within this economy: the three field system largely replaced the two field system on non-marginal soils in the 11th and 12th centuries. Moreover, had the new rotation system diffused more widely in the 13th century, it is highly likely that the 14th century depression would not have been so devastating.

One possible way to approach this question is to suggest that the open field system helped to solve some organizational problems for society while it created others. Once the open field system was established it slowed the pace of technological change simply because it was a common property, common decision making system. Changing to a fodder crop, supplemental feeding system required a radical restructuring of life in a agricultural community; that restructuring would benefit some and hurt others. For example, everyone would have to work more days in the year since supplemental feeding of animals required year-round attention. Those who were comfortable enough to value leisure more than greater output might not see such a change as beneficial. In addition, common pasture land was lost as fodder crops replaced fallow in the rotation system. Those with one or two animals and little land on which to grow fodder crops lose here. In other words, there might have been a stable coalition of rich peasants and poor peasants allied against those in the middle.

When decisions are made in common, if those who stand to lose have more voting power or more ability to manipulate the outcomes than those who stand to gain, then the status-quo will prevail. In this case an inefficient equilibrium may persist until those with such power are persuaded to change.

But, can we ever predict what institutional change will occur? McCloskey [1972, 1975 b] argues that enclosures were a new, more efficient institution that eventually replaced the open fields and allowed improving farmers to adopt the new rotation and animal management systems. Yet, Allen [1982], Allen and O'Grada [1988] and Grantham [1980] find that by the late 18th to late 19th centuries the new rotation systems were being widely adopted even on the remaining open fields. Allen [1982] goes so far as to suggest that returns to farmers were higher when the new rotation systems were used on the open field manors than under enclosure because rents tended to remain lower. Perhaps it simply happened that the balance of political power shifted in favor of those who wanted to enclose, even though enclosure was not a necessary condition for technological change.

It is not our intent to enter the historical debate on the English enclosure movement. Rather, we use this debate to illustrate the possible pitfalls associated with making *ex post* predictions about institutional change on the basis of efficiency arguments. It is clear from the historical record that by the late 17th to early 18th centuries, educated farmers in England saw the benefits of the new rotation systems and took steps to adopt them. To adopt the new rotation systems some institutional changes were necessary, if only because the traditional fallow period would be eliminated. What we cannot know is whether enclosures were the best and *predictable* solution. Perhaps both enclosures and the open fields with the new technology are just two of possibly many ways of improving on the old system. Moreover, we cannot determine *ex post* either which institution was more efficient or which institution should be *predicted* as the outcome of the ongoing soical decision process.

This note of caution in the application of theory to the origins of social institutions suggests that we should once again pay attention to a more evolutionary view of institutional change. Moreover, a number of economic historians have recently begun focusing on a *path dependent* approach to technological and institutional change. (See, for example, David [1985, 1987]; Kuran [1988] Puffert [1988]; and Rosenthal [1988].) In fact, two other papers at this conference support this view (Hoffman [1988] and Libecap [1988]). Each of these papers focuses on the particular evolutionary development of an institution within a particular society.

Because repeated games often have many inefficient equilibria, public goods are likely to be provided in suboptimal amounts, and public decision processes are notoriously inconsistent, we cannot develop a theory of the origins of social institutions that makes general predictions of efficient outcomes from sets of initial conditions. The best we can expect to do is to try to understand the process of institutional development within each individual society. To do so we can use economic tools to help understand the comparative statics outcomes we observe, but we cannot conclude that an institution which grows out of an obvious need and persists for a long time is necessarily efficient by any accepted definition of the word. In short, we must be historians as well as economists to do economic history credibly.

7. Conclusion

What have we learned from this brief introduction to the application of concepts from repeated games, the allocation of public goods, and public decision processes to historical analysis? First, in situations where prisoner's dilemma-type problems exist, inefficiency is not a sufficient condition for institutional change. Inefficient equilibria can and do persist for long periods of time. This is in part because the voluntary provision of public goods is likely to be suboptimal and because many public decision processes favor the maintenance of the status quo, whether efficient or not. Second, given that many inefficient equilibria exist, we cannot construct a predictive theory of institutional change. That is to say, we cannot predict when an institution will change or what new institution will evolve. We cannot even always predict the direction of change, since less efficient equilibria can replace more efficient ones if one faction begins to cheat on a cooperative agreement. The theory of repeated games only raises the possibility of an efficient equilibrium.

While this conclusion may seem negative, we are not suggesting either that theory should not be applied to history or that it is impossible to develop explanations for historical events. Rather, we are reminding economic historians that institutional developments in one society have a history which may not apply to understanding institutional developments in another society. It is one thing to use theory to understand a given set of historical events. It is quite another thing to develop a predictive theory of institutional change based on a presumption that persistent institutions are efficient and that comparative statics changes always involve replacing outmoded institutions with more efficient ones.

Summary

This paper examines an approach to the analysis of institutional persistence and change which is commonly observed in the economic history literature. In particular, it is often argued that institutions which persist must be efficient and that institutional change is a process of moving from one efficient equilibrium to another as a consequence of exogenous economic changes. Where institutions fail to achieve first-best efficiency, it is often argued that, due to transaction costs, only a second-best efficiency can be attained.

We argue that this approach fails to take account of the fact that economic equilibria cannot be presumed to be efficient in the presence of joint decision making. This argument is supported with reference to the theoretical and experimental literature on the allocation of public goods, recent literature on equilibria in repeated nonzero sum games, and the public choice literature on public decision processes. The paper ends with a review of the recent literature on the origins, persistence, and demise of the open field system in Europe. We show how the efficiency argument dominates historical analyses of the open field system and suggest that a path dependent approach might be more useful in the future.

Zusammenfassung

Dieser Artikel untersucht einen Ansatz zur Analyse der Dauerhaftigkeit und Änderung von Institutionen, der gewöhnlich in der Literatur der Wirtschaftsgeschichte angewandt wird. Insbesondere wird oft behauptet, daß Institutionen, die fortbestehen, effizient sein müssen und daß institutioneller Wandel, als Konsequenz von exogenen wirtschaftlichen Änderungen, ein Prozeß der Bewegung von einem effizienten Gleichgewicht zu einem anderen sei. Ferner wird oft gesagt, daß dort, wo Institutionen aufgrund von Transaktionskosten versagen, eine first-best Effizienz zu erreichen, nur eine second-best Effizienz erreicht werden kann.

Wir argumentieren, daß ein solcher Ansatz nicht in der Lage ist, die Tatsache in Betracht zu ziehen, daß ökonomische Gleichgewichte bei Vorhandensein von gemeinsamer Entscheidungsfindung nicht als effizient angenommen werden können. Dieses Argument wird unterstützt durch Bezugnahme auf die theoretische und experimentelle Literatur über die Allokation öffentlicher Güter, die neuere Literatur über Gleichgewichte in wiederholten Nichtnullsummenspielen und der Public Choice Literatur über öffentliche Entscheidungsprozesse. Der Artikel endet mit einem Überblick über die neuere Literatur zu den Ursprüngen, zur Dauerhaftigkeit und zum Verschwinden des Systems der offenen Felder in Europa. Wir zeigen, daß das Effizienzargument die historische Analyse des offenen Feldsystems beherrscht und weisen darauf hin, daß in Zukunft eine Pfadanalyse nützlicher sein dürfte.

References

ALLEN, R. C. [1982], "Efficiency and Distributional Consequences of Eighteenth Century Enclosures", *Economic Journal*, 92, 937–953.
ALLEN, R. C., and O'GRADA, C. [1988], "On the Road with Arthur Young: English, Irish, and French Agriculture During the Industrial Revolution", *Journal of Economic History*, 48, 93–116.

ANDERSON, T. L. and HILL, P. J. [1975], "The Evolution of Property Rights: A Study of the American West", *Journal of Law and Economics*, 18, 163–179.

ARROW, K. J. [1963], *Social Choice and Individual Values*, New York.

AUMANN, R. J. [1978], "Survey on Repeated Games", pp. 11–42, in: R. J. Aumann (ed.), *Essays in Game Theory and Mathematical Economics in Honor of Oskar Morgenstern*, Mannheim.

AXELROD, R. [1984], *The Evolution of Cooperation*, New York.

BINGER, B. R., and HOFFMAN, E. [1988], *Microeconomics With Calculus*, Glenview, IL.

CAMPBELL, B. M. S. [1983], "Agricultural Progress in Medieval England: Some Evidence from Norfolk", *Economic History Review*, 35, 26–46.

– – [1988], "The Diffusion of Vetches in Medieval England", *Economic History Review*, 41, 193–208.

CHEUNG, S. N. S. [1969], *The Theory of Share Tenancy*, Chicago.

COASE, R. H. [1960], "The Problem of Social Cost", *Journal of Law and Economics*, 3, 1–44.

DAHLMAN [1980], *The Open Field System and Beyond. A Property Rights Analysis of an Economic System*, Cambridge.

DAVID, P. A. [1985], "Clio and the Economics of QWERTY", *American Economic Review, Papers and Proceedings*, 75, 332–337.

– – [1987], "Some New Standards for the Economics of Standardization in the Information Age", in: P. Dasgupta and P. Stoneman (eds.), *Economic Policy and Technological Performance*, Cambridge.

FENOALTEA, S. [1975a], "The Rise and Fall of a Theoretical Model: The Manorial System", *Journal of Economic History*, 35, 386–409.

– – [1975], "Authority, Efficiency, and Agricultural Organization in Medieval England and Beyond: A Hypothesis", *Journal of Economic History*, 35, 693–718.

– – [1976], "Risk, Transaction Costs, and the Organization of Medieval Agriculture", *Explorations in Economic History*, 13, 129–152.

– – [1977], "Fenoaltea on Open Fields: A Reply", *Explorations in Economic History*, 14, 405–410.

– – [1987], "Transactions Costs, Whig History, and the Common Fields", *unpublished manuscript, Center for Advanced Study*, Princeton, NJ.

GRANTHAM, G. W. [1980], "The Persistence of Open-Field Farming in Nineteenth Century France", *Journal of Economic History*, 40, 124–142.

GREEN, E. and PORTER, R. [1983], "Noncooperative Collusion Under Imperfect Price Information", *Econometrica*, 52, 87–100.

HIGGS. R. [1973], "Race, Tenure, and Resource Allocation in Southern Agriculture, 1910", *Journal of Economic History*, 33, 149–169.

– – [1974], "Patterns of Farm Rental in the Georgia Cotton Belt, 1880–1900", *Journal of Economic History*, 34, 468–482.

HOFFMAN, P. T. [1988], "Institutions and Agriculture in Old-Regime France", *Journal of Institutional and Theoretical Economics*, 145.

HOFFMANN, R. C. [1975], "Medieval Origins of the Open Fields", pp. 23–71, in: W. N. Parker and E. L. Jones (eds.), *European Peasants and Their Markets*, Princeton.

ISAAC, R. M. and WALKER, J. M. [1987], "Success and Failure of the Voluntary Contributions Process: Some Evidence from Experimental Economics", *Liberty Fund Seminar on the Ethics and Economics of Charity*, San Diego, CA.

ISAAC, R. M., WALKER, J. M., and THOMAS, S. H. [1984], "Divergent Evidence on Free Riding: An Experimental Examination of Possible Explanations", *Public Choice*, 43, 113–149.

KREPS, D. M., MILGROM, P., ROBERTS, J., and WILSON, R. [1982], "Rational Cooperation in the Finitely Repeated Prisoners' Dilemma", *Journal of Economic Theory*, 27, 245–252.

KREPS, D. and SPENCE, A. M. [1985], "Modelling the Role of History in Industrial Organization and Competition", pp. 340–378, in: R. G. Feiwel (ed.), *Issues in Contemporary Microeconomics and Welfare*, Albany.

KURAN, T. [1988], "The Tenacious Past: Theories of Personal and Collective Conservatism", *Journal of Economic Behavior and Organization*, 10, 143–171.

KURZ, M. [1985], "Reconsideration of Duopoly Theory: A Cooperative Perspective", pp. 245–280, in: G. R. Feiwel (ed.), *Issues in Contemporary Microeconomics and Welfare*, Albany.

LIBECAP, G. D. [1978a], "Economic Variables and the Development of the Law: The Case of Western Mineral Rights", *Journal of Economic History*, 38, 338–362.

– – [1978b], *The Evolution of Private Mineral Rights: Nevada's Comstock Lode*, New York.

– – [1988], "Distributional Issues in Contracting for Property Rights", *Journal of Institutional and Theoretical Economics*, 145.

MARWELL, G. and AMES, R. [1979], "Experiments on the Provision of Public Goods I: Resources, Interest Group, Group Size, and the Free Rider Problem", *American Journal of Sociology*, 84, 1335–1360.

– – [1980], "Experiments on the Provision of Public Goods II: Provision Point, Stakes, Experience, and the Free Rider Problem", *American Journal of Sociology*, 85, 926–937.

MCCLOSKEY, D. M. [1972], "The Enclosure of Open Fields: Preface to a Study of its Impact on the Efficiency of English Agriculture in the Eighteenth Century", *Journal of Economic History*, 32, 15–35.

– – [1975a], "The Persistence of English Common Fields", pp. 73–119, in: W. N. Parker and E. L. Jones (eds.), *European Peasants and Their Markets*, Princeton.

– – [1975b], "The Economics of Enclosure: A Market Analysis", pp. 123–160, in: W. N. Parker and E. L. Jones (eds.), *European Peasants and Their Markets*, Princeton.

– – [1976], "English Open Fields as Behavior Toward Risk", *Research in Economic History*, 1, 124–169.

MOULIN, H. [1982], *Game Theory for the Social Sciences*, New York.

MUELLER, D. C. [1979], *Public Choice*, New York.

NORTH, D. C. and THOMAS, R. T. [1973], *The Rise of the Western World: A New Economic History*, Cambridge.

PLOTT, C. R. and LEVINE, M. [1978], "A Model of Agenda Influence on Committee Decisions", *American Economic Review*, 68, 146–160.

PUFFERT, D. J. [1988], *Standardization of Gauge and the Integration of Railway Networks in Britain and America*, Doctoral Dissertation, Stanford University.

RADNER, R. [1986], "Repeated Partnership Games with Imperfect Monitoring and no Discounting", *Review of Economic Studies*, 53, 43–57.

RADNER, R., MYERSON, R., and MASKIN, E. [1986], "An Example of a Repeated Partnership Game with Discounting and Uniformly Inefficient Equilibria", *Review of Economic Studies*, 53, 59–69.

REID, J. D., JR. [1973], "Sharecropping as an Understandable Market Respone: the Post-Bellum South", *Journal of Economic History*, 33, 106–130.

– – [1975], "Sharecropping in History and Theory", *Agricultural History*, 49, 426–440.

– – [1976], "Sharecropping and Agricultural Uncertainty", *Economic Development and Cultural Change*, 24, 549–576.

RIKER, W. H. [1982], *Liberalism Against Populism*, San Francisco.

ROSENTHAL, J.-L. [1988], *The Fruits of Revolution: Property Rights, Litigation and French Agriculture 1700–1860*, Doctoral Dissertation, California Institute of Technology.

SLICHER van BATH, B. H. [1963], *The Agrarian History of Western Europe, A. D. 500–1850*, London.

UMBECK, J. [1977a], "The California Gold Rush: A Study of Emerging Property Rights", *Explorations in Economic History*, 14, 197–226.
– – [1977b], "The Theory of Contract Choice and the California Gold Rush", *Journal of Law and Economics*, 20, 421–437.
– – [1981a], "Might Makes Right: A Theory of the Foundation and Initial Distribution of Property Rights", *Economic Inquiry*, 19, 38–58.
– – [1981b], *A Theory of Property Rights with Application to the California Gold Rush*, Ames.
WILLIAMSON, O. [1979], "Transaction-Cost Economics: The Governance of Contractual Relations", *Journal of Law and Economics*, 22, 130–150.

Brian R. Binger
Elizabeth Hoffman
Department of Economics
University of Arizona
Tucson, Arizona 85721
U. S. A.

[26]

Cambridge Journal of Economics 1989, 13, 79–101

Institutional rigidities and economic growth

Geoff Hodgson*

If we object that . . . historicizing, psychologizing and sociologizing are not the business of economics, then we must conclude that the objector thinks that long-term growth theory is not the business of economics. Herbert Simon (1984).

One of Nicholas Kaldor's most notable contributions to economic science is his theory of growth, initially developed to explain the relatively poor performance of the UK economy (Kaldor, 1966). Whilst modifications were made to this argument in the light of debate,[1] his enduring thesis was that differing national growth rates were to be explained by processes of cumulative causation based on 'increasing returns to scale', with the manufacturing sector as 'the engine of growth' (see, e.g. Kaldor, 1972, 1975A, 1985).

Briefly, Kaldor argued that manufacturing output growth promotes further growth in manufacturing productivity and productivity in the economy as a whole. In addition, growing manufacturing productivity helps to promote exports, further stimulating manufacturing output, as well as shifting the balance of payments constraint. This feedback closes a loop and provides a rationale for the notion of cumulative change. Furthermore, as the manufacturing sector grows in absolute terms, in its relative importance in the economy as a whole, and in its average level of productivity, it is deduced that both output and productivity will grow for the entire economy.

Despite the fact that much evidence has been marshalled in its support (see Thirlwall, 1983), Kaldor's theory has not found universal favour. At least two alternative theories have been proposed. The first is the theory of technological diffusion, proposed by Stanislaw Gomulka (1971, 1979). According to this idea, productivity growth is a function of the varying rates of diffusion of technology from lead to laggard nations,

*Newcastle upon Tyne Polytechnic. The author wishes to thank Dick Bailey, Ha-Joon Chang, Mike Dietrich, Robert Gausden, Ian Gough, Neil Kay, Tony Lawson, Lars Mjoset, Richard Nelson, Steven Pressman, Bob Rowthorn, Brian Snowdon, Ian Steedman, Tony Thirlwall, Arthur Walker, Grahame Wright, Nancy Wulwick and two anonymous referees for comments on earlier drafts and other invaluable assistance.

[1] After criticism from Wolfe (1968), Kaldor (1968) retracted his (1966, 1967) view that 'inelasticity in the supply of labour', due to a comparatively rapid and early exhaustion of the supply of labour power from the rural hinterland, was the 'main constraint' limiting the growth potential of the UK economy. Subsequently he was to put greater 'emphasis on the exogenous components of demand, and in particular on the role of exports, in determining the trend rate of productivity growth' (Kaldor, 1975B, p. 896). On this issue see Thirlwall (1978, 1979, 1983).

0309–166X/89/010079 + 23 $03.00/0

80   G. Hodgson

depending in turn on the 'technological gap' involved. Explicitly rejected by Kaldor (1975A), but viewed more sympathetically by John Cornwall (1976, 1977), Bob Rowthorn (1975A), Bernard Stafford (1981) and others, this alternative theory has been supported by some econometric evidence.

A second alternative can be found in the recent work of the American neo-Marxists Samuel Bowles, David Gordon and Thomas Weisskopf (1985) and their 'social' explanation of the slow growth of productivity of the US economy, again with supportive econometric tests. We are thus faced with an unresolved dispute of central importance both for economic theory and policy.

It will be suggested below that all these rival approaches point to unresolved problems in the underlying theory of the production process. An examination of the theoretical foundations of the different analyses reveals several flaws and suggests a search for a different framework. Fortunately, a promising alternative paradigm has already begun to emerge, based on the work of several economic theorists and historians, which suggests that growth and development are affected by inherited institutional structures and social practices. Whilst faults are found in parts of Kaldor's theory, the emerging alternative endorses some conclusions which are similar to his.

The following section of this article involves a critical discussion of the contending theories. Section 2 introduces an alternative approach with an empirical test of the type of theory that it implies. A conclusion is that an institutionalist model, based on indices of institutional flexibility or rigidity, is at least as successful, in both theoretical and empirical terms, as other available theories.

1. Foundations of the different analyses

Cumulative causation and increasing returns
At the core of Kaldor's analysis of economic growth is the idea of economic success breeding economic success, and failure breeding failure—or the 'survival of the fastest'. This is, of course, a direct challenge to the equilibrium theorising of orthodoxy, where it is often supposed that the market economy contains self-righting mechanisms to bring recovery from any downturn, and an effective price mechanism to compensate for imbalances in development. This central methodological difference accounts in part for the reluctance of orthodox theorists to embrace Kaldor's arguments.

Kaldor acknowledged two major influences on his formulation of this principle of cumulative causation. The first was the work of the institutionalist Gunnar Myrdal,[1] who initially formulated a model of cumulative causation in his *Monetary Equilibrium*, (published in Swedish in 1931) and repeated the idea in his classic studies of racial discrimination (1944) and of uneven regional development (1957).[2]

The second influence was an article by the American economist Allyn Young (1928). Emphasising that economic change 'propagates itself in a cumulative way' (p. 533), Young based this conclusion on the notion of increasing returns to scale. Kaldor seized upon this

---

[1] Myrdal himself dates his conversion to institutionalism from after the Second World War (Myrdal, 1978). Veblen argued as early as 1898 that the economic process should be viewed in terms of 'cumulative causation' (Veblen, 1919, pp. 64–70). Institutional economists (for example, Kapp, 1976) have typically stressed cumulative causation as an alternative to equilibrium theorising.

[2] As Shackle (1967) has argued, Myrdal's *Monetary Equilibrium* has extensive parallels with Keynes' *General Theory*.

Institutional rigidities and economic growth   81

idea, seeing the failure to recognise increasing returns as a crucial weakness of orthodoxy. The main function of markets, argued Kaldor and Young, is not merely to allocate but to create more resources by enlarging the scope for specialisation and the division of labour. Kaldor saw these increasing returns as particularly prevalent in the manufacturing sector, thus providing a justification for regarding manufacturing production as the engine of growth.

Third, there is the parallel between the work of Kaldor and the so-called 'Verdoorn Law' (1949). In his famous inaugural lecture Kaldor (1966) gave two specifications of this law, arguing that both the rate of growth of employment and the rate of growth of labour productivity were both positively correlated with, and functions of, the rate of growth of output. Kaldor saw this as resulting from 'learning by doing' and economies of scale resulting from general industrial expansion and the enlargement of markets. These important propositions have given rise to an enormous literature, and a number of unresolved issues, which are impossible to survey in detail here (see Bairam, 1987; McCombie, 1983; Thirlwall, 1983).

Nevertheless, we may consider briefly some aspects of this work. Following the criticisms of Rowthorn (1975A), Kaldor (1975B) was to argue that output was determined by demand and this should be taken as exogenous. In response, Erkin Bairam (1987) and others have pointed out that this assumption of exogeneity conflicts with the principle of cumulative causation. Furthermore, given that demand itself was a product of growth, single equation estimates of the Verdoorn Law are likely to be biased and inconsistent. A. Parikh (1978) attempted a simultaneous equation approach to the estimation of the Verdoorn Law, but John McCombie (1983) has pointed to some of its serious limitations.

Another line of enquiry has been to examine the underlying structure of the Verdoorn Law (Rowthorn, 1979; Thirlwall, 1980; Verdoorn, 1980; de Vries, 1980). Notably, Verdoorn's original (1949) formulation of the Law is based on neoclassical foundations and features a static Cobb–Douglas production function. There is no disembodied technical change, nor any 'learning by doing'. Clearly this contrasts with Kaldor's idea of 'dynamic economies of scale'.[1]

McCombie (1982) has shown that *if* the foundation of the Law is a production function of the Cobb–Douglas type then the degree of returns to scale from both static and dynamic equations should be equal. In other words, the coefficient relating the levels of productivity and output should be identical to that relating their growth. However, estimates of the static and dynamic Verdoorn coefficients (McCombie, 1982; McCombie and de Ridder, 1984) lead to an alleged 'paradox'. The static specifications give no evidence of increasing returns to scale, whereas there are significant and increasing returns in the dynamic case. Consequently, this evidence suggests that the assumption of an underlying production function of the Cobb–Douglas type is unwarranted.

Of course, Cambridge itself has produced a number of arguments against the aggregate production function, in the famous capital controversy (Harcourt, 1972). Less well-known are the earlier reservations advanced by Alfred Marshall, concerning the notion of increasing returns. In Appendix H of his *Principles*, he noted that increasing returns could undermine the conditions for an equilibrium of supply and demand.[2] An increase in the

---

[1] Verdoorn (1980, p. 385) has stated that the law that has been given his name now appears 'to be much less generally valid'.

[2] In addition, Marshall anticipates an aspect of Sraffa's famous (1926) critique by noting that under increasing returns 'whatever firm first gets a good start will obtain a monopoly of the whole business of trade in its district' (Marshall, 1920, p. 459n.). On this see Shackle (1967, ch. 3).

82   G. Hodgson

scale of production could mean a dramatic reduction in the supply price undermining the established normal or equilibrium price.[1] Notably, in the case of heterogeneous inputs or outputs, without a price framework it is difficult to establish any notion of changing (increasing or decreasing) returns.

Marshall's attempted solution was to make a distinction between 'internal' and 'external' economies of scale. The former related to a single firm, the latter to the gains made from the extension of markets and demand. Whilst Young drew inspiration from the 'external economies' idea, Frank Knight (who, like Kaldor, was one of Young's students) pointed out that they are dynamic in character, accruing in Smithian fashion through the growth of the market. Consequently, it is quite inappropriate to situate them in a static or equilibrium price theory (see Blitch, 1983). Indeed, for Knight, as it was for Piero Sraffa (1926), the very concept of 'external economies' was problematic.

Young's response was to stress the notion of disequilibrium, as consummated in his 1928 article, and in various letters to Knight in that year (see Blitch, 1983). However, Young gave no indication as to how to dispense with the fundamentals of equilibrium price theory. Sadly, a few months later Young was dead, leaving such theoretical problems unresolved to this day.

In addition to this theoretical difficulty, it is sometimes argued that the theory of cumulative causation is incomplete because it lacks a 'first cause': in terms of initial divergences in rates of growth. In Section 2 of this article it will be argued that both initial and persistent differences in growth rates can be partly explained by reference to differences in institutional ossification in the countries concerned.

The productivity enigma
For a long time the orthodox 'production function' model has faced a nagging problem in explaining considerable inter-plant and international differences in productivity. Much of this evidence has been reviewed elsewhere (Hodgson, 1982; Nichols, 1986). Despite productivity growth that is lower than in other developed capitalist countries, absolute US productivity levels are still higher than elsewhere, and in particular still well ahead of those in the UK and Japan (Maddison, 1982, 1987). Even more striking is the evidence for single industries, showing big sectoral productivity gaps between different countries (Prais, 1981).

A typical orthodox response is to suggest that such differences in productivity must be due, in the main, to differences in the inputs of the production function. In fact there is considerable evidence portraying relatively low levels of capital investment in the UK (Blackaby, 1978; Caves and Krause, 1980). However, there are serious problems in isolating these as the main cause of low productivity. For instance, studies show that the average increase in output resulting from a unit of investment expenditure has been much lower in Britain and Japan than in France, Italy, West Germany and the USA (Brown and Sheriff, 1978; Blume, 1980). Pratten (1976) found that differences in the amounts of hardware and other machinery appeared to be responsible for no more than one-fifth of the average difference in productivity found in comparable plants in Britain, the USA,

---

[1] In fact Marshall had exposed a general logical problem with neoclassical theory: of assuming what it is required to prove. The schedule of 'normal supply prices' which lies behind the supply curve requires some assumption of stability for each price, which in orthodox theory implies some notion of equilibrium for each point on the curve. In other words, the idea of equilibrium is tacit in the reasoning through which it is meant to be established.

Skouras (1981, pp. 202–4) finds a similar argument concerning the logical difficulties of supply and demand analysis in the work of Joan Robinson. For further discussions of this issue see Hodgson (1988, ch. 8; in press).

West Germany and France. Prais (1981, p. 269) argued that low UK productivity could not be attributed to low investment in machinery but to inadequate 'knowledge of how to create and operate modern machinery efficiently'. We are led to the conclusion that varied amounts of capital equipment per employee are not the main factor explaining internationally diverse levels of productivity.[1]

Of course, an inferior labour input could be blamed as well, but the 'production function' model is still in some difficulty in explaining the lack of a clear relation between outputs and capital inputs. Instead of further attempts to fit this awkward evidence into this 'meat grinder' model, where production results from the automatic or mechanical transformation of given inputs, the process of production should be conceived in a different manner. Instead of the orthodox symmetry of 'factors of production', labour should be seen as an active agency with capital goods as passive instruments. Production is a social process involving people with aspirations of their own, in structured social interaction with each other. As Richard Nelson (1981) argues, the firm is a 'social system' and not 'a machine'.

Most importantly, productivity is not mechanically dependent on the number of hours of work that is agreed between employer and employee. Owing to uncertainty and imperfect knowledge, the amount and efficiency of work has to be imperfectly specified in the contract; it depends not only on the given technology but also upon both the motivation and skill of the workforce and the organisation and supervision of management. These, in turn, depend on complex institutional structures and routines and on cultural norms that are inherited from the past. This is not, however, a deterministic view: there is space for the partial indeterminacy of action and will. In particular, the fact that the employment contract cannot be fully specified in advance means that outputs are not completely nor mechanically determined by inputs.

A 'social' model of production
In the 1980s some alternative formal models of the production process have emerged. Bowles's (1985) analysis focuses on the (costly) processes through which employers exercise power over labour, and the ability of workers to resist employer directives. An econometric test of this type of model appears in a study of the US economy by Bowles, Gordon and Weisskopf (1985). They regress productivity growth against several variables including indices of 'employer leverage over workers' and the 'quality of working conditions', using postwar annual US data. These variables are found to be highly significant.

On close inspection the Bowles–Gordon–Weisskopf model is not as radical as claimed.[2] For instance, Bowles's (1985) analysis is virtually identical, in formal terms, to that of Carl Shapiro and Joseph Stiglitz (1984): both employ the standard neoclassical assumption of maximising behaviour to determine an (unemployment) equilibrium

---

[1] See the further references in Hodgson (1982, 1984). Davies and Caves (1987) found a significant but slight relationship between productivity and the value of gross fixed capital stock per employee. In his comprehensive study Denison (1979) found that 'factor inputs', including capital stock, the educational level of the workforce, and the amount of expenditure on research and development, explained no more than a small fraction of the US productivity slowdown in the 1970s. Note, however, the criticism of the definition of investment in Denison's work by Scott (1981).

[2] Some of the ostensible radicalism of the Bowles–Gordon–Weisskopf account results simply from the use of revolutionary-romantic language. For instance, one of their significant independent variables is the relative cost of nonagricultural crude materials with respect to the price of finished goods. This is described as the level of 'popular resistance', suggesting that the price of oil, for example, has more to do with the struggles of the oilfield workers and less to do with the fortunes of geological exploration and the state of the OPEC cartel.

84   G. Hodgson

outcome. Notably, in the Bowles–Gordon–Weisskopf model the role of effective demand in promoting productivity does not have a clear and central place.[1]

An attempt by Weisskopf (1987) to extend this type of econometric analysis to eight OECD countries gives chequered results. He focuses on the level of unemployment which is supposed to increase employer leverage and work intensity. A significant short-run effect of unemployment on productivity is found in three countries only (US, UK and Italy) and a positive long-run effect simply in the case of the US. In four countries (Canada, France, Germany and Sweden) a statistically significant and *negative* relation-ship between unemployment and productivity growth is discovered, contrary to the Bowles–Gordon–Weisskopf analysis of the US. Weisskopf tries to explain this anomaly by suggesting that the 'threat' of unemployment may not be as effective in Canada, France, Germany and Sweden because of a more developed welfare state. But this auxiliary hypothesis is neither tested nor examined closely.

In addition, despite justified criticism of the neoclassical 'meat grinder' conception of production, the Bowles–Gordon–Weisskopf model replaces this with a 'stick and carrot' conception of the labour process which is only marginally more sophisticated. It relates to the model of management proposed by Frederick Taylor (1911) which has over-influenced Marxists, particularly in the US.[2]

Production, institutions and knowledge

One major reason why Taylorism is of limited efficiency is that 'scientific management' ignores the difficulties and costs involved in gathering and processing the information that is required to monitor and motivate workers. Furthermore, it ignores the importance of the information that the workers may themselves possess, and the fact that their 'practical knowledge' is highly significant but difficult to codify or evaluate. Productivity, especially in a complex process of production, is closely related to both the development of practical knowledge and to the signalling and interpretation of information within the firm.[3]

As Thorstein Veblen has elaborated (see Veblen, 1964; Dyer, 1984; Hodgson, 1988), labour is made up of congealed habits or skills, which may take some time to acquire and depend upon their institutional integument. Later writers have stressed that it is difficult to codify or readily communicate such skills, hence the references of Edith Penrose (1959) to 'unteachable' and Michael Polanyi (1957, 1967) to 'tacit' knowledge. The general social importance of routinised behaviour has been more recently emphasised by Anthony Giddens (1984) and Richard Nelson and Sidney Winter (1982). Contrary to the treatment of 'information problems' by neoclassical theorists, 'tacit' or 'unteachable' knowledge cannot be reduced simply to 'information' because it is partly embodied in routines or unconscious reflexes, and it cannot be reduced to or transmitted in a codified form.

Given that the productivity of an economy is crucially related to the transmission and interpretation of information, and the growth of different kinds of knowledge, there are important consequences for the theory of economic growth. For instance, improvements

---

[1] See the criticisms of the Bowles–Gordon–Weisskopf model in Nell (1984, pp. 246–7) and the remarks on the relationship between the pressure of demand and productivity by Matthews (1982) and Worswick (1982).
[2] For critiques of Taylor's (1911) theory of 'scientific management' see Vroom and Deci (1970). For Marxist correctives to Braverman's (1974) over-emphasis on Taylorism see Friedman (1977) and Burawoy (1985). Braverman's deskilling hypothesis is criticised in Cutler (1978) and Wood (1982).
[3] Informational considerations should be at the centre of explanations of why worker participation can improve productivity (see Hodgson, 1984; Jones and Svejnar, 1982; Stephen, 1982).

in work organisation are often designed both to facilitate the communication of information and the enhancement and transfer of skills within the plant.[1] Significant
increases in productivity can result from better deployment of tasks, a reduction of
waste, and improved organisational or other skills. These developments are not necessarily associated with an increase in the intensity of work.

This argument contrasts with a view which is found across the political spectrum: it is
the idea that increases in productivity, with given capital goods and technology, are
generally associated with enhanced managerial control and subsequent work intensification. As Craig Littler and Graeme Salaman (1982) have argued, the depiction of virtually
unqualified managerial control means that the performance of the worker is essentially
predetermined, thus removing the major reason for sustaining a distinction between
labour and labour-power, and denying many subtleties in Marx's (1976) account of the
production process.

Littler and Salaman point out that even under Taylorist managerial regimes, and even
with the most menial or routinised jobs, there is a real zone of discretion for the workers,
involving alternative courses of action and degrees of conscientiousness or consent. One of
the reasons for the existence of this zone is that the gathering together of all relevant
information and knowledge in management's hands is, contrary to Taylor, an impossible
task.

A consequence is that the behaviour of the firm is not, within the given constraints,
entirely determined by, nor entirely subject to, the decisions of its managers. Because
much of the 'expertise' of the firm is embedded in the firm's routines and the habitual skills
of its workforce, it is neither completely codifiable and communicable, nor completely
manageable from the apex of the organisation. As Nelson (1981, p. 1038) puts it: 'management cannot effectively "choose" what is to be done in any detailed way, and has only
broad control over what is done, and how well. Only a small portion of what people
actually do on a job can be monitored in detail.'

Thus any model of productivity growth which is centred on the application of, and
resistance to, 'employer leverage' will give us only part of the picture. As Nelson and
Winter (1982) and Veblen (1964) argue, the behaviour of the firm is largely routinised.
For this reason economic development can appear, for significant periods of time,
with exceptions discussed below, to be subject to inertia. An adequate theory of the
development of productive capabilities must take into account both the social culture and
institutions within which habits and routines are reproduced, and the conditions which
lead to their disruption or mutation.[2]

These considerations give us grounds to reject Kaldor's (1966, pp. 12–13) argument
against the possibility that productivity growth may be the driving force behind output
growth. He contends that the 'usual hypothesis is that the growth of productivity is mainly
to be explained by the progress in science and technology', and points out, quite rightly,
that the levels and growth rates of productivity can vary greatly from plant to plant, and

---

[1] Williamson (1975, 1985) has taken on board some of these points. For differing approaches see Beer
(1972), Emery (1977), and Rice (1958).
[2] Note also that the Veblen–Nelson–Winter idea of habits and routines amounts to some 'unity of knowing
and doing'. This is incompatible with Braverman's (1974) stress on the 'separation of conception and execution', and his idea that managers appropriate the decision-making process while the worker becomes 'an
appendage to the machine'. Capitalism displays elements of both managerial dominance and (limited) worker
autonomy, and it would be incorrect, therefore, to put exclusive stress on either idea. As Burawoy (1985, p. 41)
puts it: 'Rather than a separation of conception and execution, we find a separation of workers' conception and
management's conception, of workers' knowledge and management's knowledge'.

86   G. Hodgson

from country to country, even when the plants are controlled by common multinational corporations. But 'these must have had the same access to improvements in knowledge and know-how', so if productivity growth determined output growth we should presumably expect productivity and output to be growing at more uniform rates than are evident.

The error in this argument is clear. Plants cannot have the 'same access to improvements in knowledge and know-how' because much relevant knowledge is 'tacit', 'unteachable', 'parcellised', embodied in habit or routine, and non-codifiable. Furthermore, even codifiable information does not become knowledge independent of the context of its transmission or of the cognitive framework of the receiver.[1] Knowledge and information are not readily storable, nor transmissible from agent to agent as water flows in a pipe.

The diffusion hypothesis

Such considerations lead us directly to Gomulka's (1971, 1979) theory of productivity growth and economic development. He argues that the dominant factor in determining productivity growth is the degree of 'diffusion of innovations' from technologically more advanced countries to the relatively less developed, using productivity levels as a proxy for technological development. In addition, the impact of this diffusion depends upon the 'absorptive capacity' of the country in question. This is allegedly determined by educational levels, the institutional framework and 'a variety of social, cultural, institutional and political factors' (1979, p. 186). Thus, for example, productivity growth in Japan is said to be greater because of its remaining productivity gap with the leading nations, and because of its superior ability to absorb new technology, and its encouragement of, rather than resistance to, innovation and change.

Although the literature on technological diffusion cannot be surveyed here, it can be pointed out that one feature is almost universal; the term 'technology' is related almost exclusively to technical innovations for which there is codifiable knowledge or a 'blueprint'. Thus, given the will to assimilate the technique, there are few remaining barriers other than technical competence and education. Technology is treated as a kind of substance, whose meaning and content is independent of culture, institutions, and cognitive frames. This empiricist and technicist conception of information and knowledge is, however, unacceptable.

Contrary to the assumptions of the diffusion theorists, production does not simply depend upon well-specified innovations such as hybrid corn or the silicon chip. Productive advance is also a matter of countless ways of understanding, interpreting and doing, which are embedded in the social culture and reinforced by its routines. Furthermore, production is a social process, depending on social institutions, relations, customs and rules. Consequently, the level of productivity in a nation is not uniquely nor closely related to its technological development, as an exclusive emphasis on technological diffusion would suggest.

A crucial feature of non-codifiable knowledge is that it is not simply accessible like blueprints in a file; its full acquisition can never be immediate, nor independent of its progressive application in practice. In such instances it is crucial to recognise that knowing and doing are inseparable.

Thus Nelson (1980) has criticised the common idea that 'technological knowledge is in the form of codified how-to-do-it knowledge which provides sufficient guidance so that if

---

[1] Contrary to the Austrian view, these considerations do not necessarily imply a subjectivist, nor a purely relativist, view of knowledge. See Lawson (1985, 1987) and Hodgson (1988).

one had access to the book one would be able to do it' (p. 63). He rejects also the notion that such knowledge is expanded in volume largely by expenditure on R&D: 'If the salient elements of techniques involve special personal skills, or a personalised pattern of inter-action and cooperation among a group of individuals in an important way, then one cannot easily infer how it would work from an experiment conducted elsewhere' (p. 67).

Looked at in this way, the validity of the diffusion hypothesis would depend on considerations such as: (i) the extent to which the lead countries are developing and trans-mitting codifiable technical knowledge, (ii) the propensity of the laggard countries to absorb the knowledge, and (iii) the extent to which codifiable technical knowledge is representative of skill and technique as a whole.

For example, the hypothesis would be invalid in a situation where the country at the top of the absolute productivity league (say the US) was relying largely on substantial non-codifiable knowledge which had been accumulated and dispersed over the years, and a laggard country (say Japan) was achieving high rates of productivity growth largely by generating its own codifiable knowledge (through R&D or whatever) which had not been brought in from elsewhere. The *prima facie* evidence would then suggest that the diffusion hypothesis was valid, but the main source of advance would not in fact be diffusion itself.

The validity of the diffusion hypothesis depends on the 'balance' between codifiable and non-codifiable knowledge in the economy. Our conclusion must be that the assumed model of technological development in the diffusion hypothesis is too simple, and does too much violence to the complexities of knowledge and technology, and to the conditions of productive advance.

Manufacturing as the engine of growth
A crude distinction between codifiable and non-codifiable knowledge may provide insights regarding different rates of productivity growth in different industries or sectors of the economy. Before we consolidate this point we shall consider alternative arguments as to why manufacturing, in particular, should be regarded as the leading sector of the economy.

Kaldor's (1966) proposition to this effect is partly based on the assertion that it is in the field of manufacturing that the phenomenon of increasing returns is likely to be more prevalent. Other sectors, such as mining and agriculture, are presumed to exhibit diminishing returns. However, as indicated above, there are theoretical problems with this argument, and a strong empirical case for the presumed pattern of returns to scale has yet to be made.

Being influenced by Kaldor, John Eatwell (1982, pp. 52–3) endorses the engine of growth idea, asserting that the income elasticity of demand for manufacturing products remains high, compared, for example, with agriculture. However, whilst there may be limits to the consumption of food, there are no equivalent limits elsewhere, particularly in the service sector. There is no apparent reason why higher incomes should condemn such sectors to relative decline.

Much of Eatwell's remaining argument is based on a false reductionism; he asserts that manufactured goods are essential for other sectors of the economy and concludes that manufacturing thus has a primary importance. However, just as manufactured goods are essential to the agricultural and service sectors, so too are services and agricultural goods essential to manufacturing. To say that X is essential to Y does not necessarily give X primacy, especially if Y is also essential to X. Consequently, a good part of his argument is flawed.

88   G. Hodgson

Yet there are reasons for giving manufacturing some distinctiveness. Nelson (1980, p. 67) suggests that differences in productivity growth might be affected by 'hardware versus human organization' which in turn relates to the question of codifiability of knowledge. Codifiable knowledge is likely to be relatively more significant in a highly-mechanised sector than in one depending more on traditional craft skills and routines. Consequently, highly mechanised sectors will be relatively more responsive to R&D initiatives and technological diffusion, even if much knowledge is still non-codifiable in this sector.

Furthermore, manufacturing is generally associated with a compact spatial organisation. Productive activities are often gathered together, with relatively easy communications between the persons involved. In contrast, spatial dispersion is wider in agriculture and communications are inferior. And in services there have traditionally been smaller-scale production units. Thus manufacturing may enjoy the greatest and fastest diffusion of skills and technique.

If this argument is correct, and manufacturing has a higher 'proportion' of codifiable knowledge than other sectors, as well as more compactness facilitating diffusion or communication of skills, then its importance stems not from a causal primacy or structural position in the economy but from its ability to respond to the diffusion or internal generation of codifiable knowledge.

On the other hand, circumstances may arise in which other sectors increase their dependence on modern science and technology, and make more use of codifiable knowledge. The rapidly increasing use of codifiable knowledge in a sector which has traditionally been dominated by embedded habits and skills, may partly explain the higher productivity growth in agriculture since the Industrial Revolution. Currently, productivity in the service sector is increasing as it makes greater use of information technology and compact spatial organisation.

Manufacturing, however, has advantages in these terms which have yet to be surpassed. It still may be potentially more responsive to any development and communication of codifiable technique that is promoted by the policy-makers, and act as a kind of 'engine of growth' for this reason. But in the absence of flows of codifiable knowledge to the manufacturing sector, Kaldor-type or Verdoorn-type relationships would break down. This could occur, for instance, in the country in the technological lead, or in the event of a world slowdown in innovation or demand.

Kaldor's theory may also break down in conditions of recession for another reason. It is widely accepted that one effect of a slump may be to cause a relatively higher bankruptcy rate amongst low-productivity firms. A consequence is 'degenerate' productivity growth, where average productivity is rising but the economy as a whole is contracting in size. It is possible, therefore, for the rates of growth of productivity in both manufacturing and the economy as a whole to be *inversely* related to the rate of change of manufacturing output for a limited period. This would be in defiance of two out of three of Kaldor's laws.[1] Consequently, whilst these laws may find some empirical support in periods of sustained economic expansion, there may be problems in applying Kaldor's theory to periods of recession.

In this survey of ideas and theories concerning economic growth, the role of social institutions, and the transmission of different forms of knowledge, have been highlighted. We now turn to the development and application of this approach.

---

[1] Some members of the French *régulation* school have suggested that Kaldor–Verdoorn type relationships may have broken down since the oil shock of 1973 (Boyer and Petit, 1981).

2. Towards an institutionalist alternative

This section commences with a discussion of the concept of institutional ossification, followed by an econometric test of the theory outlined here. Although no statistical test should be taken as conclusive, the preliminary results are good.

Since 1960 there has been much research by historians as to the causes of the slow growth of the American and British economies and of much faster growth in France, Germany, Italy and Japan. A prominent theme is to explain much of the difference in growth rates by the different degrees of cultural or institutional ossification of the countries involved.

Institutional ossification

There are two aspects to these processes of ossification. The first is to do with the timing of the industrial revolution in different countries. During this period of rapid economic and social transformation, habits and patterns of work are laid down which endure after industrialisation is accomplished. Hence, in general, the most flexible period for the more rapid development of new skills and routines is during the period at which industrialisation is proceeding at the fastest pace. Consequently, the countries which industrialised some time ago pay 'the penalty of taking the lead', to use Veblen's (1915) phrase.

Marxist historians, amongst others, have initiated much of the debate about the ossification of British political and economic institutions. Thus Perry Anderson (1964, p. 50) sees Britain as 'a sclerosed, archaic society, trapped and burdened by its past successes'. Similarly, Eric Hobsbawm (1969, p. 188) argues that Britain's early industrialisation used 'methods and techniques which, however advanced and efficient at the time, could not remain the most advanced and efficient, and it created a pattern of both production and markets which would not necessarily remain the one best fitted to sustain economic growth and technological change'.

Non-Marxist analysts repeat a similar theme. For example, Ronald Dore (1973, p. 419) argues that: 'The way a country comes to industrialization can have a lasting effect on the kind of industrial society it becomes. It will be a long time before Britain loses the marks of the pioneer, the scars and stiffnesses that come from the searing experience of having made the first, most long-drawn-out industrial revolution'. Also Sir Henry Phelps Brown (1977, pp. 25–26) writes of practical minds that 'became bounded by the processes and products that they mastered in long apprenticeships'. Past success in the old methods, whilst being cossetted by the old imperial trading systems, made managers and administrators reluctant to learn the new. Britain in the twentieth century remained bounded by the methods, processes and products of the nineteenth century.

Perhaps the most extensive development of these ideas to date comes in a collection of essays edited by Bernard Elbaum and William Lazonick (1986) who attribute the relative decline of the British economy in the twentieth century to 'rigidities in the economic and social institutions that developed during the nineteenth century, a period when Britain was the world's leading economic power and British industry was highly atomistic and competitive in organisation'. (p. 2). These institutional rigidities, they argue, obstructed efforts at economic renovation. Examples include entrenched shopfloor unionism (see also Kilpatrick and Lawson, 1980), rigid financial institutions and inflexible corporate structures. Clearly, all these have since undergone considerable change, but in all cases its pace and extent has been affected by the structures which were laid down in the formative years of the nineteenth century.

If the ossification argument is accepted then a country in the throes of industrial revolution will be more flexible and open to new techniques than either a nation which industrialised long ago, or a predominantly agricultural economy which has yet to escape from its immobile traditions and structures. We are not referring here mainly to the advantage that accrues to laggard industrialising nations in their ability to learn or import (codifiable) techniques from the leaders. Instead the emphasis is on the non-codifiable aspects of economic transformation, and to the flexibility that accrues to the country that is experiencing the most disruptive phase in the transition from an agricultural to an industrialised society.

Another aspect of institutional ossification is the extent to which it has been temporarily arrested and reversed by the upheaval of revolution or war, leading to new regimes and institutions, often of a more dynamic or less conservative hue. This theme is also found in historical studies of the reasons for Britain's relative economic decline. For instance, Anderson (1964, p. 37) notes that: 'Alone of major European nations, England emerged undefeated and unoccupied from two World Wars, its social structure uniquely untouched by external shocks or discontinuities.' Whilst Anderson recognises the convulsive and reforming effects of the two World Wars, Britain was not shattered by invasion or revolution on the Continental scale.

Similarly, Phelps Brown (1977, p. 20) sees British institutions, such as trade unions, suffering from 'the extraordinary continuity of their history: they have had no revolution, no defeat in war and no foreign occupation to give them a fresh start'. Consequently, in the British case, advanced institutional ossification was not alleviated by any major disruption on home soil in modern times.

Mancur Olson (1982) proposes that 'countries whose distributional coalitions have been emasculated or abolished by totalitarian government or foreign occupation should grow relatively quickly after a free and stable legal order is established' (p. 75). In contrast, the absence of these disruptions from Britain 'made it easier from the firms and families that advanced in the Industrial Revolution and the nineteenth century to organise or collude to protect their interests' (p. 84). Like many other authors, Olson argues that sweeping radical change, particularly that resulting from internal revolution or defeat in war, has helped to promote economic growth by overcoming the inertia of ossified, growth-retarding institutions.

The two aspects of institutional ossification—relating to the timing of the industrial revolution and the degree of major disruption—are observed most graphically in Britain. Relatively speaking, the United States has enjoyed a superior economic performance. But the prime concern here is to explain differing degrees of dynamism and growth. The US faces the problem of the slowdown in productivity growth and the erosion of its share of world trade. In this case the institutional arguments again seem convincing. The United States was one of the first countries to follow Britain into industrialisation. The American Revolution was two centuries ago, followed later by the Civil War. Consequently, post-industrial ossification is relatively advanced, with few periods of major disruption to increase flexibility.

In contrast, countries such as Belgium, France, Germany and Italy have been disrupted both by several revolutions in the last two centuries and by extensive invasion and occupation. In each of these cases, industrial transformation was later than Britain. Japan's social and economic transformation was later still, developing during a period of fascism, to be greatly accelerated after the foreign occupation of 1945. From the point of view of the timing of industrialisation, Japan's economic institutions should be the most flexible, whereas the degree of disruption has been the greatest in Belgium, France, Germany and Italy.[1]

Much of the historical literature on institutional ossification captures the underlying and more durable features of the institutions and routines in a capitalist country. The particular emphasis and interpretation offered here is on the function of non-codifiable knowledge and deeply-embedded structures and routines. This provides a counterpoint to the theory of technological diffusion which is more relevant to codifiable knowledge and techniques. However, before we proceed to a statistical test of the theories discussed here, it is necessary to evaluate briefly Olson's argument to which the present discussion concerning institutional ossification bears a superficial similarity.[2]

Considerations regarding the creation and transmission of knowledge are not significant in Olson's theory, neither are habits or routines given pride of place. Instead of a focus on the development and mutation of industrial skills, attention shifts onto the allegedly 'growth retarding' effects of 'interest groups' and 'distributional coalitions'. Implicitly, Olson is making the same classical liberal assumptions that lie at the core of much neoclassical theory: that the market is an elemental or natural order, and that institutional rigidities play a largely negative and restrictive role. These assumptions are inconsistent with a perspective which sees markets themselves as institutions, and in which institutions in general have features which enable as well as restrict economic activity. In particular, institutionalised or routinised behaviour provides information on likely outcomes for decision-making agents (see Hodgson, 1988).

In a rather *ad hoc* manner, however, Olson considers the possibility of an 'encompassing' interest group which stands at the pinnacle of society and prevents other feuding interest groups from being formed. In this manner he explains the relative success of social democratic countries such as Sweden. Furthermore, and in conflict with his liberal presumptions, positive virtues have to be given to fascist countries or similar regimes, which have prevented other 'distributional coalitions' from emerging. However, as Frederic Pryor (1983) has shown, a statistical test of Olson's theory with a sample of capitalist and Communist-led countries fails to confirm that the supremely 'encompassing' interest group of a Communist Party has a positive or statistically significant effect on growth. Whilst being useful in its stress on institutions, when applied to capitalist countries Olson's theory ends up being a re-worked argument for the benevolent Hobbesian sovereign: one who will ensure that markets work but will break up interest groups and coalitions whenever they may occur.

Hypotheses for statistical testing

It is rare that theories of economic growth can be applied equally without qualification to both capitalist and non-capitalist countries. Unlike the theories of Kaldor, Gomulka or Olson, the present analysis takes differences in the knowledge-transmitting functions of economic structures and institutions directly into account. Consequently, it is not intended to be applicable, at least not without major modification, to centrally-planned economies. Our statistical test may be applied to capitalist economies only.

[1] This brings to mind the words of Harry Lime in the film *The Third Man*: 'In Italy for thirty years under the Borgias they had warfare, terror, murder, bloodshed: but they produced Michelangelo, Leonardo da Vinci and the Renaissance. In Switzerland they had brotherly love; they had five hundred years of democracy and peace, and what did that produce? The cuckoo clock.'
[2] Critiques of Olson (1982) are found in Barry (1983), Bowles and Eatwell (1983), Kindleberger (1983), Mjoset (1985), Pryor (1983), de Vries (1983), Wallis and Oates (1988) and Whiteley (1986).

92   G. Hodgson

Available OECD data reduced the sample to 16 major capitalist countries (namely Australia, Austria, Belgium, Canada, Denmark, Finland, France, Germany, Italy, Japan, Netherlands, Norway, Sweden, Switzerland, United Kingdom, United States). The foregoing discussion of institutional ossification suggests a slow, long-term process, thus cross-section data were used, with periods of more than ten years; namely 1960–73 and 1973–84, i.e. before and after the oil price shock of 1973. Four data sets were thus generated: (i) 1960–73, (ii) 1973–84, (iii) 1960–84 as a whole, and (iv) a composite sample of 32 observations made up by juxtaposing the data from 1960–73 and 1973–84 with the addition of a dummy variable to indicate pre- and post-oil shock conditions.

The OECD data presented a limited choice of dependent variables. The annual rate of growth of real GDP per person employed was selected as an index of productivity growth, and denoted by *PROD* (source: OECD, 1986, Table 3.7).

Four types of hypothesis were tested:

(a) that productivity growth was dependent both on the degree of institutional flexibility—the inverse of ossification—and the degree of institutional disruption. The derivation of these variables is discussed below;

(b) that productivity growth was dependent on the 'technological gap' between each country and the lead country—the United States—measured by the relative productivity levels involved;

(c) that productivity growth was dependent on the level of investment in each country, measured by gross fixed capital formation as a percentage of GDP;

(d) that productivity growth reflected Kaldors' third law, i.e. being positively correlated with the growth rate of the manufacturing sector and negatively with the growth rate of employment outside manufacturing.[1]

The institutional data

The derivation of the institutional data in (a) presents several difficulties and a degree of over-simplification is unavoidable in any such test. A precedent exists in the work of Kwang Choi (1983) but this is built upon Olson's conceptual framework. Choi uses a rising logistic curve to reflect the 'sclerosis' resulting from the growth of interest groups. Cyril Black's (1966) typology and dates are used to provide the timing of the logistic in each case.

Of course, any such periodisation of history is problematic and highly questionable.[2] An advantage of Black's dates is that he demarcates two relevant periods for a large number of countries: that pertaining to the 'consolidation of modernising leadership' followed by the period of 'economic and social transformation'. The former marks the transition into modernity, and the second is taken to represent a number of political, social and economic changes of which industrialisation is a part. Choi chooses the date that is said to mark the beginning of the consolidation of modernising leadership, but in the present study it is suggested that the start of the period of economic and social transformation would best locate the years when socio-economic change was proceeding apace.

Choi's use of a logistic curve reflects the Olsonian assumption that history is progressing from a market-based and interest-group-free 'state of nature' to the sclerosis of a coalition-

---

[1] The third law is chosen because it has productivity growth as the dependent variable. Note, however, McCombie (1981) where its economic significance is challenged.

[2] Inspired by Rowthorn and Wells (1987), another approach would be to take shifts in employment to or from industry, agriculture and services as time-series indicators of institutional flexibility (*FLX*) for each country. This would peak when the total rate of transition to or from these sectors was at a maximum, and this would substitute for the year *EST*. However, the Rowthorn–Wells data cover 13 countries only.

ridden world. Instead, a curve which would more accurately reflect the arguments concerning institutional flexibility would be hat-shaped. The peak level would correspond to the period when industrialisation was most rapid, when the capacity for promoting and absorbing new routines and skills was highest, and existing routines were at the highest level of malleability.

Once established, routinised actions and non-codifiable knowledge have an inertia of their own. As the pace of transformation declines, the system tends to ossify and reinforce existing routines. Thus for routines it is relevant to consider their 'date stamp', marking the time at which they were derived or laid down. The more ossification, the less the inclination to, and the greater the difficulty of, further transformation and change.

In addition, the older the institutions and routines the less the receptiveness of the system to flows of codifiable knowledge and techniques that are generated elsewhere. For instance, current R&D may not relate to older techniques and practices. Restructuring has to take place to improve the absorptive capacity for new ideas. Consequently, in the absence of major crises or disruptions which would promote the search for, and creation of, new institutions and routines, it is reasonable to assume that their contribution to productivity growth declines progressively through time after the transformational peak.

To present this idea in mathematical terms it was decided not to use a normal frequency function because it tailed off too rapidly at the extremes. Instead, the variable representing institutional flexibility (FLX) is defined as follows:[1]

$$FLX(t) = 100/[1 + 0 \cdot 002 \, (t - EST)^2]$$

where EST is the year at the start of the period of economic and social transformation and t is the year.

Choi's measure of disruption is derived from summing the number of 'years of major disruption'. Unfortunately, as well as including revolutions and foreign occupations, Choi assumes that each year under totalitarian government constitutes an instance of major disruption, whereas democracy is given no such accolade. The assumption that simply the presence of fascism and totalitarianism constitute major disruption is consistent with Olson's argument but not the thesis presented here. Contrary to Olson, totalitarianism is normally associated with multiple interest groups and nepotism on a grand scale. Disruptions worth including are revolutions or occupations leading to totalitarianism, and those leading to its removal. During such disruptions, but not the intervening period, new habits and routines can be more easily established.

The conditions here chosen to represent periods of major disruption are more restrictive than Choi's. To qualify, a period of major disruption (PMD) must be:

(i) an extensive foreign occupation of home soil, or revolution, or civil war, or year of national independence, in either case leading to significant social changes;

(ii) at least 10 years from any other PMD;

(iii) at or after the beginning of the period of 'consolidation of modernising leadership'.

The second criterion prevents over-weighting of single major disruptions which span more than one year. The third excludes disruptions which precede the inauguration of the

---

[1] The coefficient in the denominator of $FLX(t)$, and that in DIS_i (see below), were both crudely estimated by ordinary least-squares regressions on the institutional data for the 1960–84 period. Experimentation suggested that the results were not over-sensitive to changes in these coefficients. Nevertheless, some arbitrariness inevitably remains. For each period, mid-point values of these functions were used in the regressions. All data are available from the author.

94   G. Hodgson

Table 1. *Institutional data*

	EST	CML	←————— PMDs —————→				
Australia	1901	1801	1901				
Austria	1918	1848	1848	1918	1945		
Belgium	1848	1795	1813	1830	1848	1918	1945
Canada	1867	1791	1867				
Denmark	1866	1807	1945				
Finland	1919	1863	1918				
France	1848	1789	1789	1814	1830	1848	1871 1945
Germany	1871	1803	1805	1848	1918	1933	1945
Italy	1871	1805	1805	1848	1860	1922	1945
Japan	1945	1868	1868	1945			
Netherlands	1848	1795	1795	1810	1945		
Norway	1905	1809	1905	1945			
Sweden	1905	1809					
Switzerland	1848	1798	1803				
United Kingdom	1832	1649	1688				
United States	1865	1776	1783	1865			

Notes: EST: Beginning year of 'economic and social transformation'. *Source:* Black (1966, pp. 90–92); *CML:* Beginning year of 'consolidation of modernizing leadership'. *Source:* Black (1966, pp. 90–92); *PMD:* Period of major disruption, denoted by the last or most crucial year.

modern socio-economic system, which are too early to affect modern institutions and structures. Disruptions, like information, are structure-specific.

Of course, these strict criteria exclude many other disruptions which have had significant effects. However, their inclusion would involve difficult problems of relative weighting. This statistical study is mainly designed to indicate the general value of the approach, so that only the most important disruptions have been included here.

It is argued above that a large-scale disruptive event will generally create the opportunity to recast social relationships and routines and lay down more modern and progressive habits and routines. Disruption on this scale gives the opportunity of ridding the system of many old methods and arrangements and of adopting new ones.

It is assumed that major disruptions would have greater effect the more that economic and social transformation has advanced. Thus disruption in a less-developed country would have less impact than in one which was developed. Each period of major disruption is assumed to have an impact according to the following formula:

$$DIS_i = \exp[0 \cdot 002(PMD_i - EST)]$$

where DIS_i is the degree of disruption resulting from the given PMD and exp is the exponential function. The index of total institutional disruption is simply the sum of the appropriate DIS_is for each country. Black's data, and the chosen PMDs, are shown in Table 1.

Regressions

To test the technological diffusion hypothesis the following variable was taken from Maddison (1982, p. 212). Where required, an estimate was made by linear interpolation.

Institutional rigidities and economic growth   95

RPR = Relative productivity level (GDP per man-hour) as percentage of US level.

The level of investment was captured by the following:

INV = Gross fixed capital formation as a percentage of GDP (source: OECD, 1986, Table 6.8).

Kaldor's third law was tested using these variables:

MAN = Annual percentage change in real value added in manufacturing (source: OECD, 1986, Table 3.5). Data for Switzerland estimated from World Bank sources.

ENM = Annual percentage change in non-manufacturing employment (source: OECD, 1986, Tables 1.7, 1.10 and 2.11).

As a comparative test of a relatively large number of independent variables was involved, a sequential nested testing procedure was chosen, to eliminate insignificant variables one by one. The results, for all variables that are significant at a 10% level, are shown in Table 2. $SHOCK$ is a dummy variable that takes the value of 0 for the 1960–73 data and 1 for 1973–84.

The results shown in Table 2 are a confirmation of the institutionalist hypothesis (a) in all four cases. Notably, neither the country with the lowest productivity growth rate (the USA) nor the one with the highest (Japan) is an outlier in the regressions, nor are the results significantly affected by their removal.

The technological diffusion hypothesis is confirmed for 1960–73 and 1960–84, but not for the other two regressions. This could mean that the diffusion of codifiable knowledge has slowed down since 1973. Explanations of productivity growth in terms of levels of investment receive confirmation for the 1973–84 period only; in other cases the investment variable is not significant.

Kaldor's third law receives strong confirmation in 1960–73: the years of economic boom. However, during 1973–84, whilst the MAN and ENM variables are both significant, MAN has the wrong sign. Growth in productivity is thus associated with a contraction of manufacturing. This could be explained in terms of the 'degenerate' productivity growth associated with the post-1973 recession. MAN is not significant in the other regressions. It could be that whilst MAN and $PROD$ are correlated in the period of boom, in the post-1973 recession a Kaldor-type relationship has broken down.

The fourth regression suggests that the overall effect of the 1973 oil shock and its deflationary regressions is to lower the growth rate of productivity by about 2% per year. Arguably, much of the post-1973 growth slowdown is explicable in terms of the contraction in effective demand, as well as supply-side factors.[1]

Concluding remarks

In this paper an important distinction has been made between codifiable and non-codifiable knowledge. The latter is related to embedded skills and routines, and their

---

[1] The impact of effective demand on productivity growth is endorsed by contributors to the Matthews (1982) volume and by Fagerberg (1987), Lindbeck (1983) and Giersch and Wolter (1983).

96   G. Hodgson

Table 2. *Regressions*

1960–73 period $(N = 16)$

$PROD = \quad 3.06 \quad + \; 0.0465FLX + \; 0.172DIS \; - \; 0.0168RPR + \; 0.242MAN - \; 0.335ENM$
$\qquad\qquad (0.54) \quad (0.012) \qquad\quad (0.057) \qquad\quad (0.0076) \qquad\quad (0.059) \qquad\quad (0.094)$
$\qquad\qquad **** \qquad *** \qquad\qquad\quad ** \qquad\qquad\quad\; * \qquad\qquad\qquad *** \qquad\qquad\quad ***$

$\qquad\qquad\qquad\qquad R^2 = 0.978; \qquad\quad \text{adjusted } R^2 = 0.967$

1973–84 period $(N = 16)$

$PROD = - \; 0.691 + \; 0.0762FLX + \; 0.225DIS + \; 0.0833INV \; - \; 0.233MAN - \; 0.324ENM$
$\qquad\quad (0.65) \quad (0.027) \qquad\quad (0.050) \qquad\quad (0.033) \qquad\qquad (0.094) \qquad\quad (0.12)$
$\qquad\qquad\qquad\quad ** \qquad\qquad\quad *** \qquad\qquad ** \qquad\qquad\qquad ** \qquad\qquad\quad **$

$\qquad\qquad\qquad\qquad R^2 = 0.897; \qquad\quad \text{adjusted } R^2 = 0.846$

1960–84 period $(N = 16)$

$PROD = \quad 3.10 \quad + \; 0.0784FLX + \; 0.327DIS \; - \; 0.0248RPR$
$\qquad\qquad (0.39) \quad (0.0069) \qquad\quad (0.028) \qquad\quad (0.0048)$
$\qquad\qquad **** \qquad **** \qquad\qquad\; **** \qquad\qquad ****$

$\qquad\qquad\qquad\qquad R^2 = 0.973; \qquad\quad \text{adjusted } R^2 = 0.965$

1960–73 period combined with 1973–84 $(N = 32)$

$PROD = \quad 2.92 \quad + \; 0.0885FLX + \; 0.242DIS \; - \; 0.393ENM \; - \; 2.12SHOCK$
$\qquad\qquad (0.27) \quad (0.0090) \qquad\quad (0.051) \qquad\quad (0.10) \qquad\qquad (0.17)$
$\qquad\qquad **** \qquad **** \qquad\qquad\; **** \qquad\qquad *** \qquad\qquad\quad ****$

$\qquad\qquad\qquad\qquad R^2 = 0.936; \quad \text{adjusted } R^2 = 0.926$

Notes: Method of estimate: ordinary least squares. Standard errors in brackets. Levels of significance (two-tailed test): **** 0.1%; *** 1%; ** 5%; * 10%.

---

development depends upon the transformation and degress of flexibility of socio-economic institutions. For connected reasons it was argued that both the technological diffusion hypothesis and Kaldor's theory of economic growth must be qualified.

A statistical test has confirmed a very strong relationship between the institutional variables and the rate of growth of productivity. Both the technological diffusion hypothesis and Kaldor's third law fare worse after the oil shock of 1973.

It is interesting to project the regression-generated equations into the future. Taking the third regression, and making the heroic assumption that the coefficients in the model remain fixed, *RPR* is recalculated annually according to the derived productivity growth. The projection suggests that France will overtake the United States in terms of overall levels of productivity in the 1990s.[1] After its steep climb, Japan's relative productivity level reaches a peak of about 76% of the French in about 2006, and then begins to decline. British relative productivity rises, then peaks at about 67% of the French or American level in about 1990.

As *FLX(t)* declines over time, and assuming that no further periods of major disruption ensue, the variable of increasing relative influence is *DIS*. Eventually, countries begin to assume a rank order according to the degree of disruption they have experienced in

[1] Recent data in Maddison (1987, p. 651) suggest that French and Dutch productivity levels exceeded 97% of the US as early as 1984. Japan, still behind the UK, was at 55·6%.

Institutional rigidities and economic growth   97

modern times. Having experienced the greatest degree of disruption, France thus emerges as the lead nation, followed by Germany, Italy, Belgium, Austria and the Netherlands.

Of course, these projections ignore variations in performance that may result from changes in effective demand and from the transformation of the socio-economic institutions themselves, as well as the degree of statistical variability that is suggested by the regressions. However, what they do indicate is a process which assumes the form, but not the specific dynamic, of Young–Myrdal–Kaldor models of cumulative causation. Whilst the rank order changes, and some countries overtake others, the gap between the leading and the laggard nations eventually widens in absolute terms. Thus the effect of the institutional variables is to replicate some aspects of the cumulative causation process, and nullify any convergence that is implied by the diffusion hypothesis. We have, to use an old phrase, a process of 'combined and uneven development'.

Regarding policy conclusions, the argument points to an eclectic stance. First, at the international level, it endorses a worldwide expansion in effective demand. There is also some scope for policies to increase investment and to generate and infuse technological knowledge.

Whilst war and revolution may have the effect of increasing institutional flexibility, the first, at least, is not to be recommended. In addition, whilst New Right regimes, such as that experienced in the USA and Britain, may promote some restructuring, including work practices and the ownership of industry, key areas remain untouched, and are protected by a strong residual conservatism. Furthermore, New Right restructuring relies on a crude and misplaced Darwinism and often fails to promote long-term initiatives, in contrast with an interventionist policy in a more favourable economic environment.

Instead, the emphasis must be the kind of 'deep' institutional transformation that is implied by a radical industrial policy, but its outlines will have to await the results of further study.[1] As far as policy recommendations for Britain are concerned, institutional economic integration with more dynamic Continental Europe is a desirable, and perhaps inevitable, outcome.

There is a challenging epilogue. Maddison's sweeping (1982) study of three centuries of capitalist development suggests all too precise correlations between the overall level of productivity within a country and its world hegemonic position in politico-economic terms. We must thus anticipate the political disruption that may result from a loss of economic leadership by the United States, and the shift of the focus of capitalist development back again to its ancient Western European homeland.[2] And if disruption is to result, who can foretell the institutional outcomes? We are condemned, as the Chinese say, to live in interesting times.

Bibliography

Anderson, P. 1964. Origins of the present crisis, *New Left Review*, no. 23, January–February. Reprinted in Anderson and Blackburn (eds) (1966)
Anderson, P. and Blackburn, R. (eds) 1966. *Towards Socialism*, London, Collins
Bairam, E. I. 1987. The Verdoorn Law, returns to scale and industrial growth: a review of the literature, *Australian Economic Papers*, vol. 26, June
Barry, B. 1983. Some questions about explanation, *International Studies Quarterly*, vol. 27, no. 1, March
Beckerman, W. (ed.) 1979. *Slow Growth in Britain: Causes and Consequences*, Oxford, OUP

[1] Interventionist industrial policies are discussed by Best (1986), Carter (1981), Cowling (1987), Gruchy (1984) and Hughes (1986).
[2] This possibility, amongst others, is considered, with some scepticism, in Kennedy (1988).

98   G. Hodgson

Beer, S. 1972. *Brain of the Firm*, London, Allen Lane

Best, M. H. 1986. Strategic planning, the new competition and industrial policy, in Nolan and Paine (eds) (1986)

Black, C. E. 1966. *The Dynamics of Modernization: A Study in Comparative History*, New York, Harper and Row

Blackaby, F. (ed.) 1978. *De-Industrialisation*, London, Heinemann

Blitch, C. P. 1983. Allyn Young on increasing returns, *Journal of Post Keynesian Economics*, vol. 5, no. 3, Spring

Blume, M. E. 1980. The financial markets, in Caves and Krause (eds) (1980)

Bowles, S. 1985. The production process in a competitive economy: Walrasian, neo-Hobbesian, and Marxian models, *American Economic Review*, vol. 75, no. 1, March

Bowles, S. and Eatwell, J. 1983. Between two worlds: interest groups, class structure and capitalist growth, in Mueller (ed.) (1983)

Bowles, S., Gordon, D. M. and Weisskopf, T. E. 1985. *Beyond the Waste Land: A Democratic Alternative to Economic Decline*, London, Verso

Boyer, R. and Petit, P. 1981. Progrès technique, croissance et emploi: un modèle d'inspiration kaldorienne pour six industries européennes, *Revue économique*, vol. 32, no. 6, November

Braverman, H. 1974. *Labor and Monopoly Capital: The Degradation of Work in the Twentieth Century*, New York, Monthly Review Press

Brown, C. J. F. and Sheriff, T. D. 1978. 'De-industrialisation in the UK: Background Statistics', NIESR Discussion Paper

Burawoy, M. 1985. *The Politics of Production: Factory Regimes Under Capitalism and Socialism*, London, Verso

Carter, C. (ed.) 1981. *Industrial Policy and Innovation*, London, Heinemann

Caves, R. E. and Krause, L. B. (eds) 1980. *Britain's Economic Performance*, Washington DC, The Brookings Institution

Choi, K. 1983. A statistical test of Olson's model, in Mueller (ed.) (1983)

Coates, D. and Hillard, J. (eds) 1986. *The Economic Decline of Modern Britain: The Debate Between Left and Right*, Brighton, Harvester

Cornwall, J. 1976. Diffusion, convergence and Kaldor's laws, *Economic Journal*, vol. 86 (ed.) no. 2, June

Cornwall, J. 1977. *Modern Capitalism: Its Growth and Transformation*, Oxford, Martin Robertson

Cowling, K. 1987. An industrial strategy for Britain: the nature and role of planning, *International Review of Applied Economics*, vol. 1, no. 1

Cutler, A. 1978. The Romance of 'Labour', *Economy and Society*, vol. 7, no. 1, February

Davies, S. and Caves, R. E. 1987. *Britain's Productivity Gap*, Cambridge, CUP

Denison, E. 1979. *Accounting for Slower Economic Growth*, Washington DC, The Brookings Institution

Dore, R. 1973. *British Factory-Japanese Factory: The Origins of National Diversity in Industrial Relations*, London, George Allen & Unwin

Dyer, A. W. 1984. The habit of work: a theoretical exploration, *Journal of Economic Issues*, vol. 18, no. 2

Eatwell, J. 1982. *Whatever Happened to Britain? The Economics of Decline*, London, BBC

Elbaum, B. and Lazonick, W. 1986. An institutional perspective on British decline, in Elbaum and Lazonick (eds) (1986)

Elbaum, B. and Lazonick, W. (eds) (1986) *The Decline of the British Economy*, Oxford, OUP

Emery, F. E. 1977. *The Future We Are In*, Leiden, Martinus Nijhoff

Fagerberg, J. 1987. A technology gap approach to why growth rates differ, *Research Policy*, vol. 16, nos 2–4, August

Friedman, A. L. 1977. *Industry and Labour: Class Struggle at Work and Monopoly Capitalism*, London, Macmillan

Giddens, A. 1984. *The Constitution of Society: Outline of the Theory of Structuration*, Cambridge, Polity Press

Giersch, H. and Wolter, F. 1983. Towards an explanation of the productivity slowdown: an acceleration-deceleration hypothesis, *Economic Journal*, vol. 93, no. 1, March

Gomulka, S. 1971. *Inventive Activity, Diffusion, and the Stages of Economic Growth*, Aarhus, Aarhus Institute of Economics

Institutional rigidities and economic growth   99

Gomulka, S. 1979. Britain's slow industrial growth—increasing inefficiency versus low rate of technological change, in Beckerman (ed.) (1979)

Gruchy, A. G. 1984. Uncertainty, indicative planning, and industrial policy, *Journal of Economic Issues*, vol. 18, no. 1, March

Harcourt, G. C. 1972. *Some Cambridge Controversies in the Theory of Capital*, Cambridge, CUP

Hobsbawm, E. J. 1969. *Industry and Empire*, Harmondsworth, Penguin

Hodgson, G. M. 1982. Theoretical and policy implications of variable productivity, *Cambridge Journal of Economics*, vol. 6, no. 3, September

Hodgson, G. M. 1984. *The Democratic Economy*, Harmondsworth, Pelican

Hodgson, G. M. 1988. *Economics and Institutions: A Manifesto for a Modern Institutional Economics*, Cambridge, Polity Press

Hodgson, G. M. (in press). Post Keynesianism and institutionalism: the missing link, in Pheby (ed.) (in press)

Hughes, A. 1986. Investment Finance, Industrial Strategy and Economic Recovery, in Nolan and Paine (eds) (1986)

Jones, D. C. and Svejnar, J. (eds) 1982. *Participatory and Self-Managed Firms*, Lexington, Mass., Heath

Kaldor, N. 1966. *Causes of the Slow Rate of Economic Growth in the United Kingdom: An Inaugural Lecture*, Cambridge, CUP. Reprinted in Kaldor (1978)

Kaldor, N. 1967. *Strategic Factors in Economic Development*, New York, Cornell University Press

Kaldor, N. 1968. Productivity and growth in manufacturing industry: a reply, *Economica*, vol. 35, no. 4, November. Reprinted in Kaldor (1978)

Kaldor, N. 1972. The irrelevance of equilibrium economics, *Economic Journal*, vol. 82, no. 4, December. Reprinted in Kaldor (1978)

Kaldor, N. 1975A. What is wrong with economic theory?, *Quarterly Journal of Economics*, vol. 89, no. 3, August. Reprinted in Kaldor (1978)

Kaldor, N. 1975B. Economic growth and the Verdoorn Law: a comment on Mr Rowthorn's article, *Economic Journal*, vol. 85, no. 4, December

Kaldor, N. 1978. *Further Essays on Economic Theory: Collected Economic Essays Vol. 5*, London, Duckworth

Kaldor, N. 1985. *Economics Without Equilibrium*, Cardiff, University College Cardiff Press

Kapp. K. W. 1976. The nature and significance of institutional economics, *Kyklos*, vol. 29, Fasc. 2

Kennedy, P. 1988. *The Rise and Fall of the Great Powers: Economic Change and Military Conflict from 1500 to 2000*, London, Unwin Hyman

Keynes, J. M. 1936. *The General Theory of Employment, Interest and Money*, London, Macmillan

Kilpatrick, A. and Lawson, A. 1980. On the nature of the industrial decline in the UK, *Cambridge Journal of Economics*, vol. 4, no. 1, March

Kindleberger, C. P. 1983. On the rise and decline of nations, *International Studies Quarterly*, vol. 27, no. 1, March

Lawson, T. 1985. Uncertainty and economic analysis, *Economic Journal*, vol. 95, no. 4, December

Lawson, T. 1987. The relative/absolute nature of knowledge and economic analysis, *Economic Journal*, vol. 97, no. 4, December

Lindbeck, A. 1983. The recent slowdown in productivity growth, *Economic Journal*, vol. 93, no. 1, March

Littler, C. R. and Salaman, G. 1982. Bravermania and beyond: recent theories of the labour process, *Sociology*, vol. 16, no. 2, May

Maddison, A. 1982. *Phases of Capitalist Development*, Oxford, OUP

Maddison, A. 1987. Growth and slowdown in advanced capitalist economies: techniques of quantitative assessment, *Journal of Economic Literature*, vol. 25, no. 2, June

Marshall, A. 1920. *Principles of Economics: An Introductory Volume*, 8th edn, London, Macmillan

Marx, K. 1976. *Capital*, vol. 1 (translated by B. Fowkes from the fourth German edition of 1890), Harmondsworth, Pelican

Matthews, R. C. O. 1982. Introduction: A Summary View, in Matthews (ed.) (1982)

Matthews, R. C. O. (ed.) 1982. *Slower Growth in the Western World*, London, Heinemann

McCombie, J. S. L. 1981. What still remains of Kaldor's laws? *Economic Journal*, vol. 91, no. 1, March

100   G. Hodgson

McCombie, J. S. L. 1982. Economic growth, Kaldor's laws, and the static-dynamic Verdoorn Law paradox, *Applied Economics*, vol. 14, pp. 279–94

McCombie, J. S. L. 1983. Kaldor's Laws in retrospect, *Journal of Post Keynesian Economics*, vol. 5, no. 3, Spring

McCombie, J. S. L. and de Ridder, J. P. 1984. The Verdoorn Law controversy: some new empirical evidence using the US state data, *Oxford Economic Papers*, vol. 36, no. 2, June

Mjoset, L. 1985. The limits of neoclassical institutionalism, *Journal of Peace Research*, vol. 22, no. 1

Mueller, D. C. (ed.) 1983. *The Political Economy of Growth*, New Haven, Yale University Press

Myrdal, G. 1939. *Monetary Equilibrium*, London, Hodge

Myrdal, G. 1944. *An American Dilemma: The Negro Problem and Modern Democracy*, New York, Harper and Row

Myrdal, G. 1957. *Economic Theory and Underdeveloped Regions*, London, Duckworth

Myrdal, G. 1978. Institutional economics, *Journal of Economic Issues*, vol. 12, no. 4, December

Nell, E. J. 1984. Conclusions—cowboy capitalism: the last round-up', in Nell (ed.) (1984)

Nell, E. J. (ed.) 1984. *Free Market Conservatism: A Critique of Theory and Practice*, London, George Allen & Unwin

Nelson, R. R. 1980. Production sets, technological knowledge, and R&D: fragile and overworked constructs for analysis of productivity growth?, *American Economic Review (Papers and Proceedings)*, vol. 70, no. 2, May

Nelson, R. R. 1981. Research on productivity growth and productivity differences: dead ends and new departures, *Journal of Economic Literature*, vol. 29, September

Nelson, R. R. and Winter, S. G. 1982. *An Evolutionary Theory of Economic Change*, Cambridge Mass., Harvard University Press

Nichols, T. 1986. *The British Worker Question: A New Look at Workers and Productivity in Manufacturing*, London, Routledge & Kegan Paul

Nolan, P. and Paine, S. (eds) 1986. *Rethinking Socialist Economics*, Cambridge, Polity Press

OECD 1986. *Historical Statistics, 1960–1984*, Paris, OECD

Olson, M. 1982. *The Rise and Decline of Nations: Economic Growth, Stagflation, and Social Rigidities*, New Haven, Yale University Press

Parikh, A. 1978. Differences in growth rates and Kaldor's laws, *Economica*, vol. 45, no. 1, February

Penrose, E. T. 1959. *The Theory of the Growth of the Firm*, Oxford, Basil Blackwell

Pheby, J. (ed.) in press. *New Directions in Post Keynesian Economics*, Aldershot, Edward Elgar

Phelps Brown, H. 1977. What is the British predicament?, *Three Banks Review*, no. 116, December. Extracted in Coates and Hillard (eds) (1986)

Polanyi, M. 1957. *Personal Knowledge: Towards a Post-Critical Philosophy*, London, Routledge & Kegan Paul

Polanyi, M. 1967. *The Tacit Dimension*, London, Routledge & Kegan Paul

Prais, S. J. 1981. *Productivity and Industrial Structure: A Statistical Study of Manufacturing Industry in Britain, Germany and the United States*, Cambridge, CUP

Pratten, C. F. 1976. *Labour Productivity Differences in International Companies*, Cambridge, CUP

Pryor, F. L. 1983. A quasi-test of Olson's Hypothesis, in Mueller (ed.) (1983)

Rice, A. K. 1958. *Productivity and Social Organization: The Ahmedabad Experiment*, London, Wiley

Rowthorn, R. E. 1975A. What remains of Kaldor's Law?, *Economic Journal*, vol. 85, no. 1, March

Rowthorn, R. E. 1975B. A reply to Lord Kaldor's Comment, *Economic Journal*, vol. 85, no. 4, December

Rowthorn, R. E. 1979. A Note on Verdoorn's Law, *Economic Journal*, vol. 89, no. 1, March

Rowthorn, R. E. and Wells, J. R. 1987. *De-industrialization and Foreign Trade*, Cambridge, CUP

Scott, M. F. 1981. The contribution of investment to growth, *Scottish Journal of Political Economy*, vol. 28, no. 3, November

Shackle, G. L. S. 1967. *The Years of High Theory: Invention and Tradition in Economic Thought 1926–1939*, Cambridge, CUP

Shackleton, J. R. and Locksley, G. 1981. *Twelve Contemporary Economists*, London, Macmillan

Shapiro, C. and Stiglitz, J. E. 1984. Equilibrium unemployment as a worker discipline device, *American Economic Review*, vol. 74, no. 3, June

Simon, H. A. 1984. On the behavioural and rational foundations of economic dynamics, *Journal of Economic Behavior and Organisation*, vol. 5, no. 1

Skouras, A. 1981. The Economics of Joan Robinson, in Shackleton and Locksley (1981)

Sraffa, P. 1926. The laws of returns under competitive conditions, *Economic Journal*, vol. 36, no. 4, December

Stafford, G. B. 1981. *The End of Economic Growth?: Growth and Decline in the UK Since 1945*, Oxford, Martin Robertson

Stephen, F. H. (ed.) 1982. *The Performance of Labour-Managed Firms*, London, Macmillan

Taylor, F. W. 1911. *The Principles of Scientific Management*, New York, Harper

Thirlwall, A. P. 1978. The UK's economic problem: a balance of payments constraint, *National Westminster Bank Quarterly Review*, February

Thirlwall, A. P. 1979. The balance of payments constraint as an explanation of international growth rate differences, *Banca Nazionale del Lavoro Quarterly Review*, no. 128, March

Thirlwall, A. P. 1980. Rowthorn's interpretation of Verdoorn's Law, *Economic Journal*, vol. 80, no. 2, June

Thirlwall, A. P. 1983. A plain man's guide to Kaldor's growth laws, *Journal of Post Keynesian Economics*, vol. 5, no. 3, Spring

Veblen, T. B. 1898. Why is economics not an evolutionary science? *Quarterly Journal of Economics*, vol. 12, no. 3, July. Reprinted in Veblen (1919)

Veblen, T. B. 1915. *Imperial Germany and the Industrial Revolution*, New York, Macmillan

Veblen, T. B. 1919. *The Place of Science in Modern Civilisation and Other Essays*, New York, Huebsch

Veblen, T. B. 1964. *The Instinct of Workmanship*, New York, Augustus Kelley

Verdoorn, P. J. 1949. Fattori che regolano lo sviluppo della produttività del lavoro, *L'Industria*, 1

Verdoorn, P. J. 1980. Verdoorn's Law in retrospect: a comment, *Economic Journal*, vol. 90, no. 2, June

Vries, A. S. W. de 1980. The Verdoorn Law revisited, *European Economic Review*, vol. 14

Vries, J. de 1983. The rise and decline of nations in historical perspective, *International Studies Quarterly*, vol. 27, no. 1, March

Vroom, V. H. and Deci, E. L. (eds) 1970. *Management and Motivation*, Harmondsworth, Penguin

Wallis, J. J. and Oates, W. E. 1988. Does economic sclerosis set in with age? An empirical study of the Olson hypothesis, *Kyklos*, vol. 41, Fasc. 3

Weisskopf, T. E. 1987. The effect of unemployment on labour productivity: an international comparative analysis, *International Review of Applied Economics*, vol. 1, no. 2, June

Whiteley, P. 1986. *Political Control of the Macroeconomy: The Political Economy of Public Policy Making*, London, Sage

Williamson, O. E. 1975. *Markets and Hierarchies: Analysis and Anti-Trust Implications: A Study in the Economics of Internal Organization*, New York, Free Press

Williamson, O. E. 1985. *The Economic Institutions of Capitalism: Firms, Markets, Relational Contracting*, London, Macmillan

Wolfe, J. N. 1968. Productivity and growth in manufacturing industry: some reflections on Professor Kaldor's inaugural lecture, *Economica*, vol. 35, no. 2, May

Wood, S. (ed.) 1982. *The Degradation of Work? Skill, Deskilling and the Labour Process*, London, Hutchinson

Worswick, G. D. N. 1982. The relationship between pressure of demand and productivity, in Matthews (ed.) (1982)

Young, A. A. 1928. Increasing returns and economic progress, *Economic Journal*, vol. 38, no. 4, December

[27]

Public Choice **62**: 155–172, 1989.

The evolution of economic institutions as a propagation process

ULRICH WITT*

Faculty of Economics, University of Freiburg, Europaplatz 1, D-7800 Freiburg, FRG

Abstract. Based on some notions from recent game theoretic approaches to explain the emergence of institutions, a model is put forward which implies some generalizations and extensions. First, the evolution of institutions is interpreted as a diffusion process. This interpretation provides a general formal framework to cover both, the case of strategic and that of non-strategic interaction. Second, different forms of interdependency effects between the individuals involved are identified as making the crucial difference between the case where institutions emerge spontaneously in an unorganized form and the case where they do not.

1. Introduction

The focus of the present paper is on general, abstract regularities in the evolution of socioeconomic institutions. In its orientation, the paper follows recent contributions by Taylor (1976), Ullmann-Margalit (1978), Thompson and Faith (1981), Schotter (1981, 1986) that have been inspired by game theory. Although they differ in method, these recent contributions all follow more or less explicitly the tradition of what will be labeled here the *Smith-Menger-Hayek conjecture* of a 'spontaneous', i.e., unintended and unplanned, emergence of institutions. Adam Smith's notion of the "invisible hand" and Adam Ferguson's conjecture that institutions are "the result of human action but not of human design" express the basic idea. It has been restated independently by Menger (1883) and, more recently, has been extensively elaborated by Hayek (e.g. 1967, for a survey see Vanberg, 1986).

In what follows, an attempt is made to generalize the recent, game-theory-oriented debate in two directions. First, the theoretical background is extended so that cases where there is no strategic interaction at the basis of socioeconomic institutions can also be covered. This is achieved by interpreting the evolution as a diffusion process. It turns out that, in this process, the crucial, general regularies are interdependency effects between the decisions of the individuals involved. They take on systematically varying forms for different institutions.

* The author is grateful to J. Irving-Lessman, T. Kuran, D.C. Mueller, J. Nugent and V. Vanberg for valuable comments on an earlier draft.

156

Second, on this basis an effort is made to subsume what may be labeled the *Olson-Buchanan-Tullock conjecture* on the emergence of institutions. According to this, certain institutions cannot be expected to emerge in the way assumed by the alternative conjecture: the interests pursued by the individuals involved do not necessarily lead them to 'spontaneously' create or support an institution. In this case, for the institution to actually emerge, some kind of collective action would be required. The basic idea has been outlined in the influential book of Olson (1965) and it also figures prominently in the Virginia School of economic thought (see, e.g., Buchanan 1965 and 1975; Tullock 1974).

The paper proceeds as follows. In Section 2 the propagation of an institution is modeled on the basis of some simple assumptions and the notion of the frequency-dependency effect is explained. Section 3 discusses the case of 'spontaneous' emergence of institutions where strategic interaction is absent. In Section 4, situations with strategic interaction are shown to be special cases of the suggested model. Section 5 is devoted to discussing the class of institutions whose propagation requires special forms of collective action. In the concluding section the results are used for a straightforward interpretation of institutional change.

2. Propagation of institutions and the frequency-dependency effect

The approach chosen in this paper is individualistic, that is, an attempt is made to reconstruct the theory of institutions from decision-making or, more generally, behavior at the level of the individual agent. Since the approach is intended as a general one, including both situations in which institutions result from strategic interaction and those where the individuals involved do not notice that their own decisions affect those of others, institutions are broadly defined as follows.

> *Definition*: An institution is a unique behavioral regularity spread out among individuals or a pattern of diverse, but coinciding, possibly even mutually dependent, behavioral regularities. It is displayed whenever the involved individuals are faced with the same constituent situation of choice.

Under this definition, many different forms of institutions can be imagined: those in the realm of markets (division of labor, exchange, use of money, and more specific organizational forms such as e.g., department stores, supermarkets etc.); those in the realm of non-market behavior (e.g., rules and mores, education, family conduct, hierarchical division of labor as in corporations, etc.); or those based on explicit agreements and regulations (e.g., interaction rules, traffic regulation, laws, standing orders, etc.). In any case, the fact that the regularities may be more or less spread out in a population of individuals (or of groups of interacting individuals) points to a crucial feature of institutions, their varying degree of propagation or relative frequency of adoption. For expository convenience assume that the decision to adopt (a) or not to adopt (n) is fully informed with respect to what kind of behavior is required, be it a unique and independent regularity or one that has, in a division of activities, to contribute to a pattern of coinciding regularities. The respective behavior may be adopted by none, some, or all of the involved individuals. Accordingly, if F(a) indicates the relative frequency of adoption, the propagation of an institution can be measured by F(a) on the unit interval.

The emergence and propagation of institutions are interpreted in this paper similarly to those of ordinary behavioral innovations, possibly ones that require coincident innovations on the part of other individuals. Since the focus is on the propagation rather than on the emergence of novelty, let us assume that the idea of a new behavioral regularity, the nucleus of a new institution, has somehow emerged. Its actual propagation depends, then, first on the particular communication processes by which the knowledge of the new form of behavior (new option of choice) is diffused throughout the population. Second, it depends on whether the new option is in fact chosen, i.e., the regularity is individually adopted (the institution supported, complied to etc.).

The first process may be a spontaneous, unguided diffusion along established communication networks between the individuals, or it may result from the activities of one or more "diffusion agents" (Brown, 1981) who, for self-interested motives, try to convince the potential adopters of the benefits of adopting the respective regularity. An obvious difference between the two cases is that, in the former, in contrast to the latter, the decisions on the part of potential adopters can be viewed as independent in the sense that no suasion, negotiations, or organizational measures take place. Let us start here by assuming the former situation (the 'independent' choice; we will come back to the latter in Section 5).

With respect to the question of whether the new behavioral regularity is actually adopted or not, an individualistic approach suggests to assume that an individual is more likely to decide in favor of the new option (rather than not conforming) the more he can expect to improve his position by doing so, given his current preferences, his perception of the choice set, and, where relevant, his assessment of the extent to what others contribute/comply to. More precisely:

Assumption 1: The individual probability of adopting a new behavioral regularity f(a) is the larger, the larger the individual net benefit from choosing a rather than n is assessed provided the net benefit is positive; otherwise f(a) = 0.

This hypothesis can be considered as a statistical reformulation of the standard (deterministic) opportunity cost theory according to which individuals always

158

choose the best available alternative, no matter how much better it is compared
to the next best alternative(s). A second hypothesis, crucial for the argument
in this paper is:

> *Assumption 2*: The extent to which an individual is able to improve his posi-
> tion by adopting a behavioral regularity depends on the relative frequency
> F(a) with which other individuals in the population have already adopted (or
> in certain cases can be expected to adopt) the respective regularity or
> regularities.

This assumption is quite evidently satisfied wherever there are interdependencies among decision-makers.[1] Obviously, this is the case where the individuals
have to contribute to a pattern of coinciding, mutually dependent behavioral
regularities in order to successfully establish the institution. But even where a
division of activities is not required, where, in fact, purely stereotypic behavior
is concerned, there seem to be reasons why frequency-dependency may matter.
For instance, whether a business man opens the first or the tenth supermarket
in a small town makes a difference to the benefits he receives; but joining a
production cooperative may be more beneficial if it has already a significant
number of members. Furthermore, adopting *new* modes of behavior, i.e., behavior that deviates from previously established forms, may, as such, induce
disapproving or even hostile (sometimes possibly also sympathetic) reactions
from the environment. These reactions tend to fade away the more common
the new mode becomes, that is, the more frequently it is adopted by the population.

If, for expository convenience, agents are assumed to behave identically, the
probability f(a) of adopting a new behavioral regularity thus depends for each
individual on the extent to what the respective regularity (or the pattern of
regularities) is already represented in the population, i.e., on F(a). Written as
a function:

$$f(a) = \phi [F(a)]. \tag{2.1}$$

For the population as a whole, however, each individual decision in favor of
option a changes the composition of adopters and non-adopters. Since the outcome of each individual decision is assumed to be f(a) we have

$$\Delta F(a) = \psi (f(a) - F(a)) \tag{2.2}$$

where $\Delta F(a)$ is the change of the composition of adopters and non-adopters in
the population and ψ some monotonous, sign-preserving function such that the
change of the composition is a function of the composition itself.

3. Frequency-dependency under non-strategic behavior

The assumptions in the previous section imply that the propagation of an institution is governed by the utility or the benefits to the potential adopters from taking on the constituent behavioral regularities. The utility has been argued to depend on the relative frequency of adopters in the population. It will now be shown that the kind of dependency may vary strongly between institutions so that they differ systematically with respect to the way and the extent to which they propagate. The exposition starts with the more easily handled situation where the agents do not strategically interact.

Assumptions 1 and 2 together imply the adoption function (2.1). Since, by the first assumption, f(a) monotonically varies with the individual net benefit from choosing a over n, various cases can be plausibly imagined as characterized by the following alternative assumptions:

Assumption 3a:ϕ [F(a)] > 0 for F(a) = 0 and in the entire interval [0,1]
   (i) $\phi' > 0$, or
   (ii) $\phi' < 0$, or
   (iii) $\phi' = 0$.

Assumption 3b:ϕ [F(a)] = 0 for F(a) = 0 and $0 \leq \phi' < 1$ in the neighborhood of F(a) = 0 such that the graph of ϕ [F(a)]
   (iv)   remains below the 45°-line in the interval [0,1] or
   (v)   intersects the 45°-line from below at a point F**, $0 < F^{**} \leq 1$.

The different cases can be illustrated by diagrams in which the graph of (2.1) is depicted for the different specifications such as in Figures 1–3. For expository convenience let us assume that the composition of the population changes continuously so that (2.2) becomes dF(a)/dt = f(a) − F(a). Figures 1–3 can then be interpreted analogously to the phase diagram of this first-order differential equation. Accordingly, all points on the 45°-line represent situations in which, in the mean, the prevailing relative frequency F(a) is just maintained by the individual decision, i.e., propagation equilibria F* of an institution. At all points on a graph above (below) the 45°-line the individual adoption probability is greater (smaller) than the already existing relative frequency of a, so that the latter in the mean increases (decreases) by the individual's decision. These tendencies are indicated by arrows on the graphs that have been depicted for exemplary purposes in the diagrams.

Consider Figure 1, where case (i) is exemplified. Adopting the behavioral regularity yields a net benefit to everybody from the very beginning. The further the institution propagates the more attractive it becomes, e.g., because of increasing reputation or some positive scale effects. As an example for this

160

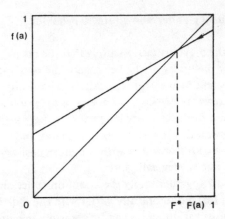

Figure 1. Propagation of an institution in case (i).

case, think of education or the use of some particular exchange medium (money). Depending on the absolute magnitudes the behavior constituent for the institution is, as shown in the figure, not necessarily adopted by the entire population. It is possible that a share 1-F* of the individuals finds alternative n more attractive after a share F* of the population has already chosen a. For instance, education might be a case in point. A differentiation of the educational system would have to be expected.

In Figure 2, representing case (ii), the net benefits develop differently in the propagation process: they steadily decline from an initially high value so that the individual probability of adoption is decreasing the more adopters there are already. Many market institutions seem to fall under this case as increasing adoption may mean increasing competition if the population is made up of the individuals on one side of the market. Department stores (on the supply side) or joint stock companies (on the demand side of the capital market) may be given as examples. The implication is, in general, only a partial propagation of the institution. The same holds true for the limiting case (iii) which is not depicted here. Taken together we obtain:

Proposition 1: Given the cases of assumption 3a, an institution spontaneously propagates without any measures being taken and establishes itself in the population in the sense that any random deviation from F* resulting, e.g., from fluctuations in the population will be compensated for, i.e. F* $\leq$ 1 is a stable propagation equilibrium.

Now consider Figure 3 where a dotted graph is depicted for case (iv). The individual net benefit from adoption would still be increasing with the number of adopters but ϕ [F(a)] < F(a) for all F(a) > 0. The obvious consequence is

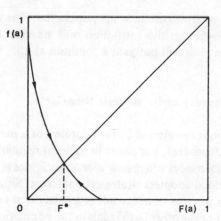

Figure 2. Propagation of an institution in case (ii).

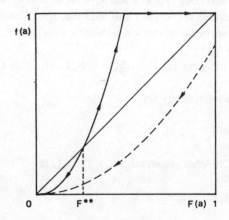

Figure 3. Propagation of an institution in case (iv) and (v).

that such an institution cannot gain a foothold in the population. By contrast, the solid curve, representing case (v), shows values of ϕ [F(a)] > F(a) for all F(a) > F**, F** therefore indicates a 'critical mass' or critical relative frequency: once F(a) happens to exceed F** it will propagate completely. (If the function is bounded from above such that it intersects the 45°-line at some F*, F** < F* < 1, from above, the relative frequency may also settle at an equilibrium level smaller than 1.)[2]

Clearly differing from the cases (i)–(iii) we now find:

Proposition 2: Given the cases of assumption 3b an institution will not spontaneously propagate unless the critical frequency F** is somehow exceeded. F** is an unstable propagation equilibrium which is not restored once F(a)

162

deviates because of fluctuations in the population. The direction of deviation determines whether the institution will be established at a stable equilibrium $F^* \leq 1$ or will not gain a foothold at all.

4. Frequency-dependency under strategic behavior

Where an institution is constituted by the adoption of a pattern of coinciding, possibly mutually dependent, but divers behavioral regularities on the part of a group of agents, as in cases where a division of activities is required, it is most likely that the potential adopters strategically interact. Situations in which individuals decide on whether or not to adopt a behavioral regularity in view of the possible choices of the other individuals in the population are slightly more complicated. With some simplifications, it is not difficult to show, however, that systematically differing types of institutions as characterized by the various cases in the previous section are implied here, too. Consider a population of m agents involved in the m-person non-zero sum game

$$\Gamma = \{ (1, \ldots, i, \ldots, m), (S_1, \ldots, S_i, \ldots, S_m), (\Pi_1, \ldots, \Pi_i, \ldots, \Pi_m)\} \quad (4.1)$$

in which agent i has a strategy set

$$S_i = \{a, n\}, i = 1, \ldots, m, \quad (4.2)$$

and his pay-off, if he chooses strategy $s_i \in \{a, n\}$, is

$$\Pi_i = \Pi_i \{s_1, \ldots, s_i, \ldots, s_m\}. \quad (4.3)$$

As a simplification underlying the following considerations assume (4.3) is identical for all $i = 1, \ldots, m$, that is, Γ is a symmetrical game. For any two agents i and j in the population, $i \neq j$, the game situation can then partially be represented in normal form by the 2×2 matrix

j

		a	n
i	a	$\Pi(a, a)$ $\Pi(a, a)$	$\Pi(a, n)$ $\Pi(a, n)$
	n	$\Pi(n, a)$ $\Pi(n, a)$	$\Pi(n, n)$ $\Pi(n, n)$

Assuming random pairing for expository convenience, the expected pay-offs of the two strategies a (adopting the behavioral regularity constituent for the institution) and n (not adopting) are conditional on the relative frequency with which the strategies will elsewhere be adopted in the population:

$$E\ [\Pi_i\ (s_i = a\ |\ F(a))] = F(a)\ \Pi(a, a) + [1-F(a)]\ \Pi(a, n) \qquad (4.4)$$

and

$$E\ [\Pi_i\ (s_i = n\ |\ F(a))] = F(a)\ \Pi(n, a) + [1-F(a)]\ \Pi(n,n). \qquad (4.5)$$

Analogously to assumption 1, agent i is supposed the more likely to decide in favor of strategy a the higher the (positive) net benefit from choosing a rather than n. Hence the difference between (4.4) and (4.5) can be used as a criterion function that determines the individual probability of adoption f(a). Setting $\Pi_i(a, a) - \Pi_i(n, a) = D_a$ and $\Pi_i(a, n) - \Pi_i(n, n) = D_n$ we obtain:

$$f(a) \begin{cases} = \min\ [D_n + (D_a - D_n)\ F(a),\ 1]\ \text{as long as } f(a) > 0, \\ = 0\ \text{otherwise.} \end{cases} \qquad (4.6)$$

This is a special, piecewise linear form of (2.1).

On the basis of (4.6) we are now in the position to investigate the propagation of a certain strategy in symmetrical m-person games as a special case of the propagation of an institution. The analysis is similar to recent adaptations of game theory to the context of biology (see Maynard Smith, 1982, for an introduction) though the interpretation differs. In fact, for the symmetrical situation chosen here, any stable propagation equilibrium F* > 0 represents what is labeled an evolutionary stable strategy (see Maynard Smith, 1982: 10–20; and Selten, 1983, for the latter) in pure strategies in the context of biological game theory.

In order to substantiate the above claim that institutions show similar differences with respect to their propagation conditions under non-strategic as well as strategic behavior let us now briefly review some numerical examples of well-known prototype games (see Ullmann-Margalit, 1978; Schotter, 1981, or the elementary text by Hamburger, 1979, for the taxonomy of games). Inserting the specification of the *convergence game* illustrated below (strategy a may, e.g., be product innovation, strategy n no product innovation) into (4.6)[3] yields the graph in Figure 4 and, thus, in almost trivial form, a stable propagation equilibrium F* = 1 corresponding to the unique equilibrium in the underlying game.

164

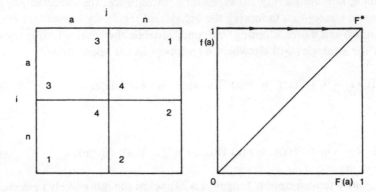

Figure 4. Pay-offs and propagation function for the convergence game.

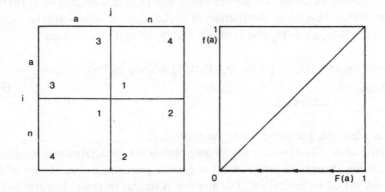

Figure 5. Pay-offs and propagation function for prisoners' dilemma game.

The *prisoners' dilemma game* with strategies a: cooperate, n: not cooperate, is represented in Figure 5 which exemplifies that, as expected, the cooperative strategy a cannot propagate in the population. Again, the equilibrium of the underlying game obtains in trivial form. For both games, covering case (iii) in the previous section, the frequency-dependency does not play a role.

More interesting insights can be gained from investigating games with less clear-cut equilibrium features as, for example, the *'chicken' game* (Figure 6) where strategy a might mean following some new form of honest trade convention as opposed to keeping to an established but somewhat corrupted form n. The game has two equilibria in pure strategies off the principal diagonal. As can easily be reconstructed, the propagation function $f(a) = 1 - 2F(a)$ intersects the 45°-line at a stable propagation equilibrium F^*, $0 < F^* < .5$, a situation similar to case (ii) in the previous section.

The *'pure' coordination game* where a may represent some set of conven-

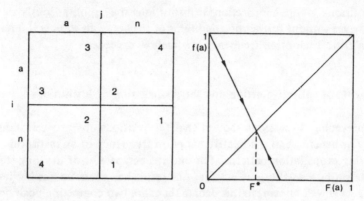

Figure 6. Pay-offs and propagation function for the 'chicken' game.

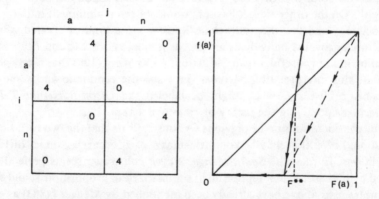

Figure 7. Pay-offs and propagation function for the pure coordination game.

tions (weights and measures, language, manners, traffic, etc.) and n another has no dominant strategies but two equilibria in pure strategies. The corresponding propagation function $f(a) = -4 + 8F(a)$ yields a positive branch which intersects the 45°-line from below in an unstable propagation equilibrium F^{**}, a critical frequency point, as depicted in Figure 7. Two stable equilibria situations prevail in $F(a) = 0$ and the stable propagation equilibrium $F^* = 1$. Note that the numerical specification is crucial for the existence of the critical frequency phenomenon. If 1 is inserted instead of 4, the propagation function remains below the 45°-line except in the unstable equilibrium point at $F(a) = 1$ (the dotted graph in Figure 7). This means that convention a cannot gain a foothold. With its varying specification, the game provides a piecewise linear analog to the cases (iv) and (v) discussed in the previous section.

As demonstrated, in the propagation of institutions under conditions of strategic interaction, two different modes can be distinguished analogously to the

166

propositions 1 and 2 in Section 3: institutions may spontaneously establish themselves without further preconditions or they may do so only if it happens that a critical adoption frequency is somehow exceeded.

5. Agents of collective action and the propagation of institutions

The preceding discussions showed that the relationships between individual utility or benefits and the relative adoption frequency of an institution imply differing propagation patterns. Put into the perspective of the long-standing debate on how institutions emerge, this result has some interesting implications. As is well known, in this debate there are two competing positions. On one side, the *Smith-Menger-Hayek conjecture* of a spontaneous emergence of institutions holds that they are "the result of human action but not of human design". On the other side, it has traditionally been maintained, in particular in sociology and law theory, that institutions are a kind of created, shaped structure or corpus. Individuals are seen as joining in order to constitute an institution in a purposeful, organized action. As Vanberg (1983) has nicely pointed out, this interpretation becomes, in a specific economic and somewhat pessimistic blending, what might be labeled the *Olson-Buchanan-Tullock conjecture* underlying the theory of collective action.

The considerations in the previous sections indicate that the two forms of institutional evolution may be complementary, each occurring under different conditions. In fact, the *Smith-Menger-Hayek conjecture* seems perfectly covered by the cases in assumption 3a as summarized in proposition 1, and some examples used above have already been mentioned by Menger (1883) as cases in point. In this section it remains to be explained how the cases in assumption 3b and their properties as given in proposition 2 are indeed dependent on collective action and to which extent the rather pessimistic *Olson-Buchanan-Tullock conjecture*, which predicts an insufficient development of such institutions, applies.

The last sections have offered little which can explain the actual process of how institutions come about under the conditions of assumption 3b. From the graphs of the propagation functions in the Figures 3 and 7 it is clear, however, that it would be advantageous to all or most of the agents in the population if they adopted the new institution once the critical frequency F^{**} is exceeded, an advantage that would induce them to support and maintain the institution in their own interest. (In the game version, this is equivalent to saying that the propagation equilibrium F^* is an equilibrium point of the game from which nobody has an incentive to deviate.) Up to that point there is, however, a problem. For a new institution to be successful, it has first to reach F^{**}, despite the fact that, up to this point, self-interest dictates that the new institution should not be adopted or supported. How is this problem overcome?

The answer suggested here is simple: by a special form of collective action being organized. The outlook for future self-reinforcement may attract organizers, leaders, agitators, moralists, intriguers, political entrepreneurs, in short agents who, for the most diverse motives, specialize in eliciting and arousing interest, producing agreements, and arranging alliances. They operate as "diffusion agents", engaged in the propagation of a new institution which, in effect, means doing away with the independence and isolation of the individual adoption decision (which has so far been assumed, see Section 2). All that these agents have to achieve is to induce a sufficient number of other agents to expect that collective adoption will come about, so that the expectation becomes self-fulfilling: just a little more than the critical mass.

Unlike those institutions covered by the *Smith-Menger-Hayek conjecture*, organized, intentional pursuit of a collective action by at least some agents is thus a prerequisite for an institution of the second kind to be established. If this is true, it seems straightforward, of course, to apply the *Olson-Buchanan-Tullock conjecture* to this kind of collective action. This is to argue that, at least in large populations, such an action does not (sufficiently) occur, since it requires the agents of collective action to provide a public good. Since the path-breaking book by Olson (1965), this is a corner-stone in the theory of collective action (for a more recent summary see Hardin, 1982). And, indeed, although the agents of collective action in the present context intervene only for the limited transition phase, and although it is not unlikely that their individual motives for acting are less oriented to material cost/benefit considerations than in Olson's examples, the validity of his argument cannot wholly be denied.

Once F** is exceeded, all agents may profit without incurring the costs of attaining this. Free-riding is possible and, if the costs are substantial, there may be no or not enough agents of collective action who are willing to provide the public good of organizing the transition. Confirming Olson's original thesis, this is more likely to happen in large populations if the costs of organizing increase with the number of agents. In larger populations it is then more 'expensive' to reach F** than in smaller ones, as the absolute number of agents who have to be convinced is greater. Increasing costs may, *ceteris paribus*, curb the individual willingness to act as agent of collective action.

What is not entirely clear is the question of how the costs and benefits of the various agents are actually structured in the situation before F** is reached (i.e., in a situation supposed to require the provision of a public good). It may be argued that, even in large groups, it is, in fact, best described as a 'chicken game' (see Fogarty, 1981; Lipnowski and Maital, 1983) with strategies engage (a) or not engage (n) as has been discussed in the previous section. In that case, there may be fewer agents of collective action than desirable, but – viewed as

168

an evolving institution itself – it can be concluded from the example of Figure 6 that a significant number of them may appear: a stable propagation equilibrium may exist, which implies that in a population of potential agents of collective action, a positive share of them will in fact adopt the attitude and help in establishing institutions of the second kind.

Even under the *Olson-Buchanan-Tullock conjecture*, institutions involving some kind of organizational initiative can thus under certain conditions be expected to emerge. In a broader sense their evolution may as well be interpreted as a spontaneous one, since it depends on some individuals adopting the role of an agent of collective action which is itself a behavioral regularity of the first kind. Looking at the game-theoretic background of the institutions subsumed here under the second category, it becomes clear, however, that they consist basically of the class of coordination games (games with multiple equilibria in pure strategies in the principal diagonal of the pay-off matrix). Examples that are often given are all sorts of conventions, statutes, traffic regulations, standing orders, language rules, manners etc.

Not included are all those institutions that require a cooperative solution in a prisoners' dilemma game. This is a very large class which, certainly, is of utmost importance in the framework of the theory of collective action (see, e.g., Nabli and Nugent, 1989). Unfortunately, it is not as easily accessible with the frequency-dependency approach suggested above as the other cases that have been discussed. As shown in Figure 5, there is no critical frequency involved in the p.d.-game that would leave room for an immediate intervention of agents of collective action. The shape of the propagation function flatly turns down any hope of success, given the original pay-offs. Nevertheless, many such institutions can be empirically observed to exist. Any explanation for this (based on the assumption of individually rational behavior), it appears, has to include hypotheses that, in effect, transform the pay-off structure to make the dilemma vanish.

In this way, some more differentiated activities on the part of agents of collective action must be assumed. Imagine, e.g., an attempt is made, in a first step, to propagate retaliatory measures in case that, in a prisoners' dilemma, somebody offering cooperation has been cheated. If the attempt were successful, retaliation would reduce the offender's temptation pay-off. But, the costs of retaliatory action would have to be incurred by the victim reducing the sucker's pay-off still further compared to the original game. If the original (partial) pay-off matrix (Figure 5) were thus changed as follows:

$\Pi(a, a) = 3$	$\Pi(a, n) = 1$
$\Pi(a, a) = 3$	$\Pi(a, n) = 0$
$\Pi(n, a) = 0$	$\Pi(n, n) = 2$
$\Pi(n, a) = 1$	$\Pi(n, n) = 2$

agitation would have transformed the p.d.-game into a coordination game with a propagation function similar to the solid line in Figure 7. A critical frequency F^{**}, $0 < F^{**} < 1$, would occur that allowed room for organizing collective action in the sense above discussed.

Unfortunately, however, the attempt to overcome the prisoners' dilemma by convincing the people of the necessity of retaliatory action may itself induce a prisoners' dilemma and, thus, simply a regress. Chances for arriving at the above coordination game when starting from a p.d.-game seem bad, unless recourse to additional arguments can be made. It has been argued elsewhere that possibly genetically caused variance in individual preferences together with social learning (which is itself frequency-dependent) may ensure the transformation (Witt, 1986). Another, historical, conjecture might be that agents in command of measures of coercion that have otherwise come into existence tend to assume the role of agents of collective action. Since they often are able to extend the measures to new areas, they may be able to punish free-riding and thus to transform a prisoners' dilemma situation into a pure coordination game.

6. Conclusions: Regularities in institutional change

By interpreting the evolution of institutions as a diffusion process in which frequency dependency effects govern the adoption patterns, some characteristic differences between institutions emerging according to the *Smith-Menger-Hayek conjecture* and those resulting from collective action along the lines of the *Olson-Buchanan-Tullock conjecture* have been outlined. The discussion can easily be extended to explain regularities in institutional change. The propagation of an institution often not only means adopting or not adopting a new behavior but at the same time may imply turning away or not turning away from a previous behavioral regularity. Where this happens, an established institution n is declining according to the relation $F(a) = 1 - F(n)$ to the extent that a new institution a is propagating.

Decline, break-down, death of institutions is an almost trivial historical experience. (In fact, explaining the viability of larger economic systems may be an intricate theoretical problem; see Day, 1987.) The exposition above suggests the following: If new institutions spontaneously propagate according to case (ii) there will always be institutional pluralism (in biology this is called polymorphism). The established institution finds a niche for survival. In the cases (i), (iii), and (v) the extent to which this is possible depends on the numerical values. If, as in Figure 3 (solid curve), the critical mass phenomenon is associated with stable situations $F^* = 0$ or 1, the two institutions are mutually exclusive. A dramatic supersession can be expected to take place once the agents of

170

collective action succeed in inducing slightly more than the critical mass to adopt the new institution.

Besides such dramatic forms of change there are, of course, the various possibilities for a creeping decline in which institutions prevailing in former times may be driven out of the population as a consequence of slow shifts in the parameter values. As a consequence of changing relative prices, redistributions, technical progress, but also of changing tastes and changing attention, the propagation functions may shift in such a way that niches for the old institutions are eliminated. As far as the cases (iv) and (v) are concerned, some of the activity of agents of collective action may indeed aim at redirecting attention, providing the 'right' information, and shaping tastes in such a way that the situation (iv) is gradually shifted into a situation (v). The dotted curve in Figure 3 then rotates upwards and F^{**} moves to the left until the costs of convincing the critical mass are sufficiently low and F^{**} can be passed.

The present paper has exclusively focussed on propagation processes. A theory of evolution is somewhat incomplete, however, without also considering the process of emergence of novelty. Where the ideas for possible new behavioral regularities come from, how they are selected, and who will be motivated to try them where – as a novelty – their implications cannot fully be anticipated is left open here. Needless to say, these questions may be of considerable importance in providing a full understanding of the regularities of institutional change as such change involves more than the adaptation process modeled above.[4] Future research should thus also focus on answering these additional questions.

Notes

1. Such interdependencies can be more generally expected than they are in economics, particularly in price theory, where they are usually interpreted as being perfectly mediated by the market, i.e., prices (except in the case of 'true', i.e., non-pecuniary, externalities). Note that the outcome of individual interactions is no longer determined by the individual choices alone if there are interdependencies. The assertion that "the whole (i.e., aggregate behavior) is more than the sum of its parts" has something to it as the particular form and the sequence of interactions in historical time may shape the choices of the individuals in different ways.
2. Critical mass models have recently been given attention in various areas of economics, e.g., in the context of speculation about other individuals' behavior (Schelling, 1978), of the development of technical regimes (David, 1987), of interdependencies in consumption behavior (Granovetter and Soong, 1986), of solutions to the prisoners' dilemma by collective learning (Witt, 1986), of the stabilization of conservative attitudes against revolutionary ones (Kuran, 1987).
3. In principle, the pay-offs may be interpreted as utility indices in the usual way. In order to determine (4.6) numerically, they are, however, treated here like cardinal values. Note that the position and shape of the resulting propagation functions may change with the numerical specification of the pay-offs.

171

4. A discussion of the questions requires extensions at the foundations of economic theory and, thus, goes far beyond the present paper. The interested reader may be referred to Witt (1987) and (1989).

References

Brown, L.A. (1981). *Innovations-diffusion – A new perspective*. London: Methuen.

Buchanan, J.M. (1965). Ethical rules, expected values, and large numbers. *Ethics* 76: 1–13.

Buchanan, J.M. (1975). *The limits of liberty*. Chicago: Chicago University Press.

David, P. (1987). Some new standards for the economics of standardization in the information age. In P. Dasgupta and P.L. Stoneman (Eds.), *Economic policy and technological performance*. London: Cambridge University Press.

Day, R.H. (1987). The evolving economy. *European Journal of Operations Research* 30: 251–257.

Fogarty, T.M. (1981). Prisoner's dilemma and other public good games. *Conflict Management and Piece Science* 5: 111–120.

Granovetter, M., and Soong, R. (1986). Threshold models of interpersonal effects in consumer demand. *Journal of Economic Behavior and Organization* 7: 83–99.

Hamburger, H. (1979). *Games as models of social phenomena*. San Francisco: Freeman.

Hardin, R. (1982). *Collective action*. Washington: Resources for the Future.

Hayek, F.A. (1967). Notes on the evolution of systems of rules and conduct. In F.A. Hayek, *Studies in philosophy, politics, and economics*, 66–81. London: Kegan Paul.

Kuran, T. (1987). Preference falsification, policy continuity, and collective conservatism. *Economic Journal* 97: 642–665.

Lipnowski, I., and Maital, S. (1983). Voluntary provision of pure public good as the game of 'chicken'. *Journal of Public Economics* 20: 381–386.

Maynard Smith, J. (1982). *Evolution and the theory of games*. Cambridge: Cambridge University Press.

Menger, C. (1883). *Untersuchungen über die Methode der Sozialwissenschaften und der politischen Ökonomie insbesondere*. Wien: Braumüller.

Nabli, M.K., and Nugent, J.B. (1989). *The new institutional economics and development: Theory and applications to Tunisia*. Amsterdam: North-Holland, forthcoming.

Olson, M. (1965). *The logic of collective action*. Harvard: Harvard University Press.

Schelling, T. (1978). *Micromotives and macrobehavior*. New York: Norton.

Schotter, A. (1981). *The economic theory of social institutions*. Cambridge: Cambridge University Press.

Schotter, A. (1986). The evolution of rules. In R. Langlois (Ed.), *Economics as a process*, 117–133. Cambridge: Cambridge University Press.

Selten, R. (1983). Evolutionary stability in extensive two-person games. *Mathematical Social Sciences* 5: 269–363.

Taylor, M. (1976). *Anarchy and cooperation*. London: Wiley.

Thompson, E.A., and Faith, R.L. (1981). A pure theory of strategic behavior and social institutions. *American Economic Review* 71: 366–380.

Tullock, G. (1974). *The social dilemma*. Blacksburg: Center for the Study of Public Choice.

Ullmann-Margalit, E. (1978). *The emergence of norms*. New York: Oxford University Press.

Vanberg, V. (1983). Der individualistische Ansatz zu einer Theorie der Entstehung und Entwicklung von Institutionen. *Jahrbuch für Neue Politische Ökonomie* 2: 50–69.

Vanberg, V. (1986). Spontaneous market order and social rules. *Economics and Philosophy* 2: 75–100.

172

Witt, U. (1986). Evolution and stability of cooperation without enforceable contracts. *Kyklos* 39: 245–266.

Witt, U. (1987). How transaction rights are shaped to channel innovativeness. *Journal of Institutional and Theoretical Economics* 143: 180–195.

Witt, U. (1989). *Individualistic foundations of evolutionary economics.* Cambridge: Cambridge University Press, forthcoming.

Name Index

The International Library of Critical Writings in Economics

Future titles will include:

The Economics of Transport
Herbert Mohring

Recent Developments in the Economics of Education
Geraint Johnes and Elchanan Cohn

The Economics of Product Differentiation
Jacques-François Thisse and George Norman

Foundations of Analytical Marxism
John E. Roemer

Implicit Contract Theory
Sherwin Rosen

Markets and Socialism
Alec Nove and Ian Thatcher

Economics and Discrimination
William A. Darity, Jr

Economic Growth in Theory and Practice: A Kaldorian Perspective
John E. King

General Equilibrium Theory
Gerard Debreu

International Trade
J. Peter Neary

The Foundations of Public Finance
Peter Jackson

Labor Economics
Orley Ashenfelter

International Finance
Robert Z. Aliber

Welfare Economics
William J. Baumol and Janusz A. Ordover

Agricultural Economics
G.H. Peters

The Theory of Inflation
Michael Parkin

The Economics of Information
David K. Levine and Steven A. Lippman

The Theory of the Firm
Mark Casson

The Economics of Inequality and Poverty
A.B. Atkinson

Business Cycle Theory
Finn E. Kydland

The Economics of Housing
John M. Quigley

Population Economics
Julian L. Simon

The Economics of Crime
Isaac Ehrlich

The Economics of Integration
Willem Molle

Financial Intermediaries
M.K. Lewis

The Rhetoric of Economics
Donald McCloskey

Ethics and Economics
Amitai Etzioni

Migration
Oded Stark

The Economics of Ageing
John Creedy

The Economics of Privatization and Deregulation
Elizabeth E. Bailey and Janet Rothenberg Pack

Gender and Economics
Jane Humphries

Location Theory
Melvin L. Greenhut and George Norman

Economic Forecasting
Paul Ormerod

Macroeconomics and Imperfect Competition
Jean-Pascal Benassy

The Economics of Training
Robert J. LaLonde

The Economics of Defence
Keith Hartley and Nicholas Hooper

Transaction Cost Economics
Oliver Williamson

The Economics of Altruism
Stephano Zamagni

Long Wave Theory
Christopher Freeman

Consumer Theory
Kelvin Lancaster

Law and Economics
Judge Richard A. Posner

The Economics of Business Policy
John Kay